THE CAMBRIDGE COMPANION TO
RELIGION AND WAR

This Companion offers a global, comparative history of the interplay between religion and war from ancient times to the present. Moving beyond sensationalist theories that seek to explain why "religion causes war," the volume takes a thoughtful look at the connection between religion and war through a variety of lenses – historical, literary, and sociological – as well as the particular features of religious war. The twenty-three carefully nuanced and historically grounded chapters comprehensively examine the religious foundations for war, classical just war doctrines, sociological accounts of religious nationalism, and featured conflicts that illustrate interdisciplinary expressions of the intertwining of religion and war. Written by a distinguished, international team of scholars, whose essays were specially commissioned for this volume, *The Cambridge Companion to Religion and War* will be an indispensable resource for students and scholars of the history and sociology of religion and war, as well as other disciplines.

Margo Kitts is Professor and Coordinator of Religious Studies and East–West Classical Studies at Hawai'i Pacific University. She is the author and editor of ten books, most recently *Sacrifice: Themes, Theories, and Controversies* and *Martyrdom, Self-Sacrifice and Self-Immolation: Religious Perspectives on Suicide.*

T0384772

CAMBRIDGE COMPANIONS TO RELIGION

This is a series of companions to major topics and key figures in theology and religious studies. Each volume contains specially commissioned chapters by international scholars, which provide an accessible and stimulating introduction to the subject for new readers and nonspecialists.

Other Titles in the Series

(*continued after index*)

THE CAMBRIDGE COMPANION TO
RELIGION AND WAR

Edited by

Margo Kitts
Hawai'i Pacific University

CAMBRIDGE
UNIVERSITY PRESS

Shaftesbury Road, Cambridge CB2 8EA, United Kingdom

One Liberty Plaza, 20th Floor, New York, NY 10006, USA

477 Williamstown Road, Port Melbourne, VIC 3207, Australia

314–321, 3rd Floor, Plot 3, Splendor Forum, Jasola District Centre,
New Delhi – 110025, India

103 Penang Road, #05–06/07, Visioncrest Commercial, Singapore 238467

Cambridge University Press is part of Cambridge University Press & Assessment,
a department of the University of Cambridge.

We share the University's mission to contribute to society through the pursuit of
education, learning and research at the highest international levels of excellence.

www.cambridge.org
Information on this title: www.cambridge.org/9781108835442

DOI: 10.1017/9781108884075

First published 2023

A catalogue record for this publication is available from the British Library.

Library of Congress Cataloging-in-Publication Data
NAMES: Kitts, Margo, 1952- editor.
TITLE: The Cambridge companion to religion and war / edited by Margo Kitts, Hawai'i
    Pacific University, Honolulu.
DESCRIPTION: Cambridge, United Kingdom ; New York, NY, USA : Cambridge University
    Press, 2023. | Series: Cambridge companions to religion | Includes bibliographical
    references and index.
IDENTIFIERS: LCCN 2022050172 (print) | LCCN 2022050173 (ebook) |
    ISBN 9781108835442 (hardback) | ISBN 9781108793438 (paperback) |
    ISBN 9781108884075 (epub)
SUBJECTS: LCSH: War–Religious aspects.
CLASSIFICATION: LCC BL65.W2 C36 2023 (print) | LCC BL65.W2 (ebook) |
    DDC 201/.7273–dc23/eng20230123
LC record available at https://lccn.loc.gov/2022050172
LC ebook record available at https://lccn.loc.gov/2022050173

ISBN 978-1-108-83544-2 Hardback
ISBN 978-1-108-79343-8 Paperback

Contents

Contributors

Asma Afsaruddin is Professor of Middle Eastern Languages and Culture at the Hamilton Lugar School of Global and International Studies at Indiana University, Bloomington.

Torkel Brekke is Professor of Religion and Head of Diversity Studies at Oslo Metropolitan University

John J. Collins is Holmes Professor of Old Testament Criticism and Interpretation at Yale Divinity School.

David Cook is Professor of Religion at Rice University.

Robert Eisen is Professor of Religion and Judaic Studies at George Washington University.

Kathinka Frøystad is Professor of Religious Studies at the Department of Cultural Studies and Oriental Languages, University of Oslo.

M. Cecilia Gaposchkin is Professor of History at Dartmouth College.

Mohammed M. Hafez is Professor of National Security Affairs at the Graduate School of International and Defense Studies, Naval Postgraduate School.

Stephen Jenkins is Professor Emeritus of Religious Studies at Humboldt State University.

James Turner Johnson is Distinguished Professor of Religion and Associate of the Graduate Program in Political Science at Rutgers University.

Reuven Kimelman is Professor of Classical Rabbinic Literature at Brandeis University.

Margo Kitts is Professor and Coordinator of Religious Studies and East-West Classical Studies at Hawai'i Pacific University.

Angela M. Lahr is Associate Professor of History at Westminster College.

Osman Latiff is Honorary Research Associate at the Department of History, Royal Holloway, University of London.

June McDaniel is Professor Emerita of Religious Studies, College of Charleston.

Paul Middleton is Senior Lecturer in New Testament and Early Christianity at the University of Chester.

Anne Murphy is Associate Professor of History at the University of British Columbia.

Kaushik Roy is Reader at the Department of History, Jadavpur University in Kolkata, West Bengal, as well as a global fellow at the Peace Research Institute Oslo.

Kristin Scheible is Professor of Religion and Humanities at Reed College.

Pashaura Singh is Professor and Dr. Jasbir Singh Saini Endowed Chair in Religious Studies at the University of California at Riverside.

Barend ter Haar is Professor at the Numata Center for Buddhist Studies of the University of Hamburg.

Brian A. Victoria is Senior Research Fellow at the Oxford Center for Buddhist Studies.

Matthew J. Walton is Assistant Professor in Comparative Political Theory at the University of Toronto.

Preface

It would be an understatement to call the completion of this volume a struggle. It was a struggle not only because its chapters were planned and written during the COVID pandemic but also because two of the prospective contributors died, although of nonpandemic causes. Aside from forcing us all to contemplate our own frailty, these deaths threw a wrench into scheduling, both temporally and with regard to the topics covered. While the volume could be vastly expanded were we to take into consideration religion and war in less traditional contexts, nonetheless this remains an outstanding compilation, although somewhat traditional in scope. The twenty-three chapters included herein should offer scholars and students valuable insights into the union of religion and war under four rubrics: classical foundations, just war, religious nationalism, and featured conflicts.

Introduction: Exploring Religion and War

MARGO KITTS

The association of religion with war is as old as our earliest writings from China (Yates 2003) and the Near East (Ballentine 2015) and continues to find expression in contemporary discourse. Despite myriad laments about this association, it is indisputable that religious rhetoric has supported military aims across geographies and historical eras. While there is arguably a propagandistic dimension to some of this rhetoric, there is no good reason to suppose that warriors on the ground have been indifferent to it. For instance, it is well-known that some Christian crusaders were inspired by portents, dreams, prophecies (Housely 2008; Gaposchkin 2017) and by devotional songs (Riley-Smith 1997), and that the same have inspired passionate millennial groups in the USA and abroad (Graziano 1999; Filiu 2011; Barkun 2013; Hegghammer 2017). Even for seemingly secular wars, just war principles rooted at least in part in religious thinking (e.g., Gratian, Aquinas) seep into war's justifications, as do inspirational fighting models based on religious legends (e.g., David, Huseyn, Arjuna). However secular the aims of military leaders today, no astute historian can deny that religion has played a role in shaping the way war has been imagined for centuries. It still does so, as we see in today's strident religious nationalisms. In short, the subject matters.

This volume explores the link of religion with war under four rubrics: classical foundations; just war; religious nationalism; and featured conflicts. Part I on classical foundations, consisting of eight chapters, investigates war as conceived at the origins of eight major religious traditions. Part II addresses just war theories as lodged in religious thinking, and Part III treats various expressions of religious nationalism, a subject with special relevance to contemporary times. Part IV features conflicts that illustrate interdisciplinary approaches to religion and war, touching on rituals, poems, piety, fierce goddesses, messianic rebellions and autonomous fighting groups thriving outside the margins of the Mughal state. This essay introduces the four parts and then summarizes each chapter.

CLASSICAL FOUNDATIONS

While definitions of religion will be endlessly debated, that religion does bear on classical wars and literature about wars may be ascertained in part by art and in part by the attribution of extraordinary passions to warriors. Beyond vivid renderings of military triumph overseen by gods (Bahrani 2008) and poetic visions of gods leading battles (Kitts 2013, 2017), we have ancient reports ascribing a conspicuous religious enthusiasm to the fight, as if to elevate the fighting register. We see this, for instance, in zeal for the holy land, in righteous indignation about perceived wrongs and in devotional performances on the battlefield, all of which conceivably endow battles with the transcendent mantle of "cosmic war," as Mark Juergensmeyer has applied the term to certain terroristic impulses (2016). Rituals, both individual and communal, might confer some of this religious enthusiasm (Kitts 2010, 2018, 2022 and Chapters 19 and 20). On an individual level, bodily purifying, swearing oaths, praying and anointing weapons historically have sanctified warriors before battle, whereas communal rituals, such as marching in formation, singing, waving standards and cursing enemies have been thought to strengthen solidarity (Von Rad 1991 [1958]; Riley-Smith 1997; Hassner 2016; Gaposchkin 2017; Chapter 17). Postwar commemorations, such as passion plays, poetry, dance, art and pilgrimages, can add to the religious fervor, particularly when these celebrate victors or lionize the fallen (Sells 2003; Chapters 6 and 20). A further influence might be legends of betrayal and of the ethical dilemmas of heroes, which surely too disturb and engage audiences (Chapters 4 and 12). It would seem impossible to grasp war in religious imagination without studying these very human experiences.

At the same time, war as conceived in religious imagination can enjoy an obvious freedom from human experiences, or at least be not entirely tethered to them. Some of our earliest Near Eastern narratives, for instance, herald heavenly wars culminating in the imposition of order over chaos: Sky gods subduing riotous waters is a popular theme (Collins 2003, 2007; Fishbane 2004; Wyatt 2005; Schwemer 2007, 2008; Kitts 2013, 2017). While these violent encounters set *in illo tempore* may have signaled a feeling of relief for some audiences, others arguably were thrilled by them, as we can ascertain from reportedly regular oral performances of the Babylonian Enuma Elish and as we see on Mesopotamian cylinder seals depicting fantastic deicides, raging monsters and god-on-monster combat.[1] A certain glee in myths that violently impose order might be inferred too by the astonishing number of eschatological expectations in world religions, although such expectations are not only triumphal but can be mired in cataclysmic predictions and/or messianic hopes (see Chapters 1, 2 and 15). A diversity of aims for such narratives thus must be acknowledged, including aims to entertain as well as to comfort.

Narratives of religious war can be fantastic but also sentimental. Many religious war tales are set within cosmic schemes that emphasize mysterious forces at work in history and worldly conditions that have gone somehow awry. It is not uncommon for scriptures and classical epics to bemoan a pattern of fallen ages and to express a certain tristesse (e.g., the Heike Monogatari, the Mahabharata), qualities that make them universally appreciable and poetic. On the fantastic side, and especially within the epic genre, an effort to remediate chaos and suppress sinister foes may occasion the harnessing of supernatural weapons and godlike powers (Arjuna and his Gandiva bow come to mind). Despite the glamor to such tales, there is also a restorative theme. For instance, one Buddhist just war doctrine is rooted in the need to redeem an *a-dhammic* world through samsaric militarism until worldly *dhamma* is restored and people begin to behave morally (Frydenlund 2017). This example highlights the intersection of cosmic and human themes.

JUST WAR

As already implied, if there is a religious urge to correct worldly instabilities, it is not only poetic. We see real-time implications in just war theories that strive to clarify the conditions and modes of justified military conduct. Just war theory has roots in the earliest centuries of virtually all the religious traditions treated herein. European just war theory stems actually from pre-Christian times (e.g., Cicero) and is still

---

[1] For instance, winged monsters devour the heads of bearded men on an Old Babylonian seal (from Ishchali, dated 1800–1700 BCE; see at http://oi.uchicago.edu/OI/IRAQ/dbfiles/objects/1321.htm). On another, an open-mouthed, winged dragon rampages (Tell Agrab; ca. 1800–1700 BCE; see at http://oi.uchicago.edu/OI/IRAQ/dbfiles/objects/1277.htm). Number 15618, from Tell Asmar (dated 2300–2200 BCE), shows a monster of the hydra variety, with seven heads, four legs and flames shooting from its back, facing two gods who are severing its heads (see at http://oi.uchicago.edu/OI/IRAQ/dbfiles/objects/1065.htm). Discussed in Kitts (2017).

compelling in principle. However ancient, concerns for *jus in bello*, or the regulation of how warriors actually fight, are integrated into the Geneva Conventions, and violation of those rules today provokes feelings of outrage based on a presumed fairness whose religious roots are rarely contemplated (but see Chapters 9 and 10).

In fact, there are evolutions and historical contingencies to all just war theories. For instance, in the eleventh century Maimonides reinforced the prescriptions for biblically commanded war (Deuteronomy 20:16–18) and at the same time softened those for optional war (Deuteronomy 20:10–12), at a time when a war led by Jews had become virtually inconceivable. He famously engaged with Greek and Islamic notions as well as biblical ones (see Chapter 9). In Islamic traditions, although ideals of right conduct on the battlefield are laid out in the Qur'an, Islamic thinking on fighting evolved and adapted first when Islam expanded out from the Arabian Peninsula in contact with the multicultural empires surrounding it, and then later when it brushed up against European ideals (see Cook 2012; Chapter 11). Some contemporary dichotomies that we see in extremist thinking, such as the tension between *Dar al Harb* (abode of war) and *Dar al Islam* (abode of peace), appear to be adapted notions (Hashmi and Johnson 2012), and they diverge from the ideals of defensive war advocated in the earliest Quranic verses (Afsaruddin 2012; Chapter 3).

As for Asian traditions, some just war notions are embedded in literary classics. Indian ideals are exceedingly old and vary from text to text, but the epic poem the Mahabharata famously crystallizes religious rationalizations for war and right conduct on the battlefield (see Chapters 4 and 12). *Karmayoga* and *rajadharma* are some of the rubrics under which the ethics of fighting are explored, but there are also deeper themes, such as the imagined conflation of killing in war with killing in ritual sacrifice (Heesterman 1993; Johnson 1998; Brekke 2005; Chapter 4). As for Buddhism, the world's many Buddhist traditions do not universally reject the doctrine of just war, although they have come to terms with war in their own disparate ways (see Chapters 5, 7, 8, 13 and 18). Some just war doctrines, as represented above, are driven by a restorative theme, but others are symbolically ferocious, as we see in Buddhist tantric texts and spectacular rites designed to invoke protective deities and to shield warriors by defensive magic (Sinclair 2014). Even the most pacifistic of Buddhist doctrines is compelled to address the bloody aftermath of war, and consequently theories *jus post bellum* have resonated with some Buddhists (Chapter 13).

RELIGIOUS NATIONALISM

It may seem strange that as all of us become more globally connected in our economies and social interactions there has emerged a number of fervent religious nationalisms that seem to differ in sensibility from the old allegiances to nation-states. Whereas nation-states were once seen as guaranteeing individual liberties and freedom from constraint (per Hobbes, Hume and others; Gorski 2010), at least in the West, now in many parts of the world religious identities seem to be overwhelming national identities (Lahr 2007; Eisen 2011; Gorski and Perry 2022; Chapters 14–18). Arguably, religious fervor is not a new feature of politics, and nor, for that matter, are reports of theophanic battles led by marching gods and goddesses who rally warriors (Kitts 2013) and cradle their favorites in death (Chapter 21). Yet the merging of national and religious identities has become conspicuous today, in some cases built on foundational religious legends whose contemporary reconstructions are historically dubious. In many cases, religious nationalism is forged by conflict, such as by the flaring of antagonisms over contested religious sites (Sells 2003; Jaffrelot 2007; Hassner 2012). Collective rituals, such as pilgrimages, songs, dramatizations and also riots, tend to anchor these sites in public imagination (Van der Veer 1996; Chapter 17). Of course, many factors – economic, political, situational – can inflame religious nationalism (Juergensmeyer 2008).

FEATURED CONFLICTS

The point of Part IV is to offer a sampling of analyses of historical conflicts that cannot be understood well without consideration of religious imagination. Part IV therefore supports the aim of the entire volume through illustrations. Hence, Chapter 19 addresses the significance of liturgy and ritual for creating the mentality of earliest Christian crusaders. Chapter 20 explores how the pursuit of piety was understood to sanctify warriors before battle, as reconstructed from Islamic military history. Chapter 21 investigates the multilayered worship of Durga and Kali, Indian goddesses associated with destruction and protection, in various guises (also see Chapters 4 and 12). Chapter 22 highlights the messianic hopes of the astonishingly destructive Taiping Rebellion. Chapter 23 focuses on autonomous martial communities, violence and the state in early modern South Asia. All five chapters are authored by stellar scholars who can validate the premise of the volume, which is that religious imagination has infused and shaped the mentalities of warriors in diverse historical settings.

Following are brief summaries of each chapter.

CLASSICAL FOUNDATIONS

Chapter 1: *Biblical Paradigms of War in History and Eschatology*
John J. Collins

Part I begins with biblical paradigms for war in history and eschatology. From songs of liberation (e.g., Exodus 15) to prescriptions for genocidal violence (e.g., Deuteronomy 7–2), the Bible's views on war are diverse and complicated. John J. Collins outlines disputes about both the historicity and the morality of biblical war tales, situating the notion of covenantal loyalty as well as the most striking biblical reports of cruelty in the context of ancient Near Eastern war rhetoric. Rather than report actual genocidal violence, different biblical war narratives have been argued to serve Israelite identity formation and thus to be ahistorical. But the harnessing of such narratives to serve actual genocidal aims later – by, for instance, the American Puritans into modern times – shows the profound worldly reach of these narratives, whether initially ahistorical or not. As for eschatological violence, one victorious trope in prophetic literature is the divine devouring of Gog and Magog and various animals and birds of prey, who also are summoned to eat the flesh and drink the blood of the worldly princes (Ezekiel 39), a voracious trope that persisted into the Book of Revelation (19:17–18) to describe retribution at the end of time. Fantasies of violent retribution are likened not only to devouring flesh, but also to harvesting grain and grapes, to marketing people and to enslavement. Other apocalyptic fantasies are quietistic, wherein the faithful await divine vengeance in the age to come, although human participation in the final days can be anticipated as well, as it is in the Dead Sea War Scroll. Collins ends by exploring the diverse appeals of violent fantasies, from shaping the terms of anticipated conflicts, to offering a therapeutic repose in the face of oppression, to providing hope for the eventual restoration of righteousness.

Chapter 2: *Early Christianity and War*
Paul Middleton

In popular thinking, early Christianity severed itself from its Jewish progenitor by embracing a crucified messiah who suffered nonviolently and "whose kingdom was not of this world." These Christians reputedly extolled martyrdom, not war, as the ultimate resistance to imperial violence, at least until the Christianization of the Roman Empire under Constantine. But Paul Middleton points out that, in fact, violence is not at all absent from the New Testament. The gospel traditions about Jesus allow that, alongside the blessings on peacemakers and exhortations to nonviolence, there are threats of eschatological judgment against those who reject Jesus (Lk 10.13–16), pronouncements of vengeance upon this "evil generation" (Lk 11.49–52), as well as graphic depictions of eternal torment (Mk 9.48; Lk 19.23–28; Mt 25.21), quite in addition to representations of Jesus as the eschatological Son of Man who will descend with his army of angels to gather the elect and to unleash apocalyptic judgment on those destined for destruction (Mk 13.24–27; Mt 24.29–31). Some scholars embrace these more militant representations as consistent with a Zealot Jesus aspiring to overthrow the Romans with his heavenly army. Others examine the peace-promoting parables as insinuating that failure to act ethically now results in violent retribution later (e.g., Mt 13.24–30), a picture Paul seems to support, as his encouragement to bless one's persecutors (e.g., Rom 12; 1 Thess 5.1) is balanced by the assurance that eventually the god of peace will "crush Satan underfoot" (Rom 16.20; cf. Rom 12.19). Meanwhile, Paul deploys military metaphors to envision himself and his churches as fellow soldiers in a war against cosmic forces, whose battles, even against arguments, will be fought with divine weapons (e.g., 2 Cor 10.3–5). In the Book of Revelation, God's people engage in end-time battles as soldiers in the armies of heaven. Warrior themes continue into the martyrologies, some of which are figured as cosmic conflicts between Christians and earthly magistrates and some of which replicate the agonistic language from gladiatorial combats in the Roman arena.

Chapter 3: *Fighting and Martial Valor in Islamic Thought*

Asma Afsaruddin begins by separating the term *jihād* in contemporary discourse from its use in the Meccan and Medinan periods of Islamic history (610–622 CE and 622–632 CE, respectively) as represented in the Qur'an. Rather than "war in the path of God," *jihād* there means to struggle, to strive, sometimes to overcome one's desires and to obey God – the standard interpretation – and sometimes to preach the message of Islam, which some later scholars will enfold into military duty. But it is Quranic *qitāl* that refers specifically to "armed combat," and the Arabic word for war in general is *harb*, which is never used with the phrase "in the path of God." Nonetheless, fighting and the conduct of war do receive ample discussion in the Qur'an. In the Meccan period,

Muslims were prohibited from physically retaliating against growing aggression from Meccan polytheists; the Qur'an instead counseled forbearance until God might correct the persecutors' immoral actions. Two years after the Medinan period began, however, permission was granted to fight against those who initiated war, those who wrongfully drove believers from their homes, those who violated oaths with the Messenger and to defend victims who cried out for help. The exhortation to fight *jus ad bellum* – for just cause – with right intention and in self-defense became obligatory for first-generation Muslims, and divine assistance was assured for righteous combat. As for *jus in bello*, a number of passages proscribe aggression, initiating hostilities and fighting with rancor, while others urge proportionality once combat has been initiated and restraint if it has ceased. In contrast, some later pundits construed some passages as promoting Muslim belligerence against non-Muslims, including other Peoples of a Book, until they submitted or paid the poll tax, which contradicts earlier passages requiring that fighting be contingent on prior aggression and is forbidden against non-hostiles. The usual reasoning for this contradiction is that later verses abrogated earlier ones, but this is disputed in the long tradition of exegesis. A further corrective to popular rhetoric is that the word for martyr, *shahīd*, is never used in the Qur'an to connote one who dies in battle. Reference to those who die for a righteous cause is not restricted to a military context, and one is urged not to glorify military deaths. Hadith texts, collected over centuries, complicate this picture.

Chapter 4: *Hinduism and War*

Kaushik Roy takes issue with the popular assumption that "Hinduism," a term of nineteenth-century vintage, is and has always been a religion of peace. Taking Hinduism as a broad category nonetheless, he explores six discourses on classical violence and war. First, a ruler's duties to protect and to conduct defensive war (*rajadharma*) are traceable at least to India's great epic poems, particularly to the Mahabharata (dated between 600 and 300 BCE), where King Yudhisthira, with the counsel of family and peers, creates order in part through ritual sacrifices. Rules of *dharmik* (righteous war) are laid out, and fighting without it can result in eternal punishments. Second is the *kshatradharma*, or the duties of the warrior caste. *Kshatriyas* were to protect Hindu *dharma* (here meaning righteousness) through force, power and strength and to develop martial skills and a heroic code of honor. This apparent militarism is softened somewhat in the Mahabharata by Krishna's exhortation to practice disinterested martial violence on the battlefield and his justification of war due to cosmic purpose. Third, rituals leading to *moksha*, or freedom from earthly existence, are traceable to 700 BCE–300 CE, when texts such as the Upanishads pondered the nature of the human soul (*atman*), the enduring consequences of action (*karma*), the transmigration of souls through lifetimes (*samsara*), fate (*daiva*), large cycles of time (*kala*) and the necessity of a great annihilating war at the end of an age, when the earthly populations become overcrowded and confused. Fourth, in the Vedic worldview sacrifices maintained the cosmic and natural order, even as victims were imagined as not quite dying, but as going on to a higher plane of existence, an imagination that reveals a profound ambivalence about killing in sacrifice. The Mahabharata war itself has been deemed a symbolic ritual sacrifice, where warriors are rendered sacrificial victims, their blood the ghee running over the chariot, itself rendered as the sacrificial altar, while the cries of the dying and wounded are compared to the war ritual's conches and drums. Fifth, as for women and war, despite some arguments about sexist figurations in Indian texts, Roy points out that Draupadi, wife of the Pandava in the Mahabharata, is not only literate in the language of *dharma*, but also is figured as the goddess Sri, whose presence confers royal power on her consort. She is unabashed in negotiating with her husband, Yudhisthira, and refuses to stay silent in the face of injustice. Lastly, Roy points out how classical texts have been harnessed by nationalist parties as well as by military officers seeking rationales for war, but oddly, with a few exceptions, most have ignored the feminist potential in the Draupadi paradigm, as well as that of the goddess Durga, another powerful figure in Indian imagination.

Chapter 5: *Buddha in the Ring of Fire: The Buddhist Ethics of Warfare*

Stephen Jenkins points out that throughout history Buddhist societies have been as warlike as any other, despite misleading characterizations of Buddhism as strictly a pacifist religion. Historically there have been Buddhist doctrines of just war, wars of conquest, brutal penal codes, messianic revolts and meditative war magic, not to mention the spiritualization of combat under the Buddhist mantle of martial arts. As for its nonviolent doctrines, while it is true that Buddhist traditions unconditionally aspire to avoid harm and to promote happiness for all sentient beings, what constitutes harm must be understood in terms of multiple life perspectives, wherein killing is *not* tantamount to personal annihilation, and also in terms of competing political and religious

concerns, proportionality and what kinds of action are possible without
harmful intention. Some scholars privilege the pacifist teachings of
canonical texts against the ethos of narrative literature, but Jenkins
points out that this choice ignores many illuminating rationales for
violence. In the Jataka tales, the past lives of the Buddha show him as,
for instance, a weapons master, a warrior king, a warhorse, a war
minister defending against a siege, even as the deity Indra at war with
demigods. Some tales justify defensive warfare and preemptive strikes
against immoral enemies, as may be seen in the tale of an early Buddha
as a ship captain who kills a criminal intent on murdering everyone on
board. While thus risking his own damnation to save others, the captain
saves not only those on board the ship but the criminal himself, who is
saved from eons in hell for his would-be murderous acts. Hence there is
the matter of intention: The Buddha reputedly distinguished those who
killed with murderous intentions, who were hell-bound, from those
who killed with compassion and foresight, who were not. Much is
determined also by the status of the victim: Criminals presumably have
less karmic merit to lose if killed. A good king, or *cakravartin* (wheel-
turner), who cares righteously for his subjects should not need armed
forces, although complications to this picture are evident in the iconography of Vajrapāni, the Buddha's formidable bodyguard who wields his
vajra menacingly to protect the Buddha wherever he goes. In the tale of
King Aśoka, who is often held up as an icon of Buddhist pacifism, his
reputed remorse after a devastating battle and his subsequent conversion to Buddhism are shown to be consistent not with Buddhist pacifism, but with the advice of the Arthaśāstra and other war manuals that
encourage public mourning and a show of regret after battle in order to
mollify and better govern the conquered. Thus, layers of contextual-
ization counter a simple picture of nonviolence when it comes to
Buddhism and war.

Chapter 6: *Sikhism: Exploring the Notion of a Righteous War*
(Dharam Yudh)

Pashaura Singh describes two major themes related to war in foundational Sikh texts: the spiritual battle fought in the mind against
internal temptations such as lust, greed, anger, attachment and pride;
and actual battles fought against external enemies and foreign invaders
to defend the community and to promote justice and liberty. Actual
battles against oppressive enemies are detailed in the Adi Granth since
the time of the first guru, Guru Nanak (1469–1539), who, when
reporting an assault by Babur's Mughal army, cried out to the Creator

INTRODUCTION: EXPLORING RELIGION AND WAR   11

to show humanity to the weak and to his disciples to stand up against tyranny. The *mīrī-pīrī* Sikh philosophy (merging the domains of temporal and spiritual sovereignty) is seeded here. Martyrdom is glorified with restrictions: Only if a warrior dies fighting for heroic values, based on true honor before an immortal lord while meditating selflessly on the divine name, can one be established as a martyr. Guru Arjan (1563–1606) was first in the tradition to be so martyred. His son, Hargobind, established the martial traditions of the Sikhs (incorporating the *mīrī-pīrī* philosophy) and also began a singing tradition of nonviolent protest. But it was Guru Gobind Singh (1666–1708) who began the Khalsa, the order of spiritual warriors, and formally advanced *dharam yudh*, the concept of just war, in the secondary Sikh text known as Dasam Granth. Akal Purakh, the divine lord, came to be identified with the divine sword and was now invoked to intervene in history for just cause. Establishing the Cherished Five youths who "offered their heads" in loyalty to the *panth* and pledging his four sons and forty liberated ones, Gobind Singh inaugurated a sacrificial martyr tradition commemorated in the Ardās, a short liturgical text of prayers that, in part, memorializes those warriors who defended the *gurudwaras* ("gates of the gurus"). The mythology developed around these figures continued into the 1980s, when Sikhs in the Punjab resisted the Indian army in its attack on the Sikh Golden Complex in Amritsar. To this day the Ardās extolls those who epitomize sacrifice and martyrdom.

Chapter 7: *Religion and War in Traditional China*

Barend ter Haar points out that political rule in China was always divinely sanctioned by the Mandate of Heaven, with corresponding titles for the ruler and the ruled. The ruler's role was acknowledged too in ancestor worship and in sacrificial rites at all social levels, from the family to the nation as a whole, for which the sovereign was a figurehead. But this is not to say that there was no resistance to national figureheads, particularly under religious auspices. One famous Daoist rebellion was the Five Pecks of Rice (184–215 CE), which established a theocratic state but gradually lost its innovative character and never imposed its beliefs on its regional population. Nor did most rebellions do this, with the exception of the Heavenly Kingdom of Great Peace, a nineteenth-century rebellion that was Christian-inspired, at least in part. More typical of religious rebellions were China's messianic movements, whether Buddhist or Daoist in orientation, which anticipated approaching disasters and advocated various remedies, from following new saviors to enlisting armies of divine protectors. When actual violence did break out, some rebels doubtlessly conceived of themselves as divine protectors (e.g., the Boxers in 1900) and their enemies (Christian missionaries in the Boxer case) as demons. Extensive rituals helped confer invulnerability on some of these divine warriors. Rituals are in fact one of the most interesting facets of Chinese religiosity through the ages, from early human and animal sacrifices (e.g., among the Shang, ca. 1550–1045 BCE), to consecrating auspicious sites, tools, generals or banners of war with sacrificial blood, to heightening the power of weapons and combatants through various means of divination, such as the use of diagrams, incantations, vapors and protective amulets. There were several localized war deities, such as Chiyou, who bore the hooves of an ox, four eyes, six hands, a human body and occasionally horns and who, despite being a creator of metal weapons, was mostly a figure of chaos. As for just war or antiwar principles, neither of these appears to have been an early concern. Sovereigns could find arguments to support their warlike activities, whether just or not, and Buddhist prohibitions on killing did not seem to interfere with the aims of the state. There are famous examples of warriors who enlisted Buddhist principles to fight ably on the state's behalf, and, in contrast, at least one Buddhist advisor, Fotudeng (310–348 CE), counseled the ruling house to execute certain rogues who were impossible to reform. On the other hand, rituals for restoring good karma for a warrior who had killed might include patronage of temples and burial of enemy war dead.

Chapter 8: *Buddhism and War in Premodern Japan*

Brian A. Victoria sees Japanese Buddhism as linked with state concerns as early as the seventh century, when the Soga clan accepted Buddhist deities as state-empowering figures based on the model of flourishing Korean and Chinese civilizations. Among texts supporting this marriage of Buddhism and the state was the Sutra on the Benevolent King, which promised the protection of 100 deities or demons should a sovereign under foreign threat make 100 images of the Buddha and invite 100 priests to lecture on the Sutra. The older Shinto deities (*kami*) were subordinated to Buddhism by at least as early as the construction of Mahāvairocana's temple in Nara (eighth century), where this "sun Buddha" was symbolically identified with Amaterasu Ōmikiami, sun-goddess and mythical progenitor of the Imperial House. But it was Hachiman, originally a god of war, who most represented this trend of *kami* serving and sometimes merging with Buddhist bodhisattvas. Hachiman's double career as a bodhisattva and *kami*-protector was famously evident in the thirteenth century, when he reputedly sent two kamikaze (e.g., *kami* winds), or typhoons, to destroy the invading Mongol fleets of Kublai Khan. Kamikaze suicide pilots in the Asia–Pacific War invoked him as well, and he remains a popular *kami* of war as well as a Buddhist bodhisattva to this day. Protection was offered too by other bodhisattvas (e.g. Kannon), by buddhas and by emperors who, upon death, strove to become saviors of sentient beings. While divinities might be imagined as supporting the state, the *sōhei*, warrior-monks, actually supported it, as combat warriors in the Heian period in Japan from the eighth century. Competing loyalties among Buddhist sects, differing clan loyalties and the rationale of resorting to violence in order to protect Buddhist *dharma* at temple sites, led to internecine strife among the various sects of warrior-monks by the tenth century and into the twelfth. Late in the twelfth century the larger samurai class seized control of the state, although they were careful to leave the emperor as state figurehead. Instead of conflicts between competing Buddhist temples, there was now conflict between warrior clans, who absorbed different groups of warrior-monks. The Zen sect was introduced to Japan in the late twelfth century and made itself indispensable to warrior-monks by introducing the practice of meditation and the pursuit of *samadhi* (making one's mind one-pointed), which, in effect, freed warriors from moral regret on the battlefield. In addition, the True Pure Land sect, based on different Buddhist principles, cultivated its own fighters from a wide swath of society.

JUST WAR

Chapter 9: *Judaism and the Ethics of War*
Reuven Kimelman
The Bible and rabbinical commentaries continue to influence discussions of Jewish just war. As Reuven Kimelman points out, two biblical categories of mandatory wars – those against the seven Canaanite nations and the one against Amalek – are operationally defunct, given the historical circumstances that vitiated both, although the second continues to inspire thinking about premessianic struggles and metaphoric battles against genocidal evil. Rationales for reactive defensive wars (labeled mandatory) and expansionary wars (classified as discretionary) continue to be argued, as do those for preventative, anticipatory and preemptive wars. Whether preemptive wars can be deemed mandatory or discretionary has been debated since the eleventh century, as have the authorization to declare war, the ethical conduct of

war and exemptions from military service. On preemptive strikes as self-defense, national self-defense is deemed a moral right. Preemptive strikes as anticipatory defense are allowed, provided that the order stems from an accepted authority, such as the Sanhedrin or its judicial equivalent, to which the citizens are bound by a pact of mutuality. Preventative war is to be launched when calculations of victory are weighed against the cost in lives and when it is deemed feasible as a deterrence from future attacks. Rules for a siege include weighing whether a city can be captured without destroying it; whether emissaries of peace have been sent to a hostile city three days in advance; whether negotiations for peace have preceded subjection of a city to hunger, thirst and disease for purposes of exacting a settlement; and even after the siege is laid, no direct cruelties may be inflicted and an escape route must be left open for those who would flee. Excessive military zeal, with its concomitant aimless violence or wanton destruction, is always to be avoided. Much of the discussion about avoiding wanton destruction derives from the biblical prohibition against axing fruit-bearing trees during a siege (Deuteronomy 20:19–20), a seeming mercy that extends to people who, unlike the tree without feet, would flee by foot if given the chance. Hence also the mandate to leave a fourth side of the city open for escape, which of course is practical as well, since a cornered people will desperately seek to avenge themselves before they die. Avoiding brutalization of the enemy also avoids brutalizing the soldier's character, as has been realized since Philo of Alexandria, who warned against slaying the defenseless for its cost on the soul of the soldier. Similarly, the Israeli Defense Force today has upheld the doctrine of purity of arms, which in theory limits killing to necessary and unavoidable situations and safeguards not only the humanity of the enemy, but also the moral stature of the soldier.

Chapter 10: *The Idea of Just War in Christian Thought from the Age of Augustine through the Early Modern Period*

As James Turner Johnson points out, Augustine of Hippo (354–430), widely thought to be the first Christian just war thinker, did not offer a systematic treatment of just war. His brief passages dealing with the topic were not systematized until Gratian in 1149 and his successors in the late twelfth and early thirteenth centuries. It was Thomas Aquinas who, in his 1270s Summa Theologiae, formalized the idea of just war based on three requirements: the sovereign authority of a secular leader; just cause in defense of justice and remediation of injustice; and right intention toward the establishment of peace and against the perpetration of evil. Given these three conditions, killing in war was not always sinful, which Aquinas supported with Paul's letter to the Romans (13.4) attesting that princes were God's ministers and avengers against evil. Canon law from this period also produced notions of noncombatant immunity, the ban on fighting on holy days and the ban on pernicious weapons, which evolved, by the fifteenth century, into a cultural consensus on *jus ad bellum* and *jus in bello*, or when to wage legitimate war and the limits on how to wage it. Complications were further addressed in the modern period. For instance, sixteenth-century Catholic theologian Francisco de Vitoria, responding to reports of the conquest of the New World, asked whether it was licit to baptize children against the wishes of their unbelieving parents. This evolved into questioning whether wars based on religion were ever just and the advocation that, even when not, moderation should always be followed in war (*jus in bello*). The one and only just cause for commencing a war was a wrong received, and never was just war legitimated by the desire to expand empire. Hence, defensive war was legitimate, whether the outrage be on Native Americans resisting Christians or Christians resisting Turks and Saracens. Grotius in the seventeenth century shifted the focus to international wars, with the understanding that all international wars could be understood as just. What made a war just or "solemn" were rites and formalities such as a formal declaration of war, with the publication of just causes by a national sovereign and a formal response from an opposing sovereign. Following the Thirty Years War, much of this was institutionalized in the Peace of Westphalia. During the Reformation, Martin Luther rejected the Catholic doctrine of two swords, one for the Church and one for temporal rulers, and argued for the extension of worldly authority to secular powers only, basing this on God's sanction of human government in the beginning of time. Sin was accrued in war when violence was practiced against the orders of temporal authorities. Calvin, following Augustine, emphasized restraint and humanity in war, even when the cause was just. Contemporary thinking is extraordinarily rich on all these subjects.

Chapter 11: *Islam and the Just War Tradition: Post-Classical Developments*

David Cook begins his treatment of traditions and legal precedents concerning Islamic just war in the tenth to twelfth centuries CE, when prophetic traditions concerning warfare were collected and published as the legal bases for *sharī'a* (law) and used as authoritative bases for practical situations. Prior to this, when the Muslim world had enjoyed an apogee of territorial, cultural and religious influence, Sunni jurists

had formulated their views on sacral warfare from a position divorced
from actual battlefields, looking to the prophetic examples in the
Qur'an and hadith. But now, when threatened on their own frontiers
by non-Muslims, the religious tenor to fighting was heightened, and
these battles became religious conquests. The real test came with the
Christian Crusades, a series of papally initiated invasions targeting the
Levant, southern Italy and Sicily and beginning the Spanish
Reconquista. Initial failure on the Muslim side was seen as due to
insufficient moral character on the part of leaders, until the twelfth-
century successes of Nur al-Din and Saladin, both ostentatiously devout
Sunni Muslims. Crusader encounters also led to questions regarding
tactics: Whereas previously there was a total ban on killing civilians,
burning bodies and other terror tactics, questions now arose about the
legitimacy of the mangonel, a type of catapult delivering a payload of
rocks or other weapons into a city, which allowed for indiscriminate
killing of women, children and unarmed enemies. Jurisprudent Ibn al-
Munāṣif rationalized such tactics as based on the need to terrorize
enemy noncombatants, provided no Muslims were among them. His
views were considerably harsher than those in classical Muslim legal
literature. When the initially non-Muslim Mongols invaded in the thirteenth century, the Turkish Mamluks stood up to defend Islamic territory, and given that the Mongols were superior in number to anything
Muslims had encountered before, new thinking about war was required
again. Before fighting Christians or Crusaders, Mamluks made public
displays of Muslim moral codes, such as prayer and prohibitions on
alcohol. When a number of Muslims ended up fighting on the Mongol
side, it was determined that they were no longer Muslims but apostates,
and so they could be killed. Ibn Taymiyaa, a refugee from the Mongols
to the Mamluks, hardened this position, rationalizing the view that
imposing Sunni Islamic norms on a society constituted a just war.
Martyrdom was a more complicated matter. Because Islam prohibits
suicide in all forms (e.g., Q4:29), intentional death in battle was not
endorsed, except on the rare and contested case of a single fighter
weaking havoc on a much larger group, a situation extrapolated from
the model of the Ismaili assassins. After a time, the ideal of the heroic,
self-sacrificing warrior was replaced by reverence for professionals, such
as engineers and archers and perpetrators of siege warfare.

Chapter 12: *Is There a Hindu Just War?*

Torkel Brekke points out that Indian concepts of war do not comport smoothly with European concepts, wherein the sovereign state is

the primary actor. Within the enormous scope of Hindu literary tradition, two concepts might be deemed key to Hindu understandings of
just war: *dharma* and *artha*. *Dharma*, referring to the right order in
nature and society, may be traced back to the ancient Dharma Sutras
(dated ca. 400–100 BCE), which were designed to convey clear rules
about the rights and obligations of persons according to social class,
age and sex. These discuss, among other things, the duties and rights of
warriors and specifically of kings. For example, we read that a king
should protect subjects and ensure victory in battle, but he should also
avoid killing noncombatants, such as those who have lost their horses
or armor, who flee the battlefield, who have surrendered and who have
gone mad. But it is the beloved epic Mahabharata, an oral poem crystal-
lized about 400 BCE, that has transmitted the key moral quandaries of
warriors through the ages. It asks, for instance, how to justify war
against family members, how a brave warrior should and should not
fight and whether one may use deceit in warfare and under what conditions. Famously in its Bhagavadgita (Song of the Lord), the god Krishna
reveals himself as having become incarnate on Earth to ensure that
dharma prevails in the upcoming war between the Pandava and
Kaurava cousins. He counsels Arjuna, the distraught Pandava assigned
with initiating battle, that it is Arjuna's *dharma* to fight and, among
other things, how to fight without attachment to the fruit of his labor,
with perfect evenness of mind – that is, in the way of *karmayoga*.
Fought in this way, a battle may be seen as a religious duty, a notion
that continues to animate moral and political debate in India to this day.
But it is Book 10, the Massacre by Night, that speaks to the ambivalent
morality of warfare. There, driven by personal anguish and an insup-
pressible desire for vengeance, Ashvatthaman invokes ancient ideals of
artha, of statecraft, to justify attacking the other side by night. The
artha traditions, while sometimes in tension with *dharma*, are in the
main pragmatic and goal-oriented. As seen in the Arthaśāstra, the king
should strive to dominate his enemies by a variety of strategies with no
moral value attached to any of them. A genre of animal fables, such as
the Pancatantra (composed ca. 300 CE), also disseminates *artha*, but in
entertaining and instructive ways. Political thinkers in late colonial
India made great use of these various precedents, as well as the cult of
the Indian Great Goddess, to promote resistance to British Home Rule.

Chapter 13: *Buddhist Just War Traditions*

In search of Buddhist just war theory, Kristin Scheible wades
through the plethora of authoritative sources on Buddhist *dharma*. To

start, conflict informs the personal narrative of Siddhartha Gautama in that his father, king of the Śakyas, anxious that his son should become a temporal rather than spiritual *cakravartin*, prohibited him from experiencing anything that would arouse a desire to find a solution to worldly sufferings, to renounce his comfortable environs and to become an awakened *buddha*. His father's quest failed, and Buddha went on to formulate the four noble truths, which lay out the foundations of suffering and its cure: that life is *duḥkha* (consisting of mental and physical agitation); caused by *tanhā* or *tṛsnā* (craving or thirst); and that a sublime end (*nirvana*) is achievable through the practical eightfold path: right view, right thought, right speech, right action, right livelihood, right efforts, right mindfulness and right concentration. From a Buddhist perspective, *duḥkha* is rampant in *samsāra* (the cycle of birth–life–death–rebirth) and is both the driver and the experience of war, but the ways it is addressed vary according to text, doctrine and even metaphor. One core text, the Dhammapada, wholly rejects violence, as "in this world hostilities are *never* appeased by hostility." Despite Buddhism's pacifistic aspirations, there are problems with imposing absolute categories such as just and unjust war on human experience over the kaleidoscope of multiple lifetimes, where karmic outcomes for violence carry varying weights. Nonetheless, it is a paramount Buddhist doctrine to dissect the root causes of suffering and to study actions and their effects. This includes the study of war, whether as practiced or sanctioned. Of the five Buddhist moral precepts, *ahimsā/avihimsā*, or nonharm, leading to compassion, is foremost, and inevitably it is violated during war. Even the spoken acts of justifying war perpetuate *duḥkha*. And yet metaphors of war penetrate the earliest Buddhist discourses. The Buddha is understood to have *vanquished* defilements and to have earned the title of *Jina*, or conqueror, because he defeated Māra, a grisly antagonist who threatened to derail his awakening and subsequent teaching of the *dharma* to the world. The metaphor of war is enlisted to battle one's own inner demons in the Dhammapada, where winning the inner battle is deemed superior to conquering thousands on a battlefield. At the same time, holding on to inner desires for vengeance is deemed defiling. Violent thought, discourse and action are proscribed as insufficient reasons for *jus ad bellum*. Buddhist *jus in bello* over the ages has included fantastic methods such as tantric war magic and mantras, speech acts that might, for example, freeze hostile armies on the battlefield. Perhaps most compelling, however, is Buddhist *jus post bellum*, which requires concerted efforts to assuage those harmed by war and that fighters perform reparations with good intentions.

RELIGIOUS NATIONALISM

Chapter 14: *War in Religious Zionism*

Robert Eisen points out that the state of Israel has had to grapple with the issue of war since 1947, when the United Nations voted to establish the state. While some Jews deemed this a triumph guaranteeing them a homeland after 2,000 years of exile, it was an affront to the Palestinians who had thrived in the land for centuries, as well as to their Arab neighbors. Three wars followed, resulting in an uneasy tension between Israel and its neighbors, but prodding some Israelis to take stock of traditional sanctions for controlling the land and fighting for it. Despite its biblical name (Zion), modern Zionism began as a staunchly secular movement advocating for a state where Jews could live and flourish without oppression, after the French Revolution failed to guarantee protections for Jewish citizens in Europe. Secular Zionism overall rejected the traditional Jewish belief that Jews would return to their homeland only if they observed God's 613 commandments and awaited a messiah to lead them. As for religious Zionism, two versions can be traced back to the nineteenth century: One (that of Rabbi Isaac Jacob Reines) argued that Jews needed their own state as a refuge from both physical and spiritual dangers; and the other (that of Rabbi Abraham Isaac Kook) argued that the Zionist settlement of the land of Israel would trigger the messianic redemption, when God would send his messiah to bring all Jews home. Initially, religious Zionists distinguished the violence necessary to defend against Palestinian aggression, which they accepted, from the exercise of violence in the service of state-building, which they rejected. After the Six-Day War of 1967, however, Tsevi Yehudah Kook, the son of the aforementioned Rabbi Kook, became certain that a divine impulse lay behind Israeli successes on the battlefield and advocated that the secular Israeli state had now become holy in itself, as were its armies and the battles necessary to extend Jewish geography to the boundaries promised to Abraham in the Bible. Returning territory to those Palestinians who formerly occupied it was seen as untenable, and Jewish settlements were established within the occupied territories, largely sponsored by the Gush Emunim (Bloc of the Faithful), which sought to fulfill Kook's vision. Today, whereas religious Zionists exercise an outsized voice in the political trajectory in Israel, they constitute only 10 percent of the Israeli population, and they have faced mounting opposition from secular Israelis, who fail to see the messianic mission in recent wars and who would trade land for peace in the occupied territories. Further, scholars who plumb the biblical and later Jewish traditions for lessons regarding war and prophecy find a great many contextual nuances that diminish the urgency to any messianic hopes.

Chapter 15: *Christian Nationalism and Millennialism in the USA*

Angela M. Lahr traces American millennial hopes from the American Revolution through today. Christian eschatological dreams, whether for the promised 1,000 years of peace or for a cataclysmic end of times, have infused the USA's self-conceptions since its beginnings. At the time of the American Revolution, postmillennialist thinking (e.g., that a 1,000-year perfection of society in the New World would bring about Christ's return) combined with nationalist rhetoric about American exceptionalism, to promote the idea that America was destined for greatness, was God's glorious Church on Earth. This notion of "manifest destiny" shifted during the Civil War, but Americans on both sides of that war continued to insist that their side alone was the proper guardian of this destined glory. The Battle Hymn of the Republic captures this millennial hope, as well as its militancy, in prophesying the "glory of the coming of the Lord" who "hath loosed the fateful lightning of his terrible swift sword." Newly emancipated African Americans saw the millennial significance of the war a bit differently: Despite lingering White resistance, they highlighted freedom tropes from the biblical Day of Jubilees and saw their emancipation as proof that they had a role to play in God's ultimate plan. Native Americans too syncretized Christian prophetic convictions with their own, leading to the tragic Ghost Dance massacre of 1880. At the start of World War I, President Wilson portrayed the USA's adoption of neutrality as a model of liberty for the rest of the world, but when the USA finally joined the Allies in 1917, its role was seen as pivotal in having saved the world when the war ended in 1918. Whereas recognition of the atrocities of World War II forced upon the US a sober dose of realism, the establishment of the United Nations revitalized a sense of millennial mission for those who lauded the American "way of life" against the "godless" communists. This implicit battle was highlighted in the Cold War rhetoric of Protestant premillennialists, who interpreted II Peter 3:10 ("the heavens shall pass away with a great noise . . .") as speaking to the nuclear threat as a fulfillment of prophecy and a warning to those who had strayed from the divine path. When Israel was established as a nation in 1948, dispensational premillennialists – those who saw a divine timeline of successive ages ending with a seven-year tribulation before Christ returned – interpreted the establishment of Israel as fulfilling the Christian mission. Whereas earlier Christian millennialists emphasized the USA as the new Israel covenanted by God, Christian Zionists now looked to the state of Israel as the sacred locus for Christ's return. As seen too in the Cuban Missile Crisis and subsequently, millennialist-inspired Christian thinking continued to offer models for US self-understanding.

Chapter 16: *The Elusive Dream of Pan-Islamism*

Mohammed M. Hafez points out that the dream of pan-Islamic solidarity has inspired Muslim reformers since the 1880s, when Muslim leaders confronting orientalism, imperialism and colonialism sought to modernize their collective Islamic identity and to defend against Western cultural encroachment. Due in part to governmental instabilities, factionalism and economic injustices, this pan-Islamic nationalist movement largely failed, which opened the door to a different kind of pan-Islamic movement, starting conspicuously in 1979, when the Iranian Revolution gave voice to an oppressed minority who saw itself as the righteous challenger of a secular and authoritarian regime. Around the same time, the Soviet invasion of Afghanistan inspired transnational fighters to join in the Afghan *jihād* against communist occupiers. Islamist movements since have been inspired by this victorious struggle, but none have been particularly successful in establishing pan-Islamism, given their propensity for "[s]sectarian fragmentation, factional infighting, and ideological hairsplitting." Islamists as a whole may be divided into three groups: political Islamists, who seek to influence state institutions through electoral politics and civic engagement; revolutionary Islamists, who seek to replace existing secular nations with Islamic ones; and transnational jihadism, which seeks to attack enemies from afar and institute a global Islamic caliphate. Of this last group, Jihadi Salafists aspire to the fabled golden age of the first three generations of Muslims, conceived as having created a utopian state extending beyond the Arabian Peninsula. Therein Islamic law (*sharī'a*) guaranteed justice and fairness for all, and erudite Islamic scholars gathered hadith traditions for posterity. Several key notions inspire Jihadi Salafists today. First are *tawhid* and *hakimyat Allah*: the oneness of God, or Allah, who alone can define right and wrong, good and evil, etc. Secular authorities cannot. Another is *takfir*, which controversially entitles Salafist Muslims to declare other Muslims, both individuals and communities, unbelievers, and so to expel them from the Islamic *ummah*. Related, *al-Wala' A-Bara'* is a matter of showing devotion to the Salafist worldview to the extent of disavowing unbelievers and impious family members. Next is *jihād* which, rather than an internal spiritual struggle to submit to God, in this context is equated to a military mandate to capture lands that once lay within the abode of Islam. Then, *istishhad*, or martyrdom, is a euphemistic title for those who commit suicide attacks in the name of Islam, despite the clear Quranic prohibition on suicide. This euphemistic title enables Jihadi Salafists to align their own suicide missions with those of the early companions of the Prophet who reputedly charged into battle to hasten their own demise. Last is the *Al-Ta'ifa al-Mansoura*, or Victorious Sect, a prophesized group of warriors who, because of their adherence to all the notions above, will be able to establish the Islamic caliphate on Earth.

Chapter 17: *Killing for the Hindu Nation: Hindu Nationalism and Its Violent Excesses*

Kathinka Frøystad begins with the 2019 musical call to "send to the graveyard" anyone who does not believe in Lord Ram, a message resonant with calls for Muslims to leave India or face the graveyard during the Ayodhya Mosque controversy in the 1990s. Although Hindu nationalist fervor has gripped India since the 2014 election, its roots stem back to British colonialism in the 1800s. Whereas some Indians had embraced British opportunities, resentment against colonial influence arose in the shape of religious reform movements in Kolkata, Mumbai and Chennai. Most consequential of these were the Brahmo Samaj (since 1828) and the Arya Samaj (since 1875), who revered Hinduism's Vedic past and promoted Hindu identity over sectarian and caste differences. As the independence movement against the British matured in the early twentieth century, fissures emerged regarding methods of resistance (violent or passive?) and religious affiliations (what to do about the 22 percent Muslim minority?). After a scarring civil war in 1947, British India divided into Muslim-majority provinces in the west and east and what is presently twenty-nine Indian states and seven territories in the middle of the subcontinent extending to the southern tip. The partition neither solved ethnic tensions nor eradicated painful memories, although India's first prime minister, Jawajarlal Nehru, and his Congress Party did advance a form of civic nationalism that promoted "unity in diversity" and religious freedom for all. In 1985, the Congress Party's religious plurality laws (different legal systems per religious population) were challenged when the elderly Shah Bano was declared eligible to receive support from her separated husband. This privilege alienated conservative Muslims fearing for their religious autonomy. The Congress Party responded by enacting a new law that absolved Muslim husbands from spousal support after a two-year waiting period, which then drew criticism from Hindu nationalists who saw it as supporting religious plurality in the face of questionable outcomes for women. Also in the 1980s, a Hindu nationalist uprising was kindled around the Muslim mosque in Ayodhya, a site claimed by the Hindu majority as the birthplace of the god Ram. Mob violence resulted in the demolition of the 250-year-old mosque and in anti-Muslim riots that killed approximately 2,000 people in 1992. Stereotypes about Muslims as rapacious vestiges of the Mughal Empire were rife in the decades preceding 2014, when the Bharatiya Janata Party won control of Congress on a platform of Hindu *rashtra* and strove to transform India into a Hindu state with identitarian sensibilities. There is little uniformity among the myriad organizations and personalities that have shaped these sensibilities, but Hindu nationalism generally may be said to express fear of a diluted cultural identity in the face of changing demographics and phantasmagorical rumors of past religious crimes.

Chapter 18: *Nationalism, Violence, and War in Myanmar's* Theravāda *Buddhist Context*

Matthew J. Walton begins his chapter by distinguishing our contemporary concept of nation from the Buddhist premodern notion of the *sāsana*, which in theory potentially includes all Buddhists and is not temporally anchored to the present. Despite its apparent timelessness, the *sāsana* itself is considered subject to impermanence. As Walton puts it, while the *sāsana* reflects what are understood to be "ultimate and abiding truths of existence, the awareness of those truths is predicated on the emergence of a Buddha who can discover and reveal them, which happens in a recurring cycle, but necessarily implies that there will be periods of ignorance regarding these truths, where *sāsana* ceases to exist, or exists only as potentiality." This impermanence and the anticipation of a Buddha have injected what might be called an anxiety into Buddhist interactions with premodern as well as contemporary polities: The *sāsana* conscientiously attempts to embody Buddhist truths in order to extend the *sāsana's* existence until a new Buddha emerges. These underlying cosmological notions complicate the way the *sāsana* has interacted with politics. For instance, Theravādan Buddhist tropes of purifying or defending the *sāsana* were used to justify royal conquests, defensive wars and internal struggles before the emergence of states in Southeast Asia. Today, Myanmar's contemporary and protracted civil war is often framed in terms of ethnic divisions, but a shared Buddhist identity underlies the conflict between some of these competing ethnic groups. The same identity is invoked by the military in its violent campaign to protect and purify the Buddhist *sāsana* ostensibly against communists and other leftists. Protection of the *sāsana* is invoked also by the Ma Ba Tha group in Myanmar in its claim to "protect race and religion" from Rohingya Muslims in the Rakhine state, although different arms of the Ma Ba Tha vary in the degree to which they recognize the historical role of Rakhines in defending Myanmar's western border. In 2021, Myanmar underwent a military coup that led to widespread protests and the development of underground resistance groups, whom the military, claiming the mantle of *sāsana*-protectors, charged with killing monks, being closet Muslims and striving to undercut the Buddhist nature of the nation. Despite the military's apparent Buddhist mantle, opposition to the military has ignited criticism of Myanmar's anti-Muslim policies and even self-criticism on the part of Burman Buddhists who apologize for the persecutions of the Rohingya over the last decade. Today, while the *sāsana* is unlikely to dissipate as part of Myanmar's Buddhist identity, the *sāsana* is also intersecting with ethnic and other identities and so is, once again, shifting in shape and impermanent in essence.

FEATURED CONFLICTS

Chapter 19: *Christian Crusading, Ritual, and Liturgy*

M. Cecilia Gaposchkin describes the ritualistic, liturgical and theological foundations for Christian crusading from the time of the First Crusade, which began badly but was revitalized when Christian supplicants circled the city of Jerusalem, chanting and beseeching God for forgiveness of sins and gifts of worldly needs and heavenly salvation. This circumambulation replicated holy models such as that of Joshua (e.g., at Jericho) and included visits to holy sites around the city, likely concluding with the well-known petition to destroy pagan peoples and to humiliate enemies of the church. The Franks attributed their success in 1099 directly to God, who had responded to their petitions to help them achieve victory on Earth, a moment commemorated in the liturgical calendar as the liberation-feast of Jerusalem. The First Crusade was saturated with rituals and devotions to expiate sin, understood as the reason for failure, and also with anticipations of the Second Coming, when the holy city would become the site for Christ's return. For more than four centuries afterward, Christians conceived of the Crusades as holy wars fought for religious reasons, against religious enemies far and near, on the authority of the pope and earning religious merit for those who fought in the army of the Cross. Merit was earned against enemies who were construed as both the devil in an eschatological battle and as the devil's minions on Earth. A number of liturgical rituals – prayers, blessings, ablutions – were conceived as expiating sin and as inaugurating the holy mission, but the eucharistic mass was especially salient: In effect, it collapsed space and time, brought the penitent community into contact with heaven and endowed battles with a sacramental register. Other rituals conferred the status of pilgrim on crusaders, those rituals including priestly blessings on the scrip and walking staff, on the sword and especially on the cross, which invoked Christ's suffering and passion ("take up the Cross and follow me" [Mt 16.25]) and anticipated Christ's triumph at the end of time. Over time, ritual blessings of a new knight, whether for Crusading or other types of warfare, grew increasingly elaborate (sacralizing the sword, shield, breastplate, spurs, battle standard), and these rituals, especially sacralizing the sword, not only constructed knighthood as a devotional ideal, but also endowed the knight with a means of enforcing God's justice on Earth, on behalf of women and orphans, amongst others. In 1187, individual blessings gave way to collective ones, when the loss of the Holy Cross on the battlefield was understood to signify collective Christian unworthiness. Then special prayers, including a clamor during mass (see Psalm 78), begged God to aid his Christian army, and similar prayers and penitential processions became "invisible weapons" to safeguard the people against variously construed agents of the end-times.

Chapter 20: *A Paradigm of Righteous* Jihād *in the Muslim Ethos*

Osman Latiff points out the inner quality of Muslim piety that is to culminate in closeness to God. According to the Qur'ān, one's *nafs* (inner self) is understood both to resonate with pietistic urges as well as potentially to undercut these, and therefore one's inner *nafs* must be cultivated. Consciousness of God is especially to be cultivated in times of *jihād*, such as at the Battle of Badr, a paradigmatic battle in which believers, nearly overwhelmed by a larger and better-equipped enemy, remembered God in the course of battle and thereby triumphed over not only unbelievers but their inner selves. On this inner battle, the Prophet is reported to have said, "The *mujāhid* is he who struggles against himself in obedience to God" (al-Albānī 1985: 2:81). Subsequent reports emphasized this inner "spiritual armament" as a pious means of invoking divine assistance and, should fighters doubt this assistance, they were assured that battlefield martyrs were not really dead, but alive in a way fighters did not perceive. *Jihād* against the Franks was especially saturated with piety in the form of poetry, which was more than a rousing literary vehicle for fighters at key historical moments. It was also a political commentary integral to reinforcing Islam's destinations, enemies and champions, and it could function both to adulate and to critique. During a time when Sufism was flourishing, Nūr al-Dīn Zengī was thought to have united pietistic concern with military struggle for his entourage of holy warriors, but he was poetically censured for misappropriating taxes and for overlooking his army's displays of religious negligence, such as enjoying wine and music. Salāh al-Dīn, by all accounts a successful military leader, endeavored to memorize inspirational religious texts, but he too was poetically censured for not considering the consequences of his actions in light of the hereafter. Poetry could thus be a boon and a weapon both. That the Sufis enjoyed a special place in this poetics of adulation and critique is evident when Nūr al-Dīn was advised to cease supporting the Sufis (and others) by stipend in favor of the army, but he retorted that the first group fought for him in their sleep, whereas the second fought by arrow only when he was awake and watching (paraphrasing). The point was clear: The spiritual ethos of *jihād* could not be forfeited in favor strictly of the military. This ethos related not only to boosting the "spiritual armament" of fighters in battle, but also to showing penitence when a population was felt to be lacking divine succor, as when the population of Damascus wept, sprinkled their heads with ashes and humbled themselves during the Second Crusade. God is reported to have heard their prayers and rewarded their humility.

Chapter 21: *Fierce Goddesses of India: Durga and Kali*

June McDaniel points out that, although Indian warriors through the centuries were largely male, the great deities of war were female. While both are fearsome, Durga and Kali have unique domains of violent protection, and they also vary in their iconography and mythology. Durga, a warrior goddess whose name means "beyond defeat," is pictured slaying a buffalo by as early as the fourth century CE. She comes into her own in the Devi Mahatmya, where she acts as a created being granted power to defeat a demon who could never be killed by a man, and also as Prakriti, a primordial, creative force stronger than the inert Purusha: "She creates this entire universe, both moving and unmoving ... when propitious, becomes a boongiver to human beings for the final liberation ... the sovereign over all lords." She emanates other goddesses, such as the fierce *matrikas* or Mothers, and they collectively defeat demon armies. Once having saved the world and absorbed her mother goddesses back into herself, she promised followers to incarnate when necessary, offering protection and destruction of foes in response to the prayers of her devotees, and finally to destroy the world at the end of the age. Durga's worship in India is vast, representing primarily the power of good over evil, of virtue over lust, but she has lingered too as a goddess of war, presiding over military activities until Indian independence. Today she is invoked for conflicts of all sorts, against pollution, against sexual crimes, against foreign invaders who would occupy Mother India and in service of religious nationalists. Kali, on the other hand, has tended to flourish in regional contexts, and to have various virtues and domains of power. She figures as an ancestress, a tantric goddess and a protective mother as well as a goddess of death and destruction. She appears in ancient Vedic texts as negative and devouring, if not of demons, then of humans. She is sometimes an emanation from Durga, sometimes a manifestation of Shiva's consort, Parvati. Her older appearance is generally fearsome, with her necklace of skulls, her blood-red eyes and hair matted with snakes, and she is depicted as mounting Shiva's corpse in reverse intercourse. She roars. While she traditionally threatens earthly stability, she also represents a transcendent order, however morally ambiguous. To her devotees, she is lovely and will appear to you when you die, taking you to dwell forever on her lap in her special heaven, which incidentally is only open to those in female form. To the modern *bhakti* poets this lovely form is the real one, and death under her auspices is gratifying. But for her enemies she is the black Kali who will drink your blood at the burning ground.

Chapter 22: *The Demonological Framework of the Heavenly Kingdom of Great Peace*

Barend ter Haar points out that the nineteenth-century Taiping Rebellion in China, or Heavenly Kingdom of Great Peace, was one of the most violent events in human history, with victims ranging in number from 20 to 70 million out of an estimated population of 400–450 million. Active initially in the southern province of Guangdong, the movement was grounded in a complex mix of Protestant Christianity, the visions of one Hong Xiuquan – a self-proclaimed Younger Brother of Jesus, of Hakka provenance – and traditional hopes for an All-Under-Heaven world as

understood by most Chinese at the time, with that world being permeated
by Confucian and Buddhist beliefs. One of the most interesting features of
the movement was its anticipation of an imminent apocalypse caused by
the world's moral decline. In an effort to cleanse the world, Heavenly
Kingdom armies attacked preexisting icons of ancestral and Confucian
cults, which they saw as representing demons, and eventually extended
their demonological targets to local enemies in Guangxi and then to the
Manchus who ruled the empire from Beijing. Inspired by dreams and
visions and fueled by ritual exorcisms and mystical encounters with
auspicious persons (such as Heavenly Father, an old man with a golden
beard, and Elder Brother, or Jesus), Hong Xiuquan produced poems and a
prophecy inducing followers to throw away statutes of deities and
Confucian tablets. Based on his iconoclasm and a preexisting demonological cultural current, he drew followers who were even more inspired,
such as one Xiao Chaogui, who seems to have acclimated the visions to a
more Chinese context. Hence the Heavenly Father merged into the Jade
Emperor and was in charge of punishing humans for their moral decline,
while mediumistic healers mimicked not only Jesus but also indigenous
healers. Nonetheless, the Old Testament's dire genocides and warnings fit
well with the demonological worldview of traditional Chinese culture at
the time and provided prototypes for conflicts between ethnic groups.
Drawing from what were perceived as Christian narratives, there was a
focus on willing self-sacrifice and aspirations for ascent to heaven after
dying in meritorious battle. This was not only a war of visions, though.
Through violent conflict, Heavenly Kingdom supporters managed to
extend their territory from Guangdong into Hunan and Jinagxi and to
conquer the city of Nanjing, which they made their Heavenly Capital.
The movement's success was relatively short-lived, as it was born in
1851 and exterminated by the Qing government in 1864. While some
Christians have extolled the movement as indicating the potential
Christianization of China, scholars grounded in traditional Chinese
thinking have tended to see the movement instead as a combustion of
traditional Chinese utopian hopes with an opportunistic reading of
Christian narratives. The movement is notable not only for its
iconoclasm and traditional demonology, but for the way it harnessed
ethnic tensions, as between the Hakka and the Punti.

Chapter 23: *War Outside the State: Religious Communities,
Martiality, and State Formation in Early Modern South Asia*

Anne Murphy begins by dispelling the notion that war must be
associated with states, as many conflicts in Indian history have

involved diverse kinds of nonstate actors. She focuses on the martial landscape of the Mughal Empire (1526–1858), beginning by stressing that the "system of layered sovereignty allowed for martial action and participation by religious communities in complex ways that elude modern notions of all-encompassing power of the state and its monopolization of violence." In the military labor market of the sixteenth to eighteenth centuries, unique martial religious communities emerged, some involving peasantry, but some also involving persons from ascetic communities, such as from the early Sikh Khalsa and the Vaishnava and Śaivite religious orders. Since both ascetics and soldiers require rigorous self-discipline and training in facing adversity, it is not surprising that ascetics might be harnessed for military pursuits, as we see in the Mahābhārata and Kautilya's Arthaśāstra. The chapter points out that ascetics had a reputation for being useful to the state in a variety of roles, including as spies and assassins. In the seventeenth and eighteenth centuries, thousands of *nāgā sannyāsīs*, or "naked ascetics," were famed as mercenaries and comprised consolidated military units who later became wealthy bankers and traders, dispelling the notion that the religious sphere was by definition antithetical to the commercial or any other. Similarly, "Sword and Scripture" married well together in traditions that became associated with *bhakti*, or devotional sects; martial asceticism and *bhakti* were not seen by the *nāgās* as inherently contradictory. Thus, a wide range of theological and communitarian commitments may be found among martial communities, including among Muslims, who in the seventeenth century were very similar to *sannyāsīs* and joined with them in martial endeavors. There were other alliances, if not always formal. Inscriptional evidence shows that Śaiva leaders participated in martial pursuits in conjunction with state interests, and Śaiva rites that conferred Śiva's agency on gurus also conferred the numen of royalty. Sufi charismatic leaders too shared symbolic and linguistic vocabularies with courtly powers, being part of a "wider literary and cultural ecumene in which kings and saints shared centre-stage together" (Green 2006: 28). Sikhs too during the Mughal period were not world-denying ascetic warriors but rather negotiated household sovereignty, community obligations and renouncer traditions. The fusion of state and religious interests was pervasive during the Mughal period until the onset of British rule. In sum, "[w]ar was, ... religious business for many in early modern South Asia, and we see synergies in broad terms between the religious and the political, in various kinds of relationships to state sovereignty."

References

Afsaruddin, Asma. 2012. "In Defense of All Houses of Worship? Jihad in the Context of Interfaith Relations." In *Just Wars, Holy Wars, and Jihads: Christian, Jewish and Muslim Encounters and Exchanges*. Edited by Sohail H. Hashmi. Oxford University Press. 47–68.

al-Albānī, Muḥammad. 1985. *Silsilat al-aḥādīth al-ṣaḥīḥa*. Mu'assasat al-Kutub al-Thaqāfiyya.

Bahrani, Zeinab. 2008. *Rituals of War: The Body and Violence in Mesopotamia*. Zone Books.

Ballentine, Deborah Scoggins. 2015. "The Conflict Topos in Extant Narratives." In *The Conflict Myth and the Biblical Tradition*. Oxford Scholarship Online. 1–76.

Barkun, Michael. 2013. *A Culture of Conspiracy: Apocalyptic Visions in Contemporary America*. University of California Press.

Brekke, Torkel. 2005. "Between Prudence and Heroism: Ethics of War in the Hindu Tradition." In *The Ethics of War in Asian Civilizations*. Edited by Torkel Brekke. Routledge. 113–147.

Collins, John J. 2003. "From Prophecy to Apocalypticism: The Expectation of the End." In *The Continuum History of Apocalypticism*. Edited by John J. Collins, Bernard McGinn and Stephen J. Stein. Continuum. 64–89.

2007. "Apocalyptic Eschatology in the Ancient World." In *The Oxford Handbook of Eschatology*. Edited by Jerry Walls. Oxford University Press. 40–55.

Cook, David. 2012. "Fighting to Create the Just State: Apocalypticism in Radical Muslim Discourse." In *Just Wars, Holy Wars, and Jihads: Christian, Jewish and Muslim Encounters and Exchanges*. Edited by Soheil H. Hashmi. Oxford University Press. 364–382.

Eisen, Robert. 2011. *The Peace and Violence of Judaism, from the Bible to Modern Zionism*. Oxford University Press.

Filiu, Jean-Pierre. 2011. *Apocalypse in Islam*. University of California Press.

Fishbane, Michael. 2004. *Biblical Myth and Rabbinic Mythmaking*. Oxford University Press.

Frydenlund, Iselin. 2017. "Buddhist Militarism Beyond Texts." *Journal of Religion and Violence* 5(1): 27–47.

Gaposchkin, M. Cecilia. 2017. *Invisible Weapons: Liturgy and the Making of Crusade Ideology*. Cornell University Press.

Gorski, Philip S. 2010. *Civil Religion Today (ARDA Guiding Paper Series)*. Association of Religion Data Archives at The Pennsylvania State University, from www.thearda.com/rrh/papers/guidingpapers.asp

Gorski, Philip S. and Samuel L. Perry. 2022. *The Flag and the Cross: White Christian Nationalism and the Threat to American Democracy*. Oxford Scholarship Online.

Graziano, Frank. 1999. *The Millennial New World*. Oxford University Press.

Green, Nile. 2006. *Indian Sufism since the Seventeenth Century: Saints, Books and Empires in the Muslim Deccan*. Routledge.

Hashmi, Soheil H. and James Turner Johnson. 2012. "Introduction." In *Just Wars, Holy Wars, and Jihads: Christian, Jewish and Muslim Encounters and Exchanges*. Edited by Soheil H. Hashmi. Oxford University Press. 3–22.

Hassner, Ron E. 2012. "Conflicts over Sacred Ground." *Oxford Handbook of Religion and Violence*. Edited by Mark Juergensmeyer, Margo Kitts and Michael Jerryson. Oxford University Press. 324–331.

2016. *Religion on the Battlefield*. Cornell University Press.

Heesterman, Jan. 1993. *The Broken World of Sacrifice: An Essay in Ancient Indian Ritual*. University of Chicago Press.

Hegghammer, Thomas. 2017. *Jihadi Culture: The Art and Social Practices of Muslim Militants*. Cambridge University Press.

Housely, Norman. 2008. *Religious Warfare in Europe 1400–1536*. Oxford University Press.

Jaffrelot, Christophe, ed. 2007. *Hindu Nationalism: A Reader*. Princeton University Press.

Johnson, William J. trans. 1998. *The Sauptikaparvan of the Mahabharata: The Battle by Night*. Oxford University Press.

Juergensmeyer, Mark. 2008. *Global Rebellion: Religious Challenges to the Secular State, from Christian Militias to Al Qaeda*. University of California Press.

2016. "Cosmic War." In *Oxford Research Encyclopedia of Religion*. Available at https://doi.org/10.1093/acrefore/9780199340378.013.65

Kitts, Margo. 2010. "The Last Night: Ritualized Violence and the Last Instructions of 9/11." *Journal of Religion* 90: 283–312.

2013. "The Near Eastern *Chaoskampf* in the River-Battle of Iliad 21." *Journal of Ancient Near Eastern Religions* 13(1): 86–112.

2017. "Ancient Near Eastern Perspectives on Evil and Terror." In *Cambridge Companion to The Problem of Evil*. Edited by Chad Meister and Paul Moser. Cambridge University Press. 165–192.

2018. *Cambridge Elements of Ritual and Violence*. Cambridge University Press.

2022. *Sacrifice: Themes, Theories, and Controversies*. Cambridge University Press.

Lahr, Angela. 2007. *Millennial Dreams and Apocalyptic Nightmares: The Cold War Origins of Political Evangelism*. Oxford University Press.

Riley-Smith, Jonathan. 1997. "State of Mind of Crusaders to the East 1098–1300." In *Oxford Illustrated History of the Crusades*. Edited by Riley Smith. Oxford University Press. 66–90.

Schwemer, Daniel. 2007. "The Storm God of the Ancient Near East, Part I." *Journal of Ancient Near Eastern Religions* 7(2): 121–168.

2008. "The Storm God of the Ancient Near East, Part II." *Journal of Ancient Near Eastern Religions* 8(1): 1–44.

Sells, Michael 2003. "Crosses of Blood: Sacred Space, Religion, and Violence in Bosnia-Hercegovina." *Sociology of Religion* 64(3): 309–331.

Sinclair, Iain. 2014. "War Magic and Just War in Indian Tantric Buddhism." *Social Analysis* 58(1): 149–166.

Van der Veer, Peter. 1996. "Riots and Rituals: The Construction of Violence and Public Space in Hindu Nationalism." In *Riots and Pogroms*. Edited by Paul R. Brass. New York University Press. 154–176.

Von Rad, Gerhard. 1991 [1958]. *Holy War in Ancient Israel*. Trans. Marva J. Dawn. Eerdmans.

Wyatt, Nicholas. 2005. *Mythic Mind: Essays on Cosmology and Religion in Ugaritic and Old Testament Literature.* Equinox.

Yates, Robin. 2003. "Human Sacrifice and the Rituals of War in Early China." *Sacrifices humains: Perspectives croisées et représentations* [online]. University Press of Liege. https://doi.org/10.4000/books.pulg.8173.

Electronic Sites

http://oi.uchicago.edu/OI/IRAQ/dbfiles/objects/1321.htm
http://oi.uchicago.edu/OI/IRAQ/dbfiles/objects/1277.htm
http://oi.uchicago.edu/OI/IRAQ/dbfiles/objects/1065.ht

Part I

Classical Foundations

1 Biblical Paradigms of War in History and Eschatology

JOHN J. COLLINS

War, in the Bible as in life, is a complex and variegated phenomenon. When the Song of the Sea in Exodus 15 celebrates YHWH, the God of Israel, as "a man of war," the context suggests wars of liberation. YHWH has just brought the Israelites out of slavery in Egypt and, at least symbolically, overthrown the Pharaoh. Another celebrated war of liberation would be waged by the Maccabees at the end of the biblical period. In these contexts, it is possible to celebrate the violence as morally justified, even by modern standards. Other cases are more problematic, and none more so than the command to utterly destroy the Canaanites in Deuteronomy 7:1–6 and its implementation in the Book of Joshua (Dawkins 2006: 247; Dawkins indicts the morality of the Bible, especially that of the Old Testament or Hebrew Bible, as "obnoxious," 2006: 237).

THE CONQUEST OF CANAAN

The command is stark:

> When the Lord your God brings you into the land that you are about to enter and occupy, and he clears away many nations before you ... and when the Lord your God gives them over to you and you defeat them, then you must utterly destroy them. Make no covenant with them and show them no mercy ... For you are a people holy to the Lord your God.
>
> (Deut 7:1–6)

According to Joshua 11:16–23:

> Joshua took all that land: the hill country and all the Negeb and all the land of Goshen and the lowland and the Arabah and the hill country of Israel and its lowland, from Mount Halak, which rises toward Seir, as far as Baal-gad in the valley of Lebanon below Mount Hermon ... So Joshua took the whole land, according to all

that the Lord had spoken to Moses; and Joshua gave it for an inheritance to Israel ...

While there are some qualifications – most notably in Judges 1 – that indicate that the extermination of the indigenous people was not complete, the account in Joshua stands as the primary biblical account of how Israel came to be in possession of the land: by violent military conquest.

The account of the conquest is not condemned as violent in the biblical record. It is not labeled as "violent" in the sense that violence is associated with oppression or wrongdoing. Matthew Lynch notes that "we must reckon with the fact that calling these acts 'violent' involves the use of a non-indigenous evaluative category. The writers of Joshua never refer to the 'ban' or the conquest as 'violent' and do not seem to present the conquest in these negatively charged terms" (Lynch 2020: 9). In the history of interpretation, misgivings on ethical grounds were routinely dismissed. John Calvin famously wrote in his commentary on Joshua: "When it is added that God so commanded, there is no more ground for obloquy against him than there is against those who pronounce sentence on criminals" (Calvin 1949: 163). It is only in recent years that scholars have come to view this dispossessing of another people as a crime (Whitelam 1996) and to speak of this conquest as genocide and see it as comparable, in intention if not in scope, with some of the horrific genocidal acts of modern times (Seibert 2012: 95–112; Lemos 2015). Critics have also become acutely conscious of the discrepancy between this campaign of extermination and other, humanitarian values in the Bible, even in the Book of Deuteronomy (Collins 2015a: 183–97).

Violent conquest was not exceptional in the ancient world. On the contrary, it was the norm. Israelites were more often the victims than the perpetrators, especially at the hands of the Assyrians and Babylonians. Powerful kings conquered weaker ones because they could, to satisfy their greed for plunder. But no one admitted to such base motives. Rather, in the words of Carly Crouch, "war is a mutual obligation of both the divine and the human king; the requirement that they go to war ... is perceived as an inherent function of the kingship embodied by each" (Crouch 2009: 25). Crouch emphasizes that the idea of a divine warrior "inherently implies a synchronized historical human agent" (Crouch 2009: 26). Appeals to a warrior god may be intended to relieve human actors of responsibility, but warfare is inevitably a human activity, regardless of how it is rationalized.

Crouch has emphasized the importance of the mythology of cosmic conflict as the background for the ancient Near Eastern, and specifically the Assyrian, royal ideology:

> [T]he articulation of the Assyrian military endeavour in terms of and as part of a cosmological struggle for order and against chaos, in which the gods themselves were involved on both a cosmic and historical plane, was fundamental in framing the Assyrian imperial and military project.
>
> (Crouch 2009: 27; compare Otto 1996: 53–4)

The enemies of Assyria were the enemies of its gods. To attack and defeat them was not only permissible, but a moral imperative. What was at stake was the preservation of right order in the world. Similar ideas can be documented for ancient Egypt (Otto 1996: 50–2). This was also true in Israel. The Song of the Sea in Exodus 15, the original proclamation of YHWH as a warrior, has distinct echoes of Canaanite myth (Cross 1973: 112–44). Presumably, the authors of Deuteronomy and Joshua also assumed that the enemies of Israel were the enemies of its God and therefore the enemies of true cosmic order.

In the case of Assyria, the religious justification of war provides only a thin veneer of covering for the exercise of power in the service of greed. The case of Israel is more complex, simply because the Israelites seldom if ever had the requisite power to conquer their neighbors. Moreover, it now appears that the account of violent conquest in the time of Joshua is largely if not entirely fictional (Finkelstein and Silberman 2001: 72–96; Dever 2003: 227–8, 2017: 187–8). In the mid-20th century there was a sustained attempt by archeologists to verify the destruction wrought by Joshua, but the project backfired. The showpiece of the conquest story was the capture of Jericho, where the walls allegedly came tumbling down. Kathleen Kenyon showed that there was no evidence of a town at Jericho in the Late Bronze Age (1500–1400 BCE) and scant evidence of occupation in the following centuries (Kenyon 1957; for a summary, see Moorey 1991: 94–9). There had only been a small, unwalled settlement at Jericho in the time of the supposed conquest. The neighboring site of Ai, also supposedly destroyed by Joshua, had been uninhabited for about 1,000 years. Of nearly twenty identifiable sites that were captured by Joshua or his successors according to the biblical account, only two, Hazor and Bethel, were destroyed in the appropriate period. Even in those cases there is no direct evidence that the destruction was caused by the Israelites. (The Philistines were moving into the coastal area of Palestine around the same time.) Hazor is also problematic because, although we are told that Joshua destroyed it, it still appears to be in Canaanite hands in the Book of Judges. Consequently, at the present time there is a consensus that the account of the conquest in the Book of Joshua is largely if not entirely fictitious. In the words of the archeologist William Dever: "There is little we can salvage from Joshua's stories of the rapid, wholesale destruction of Canaanite cities and the annihilation of the local population. It simply did not happen; the archeological evidence is indisputable" (Dever 2003: 227–8; see further Collins 2005: 41).

Some scholars actually greeted this finding with relief, since it meant that the ancient Israelites could not be charged with genocide (Bernat and Klawans 2007: 7–10), but the problems of the text remain. As James Barr astutely remarked: "[T]he problem is not whether the narratives are fact or fiction, the problem is that, whether fact or fiction, the ritual destruction is *commended*" (Barr 1993: 209, emphasis in original). Most immediately, the question arises as to why someone would have invented such an account.

Many theologically interested scholars have argued that the story represents divine judgment on the Canaanites. John Calvin argued that it was because the wickedness of the Canaanites had reached its height that God had determined to destroy them (Calvin 1949: 174). The claim is often echoed in modern scholarship. George Ernest Wright claimed that "the Canaanite civilization and religion was one of the weakest, most decadent, and most immoral cultures of the civilized world at that time" (Wright 1960: 109). The actual evidence for the wickedness of the Canaanites consists of a few passing comments in biblical texts (Gen 15:13–16; Deut 9:5). Gary Anderson takes the story as an illustration of the logic of the covenant. In Deuteronomy, Israel's possession of the land is conditional on clear moral principles: "Israel's possession of the land is conditioned on the grace of God and the moral stature of the people" (Anderson 2011: 277). He continues: "The text does not award a land to Israel in a manner that immorally voids all previous claims. Quite the opposite, the gift of the land to Israel can only take place when the sins of the Canaanites will be of sufficient number and magnitude so as to justify their expulsion" (Anderson 2011: 282). Israel would likewise lose the land in time as punishment for its sins. But this whole line of reasoning collapses if we acknowledge that the story is not historically reliable. As Nicholas Wolterstorff pointed out in his response to Anderson, "if there never was a foreign people invading the land of Canaan and taking it by conquest, then there was also no such thing as God mandating a foreign people to do so" (Wolterstorff 2011: 284).

The whole idea of divine judgment on the Canaanites is just as fictional as the collapse of the walls of Jericho.

The commandment in Deuteronomy 7 provides two warrants for the extermination of the indigenous inhabitants of the land. One is the demand that Israel worship only one god, YHWH, and the other is the claim that the land has been given to Israel by divine grant. Some modern scholars have tended to place the blame on monotheism, or "intolerant monolatry." So, for example, Regina Schwartz refers in her subtitle to "the violent legacy of monotheism," but she admits that monolatry or henotheism is more appropriate for Deuteronomy (Schwartz 1997: 17; for the expression "intolerant monolatry," see Pakkala 1999). For Jan Assmann, the problem lay in "the Mosaic distinction" between true and false religion: "[T]here is no natural way leading from the error of idolatry to the truth of monotheism" (Assmann 1997: 7). "Cultural or intellectual distinctions such as these," he argued, "construct a world that is not only full of meaning, identity, and orientation, but also full of conflict, intolerance, and violence" (Assmann 1997: 1).

Obviously, polytheistic people such as the Assyrians were no less violent than Israel, even Israel as fantasized in Deuteronomy and Joshua. What is at issue in the Hebrew Bible is not monotheism as such; it is rather the claim that the one God has chosen one people and granted them a land hitherto inhabited by others. This claim is subject to the same kind of objection as the divine judgment on the Canaanites. It is too obviously self-serving and unverifiable to be credible.

IDENTITY FORMATION

Scholars have increasingly come to recognize that the divine command in Deuteronomy and the story of the conquest are constructs to advance identity formation in Israel and Judah (Crouch 2014b: 105–225). The Book of Deuteronomy had its origin in the reform of King Josiah in 621 BCE, a century after the destruction of the northern kingdom of Israel by the Babylonians. The kingdom of Judah had been subject to Assyria for most of that century. The fall of Assyria provided a rare moment of opportunity for the assertion of Judahite independence.

In the formulation of Deuteronomy, Israel is defined by a covenant with its God, YHWH. It is widely agreed that this covenant is modeled on Assyrian vassal treaties, as exemplified by the Vassal Treaties of Esarhaddon, henceforth VTE (Weinfeld 1972: 59–129; Otto 1998; pace Crouch 2014a). The Esarhaddon "treaty" was essentially an oath of loyalty imposed on Assyria's vassals to ensure that they would recognize Esarhaddon's son, Ashurbanipal. They were commanded to "love" Ashurbanipal as themselves: "[Y]ou shall hearken to whatever he says and do whatever he commands, and you shall not seek any other king or other lord against him" (VTE 195-7). They were to teach these provisions to their sons and grandsons. Deuteronomy demands similar loyalty towards YHWH:

> Hear O Israel: YHWH is our God, YHWH alone. You shall love YHWH your God with all your heart, with all your life and with all your might ... Keep these words that I am commanding you today on your heart and teach them to your sons.
>
> (Deut 6:4–7)

The VTE issued strict injunctions against seditious talk. Deuteronomy warns against prophets who urge people to worship other gods. The two texts also threaten those who do not comply with similar curses. Deuteronomy proposed a new model for Judean identity, adapting the Assyrian demand for total loyalty and substituting YHWH for the Assyrian king. This is not so much subversion of Assyrian authority, which was already in decline when Deuteronomy was composed, as postcolonial mimicry (Collins 2017: 35). The Deuteronomists sought to adapt the methods of empire to the formation of the Judean state, as one characterized not necessarily by monotheism but by intolerant monolatry.

Postcolonial mimicry is also very probably at work in the account of the conquest. The Assyrians were notoriously cruel in warfare. Like many imperial powers they relied on terror to grind down their subjects (Younger 1990; Dozeman 2015: 67–72). According to the biblical account, the Israelites and their God likewise imposed terror on the indigenous population. The prostitute Rahab tells the Israelite spies: "I know that the Lord has given you the land, and that dread of you has fallen on us, and that all the inhabitants of the land melt in fear before you" (Josh 2:9; compare Exod 15:14–16). In the case of Deuteronomy and Joshua, the objective was not to subjugate actual Canaanites but to subjugate Judeans and Israelites who resisted Josiah's policies. In the context of the composition of these books, the objective was not to incite violence against ethnic outsiders but to put the fear of God, so to speak, into the native Israelite/Judean population (Rowlett 1996: 12–13).

In fairness to the Deuteronomists, their fantasized conquest was not as ruthless as that of the Assyrians. The rules for warfare in Deuteronomy 20 place some restraints on the conduct of war: a requirement that terms of peace be offered before an attack on a town and a prohibition of cutting down fruit trees. Writing in 1886, August Dillmann claimed that these laws counter "the wild barbarism and brutality with which many ancient peoples, especially the Assyrians, fought wars," and they affirm the "higher moral spirit of Yahwism, the basic principles of leniency and clemency" (Dillmann 1886: 334–5; trans. Wright 2008: 426). These rules are sometimes construed as a protest against the ruthlessness of Assyrian warfare (Otto 1999: 100; Wazana 2008: 295). In the case of the requirement to offer terms, this leniency may be exaggerated. It was not unusual to offer terms in the ancient world, since siege warfare was expensive (Wright 2008: 431–2). In Deuteronomy 20:15, the terms are only offered to towns that are far away (possibly a revision of a more lenient law; see Rofé 1985: 29). The terms to be offered are severe, requiring forced labor. If a town does not submit, all of the males must be put to the sword and the women, children, and livestock taken as booty. The restraint with regard to trees, however, stands in contrast to the spirit of Assyrian warfare and is in accordance with the more humane side of Deuteronomy. (Compare the command that a mother bird not be taken with its fledglings in Deut 22:6.) The overall impression, nonetheless, is one of terror.

As applied to dissenting Israelites or Judeans, the laws of destruction were largely symbolic. We are told in 2 Kings 23 that Josiah destroyed all vestiges of the worship of any deity other than YHWH, but we are not told that he massacred their devotees. Since the story apparently serves a symbolic purpose, some apologetically minded scholars see an opportunity to acquit the Bible of the charge of promoting violence. So Douglas S. Earl argues that the command to annihilate the Canaanites "should not be understood in terms of a description of the ethics and practice of ancient warfare, or as a 'model' to follow and 'act out'" (Earl 2010: 29). Instead, "a myth such as Joshua may be understood originally to be concerned with the juggling of identity construction within the society of ancient Israel – who are 'insiders' to the community ('true' Israelites) and who are the 'outsiders'?" (Earl 2010: 36–7). He continues:

> Although the story is set in the context of conquest, it is not really about conquest. Conquest is the backdrop for stories that make one think carefully about the construction of the identity of the community of those who worship Yahweh ... Joshua thus raises the question of what attitude the community of Israel ought to have towards itself and towards others .... It is *not about genocide.*
>
> (Earl 2010: 82–3, emphasis in original)

Especially important for Earl are the stories of Canaanites who are accepted by the Israelites (Rahab in Josh 2 and the Gibeonites in Josh 9) on the one hand and the Israelite who is condemned on the other (Achan in Josh 7).

The view that the book is concerned with defining Israelite identity goes back at least to the 1938 commentary of Martin Noth. But to get from there to the conclusion that Joshua is not a conquest story and is not about genocide requires a considerable sleight of hand. (For a fuller critique of Earl, see Collins 2014.) As the Native American scholar Robert Warrior commented: "People who read narratives read them as they are, not as scholars and experts would like them to be read and interpreted. History is no longer with us. The narrative remains" (Warrior 2006: 277). Rahab and the Gibeonites, as acceptable Canaanites, are very much the exceptions, and the Gibeonites are only grudgingly accepted. There are loose threads in the story that allow for a deconstructive reading, such as admissions that Joshua did not wipe out everyone, but the overall impression is still one of utter destruction (see Josh 11:16–23). The fact that Achan is excluded from Israel for immoral behavior is not very reassuring either when one considers the fate assigned to him and his family, and even his oxen, donkeys, and sheep. It is true that the story is not an accurate historical description of Israelite history and that it was not used as a warrant for genocide when it was promulgated in the time of Josiah or later. Nonetheless, it can hardly have done much to foster neighborly relations with the Gentiles, or even with Judeans who were considered deviant.

Religious traditions have dealt with the violence of the conquest story in various ways. Rabbinic Judaism held that the command of destruction applied only to the specific nations mentioned in the biblical text. Since these nations no longer existed, the commandments were moot (Greenberg 1995; Zoloth 2021). Careful attention to the biblical text could even promote resistance to violence that was not explicitly commanded (Weiss 2021). Christian theologians such as Origen had recourse to allegorical interpretation. Vices, not Canaanites, should be rooted out (Johnson 2001: 4–5; Earl 2010: 14). Some recent apologists have argued that "words in themselves are not dangerous." Scripture can be read reverentially without being taken literally (Fodor 2021). But the fact remains that the biblical commandments and examples have often been taken to legitimate violence (Bainton 1960; Collins 2004: 17–20). The story of Phinehas, who killed an Israelite man and a Midianite woman in the act of copulation in Numbers 25, was invoked as a model already in 1 Macc 1:26, by Mattathias, when he killed a Jew who was offering sacrifice to a pagan deity. Phinehas became paradigmatic for the zealots who fought against Rome in the 1st century CE. He was still invoked as a model in 2015 by modern zealots for an attack on a Pride parade in Jerusalem (Clenman 2021). The English Puritans led by Oliver Cromwell drew a parallel between their revolution and the exodus, and they proceeded to treat the Catholics of Ireland as the Canaanites. Cromwell even declared that "there are great occasions in which some men are called to great services in the doing of which they are excused from the common rule of morality," as were the heroes of the Old Testament (Bainton 1960: 151). A generation later, the Puritans of New England applied the biblical story of the conquest to their own situation, casting the Native Americans as Canaanites and Amalekites. This kind of rhetoric persisted in American Puritanism through the 18th century, and biblical analogies continue to play a part in American political rhetoric down to modern times. Many other examples could be cited, from South Africa and modern Israel, among other places.

We need not suppose that the biblical command or story is ever the primary motivating factor in actual violence. There are always other factors at work, such as racism or colonial ideology. The influence of scripture is more subtle. It can shape predispositions and lend legitimacy to actions that were undertaken for other reasons. To say that "words in themselves are not dangerous" is either very naive or disingenuous. And while it may be possible to circumscribe the potential for violence by careful interpretation, the claim that divine commands to violence can actually make people less violent is dubious in the extreme. The divine command to annihilate the Canaanites and the account of its execution by Joshua, even if fictional, remain a troubling biblical legacy that can be, and often has been, put to nefarious use.

ESCHATOLOGICAL VIOLENCE

The main accounts of violent action in the Bible are found in the story of the conquest in early Israel and in the books of Maccabees, which are not part of the Hebrew Bible but are preserved with the Greek scriptures and are classified as Deutero-Canonical in the Roman Catholic tradition. For most of history, Israel and Judah were the victims of violence rather than the perpetrators. Nonetheless, their literature is often marked by fantasies of violence, exacting vengeance on their enemies by the power of their God (Collins 2015b, 2015c).

A few examples may suffice. Ezekiel chapters 38 and 39 contain an oracle against "Gog of the land of Magog," a fictional figure, possibly based on the famous King Gyges of Lydia (Cook 2018: 74). Gog, we are told, would invade Israel, but the Lord would strike the bow from his hand and make his arrows drop. Then:

> You shall fall upon the mountains of Israel, you and all your troops and the peoples that are with you. I will give you to birds of prey of every kind and to the wild animals to be devoured.
>
> (Ezek 39:4)

He goes on to summon the birds and wild animals to "eat the flesh of the mighty, and drink the blood of the princes of the earth" (39:18). This fantasy has had a long afterlife. It was adapted in the Book of Revelation, where birds are summoned to "the great supper of God, to eat the flesh of the mighty, the flesh of horses and their riders – flesh of all, both free and slave, both small and great" (Rev 19:17–18), and Gog and Magog are nations deceived by Satan (20:8). In the bestselling *Left Behind* novels of Tim LaHaye and Jerry Jenkins there are two Gog/Magog wars. The first is when Russia (Gog) attacks Israel and is miraculously defeated. The second is at the end of the millennial reign of Christ, when Satan's followers attack Jerusalem before he is cast into the lake of fire (LaHaye and Jenkins 1995–2007).

Another violent fantasy is found in the prophet Joel:

> When I restore the fortunes of Judah and Jerusalem, I will gather all the nations and bring them down to the valley of Jehoshaphat, and I will enter into judgment with them there, on account of my people and my heritage Israel.
>
> (2:1–2a)

The judgment is likened to a harvest:

> Put in the sickle for the harvest is ripe;
> Go in, tread, for the wine press is full.
> The vats overflow, for their wickedness is great.
>
> (3:13)

The people of Judah had plenty of grievances for which they wanted vengeance. Joel is quite specific: "[T]hey have divided my land, and cast lots for my people, and traded boys for prostitutes, and sold girls for wine, and drunk it down" (3:2b–3). Now, in return, "I will sell your sons and your daughters into the hand of the people of Judah, and they will sell them to the Sabeans, to a nation far away" (3:7b–8). It is notable, however, that in both Ezekiel and Joel the Gentiles are condemned indiscriminately, whether they had had any dealings with Judah or not.

Scholars evaluate these fantasies of violence in different ways. On the one hand, Elisabeth Schüssler Fiorenza points out that the Book of Revelation is "clearly on the side of the poor and oppressed" (Schüssler Fiorenza 1981: 173). Even less sympathetic critics, such as Scott Appleby, grant that such fantasies can have a therapeutic role for the wretched of the Earth (Appleby 2002). On the other hand, David Frankfurter (2007) sees a text like Revelation as a source for violence and combative self-definition in Christian history. Mark Juergensmeyer, in his study of religion and terrorism, argues that many terrorists are inspired by an image of cosmic war:

> What makes religious violence particularly savage and relentless is that its perpetrators have placed such religious images of divine struggle – cosmic war – in the service of worldly political battles. For this reason, acts of religious terror serve not only as tactics in a political strategy but also as evocations of a much larger spiritual confrontation.
>
> (Juergensmeyer 2003: 148–9)

APOCALYPTIC QUIETISM

Even Frankfurter admits that there is little evidence to link eschatological fantasies to actual physical violence (Frankfurter 2007: 125). Quite typically, this literature is quietistic: Action is deferred in anticipation of divine intervention. The visionaries of the Book of Daniel famously regarded the Maccabees as "little help" (Dan 11:14). The more important battle was between the Archangel Michael, "Prince of Israel," and the angelic princes of Greece and Persia. In the end, Michael would arise in victory (Dan 12:1). The important thing for the Jewish people was to understand what was happening, remain faithful, and keep themselves pure. In another Jewish apocalyptic text, the Testament or Assumption of Moses, a man called Taxo takes his seven sons into a cave to purify themselves and die, for, if they do so, their blood will be avenged by the Lord, as promised in Deuteronomy 32: 43 (Test Moses 9:7; Licht 1961). The episode seems to be modeled on the pious Jews in 1 Maccabees 2:29–38, who let themselves be killed rather than violate the Sabbath by resisting. (The Maccabees, in contrast, decided to fight on the Sabbath, reasoning that if they did not, they would be wiped out.) The Book of Revelation, too, prohibits violent resistance: "[I]f you are to be taken captive, into captivity you go; if you kill with the sword, with the sword you must be killed"

(Rev 13:10; Yarbro Collins 1996: 198–217). One of the main differences between the Christian apocalypse and its Jewish prototypes is the exemplary role of the death of Jesus and the insistence that victory is achieved by "the blood of the lamb" (Collins 1997: 115–27). We find a similar combination of present restraint in hope of future vengeance in rabbinic tradition (Schremer 2002). So, for example, the *Mekhilta de Rabbi Ishmael*, Shirta 5, insists that Exodus 15:6 does not say that God has shattered the foe, but will shatter them in the Age to Come.

Apocalyptic fantasies are not incompatible with violence. The Animal Apocalypse in 1 Enoch 85–90 seems to exalt Judas Maccabee as a horned ram (90:9–10). The sectarians of the Dead Sea Scrolls pledged to avoid conflict with "the men of the Pit" until the day of vengeance (1QS 10:19), but it is clear from the War Scroll that they hoped to play a part in the final battle, even if they mainly relied on divine aid. As Krister Stendahl astutely remarked: "[W]ith the Day of Vengeance at hand, the proper and reasonable attitude is to forego one's own vengeance and to leave vengeance to God. Why walk around with a little shotgun, if the atomic blast is imminent?" (Stendahl 1962: 344–5). Revelation expected that Jesus would come from heaven on a white horse and strike down nations with the sword of his mouth (Rev 19:11–16). It is not clear whether his followers would join in the slaughter. There have been numerous instances in Christian history of people who took it upon themselves to "force the end" by violent action. Notable examples from the Reformation period include Thomas Müntzer and the Peasants' Revolt, and John of Leyden, the messiah of Münster (Cohn 1970: 198–280). Likewise, Cromwell's English Puritans, who saw themselves as "the fifth monarchy men" or "saints of the Most High" of Daniel 7, "saw it as the responsibility of believers to help bring on the final and most perfect historical age through militant action" (Barnes 1998: 163). These people did not rely just on the apocalyptic books of Daniel and Revelation, but on an apocalyptic reading of the whole Bible.

THE FUNCTION OF VIOLENT FANTASIES

Even when violent scriptural fantasies are not taken as mandates for action, they may still be implicated in violence because of the attitudes they form. Scott Appleby comments:

> A hallmark of the discourse of religious extremists is the calculated ambiguity of their leaders' rhetoric about violence. An extremist

preacher's standard repertoire – the constant use of metaphor and veiled allusion, apocalyptic imagery, and heated rhetoric not always meant to be taken literally or obeyed as a concrete set of directions – allows the preacher to evade accountability.

(Appleby 2002: 77)

Eschatological fantasies are not necessarily always used in this way, but they certainly have potential in this regard, especially because of the polarizing effect of dualistic oppositions.

We must also allow, however, that fantasized violence can sometimes have a therapeutic effect. It enables people to dissent from an oppressive culture when they lack the power to change it. The people of Judea could not bring about the destruction of Rome, but they could fantasize about it, and the fantasy provided some relief. This kind of resistance does not necessarily lead to violent revolution, but it provides a refuge against despair and enables people to preserve their values despite their powerlessness (Daschke 2010: 187–97). Wolgang Schivelbusch has written of "a culture of defeat" that affects the victims of military conquest: "Defeat follows war as ashes follow fire. At the heart of both . . . lies the threat of extinction, a threat that resonates long past the cessation of hostilities" (Schivelbusch 2001: 5). He continues: "[E]very society experiences defeat in its own way. But the varieties of response within vanquished nations – whether psychological, cultural or political – conform to a recognizable set of patterns or archetypes that recur across time and national boundaries. A state of unreality – or dreamland – is invariably the first of these" (Schivelbusch 2001: 10).

Eschatological visions, including ones that are violent and vengeful, are a way of maintaining hope in desperate situations. They usually entail destruction, but that is never an end in itself. There is always a new beginning to follow, whether in this world or in the next. To be sure, this may not be the ideal solution to social and economic crises. It might be better to find more practical ways of addressing problems. But apocalyptic visions are written for times when practical solutions seem beyond reach. Even a hope that most people might regard as illusory may be better than having no hope at all.

References

Anderson, Gary A. 2011. "What About the Canaanites?" In *Divine Evil? The Moral Character of the God of Abraham*. Edited by Michael Bergmann, Michael J. Murray, and Michael C. Rea. Oxford University Press. 269–82.
Appleby, Scott. 2002. "The Unholy Uses of Apocalyptic Imagination: Twentieth Century Patterns." In *Apocalypse and Violence*. Edited by Abbas Amanat

and John J. Collins. The Yale Center for International and Area Studies and the Council on Middle East Studies. 69–87.

Assmann, Jan. 1997. *Moses the Egyptian: The Memory of Egypt in Western Monotheism*. Harvard University Press.

Bainton, Roland. 1960. *Christian Attitudes towards War and Peace: A Historical Survey and Critical Re-evaluation*. Abingdon.

Barnes, Robin. 1998. "Images of Hope and Despair. Western Apocalypticism ca. 1500–1800." In *The Encyclopedia of Apocalypticism, Vol. 2: Apocalypticism in Western History and Culture*. Edited by Bernard McGinn. Continuum. 143–84.

Barr, James. 1993. *Biblical Faith and Natural Theology*. Clarendon Press.

Bernat, David A. and Jonathan Klawans. 2007. *Religion and Violence: The Biblical Heritage*. Sheffield Phoenix Press.

Calvin, John. 1949. *Commentaries on the Book of Joshua*. Translated by H. Beveridge. Eerdmans.

Clenman, Laliv. 2021. "Texts and Violence in Modern Israel: Interpreting Pinchas." In *Scripture and Violence*. Edited by Julia Snyder and Daniel H. Weiss. Routledge. 60–75.

Cohn, Norman. 1970. *The Pursuit of the Millennium*. Oxford University Press.

Collins, John J. 1997. "The Christian Adaptation of the Apocalyptic Genre." In *Seers, Sibyls, and Sages in Hellenistic–Roman Judaism*. Edited by John J. Collins. JSJ Sup. 54. Brill. 115–27.

2004. *Does the Bible Justify Violence?* Fortress Press.

2005. *The Bible after Babel: Historical Criticism in a Postmodern Age*. Eerdmans.

2014. "The God of Joshua." *Scandinavian Journal of the Old Testament* 28: 212–28.

2015a. "The Agonistic Imagination. The Ethics of War in Deuteronomy." In *Worship, Women and War: Essays in Honor of Susan Niditch*. Edited by John J. Collins, T. M. Lemos, and Saul M. Olyan. SBL Press and Brown Judaic Studies.

2015b. "Cognitive Dissonance and Eschatological Violence: Fantasized Solutions to a Theological Dilemma in Second Temple Judaism." In *Apocalypse, Prophecy, and Pseudepigraphy: On Jewish Apocalyptic Literature*. Eerdmans. 308–25.

2015c. "Radical Religion and the Ethical Dilemmas of Apocalyptic Millenarianism." In *Apocalypse, Prophecy, and Pseudepigraphy: On Jewish Apocalyptic Literature*. Eerdmans. 326–42.

2017. *The Invention of Judaism. Torah and Jewish Identity from Deuteronomy to Paul*. University of California Press.

Cook, Stephen L. 2018. *Ezekiel 38–48: A New Translation with Introduction and Commentary*. Yale University Press.

Cross, F. M. 1973. *Canaanite Myth and Hebrew Epic*. Harvard University Press.

Crouch, Carly L. 2009. *War and Ethics in the Ancient Near East: Military Violence in Light of Cosmology and History*. De Gruyter.

2014a. *Israel and the Assyrians: Deuteronomy, the Succession Treaty of Esarhaddon, and the Nature of Subversion*. SBL Ancient Near East Monographs 8. Society of Biblical Literature.

2014b. *The Making of Israel. Cultural Diversity in the Southern Levant and the Formation of Ethnic Identity in Deuteronomy.* VT Sup. 162. Brill.

Daschke, Dereck. 2010. *City of Ruins: Mourning the Destruction of Jerusalem through Jewish Apocalypse.* Brill.

Dawkins, Richard. 2006. *The God Delusion.* Houghton Mifflin.

Dever, William G. 2003. *Who Were the Ancient Israelites and Where Did They Come from?* Eerdmans.

2017. *Beyond the Texts. An Archaeological Portrait of Ancient Israel and Judah.* Society of Biblical Literature.

Dillmann, August. 1886. *Numeri, Deuteronomium und Josua.* 2nd ed. EHAT. Hirzel.

Dozeman, Thomas B. 2015. *Joshua 1–12: A New Translation with Introduction and Commentary.* AYB 6B. Yale University Press.

Earl, Douglas S. 2010. *A Joshua Delusion? Rethinking Genocide in the Bible.* Cascade.

Finkelstein, Israel and Neil Asher Silberman. 2001. *The Bible Unearthed: Archeology's New Vision of Ancient Israel and the Origin of Its Sacred Texts.* The Free Press.

Fodor, Jim. 2021. "Reading Scripture Reverentially but Not Univocally: Why Words in Themselves Are Not Dangerous." In *Scripture and Violence.* Edited by Julia Snyder and Daniel H. Weiss. Routledge. 111–23.

Frankfurter, David. 2007. "The Legacy of Sectarian Rage: Vengeance Fantasies in the New Testament." In *Religion and Violence.* Edited by David Bernat and Jonathan Klawans. Sheffield Phoenix Press. 114–29.

Greenberg, Moshe. 1995. "On the Political Use of the Bible in Modern Israel: An Engaged Critique." In *Pomegranates and Golden Bells: Studies in Biblical, Jewish, and Near Eastern Ritual, Law, and Literature in Honor of Jacob Milgrom.* Edited by D. P. Wright et al. Eisenbrauns. 461–71.

Johnson, Luke Timothy. 2001. "Lessons from Pre-modern Biblical Scholarship." In *Henry Luce III Fellows in Theology 2001 Conference Abstracts.* Princeton University Press. 4–5.

Juergensmeyer, Mark. 2003. *Terror in the Mind of God: The Global Rise of Religious Violence.* University of California Press.

Kenyon, Kathleen M. 1957. *Digging Up Jericho: The Results of the Jericho Excavations, 1952–1956.* Praeger.

LaHaye, Tim and Jerry B. Jenkins. 1995–2007. *Left Behind: A Novel of the Earth's Last Days.* 12 vols. Tyndale.

Lemos, T. M. 2015. "Dispossessing Nations: Population Growth, Scarcity, and Genocide in Ancient Israel and Twentieth-Century Rwanda." In *Ritual Violence in the Hebrew Bible: New Perspectives.* Edited by Saul M. Olyan. Oxford University Press. 27–65.

Licht, Jacob. 1961. "Taxo, or the Apocalyptic Doctrine of Vengeance." *Journal of Jewish Studies* 12: 95–103.

Lynch, Matthew. 2020. *Portraying Violence in the Hebrew Bible: A Literary and Cultural Study.* Cambridge University Press.

Moorey, P. R. S. 1991. *A Century of Biblical Archaeology.* Westminster John Knox.

Noth, Martin. 1938. *Das Buch Josua.* Mohr.

Otto, Eckart. 1996. "Krieg und Religion im Alten Orient und im alten Israel." In *Kontinuum und Proprium: Studien zur Sozial- und Rechtsgeschichte des Alten Orients und des Alten Testaments*. Edited by Eckart Otto. Orientalia Biblica et Christiana Harrassowitz. 49–58.

  1998. "Die Ursprünge der Bundestheologie im Alten Testament und im Alten Orient." *Zeitschrift für altorientalische und biblische Rechtsgeschichte* 4: 1–84.

  1999. *Krieg und Frieden in der hebräischen Bibel und im Alten Orient*. Theologie und Frieden 18. Kohlhammer.

Pakkala, Juha. 1999. *Intolerant Monolatry in the Deuteronomistic History*. Vandenhoeck & Ruprecht.

Rofé, Alexander. 1985. "The Laws of Warfare in Deuteronomy: Their Origins, Intent and Positivity." *Journal for the Study of the Old Testament* 32: 23–44.

Rowlett, Lori M. 1996. *Joshua and the Rhetoric of Violence: A New Historicist Analysis*. Journal for the Study of the Old Testament Supp. 226. Sheffield Academic Press.

Schivelbusch, Wolfgang. 2001. *The Culture of Defeat: On National Trauma, Mourning and Recovery*. Metropolitan.

Schüssler Fiorenza, Elisabeth. 1981. *Invitation to the Book of Revelation*. Doubleday.

Schremer, Adiel. 2002. "Eschatology, Violence, and Suicide: An Early Rabbinic Theme and Its Influence in the Middle Ages." In *Apocalypse and Violence*. Edited by Abbas Amanat and John J. Collins. The Yale Center for International and Area Studies and the Council on Middle East Studies. 19–42.

Schwartz, Regina M. 1997. *The Curse of Cain: The Violent Legacy of Monotheism*. University of Chicago Press.

Seibert, Eric A. 2012. *The Violence of Scripture: Overcoming the Old Testament's Troubling Legacy*. Fortress Press.

Stendahl, Krister. 1962. "Hate, Non-retaliation, and Love: 1QS X, 17–20 and Rom 12:19–21." *Harvard Theological Review* 55: 343–55.

Warrior, Robert A. 2006. "A Native American Perspective: Canaanites, Cowboys, and Indians." In *Voices from the Margin: Interpreting the Bible in the Third World*. Edited by R. S. Sugirtharajah. Orbis. 277–85.

Wazana, Nili. 2008. "Are the Trees of the Field Human? A Biblical War Law (Deut. 20:19–20) and Neo-Assyrian Propaganda." In *Treasures on Camels' Humps: Historical and Literary Studies from the Ancient Near East Presented to Israel Ephcal*. Edited by Mordechai Cogan and Dan'el Kahn. Jerusalem Magnes. 275–95.

Weinfeld, Moshe. 1972. *Deuteronomy and the Deuteronomic School*. Oxford University Press.

Weiss, Daniel H. 2021. "'And God Said': Do Biblical Commands to Conquer Land Make People More Violent, or Less?" In *Scripture and Violence*. Edited by Julia Snyder and Daniel H. Weiss. Routledge. 32–46.

Whitelam, Keith W. 1996. *The Invention of Ancient Israel: The Silencing of Palestinian History*. Routledge.

Wolterstorff, Nicholas. 2011. "Comments on 'What About the Canaanites?'" In *Divine Evil? The Moral Character of the God of Abraham*. Edited by Michael Bergmann, Michael J. Murray, and Michael C. Rea. Oxford University Press. 283–8.

Wright, George Ernest and Reginald Horace Fuller. 1960. "The Old Testament." In *The Book of the Acts of God*. Duckworth. 39–196.

Wright, Jacob L. 2008. "Warfare and Wanton Destruction: A Reexamination of Deuteronomy 20:19–20 in Relation to Ancient Siegecraft." *Journal of Biblical Literature* 127: 432–58.

Younger, Lawson Younger. 1990. *Ancient Conquest Accounts: A Study in Ancient Near Eastern and Biblical History Writing*. Sheffield Academic Press.

Yarbro Collins, Adela. 1996. "The Political Perspective of the Revelation to John." In *Cosmology and Eschatology in Jewish and Christian Apocalypticism*. Brill. 198–217.

Zoloth, Laurie. 2021. "'There Never Was and Never Will Be': Violence and Interpretive Erasure in the Jewish Tradition." In *Scripture and Violence*. Edited by Julia Snyder and Daniel H. Weiss. Routledge. 98–110.

2 Early Christianity and War

PAUL MIDDLETON

From Marcion (c. 110–160 CE) onwards, many Christians have perceived a marked difference in the level of violence in the New Testament compared to the Hebrew Bible. While Biblical Israel engaged in holy warfare to claim, maintain, and regain the Promised Land, Christians were committed to an eschatological rather than temporal kingdom. As nascent Christianity was developing, other Jews understood the Roman occupation of the Promised Land as an indignity that could only be solved by war. Indeed, in addition to the Yahweh Wars of the Hebrew Bible, first-century Jews could look to the recent example of the successful Maccabean wars of independence as both reinforcement of Holy War theology and inspiration for the war against the Romans. While early successes raised hopes that God would bring them victory, Jewish holy war ideology was dealt severe blows by the fall of Jerusalem in 70 CE and the unsuccessful Bar Kochba uprising (132–135 CE).

Therefore, it is said, while early Christianity was indebted to Second Temple Judaism for much of its theology and practice, a lack of commitment to land, and following a crucified Messiah, "whose kingdom is not of this world," there was a radical break in understanding what it meant to be the people of God. Such accounts of early Christianity see discipleship exemplified in following Jesus' model of non-violent suffering, even if it leads to martyrdom. Martyrdom is interpreted as the ultimate expression of non-violent resistance against the violence of imperial or national ideology and practice.

Of course, even those who believe there is a contrast between the violence of the Hebrew Bible and something akin to pacifism in the New Testament acknowledge that this non-violent ideal did not survive the Christianisation of the Roman Empire. After Constantine's conversion, Christians embraced the apparatus of the State, eventually engaging in violent repression of Jews, pagans, and heretics. Augustine's refinement of the just war tradition did not exclude correctional violence and would prepare the way for centuries of Christian empires engaging in Holy Wars, such as the mediaeval Crusades. For some readers of early Christianity, the paradigm shift between pre- and post-Constantine Christianity marks a no less significant shift in attitudes to violence and war as from the Hebrew Bible to the New Testament. So a particular account of Christian history (found with greater or lesser sophistication) runs that the violence of the Hebrew Bible is replaced by a non-violent New Testament, which informs the early Christianity, until that "Old Testament" violence is adopted once again with Constantinian Christianity. That is to say, there is a "pure" non-violent form of Christianity that existed for a few centuries before Christians fell victim to the temptation to wield the power of the State (e.g. Howard-Brook 2016).

However, this idealist position is undermined by several factors. Firstly, violence is far from absent in the New Testament, especially the Book of Revelation. Secondly, it is far from clear that early Christians did adhere to pacifism. Different attitudes to service in the Roman army are found among Church Fathers. Thirdly, and perhaps most significantly, the language of warfare was deeply embedded in the Christian psyche. Early Christians saw themselves as engaged in cosmic warfare in which they were active combatants in God's Holy War against evil. Martyr literature in particular embraces agnostic metaphors, such that the language attributed to what could otherwise be interpreted as an act of supreme non-violent resistance engages in apocalyptic fantasy violence (Frilingos 2004; Frankfurter 2009). In these "spiritual" battles, Christians were not simply victors; they imagined their defeated persecutors to be subjected to violent torture, not all of it post-mortem. Therefore, this chapter will argue that early Christians did not eschew the violence of the Hebrew Bible Yahweh War; rather, it was eschatologically transferred. Christian language of warfare fuelled negative attitudes to outsiders that justified violence when it could be actualised in changed circumstances. In short, in the first three centuries of the Church, Christian violence was only temporally and temporarily displaced.

VIOLENCE AND WARFARE IN THE NEW TESTAMENT

In recent years, there has been growing scholarly concern over dealing with the "problem" of violence in the Bible (e.g. de Villiers and van Henten 2012; Zehnder and Hagelia 2013). Most studies that deal with the Christian canon in its entirety usually consciously or unconsciously work harder with the Hebrew Bible than the New Testament. Hays suggests that "the greatest intra-canonical challenge to the witness of the Sermon on the Mount concerning nonviolence and love of enemies comes not from any New Testament text but from the Old Testament, particularly the holy war texts" (Hays 1997: 336). Ultimately, Hays concedes that "the Old Testament obviously validates the legitimacy of armed violence by the people of God under some circumstances," but for Christians, "the New Testament's witness is finally normative ... The New Testament vision trumps the Old Testament" (Hays 1997: 337; see also Yoder 1972; Wink 1984, 1986, 1992, 2003).

However, Desjardins, in her important study on New Testament violence, is more balanced: "I am unable to reduce the evidence either to one option, 'the New Testament is fundamentally peace-promoting' or to the other, 'the New Testament encourages people to be violent.' The strong presence of both is striking and intriguing" (Desjardins 1997: 11). In the last few decades, many volumes have appeared on violence in the Bible from both apologetic (e.g. Creach 2013; Zehnder and Hagelia 2013; Paynter and Spalione 2020; Nickel 2021) and more equivocal perspectives (e.g. Matthews and Gibson 2005; Boustan et al. 2010; de Villiers and van Henten 2012).

Jesus and the Gospels

Jesus is generally held up as a model of pacifism and non-violent resistance, in both word – especially the Sermon on the Mount (Mt 5–7) – and deed, exemplified by his acceptance, even embrace, of suffering and death. Of course, recovering the historical figure of Jesus from the gospel tradition is notoriously difficult. Alongside synoptic teaching on the blessedness of the peacemakers (Mt 5.9), non-retaliation (Mt 5.38–39a), and love of enemies (Mt 5.43–45//Lk 6.27–29) are threats of eschatological judgement against those who reject Jesus (Lk 10.13–16) and vengeance upon his "evil generation" (Lk 11.49–52), not to mention graphic depictions of eternal torment (e.g. Mk 9.48; Lk 19.23–28; Mt 25.41). Moreover, the Jesus of the gospels imagines himself as the eschatological Son of Man who will come from heaven with an army of angels to unleash apocalyptic judgement and separate the elect for salvation from those destined for destruction (Mk 13.24–27//Mt 24.29–31; cf. Lk 21.25–28). Some scholars see an intolerable and irreconcilable tension between Jesus' call to love one's enemies while at the same time appearing to wish violent eschatological destruction upon them, and so they dismiss the apocalyptic material as a later, non-authentic tradition – a move associated particularly with the Jesus Seminar (Funk and Hoover 1993; see also Joseph 2014: 71–89). They promote a sapiential non-apocalyptic Jesus who eschewed the violence of his day, whether Roman imperial violence or Jewish Davidic militaristic messianism (e.g. Crossan 2009).

While the non-violent figure that emerges is attractive, such accounts are not unproblematic. They fall victim to a theological tendency towards making Jesus an exceptional figure in 1st-century Judaism. Josephs goes so far as to suggest Jesus' non-violence "scandalized his contemporaries" who were still committed to Davidic revolt against the Romans (Josephs 2014: 229–230; Wright 1996: 446–450). However, the consensus, such as it is in Historical Jesus studies, is that he was indeed an apocalyptic teacher (Allison 1998; Ehrman 1999), and any tension with the non-violent teaching of the Sermon on the Mount remains (cf. Nickel 2021).

However, at the other end of the spectrum, some reconstructions of the historical figure of Jesus have placed him in the tradition of the zealots in seeking to overthrow the Romans (Brandon 1967; Maccoby 1973; Bammell 1984; Ellens 2004; cf. Nickel 2021). In support of a more apocalyptic version of this thesis, Martin (2014) notes the fact that the assault by one of Jesus' followers on the arresting party in Gethsemane clearly demonstrates at least some of Jesus' followers were armed, an incident the early Church is unlikely to have created. Martin argues that this combined with the anti-Temple gospel tradition suggest that Jesus expected his followers to participate in a revolt against the Romans and Temple authorities, accompanied by a heavenly army. However, if this were the case, it is not clear why there were not more arrests. In any case, it is not impossible to explain why the incident could have been created; it demonstrated that the Jesus movement was not a threat to Roman peace and security. Furthermore, this theory leads to the opposite problem from pacifist readers: how to account for the strong non-retaliation tradition.

If some modern commentators have difficulty reconciling the non-violent and apocalyptic traditions, this is not a problem shared by the evangelists. Furthermore, the reason given for not resisting evil-doers reflects the fact that God currently sends blessing on good and bad alike (Mt 5.45//Lk 6.35). Nonetheless, the ultimate fate of evil-doers is judgement. In the parable of the wheat and the tares (Mt 13.24–30), both are permitted to grow together until the eventual destruction of the latter. Indeed, in the parable of the sheep and the goats (Mt 25.31–36), the failure to act ethically results in violent eternal punishment. The earliest Christian writers clearly had no issue maintaining an ethic of non-retaliation in the present with violent retribution in the future.

While Marshall (1985: 115) is surely correct to note that the New Testament does not directly address the issue of war, the appropriation of the Jewish revolt within the gospels' eschatological scheme is not unlike the conviction found in the Hebrew Bible that God directs human wars, even when his people are on the losing side. The Roman siege and destruction of Jerusalem appear in the apocalyptic discourse (Mk 13.2, 14//Mt 24.2, 15), explicitly so in Luke (21.5, 20). The gospels also demonstrate that Roman military action against the Temple is God's judgement on the people through juxtaposing the cursing of the fig tree with Jesus' Temple action (Mk 11.11–25//Mt 21.12–21). In the parables, the link is even clearer. In the parable of the wicked tenants (Mk 12.1–12//Mt 21.33–46//Lk 20.9–19), the people are destroyed (Mk 12.9//Mt 21.41// Lk 20.6), with Matthew adding that the vineyard, which he interprets as the Kingdom of God, will be given to another people (Mt 21.41, 43). Matthew is even more explicit in his version of the parable of the wedding banquet (Mt 22.1–14; cf. Lk 14.15–24). After his invitations are refused and his servants abused, the enraged king "sent his troops ... and burned their city" (Mt 22.7). The clear implication of Matthew's redactional activity is his belief that God used the Roman military in order to bring judgement on the people of Israel for rejecting Jesus. While it has had a catastrophic history of interpretation, the destruction of the Temple is also probably in view in the Jewish people's curse that Jesus' blood be on them and their children (Mt 27.25). For the evangelists, then, the Roman military machine was the agent through which God executed temporal judgement. Therefore, even if it had been practical, Jesus' followers had no need to live and die by the sword (Mt 26.52), for they believed God would ultimately deal with their enemies.

In John's gospel, Jesus tells Pilate that his kingdom is not from the world, adding "if my kingship were of this world, my servants would fight, that I might not be handed over to the Jews" (Jn 18.36). Moreover, despite the apparent lack of resistance from Jesus, John's insists Pilate's power is limited to that which has been given to him (Jn 19.11), a point made clear when Jesus can only be arrested in the garden after he consents (Jn 18.4–9). It is the necessity of his arrest that appears to be the primary motivation for Jesus instructing Peter to put away the sword (Jn 18.11). Even in Matthew, Jesus does not require to be defended by the unknown disciple, as he could command a legion of angels to protect him (Mt 26.53). In each of the gospels, the primary motivation for non-resistance at Jesus' arrest is the prophetic necessity of the cross (e.g. Mt 26.54), rather than any clear prescriptive objection to violence.

Paul

Paul does not address war directly. He does, however, have a version of the non-retaliation maxim: "[s]ee that none of you repays evil for evil, but always seek to do good to one another and to all" (1 Thess 5.15). An expanded version is found in Romans, where in addition to noting repaying evil for evil (Rom 12.17), he urges his readers to "bless those who persecute you; bless and do not curse them" (Rom 12.14). Nonetheless, the general injunction to "live peaceably with all" (Rom 12.18) is found alongside the expectation of eschatological judgement: "never avenge yourselves, but leave room for the wrath of God; for it is written 'Vengeance is mine, I will repay, says the Lord'" (Rom 12.19). Clearly the implication is that Paul's readers can "overcome evil with good" (Rom 12.21), not only by shaming their assailants (Rom 12.20), but sure in the knowledge that God will take vengeance on them.

Paul, also in common with the gospels, has no difficulty with combining a non-retaliatory ethic with a belief in violent eschatological judgement. As well as there being little alternative for the early Jesus movement living in the midst of sometimes-hostile neighbours (Hurtado 1999; Middleton 2020), Paul sees the good example set by his readers as crucial for the spread of the gospel. However, while peace is a common Pauline concept (Swartley 1996: 2434–2435), often attributed to God (e.g. Rom 15.22; 1 Cor 14.33; 2 Cor 13.11; Phil 4.9; 1 Thess 5.23), it is this God of peace who will ultimately crush Satan underfoot (Rom 16.20). While Paul advocated peace between believers and, at least in the present, with those outside the churches, he conceived of the Christian battling against cosmic forces in a war against spiritual forces and even death itself (e.g. Rom 8.37–39; 1 Cor 15.24–28, 51–57). For this struggle, Paul liberally deploys military metaphors; Christians are soldiers (1 Cor 9.7; Phil 2.25; Phlm 23; cf. 1 Tim 1.18; 2 Tim 2.3–4), dressed in the armour of light (Rom 13.12; 1 Thess 5.8), with the metaphor developed most fully in the post-Pauline letter to the Ephesians (6.10–18).

While Paul imagines himself and his churches to be fellow soldiers in war against cosmic forces, he is also capable of turning this war language on his own readers, as he does in his correspondence with the Corinthians (2 Cor 10.1–6; see Roeztel 2010). In defending his apostolicity against challenge, he deploys ferocious bellicose language, warning his readers that although he is human

> [w]e do not wage war according to human standards; for the weapons of our warfare are not merely human, but they have divine power to

destroy strongholds. We destroy arguments and every proud obstacle raised up against the knowledge of God.

(2 Cor 10.3–5)

Paul ends with the threat that these weapons of war will be turned on his readers unless they accept his authority: "[w]e are ready to punish every disobedience when your obedience is complete" (2 Cor 10.6). Having launched his assault, Paul, perhaps unconvincingly, reassures his readers that he is not trying to frighten them (2 Cor 10.9)! To be sure, this, and indeed all of Paul's military language, is metaphorical. Nonetheless, given that Paul and his readers would no doubt have believed in God's coming eschatological judgement, this threatening militaristic language would have had real effects.

Revelation (The Apocalypse of John)

Even if one accepts the claim – metaphorical warfare notwithstanding – that the New Testament is generally non-violent and does not imagine war as a legitimate option for Christian communities, the Book of Revelation presents a particular challenge. While more non-violent readings have been advanced (Blount 2005, 2009; Johns 2003, 2005), in the Apocalypse, God's people are depicted as engaging in the end-time war as part of the armies of heaven (Rev 7.1–8, 14.1–5, 19.11–14), to the extent that the book has been dubbed a "Christian war scroll" (Bauckham 1998). The verb "to make war" (polemeō) and the noun "war" (polemos) occur fifteen times in the Apocalypse, compared with eight in the rest of the New Testament: "wars and rumours of war" in the synoptic Apocalypse (Mt 24.6//Mk 13.7//Lk 21.31); a parable about preparedness in Luke (14.31); Paul's metaphor of the necessity of a clear bugle sound to call armies to war (1 Cor. 14.8); the roll call of war heroes in the heavenly witnesses in Hebrews (11.34); and finally representing internal strife in the community and body in James 4.1–2, the only other occurrence of the verb outside Revelation.

In Revelation, there are various actors involved in war. First, the forces of evil, led by the Beast, make war on the saints (11.7, 12.17, 13.7; cf. 13.4), and although he is successful in killing them (11.7, 13.7), it is only because he is permitted to do so, but in any case, through death, the saints conquer him (12.11, 15.2). Second, there is the war in heaven between Michael and the Dragon with their respective angelic armies resulting in the expulsion of Satan from heaven (12.7–9). This is the backstory to the current conflict between the forces of evil and John's readers (12.13–17). Third, there are wars between Jesus and various cosmic and human forces (16.14, 17.14), culminating in the great battle in which Christ appears as a rider on a white horse:

> Then I saw heaven opened, and there was a white horse! Its rider is called Faithful and True, and in righteousness he judges and makes war. His eyes are like a flame of fire, and on his head are many diadems; and he has a name inscribed that no one knows but himself. He is clothed in a robe dipped in blood, and his name is called The Word of God. And the armies of heaven, wearing fine linen, white and pure, were following him on white horses. From his mouth comes a sharp sword with which to strike down the nations, and he will rule them with a rod of iron; he will tread the wine press of the fury of the wrath of God the Almighty.
>
> (Rev 19.11–15)

As in much early Christian tradition, Christ takes over the role of judge from God, and there are clear parallels here with the warrior God who judges righteously (e.g. Isa 63.1–6; Pss 75.2, 96.13, 98.9). Judgement in this scene is portrayed as the final battle that has been anticipated throughout Revelation (16.12–16, 17.12–14), and Jesus lines up with the heavenly army, including the white-robed martyrs (cf. Rev 6.9–11), against the Beast, the kings of the Earth, and their armies (Rev 19.19). As John has already intimated that Christ has conquered them (Rev 17.14), the war itself is not described in any detail, and is an anti-climactic rout. The Beast and the false prophet are captured and thrown into the lake of fire (Rev 19.20), and "the rest were killed by the sword of the rider on the horse, the sword that came from his mouth; and all the birds were gorged with their flesh" (Rev 19.21). While some commentators take the lack of description of the final battle to mean one did not actually take place (Neville 2011: 76–77) or argue that the fact that the sword comes from the rider's mouth means that he was victorious through a "war of words" rather than violence (e.g. Blount 2009: 354), the macabre description of birds gorging on the slain on the battlefield (Rev 19.21; cf. Ezek 39.17–20) renders these efforts unpersuasive. God wields the sword of judgement throughout the Hebrew Bible (e.g. Deut 32.1; 1 Chr 21.12; Ps 17.13; Isa 27.1, 66.1; Jer 9.16, 47.6; Ezek 29.8–9, 30.24; Zech 13.7), and elsewhere in the New Testament, Christ slays the lawless one by the breath of his mouth (2 Thess 2.8). There is one further reprise of the final battle when Satan is loosed after his 1,000-year imprisonment, which is narrated equally briefly (Rev 20.7–10). The armies that surround the holy city are destroyed by fire from heaven (Rev 20.9).

One further instance of warring is noteworthy. In a clear threat to insiders, John warns his churches that Jesus will come and war against deviant belief and action among the churches to which he writes (2.16). While the Apocalypse may be read principally as less-than-gentle encouragement to John's readers to remain faithful, in general Christians are issued with a call to conquer (2.7, 11, 17; 3.5, 12, 21) in the same way as Christ has conquered (3.21). Like the language of warfare, the concept of conquering is also concentrated in the Apocalypse, and it is explicitly linked to martyrdom in Revelation (12.11, 15.2), just as Christ's conquering is also strongly linked to his death through the image of the slaughtered lamb (5.5–6). While some commentators see this act of conquering as non-violent passive resistance (Hays 1997: 332), the death of the martyrs is not the end of the story. Martyrs are enlisted in the army of the Lamb and are raised in order to reign with Christ, and, significantly, they are given authority to participate in divine judgement (20.4–6). Whether the literary world of the Apocalypse imagines all of the faithful will be martyred (Middleton 2018) or merely prepared to undergo martyrdom (van Henten 2012), it is clear that, following death, conquering martyrs are vindicated and exalted.

Finally, the central image of the slaughtered lamb as the ultimate symbol of conquering in Revelation has often functioned as an exegetical antidote to what is perceived as the problematic violence of the Apocalypse. John is told "the Lion of the tribe of Juda, the Root of David has conquered" (Rev 5.5), and he then sees "a lamb standing, as though it had been slain" (Rev 5.6). There is voluminous literature on the apparent incongruently of the juxtaposition of the militaristic lion and sacrificed lamb (see Middleton 2018: 65–96), with many commentators arguing that the image of suffering weakness of the lamb overcomes the militaristic overtones of the Lion of Judah (e.g. Bauckham 1993: 74; Barr 2003; Johns 2003; Koester 2014: 388–389). However, the lamb is the dominant symbol for Christ in the Apocalypse, and he undertakes activities that are entirely consistent with the conquering Judaic lion imagery: the peoples of the Earth plead to be spared from the day of wrath of the lamb (6.12–17), the wicked are tormented in his presence (14.10), and he conquers an army in war (14.10). While non-violent interpreters focus on the lamb's death, it should be noted that the lamb is "standing"; the image presupposes the resurrection and exaltation (Hurtado 1985: 117). In the Apocalypse, Christ is *already* the faithful witness, the firstborn of the dead, and the ruler of the kings of the Earth (Rev 1.5); like the martyrs, his death was not the end of the story, but the means through which he attained glory and power (Rev 5.10–11) and the authority to stand as the eschatological judge, who will destroy his enemies with his faithful armies.

Therefore, although the New Testament does not deal with war directly, we find metaphors of war and conflict used to interpret the Christian struggle against evil or sin. There are also violent images of eschatological judgement alongside ethical injunctions to non-violence or non-retaliation. The Jewish revolt is reflected in the text and is positively interpreted as God's judgement in line with Hebrew Bible ideology. In the Book of Revelation, these images of war and judgement are particularly concentrated and expanded, but martyrdom is the means by which Christians conquer the forces of evil. To be sure, the Apocalypse is non-violent in the sense that it does not instruct Christians to take up arms in what would be a futile battle with the Romans, but it did encourage its readers to see themselves as participating in an eschatological holy war in which they would end up as agents of divine judgement. Moreover, John depicts those outside his believing communities as mere objects of and legitimate targets of divine wrath. In this respect, the Apocalypse is not alone in the New Testament. These twin themes of "othering" opponents and participation in holy war, especially through martyrdom, would develop in Christian thought over the forthcoming centuries.

MARTYRDOM AND HOLY WAR

Themes of persecution and martyrdom were important for Christian self-understanding in the first three centuries CE, as the Church represented itself as a "suffering body," following the pattern set by Jesus through his passion and death (Perkins 1995). While there is now general agreement that anti-Christian persecution was far less extensive and systematic than was once thought (Moss 2013), there were sufficient pockets of local hostility for Christians to interpret their experiences as imperial persecution (Middleton 2021).

Pacifist interpretations of early Christianity often point to the phenomenon of martyrdom as the ultimate act of non-violent resistance, with Crossan dubbing it "the final act of ethical eschatology" (2009: 289). Other writers have similarly enlisted early Christian martyrs to the history of civil obedience (e.g. Fergusson 1993). However, Crossan recognises that even martyrdom, if it is overly desired, colludes with the violence it opposes. Such collusion may entail minimally, desiring or provoking martyrdom (but every martyr needs a murderer). It may entail, maximally, the hunger-striker or the suicide attacker. Such collusive actions are not eschatologically ethical.

(2009: 285)

Other writers are similarly sensitive to any comparison between the passive acceptance of the early Christian martyr and violent acts associated with, for example, some contemporary Islamic manifestations of martyrdom, in which the martyr seeks their own death through suicide attack (e.g. Wicker 2006). However, there are many examples of early Christians actively seeking out martyrdom, who "participate in the violence provided by the Roman Empire" (Koscheski 2011: 105) – the so-called voluntary martyrs. While a generation of scholars simply dismissed these martyrs as heretical or abnormal, more recent studies have demonstrated that enthusiasm for martyrdom, "volunteerism," and sometimes even suicides are found and recognised as martyrdom in the early church (de Ste. Croix 1963; Middleton 2006; Moss 2012).

While it is the case that the early Christians never took up arms against Rome, to insist that this lack of physical retaliation is evidence of pacifism is to set the bar very low. Not only was there the example of the consequences of the disastrous Jewish revolt, early Christians did not have the hardware to launch any kind of military action against Rome, such as an army with which to attack or a homeland to defend, so while they inherited an apocalyptic war tradition of Second Temple Judaism, early Christians spiritualised the tradition in their martyrologies and shifted the conflict to the cosmic realm (Middleton 2006: 133; Koshecki 2011). The confrontation with earthly magistrates was reconceived as a cosmic conflict in which they were God's soldiers against their Roman enemy. In the fulcrum of this battle, the devil sought to sway the Christian from their martyr's confession and thus save their life (cf. Mk 8.34–38). Therefore, in order to win on the battlefield, martyrs had to hold fast to their confession – "I am a Christian" – and win the war through their own death. As Tertullian wrote:

Serving as a soldier under this oath, I am challenged by the enemy. If I surrender to them, I am as they are. In maintaining this oath, I fight furiously in battle, am wounded, hewn in pieces, slain. Who wished this fatal issue to his soldier, but he who sealed him by such an oath.

(Scorp. 4.5)

Parallels between the oaths of the martyr and the gladiator (*sacramentum gladiorum*) have been noted (e.g. Barton 1994: 56), as Christians liberally deployed agonistic language from the arena for their struggle, especially as the games became an important setting for many Christian martyr stories. Tertullian merged the images of gladiator and soldier in much of his reflection on martyrdom; the Holy Spirit used the prison as both soldiers' barracks and training ground (*Ad Mart.* 3) for the "most accomplished gladiators" (*Ad Mart.* 1) awaiting trial. Similarly, he claims that the Christian desires to suffer in the same way a soldier longs for war, and conquers through dying (*Apol.* 50).

This image of the potential martyr participating in battle as a soldier is found throughout the early Fathers and martyrologies (Hartog 2020: 110–111). Origen opens his *Exhortation to Martyrdom* by interpreting the Christian facing persecution in militaristic terms. His aim in writing is to "animate the soldiers of Christ" (Pref. 1), who constitute "an army established in the heavenly camp" (Pref. 2). He warns that the devil wages a war against the Christians, seeking to "find Christ's soldier unprepared" and defeat him, but those who continue to confess Christ will never be conquered (Pref. 2; also 5.36, 5.44). Cyprian also calls Christians "soldiers of Christ" (e.g. *Ep.* 8, 10, 15, 24), who are trained on the battlefield (*Ep.* 50, 55, 80), and he contends that the Devil similarly trains his army in opposition to the Christians (*Ep.* 10). The same idea is also reflected in the Christian martyr acts, such as the *Martyrs of Lyons*, in which the Devil is said to "train and prepare his minions against God's servants" (1.5; also 1.16, 23, 25, 27, 35; cf. e.g. *Mart. Polycarp* 3.1, 17.1; *Mart. Carpus* 17; *Mart. Justin* rec. C 1.1). In the *Passion of Perpetua*, the eponymous heroine realises that although she is condemned to die *ad bestias*, "it was not with the wild animals that I would fight but with the Devil, but I knew I would win the victory" (10.14). The moment of death is the decisive victory, as Tertullian remarked: "[t]he Christian is snatched by faith from the jaws of the devil, but by martyrdom he fells to the ground the enemy of his salvation" (*Scorp.* 6).

As martyrdom is often interpreted as a notable example of non-violent resistance, the violence inherent in the act is almost always interpreted as going in one direction: the persecutor on the persecuted. However, we have noted that in many early Christian texts martyrdom is interpreted as an act of cosmic combat, in which members of the early Church (at least so far as the martyr accounts are concerned) embraced or even in some cases sought it out. Martyrdom was conceived in pugilistic terms, with the martyrs conquering not only their human but their cosmic opponents. But there is also another locus of violent activity found in accounts of martyrdom and persecution: eschatological violence upon the persecutors.

Often, the persecutors' actions against the Church and their fates are inextricably linked, so Polycarp compares the short time that his burning will take with the eternal fire being prepared for those who condemn him (*Mart. Polycarp* 11.2). In the *Passion of Perpetua*, the martyr Saturnus tells the gathered crowd to look carefully at their faces, so they will recognise them on the day of judgement (17). Sometimes, the anticipation of the violent judgement that will await the wicked is barely tempered. Tertullian argued that Christians should not attend the Roman games on the grounds that their dedication to the gods made them idolatrous (*On the Games* 4–6), but also that the violent blood sport could have a negative effect on the soul of the Christian (*On the Games* 14–16). However, he is far less squeamish imagining the fate of non-Christians when they face their own time in the arena come the Day of Judgement:

> But what a spectacle is that fast-approaching advent of our Lord … Yes, and there are other sights: that last day of judgment, with its everlasting issues; … when the world … shall be consumed in one great flame! How vast a spectacle then bursts upon the eye! What there excites my admiration? what my derision? Which sight gives me joy? which rouses me to exultation? – as I see so many illustrious monarchs, whose reception into the heavens was publicly announced, groaning now in the lowest darkness with great Jove himself, and those, too, who bore witness of their exultation; governors of provinces, too, who persecuted the Christian name, in fires more fierce than those with which in the days of their pride they raged against the followers of Christ.
> (On the Games 30)

Tertullian effectively turns the tables on the Christians' tormentors. He imagines that it will be the persecutors and the crowds who urged them on who will now be in the arena as the army of Christians sit watching the bloodthirsty spectacle of judgement. They will revel in the sight of kings groaning in despair, and their persecutors getting a taste of their own medicine in even fiercer fires will provoke joy and exultation. Martyrdom not only wins salvation for the Christian – it effectively damns the persecutor.

The most graphic account of this type of retribution is Lactantius' *On the Deaths of the Persecutors*, in which God does not wait until the eschaton to judge the tormentors of the Church. Lactantius runs through the persecuting emperors and argues that their deaths were a result of divine punishment. After describing the fates of selected emperors from Nero to Valerian (2–5), he wonders how after numerous examples of divine retribution falling on the persecuting emperors anyone would move against God's people. This is a prelude to a lengthy consideration of the Great Persecution, in which the description of both tortures of the Christians and the deaths of the emperors is particularly graphic, notably that of Galerius (33). Therefore, in the minds of the Christians, the Holy War brought salvation for the martyrs and defeated their cosmic enemies. However, persecuting the Church also had consequences for the persecutors. Frend was right that martyrdom was not only a means of victory – it was "in itself an act of vengeance" (1965: 38).

So far, we have considered the metaphorical use of war rhetoric in early Christianity. In at least some strands of early Christianity, the rhetoric of martyrdom was played out in a cosmic war with violent pugilistic metaphors deployed not only to frame the victory of martyrdom, but also to imagine the ultimate defeat of Christians' persecutors. Therefore, "although the early Christians did not resist persecution with physical violence, violence was very much on their minds" (Shafer 2004: 215). We now turn to ways in which that rhetoric of eschatological violence and holy war could be actualised, first through considering Christian involvement in the army and then the beginnings of Christendom when Constantine made Christianity the religion of the Roman Empire.

CHRISTIANS AND THE ROMAN ARMY

As we have noted, much scholarly discussion around Christianity and violence or the Church and warfare tends to be refracted through more modern theological and ethical concerns. Helgeland, in his extensive study on Christians in the army, suggests that this "interference" (in both pacifist and non-pacifist directions) stems from the impulse to take "the thoughts and conduct of Christians in the first three centuries as normative for the contemporary church" (1979: 732–733; see also Charles 2010: 22). However, even if this prescriptive claim for the early Church was uncontentious, as we will see, as important as the Fathers have become for modern ethical reflection on peace and war, Christian involvement in the Roman army does not appear to have been a major issue for the early Church. We know for sure that there were Christians serving in the army, not least because there are a number of Christian soldiers who became martyrs.

As Christianity began to spread rapidly across the Roman Empire, Christians were found in nearly every aspect of the Empire's life. Inevitably, this included the army. Many early Christian thinkers simply take this for granted. Clement of Alexandria advises sailors to look to the heavenly pilot, while soldiers should "listen to the Commander who orders what is right" (*Protrepticus* 100; cf. *Paed* 12). Tertullian, whose early writings are more positive about the army than his Montanist works, recounts the story of the so-called Thundering Legion: Christian soldiers under Marcus Aurelius, whose prayers ended a drought in Germanica. As a result, the Emperor forbade any accusations against the Christians (*Apol.* 10; cf. Eusebius *H.E.* 5.5). Cassius Dio (82.8.1–10.5) recounts a similar story, but the credit is given to an Egyptian magician (Helgeland 1979: 769–772; Shafer 2004: 225); obviously, if Christians were present in Marcus' army, then they must have been there for some time.

Nonetheless, there is evidence that some early Christian thinkers did oppose participation in the Roman army. In his early career, Tertullian had been content to pray for the army against invaders (*Apol.* 30.4), and he suggests that at least some Christians served in the army: "[w]e sail together with you, we go to war ... our efforts are at your service" (*Apol.* 42.3). Like Justin before him, Tertullian's *Apology* argues that Christians played a positive role in and were not a threat to the Empire. To substantiate this claim, he maintains that Christians participate in every walk of life, other than in idolatry. However, Tertullian later became more hard-line in his opposition to the presence of Christians in the army. This may be due to the ethical rigorism of his Montanist phase, or that the number of Christians enlisting or soldiers converting brought the issue into focus (Gero 1970). Yet Tertullian addresses the question of military service in any significant way in just two pieces of writing: *On Idolatry*, in which military service is dealt with in passing, and the more substantial treatment in *On Crowns*.

Tertullian's treatise *On Idolatry* concerns what he calls "the principal crime of the human race" (1), and he is rigorist in his approach. Even the appearance of idolatry, such as wearing clothes associated with festivals and honouring the gods, is to be avoided, even if one is not participating in the rites (17–18). He then applies this principle to military service, which he regards as necessarily idolatrous (19). In the face of potential counterargument, such as those of lower rank who would not necessarily have to offer sacrifice to the gods, he responds: "there is no agreement between the divine and the human sacrament (*sacramentum divinum, sacramentum humanum*), the standard of Christ and the standard of the devil ... One soul cannot be due to two masters – God and Caesar" (19). Even the potentially stronger objection that John the Baptist did not ask the soldiers to leave their profession is dismissed by appeal to Jesus' demand to Peter to put away his sword. Tertullian reasons that, by disarming Peter, Christ disarmed every soldier. This final argument offers what appears to be a more pacifist reason set alongside the principal argument of idolatry.

The treatment in *On Crowns* is more extended, and it is occasioned by the example of a Christian soldier who has been imprisoned for refusing to wear the military crown. Tertullian argues that Christianity is incompatible with military service on the grounds both that Jesus admonished Peter for attempting to rescue him with the sword and due to the constant danger of idolatry, of which he provides an extensive list, such as serving on the Lord's Day, guarding pagan temples, eating idol meat, and sacrificing to the gods or the Emperor (11.4). Nonetheless, while it is clearly Tertullian's preference that Christians should not serve in the army, he recognises that for some soldier converts desertion was not an option. A similar concession is found in Hippolytus:

> A soldier of the civil authority must be taught not to kill men and to refuse to do so if he is commanded, and to refuse to take an oath; if he is unwilling to comply, he must be rejected. A military commander or civic magistrate that wears the purple must resign or be rejected. If a catechumen or a believer seeks to become a soldier, they must be rejected, for they have despised God.
>
> (Apostolic Tradition 16.17–19)

It is not clear whether the injunction against killing relates to any warfare or is restricted to execution, but it is clear enough that there is a significant antipathy to service in the army, although falling short of an outright ban. It should be noted that Hippolytus does not single out the military in this section; this is merely one of a long list of occupations he that finds unsuitable for new converts, including sculptors or painters if they make idols, actors, teachers, charioteers, gladiators, or huntsmen (*Apostolic Tradition* 16.9–15).

When Origen considered the issue, he was facing the accusation familiar to apologists that Christians were a threat to the social order and security of the Empire. While Tertullian's first approach was to point to the fact that Christians played a role in civic and military service, only later changing his position, Origen faces both ways simultaneously. He insists Christians are peace-loving, as distinct from their Jewish forerunners (*Against Celsus* 5.33). Nonetheless, when pushed by Celsus, he notes that there are Christians in the army, but even those who do not serve pray for the Empire's armies, and in doing so they contribute as much as those who actually engage in battle:

> [T]he more anyone excels in piety, the more effective help does he render to kings, even more than is given by soldiers, who go forth to fight and slay as many of the enemy as they can ... And none fight better for the king than we do ... we fight on his behalf, forming a special army – an army of piety – by offering our prayers to God.
> (*Against Celsus* 8.73)

He further argues that Christian abstentionism where it is found is similar, albeit more effective, than that of the pagan priests who are exempt from military service.

It is clear that the question of military service was not an issue that generally exercised the earliest Fathers, and where it did, they tended to treat the question briefly and with some ambivalence. To be sure, there is no enthusiastic embrace of the military, yet apologists in particular would use the presence of Christian involvement defensively. Pulling in the opposite direction were the non-retaliatory words of Jesus, which led to more pacifistic arguments against involvement. However, for the most part, the strongest objection concerned the danger of idolatry. Significantly, even where the most negative judgements are found, such as with Tertullian, this view was clearly not universally held, for he has to acknowledge that, despite his wishes, Christians continued to serve (e.g. *Flight* 13). Even in his most extensive reflection (*On Crowns*), Tertullian must face the fact that the "soldier of God" was not the only Christian present when the martyr-soldier was singled out for refusing to wear the soldier's crown; the rest, presumably like the growing number of Christian soldiers in the army, *were* able to accommodate the competing demands of loyalty to Caesar and Christ.

As Christians experienced sporadic bouts of repression from the mid-3rd century, soldiers were among those who were martyred, such as Marinus, Maximillian, and Marcellus (see Musurillo 1972: 240–243, 244–249, and 250–259, respectively). After the outbreak of the 'Great Persecution' in 303 CE, Diocletian purged the army of Christians (Lactantius, *Death* 10), leading to further martyr-soldier stories, including Julius the Veteran and Dasius (Musurillo 1972: 260–265, 272–279).

Julius' defence against the demand to offer sacrifice is that he had served for twenty-seven years and had never been regarded as a troublemaker, demonstrating the established position of Christians in the army (Helgeland 1979: 820–829). However, Christians' precarious position in the army changed after Constantine's victory over Maxentius at the Milvian Bridge in 312 CE and his "Edict of Milan" in the following year, first granting toleration to Christians and restoring confiscated property, then Christianising the Empire.

Famously, Constantine's "conversion" was the result of a religious experience prior to his victory, in which, according to Eusebius, he saw "a cross-shaped trophy formed from light and a text attached to it which read, 'by this conquer'" (*Life* 1.28.2; trans. Cameron and Hall 1999). Although Eusebius claims to have received this account directly from the Emperor, there are good reasons to be cautious (Barnes 1981: 140–147), given his unqualified belief that God was behind Constantine's rise. Lactantius also recounts this event, although slightly differently: Constantine saw the "heavenly sign" to be fixed to his soldiers' shields in a dream (*Death* 44). While both Eusebius (*Life* 1.39) and Lactantius (*Divine Institutes* 1.1) believed Constantine's conversion as a sure sign of God's providence, there is evidence that Constantine was careful and more political in implementing reforms (Barnes 1981; but cf. Drake 2000), particularly in the army, since he would not have wanted to alienate his non-Christian soldiers before his battle with Licinius in 324 CE (Helgeland 1979: 814–816). Nonetheless, Eusebius recounts that he introduced observance of Sundays (*Life* 4.18, 19), placed the *labarum* on his armies' shields (4.21), ordered the cessation of sacrifice (4.23), and eventually ordered that only Christians could be promoted to the highest ranks (4.52). Eventually, less than a century later, only Christians were permitted to serve in the imperial army. Pacifist scholar Walter Wink complains:

> In the year 303 CE, Diocletian forbade any member of the Roman army to be a Christian. By the year 413, no one could be a member of the Roman army *unless* he was a Christian.
>
> (2004: 54, emphasis in original)

Now with imperial apparatus behind it, the Church could prosecute its holy war against not only spiritual principalities and powers, but also their earthly manifestations, generally heretics, Jews, and "pagans." The Donatists would be first to experience the full weight of the new Christian state (Frend 1985: 141–168; Tilley 1996; Gaddis 2005: 103–130), as for the first but not the last time Christians would create other Christian martyrs. For Donatists, of course, this was nothing more than the continuation of the Great Persecution as they sought to portray the Christian state as persecutors. The Donatist Petilian accuses "you who call yourself a Christian" of "imitating the dreadful deeds of the Gentiles," arguing "God does not have butchers for his priests" (Augustine, *Answers to Petilian* 2.42). Augustine dismissed this complaint with the retort that the Donatists brought their plight upon themselves (2.32, 64–65), and violence against them was not persecution, but correction (Brown 1964; Gaddis 2005: 131–150; Dunn 2017):

> There is a persecution of unrighteousness which the impious inflict upon the Church of Christ; and there is a righteous persecution, which the Church of Christ inflicts upon the impious ... She persecutes in the spirit of love; they in the spirit of wrath; she that she might correct; they that they might overthrow.
>
> (Ep. 185.2.11)

Other heretics (Gaddis 2005: 68–102) and Jews in particular would suffer similar repression in the Empire. Conversion to Judaism was outlawed (*Cod. Theod.* 16.8.7), and the Jews' right to public gathering was increasingly restricted (*Cod. Theod.* 16.8.16, 24). Ambrose of Milan famously defended a Christian mob who, led by the local bishop, had attacked a synagogue in Callinicum against Emperor Theodosius' demand for restitution (McLynn 1994: 198–307).

Augustine, building on Ambrose and Cicero (*On Duties*), effectively legitimised war through his development of the just war doctrine (*jus ad bellum*; *Against Faustus* 22.69–76; Markus 1983; Ramsey 1992; Syse 2007). Ambrose regarded defence of the Empire as essential in defending Christianity (*On the Faith* 2.14.136–143). Similarly, he argued that defending others with force is demanded, using positively the example of Moses killing the Egyptian in defence of his fellow Hebrew, such that not intervening makes one as guilty as the assailant (Exod 2.11–15; *De Off. Min.* 1.36.178–179). Ambrose had not, however, applied the same logic to the Jews who had suffered in Callinicum. He insisted that "the maintenance of civil law should be secondary to religion" (*Ep.* 40.14). Augustine similarly regarded any instruction by God to engage in war to be sufficient cause, citing Moses' military adventures (*Questions* 6.10). While war should be for the aim of peace (*Ep.* 189) and be a means of bringing justice (*Questions on heptateuch* 6.10), Christians were now given positive reasons to join the battlefield: "Christians will engage in war to secure the earthly peace and will suffer war as a means to heavenly peace" (*City* 19). While Augustine's ultimate aim was to limit the justification for war, he effectively provided Christian blessing for warfare, which would have consequences he could never have imagined.

CONCLUSION

Constantine's reign is often seen as a turning point for Christianity's relationship with violence and war, when "Christian objection to military service evaporated" (Shafer 2004: 236). However, it is clear that any Christian objections to serving in the army prior to the Christianisation of the Empire were not universally held, and these tended to stem from a concern about idolatry rather than a commitment to pacifism. Moreover, Christians from the New Testament onwards made liberal use of pugilistic language, with martyrdom seen as a potent weapon in a holy war against the forces of Satan, and in the process "Satanized" the people of the Empire (Koscheski 2011: 105). While the non-retaliation strand in Jesus' teaching meant that Christians were not encouraged to take up arms in this struggle, it sat alongside the eschatological tradition, inspiring the belief that God would not only vindicate the suffering Christian, but punish those who persecuted them through eschatological violence. Adolf von Harnack (1981) recognised the problem that this commitment to eschatological judgement meant that Christians could not ultimately shake off a violent impulse.

Finally, while it may frustrate those looking for a uniform prescriptive attitude to war in early Christian tradition, the evidence is clearly mixed. Even if the historical Jesus was not an eschatological figure and was entirely consistent in his teaching on non-violence, before the first extant Christian text came to be written, apocalyptic beliefs had already been attached to the movement. By the time that the gospels came to be written, parables containing judgement and violence had been attached to Jesus. With Krieder (2003: 423), we should surely accept there is no single "Christian attitude" to war in the early centuries. Origen was probably the first Christian thinker to imagine what the world might look like were the whole Empire to convert. He thought that if all of the Romans embraced the Christian faith, there would be no more war (*Against Celsus* 8.70); in this, he was clearly wrong.

References

Allison, Dale. 1998. *Jesus of Nazareth: Millenarian Prophet*. Fortress Press.
Bammel, Ernest. 1984. "The Revolutionary Theory from Reimarus to Brandon." In *Jesus and the Politics of His Day*. Edited by E. Bammel and C. F. D. Moule. Cambridge University Press. 11–68.
Barnes, Timothy D. 1981. *Constantine and Eusebius*. Harvard University Press.

Barr, David L. 2003. "Doing Violence: Moral Issues in Reading John's Apocalypse." In *Reading the Book of Revelation: A Resource for Students.* Edited by David L. Barr. Society for Biblical Literature. 97–108.

Barton, Carlin A. 1994. "Savage Miracles: The Redemption of Lost Honor in Roman Society and the Sacrament of the Gladiator and the Martyr." *Representations* 45: 47–71.

Bauckham, Richard. 1993. *The Theology of the Book of Revelation.* Cambridge University Press.

     1998. "The Book of Revelation as a Christian War Scroll." *Neotestamentica* 22: 17–40.

Blount, Brian K. 2005. *Can I Get a Witness? Reading Revelation through African American Culture.* John Knox Press.

     2009. *Revelation: A Commentary.* New Testament Library. John Knox Press.

Boustan, Raʻanan S., Alex P. Jassen, and Calvin J. Roetzel, eds. 2010. *Violence, Scripture, and Textual Practice in Early Judaism and Christianity.* Brill.

Brandon, Samuel George Frederick. 1967. *Jesus and the Zealots: A Study of the Political Factor in Primitive Christianity.* Charles Scriber's Sons.

Brown, Peter. 1964. "St. Augustine's Attitude to Religious Correction." *Journal of Roman Studies* 54: 107–116.

Cameron, Avril and Stuart G. Hall. 1999. *Eusebius: Life of Constantine.* Clarendon Press.

Charles, J. Daryl. 2010. "Pacifists, Patriots, or Both? Second Thoughts on Pre-Constantinian Early-Christian Attitudes towards Soldiering and War." *Logos* 13(2): 17–55.

Creach, Jerome F. D. 2013. *Violence in Scripture.* Westminster John Knox.

Crossan, John Dominic. 1999. *The Birth of Christianity: Discovering What Happened in the Years Immediately after the Crucifixion of Jesus.* T&T Clark.

     2009. *Jesus: A Revolutionary Biography.* HarperOne.

de Ste. Croix, Geoffrey E. M. 1963. "Why Were the Early Christians Persecuted?" *Past and Present* 26(1): 6–38.

de Villiers, Pieter G. R. and Jan Willem van Henten, eds. 2012. *Coping with Violence in the New Testament.* Brill.

Desjardins, Michel. 1997. *Peace, Violence and the New Testament.* Sheffield Academic Press.

Drake, Harold A. 2000. *Constantine and the Bishops: The Politics of Intolerance.* John Hopkins University Press.

Dunn, Geoffrey D. 2017. "Discipline, Coercion, and Correction: Augustine against the Violence of the Donatists in *Epistula* 185." *Scrinium* 13: 114–130.

Ehrman, Bart D. 1999. *Jesus: Apocalyptic Prophet of the New Millennium.* Oxford University Press.

Ellens, Harold J. 2004. "The Violent Jesus." In *The Destructive Power of Religion: Violence in Judaism, Christianity, and Islam. Vol. 3: Models and Cases of Violence in Religion.* Edited by J. Harold Ellens. Praeger. 15–37.

Fergusson, Everett. 1993. "Early Christian Martyrdom and Civil Disobedience." *Journal of Early Christian Studies* 1: 73–83.

Frankfurter, David. 2009. "Martyrology and the Prurient Gaze." *Journal of Early Christian Studies* 17(2): 215–245.

Frend, William H. C. 1965. *Martyrdom and Persecution in the Early Church: A Study of a Conflict from the Maccabees to Danatus*. Blackwell.

1985. *The Donatist Church: A Movement of Protest in Roman North Africa*, revised edition. Oxford University Press.

Frilingos, Chris. A. 2004. *Spectacles of Empire: Monsters, Martyrs and the Book of Revelation*. University of Pennsylvania Press.

Funk, Robert and Roy W. Hoover. 1993. *The Five Gospels: The Search for the Authentic Words of Jesus*. Maxwell Macmillan International.

Gaddis, Michael. 2005. *There Is No Crime for Those Who Have Christ: Religious Violence in the Christian Roman Empire*. University of California Press.

Gero, Stephen. 1970. "'Miles Gloriosus': The Christian and Military Service according to Tertullian." *Church History* 39(3): 285–298.

Hartog, Paul A. 2020. "Themes and Intertextualities in Pre-Nicene Exhortations to Martyrdom." In *The Wiley Blackwell Companion to Christian Martyrdom*. Edited by Paul Middleton. Wiley Blackwell. 102–119.

Hays, Richard. 1997. *The Moral Vision of the New Testament*. T&T Clark.

Helgeland, John. 1979. "Christians and the Roman Army from Marcus Aurelius to Constantine." In *Aufstieg under Niedergang der Römischen Welt II.23.1*. De Gruyter. 724–834.

Hurtado, Larry W. 1985. "Revelation 4–5 in Light of Jewish Apocalyptic Analogies." *Journal for the Study of the New Testament* 25: 105–124.

1999. "Pre-70CE Jewish Opposition to Christ-Devotion." *Journal of Theological Studies* (new series) 50: 35–58.

Howard-Brook, Wes. 2016. *Empire Baptized: How the Church Embraced What Jesus Rejected (Second to Fifth Centuries)*. Orbis Books.

Johns, Loren J. 2003. *The Lamb Christology of the Apocalypse of John*. Mohr Siebeck.

2005. "Conceiving Violence: The Apocalypse of John and the Left Behind Series." *Direction* 34: 194–214.

Joseph, Simon J. 2014. *The Nonviolent Messiah: Jesus, Q, and the Enochic Tradition*. Augsburg Fortress.

Koester, Craig. 2014. *Revelation: A New Translation with Introduction and Commentary*. Anchor Yale Bible Commentary 38A. Yale University Press.

Koscheski, Jonathan. 2011. "The Earliest Christian War: Second- and Third-Century Martyrdom and the Creation of Cosmic Warriors." *Journal of Religious Ethics* 39(1): 100–124.

Krieder, Allan. 2003. "Military Service in the Church Orders." *Journal of Religious Ethics* 31(3): 415–442.

Maccoby, Hyam. 1973. *Revolution in Judaea: Jesus and the Jewish Resistance*. Ocean Books.

Markus, Robert Austin. 1983. "Saint Augustine's Views on the 'Just War'." In *The Church and War*. Edited by W. J. Sheils. Blackwell. 1–13.

Marshall, I. Howard. 1985. "New Testament Perspectives on War." *Evangelical Quarterly* 57: 115–132.

Martin, Dale B. 2014. "Jesus in Jerusalem: Armed and Not Dangerous." *Journal for the Study of the New Testament* 37(1): 3–24.

Matthews, Shelley and E. Leigh Gibson, eds. 2005. *Violence in the New Testament*. T&T Clark.

McLynn, Neil B. 1994. *Ambrose of Milan: Church and Court in a Christian Capital*. University of California Press.

Middleton, Paul. 2006. *Radical Martyrdom and Cosmic Conflict in Early Christianity*. T&T Clark.

2018. *The Violence of the Lamb: Martyrs as Agents of Divine Judgement in the Book of Revelation*. T&T Clark.

2020. "Martyrdom and Persecution in the New Testament." In *The Wiley Blackwell Companion to Christian Martyrdom*. Edited by Paul Middleton. Wiley Blackwell. 51–71.

2021. "Were the Early Christians Really Persecuted?" In *Tolerance, Intolerance, and Recognition in Early Christianity and Early Judaism*. Edited by Outi Lehtipuu and Michael Labahn. Amsterdam University Press. 229–250.

Moss, Candida. 2012. "The Discourse of Voluntary Martyrdom: Ancient and Modern." *Church History* 81: 535–551.

2013. *The Myth of Persecution: How Christians Invented the Story of Martyrdom*. HarperOne.

Moyise, Steve. 2001. "Does the Lion Lie Down with the Lamb?" *Studies in the Book of Revelation*. Edited by Steve Moyise. T&T Clark. 181–194.

Musurillo, Herbert. 1972. *Acts of the Christian Martyrs*. Clarendon Press.

Neville, David J. 2011. "Faithful, True, and Violent? Christology and 'Divine Vengeance' in the Revelation of John." *Passionate Eschatology: The Future as Friend*. Edited by Ted Grimsrud and Michael Hardin. Cascade Books. 56–84.

Nickel, Jesse P. 2021. *The Things That Make for Peace: Jesus and Eschatological Violence*. De Gruyter.

Paynter, Helen and Michael Spalione, eds. 2020. *The Bible on Violence: A Thick Description*. Sheffield Phoenix.

Perkins, Judith. 1995. *The Suffering Self: Pain and Narrative Representation in the Early Christian Era*. Routledge.

Ramsey, Paul. 1992. "The Just War according to St. Augustine." In *Just War Theory*. Edited by J. B. Elshtain. Blackwell. 8–22.

Roeztel, Calvin J. 2010. "The Language of War (2 Cor. 10:1–6) and the Language of Weakness (2 Cor. 11:21b–13:10)." In *Violence, Scripture, and Textual Practice in Early Judaism and Christianity*. Edited by Ra'anan S. Boustan, Alex P. Jassen, and Calvin J. Roetzel. Brill. 77–98.

Shafer, Grant R. 2004. "Hell, Martyrdom, and War: Violence in Early Christianity." *The Destructive Power of Religion: Violence in Judaism, Christianity, and Islam. Vol. 3: Models and Cases of Violence in Religion*. Edited by J. Harold Ellens. Praeger. 193–246.

Swartley, William M. 1996. "War and Peace in the New Testament." In *Aufstieg under Niedergang der Römischen Welt 26(3)*. De Gruyter. 2298–2408.

Syse, Henrik. 2007. "Augustine and Just War: Between Virtue and Duties." In *Ethics, Nationalism, and Just War: Medieval and Contemporary Perspectives*. Catholic University of America Press. 36–50.

Tilley, Maureen A. 1996. *Donatist Martyr Stories: The Church in Conflict in Roman North Africa*. Liverpool University Press.

van Henten, Jan Willem. 2012. "The Concept of Martyrdom in the Book of Revelation." In *Die Johannesapokalypse: Kontexte–Konzepte–Rezeption*. Edited by Jörg Frey, James A. Kelhoffer, and Franz Tóth. Mohr Siebeck. 587–618.

von Harnack, Adolf. 1981. *Militia Christi: The Christian Religion and the Military in the First Three Centuries*. Fortress Press. (German original, 1905.)

Wicker, Brian. ed. 2006. *Witnesses to Faith? Martyrdom in Christianity and Islam*. Ashgate.

Wink, Walter. 1984. *Naming the Powers: The Language of Power in the New Testament*. Fortress Press.

    1986. *Unmasking the Powers: The Invisible Forces That Determine Human Existence*. Fortress Press.

    1992. *Engaging the Powers: Discernment and Resistance in a World of Domination*. Fortress Press.

    2003. *Jesus and Nonviolence: A Third Way*. Augsburg Fortress.

    2004. "Beyond Just War and Pacifism: Jesus' Nonviolent Way." In *The Destructive Power of Religion: Violence in Judaism, Christianity, and Islam. Vol 4: Contemporary Views on Spirituality and Violence*. Edited by J. Harold Ellens. Praeger. 53–76.

Wright, Nicholas Thomas. 1996. *Jesus and the Victory of God*. SPCK.

Yoder, John H. 1972. *The Politics of Jesus*. Eerdmans.

Zehnder, Markus and Hallvard Hagelia, eds. 2013. *Encountering Violence in the Bible*. Sheffield Phoenix.

3 Fighting and Martial Valor in Islamic Thought

ASMA AFSARUDDIN

Fighting and the conduct of warfare are important topics in the Islamic milieu, and considerable attention has been paid to them by Muslim authors from the earliest centuries of Islam. Fighting or war is often reduced to the Arabic word *jihād* by both Muslim and non-Muslim authors. Such a conflation, however, elides a broader semantic landscape for the term *jihād* as indicated in a number of Islamic sources; this landscape will be resurrected to a considerable extent in the discussion below by consulting a broad range of primary Arabic sources. Such sources include primarily the Qur'an, Qur'an commentaries (*tafsīr*), and collections of *ḥadīth*, which record the sayings of the Prophet Muḥammad.

As part of *jihād*, fighting for a legitimate, just cause is valorized within the Islamic tradition, and those who exhibit martial valor on the battlefield in the service of such a cause earn high praise in the relevant literature. In these literary sources, this attribute is particularly assigned to, beside the Prophet, some of his closest associates, called Companions, especially those who were considered to be qualified for positions of leadership. The content of this praise literature will be discussed briefly in the final section of this chapter.

THE QUR'ANIC DISCOURSE

Any discussion of fighting and the conduct of warfare must, of course, start with the Qur'an – the central sacred text of Islam that Muslims regard as divinely revealed scripture. Although *jihād* is the term frequently used in Western sources to narrowly connote war waged for a religious purpose, the word's basic meaning is "struggle," "striving," "exertion" in the broadest sense. When the word *jihād* (or its derivatives) is joined to the phrase *"fī sabīl Allāh"* (lit. "in the path of God"), the full expression in Arabic, *al-jihād fī sabīl Allāh*, means "struggling/striving for the sake of God." The Qur'an uses a different term – *qitāl* – to refer specifically to "fighting" or "armed combat" that is permitted under certain conditions. *Ḥarb* is the Arabic word for war in general. It is, however, never used in the Qur'an with the phrase "in the path of God" and has no connection with the concept of *jihād*.

Muslim scholars divide the Qur'anic revelations into two main periods, corresponding to the two phases of Muḥammad's prophetic career. The first is the Meccan period between 610 and 622 CE when Muḥammad lived and preached in Mecca in the Arabian Peninsula. The second is the Medinan period that began in 622 CE when Muḥammad and his followers emigrated to Medina, a city to the north of Mecca about 200 miles away. This period lasted until the death of the Prophet in 632 CE.

MECCAN PERIOD

Although the term *jihād* has come to be used almost exclusively in a military sense in both academic and popular discourses and this understanding is then projected back to the Qur'an, a careful examination of Qur'anic verses themselves provides an important corrective to this usage. *Jihād* and related terms frequently occur in the Qur'an in a nonviolent sense during both time periods. During the Meccan period when no fighting was allowed, Muslims were allowed to engage only in nonviolent struggle against their pagan Meccan persecutors. In roughly 610, when Muḥammad publicly began preaching his message of monotheism to Meccans who were polytheistic idol-worshippers, he frequently faced hostile resistance from the latter. When the number of his followers began to grow, they too began to face persecution from the Meccan polytheists. Despite the growing aggression, Muslims were not granted permission to physically retaliate against their persecutors during this period. Instead, the Qur'an counseled them to forgive those who caused them harm and to bear with patience the trials and tribulations that were visited upon them. Qur'an 42:43 states: "Whoever is patient and forgives, that is indeed the best resolution of affairs." Another verse (Qur'an 3:200) counsels: "O those who believe, be patient and forbearing, outdo others in forbearance, be firm and revere God so that you may succeed" (Afsaruddin 2020: 448–450).

In these and other verses, the Qur'an highlights "patient forbearance," termed *ṣabr* in Arabic, as a highly significant, nonmilitant dimension of struggling against wrongdoing (and, therefore, of *jihād*) in this early period. Qur'an 42:40–42 further amplify this nonviolent aspect of *jihād*; they state:

The requital of evil is an evil similar to it: hence, whoever pardons
and makes peace, his reward rests with God – for indeed, He does
not love evil-doers. Yet surely, as for those who defend themselves
after having been wronged – no blame whatever attaches to them:
blame attaches but to those who oppress people and behave
outrageously on earth, offending against all right; for them is
grievous suffering in store!

Nonviolent struggle against wrongdoing is not the same as passiv-
ity, however, which, when displayed in the face of grave oppression and
injustice, is clearly marked as immoral in the Qur'an (4:95).

The term *jihād* itself is also used in the Qur'an during the Meccan
period in a noncombative sense. Two important verses may be cited
in this context as examples. The first is Qur'an 22:78, which states:
"Strive (*jāhidū*) in regard to God a true striving as is His due"; the
second is Qur'an 29:69, which states: "As for those who strive in
regard to us (*jāhadū fīnā*), we will surely guide them to our paths,
indeed God is with those who do good." Early exegetes from before
the 10th century, like Muqātil ibn Sulaymān (d. 767), understood the
Arabic verbs *jāhidū* and *jāhadū* in Qur'an 22:78 and Qur'an 29:69,
respectively, to refer to the general striving of believers to obey God
in their actions and to please Him. These exegetes also emphasized
that since these verses are Meccan, they are not to be understood as
referring to the military *jihād*. Later scholars, like the celebrated
exegete Muḥammad ibn Jarīr al-Ṭabarī (d. 923), however, assign military meanings to these verses. After al-Ṭabarī, influential exegetes
like Fakhr al-Dīn al-Rāzī (d. 1210) and Muḥammad al-Qurṭubī
(d. 1273) attach both combative and noncombative meanings to these
verses. With regard to Qur'an 22:78, these last two exegetes understand two types of exertion to be implied in the verse: (1) the spiritual
exertion required to overcome one's base desires in order to obey God;
and (2) the general, physical exertion required to carry out one's
religious obligations, including military activity. With regard to
Qur'an 29:69, al-Rāzī additionally understands this verse to be a
reference to the intellectual effort of the believer to increase in knowledge of God.

Another critical Meccan verse is Qur'an 25:52, which states: "Do
not obey the unbelievers and wage a mighty struggle (*jihād kabīr*) with
it (*bihi*)." An overwhelming majority of the exegetes understand this
striving to be carried out by means of the Qur'an, referred to in the
enclitic pronoun "it." One exegete explains that the Arabic phrase *jihād*

kabīr ("a mighty struggle") in the verse refers to *jihād* of the tongue; that is to say, the struggle to preach the message of Islam.[1]

MEDINAN PERIOD: ESTABLISHING JUST CAUSE FOR MILITARY COMBAT

Specific just causes (*casus belli*) for which recourse to military force may be sanctioned are mentioned in the Qur'an. Roughly two years after the emigration to Medina, two Qur'anic verses (22:39–40) permitting fighting (*qitāl*) were revealed. These verses state:

> Permission [to fight] is given to those against whom war has been initiated;
>
> indeed, God has the power to help them: those who have been driven from their homes unjustly for no other reason than their saying, "Our Provider is God!" For, if God had not enabled people to defend themselves against one another, monasteries, churches, synagogues, and mosques – in all of which God's name is abundantly glorified – would surely have been destroyed.

As we may recall, the previously cited Qur'an 42:40–42 had allowed nonviolent self-defense for the following reasons: the wrongful conduct of enemies and their oppressive and immoral behavior on Earth. In Qur'an 22:39–40, two more explicit reasons are given: the initiation of fighting by the enemy and the wrongful expulsion of people from their homes for peacefully affirming their belief in one God. Furthermore, these verses assert, if people were not allowed to defend themselves against aggressive wrongdoers, all the houses of worship – it is noteworthy that Jewish and Christian places of worship are included alongside Muslim ones – would be destroyed and thus the word of God extinguished. It is reasonable to infer from this verse that Muslims may resort to defensive combat also on behalf of non-Muslim monotheists who come under attack by hostile forces.

Additional reasons that legitimate an armed response to the adversary are contained in another important group of verses – Qur'an 9:12–13 – which state:

---

[1] For a detailed discussion of Qur'an 22:78; 29:69; and 25:52 and their exegeses, see Afsaruddin 2013: 16–25.

If they break their pacts after having concluded them and revile your religion, then fight the leaders of unbelief. Will you not fight a people who violated their oaths and had intended to expel the Messenger and commenced [hostilities] against you the first time?[2]

The overwhelming majority of exegetes stress that the violation of pacts by the polytheists, their denigration of Islam, hostile intent toward Muḥammad, and their initial act of aggression against Muslims had made fighting necessary against them.

Therefore, when both just cause and right intention exist, fighting in self-defense against an intractable enemy may become obligatory. Qur'an 2:216 states:

Fighting (al-qitāl) is prescribed for you, while you dislike it. But it is possible that you dislike a thing which is good for you, and that you love a thing which is bad for you. God knows and you know not.

Although this verse when taken out of its historical context may imply that fighting was henceforth to be considered obligatory for Muslims in perpetuity, the commentary literature makes clear that a majority of the medieval exegetes understood these verses to be applicable only to the time of the Prophet and his Companions and to have no further applicability beyond the first generation of Muslims (Afsaruddin 2013: 65–71). Another verse – Qur'an 48:17 – grants exemption from armed combat to those who have physical disabilities but warns of punishment for those who willfully refuse to fight in a legitimate battle in spite of their ability to do so. Those who take part in such a legitimate battle are assured of divine assistance through angels who fight on the side of the righteous warriors (Qur'an 3:124–126; 8:9). In one verse associated with the Battle of Badr fought in 624 CE, in which the pagan Meccans were routed and suffered severe losses, the Qur'an (8:17) declares that "it was not you but God himself who slew them."

In addition to self-defense, the Qur'an states that Muslims may fight to defend those who are oppressed and who call out to them for help (4:75), except against a people with whom the Muslims have concluded a treaty (8:72). The Qur'an also has specific injunctions with regard to the initiation of hostilities and conduct during war (jus in bello). Qur'an 2:190, which states: "Fight in the cause of God those who fight you, but do not commit aggression, for God loves not aggressors," forbids Muslims from commencing hostilities and affirms that fighting can

---

[2] For an extensive discussion of the exegeses of this verse, see Afsaruddin (2013: 58–64).

only be undertaken in response to a prior act of aggression by the opposite side. The Qur'an further counsels (5:8): "Let not rancor towards others cause you to incline to wrong and depart from justice. Be just; that is closer to piety." This verse warns against succumbing to unprincipled and vengeful desires to punish and inflict disproportionate damage. Proportionality is explicitly stressed in Qur'an 2:194, which states: "Whoever attacks you attack him to the extent of his attack."

Other verses in the Qur'an make clear that fighting is defensive and limited in nature and must cease when the other side lays down arms. Two significant verses (Qur'an 60:8–9) mandate kind and just interactions with those who are peaceful, regardless of their religious beliefs, in contrast to those who willfully commit aggression:

> God does not forbid you from being kind and equitable to those who have neither made war on you on account of your religion nor driven you from your homes; indeed God loves those who are equitable. God forbids you however from making common cause with those who fight you on account of your religion and evict you from your homes and who support [others] in driving you out.

Similarly, Qur'an 4:90 states: "If they hold themselves aloof from you and do not wage war against you and offer you peace, then God does not permit you any way against them."

Al-Ṭabarī in his exegesis of Qur'an 60:8–9 affirms that these verses clearly permit Muslims to be kind to all those who bear no ill will towards them, regardless of their religion and creed, for God, he says, loves those who are equitable, who give people their due rights, who are personally just to them, and who do good to those who are good to them (al-Ṭabarī 1997: 12: 62–63). These views were repeated by practically all of the exegetes who came after him; among the later exegetes, the 13th-century Andalusian exegete al-Qurṭubī is the most adamant in maintaining that the exhortation in Qur'an 60:8 to be kind to those who had caused Muslims no harm was applicable to everyone who belonged in this category, regardless of religious affiliation, and that the command was unambiguous and valid for all times (al-Qurṭubī 2001: 18: 54–55).

Another important verse – Qur'an 8:61 – requires Muslims to cease fighting when the other side desists from fighting and makes peaceful overtures. The verse states: "And if they should incline to peace, then incline to it [yourself] and place your trust in God; for He is all-hearing and all-knowing." This point is stressed by al-Ṭabarī, who comments that when a people enters into Islam, pays the *jizya* (a kind of poll tax), or establishes friendly relations with Muslims, then Muslims should do the same "for the sake of peace and peacemaking" (al-Ṭabarī 1997: 6: 278).

But there were other scholars and authorities in later centuries, particularly during the Mamluk period (1250–1517), who wished to promote the view that the Qur'an mandates continuous warfare against non-Muslims *qua* non-Muslims and that fighting in the Qur'an was not only defensive but offensive as well. Two verses in particular are cited by the proponents of this view: Qur'an 9:5, which is understood by these authorities to mandate fighting against all non-Abrahamic non-Muslims until they convert; and Qur'an 9:29, which is understood to require fighting against the People of the Book (mainly Jews and Christians) until they either submit to Muslim rule, signified by their payment of the poll tax, or embrace Islam. Since the previously cited verses – Qur'an 2:190, 60:7–9, 4:90, and 8:61 – taken together clearly establish that fighting was contingent on the prior aggression of the enemy and that peaceful people, regardless of their religion, could not be attacked under any circumstance, these more "hawkish" scholars had to develop an interpretive tool or principle for effectively "canceling" these verses. This interpretive tool or principle is known in Arabic as *naskh*, which is usually translated as "abrogation." According to this principle of abrogation, later verses in the Qur'an, such as 9:5 and 9:29, may be understood as superseding earlier verses – such as 60:7–9 and 8:61 – whose texts taken together may appear contradictory. These views did not go uncontested; our brief discussion of these two verses below conveys the tenor of some of these contestations.

Qur'an 9:5 states:

> When the sacred months have lapsed, then kill the polytheists (*al-mushrikīn*) wherever you may encounter them. Seize them and encircle them and lie in wait for them. But if they repent and perform the prayer and give the *zakat* [obligatory alms], then let them go on their way, for God is forgiving and merciful.

Premodern exegetes from before the Mamluk period (that is, from before the mid-13th century) typically restrict the applicability of this verse to the Arab polytheists with whom the Muslims had no pact. They also do not maintain that Qur'an 9:5 had abrogated other verses in the Qur'an that counsel good relations with peaceful people, regardless of their religious affiliation. For example, the 12th-century exegete al-Zamakhsharī (d. 1144) identifies the intended polytheists in Qur'an 9:5 as specifically those who break their pledges and display *a priori* hostility to Muslims – not polytheists as a general collectivity. Like al-Ṭabarī before him in the 9th century, he does not consider this to be an abrogating verse (al-Zamakhsharī 1998: 3: 13–14). Similarly, al-Qurṭubī in the 13th century considers the verse to be neither abrogated nor abrogating (al-Qurṭubī 2001: 8: 70). It is also highly significant that none of these exegetes up to al-Qurṭubī had specifically dubbed this verse the "sword verse" (in Arabic *āyat al-sayf*), which is the name given to it in later commentaries, such as the one by the 14th-century exegete Ibn Kathīr (Ibn Kathīr 1990: 2: 322). Ibn Kathīr's commentary on this verse indicates to us that a partiality had developed by the Mamluk period for the derivation of an expansive general mandate from otherwise historically circumscribed Qur'anic verses (as so understood by earlier exegetes) to fight or punish all those deemed enemies of Islam – in Ibn Kathīr's time, these were the Crusaders as well as the Mongols (Afsaruddin 2013: 71–75).

Qur'an 9:29 also came to be understood by a number of influential exegetes from roughly after the 8th century as granting permission to Muslims to fight a different group of non-Muslims – the People of the Book – who refuse to accept Islam or submit to Muslim political rule. The verse states:

> Fight those who do not believe in God nor in the Last Day and do not forbid what God and His messenger have forbidden and do not follow the religion of truth from among those who were given the Book until they offer the *jizya* with [their] hands in humility.

The early 8th-century exegete Mujāhid ibn Jabr (d. 722) understands this verse to refer specifically to the Byzantines, who are said to have amassed their forces on the Syrian border in preparation for an attack on Muslims in the year 630. This event is referred to as the Battle of Tabūk in the sources, although no battle was actually fought since the Byzantine forces failed to materialize (Mujāhid ibn Jabr 2005: 99). Exegetes after Mujāhid, however, routinely identify the referents in this verse as Jews and Christians in general who are expected to pay the *jizya* humbly in return for their protection by Muslim rulers. Al-Ṭabarī acknowledges that the historical context for the revelation of this verse was the campaign of Tabūk. But unlike Mujāhid, who specifically identifies the warring Byzantine Christians as the referent in this verse, al-Ṭabarī understands this verse to refer in general to Jews and Christians who must pay the *jizya* as a marker of their inferior legal and social status (al-Ṭabarī 1997: 6: 349–350). Al-Ṭabarī's views are consistently replicated by later exegetes, with the notable exception of al-Qurṭubī, who pleads for respectful and compassionate treatment of the People of the Book in his Andalusian milieu (Afsaruddin 2013: 75–79).[3]

At the same time, al-Ṭabarī and other influential exegetes maintain in their commentaries that these verses (9:5; 9:29) do not abrogate the peaceful, conciliatory verses in the Qur'an and dismiss the views of others who adhere to this position. Al-Ṭabarī thus notes that Qatāda ibn Di'āma (d. 736), who was a Successor (from the second generation of Muslims), had stated that Qur'an 8:61 (which exhorts Muslims to incline to peace when the other side does) had been abrogated by Qur'an 9:5. Al-Ṭabarī dismisses this interpretation as insupportable on the basis of the Qur'an, the *sunna* (referring to the practices and customs of Muḥammad), or reason (al-Ṭabarī 1997: 6: 278–279). The unabrogated status of the verse was similarly affirmed by a majority of exegetes after him (Afsaruddin 2013: 90–93). The invocation of the principle of abrogation by some scholars testifies to the ingenuity of a belligerent faction that was determined to find scriptural sanction for wars that may be fought offensively, thereby overriding the categorical Qur'anic prohibition against the initiation of fighting (especially in Qur'an 2:190).

GLORIFICATION OF FIGHTING AND MILITARY MARTYRDOM IN ISLAMIC TEXTS

Martyrdom in the Qur'an

It is commonly assumed in both academic and nonacademic circles that military martyrdom is highly valued within the Islamic tradition and that there are foundational texts that exhort adult male Muslims to seek this kind of martyrdom should the opportunity present itself. It therefore tends to come as a surprise when one discovers through a careful reading of the Qur'an that it does not actually have a single, unambiguous word to connote "martyr" or "martyrdom" in the military or non-military sense. The common Arabic word for martyr outside of the Qur'an became *shahīd*. The Qur'an itself does not use this word (and its plural *shuhadā'*) for a martyr; rather, it is only used to refer to a legal witness or eyewitness. Only in the later extra-Qur'anic tradition does this word acquire the specific meaning of "one who bears witness for the faith," particularly by laying down their life. An extraneous, especially Christian influence may be suspected here. There is evidence for

---

[3] For further discussion of the exegeses of Qur'an 9:29, see Abdel Haleem (2012: 72–89).

the influence of the related Syriac word for martyr-witness *sahēd* on the Arabic *shahīd* and the latter's subsequent acquisition of the secondary meaning of "martyr" (Jeffrey 1938: 187).

The Qur'an instead uses the phrase "those who were/are slain in the path of God" (in Arabic *man qutila fī sabīl Allāh*) to refer broadly to people who die for a righteous cause and/or in a righteous manner; this may include dying in battle but is not necessarily restricted to this meaning. One Qur'anic verse (3:169) that has been understood to refer to the special status of the military martyr states: "Do not think that those who were slain in the path of God are dead. They are alive and well provided for by their Lord." In his exegesis of this verse, which does not explicitly refer to any military activity, al-Ṭabarī relates it specifically to those Companions who were killed at the Battle of Uhud, fought in the year 634 after the emigration to Medina. He comments that the verse serves to inform Muḥammad that he should not regard them as dead; rather, they are to be regarded as being alive in the presence of God, exulting and rejoicing in what God grants them from His generosity and mercy (al-Ṭabarī 1997: 3: 513).

One Qur'anic verse (22:58), however, contains a firm stricture against the glorification of military martyrdom. This verse states: "Those who emigrated in the path of God and then were slain or died [of natural causes], God will provide handsome provisions for them; indeed God is the best of providers." In his exegesis of this verse, al-Ṭabarī states that this verse was revealed specifically in regard to certain Companions who differed regarding the status of those who had perished in the path of God. Some were of the opinion that the one who was slain and the one who died naturally were of the same status, while others maintained that the one who was slain had achieved greater merit. Then God revealed this verse, continues al-Ṭabarī, in which He informed Muḥammad that both the one who is slain and the one who dies in the path of God attain the same reward in the hereafter (al-Ṭabarī 1997: 9: 182).

Other exegetes after him offer similar exegeses. The late 12th-century commentator al-Rāzī cites a *ḥadīth* in explanation of this position that states: "The one who is slain in the path of God the Exalted and the one who dies [of natural causes] in the path of God are the equal of one other in regard to the blessings and reward [that they are entitled to]" (al-Rāzī 1999: 8: 244). In his exegesis of Qur'an 22:58, al-Qurṭubī in the 13th century notes that some scholars were of the opinion that the one who is slain in the path of God is better than the one who dies of natural causes, but the revelation of this verse affirmed that both were equal in status and equally assured of a handsome provision in the hereafter. Al-Qurṭubī notes that Islamic law, however, came to indicate the superior status of the battlefield martyr in spite of Qur'an 22:58, which makes no *prima facie* distinction in status between the naturally deceased and the fallen in battle (al-Qurṭubī 2001: 4: 262–267).

Martyrdom in *Ḥadīth* Works

After the Qur'an, the *ḥadīth* literature containing the sayings of Muḥammad is the most important source of law, ethics, and morality for Muslims. One early *ḥadīth* work from the first half of the 9th century is particularly helpful for us in tracing the debates among early Muslims concerning the purview of *jihād* and martyrdom. This work is titled *al-Muṣannaf* by 'Abd al-Razzāq al-Ṣan'ānī (d. 827), and it contains reports attributed not only to Muḥammad but also to his Companions, as well as to the next generation of Muslims known as the Successors, who speak on their own authority. As a result, these works preserve for us a broader range of highly significant reports containing multiple, contested perspectives on *jihād* and martyrdom that are often missing from later works.

The multiple ways of carrying out *jihād* are heralded in a noteworthy report recorded in 'Abd al-Razzaq's *Muṣannaf*, which relates that a number of the Companions were sitting with the Prophet when a man of muscular build, apparently a pagan from the tribe of Quraysh, came into view. Some of those gathered exclaimed, "How strong this man looks! If only he would exert his strength in the way of God!" The Prophet asked, "Do you think only someone who is killed [sc. in battle] is engaged in the way of God?" He continued, "Whoever goes out in the world seeking licit work to support his family is on the path of God; whoever goes out in the world seeking licit work to support himself is on the path of God. Whoever goes out seeking worldly increase has gone down the path of the devil" (al-Ṣan'ānī 2000: 5: 183). This report is noteworthy for at least two reasons. Firstly, it contains a clear rebuttal to those who would understand "striving in the way of God" in primarily military terms. It praises instead the daily struggle of the individual to live their life "in the way of God," which endows even the most mundane of licit activities with moral and spiritual significance. Secondly, the report emphasizes the importance of personal sincere intention in determining the moral worth of an individual's act. One may therefore understand this report to be counseling caution against assuming that what appears to be a pious activity to humans will be deemed as such by God, who alone can know the true intention of the individual.

There are additionally several reports in the *Muṣannaf* that record the displeasure of certain Companions at the military adventurism of the Umayyad rulers, who were widely perceived as immoral and unscrupulous rulers by pious Muslims. The Umayyads, whose political base was in Syria, ruled between 661 and 750 CE and were engaged in constant border warfare with the Byzantines; no doubt, there was a perceived need on the part of the Umayyads to justify these military campaigns on a theological and legal basis, to which there appears to have been considerable pushback among the piously minded. One report specifically warns the pious not to join in the military campaigns of those "who fight seeking [the gains of] the world" – here a pointed reference to the Umayyads – for then they would forfeit their "portion in the hereafter" (al-Ṣanʿānī 2000: 5: 189).

In general, we often see a regional division between the supporters and opponents of the Umayyads, with mostly Syrian scholars, like Makḥūl al-Shāmī (d. ca. 730), expressing support for offensive *jihād*, while non-Syrian scholars, often based in Mecca and Medina (called the Ḥijāz), expressed opposition to it (Mottahedeh and al-Sayyid 2001: 23–29). Thus, pious Ḥijāzī scholars like ʿAbd Allāh ibn ʿUmar (d. 693) and ʿAṭāʾ ibn Abī Rabāḥ (d. 733) are on record as having opposed what must have appeared to them as unseemly glorification of military activity in pro-Umayyad circles at the expense of the cultivation of the usual noncombative religious virtues and duties. According to one significant report, the Ḥijāzī scholar ʿAbd Allāh ibn ʿUmar was once asked by a young man why he did not take part in the military *jihād*. Ibn ʿUmar is said to have first turned away from him and then responded after his initial silence:

> Indeed Islam is founded upon four supports – performance of prayer, giving of the required alms – and no distinction is made between the two; fasting during the month of Ramadan; and pilgrimage to the Kaʿba for the one capable of undertaking it. *Jihād* and non-obligatory charity (*ṣadaqa*) are among the good voluntary activities.
>
> (al-Ṣanʿānī 2000: 5: 189)

In this report we discern a sharp critique of the promotion of the combative *jihād* by some as a religious obligation and an affirmation instead of the position that fighting is at best a voluntary and optional activity. Early reports such as this convey to us that a cult of the military *jihād* and martyrdom that is clearly taking shape during the Umayyad period did not go unchallenged, nor was it fully formed during the first and second centuries of Islam (Blankinship 1994).

With regard to the notion of martyrdom that is connected with the military *jihād*, we find that there are multiple, competing definitions of who qualifies as a martyr, invariably called *shahīd* in the *ḥadīth* literature in contrast to the Qur'an. The *Muṣannaf* of 'Abd al-Razzāq contains a number of reports that relate competing definitions of *shahīd*. One report attributed to the famous Companion Abū Hurayra states that the *shahīd* is one who, were he to die in his bed, would enter heaven (al-Ṣan'ānī 2000: 5: 268). Another 8th-century *ḥadīth* compilation records multiple significations of the term *shahīd*. The *Muwaṭṭa'* of the famous jurist Mālik ibn Anas (d. 795) records that the Prophet identified seven kinds of martyrs, in addition to those who died from fighting in God's way. Thus:

> He who dies as a victim of an epidemic is a martyr; he who dies from drowning is a martyr; he who dies from pleurisy is a martyr; he who dies from diarrhea is a martyr; he who dies by [being burned in] fire is a martyr; he who dies by being struck by a crumbling dilapidated wall is a martyr; and the woman who dies in childbed is a martyr.
>
> (Mālik ibn Anas 1994: 1: 366–367)

This report therefore draws attention to the suffering of the believer – whether on account of debilitating illnesses or other afflictions in life, including undertaking the arduous task of defending Muslims on the battlefield – as the core ingredient of martyrdom rather than the manner of dying itself.

Compared to this early work, later *ḥadīth* compilations, such as the famous collection of al-Bukhārī (d. 870) called *Ṣaḥīḥ* (referring to "sound" and therefore reliable *ḥadīths*), record more reports attributed to the Prophet that contain effusive praise of the military *jihād*, with generous posthumous rewards promised to the military martyr. One such *ḥadīth* states that there is an "abode of martyrs" (*dār al-shuhadā'*) that is the best and most excellent of abodes in the hereafter (al-Bukhārī n.d.: 4: 409). Another *ḥadīth* quotes the Prophet as saying that "[c]oming and going in the path of God (referring to military activity) is better than the world and what is in it" (al-Bukhārī n.d.: 4: 410).

Some *ḥadīths* warn, however, that the exalted status of the warrior should not lead to the deliberate courting of martyrdom on the part of the faithful by seeking to confront the enemy. One such *ḥadīth* relates that, during military campaigns, Muḥammad would customarily wait until the sun had tilted toward the west and then address his troops thus: "Do not wish to meet the enemy, O People, and ask forgiveness of

God. When you meet them, be forbearing and know that paradise lies below the shade of the swords" (al-Bukhārī n.d.: 4: 481–482).

Notions of *jihād* as a moral and spiritual struggle, however, continue to be preserved along with the notion of *jihād* as military activity in most *hadīth* collections. In a number of these reports that focus on *jihād* as a moral and spiritual endeavor, the emphasis is on charity and prayer and on nonmilitant acts of courage, such as speaking the truth before a tyrant even at the cost of imperiling one's life (Abū Dāwūd 1988: 4: 122). These meanings are consistent with the famous prophetic *hadīth* that describes the various means of carrying out *jihād*: by the hand, the tongue, and intent (that is, silently with the heart; al-Nawawī 1997: 110).

The two main dimensions of *jihād* that are evident in the Meccan and Medinan chapters of the Qur'an – *ṣabr* and *qitāl* – are renamed in the *hadīth* literature as *al-jihād al-akbar* ("the greater struggle") and *al-jihād al-asghar* ("the lesser struggle"), respectively, with the former referring to the continuous internal, spiritual struggle (*jihād al-nafs*) and the latter to conditional armed combat (*jihād al-sayf*). This later typology became pervasive in various kinds of edifying and mystical literature, where *ṣabr* as the ongoing spiritual struggle to overcome one's base desires is exalted as the highest form of warfare to be waged by the righteous individual. This is eloquently expressed by the famous Muslim theologian Abū Ḥāmid al-Ghazālī (d. 1111) when he remarks:

> Patience is an expression of the perseverance of the religious impulse in its confrontation with the impulses present in the lower self. If it [the religious impulse] perseveres until it overcomes and prevails over the opposed baser instincts, then the party of God has triumphed and becomes affiliated with the patient ones (*al-ṣābirīn*). If it should flag and weaken so that the baser instincts vanquish it and it does not resolutely repel it, then it becomes affiliated with the followers of devils.
>
> (al-Ghazālī n.d.: 4: 87)

The external cosmic battle between the forces of good and evil that will persist until the last times has been completely internalized by al-Ghazālī and transferred to the "battleground" of the human heart. In al-Ghazālī's discussion of the basic human duty to strive in the path of God, the external military *jihād* of the jurists pales beside the relentless spiritual war constantly being waged by the pious Muslim against the incitements of the lower self.

EXTOLLING MILITARY VALOR IN LITERARY SOURCES

According to a report found in the *Muṣannaf* of 'Abd al-Razzāq, a man once came to Muḥammad and lamented, "I am a timid man; I cannot bear [the idea] of encountering the enemy." The Prophet replied, "Shall I not indicate to you a *jihād* in which there is no fighting?" When the man expressed eagerness to learn what it was, Muḥammad responded, "The greater and the lesser pilgrimage are incumbent upon you." In a variant report, the Prophet describes the pilgrimage as "a *jihād* which requires no physical strength" (al-Ṣan'ānī 2000: 5: 120). It is worth noting that this original report undergoes a dramatic transformation when recorded in later standard *ḥadīth* works; in such works, the report now counsels only *women* to substitute the pilgrimage for the military *jihād*.

The later version is reflective of the fact that in certain literary sources produced from the third Islamic century onward martial prowess and valor on the battlefield came to be promoted as desirable features of virile manhood. Above all, such valor was associated with the ideal sociopolitical leader who thereby proved himself to be worthy of the office of "the Commander of the Faithful." This development is clearly manifested in the literature that discusses the qualifications of the early male Companions, particularly Abū Bakr and 'Alī, for the office of the caliphate.

The supporters of 'Alī, who became known as the *Shī'at 'Alī* (partisans of 'Alī; shortened to Shī'a) are depicted in these literary sources as having argued on behalf of 'Alī's greater claims to the caliphate by pointing to his impressive track record of martial prowess on the battlefield, among other praiseworthy attributes. Later Shī'ī authors continued to replicate these arguments in their works to impugn the views of Sunnī authors who supported Abū Bakr's claims to the caliphate. These Shī'ī scholars typically underscore that in several *ḥadīths* the Prophet is known to have praised 'Alī's valor and exceptional fighting ability, which places the latter in a special league all by himself. Probably the most famous *ḥadīth* in this regard is the one that states: "Gabriel, peace be upon him, used to cry out, 'there is no sword but Dhū'l-Fiqār [the name given to 'Alī's sword] and no valiant youth except 'Alī.'" The 14th-century Shī'ī author al-'Allāma al-Ḥillī (d. 1325) lauded 'Alī's exemplary courage in the various military campaigns of Islam. He declares 'Alī to be the most courageous of men (*ashja' al-nās*) for "he made firm the foundations of Islam with his sword and propped up the pillars of faith, never suffering defeat in any place . . ." (al-'Allāma al-Ḥillī 1962: 181–182).

The supporters of Abū Bakr also tend to portray him as a valiant man who rendered important martial services to early Islam, although admittedly not at the level of 'Alī. For example, the 9th-century author 'Amr ibn Baḥr al-Jāḥiẓ (d. 829) in an influential treatise on the caliphate comments that although Abū Bakr was not known for having possessed extraordinary military skill, he had exercised considerable influence during the battles in which he accompanied the Prophet. Al-Jāḥiẓ chronicles the events in which Abū Bakr showed exceptional bravery in confronting the enemy, in word and in deed. During the Battle of Badr in 624, for instance, Abū Bakr was the first to speak out and encourage the Muslim forces to strike at the enemy (al-Jāḥiẓ 1955: 62 ff.).

In another treatise, the well-known 13th-century scholar al-Muhibb al-Ṭabarī (d. 1295) states that none other than 'Alī ibn Abī Ṭālib himself testified to the exceptional martial valor of Abū Bakr. On one occasion when 'Alī was with a group of people, he asked them:

> "Who is the most courageous of people?" They replied, "You are, O Commander of the Faithful." He said, "As for me, I only rose to fight one man to avenge him but the most courageous of people is Abū Bakr. When it was the day of Badr we set up a booth for the Messenger of God, peace and blessings be upon him, and we asked, 'Who will be with the Prophet, peace and blessings be upon him, so that no one from among the polytheists can reach him?' And by God, no one from among us approached him except Abū Bakr with his sword drawn over the head of the Messenger of God, peace and blessings be upon him ..."
>
> (Al-Muhibb al-Ṭabarī n.d.: 1: 164)

At the same time, there were those who downplayed the attribute of martial prowess by itself and valorized instead other kinds of courage, particularly as displayed in the face of inordinate suffering and worldly affliction. The aforementioned al-Jāḥiẓ comments in the context of debates about the caliphate that fighting heroically on the battlefield and slaying the enemy do not automatically guarantee exceptional merit, for if that were the case, such men would surpass the Prophet, who rarely took part in actual combat. This could not be possible since "we know there was no one more steadfastly enduring, and [confronted with] greater trials, nor more manifestly virtuous than he, God's blessings be upon him" (al-Jāḥiẓ 1955: 45–48).

The 15th-century Sunnī scholar Muḥammad ibn Khalīl al-Maqdisī (d. 1483) takes issue with those who declare that 'Alī was more morally excellent than Abū Bakr because he was better known for his military prowess on the battlefield. Al-Maqdisī says that this view is erroneous since *jihād* is of three types: (1) inviting people to God with the tongue; (2) defending Islam through sound judgment and carefully considered opinions; and (3) defending Islam through physical combat. With regard to the first type, al-Maqdisī stresses that, due to his persuasive speech, Abū Bakr is widely acknowledged to have brought more people into the fold of Islam than any other Companion during the Meccan period. With regard to the second type, Abū Bakr, along with 'Umar ibn al-Khaṭṭab (the second caliph), also eclipsed the other Companions in their ability to convince people of the truth of Islam's message through their cogent reasoning. 'Alī, once again, was not known to have excelled in this form of discursive *jihād*. With regard to the third type, al-Maqdisī states that this is the least important aspect of *jihād*. When we look at the Prophet himself, he says, we realize that the majority of his actions fall into the first two categories, and although he was the most courageous of all human beings, he engaged in little physical combat (al-Maqdisī 1989: 99–100). Al-Maqdisī's views were fairly common particularly among scholars who, not surprisingly, valued discursive and intellectual efforts to explain the truth and defend Islam as a higher, more effective form of *jihād* compared to the military activity of warriors, which represented its lesser dimension.

CONCLUSION

Fighting, the conduct of warfare, and martial valor have received due attention in a number of Islamic genres – scripture, exegesis, *hadīth*, and praise literature, among others. The Qur'an carefully demarcates the boundaries between legitimate and illegitimate violence, allows fighting in justified self-defense against prior acts of aggression, and imposes critical restraints on unprincipled recourse to violence. Comparison of early *hadīth* literature from before the 9th century with the later collections allows us to trace a trajectory of increasing valorization of the military *jihād* fought for both God and empire. A similar trajectory can be discerned in the prolific Qur'an commentary literature composed in different centuries that records the voices of various authorities who debated the valences of war and its influence on the construction of religious and gendered identities through time. Martyrdom, which had an expansive meaning in the early period, increasingly came to refer to dying on the battlefield, and martial valor came to be considered an essential trait in the virile adult male.

Such perspectives continued to be debated and contested through time and were challenged particularly by those scholars who praised the merits of the internal spiritual *jihād* that, although bloodless, was deemed to be more arduous and exacting, and indispensable for the moral formation of the individual. Other scholars considered intellectual pursuits to be a more worthy manifestation of the holistic struggle that all humans must wage in this world to promote what is right and prevent what is wrong – a fundamental ethical imperative within the Islamic tradition and a primary objective of *jihād*. Recuperation of these diverse and contested views helps us realize that *jihād* is a many-splendored thing and provides a discursive template for contemporary Muslims – as it did for their premodern predecessors – to air their sociopolitical concerns and articulate a moral worldview that has to be constantly negotiated in varying sociohistorical contexts.

References

Abdel Haleem, M. A. S. 2012. "The *jizya* Verse (Q. 9:29): Tax Enforcement on Non-Muslims in the First Muslim State." *Journal of Qur'anic Studies* 14(2): 72–89.

Abū Dāwūd 1988. *Sunan*. Dār Jīl.

Afsaruddin, Asma 2013. *Striving in the Path of God: Jihad and Martyrdom in Islamic Thought*. Oxford University Press.

   2020. "Jihad in Islamic Thought." In *Cambridge World History of Violence*, vol. 2. Edited by Philip Dwyer et al. Cambridge University Press. 448–469.

al-ʿAllāma al-Ḥillī 1962. "Minhāj al-karāma." In Ibn Taymiyya, *Minhāj al-sunna al-nabawiyya*. Edited by Muḥammad Rashād Sālim. Jāmiʿat al-Imām Muḥammad ibn Suʿūd al-islāmiyya. 75–200.

Blankinship, Khalid Yahya 1994. *The End of the Jihād State: tTe Reign of Hishām Ibn ʿAbd al-Malik and the Collapse of the Umayyads*. State University of New York Press.

al-Bukhārī, Muḥammad ibn Ismāʿīl n.d. *Ṣaḥīḥ*. Edited by Qāsim al-Shammāʿī al-Rifāʿī. Dār al-qalam.

al-Ghazālī, Abū Ḥāmid n.d. *Iḥyāʾ ʿulūm al-dīn*. Edited by ʿAbd Allāh al-Khālidī. Shirkat Dār al-Arqam Ibn Abī al-Arqam.

al-Jāḥiẓ, ʿAmr ibn Baḥr 1955. *Kitāb al-ʿUthmāniyya*. Edited by ʿAbd al-Salām Hārūn. Maktabat al-Khānjī.

Ibn Kathīr, Muḥammad 1990. *Tafsir al-qurʾan al-ʿazim*. Dar al-Jil.

Jeffrey, Arthur 1938. *The Foreign Vocabulary of the Qurʾan*. Oriental Institute.

Mālik ibn Anas 1994. *Al-Muwaṭṭaʾ*. Edited by Bashshār ʿAwad Maʿrūf and Maḥmūd Muḥammad Khalīl. Muʾassasat al-risāla.

al-Maqdisī, Muḥammad ibn Khalīl 1989. *Al-Radd ʿalā al-rāfiḍa*. Edited by Aḥmad Ḥijāzī al-Saqqā. Maktabat al-Thaqafī,

Mottahedeh, Roy and Ridwan al-Sayyid 2001. "The Idea of the Jihad in Islam before the Crusades." In *The Crusades from the Perspective of Byzantium and the Muslim World*. Edited by Angeliki E. Laiou and Roy Parviz Mottahedeh. Dumbarton Oaks Research Library and Collection. 23–29.

Al-Muḥibb al-Ṭabarī n.d. *Al-Riyāḍ al-naḍira fī manāqib al-ʿashara*. Edited by Muḥammad Muṣṭafā Abū al-ʿAlā'. Maktabat al-jundī.

Mujāhid ibn Jabr 2005. *Tafsīr*. Edited by Abū Muḥammad al-Asyūṭī. Dār al-kutub al-ʿilmiyya.

al-Nawawī, Yaḥya ibn Sharaf 1997. *Forty Hadith*. Translated by Ezzeddin Ibrahim and Denys Johnson-Davies. Islamic Texts Society.

al-Qurṭubī, Muḥammad 2001. *Al-Jāmiʿ li-aḥkām al-qurʾān*. Edited by ʿAbd al-Razzāq al-Mahdī. Dār al-kitāb al-ʿarabī.

al-Rāzī, Fakhr al-Dīn 1999. *Al-Tafsīr al-kabīr*. Dar ihya' al-turath al-ʿarabi.

al-Ṣanʿānī, Abd al-Razzāq 2000. *Al-Muṣannaf*. Edited by Ayman Naṣr al-Dīn al-Azharī. Dār al-kutub al-ʿilmiyya.

al-Ṭabarī, Muḥammad ibn Jarīr 1997. *Jāmiʿ al-bayān fī tafsīr al-qurʾān*. Dār al-kutub al-ʿarabī.

al-Zamakhsharī, Maḥmūd ibn ʿUmar 1998. *Al-Kashshāf ʿan haqāʾiq ghawāmiḍ al-tanzīl wa-ʿuyūn al-aqāwīl fī wujūh al-taʾwīl*. Edited by ʿĀdil Aḥmad ʿAbd al-Mawjūd and ʿAl Muḥammad Muʿawwid. al-ʿUbaykā.

4 Hinduism and War

KAUSHIK ROY

The dominant idea holds that Hinduism is a religion of peace. This is a product of the formulations put forward by Mohandas Karamchand Gandhi (1869–1948) and the 19th-century Orientalists. Gandhi argues in his works that the use of martial imagery and rhetoric in Hinduism is merely a ploy, an allegory for the features related to rituals and the inner agony of the souls of individuals. In fact, Gandhi largely derived his theory of *satyagraha* (peaceful noncooperation with the oppressor and the search for the ultimate truth) and *ahimsa* (nonviolence) from the *Bhagavad Gita*. Besides Gandhi, Swami Vivekananda (1863–1902), like the Orientalists during the 18th century and the first half of 19th century, assumed that Hinduism was an idealist, otherworldly, nonmaterialistic religion focusing on spiritual rather than material supremacy (Inden 2006: 13–60).

This chapter takes a different tack and argues that there are different layers within Hinduism. In the various texts generated under the umbrella term "Hinduism" in ancient India, there exists a subtle, intricate and intimate relationship between violence, sacrifice, rituals and salvation. Moreover, certain strands within ancient Hinduism are highly materialistic. First of all, it should be noted that the term "Hinduism" is of 19th-century vintage. In ancient times, the term used was either "Brahmanism" or "Sramanism." For the sake of brevity, this chapter will use the term "Hinduism," but whereas the West is accustomed to regarding Hinduism as a religion, Hinduism or Hindu *dharma* is not a religion per se but an all-encompassing canopy for its followers. *Dharma* does not mean religion but way of life. Situating an origin to the notion of *dharma* is also complicated. It is not possible to date precisely any of the ancient Sanskrit works that discuss Hindu *dharma* (all of which are polysemic in nature), nor can we be certain about their authorship.

On the subject of violence, the ancient Hindu texts use three different terms: *yuddha* (war), *vigraha* (internal conflicts) and *kalaha* (tension and enmity leading to a low level of violence). This chapter will use the term "violence" to denote all types of conflicts. It will deal with four interrelated themes. The first theme discusses the role of the raja (Hindu ruler) and *rajadharma* (duties of a ruler). Violence constitutes an important component of the raja's duty. The second theme revolves around the Kshatriyas, the warrior order of Hinduism. The third section of the chapter focuses on the interrelation between violence, salvation and rituals. The fourth section outlines the relationship between gender and war in the Hindu scriptures. And the last section discusses the impact of Hindu religion on the theory and praxis of Indian security policy (broadly defined) in the present times.

RAJA AND *RAJADHARMA*

Traditional Hindu society is composed of four *varnas* (orders), and this term is translated as "castes." The four orders are as follows: Brahmins at the top, Kshatriyas second, then Vaishyas and, finally, the Shudras at the bottom. One of the hymns of the *Rig Veda* tells us that *Purusa* (the primeval man from whom humanity descended) created the four *varnas*. While the Brahmins should aim for wisdom, continues the hymn, the Kshatriyas should aspire for glory, the Vaishyas for making profits and the Shudras are to serve the higher orders by performing laborious tasks. The Brahmins are to focus on religious rituals and act as advisors to the rajas, or kings. The Kshatriyas are soldiers, commanders and rulers. The Vaishyas are supposed to be concerned with trade and commerce. The Shudras, in accordance with the scriptures, are associated with agriculture. The Brahmins and the Kshatriyas are regarded as twice born, and they dominate the *varna* system. They were originally the Proto-Indo-European (PIE) people who intruded into the Indian subcontinent after the collapse of the Indus Valley Civilization (Chatterji 2007: 24).

The notions of war and religion in ancient India can be traced back to *Rig Veda* as this work was composed when the "Aryans" were entering India and fighting the "Dravidians." The term *Rig Veda* means "to know" or "knowledge" (Nandi 2018: 1–3). The *Rig Veda Samhita* is composed of 10,000 stanzas, which are products of bardic composition and have been added over several centuries (roughly 1400–800 BCE). Some of the hymns address the issue of *kshatra* (sovereign power), which requires armed expeditions on the part of the Aryan tribal clan chiefs known as *rajans*. The Aryans (the term *arya* refers to nobleman) or the PIE speakers organized in tribes who came to India from Central

Asia and Iran through Afghanistan and the North-West Frontier in around 1500 BCE. The PIE speakers were equipped with *naracha* (iron arrows) and iron swords and fought from horse-drawn chariots, giving them a military advantage over the indigenous inhabitants. The *Rig Veda* mentions that the *rajans* conducted raids and subjugated the dark-skinned *Dasas* and *Dasyus* (Dravidians who were the original inhabitants of India). The *Rig Vedic* hymns tell us that the *rajans* ruled from their citadels (Nandi 2018: 13, 26). For instance, the *Ramayana* (one of the epics of Hinduism) speaks of the city of Ayodhya (from where King Dasaratha and later his eldest son, the hero Rama, ruled), which is surrounded by towers for defensive purposes (Srivastava 1985: 60).

The citadels, which were actually protected cow pens, gradually were transformed by the rulers into cities with rudimentary defensive works. Initially, raids were conducted for collecting valuables like gold and silver, women and cows, as the Aryans were pastoral people. Later, with the rise of cities and the expansion of agriculture, the hitherto mobile tribes settled down, and gradually there emerged *janapadas* (polities that included cities and were surrounded by agricultural lands). The spread of iron technology resulted in the felling of forests in the Ganga-Yamuna Doab and resulted in huge surpluses of crops. Production of agricultural surplus, urbanization, development of long-distance trade and a money economy that replaced barter all allowed for the emergence of bureaucracies and standing armies (dominated by the Kshatriyas), an elaborate priestly class (Brahmins) and traders (Vaishyas). All of these activities occurred within the ambit of a peasant society composed mostly of Shudras. The *rajan* then became the *raja* (Hindu king: ruler of a settled agrarian community or kingdom). The *janapadas* fought against each other, giving rise to *mahajanapadas* (big kingdoms), which finally gave way to the Nanda and then the Maurya empires. These empires had elaborate defensive structures for protecting their cities (Thapar 1971: 408–412). This process was completed between 800 and 300 BCE.

There are two main Hindu epics: the *Ramayana* and the *Mahabharata*. The latter is the longest poem in the world. While the *Ramayana* deals with the achievements of the Aryan King Rama of Ayodhya's exploits against the Dravidians, the *Mahabharata* depicts the ritual aspects of *rajadharma* in great detail. The date of composition of these two epics is surmised to be between 600 and 300 BCE. However, the *Mahabharata* deals with an earlier era. The *Mahabharata* deals with the conflict between two Aryan clans, the Kauravas against the Pandavas, which ultimately draws in other powers and becomes an all-encompassing war. In the *Mahabharata*, Yudhistira's (the eldest among the five Pandava brothers) transition from a *dharmaraja* (a just king) to the paramount ruler is portrayed. Such an epic king occupies the spiritual office of a sacrificer – he is a figure who creates order through performing ritual sacrifices. Kingship is related to war and sacrifice in both Vedic and Epic texts (1500–300 BCE).

Horses are an important aspect of Hindu kingship and a means for expanding territory. The *Brhadaranyaka Upanishad* (700 BCE) refers to the *Aswamedha Yagna* (Horse Sacrifice Ritual; Olivelle 1998: 5), wherein a specially selected horse is allowed to roam freely outside the domain of the ruler. If it can move across the domains of other rulers without any opposition, then these rulers theoretically become the vassals of the ruler who performs the *Aswamedha Yagna*. If the horse is stopped by a neighboring ruler, it signifies opposition to the ruler performing the *Yagna*. Then, the patron ruler of the *Aswamedha Yagna* is forced to fight the ruler who has imprisoned the sacrificial horse. After a certain time, the horse is ritually sacrificed. In the *Mahabharata*, Yudhistira performs the *Aswamedha* sacrifice after being crowned ruler.

The idea of kingship as narrated in the epics is a performative one as kingship is not merely an office but an activity that requires continuous performances of ritualized sacrifices. Kingship in the *Mahabharata* is not autocratic but what may be termed "fraternal." The king is advised and guided by chiefs, brothers and even his wife. In the *Mahabharata*, Yudhistira, coronated at Hastinapura, initially shares power with his uncle, Dhritarashtra, and then with Lord Krishna (McGrath 2017: 1–2). Even as early as the *Rig Veda* there are references to popular assemblies like the *sabha* and the *samiti* that somewhat limit the power of the ruler (Chousalkar 2018: 38). However, the idea of kingship was transformed in the post-epic works like the *Arthashastra*.

In contrast to the *Mahabharata*, Kautilya's *Arthashastra* (composed in 300 BCE–300 CE) advocates an instrumental approach towards kingship. The *Arthashastra* means the science of kingship: the art of maintaining the *rajya* (kingdom). Economic management constitutes one of the principal aspects of kingship. For Kautilya, economics and politics (especially power) constitute a seamless unity (Trautmann 2012: 2–3). The most important element of *artha* is the acquisition of power. For R. P. Kangle, the term *artha* refers to the establishment of control over *prithivi* (earth), and the *Arthashastra* stands for the science of dealing with the acquisition and consolidation of power (Kangle 1992: 1). Kautilya is a realist and a theorist of power. In Hinduism, this school of thinking is called the Carvakas or Lokayata stream of thought. Lokayata philosophy is materialist rather than spiritual in nature and believes in the direct evidence of the senses, emphasizing reason and rejecting the authority of the *Vedas*. *Lokayatavidya*, which separates political theory from theology, is transformed into the art of politics in the *Arthashastra* (Chousalkar 2018: 3, 9). Kautilya's *Arthashastra*, which pays only lip service to Vedic *dharma*, remained very influential among the Indian ruling class until the 12th century (Boesche 2017: 8) when the Hindus lost power to the Islamic Turks who came from Afghanistan and established their principalities in Hindustan.

In contradistinction to the *Mahabharata*, the *Arthashastra* encourages the *vijigishu* (ambitious ruler) to become the *ekarat* (sole ruler) and *samrat* (ruler of the whole Indian subcontinent). The *Arthashastra* speaks of three kinds of war that the *vijigishu* should wage: open war, concealed war and silent war. Open war involves battles and sieges with regular armies; concealed war is guerrilla war; and silent war means conducting acts of terrorism (assassination, subversion, use of misinformation and conducting disinformation campaigns against enemy polities, etc.) through the government's secret agents (Boesche 2003: 22). In modern terminology, silent war is equivalent to fifth-generation warfare. The last two types of war are examples of Kautilya's *kutayuddha* (war involving unjust means). Unlike in the *Vedas*, sacrifices and rituals play no role in Kautilya's thinking about *kutayuddha*. The *Arthashastra* informs us that a king should use holy men, women and children as spies and assassins. This book gives details about the various types of spies, different types of tortures and techniques of subversion to be used for maintaining the authority of the king and the power of the state.

The *Mahabharata*, in contrast, speaks only of open war, which is considered *dharmik* (just/righteous). When the Kshatriyas break rules during combat, then they become fallen Kshatriyas because of their *adharma* (unjust/nonrighteous actions). Drona's son, Aswathama, carries out a night attack to kill sleeping Pandava soldiers (Mahabharata 2015: 8: 1–13), which is explicitly against the rules of war in the *Mahabharata*. Aswathama was punished by Krishna for this dastardly act. He was banished to the Himalayas for eternity. However, in the *Arthashastra*, nocturnal commando raids become an essential feature of the *vijigishu*'s military strategy.

KSHATRIYAS AND *KSHATRADHARMA*

The *Aitareya Brahmana* (dated to ca. 600 BCE) says that the Kshatriyas represent force, power and strength (Chatterji 2007: 27). The Kshatriya caste was considered essential for the protection of Hindu *dharma*. However, the Kshatriyas' social composition somewhat changed with time. Initially, the Vaishyas and the Shudras were Dravidians who were subjugated by the incoming Aryans. Outside of the *varna* system are the untouchables. They initially were the hunting and gathering tribes who inhabited the forests. They are also called *nishadas* in ancient Sanskrit literature. According to the ancient Hindu texts, they deal with "unclean menial jobs" like working with leather, killing animals, burning dead bodies, etc. For maintaining the purity of the upper three *varnas*, the untouchables are to live outside the borders of the cities and the villages. With the passage of time, intermarriages between the four *varnas* occurred despite the strictures of the scriptures, and by 100 BCE, society became more complex. Hence, the *acharyas* (Hindu religious teachers) came up with the formulation of various subcastes (mixed *varnas*).

Another group of outsiders are termed as *mleccha* by the Sanskrit works. The designation of the groups termed as *mleccha* changed with time. The term first appears in *Satapatha Brahmana* (composed in 800–600 BCE), which assigns the term to those groups whose languages were different from Sanskrit. Frontier tribes and forest tribes are called *mlecchajatis* (*mleccha* communities) by Kautilya. The *Arthashastra* urges that these communities should be manipulated and utilized by the *vijigishu* against enemy kings. After the beginning of the Common Era, foreign invaders like the *Yavanas* (Greeks), Sakas, Parthians and Kushanas are also brought under the term *mleccha*. The Sanskrit texts advise the rajas to utilize *mleccha* troops as their martial capabilities are exemplary. So it can be seen that in the ancient Sanskrit literature, like the *nishadas*, the ritual status of the *mleccha* is low (Parasher 1979: 109–120). However, unlike the *nishadas*, the *mleccha* communities enjoyed more power. Hence, by 300 CE, many *mleccha* communities were given the status of Kshatriyas, and they became defenders of Hinduism.

Kshatriyas represent the traditional martial caste of ancient India. The Kshatriyas' duty is to pursue *Kshatriyadharma* (way of life of the warriors), which means fighting. To an extent, the *Kshatriyadharma* is somewhat similar to the *Bushido* of the *samurai* and the chivalry of the medieval knights. The *Atharva Veda* (composed in 1000–900 BCE) says that the Kshatriyas are not afraid of death and possess fire within them. Moreover, the text also hints at the Kshatriyas' mastery with horses (probably horse-drawn war chariots). Some of the verses of the *Atharva Veda* about the Kshatriyas are as follows: "He who knoweth the fuel of him, piled on the Kshatriya – he seek ... unto death ... He goes not down to the dead – the Kshatriya who, knowing, takes the name of Agni unto length of life ... The earth hath stood ... I have made the horses stand in their station" (*Atharva Veda* 1993: 338–339). The *Arthashastra* notes the duty of the Kshatriyas as follows: "performing sacrifices for self ... living by (the profession) of arms and protecting beings" (Kangle 1992: 7).

The Kshatriyas' favorite weapons in ancient India, as mentioned in works like the *Ramayana*, the *Mahabharata* and the *Arthashastra*, are bows and arrows, and the Kshatriyas fight from *rathas* (horse-drawn chariots). The *Arthashastra* mentions that bows are to be constructed from bamboo, palmyra and bone and horn (Srivastava 1985: 31). Though *rathas* remain the queens of the Kurukshetra battlefield, the *Mahabharata* also mentions the use of elephants in war (Das 1986: 8, 11). After 300 BCE, elephantry became very important on Indian battlefields.

Torkel Brekke asserts that the ancient Hindus had no concept of war as a public business. Brekke continues that, for the Kshatriyas, war remained a spectacle of private violence, a heroic martial sport of a sort (Brekke 2005: 59–86). True, the *Mahabharata* depicts the heroes of opposing sides, like Arjuna of the Pandavas fighting against Karna of the Kauravas. The heroes of the *Mahabharata* who are related by blood ties (Karna is the elder half-brother of Arjuna) fight private duels with each other. The epic heroes have a concept of fighting private duels in support of the greater war that is being fought between two camps with opposing ideologies. The Pandavas are fighting for *dharma* against the Kauravas whose objective is to crown Duryodhana as the absolute ruler of an unitary polity.

The concept of *yuddha*, being organized violence that was conducted by an impersonal organization such as the state for public interest, is further developed in the *Arthashastra*. Kautilya speaks of statist violence. The *Arthashastra* details how the infantry with chariots, warhorses and elephants should be organized on the battlefield in *vyuhas* (tactical formations) as part of the army's combined arms tactics (Das 1986: 21–22). The role of war being an affair of state rather than of individual heroes is more developed in the *Arthashastra* than in the *Mahabharata*. This is because the *Mahabharata* refers to the period of fluctuating tribal domains in the era of pastoral nomadism, while the core of the *Arthashastra* came into existence under the Maurya Empire (322–185 BCE), which was a strong unitary bureaucratic entity with a vast standing army spawned by an expanding settled agrarian society.

The *Bhagavad Gita*, which marks the beginning of *Bhakti* (devotional) ideology that focused on love to God and one's lord, somewhat dampens the Kshatriyas' ardor for war. The *Bhagavad Gita* emphasizes war as a last resort. In general, killing human beings is not encouraged, but it is considered a necessity in exceptional circumstances. War itself, according to the *Mahabharata* (of which the *Bhagavad Gita* is a part), is a part of God's *lila* or spiritual pastime. Despite the fact that Duryodhana is the Kali Purusha (demon Kali in human form) and Draupadi (collective wife of five Pandava brothers) insists on war, the god Krishna does not easily acquiesce to this warmongering policy. Krishna repeatedly stresses the point in the *Bhagavad Gita* that war should never be waged for revenge, against personal insult or to vent anger. However, Krishna does not agree with Yudhistira's reasoning that the pursuit of *Kshatriyadharma* results only in pain and regret. Krishna highlights that in these specific circumstances the Pandavas would have to fight the good war only to end all wars (Rosen 2007: 22–25). To fight a righteous war, warriors need to be like ascetics. They fight for the greater good and must be uninterested in making any personal gains. In such circumstances, *himsa* (violence) against others actually becomes *ahimsa* (Vidal et al. 1994: 196–213).

Ironically, Duryodhana, the leader of the Kauravas, a typical anti-hero and the principal villain in the *Mahabharata*, reaches heaven before Yudhistira. This is because of the physical and moral courage of Duryodhana, who refuses to give up the struggle. In fact, like a true Kshatriya, Duryodhana continues to fight until his death. Finally, when the mortally wounded Duryodhana dies, the gods shower flowers on him and the Gandharvas play musical instruments in his honor (Kane 1968: 385). The Pandava brothers have to trek through the snowy and dangerous Himalayan Mountains to reach heaven. Draupadi and all of the brothers except Yudhistira die before reaching heaven. After reaching heaven, Yudhistira learns that his brothers are in hell. The god Indra explains to Yudhistira that this is because Duryodhana fought heroically like a true warrior who never broke the *dharmic* code of conduct during battle, but the four Pandava brothers had occasionally transgressed *Kshatriyadharma* while fighting the Kaurava warriors. And Draupadi was punished because instead of treating all of her husbands equally, she was partial to Arjuna.

MOKSHA AND VIOLENCE

Moksha means *mukti*/freedom from earthly existence – the ultimate goal of a Hindu. *Moksha* is related to sacrifice in *yuddha*. The three ideas of sacrifice, violence and *moksha* (salvation) are interrelated and pervade Hinduism. Hindu scriptures propagate the theory of continuous rebirth (i.e., of transmigration of souls). The idea of merit or *karma* (*tapas*) as something to be earned, accumulated, occasionally transferred and eventually realized, says Wendy Doniger, owed much to the post-Vedic monied economy. Overall, the emergence of a monied economy accelerated the transformation of war from being a struggle between the epic heroes to a state-dominated public business. Traders and merchants had heavily subsidized Buddhism, starting in the 6th or 5th century BCE, and indirectly supported trade and commerce. Hindu *dharma* responded by creating new texts like the *Upanishads*. The *Upanishads* came into existence between 700 BCE (when the *Aranyakas* were composed) and 300 CE (when the *Grihya Sutras* came into being). When the early *Upanishads* were being created, Buddha was preaching in Magadha. Buddha died in around 450 BCE, and at that time the *Brihadaranyaka*, the *Taittiriya* and the *Chandogya* works were in circulation (Kosambi 2001: 176–197; Doniger 2015: 164–167).

The *Upanishads* teach that the individual self/soul is *atman*, which is part and parcel of the *brahman* (not to be confused with Brahmin), the composite soul of the cosmos. A human becomes good through good *karma*, but a human becomes something inferior if they perform bad *karma*. *Karma* means action or morally charged action that has consequences for the soul in the future. So, *karma* determines the future rebirth of all people. To an extent, *karma* is also the product of past lives. So, through the theory of *karma*, past, present and future are intertwined together. Occasionally, the results of good and bad *karma* can be transferred from one person to another under special circumstances. For instance, such transference can occur between parent and children and between the sacrificial priest and the patron of the *yagna* (religious rituals). Such transference can occur intentionally as well as unintentionally. As the *Chandogya Upanishad* tells us, the reward for good *karma* is a better and more pleasant life in the next rebirth and the punishment for bad *karma* is a lower, sorrow-filled rebirth. Only a few *atmans* (souls) can escape the continuous cycle of rebirth by freeing themselves from all desires. Instead of being born again, these select few become part of the *brahman* (eternal soul/cosmic consciousness). The *Brhadaranyaka Upanishad* notes: "This innermost thing, this self (*atman*) ... it is dearer than anything else ... When a man regards only his self as dear to him, what he holds dear will never perish" (Olivelle 1998: 49). However, such a path is not open to the majority. The *karma* theory is based on the theory of the continuous reincarnation of souls or repeated rebirth. Indirectly, here lies the idea of the necessity of a great war. When the Earth is overcrowded and bad *karma* prevails among a majority, a great war resulting in massive numbers of deaths (like the Mahabharata War) becomes a just necessity (Doniger 2015: 168–176). In addition to human agency, *daiva* (fate) also plays a role in causing war.

The Kshatriyas are not always blamed in the Sanskrit works for pursuing violence. Vyasa, the purported author of the *Mahabharata*, suggests that time (*kala*) is ultimately responsible for the large-scale slaughter on the battlefield of Kurukshetra where the Mahabharata War occurs. In the *Bhagavad Gita*, Krishna says to Arjuna that he himself represents time and Arjuna need not worry about the consequences of his actions on the battlefield. At another level, the *Mahabharata* speaks of a trinity that results in genocidal war: *daiva* (policy of the gods and also something left in the hands of fate), *kala* (time) and *purusakara* (autonomous human action; Brodbeck and Black 2007: 5–6). Towards the end of the *Mahabharata*, King Dhritarashtra, father of the Kauravas, blames Duryodhana (his eldest son) for the debacle of the devastating war and also blames himself (out of self-pity) for failing to stop Duryodhana from going towards the path of *adharma*, destruction and infamy. But sage Sanjaya tells Dhritarashtra that even a person with superior wisdom cannot avert fate caused by *daiva*.

The *Mahabharata* speaks of three kinds of *kala*: cosmological time (*kala* as the creator and destroyer of all beings in the world), sequential time (past, present and future time relative to the sequence of events in the *Mahabharata* narrative) and consequential time (the inextricable link between past, present and future and between acts and consequences; Hudson 2007: 36–39). *Kala* (time) stands for long-term impersonal structural factors. For instance, the Earth is sinking under the sin and weight of the *asura* (demon) kings like Duryodhana. Hence, to vanquish them, the Mahabharata War involving mass slaughter becomes necessary. *Purusakara* represents human agency, which binds sequential and consequential time. The Mahabharata War is the product of human agency (sequential and consequential time) linked with *daiva* (cosmological time and fate). Thus, the *Mahabharata*'s trinity is an admixture of impersonal long-term structural factors, human agency and *daiva*.

The *Mahabharata* is considered as a *rana yajna* (war ritual). Duryodhana says that the war chariot represents the sacrificial ground, the mace is the oblation spoon and the arrows are the *dhurba* grass (required in certain rituals). Karna reflects that the blood of the soldiers represents *ghee* (clarified butter) used for Vedic sacrifice, and the cries and howls of the wounded and dying soldiers are conches and drums used during rituals. Finally, the weapons represent the bricks of the sacrificial altar. The fallen warriors are *pasu* (sacrificial victims). So, the Mahabharata War is a *naramedh yagna* (human ritual sacrifice) on a large scale. One important feature is that *naramedh yagna* requires victims to be willing to undergo sacrifice; the warriors in the *Mahabharata* willingly entered the battle to fight and die. Duryodhana, by dying in war, sacrifices himself, and the Pandavas are the high priests who conduct the sacrificial ritual under the watchful eyes of Lord Krishna. The Earth is replenished by the rotting corpses of the soldiers. Kurukshetra is *dharmakshetra* and the war is an example of *dharmayuddha*, which is necessary to maintain *rta* and *dharma* (higher cosmic order). This harks back to the Purusa Sukta hymn of *Rig Veda* where the world is created out of the sacrifice of the primordial giant. After all, Lord Krishna takes steps to make the Mahabharata War inevitable, and this is a cosmic design to save Earth from overpopulation. The *Mahabharata* represents the destruction of all lineage-based Kshatriya clans. Actually, the transformation of pastoral society into an agrarian society resulted in the replacement of lineage-based clannish rule with the emergence of monarchical polities between 600 and 300 BCE. This sociopolitical shift is portrayed in the *Mahabharata* (Jatavallabhula 1999: 69–103).

In the Vedic worldview, sacrifices are necessary for maintenance of the cosmic and natural order. Vedic rituals involve violence. Occasionally, human beings are sacrificed. Animals are sacrificed on a large scale even now, but in many cases animals may be replaced with grain. The sacrificed animals and plants are said to be reborn again, but this rebirth requires violent killing. However, killing for Vedic sacrifice is justified by considering it not to be real killing because the sacrificed victims go to a higher plane of existence. The *Manavadharmashastra* (*Manusmriti*), which was composed around the beginning of the Common Era, says that killing is *himsa* (violence), but killing for Vedic rituals is *ahimsa* (nonviolence). By this same logic, just war, which is regarded as a sacrifice, and killing in combat become *dharmik* (holy/sacred) actions. *Ahimsa* is derived from *ahimsayai* (to avoid injury). With the passage of time, the trend in Hinduism has been to minimize the role of violence while performing Vedic rituals. Similarly, even when a just war is fought, to maintain *dharma*, the aim is to reduce killing to the lowest possible quotient. However, violence cannot be totally relegated from life and rituals. Violence is the apogee of the Kshatriyas' way of life just as sacrifice during rituals is the battleground of a violent world where the *asuras* and the gods are fighting each other. The Mahabharata War is depicted as the *devayajana* (*yajna* here means battle) of the gods (Heesterman 1984: 119–127).

Himsa (violence, cruelty) and *ahimsa* appear frequently in the ancient Sanskrit texts. Upinder Singh writes that *himsa* refers to the excessive, unjust, unethical and disproportionate infliction of violence (Singh 2017: 8). *Ahimsa*, rather than absolute nonviolence, means non-injury to others, displaying an attitude of compassion and empathy. In the pre-Upanishadic texts, *ahimsa* refers to security and safety. In later texts, *ahimsa* refers to pacifism, vegetarianism and rejection of hunting, which was an essential component of *rajadharma* and a necessary form of training for waging war. In the post-Vedic literature, *himsa* is personified as the wife of *adharma* (unrighteousness) and *ahimsa* as the wife of *dharma* (righteous law). However, pacifism is not applied to the case of the Kshatriyas, whose caste duty involves the pursuit of violence. *Ahimsa* as it appears in the *Dharmasutras* (composed in 600–200 BCE) is related with asceticism, renunciation and pacifism. For the Kshatriyas, *himsa* is justified by arguing that their killing is not real killing because they are engaged in *rana yagna* (battle rituals), and that only the body can be destroyed but the *atman* (soul) that resides in each person cannot be destroyed (Bodewitz 1999: 17–44).

WOMEN AND WAR

Superficially, it seems that women appear as marginal and sexual playthings in the high Sanskrit literature of ancient India generated by the "patriarchal and misogynistic" male *acharyas*. Jarrod Whitaker writes that sexualized and sexist imagery permeates the *Rig Vedic* hymns. The *Rig Veda*'s weapon hymns, which praise a king's army and weapons, are militaristic in nature. A warrior firmly holding a bow is equated with a male lover closely embracing his female partner. A powerful arrow discharged from a strongly charged bow represents male anatomy and stands for heroic masculine virility and sexual desire. A warrior should dominate the battle and control his weapons just as he dominates and controls his female partner while having sex. Whitaker continues by saying that masculine power and military prowess are equated by the hymns' composers (Whitaker 2019: 127–143). Women appear to be represented as the dominated gender.

However, certain women are important figures due to their gender and identity. Queen Draupadi, who is literate in the discourse of *dharma*, is the manifestation of the goddess Sri. Sri is connected with royalty, and her presence bestows royal power upon her consort. The prosperity of a king is dependent on the graceful presence of Sri. So, the presence of Sri in the figure of Draupadi legitimizes the Pandavas and especially their elder brother Yudhistira's claim to royalty (Black 2007: 62–71). When Yudhistira in the *Mahabharata* rules as a king for a brief time before losing his kingdom, Draupadi manages the household affairs and expertly partakes in the general administration of the royal domain as well as the treasury. Moreover, Draupadi is an independent woman. She is the *sakhi* (girlfriend) of Lord Krishna, who is her *sakha* (boyfriend; Hiltebeitel 2007: 126–127). Laurie L. Patton writes that Draupadi emerges in the *Mahabharata* as an *adi*-superwoman (Patton 2007: 97–109).

This ancient superwoman is humiliated when Dushasana brings her to an open court after grabbing her hair after her husband has lost a dice match with Sakuni (the maternal uncle of Duryodhana). Duryodhana has challenged Yudhistira to a dice match and he, being a Kshatriya, must accept such a challenge. In this match, Yudhistira gambles everything: his kingdom, his life and the lives of his four brothers plus his wife. After losing the dice match to Sakuni, who plays on Duryodhana's behalf, the *Mahabharata* narrates that Yudhistira's brothers and Draupadi are legally slaves of the victor: the Kauravas. At that time, Draupadi is menstruating and wears only one piece of cloth. Karna, the son of the Sun God, tells Dushasana to disrobe her in public because she is a whore who has married five Pandava brothers. According to Hiltebeitl's nature myth analogy, disrobing Draupadi on the orders of Karna also symbolizes a greater climatic shift. The overbearing climate of the hot season due to the scorching sun (Karna) lays the Earth bare, much like Draupadi (Sri) being disrobed. While being disrobed, Draupadi prays to Hari (Krishna), who covers her bare body. Krishna's color is black, the color of earth. By this nature myth analogy, the black earth has its own power of renewal. In the end, Karna, son of the Sun God, will be killed by Arjuna, son of Indra, God of Rain. The nature mythology linked with Draupadi's disrobing scene in the *Mahabharata* represents that when *adharma* (due to Duryodhana's actions) flourishes on Earth, then the Earth becomes infertile. The bounty of Earth is restored with the rule of a *dharmik* (just) king (Hiltebeitel 1980: 97–112).

When Yudhistira loses his kingdom after the dice match and retires to the forest, Draupadi emphasizes to Yudhistira that since his royal status has been lost, their husband–wife relationship needs to be renegotiated. Several times Draupadi challenges her husband Yudhistira's policy decisions, especially regarding war with the Kauravas. Instead of being a silent, loyal and dedicated wife as Sita is to Rama (the hero of the *Ramayana*), Draupadi accuses Yudhistira that he cares more for *dharma* than for the sufferings of his brothers and wife. When Yudhistira says to Draupadi that all human beings' actions and follies are part and parcel of the divine plan, Draupadi challenges this so-called divine justice. Draupadi indirectly starts accusing the gods of using human lives like rag dolls in a play. Draupadi refuses to remain a silent spectator and sufferer and condemns Yudhistira for refusing to display *manyu* (spirit of anger against unjust actions). Yudhistira accuses Draupadi of being a *nastik* (heretic) and, in response, Draupadi tells Yudhistira that he is suffering from delusions and openly proclaims that until the Kauravas are defeated she will consider that she has no husbands; that means she will neither sleep with the five Pandava brothers nor perform the duties traditionally associated with a wife (Malinar 2007: 80–94).

Women may not have participated directly in combat, but they play a very important role in the origins and consequences of war. It would be wrong to assume that all female characters in ancient Sanskrit literature represent antiwar attitudes. In fact, Kunti (mother of the five Pandava brothers) and Draupadi in the Pandava camp are the two principal advocates of war with the Kauravas. The dark and fiery Draupadi who is born from fire, is a goddess in human form, united through marriage with Arjuna, who represents the yogic and ascetic power of Lord Shiva (the god of destruction) in the epic. Just before Krishna sets off as a *duta* (envoy) to the Kaurava Court before the Mahabharata War begins, Draupadi tells Krishna that she wants Dushasana's dark arm to be cut off and laid in dust. When Kripacharya requests that Duryodhana make peace with the Pandavas, Duryodhana, while musing over his fate, responds that Draupadi would never allow the Pandavas to pursue a peace policy with the Kauravas because of her humiliation in the Kaurava court. In fact, Draupadi undergoes fierce *tapas*, praying for the destruction of the Kauravas (Hiltebeitel 1985: 71–77).

Collectively, Hindu women are not portrayed as antiwar in the early Hindu works as well. Thanks to *Kshatriyadharma*, maternal child protection is of low priority for the Kshatriya women, as they willingly send their sons to possible death in battles, as depicted in the *Mahabharata* (Brodbeck 2007: 145). In the early Hindu texts, there is evidence of wives calling their husbands by their first names (Hiltebeitel 1998: 399), which implies equal or familiar status. But with the emergence of large agrarian bureaucratic empires, Hindu society became more conservative. This was due in part to the repeated foreign invasions that occurred. *Manavadharmashastra (Laws of Manu*, which codified Hindu laws) relegates women to the background, and under the Gupta Empire (319–542 CE), the social, political and economic positions of women declined.

CONCLUSION: HINDUISM FAST-FORWARD

Instead of summing up the arguments of this chapter in traditional style, this section looks forward, toward the enduring impact of the ideas discussed above in the modern period. Though the bulk of the Indian nationalists from the late 19th century believed that Hinduism stood for peace, a small minority among the nationalist leaders asserted that ancient Hindu texts also advocated violence in order to root out internal as well as external enemies. Bal Gangadhar Tilak (1856–1920), a right-center Hindu nationalist who operated from west India before Gandhi, found in the *Bhagavad Gita* the necessity of using limited violence under certain conditions (Houben and Van Kooij 1999: 5). Similarly, in the late 20th century, right-wing Hindus, presently members of the Bharatiya Janata Party (BJP; previously Jan Sangh), believed in a similar interpretation. They relied on the paradigm of the Kaurava General Dronacharya's son, Aswathama, who used the *brahmastra* as a weapon of last resort when pushed to the wall and when the Kaurava camp was facing destruction. In the late 1980s, the BJP argued for a Hindu atomic bomb to meet the challenge of an Islamic atomic bomb that was being pursued by Pakistan. The BJP argued that India needed *brahmastras* (weapons of mass destruction or WMDs), which, at present, means nuclear weapons. Following the *Arthashastra*, the "hawks" within the Indian security establishment argued that when *adharma* prevails (in this case the actions of Pakistan in supporting insurgencies in Kashmir), Hinduism allows the pursuit of *kutayuddha* (war involving unjust techniques). If the enemy uses WMDs, a nuclear response to the use of such weapons and covert actions in self-defense become parts of a just war (righteous war). The point to be noted is that even the hawks do not argue for first use of WMDs or the use of tactical nuclear weapons on the battlefield. WMDs, conclude the hawks, should be used for maintaining deterrence, and if deterrence fails and the enemy launches a nuclear attack, only then should *brahmastras* rain down upon them (Young 2004: 277–320).

From the late 20th century onwards, a group of Indian military officers started paying attention to the classical Hindu texts in order to assess their relevance for present and future conflicts. This trend is consonant with Chinese military thinkers searching Sun Tzu's *The Art of War* and Pakistani military officers rummaging through the *Koran* in order to distill the principles of war for application in modern conflicts. As regards the *Mahabharata*, Lieutenant-Colonel G. D. Bakshi of the Indian Army writes in his monograph: "We need to look at the *Mahabharata* ... because it has a lot to offer. The weapon systems and technologies change – the basic maneuvers and strategies of war seem to remain constant" (Bakshi 1990: 72). Bakshi continues that while Bhisma represents the art of symmetrical response, Krishna advocates the art of nonsymmetrical response on the battlefield. Krishna's approach flowered as the art of *kutayuddha* in the *Arthashastra* (Bakshi 1990: 73).

From the 7th century CE onwards until the present day, the *Mahabharata* has been a work for popular education among Hindus and has been recited before general audiences. It is regarded as a work of *ithihasa* (history), while the *Ramayana* is regarded as a *kavya* (poem) (Kane 1968: 355–356). Knowledge of the Great Bharata War (Mahabharata War) has shaped the consciousness of the common Hindus through the ages. To give an example, the sepoys (Indian soldiers) who joined the British-officered Indian Army in colonial India, while fighting in the trenches of France during 1914–1915, conceived of the mass slaughter of this industrial war as a repeat of the Mahabharata War's grand slaughter.

Ancient Indian tradition gave birth to two types of role models for Hindu women. One is the Sita-type model where the wife is *pativrata* (loyal to the husband under all circumstances) and docile (meekly succumbing to the whims and decisions of the patriarch-husband). This trend gave rise to the following idea: *patir punya satir punya* (the greatness of a wife depends on supporting her husband under all circumstances). The wife becomes a devotee of the husband (her lord/god), an idea somewhat akin to the *Bhakti* ideology whose seeds can be traced back to the *Bhagavad Gita* and that spread later in medieval India. The other model is Draupadi, where the woman, though a wife, emerges as an independent actor and a key decision-maker and at times challenges her husband forcefully and rationally. In the Draupadi model, the position of a wife is neither predetermined nor static but continuously evolving through negotiations and renegotiations due to ever-changing circumstances. She can have multiple partners. During India's struggle for freedom against the British Empire, Gandhi supported the Sita-like model for Indian women joining the nationalist movement. In Gandhi's paradigm, women provided logistical support silently under the leadership of men. But Subhas Chandra Bose (1897–1945) adopted the goddess Durga (war goddess) and Draupadi model, as he inducted female combatants in his *Azad Hind Fauj* (Indian National Army). These female combatants lived outside the institution of marriage and chose their own male partners.

Strangely, the Draupadi model remains neglected by Indian feminists, even today. However, the rise to power of the BJP as well as the increase in unconventional intrastate conflicts in the subcontinent and nuclear rivalry suggest that the use of ancient Hinduism's imagination of war will only increase among scholars and strategic security managers in the near future.

References

Atharva Veda 1993. *Samhita Vol. 1.* Translated into English with critical and exegetical commentary by William Dwight Whitney. Revised and edited by Charles Rockwell Lanman. Motilal Banarasidass Publishers.

Bakshi, Lieutenant-Colonel G. D. 1990. *Mahabharata: A Military Analysis.* Lancer International.

Black, Brian. 2007. "Eavesdropping on the Epic: Female Listeners in the *Mahabharata.*" In *Gender and Narrative in the Mahabharata.* Edited by Simon Brodbeck and Brian Black. Routledge. 53–78.

Bodewitz, Henk W. 1999. "Hindu *Ahimsa* and Its Roots." In *Violence Denied: Violence, Non-violence and the Rationalization of Violence in South Asian Cultural History.* Edited by Jan E. M. Houben and Karel R. Van Kooij. Brill. 17–44.

Boesche, Roger. 2003. "Kautilya *Arthashastra* on War and Diplomacy in Ancient India." *Journal of Military History* 67(1): 9–38.

2017. *Kautilya: The First Great Political Realist.* HarperCollins.

Brekke, Torkel. 2005. "The Ethics of War and the Concept of War in India and Europe." *NUMEN* 52(1): 59–86.

Brodbeck, Simon. 2007. "Gendered Soteriology: Marriage and the *Karmayoga.*" In *Gender and Narrative in the Mahabharata.* Edited by Simon Brodbeck and Brian Black. Routledge. 144–175.

Brodbeck, Simon and Brian Black. 2007. "Introduction." In *Gender and Narrative in the Mahabharata.* Edited by Simon Brodbeck and Brian Black. Routledge. 1–34.

Chatterji, Madhumita. 2007. *The Kshatriyas in Ancient India.* Munshiram Manoharlal Publishers.

Chousalkar, Ashok S. 2018. *Revisiting the Political Thought of Ancient India: Pre-Kautilyan Arthashastra Tradition*. SAGE.

Das, Harish Chandra. 1986. *Military History of Kalinga*. Punthi Pustak.

Doniger, Wendy. 2015. *The Hindus: An Alternative History*. Speaking Tiger Books.

Heesterman, Jan C. 1984. "Non-Violence and Sacrifice." *Indologica Taurinensia* 12: 119–127.

Hiltebeitel, Alf. 1980. "Draupadi's Garments." *Indo-Iranian Journal* 22: 97–112.

——— 1985. "Two Krsnas, Three Krsnas, Four Krsnas, More Krsnas: Dark Interactions in the '*Mahabharata*'." *Journal of South Asian Literature* 20 (1): 71–77.

——— 1998. "Empire, Invasion, and India's National Epics." *International Journal of Hindu Studies* 2(3): 387–421.

——— 2007. "Among Friends: Marriage, Women, and Some Little Birds." In *Gender and Narrative in the Mahabharata*. Edited by Simon Brodbeck and Brian Black. Routledge. 110–143.

Houben, Jan E. M. and Karel R. Van Kooji. 1999. "Introduction." In *Violence Denied: Violence, Non-violence and the Rationalization of Violence in South Asian Cultural History*. Edited by Jan E. M. Houben and Karel R. Van Kooij. Brill. 1–15.

Hudson, Emily T. 2007. "Listen but Do Not Grieve: Grief, Paternity, and Time in the Laments of *Dhrtarashtra*." In *Gender and Narrative in the Mahabharata*. Edited by Simon Brodbeck and Brian Black. Routledge. 35–52.

Inden, Ronald. 2006. *Texts and Practice: Essays on South Asian History*. Oxford University Press.

Jatavallabhula, Danielle Feller. 1999. "*Ranayajna*: The Mahabharata War as a Sacrifice." In *Violence Denied: Violence, Non-violence and the Rationalization of Violence in South Asian Cultural History*. Edited by Jan E. M. Houben and Karel R. Van Kooij. Brill. 69–103.

Kane, Pandurang Vaman. 1968. *History of Dharmasastra (Ancient and Medieval Religious and Civil Law in India), Vol. 1, Part I*. Bhandarkar Oriental Research Institute.

Kangle, R. P. 1992. *The Kautilya Arthashastra, Part II, An English Translation with Critical and Explanatory Notes*. Motilal Banarasidass Publishers.

Kosambi, D. D. 2001. *The Culture and Civilisation of Ancient India*. Vikas.

Mahabharata. 2015. *Vol. 8 (Sections 78–86)*. Translated by Bibek Debroy. Penguin.

Malinar, Angelika. 2007. "Arguments of a Queen: Draupadi's Views on Kingship." In *Gender and Narrative in the Mahabharata*. Edited by Simon Brodbeck and Brian Black. Routledge. 79–96.

McGrath, Kevin. 2017. *Raja Yudhistira: Kingship in Epic Mahabharata*. Orient Blackswan Private Limited.

Nandi, Ramendra Nath. 2018. *The Rgveda in Its Historical Setting*. PRIMUS.

Olivelle, Patrick. 1998. *The Early Upanishads: Annotated Text and Translation*. Oxford University Press.

Parasher, Aloka. 1979. "The Designation *Mleccha* for Foreigners in Early India." *Proceedings of the Indian History Congress* 40: 109–120.

Patton, Laurie L. 2007. "How Do You Conduct Yourself? Gender and the Construction of a Dialogical Self in the *Mahabharata*." In *Gender and Narrative in the Mahabharata*. Edited by Simon Brodbeck and Brian Black. Routledge. 97–109.

Rosen, Steven J. 2007. *Krishna's Song: A New Look at the Bhagavad Gita*. Praeger.

Singh, Upinder. 2017. *Political Violence in Ancient India*. Harvard University Press.

Srivastava, A. K. 1985. *Ancient Indian Army: Its Administration and Organization*. Ajanta Publications.

Thapar, Romila. 1971. "The Image of the Barbarian in Early India." *Comparative Studies in Society and History* 13(4): 408–436.

Trautmann, Thomas R. 2012. *Arthashastra: The Science of Wealth*. Allen Lane.

Vidal, Denis, Gilles Tarabout and Eric Meyer. 1994. "On the Concepts of Violence and Non-violence in Hinduism and Indian Society." *South Asia Research* 14(2): 196–213.

Whitaker, Jarrod. 2019. "Women, Weapons, and Words: Gender and Sexuality in the *Rgveda*'s Weapons Hymn (6.75)." In *Self, Sacrifice, and Cosmos: Vedic Thought, Ritual, and Philosophy*. Edited by Lauren M. Bausch. PRIMUS. 127–143.

Young, Katherine K. 2004. "Hinduism and the Ethics of Weapons of Mass Destruction." In *Ethics and Weapons of Mass Destruction: Religious and Secular Perspectives*. Edited by Sohah H. Hashmi and Steven P. Lee. Cambridge University Press. 277–320.

5 Buddha in the Ring of Fire: The Buddhist Ethics of Warfare

STEPHEN JENKINS

This chapter approaches Buddhist ideologies of warfare by first acknowledging that, both in the contemporary and ancient world, Buddhist societies have been as warlike as others. It does so by briefly surveying the expanding contemporary scholarship on Buddhist-inspired violence. It then asks how the common conception of Buddhist pacifism arose, pointing to Buddhist missionaries and certain approaches to texts in modern scholarship. This question deserves a book-length study, but for present purposes it is important to emphasize that the subject requires heightened critical self-awareness. The chapter then addresses supporting evidence for Buddhist pacifism, while ultimately arguing that this has been a misleading conception that eclipses valuable Buddhist thought on the ethics of warfare. The distorting effect of mistranslating "*ahiṃsā*" as Gandhian "nonviolence" is highlighted. The chapter closes by examining Buddhist lore regarding great kings, particularly Aśoka, a touchstone for Buddhist pacifist ideals, and Duṭṭhagāmaṇi, an apparently shocking exception to stereotypes of Buddhist values. New research is offered that shows that Aśoka's famous expression of remorse for warfare is standard Indian statecraft. Regarding Duṭṭhagāmaṇi, the infamous statement that his victims were mere animals is shown to be far more complex than it appears and consistent in ways with Buddhist ideals.

SURVEYING BUDDHIST WARFARE

Despite continuing debate regarding Buddhist ethical thought on "violence," it has become increasingly undebatable that in penal codes and warfare ancient Buddhist cultures were no more historically pacifist than they have been in recent times. Let us glance at recent scholarship: Michael Jerryson has illuminated the conflicts in Southeast Asia including those with Muslim populations in Myanmar and Thailand (Jerryson 2011; 2013; 2018); these current wars are preceded by a long history of wars of conquest by Burmese, Mon, Khmer, and Thai monarchs. Brian Victoria has drawn attention to Japanese Zen and Pure Land support for World War II (WWII) as the "Great Compassionate War," including campaigns of terrorist assassinations led and supported by Zen practitioners (Victoria 2006; 2020); this history has long antecedents in the militarization of monasteries up until their defeat by the Samurai warlords that united Japan under the Shogunate. There is no referent for a pacifist Japanese Buddhism prior to the end of WWII; Buddhism was long associated with its own military power and its support of state militarism. So, as in other contexts, this is not a matter of an initially pacifist Buddhism gone wrong at some historical juncture.

Regarding China, Buddhist values supported both state-sponsored violence and mass uprisings often based on messianic expectations for the descent of the savior Maitreya. Xue Yu has documented Buddhist organized guerilla warfare and assassination campaigns during the Japanese invasion (Xue 2012). Under the Communist regime, Buddhist rationalizations of warfare were deployed to encourage Chinese to fight in the Korean War, while similar texts were referenced in South Korea in support of fighting Communists (Rhi 1976; Xue 2012). Tibet has a long and well-documented history of Buddhist-inspired warfare and war magic up to the recent CIA-sponsored guerilla warfare (Maher 2010; Bellezza 2020). Elliot Sperling presents pacifism as a dubious feature of orientalist imaginations of Tibet (Sperling 2001). Although the current Dalai Lama has rightly been an icon of compassion, the popular and academic misunderstanding of what he means by "nonviolence" has been a key factor in the distortion of Buddhist war ethics (Jenkins 2021a).

Indian Buddhist traditions remember many Buddhist *rājas*, including Aśoka, for their mass violence against "outsiders" perceived as enemies of Buddhist tradition or for wars of conquest supported by Buddhist ideals (Jenkins 2016). Scholarly treatment of Indian warfare often begins with naive readings of the Aśokan edicts, to which we will return below, which fail to heed John Strong's advice to treat them as propaganda (Strong 1994). It will be shown here that Aśoka's famous expression of remorse is in accord with standard Indian statecraft. Sri Lanka has been a great focus of attention on this subject, particularly the apparently shocking case of King Duṭṭhagāmaṇi, who made war to unite the island under a Buddhist "dispensation," *Sāsana*. This chapter sheds new light on this character who has been both celebrated as a role model and treated with apologetic horror. It will attempt to normalize the legend of Duṭṭhagāmaṇi. We discuss below how even the Buddha is regarded as having used fire, storms, and weapons to ethnically cleanse Sri Lanka of its original inhabitants.

WHENCE BUDDHIST PACIFISM

This leads to a seldom-asked question. As Richard Gombrich put it, "[w]hen one looks at the historical record one begins to wonder how anyone ever came by the idea that Buddhists are any less violent than other cultures" (Gombrich 2006: 31). Gombrich has suggested academic fundamentalism as a cause; that is, a retreat from history and later texts and commentarial interpretations towards "fundamental values" represented by a core body of early texts. He notes that Buddhist tradition itself was never fundamentalistic in this way. This fundamentalist approach excludes a vast body of literature that is rich in examples that contradict notions of pacifism. There is a well-known orientalist tendency for modern scholars to idealize a golden age represented by texts that they curate, and then they regard the living tradition as a disappointment of their fantasies.

Such academic fundamentalism may also be a reaction to increasing evidence of violence in texts and historical practice. As it becomes difficult to uphold an image of pacifist Buddhism in the light of historical practice, or even in the textual corpus of the living tradition, that image must be relocated in "early" canonical texts. An essay by Rupert Gethin on Buddhist violence speaks of the "fundamental Buddhist attitude" found in the canonical literature, brushing aside *jātakas*, authoritative texts like the *Milindapañha*, and later postcanonical tradition (Gethin 2007: 60, 67, 69). These texts are classified as noncanonical and often represent later historical layers, but they are also the sources that do the work of addressing social ethics, especially those related to warfare and punishment. Much of the narrative literature is centered around the conduct of kings. To categorize this literature in a way that suggests it is not "fundamental" to understanding Buddhist values secures an untainted textual core and excludes the functional canon of the living tradition.

In perhaps the only publication dedicated to Gombrich's question, Iselin Frydenlund points to the early Buddhist missionaries to the West, particularly Dharmapala, who, at the World's Parliament of Religions in 1893, presented Buddhism as a religion of peace that had "made Asia mild" (Frydenlund 2017). Ironically, Dharmapala is also blamed for glorifying the violent King Duṭṭhagāmaṇi in ways that stimulated the Sri Lankan Civil War (Grant 2009). Walpola Rahula was a 20th-century

Sri Lankan monk who served as an American professor. His *What the Buddha Taught* served as a standard primer in Buddhist Studies courses for decades. There he made the oft-repeated claim that "there is not a single example of persecution or the shedding of a drop of blood in converting people to Buddhism, or in its propagation during its long history of 2500 years" (Rahula 1982: 5). In addition to whitewashing and distorting Buddhist history, such claims served a variety of purposes. They allowed colonized Buddhists to take the moral high ground from their exploiters and explain away their domination as a result of their higher religious ideals. They allowed Hindus in the Indian independence movement to blame Jains and Buddhists for making India weak. For historians, Buddhist pacifism helped explain the extinction of Buddhism in India. Today's Tibetan refugee youth even blame their ancestors' perceived pacifism for the loss of their homeland (Jenkins 2011; 2021a).

SUPPORTING EVIDENCE FOR PACIFISM

One problem consistently noted in scholarship is that Buddha is generally unforthcoming about warfare. For instance, he must be asked three times by warriors about the fate of those who die in battle (Bodhi 2000: 1335). In situations calling for jeremiads about the horrors of war, such as the conflict between Kings Pasenadi and Ajātasattu, he merely offers lessons about winning, losing, and the dangers of enduring enmity. When asked by Ajātasattu for advice about war against the Vajjis, rather than deploring warfare, Buddha says they will never be defeated as long as they stay united. This suggests military advice to Ajātasattu. Sowing dissent among enemies by subterfuge is one of a standard set of Indian techniques for conquest, and Ajātasattu successfully does so (Wu 2015). Traditional commentaries noticed Buddha's silence as well. On Buddha's meeting Pasenadi after a successful campaign putting down and impaling rebels, the commentator suggests Buddha withheld comment in order to avoid alienating the King (Bodhi 2000: 410 note 257).

There are good reasons for perceiving Buddhism as pacifist. Buddhist traditions are unconditionally against harm and harmful intentions and value the happiness and well-being of all sentient beings. As discussed below, the complicating issues are what constitutes harm, how to navigate competing concerns for and proportionality of harm, and what types of action are possible without harmful intentions. For instance, these are questions that have to be considered from a multiple-life perspective. Killing is not annihilation, and one's motivation for killing may be to prevent greater harm in future lives.

Concern to avoid harm is shown in many ways. The Buddha asked the laity to abstain from arms trafficking. Descriptions of ideal kingdoms, which include excellent armed forces, are also without butchers, fishermen, and poulterers. Vegetarianism was never universal but often encouraged. Monks filter water to avoid killing microbes; honey gathering and sericulture produced angst about robbing and killing insects. One should ask trees for permission before cutting them.

It seems never to have been the case, but texts often call for moderation in penal codes and abstention from capital punishment. Although Buddha never condemned military service by the laity (again, the ideal society has excellent armed forces), monks are discouraged from associating with military camps, parades, and battles. Even killing in self-defense or to defend a friend is unwholesome and rooted in defilement (Schmithausen 1991: 45). Encouraging euthanasia or asking for a torture victim to be killed quickly may result in a monk's expulsion (Schmithausen 1991: 46). Wars of conquest and pillage are condemned. *Temiya Jātaka*, one of Buddha's most enduringly famous past lives, tells of a prince who feigned disability to avoid the horrific karma entailed by the duties of a king to protect and punish (Cowell 2005: 1). This is often cited to support the view that one would be better off not to become a king. From the earliest texts to late tantric *rituals* for killing, engaging in violence entails great moral peril, even when justified.

Abhorrence for harm is not just expressed textually. Sacred sites prominently feature sculptural depictions of narratives that daringly challenge the violence of kings. Depictions of King Udena firing arrows at Queen Śyāmavatī, falsely accused of assassination, are common in India. When Śyāmavatī manifested a mind of loving kindness, *mettacitta*, the king's arrows turned back at him. This demonstrates the dangers of rash injustice and the central idea that compassion has protective power. There are tales of kings being arrow-proof as long as they maintain a mind of loving kindness, and this bears directly on concerns to maintain such attitudes even in battle (Jenkins 2021b). Artistic representations of King Māndhātar, a king who conquered his way all the way to heaven only to fall from glory on his first thought of unrighteous conquest, are among the most common in India.

THE APPARENT BIFURCATION OF DHARMA ROOTED IN OUR APPROACH TO SOURCES

Buddhist concern to avoid harm is so uncompromising that it seems impossible to reconcile it with the sources and practices that reflect situational adaptation to contexts and conditions. The precept not to kill and the general abhorrence for harm are in sharp contrast with historical practice and with many sources that validate violence. In response, scholars have suggested a bifurcation of Dharma correlating with distinctions between canonical and noncanonical, earlier and later sources, and between "fundamental values" and actual practice (Collins 1998: 419–420, 451–466; Schmithausen 1999: 53; Gethin 2007: 69). This bifurcation of Dharma also parallels the dissonance between Western expectations of pacifism and historical reality.

This apparent contradiction, of which Buddhists seem unaware, suggests a problem in our own understanding. Part of the problem may be the way we read Buddhist texts. For instance, in *Temiya Jātaka* a prince goes to great lengths to avoid being a king because this will entail inflicting harm in the roles of warrior and punisher. It is one of ten narratives cherished for recounting the last ten lives before Buddhahood. These last rebirths are the pinnacle of countless lives of moral cultivation. In any South Asian temple, one may find them portrayed as a set. They should be read together as a body of moral studies, rather than as singular proof texts. In all but one of these ten stories, the Buddha is either king or war minister, hardly consistent with the view that a Buddhist should avoid being king. In the only rebirth in which he is not a king, he trains a king in royal duties, who subsequently "swells the hosts of heaven" by leading his subjects in virtue (J.540; Cowell 2005: 38). In *Ummagga Jātaka*, to which we will return, the Buddha is a war minister and spymaster actively engaged in deadly warfare (J.546; Cowell 2005: 197–198). In *Nimi Jātaka*, the king learns from Indra that both giving alms and renunciation (i.e. being a king and being a renunciant) are important (J.541; Cowell 2005: 53). Refusing to stay in heaven, he returns to Earth for the opportunity to do good as a king. The tension between the roles of king and renunciant are resolved by taking a page from the Hindu life phase (*āśrama*) system. A king should play his role until reaching old age and then become a renunciant. In *Mahānārada Jātaka*, Buddha incarnates as the deity Brahma and convinces a king of karmic rebirth, and so influences him to renew social welfare programs (J.544; Cowell 2005: 114).

Each of these stories does a particular kind of work, and within each narrative whatever value is being emphasized is treated hyperbolically, whether it is skill in warfare or horror at the moral hazards of warfare. These are simultaneously valued, but each one taken individually could be misleading. Rather than developing a paralyzing ethical tension, the tradition values kings who are simultaneously reticent, reluctant, deliberate, cognizant of their moral peril, martially effective, and productively remorseful in terms of subsequent merit-making that benefits the monastic community. We will see this repeatedly expressed in ideal characters and in historical behavior.

Another methodological issue involves how we categorize sources. Mahinda Palihawadana writes that "nowhere in the canonical texts can we find an instance where the use of military force is justified or the role of the fighter is idealized" (Palihawadana 2006: 72). Similarly Peter Harvey writes that "within the Theravāda, no canonical text can be found justifying violence" (Harvey 2000: 255). Both these statements are disproven below, but we should note their use of sources. Their claims are restricted to canonical texts, as if this designates the fundamental values of Buddhism. This bifurcates the textual tradition in a way that devalues the central resources of Buddhist ethical thought, those that show how the living tradition actually understood its values. A parallel disjunct to that between "canon" and historical behavior is found between the "canonical" and narrative literature, chronicles, and hagiographies. As Gombrich notes, the tradition was not fundamentalistic, and this broader literature played a vital role.

The noncanonical *jātaka* tales of the early Mainstream[1] narrative traditions abound in warfare, featuring Buddha in past lives as a weapons master, a warrior king, a warhorse, an execution elephant, a *yakṣa* praising a successful military campaign, an elephant mahout participating in a siege, a war minister defending against a siege, even the deity Indra at war with the demigods, etc. (Jenkins 2017). In one *jātaka*, King Pasenadi, considered good in comparison to his patricidal enemy Ajātasattu, is ridiculed by monks for his military incompetence. Agents of Pasenadi overhear monks talking about combat strategy, which he promptly employs to capture Ajātasattu alive. The tale relates this to a past life in which the wise monk was a boar who organized his community to kill a tiger. The boars then pursued the evil ascetic who controlled the tiger, thinking he would soon employ another. They knocked down the tree where he took refuge and tore him apart. Buddha is represented here by a *yakṣa*, who applauds their success (Jenkins 2017). Both defensive warfare and a preemptive strike against an immoral enemy are modeled here.

[1] The term "Mainstream" refers to the broad range of non-Mahāyāna traditions, including Theravāda, and avoids the term "*hīnayāna*," which is a calculated insult deployed by the Mahāyāna in its rhetoric of superiority.

INTENTION AND RELATIVE DEGREES OF MORAL WRONG IN THE ETHICS OF KILLING

In many of these stories, warriors die heroic deaths with morbid melodrama. How does this accord with Buddha's much-cited canonical assertion that those who die in battle go to hell rather than heaven? This assertion is often mistakenly read as explaining the result of killing in battle, but here warriors go to hell because they die holding intentions to kill.

> When, headman, a mercenary is one who strives and exerts himself in battle, his mind is already low, depraved, misdirected by the thought: "Let these beings be slain, slaughtered, annihilated, destroyed, or exterminated." If others then slay him and finish him off while he is striving and exerting himself in battle, then ... he is reborn in the "Battle-Slain Hell."
>
> (Bodhi 2000: 1334)[2]

The Buddha does not say here that warriors go to hell for merely participating in warfare. They go to hell because they are killed while filled with murderous intentions. In Buddhism, intention is determinative for karmic outcomes. In Mainstream, Mahāyāna, and Tantric texts, it is often possible to do things that are normally considered morally wrong if they are done with righteous intentions (Jenkins 2010a; 2010b). In later explanations of ethical killing, it is crucial that the intention be compassion. The warriors' rebirth in hell reflects a common Indian belief about the power of *maraṇacitta*, one's dying thought, to determine the subsequent rebirth. We can also see this concern in the Mahāyāna conception of compassionate killing, where one should avoid killing when the victim is in a negative state of mind. To do so would defeat the purpose by resulting in their rebirth in hell. Clearly the composers and compilers of the *jātaka* collection, with its abundant examples of martial heroes combatting invasions and demonic individuals, did not believe hell was the necessary fate of anyone who engaged in warfare.

This brings us to the key ethical question of whether one can engage in warfare without murderous intentions, or even with compassion. Jain and Mainstream Buddhist sources sometimes depict warriors setting special intentions not to kill before battle (Schmithausen 1991: 45; Wu 2015). In Mahāyāna and tantric traditions, there is a broadly held

---

[2] The translation term "mercenary" here is misleading. A professional soldier is indicated. The term translated as "headman" is a stock term for a military chieftain.

view that compassionate killing and warfare are possible, and that soldiers who kill may make great karmic merit. It is even regarded as a moral failure to refrain from such actions when the situation calls for them (Jenkins 2010a; 2010b).

There is debate about whether compassionate killing is a Mahāyānist innovation or has some basis in Mainstream traditions. Rupert Gethin has argued that in Theravāda *abhidharmic* thought killing can never be accompanied by auspicious states of mind like compassion (Gethin 2004). He draws from *abhidharmic* analysis of a king smilingly ordering an execution. Even when unapparent, there must be some subtle unwholesome quality in his intention. This seems black and white; killing must always be inauspicious. However, it also shows there are times when inauspicious intentions in killing must be sought on a subtle level. Because the criminal has very low moral status, this is a case where the relative degree of unwholesomeness has to be sought at the extreme end of a sliding scale.

The gradation of the unwholesomeness in killing based on the moral status of the victim is a standard aspect of Indian thought that mediates between the *prima facie* principle that killing is simply wrong and the pragmatic situational balancing of competing concerns to avoid harm. Killing is forbidden in the precepts, even killing animals. However, in the monastic code, killing a crow merely requires confession from a monk, and even killing *yakṣas*, human-like beings, does not entail expulsion from the monastic community (Gethin 2004: 171–172; Jenkins 2010a: 307), while killing humans requires expulsion. However, the Theravāda Vinaya literature allows for monks to take up weapons in self-defense and exonerates them if the attackers are killed (Aono 2021: 159). The implications for the laity are obvious. The karmic retribution for killing humans further depends both on the victim's moral status and their relationship to the killer. Harming a saint or one's own parents leads without reprieve directly to hell (Silk 2007; Jenkins 2016). As discussed below, this may place criminals and enemies of the Dharma, agents of the worst possible harm, in a moral category lower than animals. This is a dangerous idea, since it can result in dehumanizing enemies, but it is also commonsensical. If we think of an animal attacking children or a terrorist threatening good people, courses of action would be informed by their relative moral status.

Those who harm a buddha or *arhat*, persons of the highest moral status, face the most extreme and immediate penalties. These crimes are called "immediates" because the killer goes to hell without any intermediate lives in which to repentantly generate merit, or even to get ordained and achieve liberation, as did the mass murderer Finger-Necklace, Aṅgulimāla. Killing one's own parent is also an "immediate," but not killing someone else's parent. In the story of Finger-Necklace, Buddha intervenes in his killing spree only after he decides to kill his own mother. If he had committed that murder, he would have been beyond hope. So one's personal relationship to the victim and the victim's moral status are determinative of karmic outcomes. Dogmatically speaking, killing one's parents is least among these, while harming a buddha is the greatest. A related set of crimes, similar to the "immediates," include things like stealing from the Saṅgha and harming a stūpa (Silk 2007).

In this relative scale of karmic outcomes the worst sort of harm is to Buddhist saints and institutions, the Sāsana. Although not an "immediate," wrong views (i.e. views that oppose Buddhist thought) also result in hell "as if someone brought you there" (Jenkins 2016). Conversely, the least negative karmic outcomes are for killing the worst possible persons, defined as enemies of the Dharma. Theravāda and Mahāyāna claims that killing such people is less negative than killing an animal or insect, discussed below, accord with this rubric. Rationalizations of violence that portray the victims as enemies of the Dharma and the killer as a defender are the most morally secure possible. Those who attack Buddhist institutions or saints have the lowest possible moral status, while protecting the Dharma represents an inversely high motivation to avoid harm. Enemies of the Dharma are in the most dangerous place possible in the Buddhist moral calculus. So the key question is not whether killing must be associated with negative intentions or excludes positive ones, but to what degree unwholesomeness is involved. In this light, killing must always be evaluated contextually and relationally, and this in no way contradicts a general abhorrence for taking life.

The Milindapañha, a canonical or "quasi-canonical" Theravāda text depending on cultural context, in which a monk instructs a king, absolves kings for punishments such as execution and dismemberment and absolves the Buddha's teaching for calling for punishment by locating the cause in the victim's karma. Criminals bring it on themselves, and the king carries no blame (Jenkins 2010a). This may help explain why Buddhist polities have almost universally had draconian penal codes including dismemberment and capital punishment. If we extrapolate to situations where any group, already bound for hell by holding and promoting false views, represents a vital threat to the Buddhist tradition, it is clear that its members have the lowest possible moral status and so the karmic repercussions for killing them are the lowest possible. There is even an argument that it is the ripening of their karma.

In 2016, Damien Keown and the author published arguments, referencing different textual resources, that there is a basis for compassionate killing in the Pali canon. Both arguments focused on painfully harsh speech motivated by compassion. Examples include parents disciplining children, teachers scolding students, or Buddha reprimanding monks for misconduct. Buddha likened his harsh words for his murderous cousin, Devadatta, to an adult compassionately pulling a stick from a choking child's throat, even if it draws blood. This is similar to an example deployed by Mahāyānists and Jains of a doctor cutting off the viper-bitten finger of a child to prevent the spread of poison. Keown pointed out another medical analogy from the *Kathāvatthu* commentary that "even the giving of an unpleasant thing – for example, bitter medicine – must be regarded as a morally good act, provided that it has its source in a beneficent state of mind (*hita-citta*)" (Keown 2016 citing Devdas 2004: 275, 423). It is no coincidence that harsh speech is often the first example in Mahāyānist discussions of compassionate transgression. The *Milindapañha* put the basic idea like this:

> The Tathāgata [Buddha], O king, wounds people but to their good, he casts people down to their profit, he kills people but to their advantage. Just as mothers and fathers, O king, hurt their children and even knock them down, thinking the while of their good; so by whatsoever method an increase in the virtue of living beings can be brought about, by that method does he contribute to their good.
> (Rhys Davids 1963: 164–165)

Keown asks: "Why is it psychologically possible to use harsh speech out of compassion, but psychologically impossible to kill out of compassion, even though both actions share identical roots? … It follows further that killing from compassion is not only psychologically possible but morally good (*kusala*)" (Keown 2016: 76). Keown acknowledges Gethin's interpretation of the *Abhidhamma* but argues it is a poor and damaging argument contradicted by other Buddhist sources. "By denying there can be circumstances in which the use of lethal force is morally justified (meaning that no bad karma is produced, not even a little), the *Abhidhamma* blocked the development of an ethics of self-defense and just war, leaving total pacifism as the only option – one routinely rejected in practice by Buddhist societies" (Keown 2016: 78).

This is an important point, but perhaps it is not the *Abhidhamma* that blocked development of such thought. Buddhist narrative literature offers abundant case studies addressing everything from the proper treatment of prisoners to the conduct of war to postwar reconciliation. One reason for the lack of modern systematic thought on war ethics, particularly by those who might have moderated the recent Sri Lankan Civil War and constructively contributed to postwar reconciliation, is the erroneous image of absolute pacifism cultivated by missionaries and cherished in scholarship. Such an image suggests that Buddhist tradition may resist war but has no constructive resources to offer on its proper conduct. Perhaps the Sri Lankan Civil War might not have ended in a massacre of civilians, and postwar processes might have included mourning and honoring the Tamil dead, rather than bulldozing their cemeteries. Standard Buddhist arguments suggest such conduct will only perpetuate multigenerational cycles of violence (Jenkins 2017: 171–172).

BUDDHIST WAR ETHICS

With few exceptions, warfare narratives valorize victory that cleverly minimizes casualties, even at the cost of the hero's life. They emphasize defensive *intentions* to protect innocents and to capture the enemy alive rather than to harm or kill. Well-trained and well-paid armed forces are considered a deterrent to aggression through intimidation. Warfare should avoid unnecessary harm, even to wildlife, vegetation, crops, and infrastructure. Warfare narratives emphasize humane treatment of prisoners and complete impassivity to hostility, abuse, and provocation. Wars of conquest are disparaged, and cases of offensive warfare are rarely depicted. Although many narratives honor the protection of others from animals, bandits, or soldiers, personal self-defense is not a justification for the use of deadly force. It is emphasized that warfare is never a solution. Violence begets violence in incessantly self-renewing multigenerational, multiple-life cycles. Such cycles of violence can only be ended by courageous gestures of friendship. For instance, in *Ummagga Jātaka*, the Buddha, in a past life as a war minister defending his besieged city, uses spies and subterfuge to lure the enemy to assault a place below the ramparts where the moat has been filled with crocodiles, and an ambush rains down deadly projectiles. In an image memorialized across modern South Asia, he captures the enemy king and brandishes a sword; but instead of killing him, he risks his own life by offering him his weapon. The result is enduring friendship and an end to war (Jenkins 2017: 168).

Mahāyāna scriptures such as the *Satyakaparivarta, Upāyakauśalya,* and *Mahāparinirvāṇa Sūtras* and a host of commentators applied

Mainstream arguments supporting compassionate punishment and harsh speech to armed struggle (Jenkins 2010a). In the touchstone case known throughout northern Asia, Buddha, as a ship's captain in a terrorist-like situation, kills a criminal who intends to murder everyone on board. In this way, he saves the murderer from the harm of eons in hell. He saves the potential victims both from being killed and from going to hell themselves for killing the criminal in a rage. Lastly, the captain benefits by making enormous merit. The tale is morally double-edged: Compassionate killing is used to save people from the karma of killing without it. The captain is depicted as willing to risk his own damnation and as having no other option. Several scholarly treatments have tried to suggest that the killing is somehow still inauspicious or that the Buddha subsequently experiences karmic repercussions. However, they fail to note that the text explicitly denies this. The auspiciousness of the act is also indisputably confirmed by accruing enormous karmic merit. The commentator Asaṅga extends the logic of compassionate transgression to stealing from thieves and unseating vicious kings and exploitative ministers (Jenkins 2010a; 2010b).

The *Satyakaparivarta Sūtra* allows a king to go to war with compassionate intentions to protect his people and stop the wanton killing by his enemy, but only after exhausting alternatives such as negotiation, intimidation, and bribes. He should fight with the intention to capture the enemy alive, but if he inadvertently kills during the struggle, he incurs no sin and makes merit instead. This also includes his armed forces. In making war, he should avoid damaging infrastructure, noncombatants, and the natural environment and treat prisoners humanely (Jenkins 2010a). These may sound like concessions to idealism, but they are each related to failures in the recent Gulf Wars that damaged American interests. In Buddhist thinking, criminals and rebels may be beaten and tortured for the sake of rehabilitation, but they should never be killed or permanently maimed. As with harsh speech, the king is said to be like a loving parent compassionately offering discipline. Tantric contexts, too, often taken as representing an extreme ethical shift, merely offer ritual technologies for doing what is allowed in Mahāyāna scriptures and commentaries. They hold the same reservations about moral peril and the crucial importance of compassionate intentions.

BUDDHIST KINGS, MYTHIC AND HISTORICAL

A response to Palihawadana's claim that the role of the warrior was never idealized in canonical texts begins with a discussion of the wheel-turning king, *cakravartin*, whose idealization includes superb armed forces. Although the highest type of *cakravartin* represents idealized militarism, because of his righteousness he has no enemies, and therefore under perfect kings war and punishment are unnecessary. This suggests that kings' use of force is directly proportional to their imperfection. From early sources through later narratives, poverty is a root cause of violence, and it is a king's responsibility to maintain prosperity and avoid economic exploitation of his subjects and other polities (Jenkins 2021b). Ideal governance requires no force, so force implies failure and casts doubt on its agent. In the *cakravartin* model, the righteous response to a *cakravartin*'s armed forces is submission. So polities resisting kings modeling themselves as *cakravartins* are in a dangerous position. Schmithausen notes that "kings in Ceylon and Southeast Asia who took the *cakravartin* ideal as their model (or, for that matter, declared themselves *Bodhisattvas*) had no scruples about conquering their neighbors by bloody force, if the neighbors were not willing to conform to the pattern of conduct described in canonical texts and submit spontaneously" (Schmithausen 1999: 55–56).

Another idealized canonical warrior is Vajrapāṇi, Buddha's armed bodyguard, who follows him everywhere according to Mainstream and Mahāyāna canonical scriptures. Vajrapāṇi is generally identified with Indra; he is the warrior king divinized and models the right use of force in support of the Buddha. In the Grecian northwest, he is artistically represented as the burly hero Heracles/Hercules. In canonical texts, he threatens to smash the head of anyone disrespecting the Buddha with his sidearm, the *vajra* (Jenkins 2010a). This canonical case of justified violence models the relationship between ideal ascetic and ideal warrior. Gethin suggests these threats are merely a statement of fact (i.e. that one's head will explode for disrespecting the Buddha; Gethin 2007: 68–69), but the canonical text and commentary describe the terror of those threatened upon seeing Vajrapāṇi, and other narratives depict Vajrapāṇi splitting mountains or blowing away competitors. There is no question this is a deadly threat (Jenkins 2016: 148–149). Ancient depictions of Vajrapāṇi accompanying Buddha are found from Taxila to Nāgārjunakoṇḍa, and images of Vajrapāṇi brandishing his fiery *vajra* above a cowering anti-Buddhist competitor are common at contemporary Theravādin sacred sites (Jenkins 2010a).[3]

---

[3] In a famous example, the assertion that Buddha's challenger refuses to acknowledge is that kings have the power to execute criminals and are worthy to do so (Jenkins 2010a).

The historical King Aśoka is an enduring icon of Buddhist pacifism. His romanticization in textbook treatments of Buddhism has been a major cause of distortion. It is important to avoid the common mistake of conflating the Aśoka of the edicts with his character in Buddhist legends. There is no evidence that later Buddhists could read the Aśokan inscriptions or remembered their content (Strong 1994: 142). Although he is remembered by Buddhists as changing from cruel to righteous, his famous edict of remorse for war atrocities plays no role in Buddhist memory. In that same edict where he expresses remorse, he warns of deadly consequences for rebellion. His is a peace that is the result of war, not its prevention. There is no hint he made restitution for the vast numbers he killed, enslaved, and displaced from their homeland.

His remorse is often thought to coincide with Buddhist conversion, but the best evidence suggests that Aśoka was a convert to Buddhism before he engaged in this war (Tambiah 1976: note 154), and so his massacre was the act of a Buddhist king. Scholars generally see the ethics of Aśoka's edicts as opposed to the *Arthaśāstra*, an Indian text on statecraft often described as Machiavellian and attributed by legend to Aśoka's own chief minister. As Tambiah put it, "Aśoka's Buddhistic proclamations on the ethics of kingship can be best understood as standing in dialectical contrast to the norms of statecraft propounded by the *Arthaśāstric* writers" (Tambiah 1976: 27). However, most of what Aśoka does after his successful campaign of conquest is in complete accord with the recommendations of the *Arthaśāstra* and Hindu *Dharmaśāstras* for a victorious king. The *Arthaśāstra* recommends a full-blown Dharma-campaign demonstrating moral superiority (Kautilya 1992: 38). The king should substitute his virtues for the defeated enemies' vices, follow pleasing policies, and attend and support festivals. (Remember Aśoka's pilgrimage tours.) He should show piety, support scholars and ascetics, and ensure devotions are held regularly in temples and ashrams. A victorious king should adopt the conquered peoples' lifestyle, language, and customs. He should please the chiefs of the country and protect their traditional rights. He should release all prisoners. The ill, helpless, and distressed should be helped (Kautilya 1992: 741). He should promote the good of his people, "because power comes from the countryside" (Kautilya 1992: 541). In sum, all practices not in accordance with Dharma should be discontinued (Kautilya 1992: 541). Even the limited restrictions on castration and the slaughter of animals found in the edicts are suggested for programs of postwar pacification.

Rather than a confessional statement of moral conversion,[4] Aśoka's expression of remorse is a standard feature of Indian statecraft, which has sophisticated concern for manipulating public opinion. The *Śāntiparvan*, a chapter of the *Mahābhārata* dedicated to statecraft, advocates that, after a conquest, a king should, like Aśoka, mourn and make a speech of regret for the death of his enemies, and only discretely praise those who did the killing (Fitzgerald 2004: 426). "After he has violently forced the inhabitants to bow down, the king should mollify them very quickly with conciliatory speeches," lest they remain eager to support his enemies at the first opportunity (Fitzgerald 2004: 413). A king "should offer compassionate relief to those in distress. He becomes the favorite of the people ... This is how an enemy is really taken!" (Fitzgerald 2004: 408). Aśoka's edict expresses concerns to pacify the conquered and avoid rebellion. His inscriptions may be the most enduringly successful public relations campaign in world history. As John Strong put it, we should "think of the rock inscriptions, not as blocks of historical fact, but political propaganda and campaign speeches" (Strong 1994: 141). Aśokan edicts should be read in light of the fact that his statements are closely aligned with norms of Indian statecraft. He is an ideal Arthaśāstric king.

Before taking this in cynical terms, it should be noted that the ideals of kingship in Buddhist sources like the *jātakas* share a skillful appeal to monarchs' self-interested desire for power and security by arguing that Dharmic rule is successful rule. Vicious, exploitative rulers fail. Buddhist appeals to kings to avoid or moderate warfare are not just based on the moral compunctions of idealistic ascetics, but rather on strong pragmatic arguments.

For instance, the extended Chinese version of the *Satyakaparivarta Sūtra* advises a king not to kill or maim defeated rebel vassals and to be moderate in the amount of their property he appropriates, explaining that this will lead others to be less likely to rebel or to surrender more quickly if they do (Xue 2012).

The reticent or regretful warrior king is a standard trope in Indian thought that is consistently related in modern scholarship to Aśoka's edict. In the Mahāyāna, it is understood that, like a doctor who must amputate a child's viper-bitten finger to save their life, the ideal actor

---

[4] Wendy Doniger speaks of Aśoka's "frankness and sincerity" and "realization that military conquest, indeed royal vainglory, was impermanent" (Doniger 2009: 54). Tambiah, despite critical reservations on the myth, still speaks of his "moral revolution" (Tambiah 1976: 55).

should regret that such violence is necessary. The king's reluctance, his successful violence, and his productive remorse, which induces massive merit-making projects, rather than being conflicted aspects of royal ethics, are all cherished as part of a consistent pattern of violence followed by dramatic enrichment of Buddhist institutions (Jenkins 2016). The reluctance and remorse are productive. They induce moderation, lead to merit-making projects, and serve a victor's political agenda by winning the hearts and minds of conquered people.

One of the confusing aspects of the Aśokan edicts is the frequency of references to *ahiṃsā*, which is routinely mistranslated as "nonviolence." Henk Bodewitz has shown that the Gandhian independence movement, intellectually rooted in Tolstoy and Thoreau, reinterpreted the concept of *ahiṃsā*, nonharm, to mean "nonviolence" in terms that it never meant in India for Jains, Hindus, or Buddhists (Bodewitz 1999). Failing to punish the wicked, to defend the state, or to perform animal sacrifice all could be considered harmful in Hindu contexts. Yet animal sacrifice is not considered harm, *hiṃsā*, because the victim goes to heaven, and warfare is homologized with sacrifice, such that war dead also attain heaven. References to *ahiṃsā* do not generally imply what moderns mean by "nonviolence," and many confusing aspects of the edicts and other texts disappear when we translate *ahiṃsā* as nonharm instead of nonviolence.

Buddhist memories of Aśoka vary dramatically from the edicts. The most positive version of Aśoka, cherished in uniquely generous Theravāda sources, takes care to absolve him of culpability for his ministers having killed Buddhist monks for failing to practice orthodox rituals (Mahānāma 1986: 46–49). The *Aśokāvadāna*, associated with the Sarvāstivādins, remembers him for slaughtering 18,000 Jains, long after his conversion to Buddhism, for an offense to a Buddha image, a crime considered in Buddhist theory to be nearly as serious as killing one's parents (Silk 2007). Scholars have claimed that, after his own brother was killed in the pogrom, he abstained from capital punishment. But later in the text, after his son, Kunāla, is blinded in a palace intrigue, Aśoka slaughtered the innocent citizens of Taxila and burned his own queen alive. In this legend, there is no point where he is "made mild" by Buddhist influences.

The 7th-century Chinese pilgrim Xüanzang reports a legend that Aśoka attempted to drown the Sarvāstivādin *arhats* in the Ganges. In an account similar to the *Mahāvibhāṣā's*, Xüanzang says Aśoka, "being unable to discern the Arhats from the ordinary monks ... had sympathy with those that he liked and supported those who were on intimate terms with him. He summoned the monks to the Ganges, intending to sink them into the deep water to kill them all. The *arhats*, realizing their lives were at stake, used their supernatural powers and flew through the air." The Sarvāstivādins fled to Kaśmīr, their historical stronghold, and refused to return (Xüanzang 1996: 102). Aśoka, routinely celebrated for religious tolerance, is remembered both by those he favored and those who fled him as involved in deadly interventions in the *Saṅgha*'s affairs as well as for massacring Jains. Theravādin sources glorify Aśoka and take pains to absolve him of his ministers' deadly persecution of delinquent monks. The Sarvāstivādins, source of the *Aśokāvadāna*'s unflattering account of his excessive violence, see themselves as well as the Jains as his victims. But even in the Sarvāstivādin sources, on his deathbed Aśoka turns down heaven and empire, aiming for even higher afterlife goals.

In legendary accounts of Buddhist kings, Aśoka's mass violence against non-Buddhists is not exceptional. Xüanzang describes his contemporary, King Harṣavardhana, as oppressed by vicious anti-Buddhist enemies who killed his father. In distress, Harṣa supplicated the celestial *bodhisattva* Avalokiteśvara, supreme embodiment of compassion, with prayers and offerings. In return for promises to overthrow the anti-Buddhist king, restore the influence of Buddhism, and rule compassionately, Avalokiteśvara empowered and sanctioned Harṣa's military conquest (Xüanzang 1996: 141; Devahuti 1998: 92–94). Harṣa's motivations are not unlike Duṭṭhagāmaṇi's and belie claims that Buddhists never went to war to spread the Dharma. The Buddhist historian Tāranātha records that Śrī Harṣa, who "was incomparable as a king," desired to destroy the doctrine of the *mlecchas* (foreigners). So, with rich offerings, he lured "12,000 experts of their doctrine" into a wooden building. After he convinced them to gather all their texts there as well, he burned them alive with their books (Chimpa 1970: 178). To "atone for his sin," Harṣa built five monasteries, each supporting a thousand monks. As usual, merit-making follows violence. It is a "win–win situation"; the enemies of Buddhism are massacred or simply disenfranchised and monks replace them in a repentant act of merit-making.

The Dharma-King Caṇḍapradyota, regarded as a contemporary of the Buddha, is a stock character appearing in Mahāyāna *sūtras*, *vinaya* texts, and *apadānas*. He is fierce, beating young monks for daring to speak to his wives, executing night-guards for falling asleep, and attempting to kill a doctor who cured him with forbidden medicine (Willemen 1994: 59–62; Saṅs-rgyas-rgya-mtsho and Kilty 2010: 117–119). In *Satyakaparivarta Sūtra*, just after being told to forgo capital punishment, he threatens to execute anyone who fails to attend an assembly with the Buddha (Jenkins 2010a). According to Michael Zimmermann, the *Mūlasarvāstivāda-Vinaya* describes him massacring 80,000 *Brāhmaṇas* (Zimmermann 2000: 180). It is notable that, despite all this terrifying behavior, he is still described as a righteous king, or *dharmarāja*, with many of the special possessions and properties ascribed to them.

A legend of the 2nd-century Emperor Kaniṣka, regarded as having gone from fierce warrior to merit-making *dharmarāja*, illustrates crucial concepts about karma still invoked today. After his conquest, Kaniṣka hears ministers whispering that he is destined to hell for his harsh actions. The king places a ring in boiling water and commands them to reach in and take it out. When they hesitate, he pours cold water into the boiling pot and takes it out himself. The cold water, he says, is analogous to his merit-making (Jenkins 2010b). This informs a recognizable historical pattern in Buddhist polities of violence followed by merit-making.

In Mainstream and Mahāyāna thought, those with great reservoirs of *karmic merit* may be able to commit grave crimes with minimal impact, while those with large amounts of negative karma may incur birth in the hell realms for minor acts. The common analogy is to adding salt to a large body of clear water, which would be unnoticeable, while adding just a little to a small amount of already salty water would make it undrinkable.[5] Kings have vast merit and the ability to make merit on a grand scale through support of the *Saṅgha* and contributions to sacred sites, while enemies of the Dharma have a contrasting low moral status that minimizes the karmic repercussion for harming them. According to another legend, Kaniṣka is still reborn as a thousand-headed fish whose heads are continually cut off. But each time an *arhat* rings the bell of the monastery he donated, it relieves his suffering, so monks continually ring the bell in relays (Rosenfield 1967: 38–39).

Rahula's claim, mentioned earlier, that not a drop of blood has been shed to propagate Buddhism seems disingenuous from someone who certainly knew the story of the Sri Lankan King Duṭṭhagāmaṇi, who expressly went to war not for conquest, but to unify the island under a Buddhist regime and to make the *Sāsana* shine. King Duṭṭhagāmaṇi's conquest of the Tamils is one of the most problematic episodes in Buddhist literature. The tale is found with some variations in chronicles

---

[5] For references to Mahāyāna and Mainstream sources, see Jenkins (2010b).

from the 5th-century *Mahāvaṃsa* to 14th-century commentaries and retranslations. The temporal range of these texts shows that the story is not just a historical anomaly revived by colonial translators; rather, it endured over centuries. It is also memorialized on a grand scale by *stūpas*. In recent times, Dharmapala, a key source for the image of Buddhist pacifism, encouraged young anticolonialists to be like King Duṭṭhagāmaṇi (Grant 2009: 77; Frydenlund 2017).

Duṭṭhagāmaṇi's origin story is wonderous. His mother, Queen Vihāradevī, having begged a dying monk to be reborn in her barren womb and then performed his funeral rites as he lay inside her, developed a craving that united merit-making and violence. She longed to eat from a giant honeycomb after offering honey to 12,000 monks,[6] and then she drank water that rinsed the bloody sword that had beheaded the Tamil champion as she stood upon his severed head (Mahānāma 1986: 1149–1151). Soothsayers explain that this is because her son would conquer the Tamils and make the *Sāsana* shine. Her desires were fulfilled, and we are presented the image of a honey-filled pregnant Queen standing on a severed head as she drinks its blood, a striking image cherished by Theravādins for centuries.

As a child, Duṭṭhagāmaṇi threw a fit when asked to vow not to attack the Tamils and, as a young man, he insulted his father for cowardice when he refused permission to attack, earning him the epithet Duṭṭha, which can mean angry or wicked. What is elevated by the name Duṭṭha is not wickedness (indeed he is lauded in the first passages that name him Duṭṭha as wise, meritorious, and bound for heaven) but his outrage at the occupation of the Tamils manifested in hostility and insulting behavior toward his father.[7]

With a relic in his scepter, Duṭṭhagāmaṇi warred to reunite Sri Lanka under a Buddhist dispensation, *Sāsana*. Like honey and blood, the relic-filled scepter symbolically unites religion and royal power, merit-making and violence. In keeping with the logic we saw in the Kaniṣka legend, it ultimately becomes the core of a great *stūpa*, covered with a mound of postwar merit-making. In addition to great monuments, Duṭṭhagāmaṇi is remembered for building eighteen hospitals and other public works (Berkwitz 2007: 248). The sources are emphatic

---

[6] According to legend, a past-life offering of honey by Aśoka resulted in his rebirth as an emperor (Mahānāma 1986: 30).

[7] Much has been made of this epithet (Gethin 2007). In its earliest occurrence, the *Dīpavaṃsa* describes Duṭṭhagāmaṇi as a wise merit-making king, with no suggestion that it indicates general wickedness (Oldenburg 2001: 210). Oldenberg adds "enlightened" to his description, which is unsupported by the Pali.

that he fought for Buddhism and not for gain. To emphasize his pure intentions, he is depicted making a "truth statement": "Not for the joy of sovereignty is this toil of mine, my striving (has been) ever to establish the doctrine of the Saṃbuddha. And even as this is truth may the armour on the body of my soldiers take the colour of fire" (Mahānāma 1986: 171).

It is clear in most sources that the war was not about ethnicity. Duṭṭhagāmaṇi's chief warrior was a Tamil defector with a backstory of killing Tamils who desecrated sacred sites (Mahānāma 1986: 155). The Tamil King Eḷāra is regarded as a just and respectful unbeliever; on accidentally damaging a *stūpa*, he offered to be executed. Ironically, the monks replied that "injury to another does our master in no wise allow" and encouraged him instead to repair it (Mahānāma 1986: 144). Still, Eḷāra is regarded as an occupying invader, and there is a general motivation that Tamils are defiling the sacred sites (Mahānāma 1986: 155; Berkwitz 2007: 166). After Duṭṭhagāmaṇi killed Eḷāra, consistent with the advice of the *Arthaśāstra*, he honored his defeated victim.

Duṭṭhagāmaṇi built up a *stūpa* commemorating his victory at the location where Buddha visited Sri Lanka and ethnically cleansed it for the sake of the Sinhalese *Sāsana*.[8] In a legend that resonates with the current situation in Myanmar, using the power of storms and fire (later commentary adds a hail of weapons; Gunawardana 1978: 55–56), the Buddha terrorized the original inhabitants and drove them out of the island (Mahānāma 1986: 4). Sri Lankan temples display images of Buddha in the center of an expanding ring of fire as characters that look like primitive tribesmen flee. The later commentary explains that they were incapable of understanding the Dharma and were opposed to the *Sāsana* (Gunawardana 1978: 56). This personal use of force by Buddha, including forced conversion, is not exceptional in Buddhist narratives and is often supported by Vajrapāṇi (Strong 1992: 26–29; Jenkins 2016: 149). Duṭṭhagāmaṇi's military unification of the island is directly correlated with Buddha's original ethnic cleansing.

Visits of the Buddha are reported across Southeast Asia. These mythical visits instantiate his abiding presence and are memorialized by *stūpas* and footprints in stone. They create a sacred landscape, incorporating an imaginal identification of the land and the Buddhist tradition that is basic to the sense of *Sāsana* and informs contemporary

---

[8] According to one source, at a place where he threw Tamil war dead into the river (Berkwitz 2007: 180).

Thai, Sinhala, and Burmese nationalist concerns about the presence of outsiders, *tīrthika*.

After Duṭṭhagāmaṇi's mass slaughter, he experiences concern for his afterlife (not remorse for his actions), but is comforted by *arhats*, including one of his heroes who has since become ordained and attained enlightenment (Berkwitz 2007: 190, 246), who tells him that he has only killed one and a half humans. One victim had taken precepts and the other had taken refuge, the rest were merely like "*pasu*" (Sanskrit *paśu*, animals). This employs the idea found in the *Vinaya* that killing animals is a lesser crime and that the moral status of a victim determines the negative karma for killing them. The Mahāyāna's *Mahāparinirvāṇa Sūtra* describes killing the morally hopeless *icchāntika* as no more a sin than killing an ant (Harvey 2000: 138). The same *sūtra* says that if one's motivation is pure, it is appropriate to kill someone who is persecuting Buddhists or deriding the Mahāyāna without incurring karmic retribution (Schmithausen 1999: 57–58 and note 60; Jenkins 2016: 146). The 13th-century Sinhalese *Thūpavaṃsa* moderated this image by reminding us that "even when killing small creatures such as … ants, nits, and lice there is sin" (Berkwitz 2007: 191). But the 14th-century *Saddharmalamkaraya* describes the slain Tamils as "morally indisciplined [sic], impure and holders of false views. Therefore they died like cattle and dogs" (Dharmakirti 1970: 253). Today this idea is employed by those persecuting Muslims in Myanmar, who are regarded as only 10 percent human (d'Elena 2021).

However, the term *pasu/paśu* is a special technical term in both religious practice and warfare. *Paśu* designates a sacrificial victim, and, due to the Hindu homologization of sacrifice and warfare, it is also a standard term for war casualties, who, like the sacrificial victim, attain heaven, and so are ultimately unharmed (Jatavallabhula 1999: 73–74). Gavin Flood recently reminded the author that Tamil Cholas were Pāśupata Saivites, self-identifying as *paśu*, so the term also has connotations of social identity. Perhaps the point was to compare Buddhists with Saivites, suggesting as well their identification as "Hindu" war dead. In any case, the passage expresses something more complex than simple identification of the dead as animals.

The contemporary Thai monk Kittivuddho reportedly argued that "to kill a communist is not demeritorious." He explains that "while any killing is demeritorious, the demerit is very little and the merit very great for such an act which serves to preserve the nation, the religion, and the monarchy. 'It is just like,' he said, 'when we kill a fish to make a stew to place in the alms bowl for a monk. There is certainly demerit in killing the fish, but we place it in the alms bowl of a monk and gain much greater merit'" (Keyes 1978: 153). Kittivuddho refers both to the idea of balancing proportionality in merit and demerit and to the concern for the relative moral status of victims. As when kings punish criminals, killing a demonized victim incurs minimal demerit. This is a logic that is generally applied to enemies of the *Sāsana*, or Buddhist tradition.

At the end of his life, Duṭṭhagāmaṇi was reborn in Tuṣita heaven, abode of Maitreya. To dispel any doubt about the auspiciousness of his life, it is declared that he will be the future Buddha Maitreya's right-hand disciple. He recalls all the beings who have been murdered out of greed, the text having reminded us many times that not greed but the glory of the *Sāsana* is his motivation. Tsunehiko Sugiki has pointed out that a central agenda in many of these narratives, both Mainstream and Mahāyāna, is to assure warriors that they will attain heavenly rebirth (Tsunehiko 2020a; 2020b). The *Mahāvaṃsa* closes his tale by saying: "He who, holding the good life to be the greatest (good), does works of merit, passes, covering over much that perchance is evil-doing, into heaven as into his own house; therefore will the wise man continually take delight in works of merit" (Mahānāma 1986: 227). The depiction of Duṭṭhagāmaṇi's remorse and the *arhat*'s response does more than just raise and dismiss his concerns. As with Hindu kings such as Arjuna and Yudhiṣṭhira, his remorse, moral concerns, and Dharma-restoring violence are all valued. It informs the building of hospitals and grand monuments. A king who exults in killing is neither good nor skillful, and, even in the *Arthaśāstra*, vicious kings fall.

CONCLUSION

Although generally speaking Buddhism is not pacifist in the usual sense, it is against harm in all forms and offers nuanced ethical thought on the conduct of warfare. There are cases where forceful action is required to minimize harm, supported by examples like surgery and disciplining children. Such actions should be performed with positive intentions and never in anger. The dehumanization of enemies and the wicked, common to Indian thought, is a dangerous feature, but the resulting relative scale of inauspiciousness overcomes the paralysis induced by an ethic of absolute values. Moral concerns for moderating warfare and avoiding the horrors of hell include: eschewing exploitation that generates internal disorder and creates foreign enemies; considering one's own culpability in creating hostile conditions; exhausting alternatives such as negotiation; setting wholesome intentions to avoid casualties and capture the enemy alive; and avoiding harm to animals, the natural environment, infrastructure, and noncombatants. Prisoners should be treated humanely and warfare should be followed by honoring enemy casualties, celebrating the culture of the defeated enemy, and a general program of postwar healing. Even when justified, warfare is never a solution; only healing the root causes of hostility can end multi-generational cycles of violence. These are not just the moral scruples of ascetics but are regarded as practical keys to political success.

References

Aono, Michihiko 2021. "Practical Knowledge for Monks to Abstain from Killing and Injuring Living Beings in Everyday Life with Reference to the Vinayapiṭaka and the Samanta-pāsādikā." *International Journal of Buddhist Thought & Culture* 31(1): 141–177.

Bellezza, John 2020. *Besting the Best: Warriors and Warfare in the Cultural and Religious Traditions of Tibet*. Lumbini International Research Institute.

Berkwitz, Stephen 2007. *The History of the Buddha's Relic Shrine: A Translation of the Sinhala Thūpavaṃsa*. Oxford University Press.

Bodewitz, Henk 1999. "Hindu Ahiṃsā and Its Roots." In *Violence Denied: Violence, Non-violence and the Rationalization of Violence in South Asian Cultural History*. Edited by Jan E. M. Houben & Karel R. Van Kooij. Brill. 17–44.

Bodhi, Bhikkhu 2000. *The Connected Discourses of the Buddha: A New Translation of the Saṃyutta Nikāya*. Wisdom.

Lama Chimpa. 1970. *Tāranātha's History of Buddhism in India*. Motilal Banarsidass.

Collins, Steven 1998. *Nirvana and Other Buddhist Felicities: Utopias of the Pali Imaginaire*. Cambridge University Press.

Cowell, E. B. and W. H. D. Rouse trans. 2005 (first 1907). *The Jātaka*. Vol. VI. Pali Text Society.

Devahuti, D. 1998. *Harṣa: A Political Study*. Oxford University Press.

Devdas, Nalini 2004. "A Study of Cetana and the Dynamics of Volition in Theravāda Buddhism." Doctoral Dissertation. Concordia University.

Dharmakirti, Devarakshita Jayabahu 1970. "Saddharmalamkaraya." Translated by Vajira Cooke and C. B. Cooke. In *An Anthology of Sinhalese Literature up to 1815*. Edited by C. H. B. Reynolds. Allen & Unwin. 233–265.

Doniger, Wendy 2009. *The Hindus: An Alternative History*. Penguin.

d'Elena, Grisel 2021. "Humanizing the Rohingya Beyond Victimization: A Portrait." In *Buddhist Violence and Religious Authority: A Tribute to the Work of Michael Jerryson*. Edited by Margo Kitts and Mark Juergensmeyer. Equinox. 91–106.

Fitzgerald, James L. 2004. *The Mahābhārata: Book 11, The Book of Women; Book 12, The Book of Peace*, Pt. 1, Vol. 7. University of Chicago Press.

Frydenlund, Iselin 2017. "'Buddhism Has Made Asia Mild': The Modernist Construction of Buddhism as Pacifism." In *Buddhist Modernities: Reinventing Tradition in the Globalizing Modern World*. Edited by Hanna Havnevik, Ute Hüsken, Mark Teeuwen, Vladimir Tikhonov, and Koen Wellens. Routledge. 204–222.

Gethin, Rupert 2004. "Can Killing a Living Being Ever Be an Act of Compassion? The Analysis of the Act of Killing in the Abhidhamma and Pali Commentaries." *Journal of Buddhist Ethics* 11: 166–202.

          2007. "Buddhist Monks, Buddhist Kings, Buddhist Violence: On the Early Buddhist to Violence." In *Religion and Violence in South Asia: Theory and Practice*. Edited by John Hinnells and Richard King. Routledge. 59–78.

Gombrich, Richard 2006. "Is the Sri Lankan War a Buddhist Fundamentalism?" In *Buddhism, Conflict and Violence in Modern Sri Lanka*. Edited by Mahinda Deegalle. Routledge. 22–37.

Grant, Patrick 2009. *Buddhism and Ethnic Conflict in Sri Lanka*. SUNY.

Gunawardana, Ranaweera Appuhamilage Leslie Herbert 1978. "The Kinsmen of the Buddha: Myth and Political Charter in the Ancient and Medieval Kingdoms in Sri Lanka." In *Religion and the Legitimation of Power in Sri Lanka*. Edited by Bardwell Smith. Columbia University Press. 53–62.

Harvey, Peter 2000. *An Introduction to Buddhist Ethics: Foundations, Values and Issues*. Cambridge University Press.

Jatavallabhula, Danielle Feller 1999. "Raṇayajña: The Mahābhārata War as a Sacrifice." In *Violence Denied: Violence, Non-violence and the Rationalization of Violence in South Asian Cultural History*. Edited Jan E. M. Houben and Karel R. Van Kooij. Brill. 69–104.

Jenkins, Stephen 2010a. "On the Auspiciousness of Compassionate Violence." *Journal of the International Association of Buddhist Studies* 33(1–2): 299–331.

          2010b. "Making Merit through Warfare According to the Ārya-Bodhisattva-gocara-upāyaviṣaya-vikurvaṇa-nirdeśa Sūtra." In *Buddhist Warfare*. Edited by Mark Juergensmeyer and Michael Jerryson. Oxford University Press. 59–75.

          2016. "Debate, Magic, and Massacre: The High Stakes and Ethical Dynamics of Battling Slanderers of the Dharma in Indian Buddhist Narrative and Ethical Theory." *Journal of Religion and Violence* 4(2): 129–157.

          2017. "Once the Buddha Was a Warrior: Buddhist Pragmatism in the Ethics of Peace and Armed Conflict." In *The Nature of Peace and the Morality of Armed Conflict*. Edited by Florian Demont-Biaggi. Palgrave. 159–178.

          2021a. "Buddhism: Confronting the Harmful with Compassion." In *Nonviolence in World Religions*. Edited by Mike Long and Jeff Long. Routledge. 39–50.

          2021b. "Compassion Blesses the Compassionate: The Basis of Human Flourishing in Buddhist Thought and Practice." In *Buddhist Visions of the Good Life for All*. Edited by Sallie B. King. Routledge. 36–53.

Jerryson, Michael 2011. *Buddhist Fury: Religion and Violence in Southern Thailand*. Oxford University Press.

2013. "Buddhist Traditions and Violence." In *The Oxford Handbook of Religion and Violence*. Edited by Mark Juergensmeyer, Margo Kitts, and Michael Jerryson. Oxford University Press. 41–66.

2018. *If You Meet the Buddha on the Road: Buddhism, Politics, and Violence*. Oxford University Press.

Kautilya 1992. *The Arthaśāstra*. Translated by L. N. Rangarajan. Penguin.

Keown, Damien 2016. "On Compassionate Killing and the Abhidhamma's 'Psychological Ethics'." *Journal of Buddhist Ethics* 23: 45–81.

Keyes, Charles F. 1978. "Political Crisis and Militant Buddhism in Contemporary Thailand." In *Religion and Legitimation of Power in Thailand, Laos, and Burma*. Edited by Bardwell L. Smith. Anima Books. 147–164.

Mahānāma 1986. *Mahāvaṃsa or the Great Chronicle of Ceylon*. Translated by Wilhelm Geiger into German. Translated into English by Mabel Bode. Asian Educational Services.

Maher, Derek F. 2010. "Sacralized Warfare: The Fifth Dalai Lama and the Discourse of Religious Violence." In *Buddhist Warfare*. Edited by Michael K. Jerryson and Mark Juergensmeyer. Oxford University Press. 77–90.

Oldenberg, Hermann 2001 (first 1879). *The Dīpavaṃsa: An Ancient Buddhist Historical Record*, 4th edition. Asian Educational Services.

Palihawadana, Mahinda 2006. "The Theravada Analysis of Conflict." In *Buddhism, Conflict and Violence in Modern Sri Lanka*. Edited by Deegalle Mahinda. Routledge. 67–77.

Rahula, Walpola 1982. *What the Buddha Taught*. Gordon Fraser Gallery.

Rhi, Ki Yong 1976. "Compassion and Violence." In *Buddhism and the Modern World*. Edited by Sun Keun Lee and Ki Yong Rhi. Seoul University.

Rhys Davids, T. W. trans. 1963 (first 1890). *The Questions of King Milinda*, Part 1. Dover.

Rosenfield, John 1967. *Dynastic Arts of the Kushans*. University of California Press.

Saṅs-rgyas-rgya-mtsho and Gavin Kilty 2010. *Mirror of Beryl: A Historical Introduction to Tibetan Medicine*. Simon and Schuster.

Schmithausen, Lambert 1991. "Buddhism and Nature." In *Studia Philologica Buddhica*. Occasional Paper Series VII. International Institute for Buddhist Studies. 1–67.

1999. "Aspects of the Buddhist Attitude to War." In *Violence Denied: Violence, Non-violence and the Rationalization of Violence in South Asian Cultural History*. Edited by J. E. M. Houben & K. R. van Kooij. Brill. 45–67.

Silk, Jonathan 2007. "Good and Evil in Indian Buddhism: The Five Sins of Immediate Retribution." *Journal of Indian Philosophy* 35(3): 253–286.

Sperling, Elliot 2001. "Orientalism and Aspects of Violence in the Tibetan Tradition." In *Imagining Tibet*. Edited by Thierry Dodin and Heinz Räther. Wisdom. 317–329.

Strong, John S. 1992. *The Legend and Cult of Upagupta*. Princeton University Press.

1994. "Images of Aśoka." In *King Aśoka and Buddhism: Historical and Literary Studies*. Edited by Anuradha Seneviratna. Buddhist Publication Society.

Tambiah, Stanley 1976. *World Conqueror and World Renouncer*. Cambridge University Press.

Tsunehiko, Sugiki 2020a. "Compassion, Self-Sacrifice, and Karma in Warfare: Buddhist Discourse on Warfare as an Ethical and Soteriological Instruction for Warriors." *Religions* 11(2): 1–22.

2020b. "Warriors Who Do Not Kill in War: A Buddhist Interpretation of the Warrior's Role in Relation to the Precept against Killing." *Religions* 11(10): 1–20.

Victoria, Brian 2006. *Zen at War*, 2nd edition. Rowman & Littlefield Publishers.

2020. *Zen Terror in Prewar Japan: Portrait of an Assassin*. Rowman & Littlefield Publishers.

Willemen, Charles, trans. 1994. *The Storehouse of Sundry Valuables*. Numata Center.

Wu, Juan 2015. "Comparing Buddhist and Jaina Attitudes towards Warfare: Some Notes on Stories of King Ajātaśatru's/Kūṇika's War against the Vṛjis and Related Material." *Annual Report of the International Research Institute for Advanced Buddhology* XVIII: 95–112.

Xüanzang 1996. *The Great Tang Dynasty Record of the Western Regions*. Translated by the Tripiṭaka-Master Xüanzang under Imperial Order. Composed by Śramaṇa Bianji of the Great Zonchi Monastery. Translated into English by Li Rongxi. Numata Center.

Xue, Yu 2012. "Buddhism and the Justification of War with Focus on Chinese Buddhist History." In *Buddhism and Violence: Militarism and Buddhism in Modern Asia*. Edited by Vladimir Tikhonov and Torkel Brekke. Routledge. 194–208.

Zimmermann, Michael 2000. "A Mahāyānist Criticism of Arthaśāstra, the Chapter on Royal Ethics in the Bodhisattva-gocaropāya-viṣaya-vikurvaṇa-nirdeśa-sūtra." In *Annual Report of the International Research Institute for Advanced Buddhology at Soka University for the Academic Year 1999*. International Research Institute for Advanced Buddhology. 177–211.

6 Sikhism: Exploring the Notion of a Righteous War (*Dharam Yudh*)

PASHAURA SINGH

Geographically and culturally, Sikhism originated more than five centuries ago in the Punjab ("five rivers") region of northwestern India, a frontier zone where the interaction between different segments of the society and cultures of the Middle East, Central Asia and India was commonplace. It was rooted in the particular religious experience, piety and culture of that period and informed by the unique inner revelations of its founder, Guru Nanak (1469–1539), who declared his independence from the other schools of thought in his day. He kindled the fire of autonomy and courage in his first disciples (Sikhs) who gathered around him at Kartarpur ("Creator's Abode"), a town that he himself founded in 1519 on the right bank of the Ravi River. His creative ideas and strategies triggered the process of institutionalization in the early Sikh tradition during the last two decades of his life. His specific ethical formulations based on "truth, love, justice and equality" became a viable model of a new social organization beyond the grip of the hierarchical caste system. In particular, Guru Nanak's rejection of the prevailing orthodoxies of both Islamic and Hindu tradition provided an alternative spiritual paradigm that became the basis of social reconfiguration according to divinely sanctioned normative principles.

The very survival of Guru Nanak's message over many generations and historical periods is a testimony to its unique qualities of continued relevance. Based initially on religious ideology, the distinctive Sikh identity was reinforced with the introduction of distinctly Sikh liturgical practices, ceremonies and holy sites and the compilation of an authoritative scripture. The fifth Guru, Arjan (1563–1606), played an extremely important role in this process of crystallization of the Sikh tradition (P. Singh 2006: 198). Most instructively, the ideology based upon the religious ideals and cultural innovations of Guru Nanak and his nine successors ultimately engendered the first of three formative elements on which the evolution of Sikhism depended. The second was the rural base of Punjabi society, comprising mainly peasantry with its martial traditions. The third significant element was the period of history of Punjab during which Sikhism evolved in tension with Mughals and Afghans in the 17th and 18th centuries. These three elements combined to produce the mutual interaction between ideology and environment in the historical development of Sikhism, making "militancy" an integral part of the tradition in self-defense. This militancy is entirely rooted in the tradition's humanitarian ethos. With unflinching faith in the Oneness of divinity, Sikhism stresses the ideal of achieving spiritual liberation from self-centeredness (*haumai*, "I-ness," "my-ness") within a person's lifetime through the practice of meditation on the divine Name (*nām simaran*). It is oriented toward action, encouraging the dignity of regular labor as part of spiritual discipline. Family life and social responsibility are important aspects of Sikh teachings.

The purpose of this study is to explore the notion of defensive warfare as it evolved through various historical junctures in the Sikh tradition. The verb *jūjhi* in classical Punjabi means "to fight or do battle," and the noun *judh* (*yudh*) stands for "war." There are two major themes related to war in the foundational text of Sikhism, the *Gurū Granth Sāhib* (GGS): first, "spiritual battle" fought in the mind itself against five internal enemies (i.e., temptations such as lust, anger, greed, attachment and pride); and second, "actual battle" fought against external enemies with military aims to defend the country from foreign invaders or to defend justice and liberty by resisting oppressive state structures. Recent research has made us aware of two divergent views on the place of warfare in the Sikh tradition. The first view is based on the framework of "early pacifism versus later militancy" discourse that has dominated in the popular writings on Sikhism. It draws attention to the apparent contradiction between the interior devotion of early Nanak-panth ("followers of Guru Nanak's path") and the militant character of the Khalsa tradition. Khushwant Singh's history of the Sikhs contains a chapter entitled, "From the Pacifist Sikh to the Militant Khalsa" (K. Singh 1999 [1963]: 76–98). Following the Orientalist paradigm, such works ignore the contextual depth and misrepresent the process of this evolution by focusing too much on the apparent contradiction between religion and politics in the Sikh tradition.

The second view has emerged more recently in the writings of Balbinder Singh Bhogal and Navdeep Mandair, who claim that canonical sources reveal a more startling view of warfare as a phenomenon that is profoundly excessive to any rationalization (Bhogal 2007: 107–135; N. Mandair 2009: 85–101). In particular, the central theme of the three goddess compositions in the *Dasam Granth* (DG; "Book attributed to the Tenth Guru") is focused on unrelentingly gruesome battles against demons, with the poet delighting in sketching images of shining swords and other weapons flashing as warriors wield them against their enemies, the sounds of swords and arrows whizzing through the air, the shrieks and cries of warriors and gaping wounds, severed body parts and flowing rivers of blood. However, the killing of demons that occurs in these battles is auspicious, even to be celebrated, for it represents a triumph of the forces of good and allows good people to live well (Rinehart 2011: 102–103). Navdeep Mandair points out the savage excesses of the goddess (Chaṇḍī/Durgā), who delights in conflict and carnage, expressing a horrid pleasure when she laughs mightily amid the bloody wreckage of battle. For him, it is the gleeful accent of this onslaught that renders it excessive – a violence that exceeds the measures strictly necessary to restore order and righteousness (*dharam*) and therefore regulated by the capricious tempo of divine play (N. Mandair 2009: 94–95). Accordingly, Sikh religious violence must be understood by taking into account its profoundly gratuitous nature and intensity, which is not irrational but incommensurate with a rationale. These are the two extreme positions based upon doctrinal readings of textual sources (P. Singh 2012: 201).

The present study offers a measured assessment of scriptural sources and follows a genealogical mode of reading by employing multiple voices to relativize all of them; in this way, no single voice becomes dominant. It examines the connection, both actual and perceived, between Sikh texts and the justification of war as divinely mandated. In the Sikh scriptures, "violence" is represented as an integral part of the human situation. The Punjabi term used for violence is *hansu* or *hinsā*, referring to the "infliction of injury" in the situation of conflict. Employing the metaphor of a "burning river" for human existence, Guru Nanak proclaims: "Violence, attachment, avarice, and wrath are four rivers of fire. Falling into these, people get burnt, O Nanak; they can be saved only through the grace of loving devotion at the Master's feet" (GGS 147). In his spiritual vision, both good and evil exist in the divine plan. In the *Mārū* hymn, for instance, *Akāl Purakh* ("Eternal One," God) is represented as both violent and benevolent: "He himself kills and rejuvenates" (GGS 1034). Unsurprisingly, love and violence, pains and pleasures, good and evil, matter and spirit are intrinsic to the human condition. The true meaning of "violence" is linked with a struggle to kill one's ego or self-centeredness (*haumai*), making self-sacrifice an inseparable part of one's spiritual discipline.

This study examines relevant scriptural bases for war, both internal and external. It argues that the Sikh notion of sovereignty is at the heart of the intersection of the religious and secular domains in defensive warfare, presenting the key concept of *mīrī-pīrī* ("secular-spiritual") as a possible explanation for understanding the imaginations of war. It also describes important ritual traditions such as the Khalsa initiation ceremony, cultural practices like the mounting of a nonviolent protest march (*chaunkī chāṛhnī*) and the celebrations of martyrdom that have shaped the way conflict has been imagined and/or performed within the Sikh tradition. It then glances forward at what understanding these traditional impulses for warfare might mean for contemporary events and discourse.

HISTORICAL CONTEXT: BABUR'S INVASIONS OF INDIA

During his invasions to secure northern India in the 1520s, the first Mughal emperor, Babur (1483–1530), achieved his final victory over Ibrahim Lodhi on April 20, 1526, in the field of Panipat. Guru Nanak had firsthand experience of warfare when he actually witnessed the third of Babur's preliminary expeditions when the Mughal army assaulted the town of Saidpur, the modern-day Eminabad in Gujranwala District in Pakistan. He commented upon the violence inflicted on innocent people in his nine hymns, collectively known as *Bābar-vāṇī* ("Arrow-like Utterances concerning Babur"; GGS 145, 360, 417–418, 721–723, 1288 and 1412), works that the present author has critically examined in light of Babur's memoirs in an earlier study (P. Singh 2020c: 5–9). In fact, these scriptural hymns provide an eyewitness account of Babur's invasion of India and throw considerable light on the devastation caused by his army. Some important themes emerge from them as follows.

First, Guru Nanak raised his voice against the foreign invader from the standpoint of truth and justice: "Nanak speaks the Word of Truth; he will always proclaim the Truth at the most appropriate moment of time" (GGS 723). This proclamation was made in the historical context of Babur's invasion of India when Guru Nanak was standing in "the city of corpses" at Saidpur in 1520–1521 CE. For the sake of Truth, as Bruce Lincoln remarks, it is essential for the "right speaker" to deliver the "right speech" at the "right time and place" before an audience, the historically and culturally conditioned expectations of which establish the parameters of what is judged "right" in all these instances. Thus, an authoritative speech has to be "supple, dynamic, and situationally adaptable" (Lincoln 1994: 116–117). Accordingly, there is no use in raising one's voice afterwards when the appropriate moment is lost. Thus, Guru Nanak laid down the foundation of a fundamental Sikh principle of "Speaking Truth to Power" for his disciples through his bold response to the political events of Babur's invasions. He inspired his disciples to stand up against any kind of injustice and tyranny (P. Singh 2020c: 3).

Second, Guru Nanak addressed Akal Purakh ("God") in *Āsā* melody: "You spared Khurasan yet spread fear in Hindustan. Creator, you did this, but to avoid the blame you sent the Mughal as messenger of death. Receiving such chastisement, the people cry out in agony and yet no anguish touches you. Creator, you belong to all. If the mighty destroy only one another, one is not grieved" (GGS 360). The principal theme in this hymn is related to the question of why the weak and innocent should suffer unmerited torment at the hands of the strong. In this respect, this hymn has obvious affinities with the Book of Job in the Hebrew Bible. God is called into account, just as Job summons him. Guru Nanak made it quite explicit that it was the Creator who sent Babur as the messenger of death to destroy the Lodhi Sultanate. He was crying out against this violence in an emotional appeal to God to remember ethics and humanness, and he underscored the point that if any mighty person attacks "the weak and unarmed" then it is a violation of an ethical norm of warfare (P. Singh 2020c: 6).

Third, Guru Nanak was responding to an actual life situation with his profound inner experience and outer observation. In tune with Akal Purakh, he reflected on the situation at hand and placed the responsibility on the shoulders of various human actors from both sides. In this context, J. S. Grewal argues that there is a moral dimension that restrains Guru Nanak from an outright condemnation of either the conqueror or the conquered (Grewal 1969: 163). Balbinder Singh Bhogal, on the other hand, underlines Guru Nanak's "powerlessness" and "blunt tone of abject resignation" in response to the devastation caused by Babur's army (Bhogal 2007: 119). This was certainly not the case. For instance, Guru Nanak described the Lodhis as "wretched dogs" for their moral failure to protect their sovereignty and the jewel-like (*rattan*) innocent people (GGS 360). On the other hand, he referred to Babur's army as the "marriage-party of evil" (*pāp kī jañj*), charging them for their moral failure of forcibly demanding a "dowry" (*dān*) from already suffering people (P. Singh 2012: 204–205). This "dowry" referred to heavy taxes collected by the Mughal army from the conquered subjects.

Fourth, Guru Nanak's response to war and suffering was not limited to his personal anguish. He held the heedlessness of Akal Purakh on the part of Lodhi rulers responsible for bringing about this retribution. In the case of the rape of women, Guru Nanak made the following comment: "The wealth and sensual beauty which intoxicated them became their enemies. The messengers of Death, under orders to persecute, strip them of their honor and carry them off" (GGS 417). He employed the Punjabi phrase "stripping of one's honor" to describe the rape of women by the Mughal army, as a violation of women's honor in Punjabi culture to the extent that it can affect a family's social standing. Some other verses represent a terrible portrait of women being raped by soldiers who did not bother to discriminate between Hindus and Muslims who were in their path: "Some lost their five times of prayer, some the time of *puja*" (GGS 417). Guru Nanak was deeply anguished over the horrible situation of women. He was cognizant of the situation of poor women, and their agony reminded him of a religious truth that unrighteousness would be punished according to divine justice.

Finally, Guru Nanak was fully aware of the relationship between the two existing domains of temporal and spiritual sovereignties (*mīrī-pīrī*) in contemporary India. He employed the key words *pīr* (saint) and *mīr* (sovereign), representing religious and secular powers in the early 16th century. In his *Āsā Aṣṭapadī* Guru Nanak claimed that the religious leaders (*pīrs*) miserably failed to halt the invader with their miraculous tricks by falsely claiming that the Mughals would be blinded when they arrived and by their lack of intelligent strategies. Hence, riding on their fast-running horses, the Mughals were able to fire their guns on the army of Pathans on their elephants (GGS 418). The *Baburnama* testifies that Sultan Ibrahim's "standing army was estimated at one hundred thousand" and that his commanders "were said to have one thousand elephants" (Thackston 1996: 329). On the whole, Guru Nanak's description of the Panipat battle was to the point, although it was largely based upon second-hand reports. He admitted the enormity of violence caused by Babur's army as part of the Mughal invasions of India, but he rendered it small from the perspective of a larger metaphysic of divine Order (*hukam*). Most instructively, Guru Nanak fully realized that unchecked political power could easily crush the religious authority of saintly people. It is no wonder that he sowed the seeds of *mīrī-pīrī* tradition in his bold resistance against the power structures of his times (P. Singh 2019: 4).

SIKH SOVEREIGNTY AND THE EVOLUTION OF THE WARRIOR CULTURE

Some scholars have raised the issue of the *Bābar-vāṇī* being the "exception" in the context of the overall emphasis of Guru Nanak's teachings of "interior devotion." This is a simplistic assertion, since Guru Nanak's critique of the political structures of his time may be seen in other works, particularly his celebrated *Japjī* (GGS 4, 6–8), *Vār Mājh* (GGS 145), *Vār Āsā* (GGS 468–469) and *Vār Malār* (GGS 1287–1288) and the opening hymn of the very first melody of *Sirī Rāgu* in the Sikh scripture (GGS 14). Our reading of Sikh canonical sources challenges the reductionist approach that defines the Sikh culture simply as a religion of interior devotion limited essentially to the private sphere without taking into account its relevance to the political, economic and social arenas of the public sphere. While appreciating the beauty and wonder of goodness in the world in his *Japjī*, Guru Nanak applauds "countless heroic warriors who bear the brunt of attack in battle" (GGS 4). He simultaneously admits the existence of evil and tyranny in the following stanza: "Countless the fools, the thieves, the swindlers; countless those who rule by force. Countless are the cutthroats and violent murderers; countless those who live evil lives" (GGS 4). Again, violence is divinely sanctioned: "When it pleases You [O divine Sovereign!], some wield swords cutting off the heads [of their enemies] as they move [in the battlefield]" (GGS 145).

Guru Nanak glorifies those warriors who die fighting for "heroic values," and their death may be constructed as the ideal of martyrdom. For him, a heroic death must be based upon the true "honor" obtained before the divine court of Akal Purakh: "Blessed is the death of heroic persons if their dying is approved of [by the Immortal Lord]. Only those people may be called true heroes who obtain true honor before the divine Court" (GGS 579–580). Such spiritual heroes who practice the discipline of meditation on the divine Name (*nām simaran*) during their lifetime receive true honor at the final moment of their death. In fact, the fourth stage on the mystic path described in the *Japjī* is the "Realm of Grace" (*karam khaṇḍ*), which is the abode of "divine heroes and mighty warriors" who pass beyond error and transmigration. They are the "real martyrs" in Guru Nanak's eyes. They are in full control of themselves, since they have conquered their "self," an achievement that goes beyond the conquest of nations and people (GGS 8). By contrast, "the noses of tyrants [who terrorize innocent people] are chopped off in disgrace and they are branded as untrustworthy in the divine Court" (GGS 1288).

To understand the intersection of religion and war at different historical junctures, there is an urgent need to begin with the notion of sovereignty from the Sikh perspective. In the modern sense the term "sovereignty" refers not only to the ability but also to the right to freely express one's lifeworld, with the "power to authorize" one's own speech. Guru Nanak always invoked Akal Purakh as *sachā pātishāh*, the "True Sovereign" (GGS 463), whose *hukam* ("divine will, order or command") supersedes all temporal authority. He bequeathed the concept of sovereignty to one and all by asserting that if God is the "True Sovereign" in the spiritual and temporal realm, then a human being as a creation of God partakes of the sovereignty of the Divine. The divinity of God is the source of the sovereignty of the human person: To be fearless is to be free, and to be free is to be sovereign. The philosophical basis for the sovereignty of a human being therefore flows from Guru Nanak's description of God as "Fearless" (*nirbhau*) and "Devoid of Enmity" (*nirvair*) in the preamble of the Sikh scripture (GGS 1; Ahluwalia 1983: 148). The Punjabi word for "sovereignty" is *pātishāhī*, which is frequently employed in the Sikh scripture (GGS 5, 48, 144, 590, 749 and 1073). For Guru Nanak, this sovereign consciousness comes only when one overcomes one's self-centeredness or ego (*haumai*) through the discipline of meditation on the divine Name: "One who is blessed with the gift of singing the praises of the Lord, O Nanak, is the king of all kings" (GGS 5). Thus, sovereign consciousness overflows with the sense of fearlessness and compassionate love for everyone.

Guru Nanak continued to exhort his audience at Kartarpur "to turn to God, the true king, the king of kings," whose "service alone is true service" (Grewal 1990: 29). He referred to the Earth (*dharti*) as the place to practice righteousness (GGS 7), and his own village was conceived as a place of justice where the divine will was carried out. The congregation assembled at the Guru's house at Kartarpur symbolized the establishment of divine sovereignty on Earth. There, Guru Nanak lived as the "spiritual guide" of a newly emerging religious community. In his view, the key discipline of meditation on the divine Name (*nām simaran*) was meant to liberate oneself from the shackles of ego or self-centeredness (*haumai*). The word *simaran* is derived from the Sanskrit root *marana*, meaning "to die" or "pass away," referring to the experience of finitude in the first place, leading to an awareness of the eternally sounding vibrations of the divine Name and making it a sacrificial practice for transforming memory by eliminating one's ego or self-centeredness.

Guru Nanak's struggle with the ego involved the practice of "warrior asceticism" in the form of a nonviolent violence, which Arvind-Pal Singh Mandair terms a "sovereign violence," a process focused on self-surrender and the loss of ego, a loss that is necessary to bring the self into harmony with the divine imperative (*hukam*). By questioning the conventional dialectic of violence and nonviolence, this idea of "sovereign violence" provides a more nuanced image of (non)violence intrinsically connected to issues of sovereignty and the relationship between Sikhism and the state during the five centuries of its history (A. Mandair 2022: iii). The use and imagery of weapons in Sikh scriptures offer a rationale for sovereign violence in its own right. The rhetoric of weaponry can provide us a window onto the reality of "how instruments of harm were understood within the complex web of social relationships that necessitated them" (Patton 2007: 13). Since the spiritual reign of the third Guru, Amar Das (1479–1574), the court poets eulogized the Gurus as the "Warriors of the divine Word" (*shabad sūr*), as kings whose rule is eternal and as warriors of truth, wielding the power of humility and fighting the battles of righteousness (*dharam*):

> Wearing the armor of absorption [in the divine Name], [the third Guru] has mounted [the horse] of wisdom. Holding the bow of righteousness, he has released [the arrows of] devotion and morality in the fight. He has wielded the lance of fear of the Fearless One; he has thrust the spear of the Guru's Word into the mind. Thus equipped, he has cut down the five demons of lust, wrath, greed, attachment and egoistic pride. The noble King Amar Das, son of Tej Bhan, has been exalted King of kings by the blessings of [Guru] Nanak. The bard Salh proclaims, verily, you have overthrown this hoard by waging such a battle.
>
> (GGS 1396)

Wielding weapons here symbolizes the cultivation of ethical virtues in the internal struggle against worldly temptations. Thus, the sword of wisdom (*giān kharag*) is meant to slay duality, the false self and its desires and delusions. It is in this sense that the scriptural words have the power to act as weapons in the battle, whether it is fought within the self or with the external enemies who are a threat to the faith (P. Singh 2012: 207).

The reality of the establishment of a divine kingdom became unmistakable during the reign of the fifth Guru, Guru Arjan: "There is no other place like the beautiful and thickly populated Ramdaspur. The divine rule prevails in Ramdaspur due to the grace of the Guru. No tax (*jizyā*) is levied, nor any fine; there is no collector of taxes" (GGS 430, 817). The administration of the town was evidently in the hands of Guru Arjan. In a certain sense, Ramdaspur was an autonomous town in the context and framework of the Mughal rule of Emperor Akbar (r. 1556–1605). Guru Arjan's claim that there was no collector of taxes at Ramdaspur points toward a reality that it came under the authority of the Guru, not under the Mughal state. In a particularly striking composition, Guru Arjan claims to have established the rule of justice and humility (halemī rāj) in the town of Ramdaspur: "The merciful Lord has now ordained a commandment that none shall be domineering over others. All shall abide in peace, prosperity and justice. The rule of justice and humility is thus established on earth" (GGS 74). Guru Arjan enacted the divine rule in actual practice in providing comfortable living to the people at Ramdaspur. His idea of divine rule was related to an ethical way of life based on the principles of truth, social justice and humility taught by Guru Nanak. This lifestyle would create the spirit of fearlessness among the contemporary Sikhs, particularly the residents of Ramdaspur, who would feel that they were directly under the protection of Akal Purakh, the King of all kings. No worldly power could disturb their peace of mind. One must not underestimate the powerful appeal of Guru Arjan's verses in their socially subversive function. The common people, particularly the peasantry of the Punjab, could easily interpret their message in political terms. For the Sikhs, Guru Arjan was indeed a "true king" (sachā patishāh), in contrast to the false rulers of the world. His personal authority and appeal rested on his charismatic ability to embody Divine Power (P. Singh 2006: 120–121).

In an early painting Guru Arjan is portrayed in the Mughal style, holding a hunting hawk on his hand. In those days a hawk was regarded as the symbol of royalty. Also, the Guru had encouraged his Sikhs to participate in the trade of horses. These developments clearly indicate that the office of the Guru provided both spiritual and temporal authority (P. Singh 2017: 67). The author of Dabistan-i-Mazahib ("The School of Religions"), a mid-17th-century Persian historian, Maubad Mobad Shah, attests that by "the reign of Guru Arjan Mal, [the Sikhs] became very numerous. Not many cities remained in the inhabited region, where the Sikhs had not settled in some number" (Grewal and Habib 2001: 66). The growing strength of the Sikh movement attracted the unfavorable attention of the ruling authorities because of the reaction of Muslim revivalists of the Naqshbandi order in Mughal India. There is clear evidence in the compositions of Guru Arjan that a series of complaints were made against him to the functionaries of the Mughal state, giving them an excuse to watch the activities of the Sikhs. On

November 4, 1598, Emperor Akbar officially visited the Sikh court at Goindval. He acknowledged Guru Arjan's "great store of spiritual love" and the selfless service of the Sikhs. At the Guru's insistence, Akbar remitted the annual revenue of the peasants of the district who had been hit hard by the failure of the monsoon. As a result of the tax remission, Guru Arjan's popularity skyrocketed in the rural peasantry of the Punjab (P. Singh 2006: 81–82).

The liberal policy of Emperor Akbar may have sheltered Guru Arjan and his followers for a time, but it could not remove the nefarious designs of the Guru's enemies for good. The effect of his policy of religious tolerance did not last long after his death in October 1605. As a matter of fact, his liberal approach was much despised by many of his more aggressive coreligionists, particularly the protagonists of the Naqshbandi revivalist movement. In the volatile atmosphere of Prince Khusrau's rebellion, Guru Arjan was tortured to death on May 30, 1606, by the orders of Emperor Jahangir (r. 1605–1628). Although the crowning cause of the capital punishment was presented as Guru Arjan's alleged blessings to the rebel Prince Khusrau, there were other urgent religious, sociocultural and economic factors that contributed to the final judgment of the absolute monarch. The Mughal administrators of Lahore who had been carefully monitoring the Sikh movement for a number of years found their opportunity to finally act against the Guru. They moved swiftly to eliminate Guru Arjan and cripple the rapidly growing Sikh movement (P. Singh 2006: 205–235).

Guru Arjan's execution empowered his followers to stand for the ideals of truth, social justice and fearlessness more boldly. A radical reshaping of the Sikh Panth took place after his martyrdom. His son and successor, Guru Hargobind (1595–1644), signaled the formal process when he traditionally donned two swords symbolizing the spiritual (*pīrī*) as well as the temporal (*mīrī*) investiture. The inscriptions on these two swords preserved at the *Toshākhānā* at Amritsar are instructive: The phrase *pātashāhī chhevīn pīrī* ("Spiritual authority of the sixth King") appears on the sword of spiritual authority (*pīrī tegh*), while the wording *amal-e-pātashāh-mīrī* ("Temporal authority of the sovereign King") appears on the sword of temporal authority (*mīrī tegh*). Also, the sixth Guru built the *Akāl Takhat* ("Eternal Throne") facing the Darbar Sahib (present-day Golden Temple), representing the newly assumed role of temporal authority. Under his direct leadership, the Sikh Panth took up arms to protect itself from Mughal hostility. It was meant to achieve a balance between temporal and spiritual concerns. Thus, Guru Arjan's martyrdom became the watershed in Sikh history, contributing to the growth of Sikh community self-consciousness, separatism and militancy.

A distinctive resistance movement in the form of a processional devotional singing march (*chauṅkī chāṛhnī*) came into being when Jahangir put Guru Hargobind into jail in the fort of Gwalior. During the Guru's absence from Amritsar at the time of his internment the elderly Sikh Baba Buddha (d. 1635) started the first processional *chauṅkī* from the *Akāl Takhat* to protest against the Mughal authorities. The author of the Persian *Dabistān-i-Mazāhib* (1640s) testifies, "during this time the Masands and the Sikhs used to go and bow down to the wall of the fort" (P. Singh 2011: 117). One Sikh would hold a torch (*mishāl*) of protest, leading the chanting Sikhs to Gwalior. It was due to the impact of such public musical processions from Amritsar to Gwalior that Emperor Jahangir released Guru Hargobind in 1612 much before the completion of the actual imprisonment of twelve years. The tradition of public musical performance has been followed for the last four centuries and has become an integral part of nonviolent Sikh protests (P. Singh 2011: 117–119).

Contemporary evidence about the transformation of the Sikh Panth at this historical juncture may be seen in the ballads (*vārs*) of Bhai Gurdas (ca. 1558–1636), who personally witnessed the peaceful days of Emperor Akbar's reign, Guru Arjan's martyrdom at the beginning of Emperor Jahangir's reign, Guru Hargobind's reaction to this major event and his armed conflict with Mughal authorities during the reign of Emperor Shah Jahan (r. 1627–1658). He "lived in a phase of Sikh history that was marked by a critical transition" (Grewal 1996: 30). He made it quite explicit in his famous stanza that Guru Hargobind's way of life was indeed different from that of his predecessors:

The earlier Gurus sat peacefully in the *dharamsāl* ("place of worship"); this one roams the land. Emperors visited their homes with reverence; this one they cast into gaol. No rest for his followers, ever active; their restless Master is afraid of none. The earlier Gurus sat graciously blessing; this one goes hunting with dogs. They composed the *bāṇī* ("inspired utterances") for listening and singing; this one neither composes [the *bāṇī*] nor sings. They had servants who harbored no malice; this one encourages scoundrels. Yet none of these changes conceals the truth; the Sikhs are still drawn as bees in the lotus. The Truth stands firm, eternal, and changeless; and pride still lies subdued.

(Vārān Bhāī Gurdās [VBG] 26:24)

Here, Bhāī Gurdās provides us with the firm evidence of the change that took place under Guru Hargobind. In the first six lines of the stanza, he poses the problem he sees in the contemporary discussion among the Sikhs, and then he provides his own answer in the remaining two stanzas. As a loyal disciple of the Guru, he defends the new martial response as "hedging the orchard of the Sikh faith with the hardy and thorny *kikkar* tree" (VBG 25:25). According to Bhāī Gurdās, "The Guru is the vanquisher of the armies, and he is such a hero who is both very brave and benevolent" (VBG 1:48).

Guru Hargobind, who fought to resist the oppression of Mughal authorities, instructed his followers that even when one is fighting in battle, one should do so without any feeling of enmity toward one's foe. In the Persian text *Dabistān-i-Mazāhib*, the Guru's contemporary Maubad Mobad Shah (ca. 1615–1670) recorded on the basis of personal knowledge: "It comes to my mind that sword-striking of the Guru was also by way of teaching, for they call the teacher a *Guru* (or that the Guru means a teacher), and not by way of anger because it is a condemned thing" (G. Singh 1940: 210, emphasis in original). After four skirmishes with Mughal troops, Guru Hargobind withdrew from Amritsar to the Shivalik Hills – beyond the jurisdiction of the Mughal state – and Kiratpur became the new center of the mainline Sikh tradition. Relations with the Mughal authorities eased somewhat under the seventh and eighth Gurus, Har Rai (1630–1661) and Har Krishan (1655–1664), although the Gurus held court to adjudicate on temporal issues within the Panth and kept a regular force of horsemen.

During the period of the ninth Guru, Tegh Bahadur (1621–1675), the increasing strength of the Sikh movement in the rural areas of the Malwa region of the Punjab once again attracted the hostility of Mughal authorities. The Guru encouraged his followers to be fearless in their pursuit of a just society: "He who holds none in fear, nor is afraid of anyone, is acknowledged as a man of true wisdom" (GGS 1427). In doing so, Guru Tegh Bahadur posed a direct challenge to Emperor Aurangzeb (r. 1658–1707), who had imposed Islamic laws and taxes on non-Muslims. According to an early narrative, when a group of Hindu *pandits* ("scholars") from Kashmir asked for the Guru's help against Aurangzeb's oppressive measures, he agreed to do whatever was necessary to defend their rights to wear their "sacred threads and frontal marks" (DG 1:70). A message was sent to the emperor saying that if Guru Tegh Bahadur could be persuaded to accept Islam, the Hindus would convert as well. Accordingly, the Guru was summoned to Delhi, and when he refused to abandon his faith, he was publicly executed on November 11, 1675. If the martyrdom of Guru Arjan had helped to bring the Sikh Panth together, the second martyrdom of Guru Tegh Bahadur helped to make "human rights and freedom of conscience" central to its identity (P. Singh 2012: 210).

THE INSTITUTION OF THE KHALSA: THE ORDER OF SPIRITUAL WARRIORS

The tenth Guru, Gobind Singh (1666–1708), was only nine years old when his father was executed, and he was sheltered by his uncle until he grew up to manhood. As a young adult he was soon involved in wars with hostile neighbors who were eventually joined by Mughal forces. His reflections on his experience of warfare against the Mughal authorities and the local Hindu hill chiefs may be seen in the DG, the secondary Sikh scripture and a principal source for understanding the idea of a "just war" (dharam yudh). For the Guru, Akal Purakh is supremely just, exalting the devout followers and punishing the wicked. In the everlasting struggle between the forces of good and evil that Mark Juergensmeyer describes as "cosmic war" (Juergensmeyer 2016), Akal Purakh intervenes in human history to restore the balance in favor of those who wage war on behalf of the good. From time to time, particular individuals are chosen to act as agents of God in the struggle against the evil forces. Defining his own mission in his autobiographical Bachittar Nāṭak ("Wondrous Drama"), the Guru firmly believed that he was such an agent of God: "For this purpose I was born in this world. The divine Guru (gurdev) has sent me to uphold righteousness (dharam), to extend the true faith everywhere, and to destroy the evil and sinful" (DG 1:74).

Guru Gobind Singh identifies Akal Purakh with the "Divine Sword": "Thee I invoke, All-conquering Sword, destroyer of evil, Ornament of the brave ..." (DG 1:53). In his celebrated Jāp Sāhib ("Master Recitation"), he proclaims: "I bow to you, the one who wields weapons that soar and fly. I bow before you, Knower of all, Mother of all the people" (verse 52). Thus, the divine Being is a great warrior who wields weapons of all kinds, with the perfect knowledge of what is right and what is wrong. And, during the battle, the divine Being does not fight savagely with anger but with the nurturing presence of the mother whose aim is to reform her children who have gone astray. On Visakhi Day of 1699 Guru Gobind Singh established his army of spiritual warriors at Anandpur by initiating the "Cherished Five" (panj piare), who formed the nucleus of the new Order of the Khalsa ("Pure"). These five volunteers, who responded to the Guru's call for loyalty and who came from different castes and regions of

India, received the initiation through a ceremony that involved sweetened water (*amrit*) stirred with a two-edged sword and sanctified by the recitation of five liturgical prayers. The Guru symbolically transferred his spiritual authority to the Cherished Five when he received the Khalsa initiation from them. With the creation of the Khalsa, the Guru infused a new spirit among his warrior-saints, who were ready to fight against injustice and tyranny. Thus, in transforming Sikhs into a self-governing warrior group, the tenth Guru set in motion a profound change in the political and cultural fabric of the Mughal province of Punjab (Dhavan 2011: 3). Most instructively, his army was never to wage war for power, for gain or for personal rancor: "The Khalsa was resolutely to uphold justice and to oppose only that which is evil" (H. McLeod 1997: 105).

Following the *mīrī-pīrī* tradition of Guru Hargobind, Guru Gobind Singh assumed characteristics of a spiritual leader as well as a temporal ruler who had the specific responsibility of protecting righteousness (*dharam*). The majority of the narrative of his life is devoted to a detailed description of a series of fierce battles. As an able spiritual and political leader, Guru Gobind Singh maintained a court at Anandpur and led an army in many battles throughout his life, some of which are described in the *Bachittar Nāṭak* section of the DG (Rinehart 2011: 66–68). In this context, Hardip Singh Syan aptly argues that the tenth Guru had transformed his estate into something more sizable and converted himself into a local monarch: "Unlike previous Gurus, Guru Gobind Singh's power was profoundly political, and given the heightened geo-political sensitivities of late 17th-century Mughal India, it was seen as overtly threatening to Mughal authority" (Syan 2013: 157). The creation of the Khalsa by Guru Gobind Singh was unique in two senses: First, it invited all Sikhs to join the Order of the Khalsa regardless of their background; and second, it had a coherent vision of political sovereignty. The tenth Guru proclaimed: "The Khalsa shall rule, no enemy shall remain. All who endure suffering and privation shall be brought to the safety of the Guru's protection" (W. H. McLeod 1989: 64). All Sikhs were encouraged to become warriors of righteousness (*dharam*) engaged in a struggle against tyranny. Thus, Guru Nanak's fundamental message of human equality, self-respect, dignity and fearlessness found its practical expression in the lived experience of the Khalsa (P. Singh 2017: 76).

The fundamental principle of warfare is described by Guru Gobind Singh in his *Zafar-nāmāh* ("Letter of Victory") that he addressed to Emperor Aurangzeb in response to his personal message. It contains

certain references to the promises made by the Mughal officials before
the evacuation of Anandpur by the Guru, who had resisted them for a
considerable length of time. These promises were not kept, and the
Guru was obliged to fight the battle at Chamkaur, in which he was
overwhelmed by a disproportionately large number of Mughal troops.
Although he himself escaped unscathed, he lost two of his sons and
many followers in the battle. Again, there is a reference to the written
and verbal messages from Aurangzeb, probably asking the Guru to
present himself before the emperor. Guru Gobind Singh wrote the
Zafar-nāmāh in the Persian language from Dina Kangar in the southern
Punjab in February 1705 when he heard the news of the execution of his
other two sons at Sirhind. The Guru was prepared to meet with the
emperor at his camp in the Deccan in south India where he was engaged
in quelling disturbances. Unfortunately, Aurangzeb died while the Guru
was on his way to the south, and thus the actual meeting never took
place (P. Singh 2012: 212).

In his insightful analysis, Louis E. Fenech has described the *Zafar-
nāmāh* as "a discursive blade in the heart of the Mughal Empire"
(Fenech 2013). In verse 22 of its text Guru Gobind Singh advocates the
doctrine that one must first try all peaceful means of negotiation in the
pursuit of justice. Only when all those methods of redress have failed is
it legitimate to draw the sword in defense of righteousness. This celebrated verse makes this point explicitly: "When all other methods have
been explored and all other means have been tried. Then may the sword
be drawn from the scabbard, [and] then may the sword be used" (DG
3:1240). Here, Guru Gobind Singh justifies the use of force in defense of
social justice when all other alternatives fail. The use of force is certainly allowed in the Sikh doctrine, but it is authorized only in defense
of justice and only as a last resort. Moreover, in the face of tyranny,
justice can be defended and maintained through sacrifices. Verse 78 of
the *Zafar-nāmāh* stresses that no sacrifice is too great for the sake of
truth and justice: "It does not matter if my four sons have been killed;
the Khalsa is still there at my back" (DG 3:1246).

The *Rahit-nāmās* ("Manuals of Code of Conduct") provide a rare
insight into the evolving nature of the Khalsa code over time. These
texts grew considerably during the 18th century in response to Mughal
campaigns and later to the Afghan menace, and they produced injunctions that were clearly aimed at protecting the Khalsa from enemies,
who were seen to be Muslims. The *Tanakhāh-nāmā* ("Manual of
Penances") is the oldest document written during the period of Guru
Gobind Singh, and its earliest extant manuscript is dated 1716 CE. The

following relevant extract from it throws considerable light on the ideology of warfare:

> He is a Khalsa who in fighting never turns his back. He is a Khalsa who slays Muslims (*turk*). He is a Khalsa who triumphs over the five [evil impulses]. He is a Khalsa who avoids another's woman. He is a Khalsa who fights face to face. He is a Khalsa who destroys the oppressors. He is a Khalsa who carries weapons.
>
> (W. H. McLeod 2003: 284)

McLeod's translation of the word *turk* as "Muslims" because of its sense of religious identity in north Indian usage is problematic. In early Sikh literature the word *turk* or *turkarā* refers to the Mughal rulers of the day or to Afghan invaders, although neither of these groups were of Turkic ethnic origin. They were perceived to be oppressors, and hence it was the fundamental duty of the Khalsa to "slay oppressors" (P. Singh 2012: 217).

The Khalsa spent most of its first century fighting the armies of Mughals and Afghan invaders. In 1799 Ranjit Singh (1780–1839) succeeded in unifying the Punjab, taking control of Lahore and declaring himself Maharaja ("Great King"). For the next four decades, the Sikh community enjoyed more settled political conditions, and with territorial expansion as far as Peshawar in the west, people of different cultural and religious backgrounds were attracted into the fold of Sikhism. After Maharaja Ranjit Singh's death in 1839, however, his successors could not withstand the pressure exerted by the advancing British forces. As a result, the Sikh kingdom was annexed to the British Empire after two Anglo-Sikh wars of 1846 and 1849. With the loss of Punjab's independence, the Sikhs were no longer the masters of their own kingdom (P. Singh 2012: 218).

TALES OF BRAVERY, MARTYRDOMS AND THE LITURGICAL PERFORMANCE OF *ARDĀS*

The notion of martyrdom is an integral part of the Sikh tradition, and the Punjabi phrase *sīs denā* ("offering of a head") was used for it in early sources and adopted in the standard Sikh Prayer (*Ardās*). However, the most popular scriptural passage that has inspired the Sikh community is the following verse by Guru Nanak: "If you want to play the game of love, step into my lane with your head on the palm of your hand. Place your feet on this path, and give your head without any fear or grumbling" (GGS 1412). To place one's "head on the palm" symbolizes the sacrifice of one's egoistic self, and loving devotion in the Sikh tradition is a matter of life and death where to love ultimately means to sacrifice one's life. This motif of love-violence may be seen in the tradition of the "Cherished Five" (*Pañj Piāre*) who offered their "heads" at the call of Guru Gobind Singh when he inaugurated the institution of the Khalsa in 1699. An enormously popular tradition involving the ultimate sacrifice of one's head is lionized in the narrative of the 18th-century martyr Baba Dip Singh (1682–1757), who supernaturally carried his own decapitated head on his palm en route to Amritsar to fulfill his religious vow. He became an icon for Jarnail Singh Bhindranwale (1947–1984) in the 1980s (P. Singh 2020a: 683).

The second section of *Ardās* recalls the contributions of the faithful members of the Panth, beginning with its nucleus of original *Pañj Piāre* who responded to Guru Gobind Singh's call for sacrifice at the founding of the Khalsa:

> The Cherished Five, the Master's four sons, and the Forty Liberated Ones; all who were resolute, devout and strict in their self-denial; they who were faithful in their remembrance of the divine Name and generous to others; they who were noble both in practice of charity and in battle; they who magnanimously pardoned the faults of others: reflect on the merits of these faithful servants, O Khalsa, and call on God, saying, *Vāhigurū* ("Hail the Guru")!

Following the *Pañj Piāre*, the four sons of Guru Gobind Singh are reverentially remembered as martyrs to their faith. The two elder sons, Ajit Singh and Jujhar Singh, fell at the Battle of Chamkaur in 1705, while the two younger sons, Zorawar Singh and Fateh Singh, were executed soon after by the Mughal governor of Sirhind. They are recalled as *Chār Sāhibzāde* ("Four Princes") in *Ardās*. During the siege of Anandpur, forty Sikhs deserted the tenth Guru and returned to their homes. Shamed by their women, they rejoined the Guru's force prior to the Battle of Khidrana (now Muktsar) later in 1705 and were all killed. In recognition of their restored loyalty and subsequent sacrifice the Guru declared them to be *Chālī Mukte* ("Forty Liberated Ones"). The *Ardāsīā* ("one who performs *Ardās*") then implores the congregation to reflect on the merits of those faithful servants who were resolute (*haṭhī*), devout (*japī*) and strict in their self-denial (*tapī*); those who were faithful in their remembrance of the divine Name and generous to others by sharing their earnings; those who were noble both in the practice of charity (*degh chalāī*) and in wielding the sword in battle (*tegh vāhī*); and those who magnanimously pardoned the faults of others (*dekh ke aṇaḍiṯh kīṯā*). In response to the *Ardāsīā*'s call for attention, the congregation exclaims in a spirited voice: *Vāhigurū*!

The third section of *Ardās* glorifies martyrdom as a religious ideal in the face of persecution. It invokes the sacrifices of those male and female members of the Khalsa (*siṅghs* and *siṅghaṇīs*) who gave their heads for their faith:

> Those loyal members of the Khalsa [both men and women] who gave their heads for their faith; who were hacked limb from limb, scalped, broken on the wheel, or sawn asunder; who sacrificed their lives for the protection of hallowed gurdwaras, never forsaking their faith; and who were steadfast in their loyalty to the uncut hair of the true Sikh; reflect on their merits, O Khalsa, and call on God, saying, *Vāhigurū*!

It recalls the martyrdoms of Bhai Mani Singh (who was "hacked limb from limb" in 1737), Bhai Taru Singh (who was "scalped" in 1745), Subeg Singh and his son, Shahbaz Singh (who were "broken on the wheel" in 1745), and Bhai Mati Das (who was "sawn asunder" in 1675). These historical events were fresh in the collective memory of the Panth in the 18th century when they made their debut in the evolving text of *Ardās*. The reference to the sacrifices made for the "protection of hallowed gurdwaras" also commemorates the struggles for the control of historical gurdwaras that took place during the years 1921–1925 under British rule. During these ordeals the servants of the Panth did not forsake their faith and remained steadfast in their loyalty to the uncut hair of the true Sikh. The *Ardās* has kept the memory of these martyrdoms alive in the hearts and minds of each generation of Sikhs that participates in its liturgical performance.

The festival of *Holā Mahallā* introduced by Guru Gobind Singh in 1701 – an organized procession of *Nihaṅgs* ("Khalsa Warriors") in the form of an army column accompanied by war drums and standard-bearers and proceeding to a particular spot to practice mock-fighting at Anandpur – is celebrated annually one day after the Hindu color festival of Holi in March with military exercises, martial arts (*gatkā*) and literary contests. It is no wonder that the representation of Sikhs in violent and militant images has been pivotal in understanding Sikhism since colonial times. The British developed their theory of the "martial races" of India during the latter part of the 19th century, in accordance with which they classified Sikhs as a martial race, thus favoring them as army recruits with the requirement of turban and Khalsa initiation. Sikh history is replete with the valor of the Sikh warrior in battle.

However, there is less attention given to the Sikh warrior in equally and perhaps more demanding nonviolent actions. Paul Wallace aptly argues that the Sikhs are not essentially violent but are militant where "militancy" does not mean violence in actions and reactions alone but also an aggressive and passionate defense of the cause of their religion and the Gurus. This nonviolent militancy is actually "sovereign violence," demonstrated in public demonstrations and active political protests. The three case studies of the Gurdwara Reform Movement during British rule from 1920 to 1925, the Punjabi *Sūbā* ("Province") Movement from 1947 to 1966 in independent India and the movement against the state of emergency imposed by Prime Minister Indira Gandhi from 1975 to 1977 highlight the strength of the nonviolent struggles and those of the actors within the Akali Dal, the main political party of the Sikhs (Wallace 2011: 85–101).

The Punjab crisis of the 1980s reflected the multidimensionality of violence, resulting in "Operation Blue Star" when the Indian army attacked the Golden Complex in Amritsar. On the one hand, the involvement of government agents of the "Third Agency" in the garb of Sikh militants in random acts of violence and guerrilla warfare was totally unwarranted and counterproductive, although it served the specific purpose of the state to take coercive action against a religious and cultural minority (P. Singh 2016: 183). On the other hand, the state allowed the "chaos of insurgency to proliferate before brutally and clinically exterminating it almost at will" (A. Mandair 2009: 220). Thus, one cannot overlook the sheer egregious and unjust acts of the state killing in the name of order, security and sheer power, especially when religious militants were the victims. Ultimately, all the principal actors in this spiral of violence paid with their own lives. A considerable mythology gathered around Jarnail Singh Bhindranwale during his lifetime. His death during the Indian army's assault on the Golden Temple in June 1984 ensured that he will always be remembered as a great hero and martyr of the Sikh Panth because he fought for Sikh sovereignty (P. Singh 2012: 221–222).

CONCLUSION

This study has shown that there is a connection between Sikh sacred sources and the justification of war as divinely mandated. Indeed, scriptural words can act as weapons to motivate people to battle against the temptations of the mind. In actual wars, these words do inspire the killing of unjust and ruthless enemies who pose a danger to the survival of the faith. Thus, a militant interpretation of these texts has been seminal in generating a warrior culture in different historical periods. Further, the sword is central to the teachings and example of Guru Gobind Singh, and the text of the *Zafar-nāmāh* is explicit in declaring that it may be drawn only in defense of righteousness (*dharam*) and only when all other means of peaceful negotiation have failed. There is no sanction for indiscriminate, unrelenting and insatiable violence in the Sikh tradition. In the face of tyranny, however, justice can be defended and maintained through sacrifices and sovereign violence. Like all religious traditions, Sikhism has its own share of violence in its history, especially in times of nationalistic fervor. The Sikh notion of sovereignty is at the heart of the intersection of religion and war. As a matter of fact, such acts of violence and nonviolence are social phenomena that take place at particular historical junctures. They cannot be described as essential features of any community (P. Singh 2020b: 641).

The liturgical performance of *Ardās* repeats the common rich heritage of the Sikh tradition within five minutes. It recalls the past trials and triumphs of the Panth in a most profound way. In one sense, the recitation of *Ardās* is central to the ongoing memorialization of sacrifice and martyrdom. It is no wonder that after performing *Ardās* many a Sikh warrior died fighting on the battlefield in defense of their faith. For them, sacrifice became the ultimate gift, and the act of dying in war became the most complete method of reenacting the sacred history of the Panth. The text of *Ardās* glorifies them not by their names but by their heroic deeds. The Sikh community has created and preserved a collective memory through the constant recitals of *Ardās*. Rituals and recitals always bridge the gap between the past and the present, where recitals of the past events are not just matters of intellectual exercise but of invocation and evocation in which historical remembrances produce subjectivities and create mentalities. If the Sikh community is responsible for shaping the text of *Ardās* in light of its lived experience, then it is equally important to underline the fact that the liturgical performance of *Ardās* has played a significant role in shaping its destiny. To maintain their sense of sovereignty Sikhs have always fought against brutal state structures, whether it be the Mughal regime, the British Raj or even the Government of India in modern times.

REFERENCE NOTES

All of the citations from the GGS are taken from the standard version of the 1,430-page text. For instance, "GGS 721" refers to a citation on page

721 of the standard volume. The DG citations are taken from the three-volume *Shabadārath Dasam Granth Sāhib*, edited by Randhir Singh. Also, the VBG citations are taken from the version edited by Bhai Vir Singh.

References

Ahluwalia, Jasbir Singh. 1983. *The Sovereignty of the Sikh Doctrine: Sikhism in the Perspective of Modern Thought*. Bahri Publications.

Bhogal, Balbinder Singh. 2007. "Text as Sword." In *Religion and Violence in South Asia*. Edited by John R. Hinnells and Richard King. Routledge. 107–135.

Dhavan, Purnima. 2011. *When Sparrows Became Hawks: The Making of a Sikh Warrior Tradition, 1699–1799*. Oxford University Press.

Fenech, Louis E. 2013. *The Sikh Zafar-nāmāh of Guru Gobind Singh: A Discursive Blade in the Heart of the Mughal Empire*. Oxford University Press.

Grewal, Jagtar Singh. 1969. *Guru Nanak in History*. Panjab University.

1990. *The New Cambridge History of India: The Sikhs of the Punjab*. Cambridge University Press.

1996. *Sikh Ideology, Polity, and Social*. Manohar Publications.

Grewal, Jagtar Singh and Irfan Habib, eds. 2001. *Sikh History from Persian Sources*. Tulka Books.

Juergensmeyer, Mark. 2016. "Cosmic War." In *Oxford Research Encyclopedia of Religion*. DOI:10.1093/acrefore/9780199340378.013.65.

Lincoln, Bruce. 1994. *Authority: Construction and Corrosion*. University of Chicago Press.

Mandair, Arvind. 2007. "The Global Fiduciary: Mediating the Violence of Religion." In *Religion and Violence in South Asia*. Edited by John R. Hinnels and Richard King. Routledge. 211–225.

2020. *Violence and the Sikhs*. Cambridge University Press.

Mandair, Navdeep. 2009. "An Approximate Difference." In *Sikh Formations: Religion, Culture, [and] Theory*. Taylor and Francis. 85–101.

McLeod, Hew. 1997. *Sikhism*. Penguin Books.

McLeod, William Hewat. 1989. *The Sikhs: History, Religion, and Society*. Columbia University Press.

2003. *Sikhs of the Khalsa: A History of the Khalsa Rahit*. Oxford University Press.

Patton, Laurie L. 2007. "Telling Stories about Harm." In *Religion and Violence in South Asia*. Edited by John R. Hinnels and Richard King. Routledge. 11–40.

Rinehart, Robin. 2011. *Debating the Dasam Granth*. Oxford University Press.

Singh, Ganda, trans. and ed. 1940. "Nanak Panthis or the Sikhs and Sikhism of the 17th Century." *Journal of Indian History* 19(2): 195–219.

trans. and ed. 1967. "Nanak-Panthis." In *The Panjab Past and Present*, Vol. I. Punjabi University.

Singh, Khushwant. 1999. *A History of the Sikhs, Vol. I, 1469–1839*. Oxford University Press. First published 1963.

Singh, Pashaura. 2006. *Life and Work of Guru Arjan: History, Memory and Biography in the Sikh Tradition*. Oxford University Press.

2011. "Musical Chaunkis at the Darbar Sahib: History, Aesthetics, and Time." In *Sikhism in Global Context*. Edited by Pashaura Singh. Oxford University Press. 102–129.

2012. "Words as Weapons: Theory and Practice of a Righteous War (*DharamYudh*) in Sikh Texts." In *Fighting Words: Religion, Violence, and the Interpretation of Sacred Texts*. Edited by John Renard. University of California Press. 200–225.

2016. "Deconstructing the Punjab Crisis of 1984: Deer, Hawks, and *Siqdārs* ('Officials') as Agents of State-Sponsored Violence." In *Sikh Formations: Religion, Culture, [and] Theory*. Taylor and Francis. 173–190.

2017. "The Sikh Gurus: Works of Art in the Kapany Collection." In *Sikh Art from the Kapany Collection*. Edited by Paul Michael Taylor and Sonia Dhami. The Sikh Foundation International in association with Asian Cultural History Program, Smithsonian Institution. 50–77.

2019. "How Avoiding the Religion–Politics Divide Plays out in Sikh Politics." *Religions* 10: 296.

2020a. "Martyrdom." In *Religious Violence Today: Faith and Conflict in the Modern World*, Vol. 2. Edited by Michael Jerryson. ABC-CLIO. 683–686.

2020b. "Sikhism: Introduction." In *Religious Violence Today: Faith and Conflict in the Modern World*, Vol. 2. Edited by Michael Jerryson. ABC-CLIO. 633–642.

2020c. "Speaking Truth to Power: Exploring Guru Nanak's Bābar-vāṇī in Light of the Baburnama." *Religions* 11, 328.

Singh, Randhir, ed. 1973. *Shabadārath Dasam Granth Sāhib*, Vols. I–III. Punjabi University.

Singh, Vir, ed. 1977. *Vārāṅ Bhāī Gurdās*. Khalsa Samachar. First published 1911.

Syan, Hardip Singh. 2013. *Sikh Militancy in the Seventeenth Century: Religious Violence in Mughal and Early Modern India*. I.B. Tauris.

Thackston, Wheeler M., trans. and ed. 1996. *The Baburnama: Memoirs of Babur, Prince and Emperor*. Oxford University Press.

Wallace, Paul. 2011. "Sikh Militancy and Non-violence." In *Sikhism in Global Context*. Edited by Pashaura Singh. Oxford University Press. 85–101.

7 Religion and War in Traditional China

BAREND TER HAAR

Military violence was an important component of all imperial regimes in Chinese history, since that is how they came to power and how they were replaced, whether through war and insurrection or a coup at the court by the imperial guard. This chapter will not make a formal distinction between different kinds of armed conflict based on political or historiographical considerations of legitimacy for armed conflict. The primary interest of this contribution will be the role of religious culture in and around actual armed conflict, rather than the pervasive role of violence in religious culture as a whole (ter Haar 2019). We will also refer briefly to philosophical and religious statements on the concept of a "just" war. Until now, relatively little work has been done on the religious dimension of armed conflict in traditional China (but cf. Graff 2002: 8–9; Yates 2005: 31).

RELIGIOUS INSPIRATIONS

The traditional Chinese ruler defined him- or herself in terms of heavenly support, the so-called Mandate of Heaven (*tianming* 天命), with the mission of establishing order in the All-under-Heaven (*tianxia* 天下) and the title Son-of-Heaven (*tianzi* 天子). Thus political rule was always religiously sanctioned rule. The emperor did not usually try to impose his or her personal belief system but definitely claimed supreme authority about all forms of worship. Since sacrifice and worship of various divine forces or ancestors were at the core of virtually all social formations, from family and village to the nation as a whole, it is only natural that the supreme ruler asserted his or her authority over these (Lagerwey 2010).

Since the Daoist-inspired rebellions of the year 184 CE, the common stereotype has been that new religious traditions have a strong potential for armed rebellion (ter Haar 1992). The relatively successful Five Pecks of Rice movement that also started in that year certainly succeeded in establishing a theocratic state, which only lasted until 215 CE. After that, it was incorporated into the northern Chinese territory of Cao Cao 曹操 (155–220) that eventually became the Wei 魏 state (220–280). In the process, it evolved into a religion supporting political legitimacy, but also a personal system of religious practices, without aiming to impose its beliefs and practices on all those in a given territory (Kleeman 2016). Traditional China rarely saw armed conflicts aimed at imposing one's worldview on the other, at least not until the 20th century (cf. Kang 2014). A major exception was the rebellion of the Heavenly Kingdom of Great Peace in the mid-19th century, which was partly Christian inspired and sought to impose its own worldview on those it conquered, at least initially.

China has a rich tradition of messianic movements, whether inspired by Buddhist beliefs in the advent of Maitreya as the Buddha of a new cosmic era and/or by more Daoist-inspired beliefs in the advent of a future king. In these often loosely structured movements, it was believed that the world was going to be hit by terrible disasters, ranging from famine, droughts and/or flooding to military incursions. There were several approaches to this kind of threat. The most common one was to follow the new savior and change one's lifestyle and/or take prophylactic measures, remaining entirely peaceful whilst awaiting the irrevocable end of time. In another approach it was believed that the new ruler would provide protection by means of divine armies under divine generals. We today might consider this ruler and their armies mythical, but they were only too real to their adherents and even to the imperial state. They were regularly employed to fight the demonic forces that threatened everyday life, from diseases to flooding (ter Haar 2019). The state often spent great expense on tracking down these figures, even if they were usually frustrated in this search. It therefore considered such prophecies violent, even if from a Western academic perspective they are clearly imagined and even though such demonological messianic incidents usually remained peaceful unless repressed by the state (ter Haar 1998, 2015).

Those few instances in which messianic views did develop into violent events were usually inspired by this demonological worldview, because given the right socioeconomic circumstances the leaders and their followers might feel stronger gratitude for the support of divine armies. Examples are the rebellions of the Red Turbans that broke out in 1351 and lasted until 1368, the martial healer–teacher Wang Lun 王倫 in 1774 and the sectarian Eight Trigrams movement in 1813 (ter Haar 2018, 2020a). The Boxers, who were not really rebels but did rise violently in 1900 against Western Christianity, conceived of themselves as Divine Soldiers (*shenbing* 神兵), using the exactly same term that is used in ritual practices that summoned up divine armies to fight demons. Their demons were the missionaries spreading the Christian faith. By carrying out extensive rituals of self-empowerment, they were convinced that they formed an invulnerable military force. Even an important part of the imperial court believed in it (Esherick 1987; Cohen 1997).

HUMAN AND ANIMAL SACRIFICE

The first written texts in Chinese history on ox scapulae and tortoise shields from the period of ca. 1200–ca. 1045 BCE show us quite clearly how essential sacrificial practice was to the political structures of the time, usually referred to as the Shang 商 dynasty (1550?–ca. 1045 BCE). Robin Yates has argued that the Shang rulers practiced war as a means to get human sacrifices. Just how important this was in ritual terms is abundantly clear from the Shang divination record and the scores of sacrificed humans in their royal graves as well as their territorial cults (Kominami 2009; Yates 2013). Whether the victims also occupied leading positions in the political units that had been defeated is unclear.

Early political units were already constructed around the worship of the soil and shared descent by the ruling families from prominent ancestors, making the rituals surrounding these extra-human agencies of great importance in armed conflict. We can see this in the ancient practice of carrying around an impersonator (*shi* 尸, which literally means corpse) of the main ancestor and a clod of earth from their Altar of the Soul on major military campaigns (Kominami 2009: 208, 218–219; Puett 2009: 704ff). From the second half of the Zhou period onwards (after 771 BCE), defeating a competing state meant destroying its ritual center, most prominently the Altars for the Soil and Millet (*shejitan* 社稷壇). This could even include sacrificing the leader of the defeated state in celebratory worship at the altars of the victorious party (Kominami 2009: 207, 222–224). Since the rule over these territorial units was in the hands of aristocratic lineages claiming a venerable depth in time, their ancestral temple was the prime location for receiving commands by the army commander with the ancestors as his witnesses (Galvany 2015: 154–155). After a campaign had been successfully concluded, sacrifice would again be offered (e.g. Kern 2009: 178). Similar rituals continued in later centuries, but they came to compete with the worship of anthropomorphic deities that could express the fears and emotions of warfare much better. Such deities also appeared in battle to provide very concrete and visible support in a way that these older rituals could not.

As Robin Yates has pointed out for ancient China and the early empire, "warfare was a great ritual, a sacrifice essential for the maintenance of the existence of the dead ancestors and the spirits, as well as for the generation of good fortune for the living, perhaps a form of thanksgiving sacrifice for victory as well as an expiatory rite for engaging in the polluting act of killing." This extended to ritual preparation for war (at least by the leaders), the right clothing, the right moment of the year and so forth (Yates 2005: 20ff). These concerns did not change fundamentally in subsequent periods.

BLOOD-SMEARING RITUALS

Ancient preparations for war included a blood-smearing ritual as part of the sacrifices. As stated by the *Zuo Tradition* (*zuozhuan* 左傳): "When the ruler travels with the army, he performs a purification sacrifice at the altar of earth, and he anoints the drums with blood (*bashe xingu*祓社釁鼓); the invocators accompany him to attend to their duties, and in this way the group crosses the borders" (Durrant et al. 2016: 1746–1747, also 450–451 and 1398–1399). In a broader ritual context, smearing the blood of sacrificial victims (called *xin* 衅/釁, or *sha* 歃) on an important building or object to provide them with further power is well attested from early on (*Liji zhengyi* 2000: 17/636, 39/1322–1323, 43/1431–1432). Drums and, as we will see further below, banners were essential instruments of war, obviously for communication and to serve as rallying points, but in the case of drums also to drown out the sounds of death (Rom 2020).

The practice of consecrating the instruments of war with the blood of live sacrifices continued into later dynasties, but in exceptional cases also using that of rebels or similar marginal figures. During the mid-8th-century rebellions that shook the Tang 唐 dynasty (618–907) to its very foundations, a certain Abuli 阿布離, headsman of the Xi 奚 ethnic group in north-east China and an ally of the rebels, was captured. After his beheading, his blood was smeared on the war drums (*Xin tangshu* 1975: 224 *xia*/6387). Already in the preceding Sui dynasty 隋 (589–617) it was common practice that, "when the imperial princes personally went on military expeditions and great generals went out with their armies, they would smear the drums with the buttocks of one boar/male swine. All [enterprises] were to be announced to the Temple of the Lord of the

Earth. After hatchet and axe had done their work, nobody was allowed to go back and sleep at home" (*Suishu* 1973: 8/163). The blood not only served to consecrate the drums, but also the generals, making them into highly charged beings that could easily cause mishap at home because of this. In exceptional cases throughout the following centuries, we continue to find the smearing of blood from human sacrifice on military banners, both among rebels or bandits and by government forces. Whether this is always an actual practice or a rhetorical statement akin to accusations of cannibalism and excessive cruelty is often difficult to ascertain (Katz 2009).

The Song 宋 dynasty (960–1127–1276) administrative records from 1001 provide a good idea of the larger ritual practice. After preparing an earthen altar,

> [the official in charge] set up a tent [on top] and placed the military horns [on top of the banners], the six banners, and spirit tablets inside. The tablets were seven *cun* 寸 square (ca. 23 cm) and three *fen* 分 (ca. 1 cm) thick. For the sacrifice he picked an uneven day (i.e. a Yang day with extra energy). He prepared the regular food offerings, using the Grand Animal Sacrifice, but replacing it with goats and pigs (which strictly speaking is the Minor Animal Sacrifice, by leaving out the ox). The [spirit] money and the military horns [on top of the banners] were white, the six banners dark, each of them one fathom and eight feet long. The Head Area Commander did the first offering, the next generals in line did the second and third offering, all dressed in military garb. After a pure fasting for one night, the officers stood in line. After the rituals had been completed, they burned the [spirit] money and smeared the drums with blood using the skin [of the sacrificial animals].
> (Songhuiyao jigao, li 禮 14/1, 39)

The smearing of blood on banners came to be transformed into a cult that was to be maintained in dedicated Temples of Flags and Banners (*Qidao miao* 旗纛廟). It was instituted by the Ming (1368–1644) at the outset of its rule and continued until the fall of the empire in early 1912 (Katz 2009: 218–219). Smearing blood to consecrate ritual objects, such as amulets or divine statues and spirit tablets, but also consuming blood mixed with an alcoholic beverage to empower the mouth when swearing an oath were common ritual practices through imperial history (ter Haar 1998: 151–167). Thus, smearing rituals in a military context would have been easily understood by all levels of the army and would certainly not have been experienced as strange or excessive.

RITUALS TO MANAGE UNCERTAINTY

Sacrifice and the consecration of drums, banners and other instruments of war served to increase the power of weapons and combatants, and through that the management of uncertainty. Equally important in this respect was the practice of divination, to ascertain the prospects of the enterprise and select the best day to set forth or engage in actual battle. The Shang oracle bones already include divination to the highest divine agencies about military campaigns and their potential fate (Keightley 2000: 45–47, 52, 63, 66–68). In subsequent periods, too, permission of the ancestral spirits and other extra-human agencies was essential to a successful campaign (Xu and Linduff 1988: 103–109; Yates 2005: 18). Throughout the imperial period divination and the interpretation of a broad range of portents as well as dreams were officially acknowledged and described in military manuals, using the entire repertoire of divination methods that was also used more generally. While some traditional authors expressed their skepticism, that does not seem to have stopped these practices (Loewe 1994; Yates 2005; Sawyer 2009). Already the earliest extant divinatory manuals from the 3rd and 2nd centuries BCE had military affairs among their concerns and regularly specified which days would have what kind of military outcome (Poo 1998: 76–78).

One form of divination that military manuals took very seriously was the observation of cosmic vapor or miasma (qi 氣). By inspecting its timing, movements, shape and color, something could be said about an army's prospects (Yates 2005: 24–31). This belief in different kinds of miasma (qi) manifesting themselves was not some kind of quaint archaic practice. In local histories of the late Ming dynasty, for instance, white miasma was seen as a positive sign and dark or black miasma as a threat. In daily life one might still fear the "deadly miasma" (shaqi 殺氣) of the recently deceased (ter Haar 2006: 214–215, 222–224, 232–234, 269–272). Some people might of course be better at observing it than others, but it is not hard to imagine that fog and low-hanging clouds might influence the prospects of an armed conflict.

Military manuals indicate quite clearly that divination remained a prominent part of war-related rituals, and Marcia Butler has argued that such practices even became more common during the Song dynasty than before. Whether this is true is hard to measure, but divination certainly took up more space in the military manuals of that time than before. Butler points out, for instance, that the creation of cosmic diagrams for positioning the army and structuring its defense and attack in line with the larger patterns of the universe were important parts of military preparation. Quite apart from how accurately such diagrams could represent battle realities, people thought that it was possible and discussed it in preparing for war. It also provided military leaders with a language and other tools to visualize their campaigns, even if they may not have applied it "literally." Moreover, and important for our next section, the belief in such cosmic diagrams further strengthened the general acceptance of an intimate connection between war and cosmic processes, as well as among the intellectual and political elites (Butler 2007, 2008, 2016).

Another way in which such diagrams may have been used is as part of ritual practices to guarantee the safety of the participants in an armed conflict. One example is the ritual used for the departure of an army, which can be traced from materials found at 1st-century CE military outposts in the north as well as Dunhuang manuscripts from the east some ten centuries later. It involved drawing a now lost diagram on the ground, chanting an incantation to guarantee safety on the road and protection against arms and stepping over the diagram. These actions were to be taken by the army general at the time of his departure (Harper 2017: 123–124ff). The *Enfeoffment of the Gods*, a late 16th-century vernacular novel depicting the wars at the transition of the Shang to Zhou dynasties, but also purporting to describe the origin of many northern deities, is full of references to battle arrays (*zhen* 陣) that are used to trap and vanquish enemy forces (Meulenbeld 2015). In northern ritual practice oil lamps were used to build similar battle arrays to vanquish demonic forces during the New Year festival and other occasions (Holm 1994). Thus, the belief that such diagrams could serve to protect against martial violence or demonic aggression was well-accepted in traditional China.

Finally, armed fighters carried with them objects that it was hoped would provide protection against enemy weapons (Yates 2005: 21; Yan 2017: 209). Early sources from the 4th to 10th centuries mention medicinal substances and protection cords for this purpose (Copp 2018: 48, 49, 80, 255–256). As late as 1857 a rich arsenal of materials was confiscated from arrested participants in the rebellion of the Heavenly Kingdom of Great Peace. These included the movement's Christian writings, but also prescriptions for manufacturing amulets to strengthen one's courage, for burning temples and government offices, a spell to avoid arms and a spell for attaining long life (*Shanhua xianzhi* 1877: 34/20b–21a). Here, the monotheistic background of the participants did not prevent them from using more traditional means of protection through amulets. The most famous recent examples are of course self-protection practices by the Boxers in 1900 and the Red Spears in the Republican period, including amulets to ward off gunshots. Modern scholarship has seen this as specific to sectarian religious traditions, but it is clear that this was inspired as well by long-standing military practices (Esherick 1987: 54–58ff).

Sacrifice took place at many points of a campaign and divination was probably also repeated at various points. Some rituals explicitly served to structure the campaign itself. It would be tedious to list all the rituals that are attested in state ritual treatises, but we can note that sacrificial and other rituals accompanied many of the important stages of a campaign (Waley-Cohen 2006: 66–88; Butler 2007). An important function of collective rituals was to create an esprit de corps, to amplify the usual military training. Rituals that transferred power from the emperor to his general as well as those that bound the army as a whole to their officers through a common oath were of special importance (Butler 2007: 92). This can be illustrated by the examples of enlistees without any prior military experience, such as the lay Buddhist Qi Biaojia 祁彪佳 (1603–1645). He was a retired civilian official, amateur landscape architect and devout admirer of the martial deity Lord Guan.[1] When the north had already fallen to the Manchu Qing (1644–1911) invaders in the summer of 1644, he set out to organize resistance forces in his Lower Yangzi region hometown. An essential ritual step for him was the worship of the military banners and Lord Guan along with his fellow commanders. First, he gave them a speech on the importance of their military enterprise. Then they killed a sacrificial ox and smeared its blood over the entire fighting force. As a result, "[t]hat day the military looked especially strong and the entire city came out to watch" (ter Haar 2017: 133–134).

DEITIES OF WAR

In the secondary literature we find frequent mention of three figures who are labeled as deities of war, namely the figures of Chiyou 蚩尤, Qi Taigong 齊太公 and Lord Guan 關公, whose worship also roughly succeeded each other in time. These modern labels do not go back to a Chinese original, such as "deity of war" (zhanshen 戰神) or "deity of the army" (junshen 軍神). The scholarly assumption of a deity designated

---

[1] Lord Guan is a still common general appellation for the divinized figure of Guan Yu 關羽, a prominent military figure of the early 3rd century CE. See ter Haar (2017).

specifically by warrior attributes has been inspired by Greek and Roman mythological expectations. Instead, Chinese warrior deities were localized; we have already seen that war rituals on a territorial level were devoted to deities protecting the soil, and on a clan or lineage level to the ancestors of that kinship unit. On the other hand, many deities had their origins in military figures and derived their power from that (ter Haar 2019).

Nonetheless, there can be no doubt that the figure of Chiyou was warlike, known for his brutal fighting and his continuous resistance to the forces of order. According to one description, he had a human body but the hooves of an ox, four eyes and six hands. Another source says that he had horns. He was also supposed to be the inventor of metal weapons (Birrell 1993: 50–53, 132–134, 192–193). In extant narratives and ritual practices he appears to be a figure of unregulated chaos (*luan* 亂) and excessive violence (*bao* 暴) – in other words, a figure who must be subdued (*Shiji*, 1/3). In one source from the 2nd century BCE, it is even specified that there is a taboo on military activity on his death day, when "it is not permitted to engage in crying and mourning, to gather the multitude, and to assemble soldiers" (Yan 2017: 232). This kind of taboo hardly seems practical within a war campaign but could have fitted in the preparatory stage.

Chiyou was indeed worshipped more narrowly as a deity of weapons (*bing* 兵, which only got its modern meaning of soldiers much later). This worship does not seem to have been institutionalized. For the Western Han (202 BCE–9 CE) we have two telling pieces of information. When Sima Qian (fl. late 2nd century BCE) in his *Record of the Scribe* describes retrospectively the rise to power of the dynastic founder Liu Bang 劉邦 (256–195 BCE), he records that early on in his rebellion Liu Bang "prayed at the Altar of the Soil at the White Elm Tree in Feng [County]" (*dao feng fenyu she* 禱豐枌榆社), which was the typical territorial sacrifice at the start of a military campaign. When he could not mobilize his followers, he went a step further and "sacrificed to the Yellow Emperor and worshipped Chiyou in the courtyard of Pei [County] and smeared blood on the drums and banners. His pennants all became deep red" (*ci huangdi, ji chiyou yu Pei ting, er xin guqi, zhi jie chi* 祠黃帝，祭蚩尤於沛庭，而釁鼓旗，幟皆赤) (*Shiji*, 8/340, 28/1378). The combined worship of the Yellow Emperor with his mortal enemy Chiyou is a bit odd, but the purpose of the sacrifice seems to have been the consecration of weapons and other instruments of war rather than the initial prayers of support that took place at the White Elm Tree. It was an additional ritual practice rather than the core of a military ritual.

We find the same combination again in the second reference by Sima Qian, when he discusses the ultimate territorial sacrifices called *Feng* 封 and *Shan* 禪 that were held at Mount Tai 泰山 by the Martial Emperor (*wudi* 武帝) in 110 BCE. Part of the ritual program included "thirdly: sacrifices to Chiyou, the Lord of the weapons" (*sanyue bingzhu ci chiyou* 三曰兵主，祠蚩尤). However, this worship did not take place in connection with actual military campaigns, whether in the Chang'an capital or on the battlefield, but at his putative grave in Dongping (*Shiji*, 28/1367). It seems that Chiyou might be worshipped as the inventor of weapons, but not as a god of war or regular military campaigns. In that capacity he could even be worshipped to provide protection against them, as recorded in a Dunhuang manuscript from the late 9th or early 10th century CE (Harper 2017: 123–124). Modern scholarship has deduced from this connection that Chiyou is the equivalent of gods of war from Roman or Greek tradition, but unlike them he does not participate in war campaigns and he is not worshipped to initiate a campaign (e.g. Birrell 1993: 50ff; Yan 2017: 233 and others).

By the early Song dynasty, the worship of Chiyou is still included in the state sacrificial canon, but only as part of a much larger repertoire of rituals devoted to war (*Songhuiyao jigao, li* 禮5: 18; *li* 7: 39; *li* 14: 88; *li* 18: 37). One example is from 980, when the Taizong emperor personally went on a military expedition. The day before the army set out, the emperor dispatched two officials to go to the Northern Suburbs to sacrifice to Chiyou 蚩尤 and to the horns that were customarily placed on top of the pole carrying the army banners. At this time, he also instructed another official to go the Altar for Inspecting Miasma in the same Northern Suburbs, accompanied by sacrifices, to worship the Heavenly King of the North (*Songhuiyhao jigao, li* 14: 9, 39 and *li* 48: 1). The directionality of these sacrifices could be explained by the fact that by this time the main enemies of the newly founded dynasty were located in the north, in the form of the Khitan Liao dynasty (916–1125). Soon after, the worship of Chiyou on the state level seems to have been discontinued, perhaps because he was the mortal enemy of the Yellow Emperor, who was construed as the ancestor of the Song imperial lineage from 1012 onwards (Cahill 1980: 23–44; Butler 2007: 76). Moreover, at least in the mythology of Guan Yu in northern China, he was constructed as a major demon who was defeated by the deity to protect the extraction of salt from a local salt lake (ter Haar 2017: 67–72).

By the Tang period, a cult was actually created for a figure who may be considered a deity of war, even if not all of its history is clear. The putative author of several military treatises and military advisor to the early Zhou dynasty (ca. 1045–256 BCE), Qi Taigong 齊太公 (fl. 11th century BCE), became the subject of a cult specifically dedicated to him. From 706 CE onwards he was the subject of worship in his own temples in Chang'an and Luoyang, which functioned as the capital and shadow capital, respectively. By 719 it is explicitly stated that generals going on campaign should take their leave at his temple and report their victories at the temple. Although this did not necessarily replace the worship of territorial divine agencies, it introduced an anthropomorphic form of worship that did not exist before. In 731 the cult was extended to the country as a whole, and in 760, during one of the worst rebellions in Chinese history, he was ennobled as a king with the title of Martial Accomplishments (wucheng wang 武成王). The cult was controversial among civilian officials, who avoided writing about it, feeling that the military element (wu 武) in the dynasty should not be given a chance to dominate the civilian element (wen 文) (McMullen 1989). Thus, his cult was often considered in tandem with that for Confucius, who was thought to represent the latter element. By then the historical philosopher's well-attested advocacy of archery and charioteering as crucial aristocratic skills or his support for blood vengeance were commonly ignored, since they conflicted with the new norm of civilian values. By the 17th century, Qi Taigong would be replaced in this tandem role by the figure of Lord Guan.

Subsequent dynasties continued the worship of Qi Taigong under his Tang official title and often in tandem with the worship of Confucius (e.g. Songhuiyao jigao, yue 3/8; li 14/1–3, 26/9–10 and so forth). When the first emperor of the newly founded Song dynasty visited the deity's temple in the capital of Kaifeng in 961, he pointed at the portrait of a 3rd-century BCE general and criticized him for his killing of thousands soldiers who had already surrendered. Not only did this lead to a revision of the temple pantheon, but it also made clear that the emperor intended a lenient policy towards the different local states that he was still fighting at that point in time (Songhuiyao jigao, li 16/5). Apparently, the temple was quite big in size with more than forty rooms and could serve to lodge large numbers of officials, but it was also used for a military school and for teaching medical texts later in the dynasty (Songhuiyao jigao, li 14/19, li 16/5; chongru 1/31, 3/29; zhiguan 14/1, 22/35). It never really became a temple of the people, nor of ordinary soldiers.

The cult was reestablished immediately after the founding of the Ming dynasty (1368–1644) as well, initially in the new capital of

Nanjing. We have already seen that this dynasty ordered the establishment of Temples of Flags and Banners all over the empire to celebrate martial values, but now in a permanent temple rather than on a temporary altar. This certainly was an important innovation, part of the initial martial direction of the dynasty (Dreyer 1982). The cult of the King of Martial Accomplishment was reestablished in explicit imitation of Song precedent, which probably reflects the general tenor of the rebellions of the 1350s and 1360s, which often harked back to Song political symbols (ter Haar 2018) and brought the Mongol Yuan dynasty (1271–1368) to its end. The early Ming Veritable Records contain a lengthy discussion on what should be adopted from ancient military rituals (junli 軍禮), and they describe the proper worship of the King of Martial Accomplishments by the nation's highest generals in great detail (MSL, Taizu shilu太祖實錄: 33: 581–590 [Hongwu 1: run 7: 12]). After the capital was moved north to Beijing, a cult for him was maintained in the military headquarters itself (MSL, Yingzong shilu 英宗實錄, 98: 1963 [Zhengtong 7: 11: 2]).

The worship of the King always retained its strictly military character (e.g. Jiankang zhi, 44: 27b–28a and Qicheng, 4: 25a). Thus, in the northern prefecture of Hejian a local military officer sometime during the mid-Ming period worried about the custom whereby sons of local garrison officials stopped practicing military affairs and went out to enjoy themselves. To remedy this, he founded a military school next to the Confucian temple, including a Temple for the King of Martial Accomplishments. Apparently, the temple lasted, for even in the middle of the 18th century people who took military examinations often prayed here (Hejian xinzhi 18: 34a–b). A late 17th-century inscription from the border garrison town of Xuanhua devoted to the King stressed the importance of caring for military affairs through his worship, next to the civilian affairs symbolized by the worship of Confucius. The author notes that the temple had been restored numerous times since the early 16th century. Now, in 1684, a new project was carried out, financed by local generals and martial elites with an interest in "righteousness" (yi 義). They invited a Daoist priest to keep the incense fire alive on a regular basis (Xuanhua xianzhi 28: 32b–33b).

On the whole, the cult for the deity did lose currency over the course of the Ming and Qing dynasties, because another cult for a martial deity became increasingly popular, devoted to Lord Guan. Precisely how this competition unrolled needs further research, but by the late Ming this highly popular deity had become the preeminent representative of martial values (*wu* 武) next to Confucius as the representative of civilian values (*wen* 文) (ter Haar 2017: 198ff). One intermediary development was the rise of local Temples for Martial Virtues (*wumiao* 武廟) associated with military activities (e.g. *Songjiang fuzhi* 13: 18a–b; *Hejian fuzhi* 3: 47b–48a; *Shuofang xinzhi* 4: 46b–47a; *Licheng xianzhi* 4: 2a), often still explicitly devoted to the King of Martial Accomplishments. At the same time Lord Guan might be worshipped at small shrines or temples directly next to the military exercise fields of most administrative units (ter Haar 2017: 95, 178, 193, 208). In the north of China this did not have major consequences for his worship, since the cult of Lord Guan had already been highly popular for several centuries, but south of the Huai River these temples would eventually become the nucleus of serious local worship, receiving a further boost during the mid-16th-century incursions of sea pirates (ter Haar 2017: 100–101). Thus, there will have been confusion between the old cult for the King of Martial Accomplishment, whose worship was largely a state affair on different administrative levels, and that of Lord Guan, who was highly popular on a much more personal level.

The creation of Temples for Martial Virtues (*wumiao*) probably was not an official decision on the national level, since from 1521 onwards the same term was one of the official ways of referring to the Martial Ancestor 武宗, the posthumous title of the Zhengde Emperor, as Zhu Houzhao 朱厚照 (1491–r. 1505–1521) came to be referred to after his death. It is therefore only in the Qing period that the Temple for Martial Virtues became an official appellation, parallel to the Temple for Civilian Virtues (*wenmiao* 文廟), which we usually refer to as the Confucian Temple. With the rise of the cult of Lord Guan to the level of the emperor in 1614 and his newly won status as the martial counterpart of Confucius at around the same time, there were of course some serious contradictions in ritual terms (ter Haar 2017: 180–181).

In 1727 the career general Li Rubai李如栢 therefore memorialized his concern about the inappropriate situation that, in the Temple of Martial Virtues, a mere king, Qi Taigong, occupied the central position, and the much higher Emperor Guan was at best among his four subordinates. He deemed this inappropriate given the honors that Lord Guan had received in the past, but also because he had been placed on the same level as Confucius by the present dynasty (i.e. the Qing itself). Here the general overlooked the fact that this development actually went back to the last decades of the Ming. General Li therefore proposed that the statues of Lord Guan in the Temple of Martial

Virtues as well as in other subordinate shrines elsewhere all be given an independent temple, or that he at least be placed on the same level as the King of Martial Accomplishments (*Shizong zhupi*, 161: 13b–15b). This memorial was subsequently carried into practice, and we find it referred to in local sources (e.g. *Yucheng xianzhi* 6: 2a; *Xingning xianzhi* 9: 11b–12a). At least one temple for Lord Guan in every administrative unit would now be designated as the Temple of Martial Virtues (e.g. *Gucheng xianzhi* 5: 13a; *Baling xianzhi* 10: 8a; *Yuxiang xinzhi* 5: 5a). As a state cult, this temple also received regular worship by representatives of the state, including the military. One further manifestation is the spread of his cult along with the military expansion of the Qing Empire to Central Asia, creating the New Territories or Xinjiang 新疆 as they are known today (ter Haar 2017: 182). And yet, unlike his sort-of-predecessors Chiyou and Qi Taigong, he remained just as much a deity of local communities and the patron saint of the Shanxi merchants, as well as a deity popular among the literati, a deity of wealth and eventually a new high deity of the late imperial pantheon in spirit writing cults (ter Haar 2017). A further attempt at ritual innovation took place during the Republican period (1912–1949), when there was a need for a military hero who was more explicitly connected to the fight against barbarian invaders – in this case, the Japanese. For this reason the worship of Emperor Guan in the Temple of Martial Virtues was expanded with the figure of Yue Fei 岳飛 (1103–1142), a hero of the early Southern Song fight against the Jurchen in the north (Wilhelm 1962). This was first and foremost an attempt by the civilian government of the Nationalist Party to create new symbols of martial and nationalist vigor, but as far as we can tell it did not achieve great popularity.

IN SUPPORT OF WAR

As in most philosophical and religious traditions, it is not difficult to point to principles that might justify (or should have justified in our eyes) tolerance and nonviolence (Ching 2004; much more skeptical is Ivanhoe 2004), but the simple reality is that all regimes relied and still rely heavily on a broad spectrum of violent activities for obtaining and maintaining control over their respective populations. Religious activities were an important part of this program.

In an important article, Mark Lewis has pointed out that in very early Chinese history warfare was the normal situation and there was no necessity to justify it (Lewis 2006). According to him, ideas about a just war (*yibing* 義兵[2]) were first developed by the philosophical trad-itions of the Warring States period, from the late 4th century onwards. While he identifies the relevant texts with the conventional Western label "philosophical," he also points out that the ruler is "the only proper source and guarantor of licit warfare" (Lewis 2006: 189). Given that the ruler in the Chinese context is defined as a "Son of Heaven" also in the relevant "philosophical" texts, thus deriving his authority from Heaven, one would think that a religious dimension is still quite fundamental here. This is also clear from an example quoted by Lewis as typical of this view of the righteous war: namely the lengthy stone inscriptions placed on top of selected mountains by the First Emperor of the Qin (r. 221–210 BCE) (Lewis 2006: 191–192). These are written in the four-character verse that is typical of court ritual poetry, and the selection of mountains is precisely because they are meeting points with Heaven. We can surmise that the First Emperor also offered exten-sive sacrifices here, minimally on top of the mountains to Heaven and most likely also at the bottom to Earth and/or local deities. Lewis goes on to show that the "just war" according to these inscriptions was supposed to take place in the name of Heaven and following the Heavenly patterns (Lewis 2006: 193–194; also Fraser 2016; ter Haar 2020b).

So-called philosophical discourse was always intended for practical application by actual rulers whose power was based on religious assumptions about the origin of their rule and with that their legitim-acy. It only appears more narrowly philosophical because modern readers have decided to study these texts whilst ignoring their larger politico-religious context, not because people in traditional China ever thought in terms of distinct categories of philosophy and religion. Even the *Analects* ascribed to Confucius does not really reject religious ritual activity, even though its protagonist is presented as less expert in that field and therefore silent on it. The Confucius whom we find in early ritual texts was in fact deeply interested in religious beliefs and prac-tices. Much the same is true of Mozi and his followers, whose work is often quoted in discussions of early attitudes towards war (ter Haar 2022). In later times, politicians would always succeed in finding argu-ments for ignoring the restrictions put upon them by the notion of a "just war" when they wanted to (Johnston 1995; Wyatt 2008).

---

[2] This uses the Western concept. The Chinese term *yi* is more commonly translated as "righteous." See also Johnston (1995).

Superficially, one might think that the Buddhist prohibition on killing would have made Buddhists oppose military and other forms of violence (Chen 2017: 209). Both historically and contemporaneously, however, it has proven quite possible to combine Buddhist beliefs and military activities (Jerryson and Juergensmeyer 2010). Chen Jinhua has pointed out the role of Buddhist monks and military chaplains and counselors in the Tang dynasty and before. They gave lectures on moral principles, but also performed rituals to achieve victory in battle or to summon up illusions to scare away the enemy. At times Buddhist monks even engaged in actual battle, most famously the monks of the Shaolin Monastery on Mount Song who supported the founding family of the Tang dynasty during a crucial moment (Demiéville 2010 [1957]; Chen 2017: 218–219). Unlike some authors, we would not want to trace back the later martial arts tradition all the way to this Shaolin monastery, but when such traditions first appear fully into history in the 1550s they do self-identify as Buddhist monks using the epithet Shaolin and participate in the actual fighting against the sea pirates who were plaguing the coast of the Lower Yangzi region (Shahar 2008). We also encountered the lay Buddhist Qi Biaojia who tried to organize armed resistance against the invading forces of the Manchu-Qing dynasty in 1644.

The most famous example of a Buddhist counsellor who was intimately associated with a warlike dynasty and its campaigns is probably the learned Buddhist monk Fotudeng 佛圖澄 (fl. 310–348, perhaps from Kucha on the Silk Road). He became the close counselor and ritual specialist of one of the houses of Turkic descent that ruled northern China from the early 4th to late 6th centuries. His role as advisor also extended to military activities, and he converted the members of this family to Buddhism as well (Wright 1948). He left us the following statement expressing a Buddhist point of view on the notion of a "just war":

> Worship of the Buddha on the part of emperors and kings lies in their being reverent in their persons and obedient in their hearts and in glorifying the Three Treasures. [It lies in] not making cruel oppressions and not killing the innocent. As to the rogues and irresponsibles whom the civilizing influence does not reform, when they are guilty of a crime, they must be put to death, and if they are guilty of an evil deed, they must be punished. You should execute only those who should be executed and punish only those who should be punished. If, cruelly and willfully you put the

innocent to death, then, even if you should pour out your wealth and devote yourself to the Dharma, there will be no escaping a bad end. I wish that the emperor might eliminate desire and cultivate compassion. If [your compassion] is broad and all pervading, then Buddhism will long prosper, and your good fortune will be prolonged.

(Wright 1948: 352)

In a much more recent period, too, Buddhist monks in China were unable and possibly unwilling to remove themselves from the mainstream events of their times. In this case, they actively supported the Chinese side in the Korean War of 1950–1953 (Yu 2010).

A recurring topic in our sources is the miraculous protection of a military unit or local community, but even of the emperor himself, by the new anthropomorphic deities who became increasingly popular from the 11th century onwards. Stories about the divine protection of fighting forces of every kind were not limited to more obviously martial deities, such as Lord Guan (Davis 2001: 65–66, 75, etc.; ter Haar 2017). In 1206 the prefecture of Xinghua in modern Fujian sent soldiers to take part in the fight against the Jurchen enemy in the north. They carried with them the incense fire of their own female deity Mazu 媽祖. During the fight to relieve the encirclement of Hefei (modern Anhui), far away from home, she manifested herself in the air with flags and pennants, raising the spirits of the soldiers and leading them to victory (*Xianchun linan zhi* 73: 15b–16a for several miracles of military support). This would hardly be the last time that she came to the help of military forces. She also appeared to support the fleet of admiral Shi Lang 施琅 on behalf of the Manchu-Qing dynasty during their final conquest of Taiwan in 1683. This remarkable event has been included in a series of exquisite temple paintings preserved in the Dutch National Museum (Ruitenbeek 1999).

THE BURDEN OF WAR

Supporting Buddhist institutions also allowed the donor to buy merit as well as peace of mind by having rituals performed or making other kinds of donations. Take, for example, the powerful official Pei Du 裴度 (765–839) who successfully co-organized a major victory over an internal threat to his dynasty in 817, at the cost of innumerable deaths. Because he was a "believer in the teachings of the Buddha" (*xin futujiao* 信浮圖教), he was afraid that he might incur misfortune, so he decided to invest his considerable rewards in the restoration of a Buddhist monastery in the capital to collect merit in compensation (*Taiping guangji*, 244: 1889–1890). Much later, prominent military leaders were among the main patrons of Taixu's famous Sino-Tibetan Buddhist Institute in Sichuan in the 1930s (Tuttle 2005: 197–198, 227). It seems likely – but it would require further study – that such military support through the ages stemmed directly from the wish to collect merit to offset the bad karma created by killing.

After a war, there would be an abundance of corpses remaining on the battlefield. While the victorious survivors might take care of their own dead, the remains of the defeated were left on the battlefield or at best buried anonymously in a burial mound for display (Halperin 1999: 75–77). Leaving corpses without sacrifice was only meaningful because sacrifice upon burial was the norm and should not be seen as a secular act. Moreover, the dead who were not cared for still constituted a major threat to those alive, since they might come to haunt people (Yan 2017: 208–209ff). From the 3rd century CE onwards, generals killed in battle could even become the focus of regular worship in order to harness their surplus force of life to protect people against other demons or even human threats to life (Stein 1979: 65, 71). Lord Guan, already mentioned above, is just one example of such a cult, and there are many others (ter Haar 2017).

As Mark Halperin has shown, by the Sui dynasty (589–617), the first Buddhist rites for the war dead appear in our sources. Both the Sui founding emperor and the second emperor of the succeeding Tang dynasty (618–907) ordered Buddhist monasteries built on their main battlefields to pacify the ghosts of the deceased in battle. Succeeding Tang rulers do not seem to have continued this practice (Halperin 1999: 77–79). However, under the Song dynasty (960–1127–1276), Buddhist rituals to bury the war dead became standard practice. After the 1127 loss of the north, Buddhist ritual practices were used to not only pacify the dead, but already during the war itself to show the munificence of the ruler and hopefully increase the willingness of the soldiers to potentially give their lives for him and his dynasty (Halperin 1999: 79–95). The anecdotal literature of the 12th century contains plenty of stories illustrating how the ongoing war against the Jürchen invaders intersected with the supernatural world, resulting in ghostly appearances and even the odd ghost pretending falsely to be a war victim in order to receive sacrifices (*Yijianzhi*, yi 3: 205–206; yi 5: 224–225; yi 6: 235–236; yi 9: 259; yi 13: 290–292; *sanxin* 3: 1407–1408; *bu* 10: 1638).

As late as the Republican period, different socioreligious institutions such as Charity Halls or more outright religiously inspired groups such as the Red Swastika Society and others took it upon themselves to take care of the dead, including ritual services. The secular tradition of creating shrines to honor loyal martyrs for the Republican cause, and after 1949 by the communist state, was part of another trend to create quasi-secular rituals that in more ways than one were religious in all but name (Nedostup 2017). Throughout Chinese history, war and religious culture were intimately connected, even if the much more specific phenomena of holy wars to impose one's faith on the other were extremely rare.

References

Baling xianzhi 巴陵縣志 (1804).

Birrell, Anne. 1993. *Chinese Mythology: An Introduction*. Johns Hopkins University Press.

Butler, Marcia. 2007. "Reflections of a Military Medium: Ritual and Magic in Eleventh and Twelfth Century Chinese Military Manuals." PhD dissertation. Cornell University.

2008. "A Hidden Time, Hidden Space: Crossing Borders with Occult Ritual in the Song Military." In *Battlefronts Real and Imagined: War, Border, and Identity in the Chinese Middle Period*. Edited by Don J. Wyatt. Palgrave Macmillan. 111–149.

2016. "Mapping Culture: Battle Array Schemas (Zhentu) in Middle Period China." *Journal of Chinese Military History* 5(1): 37–78.

Cahill, Suzanne E. 1980. "Taoism at the Sung Court: The Heavenly Text Affair of 1008." *Bulletin of Sung-Yüan Studies* 16: 23–44.

Chen, Jinhua. 2017. "A 'Villain Monk' Brought Down by a Villein-General." In *Behaving Badly in Early and Medieval China*. Edited by N. Harry Rothschild and Leslie V. Wallace. University of Hawaʻi Press. 208–230.

Ching, Julia. 2004. "Confucianism and Weapons of Mass Destruction." In *Ethics and Weapons of Mass Destruction: Religious and Secular Perspectives*. Edited by Sohail H. Hashmi and Stephen P. Lee. Cambridge University Press. 246–269.

Cohen, Paul A. 1997. *History in Three Keys: The Boxers as Event, Experience, and Myth*. Columbia University Press.

Copp, Paul F. 2018. *The Body Incantatory: Spells and the Ritual Imagination in Medieval Chinese Buddhism*. Columbia University Press.

Davis, Edward. 2001. *Society and the Supernatural in Song China*. University of Hawaʻi Press.

Demiéville, Paul. 2010 [1957]. "Le bouddhisme et la guerre." Translated as "Buddhism and War." In *Buddhist Warfare*. Edited by Michael Jerryson and Mark Juergensmeyer. Oxford University Press. 17–57.

Dreyer, Edward L. 1982. *Early Ming China: A Political History, 1355–1435*. Stanford University Press.

Durrant, Stephen W. Li Wai-yee and David Schaberg. 2016. *Zuo Tradition = Zuozhuan: Commentary on the Spring and Autumn Annals*. University of Washington Press.

Esherick, Joseph. 1987. *The Origins of the Boxer Uprising.* University of California Press.

Fraser, Chris. 2016. "The Mozi and Just War Theory in Pre-Han Thought." *Journal of Chinese Military History* 5(2): 135–175.

Galvany, Albert. 2015. "Signs, Clues and Traces: Anticipation in Ancient Chinese Political and Military Texts." *Early China* 38: 151–193.

Graff, David A. 2002. *Medieval Chinese Warfare, 300–900.* Routledge.

*Gucheng xianzhi*故城縣志 (1727).

Halperin, Mark. 1999. "Buddhist Temples, the War Dead, and the Song Imperial Cult." *Asia Major Third Series* 12(2): 71–99.

Harper, Donald. 2017. "Daybooks in the Context of Manuscript Culture and Popular Culture Studies." In *Books of Fate and Popular Culture in Early China: The Daybook Manuscripts of the Warring States, Qin, and Han.* Edited by Donald Harper and Marc Kalinowski. Brill. 91–137.

Harper, Donald and Marc Kalinowski, eds. 2017. *Books of Fate and Popular Culture in Early China: The Daybook Manuscripts of the Warring States, Qin, and Han.* Brill.

Hashmi, Sohail H. and Steven P. Lee, eds. 2004. *Ethics and Weapons of Mass Destruction: Religious and Secular Perspectives.* Cambridge University Press.

Hejian fuzhi 河間府志 (1615).

*Hejian xinzhi*河間府新志 (1760).

Holm, David. 1994. "The Labyrinth of Lanterns: Taoism and Popular Religion in Northwest China." *Minjian xinyang yu zhongguo wenhua guoji yantaohui lunwenji*民間信仰與中國文化國際研討會論文集. 797–852.

Ivanhoe, Philip J. 2004. "'Heaven's Mandate' and the Concept of War in Early Confucianism." In *Ethics and Weapons of Mass Destruction: Religious and Secular Perspectives.* Edited by Sohail H. Hashmi and Steven P. Lee. Cambridge University Press. 270–276.

Jerryson, Michael and Mark Juergensmeyer, eds. 2010. *Buddhist Warfare.* Oxford University Press.

Jiankang zhi 建康志 (1260–1264). 1990. Reprinted in *Song Yuan fangzhi congkan* 宋元方志叢刊. Zhonghua shuju.

Johnston, Alastair Iain. 1995. *Cultural Realism: Strategic Culture and Grand Strategy in Chinese History.* Princeton University Press.

Kang, David. 2014. "Why Was There No Religious War in Premodern East Asia?" *European Journal of International Relations* 20(4): 965–986.

Katz, Paul R. 2009. "Banner Worship and Human Sacrifice in Chinese Military History." In *The Scholar's Mind: Essays in Honor of Frederick W. Mote.* Edited by Perry Link. The Chinese University Press. 207–227.

Keightley, David N. 2000. *The Ancestral Landscape: Time, Space, and Community in Late Shang China, ca. 1200–1045 B.C.* Institute of East Asian Studies, University of California.

Kern, Martin. 2009. "Bronze Inscriptions, the Shijing and the Shangshu: The Evolution of the Ancestral Sacrifice during the Western Zhou." In *Early Chinese Religion, Part One: Shang through Han (1250 BC–220 AD).* Edited by John Lagerwey and Marc Kalinowski. Brill. 143–200.

Kleeman, Terry F. 2016. *Celestial Masters: History and Ritual in Early Daoist Communities*. Harvard University Asia Center.

Kominami, Ichirô. 2009. "Rituals for the Earth." In *Early Chinese Religion, Part One: Shang through Han (1250 BC–220 AD)*. Edited by John Lagerwey and Marc Kalinowski. Brill. 201–234.

Lagerwey, John. 2010. *China: A Religious State*. Hong Kong University Press.

Lagerwey, John and Marc Kalinowski, eds. 2009. *Early Chinese Religion, Part One: Shang through Han (1250 BC–220 AD)*. Brill.

Lewis, Mark E. 2006. "The Just War in Early China." In *The Ethics of War in Asian Civilizations: A Comparative Perspective*. Edited by Torkel Brekke. Routledge. 185–200.

Licheng xianzhi 歷城縣志 (1628–1644).

Liji zhengyi. Li, Xueqin李學勤 / Gong, Kangyun 龔抗雲 / Lu, Guangming 盧光明, eds. 2000. *Shisan jing zhushu, zhengliben*十三經注疏, 整理本, *Liji zhengyi* 禮記正義. Beijing daxue chubanshe.

Loewe, Michael. 1994. "Divination by Shells, Bones and Stalks." In *Divination, Mythology and Monarchy in Han China*. Edited by Michael Loewe. Cambridge University Press. 160–190.

McMullen, David L. 1989. "The Cult of Ch'i T'ai-kung and T'ang Attitudes to the Military." *Tang Studies* 7: 59–103.

Meulenbeld, Mark R. E. 2015. *Demonic Warfare: Daoism, Territorial Networks, and the History of a Ming Novel*. University of Hawai`i Press.

MSL *Ming shilu* 明實錄 (Nangang: Zhongyang yanjiuyuan lishi yuyan yanjiusuo, 1966).

Nedostup, Rebecca. 2017. "Burying, Repatriating, and Leaving the Dead in Wartime and Postwar China and Taiwan, 1937–1955." *Journal of Chinese History* 1: 111–139.

Poo, Mu-chou (Pu, Muzhou). 1998. *In Search of Personal Welfare: A View of Ancient Chinese Religion*. State University of New York Press.

Puett, Michael. 2009. "Combining the Ghosts and Spirits, Centering the Realm: Mortuary Ritual and Political Organization in the Ritual Compendia of Early China." In *Early Chinese Religion, Part One: Shang through Han (1250 BC–220 AD)*. Edited by John Lagerwey and Marc Kalinowski. Brill. 695–720.

Qicheng 齊乘 (1339). Reprinted in *Song Yuan fangzhi congkan* 宋元方志叢刊. Zhonghua shuju, 1990.

Rom, Avital Hedva, 2020. "Beat the Drums or Break Them: Bells and Drums as Communication Devices in Early Chinese Warfare." *Journal of Chinese Military History* 9: 125–167.

Ruitenbeek, Klaas. 1999. "Mazu, the Patroness of Sailors, in Chinese Pictorial Art." *Artibus Asiae* 58(3/4): 281–329.

Sawyer, Ralph D. 2009. "Martial Prognostication." In *Military Culture in Imperial China*. Edited by Nicola Di Cosmo. Harvard University Press. 45–64.

Shahar, Meir. 2008. *The Shaolin Monastery: History, Religion, and the Chinese Martial Arts*. University of Hawai`i Press.

Shanhua xianzhi 善化縣志 (1877).

Shiji Sima, Qian 司馬遷 (fl. 100 BCE). *Shiji* 史記. Zhonghua shuju, 1973.

*Shizong zhupi Shizong xianhuangdi zhupi yuzhi*世宗憲皇帝硃批諭旨. *In Yingyin wenyuange siku quanshu*景印文淵閣四庫全書. Shangwu yinshuguan, 1986.

Shuofang xinzhi 朔方新志 (1617; reprinted ca. 1670).

Songhuiyao jigao Xu, Song 徐松 (1781–1848), *Songhuiyao jigao* 宋會要輯稿. Zhonghua shuju, 1957.

Songjiang fuzhi 松江府志 (1512).

Stein, Rolf. 1979. "Religious Taoism and Popular Religion from the Second to Seventh Centuries." In *Facets of Taoism: Essays in Chinese Religions*. Edited by H. Welch and A. Seidel. Yale University Press. 53–81.

Suishu Wei Zheng魏徵 (580–643) and others. 1973. *Suishu* 隋書. Zhonghua shu ju.

Taiping guangji Li, Fang李昉 (925–996), *Taiping guangji*太平廣記. Zhonghua shuju, 1961.

ter Haar, Barend J. 1992. *The White Lotus Teachings in Chinese Religious History*. E.J. Brill.

1998. *The Ritual and Mythology of the Chinese Triads: Creating an Identity*. E.J. Brill.

2006. *Telling Stories: Witchcraft and Scapegoating in Chinese History*. Brill.

2015. "The Sutra of the Five Lords: Manuscript and Oral Tradition." *Studies in Chinese Religions* 1(2): 172–197.

2017. *Guan Yu: The Religious Afterlife of a Failed Hero*. Oxford University Press.

2018. "Rumours and Prophecies: The Religious Background of the Late Yuan Rebellions." *Studies in Chinese Religions* 4(4): 382–418.

2019. *Religious Culture and Violence in Traditional China*. Cambridge University Press.

2020a. "Giving Believers Back Their Voice: Agency and Heresy in Late Imperial China." In *Text and Context in the Modern History of Chinese Religions: Redemptive Societies and Their Sacred Texts*. Edited by Philip Clart and David Ownby. Brill. 16–54.

2020b. "A Word for Violence: The Chinese Term *bao* 暴." *Journal of Religion and Violence* 8(3): 221–241.

2022. "Harmful Ancestors or Friendly Ghosts: Looking At Our Early Evidence on the Chinese Notion of gui 鬼." *Journal of Asian History* 55: 269–307.

Tuttle, Gray. 2005. *Tibetan Buddhists in the Making of Modern China*. Columbia University Press.

Waley-Cohen, Joanna. 2006. *The Culture of War in China: Empire and the Military under the Qing Dynasty*. I.B. Tauris.

Wilhelm, Hellmut, 1962. "From Myth to Myth: The Case of Yüeh Fei's Biography." In *Confucian Personalities*. Edited by A. F. Wright and Dennis C. Twitchett. Stanford University Press. 146–161.

Wright, Arthur Frederick. 1948. "Fo-t'u-têng: A Biography." *Harvard Journal of Asiatic Studies* 11(3/4): 321–371.

Wyatt, Don J. 2008. "In Pursuit of the Great Peace: Wang Dan and the Early Song Evasion of the 'Just War' Doctrine." In *Battlefronts Real and Imagined: War, Border, and Identity in the Chinese Middle Period*. Edited by Don Wyatt. Palgrave Macmillan. 75–109.

*Xianchun lin'an zhi*咸淳臨安志 (1275–1274). Reprinted in *Song Yuan fangzhi congkan* 宋元方志叢刊. Zhonghua shuju, 1990.

Xin Tangshu Ouyang, Xiu歐陽修 (1007–1072), *Xin Tangshu* 新唐書. Zhonghua shuju, 1975.

*Xingning xianzhi*興寧縣志 (1875).

Xu, Zhuoyun and Katheryn M. Linduff, 1988. *Western Chou Civilization*. Yale University Press.

*Xuanhua xianzhi*宣化縣志 (1736).

Yan, Changgui. 2017. "Daybooks and the Spirit World." In *Books of Fate and Popular Culture in Early China: The Daybook Manuscripts of the Warring States, Qin, and Han*. Edited by Donald Harper and Marc Kalinowski. Brill. 207–247.

Yates, Robin D. S. 2005. "The History of Military Divination in China." *East Asian Science, Technology, and Medicine (EASTM)* 24: 15–43.

2013. "Human Sacrifice and the Rituals of War in Early China." In *Sacrifices humains: Perspectives croisées et representations*. Edited by Pierre Bonnechere and Renaud Gagné. Presses universitaires de Liège. Consulted at http://books.openedition.org/pulg/8173.

Yijianzhi Hong Mai 洪邁. *Yijian zhi* 夷堅志. Zhonghua shuju, 1981.

Yu, Xue. 2010. "Buddhists in China during the Korean War (1951–1953)." In *Buddhist Warfare*. Edited by Michael Jerryson and Mark Juergensmeyer. Oxford University Press. 131–156.

Yucheng xianzhi 禹城縣志 (1808).

Yuxiang xianzhi 虞鄉縣志 (1880).

8 Buddhism and War in Premodern Japan

BRIAN A. VICTORIA

INTRODUCTION

One of the chief characteristics of religion in Japan has been, and remains, the syncretic fusion of deities and Buddhas. The "deities" referred to are, of course, the innumerable animistic deities associated with what is today called "Shinto" or the "Way of the Gods." First-time visitors to Japan often marvel at, or are surprised by, the Japanese people's ability to believe in/practice two faiths at the same time. From the standpoint of the exclusivist demands of the Abrahamic faiths this dual adherence seems incongruent at best and downright heretical at worst. But for today's Japanese it is as natural as going to a Shinto shrine to celebrate life's happy events, like marriages and births, or going to a Buddhist temple for somber events like funerals and ancestor memorial rites. However, today's "peaceful coexistence" between the two faiths was not always the case, especially at the time of Buddhism's formal introduction to Japan in the mid-6th century. It was then, for the first time, that conflict, leading to actual war, enveloped the two faiths. That is to say, by the time Buddhism was introduced to Japan, the belief in the multiple animistic deities of today's Shinto had already taken root. Thus the question was: Was there room for more, especially *foreign* deities? The Mononobe clan rejected the new deities, the Soga clan accepted them.

It is important to note that both clans struggling over the acceptance or rejection of the Buddha(s) agreed that they were *kami* (i.e., animistic deities with superhuman, magical powers and personalities). This agreement would eventually lead to the well-known Japanese expressions: *shinbutsu shūgō* (unification of *kami(s)* and Buddhas) and *shinbutsu ichinyo* (*kami(s)* and Buddhas are one). Thus, the struggle was not one between two separate religions, but, instead, whether or not foreign deities, of the same character as indigenous deities, were more powerful than indigenous deities. In other words, the critical question was whether the Buddhas' alleged magical powers were superior to those of indigenous deities.

Initially, it appeared the Buddhas were the losers. When a plague subsequently broke out after the court paid homage to a gilt-bronze Buddha statue, the Mononobe clan was quick to blame the worship of foreign deities, claiming that "the *kami* (Shinto deities) of our land will be offended if we worship foreign *kami*" (Tamura 2000: 26). This resulted in the Buddha image being unceremoniously dumped in the nearby Naniwa canal. However, when still later Soga no Umako (551?–626), a pro-Buddhist leader of the Soga clan, fell ill, Emperor Kimmei's successor, Emperor Bidatsu (r. 572–585), allowed the image to be restored in hopes of curing Umako's illness. It was not until 587, however, that the issue was finally settled thanks to Soga no Umako's military defeat of the Mononobe, a feat ascribed to the protection of Buddhist deities. Thus, Buddhism prevailed in Japan by feat of arms.

BUDDHISM TAKES ROOT

The Soga clan prevailed not simply because of their embrace of Buddhism but because of their equal willingness to embrace the powerful continental civilizations of Korea and China. These countries, Japanese leaders believed, could not have become as powerful as they were without the support of equally powerful deities. As Daigan and Alicia Matsunaga note, Buddhism was "merely regarded . . . as a possible superior form of magic long practiced by the advanced civilizations they respected and sought to emulate" (Matsunaga and Matsunaga 1974: 10). Thus, it is not surprising to learn that the first Japanese emperor to personally espouse Buddhism (i.e., Yōmei, r. 585–587), did so to enlist the aid of the Medicine Buddha, Yakushi (Skt. Bhaiṣajyaguru), in curing his grave illness.

This forms the background to what the distinguished Buddhist historian Anesaki Masaharu noted was one of the salient characteristics of Japanese Buddhism (i.e., its close identification with the state and its interests from the time it was first introduced). Anesaki wrote: "A close alliance was established between the throne and the [Buddhist] religion, since the consolidation of the nation under the sovereignty of the ruler was greatly supported by the fidelity of the imported religion to the government" (Anesaki 1963: 12). Initially at least, the various Buddhas were called upon to protect the state and its officers, including their health and longevity, through the conduct of appropriate rituals, including the recitation of both efficacious sutras and *mantras* (magical spells). However, as Charles Keyes noted, "violence justified by religion has probably existed since Buddhism first became a religion supported by state authorities" (Keyes 2016: 42).

To this day, miraculous cures remain attributed in Japan to various Buddhas, bodhisattvas and even certain spiritually empowered Buddhist clerics. However, there was one additional area in which the magical powers ascribed to one or another of the Buddhas introduced to Japan was even more important than curing illness: protection of the state. This is hardly surprising in that 6th-century Japan was still a confederation of clans only nominally under the control of the Yamato clan and its head, the emperor. Concretely, this magical power could be accessed through the adoption of three sutras – the *Golden Light Sutra* (Skt. Suvarṇaprabhāsottamasūtrendrarājaḥ), the *Sutra on the Benevolent King* (Ch. Rén Wáng Jīng) and the *Lotus Sutra* (Skt. Saddharma Puṇḍarīka Sutra). Elaborate ceremonial recitations of these sutras were held, and, as Tamura notes, "[m]ost of the temples were built to ensure the Buddhas' and Bodhisattvas' protection of the nation" (Tamura 2000: 40). The *Golden Light Sutra* teaches that the Four Heavenly Kings protect a ruler who governs his country in the proper manner. This sutra was highly esteemed for the protection it offered not only in Japan, but also in China and Korea, where it was publicly recited to ward off threats and disasters. In China it was first read at a court ceremony during the Tang dynasty (618–907) in around 660 and in Korea when the state of Silla defeated the state of Paekche in 663. When, in 741, Japanese Emperor Shōmu (r. 724–749) founded provincial monasteries for monks and nuns in each province, he designated them as "Temples for Protection of the State by the Four Heavenly Kings Golden Light Sutra" (J. and Ch. 金光明經四天王護国之寺). The twenty monks who lived in each of these temples recited the *Golden Light Sutra* on a regular basis in order to protect the country.

Following Buddhism's acceptance in Japan, many powerful clans also erected their own temples. As Miyata Koichi notes: "Each clan had autonomy and the right to govern their land and people directly. The heads of the clans could make some of their people become priests without restraint and make them dwell in their clan temples to pray for the clan's prosperity" (Miyata 2001: 124). Once again, Buddhas were invoked for the decidedly worldly benefits their worship would produce. It was not until 701 that the central government was powerful enough to bring all male and female clerics under its strict control, including permission to be ordained.

The *Sutra on the Benevolent King*, known as *Inwang-gyeong* in Korean and *Ninnō-gyō* in Japanese, is purported to be a translation from Sanskrit, though it is generally believed to be an apocryphal text, first composed in China. The *Sutra on the Benevolent King* is unusual because, unlike most sutras, its target audience is not *arhats* or bodhisattvas but the kings of sixteen ancient countries in India. Further, instead of expounding on the merits of meditation and wisdom, the virtues of benevolence and forbearance – standard Indian ideas – are promoted as the most important criteria for a ruler to possess in governing. In Japan, a ceremonial lecture on the *Sutra on the Benevolent King* was first held in court in 660. Stress was placed on a passage stating that when a foreign threat appears, 100 demons or gods will protect the king if he will make 100 images of the Buddha and invite 100 priests to lecture on it. Such protection was of no idle concern to the government at the time, given that the military alliance between the governments of the Chinese Tang dynasty and the Korean state of Silla had defeated Paikche, a second Korean state, and were threatening Japan. The ceremony was thus of critical importance to the emperor and his court.

As for the *Lotus Sutra*, it is without doubt the most famous and influential sutra in East Asian Buddhism, especially in Japan. As such, it is considered to bestow innumerable benefits on believers, including protection of the state. Rōben (689–773) was the first Buddhist priest to hold a ceremonial lecture on the *Lotus Sutra* in 749, something destined to become an annual event sponsored by the government. Included in the ceremony were prayers for the prosperity of the Imperial House and noble families, security of the state and a rich harvest, all of which were integral to the protection of the state. Additionally, the *Lotus Sutra* was chanted to ensure recovery from disease, and it was used in memorial services for deceased parents and ancestors. For example, as early as 726 Emperor Shōmu ordered additional copies of the *Lotus Sutra* be made in order to pray for the recovery of his aunt, the Retired Empress Genshō (r. 715–724). When she died in 748, Emperor Shōmu ordered 1,000 copies of the *Lotus Sutra* made as part of her memorial service.

Once again, it is important to remember that these developments were far from being uniquely Japanese. On the contrary, it was only a replication of the relationship between Buddhism and the state that already existed on the Korean peninsula. As S. Keel pointed out: "Buddhism [in Korea] was available as the politico-religious ideology which would serve the cause of building a powerful centralized state with a sacred royal authority .... [It] was understood primarily as the state-protecting religion, *hoguk pulgyo* [J. *gokoku Bukkyō*] not as the supramundane truth of salvation for individuals" (Keel 1978: 16–17). It should be noted, however, that state-protecting Buddhism was but an extension of its Chinese antecedent with roots reaching back as far as India and Emperor Ashoka of the 3rd century BCE. Needless to say, protection of the state was never more important than when the state's leaders found themselves under attack whether from either domestic or foreign opponents. Buddhism was the glue used to unite the ruler and his subjects as one.

In Japan, the Sangha's subservience to the state was codified in the so-called Seventeen Article Constitution, traditionally asserted to have been promulgated by Prince Regent Shōtoku in 604. On the one hand, in Article Two of the Constitution, Shōtoku called on his subjects to "faithfully respect the 'Three Treasures,' i.e., the Buddha, Dharma, and Sangha." In Article Three, however, Shōtoku went on to say:

> Respect the Imperial commands. The ruler is analogous to heaven, the subjects to the earth. The heaven covers the earth, and the earth supports heaven; if the four seasons pass smoothly, everything functions well. But if the earth tries to dominate heaven, it crumbles into powder. For this reason heaven commands and the earth receives, and for the same reason the ruler commands and the subjects obey. Therefore, every subject should respect the Imperial commands, if not there will be confusion.
>
> (Committee for the Celebration of the 70th Anniversary of the Introduction of Buddhism to America 1963: 231)

Although a number of distinctly separate Buddhist sects would eventually develop in Japan, the one thing they always agreed on is, as stated in Article Three: "The ruler commands and subjects obey." It may be argued that, given the fragile nature of Shōtoku's only recently unified central government, beset as it was by the ever-present danger of clan warfare, his emphasis on the supremacy of the ruler was necessary to the state's survival. In this context it may also be argued that Buddhism made a positive contribution to the subsequent development of Japanese civilization by providing the newly formed state with a highly moral unifying ideology that transcended the clan divisions (and clan deities) of Shōtoku's day. What cannot be disputed, however, is that it also set the stage for the historical subservience of Buddhism to the Japanese state.

BUDDHISM AND SHINTO

One of the earliest rulers to make use of the Buddha Dharma for political purposes is Emperor Shōmu, whose reign lasted from 724 to 748. He focused on the teachings of the *Avatamsaka Sutra*, particularly its doctrine of a central celestial or cosmic Buddha (i.e., *Mahāvairocana*) surrounded by an infinite number of bodhisattvas. *Mahāvairocana's* mind was believed to pervade all of reality and be present in all things, the latter being ranked in harmonious interdependence. With this imagery in mind, Emperor Shōmu built the giant central cathedral of Tōdai-ji in Nara and enshrined a sixteen-meter-high statue of *Mahāvairocana* (J. *Dainichi*). As Anesaki has described it, this cathedral "was to be a symbolic display of the Buddhist ideal of universal spiritual communion centered in the person of Buddha, parallel to the political unity of national life centered in the monarch" (Anesaki 1963: 231).

For all intents and purposes, devotion and loyalty to this Buddha became synonymous with the same virtues directed toward the person of the emperor and the state that he embodied. The use of *Mahāvairocana* had the added benefit that as a "celestial" or "Sun Buddha" there was also a symbolic link to the indigenous Shinto "Sun Goddess," Amaterasu Ōmikami, the mythical progenitor of the Imperial House. From the outset, and unlike the Abrahamic faiths, Buddhism in Japan did not attempt to eradicate indigenous Shinto deities. Instead, Buddhism *subordinated them* to itself, as seen in the Buddhist temples it built.

The origin of this practice can be traced to the Shinto deity Hachiman. Originally a god of war, Hachiman's roots can be traced to two semilegendary rulers: Empress Jingu and her son, Emperor Ōjin (r. 270–310?). Both of these figures were regarded as avatars of Hachiman due to their great feats in both warfare and culture – Jingu for her invasion of Korea and Ōjin for inviting Chinese and Korean scholars to Japan. Hachiman's first connection to Buddhism occurred in 747 when, as the chief deity of Usa Shrine on the southern island of Kyushu, he issued an oracle expressing his wish to travel to Tōdai-ji to pay homage to the Great Buddha. A shrine maiden transported Hachiman to Tōdai-ji, where he was installed as the temple's official protector. This subsequently led to various Shinto *kami* being incorporated as protectors of Buddhist temples throughout the country. This is why, even today, small Shinto shrines are located somewhere on the grounds of most Buddhist temples, for their role is to *protect* the temple from evil spirits.

It is noteworthy that Shinto *kami* were relegated to the role of protecting Buddhist temples, not the other way around. Their role as protectors was justified on the basis that, like all sentient beings, *kami* were suffering creatures seeking to escape their present condition and attain Enlightenment. Buddhist priests created a series of tales describing the desire of various *kami* to receive Buddhist teachings, thereby overcoming the negative karma that had caused them to remain as no more than unenlightened deities. Some *kami*, it was claimed, even expressed their desire to become Buddhists by taking refuge in the Three Treasures (i.e., Buddha, Dharma and Sangha). This is similar to animistic practices that exist alongside Buddhism in many Asian countries.

In the following centuries, Shinto clergy accepted, however unwillingly, what was essentially second-class status for themselves and their deities. This included Buddhist clergy being put in control of major Shinto shrines, as embodied in the construction of *jingu-ji* (shrine-temples), built with the encouragement of the government. At these shrine-temples, Buddhist priests recited Buddhist sutras for the sake of the *kami* who had, it was claimed, decided to protect the foreign faith in hopes of spiritual advancement. However, by relegating *kami* to second-class status, Buddhism lay the groundwork for its own suppression more than 1,000 years later.

In 937, Hachiman was officially declared a bodhisattva, the first of many *kami* to be given this status. In effect, Hachiman had completed his transition to a Buddhist deity, although Shintoists continued to view him as one of their own. This resulted in Buddhist monks being given the responsibility of interpreting Hachiman's oracular proclamations. Hachiman proved so popular that he was eventually elevated to the rank of *Great Bodhisattva* (J. *Daibosatsu*), with his duties expanded to become the guardian of all Tōdai-ji's subordinate temples in the provinces. Befitting his martial image, Hachiman's symbol was originally that of a bow and arrow, the ancient weapon of choice of Japan's warriors. In his Buddhist incarnation, however, Hachiman was depicted in the form of a Buddhist priest on both scrolls and statuary.

One of Japan's greatest religious leaders was Kūkai (aka Kōbō-Daishi, 774–835), founder of the esoteric Shingon (True Word/Mantra) school of Buddhism. In 816, Kūkai was searching for a suitable spot to establish a mountain retreat on Mount Kōya. Legend states that he came across a hunter whose two dogs, one black and one white, led him to a hidden valley. The hunter was considered to be the son of the Shinto goddess Niutsu-hime (i.e., Princess Niutsu), who readily granted him permission to build a monastery on her land. This event marked Kūkai's recognition of the existence of *kami* and led to the placement of shrines throughout the mountain. These shrines were serviced by Shingon sect priests, and the deities they enshrined were, like Hachiman at Tōdai-ji, believed to protect the monastic compound. This event also contributed to the creation of similar Shinto shrines on the grounds of other Buddhist temples throughout the country.

In the 11th century, the militarily powerful Minamoto clan selected Hachiman as its tutelary deity in order to claim descent from Emperor Ōjin. Minamoto Yorinobu (968–1048) made this claim in 1046, and his son, Yoriyoshi (988–1075), strengthened the family ties to Hachiman by crediting the deity for his victory over the Abe clan in 1062. When the Minamoto and Taira clans clashed in the Genpei (aka Gempei) War of 1180–1185, Minamoto Yoritomo (1147–1199), founder of the Kamakura Shōgunate, first put on ceremonial robes and bowed toward the Iwashimizu Hachiman shrine, requesting Hachiman's protection. Hachiman's greatest alleged triumph, however, occurred at the time Japan faced repeated Mongol invasions in the late 13th century. Hachiman was credited with responding to prayers for divine intervention by sending the *kamikaze* (lit. "*kami* wind") in the form of typhoons to destroy two Mongol invasion fleets sent by Kublai Khan in 1274 and 1281.

Given this background, it is not surprising that during the Asia-Pacific War of 1937–1945, Hachiman was once again called upon to protect Japan, this time from Allied invasion. In this instance, his protection took the form of the aptly named *kamikaze* suicidal (and ultimately futile) air attacks. With some 25,000 shrines dedicated to him, Hachiman remains a popular deity to this day, both as a Shinto god of war and a Buddhist bodhisattva.

KANNON AS A "GOD OF WAR"

If Shinto *kami* could become Buddhist bodhisattvas, it is perhaps not surprising that a bodhisattva could be turned into a *kami*, at least in function. This is exactly what happened to possibly the most popular bodhisattva in East Asia, *Kannon* (Skt. Avalokiteśvara). Inasmuch as *Kannon* is the Buddhist personification of compassion, this bodhisattva would appear to be the least likely of the pantheon of Mahāyāna bodhisattvas to play the role of Hachiman (i.e., a god of war). To some extent, this transformation in Japan was foreshadowed by what had already occurred in China. In Chinese art, *Kannon* (Ch. Guānyīn) is sometimes depicted flanked by two warriors. The two warriors are the historical General Guan Yu (d. 220) of the late Han dynasty (206 BCE–220 CE) and the warrior representation of bodhisattva Skanda.[1] With *Kannon* in the center, these three figures are understood to protect both the temple they are enshrined in as well as Buddhism itself.

It is also noteworthy that according to the *Lotus Sutra*, "[if] fearful in the midst of battle, you contemplate the power of Avalokiteśvara, all enemies will flee away" (Tsugunari and Yuyama 2007: 301–302). Thus, it is not surprising that, in Japan, *Kannon* was turned into a god of war by the Minamoto clan, specifically Minamoto Yoritomo. As noted above, Yoritomo initially prayed to Hachiman for his clan's protection at the time of the Genpei War. Nevertheless, in 1189, Yoritomo had a personal temple built that became known as the Hokke-dō (lit. "Lotus Sutra hall") after his death in 1199. The main object of worship chosen by Yoritomo was a six-centimeter silver statue of *Shō-Kannon* (lit. "holy/proper *Kannon*"). Given its small size, this statue is likely the same one Yoritomo always carried under his helmet, inserted in his hair topknot, during battle.[2] Due to the alleged unity of *kami* and deified Buddhas/bodhisattvas, Yoritomo was able to enjoy the protection of figures in both religions.

The argument can be made, as Buddhist scholar John Nelson does, that in Japan, if not all of East Asia, *Kannon* is no longer a specifically Buddhist deity. Nelson states:

> *Kannon* has been so widely dispersed in Japanese culture, like the air one breathes, she has become part of the social and cultural landscape in ways that transcend sectarian doctrine .... Perhaps we are limiting the possibilities by thinking of *Kannon* as a specifically Buddhist deity. Surely it makes as much sense in the context of the Japanese religious culture to see her role as similar to

---

[1] Skanda, also known as Wei Tuo in Chinese, is a Mahāyāna bodhisattva regarded as a devoted guardian of Buddhist monasteries who also guards the teachings of Buddhism. Skanda is depicted as a young man fully clad in the armor and headgear of a Chinese general, and he is usually leaning on a *vajra* staff. Skanda may have come from Hinduism as the war deity Kartikeya, who bears the title Skanda. Skanda might also be a manifestation of Vajrapani, a bodhisattva who bears some relation to Skanda because they both wield *vajras* as weapons, are both portrayed with flaming halos and are both heavenly protectors of Buddhism. Alternatively, Skanda may be connected through Vajrapani to Greco-Buddhism, as Skanda's image is reminiscent of the Heracles depiction of Vajrapani.

[2] See reference in the "Miraculous Japanese Legends About Kannon" section of Kannon Notebook, *Buddhist Statuary*, available online at www.onmarkproductions.com/html/kannon.shtml (last accessed August 15, 2018).

that of a Shinto *kami* – specific to the situations of any place and its people, and attentive to sincere petitions.

(Nelson 2002: 160–161)

Further supporting Nelson's argument is the fact that in Shinto art yet another form of *Kannon*, *Jūichimen Kannon* (Eleven-Headed *Kannon*, Skt. Ekadasamukha), is a common choice as the Buddhist counterpart (J. *honji-butsu*) of female Shinto deities. Indeed, *Jūichimen Kannon* is one of the two most common choices as the Buddhist counterpart to the Shinto Sun Goddess Amaterasu. As previously noted, the other common Buddhist identification of the Sun Goddess is *Dainichi/ Mahāvairocana* Buddha. This raises the question: Isn't the ready identification of Buddhas and bodhisattvas with animistic *kami* problematic? For example, when Buddhas and bodhisattvas become identified with gods of war, what happens to Buddhism's first ethical precept: not to take life? At the same time, as revealed in the *Lotus Sutra*, *Kannon*'s connection to war, at least as far as offering protection against enemies, is clear. This topic will be explored further below.

BUDDHAS AS GODS OF WAR

It was not only bodhisattvas who were capable of becoming gods of war. Buddhas, especially *Amida* (Skt. Amitābha), was also capable of playing this role. The great warlord and ultimate unifier of medieval Japan, Tokugawa Ieyasu (1543–1616), exemplifies this possibility. Ieyasu was a devoted follower of the Jōdo (Pure Land) sect, the chief object of veneration of which is *Amida* Buddha. Ieyasu had the Pure Land temple of Zōjōji relocated to Edo (present-day Tokyo) in 1598. Thereafter, Zōjōji became the family temple of the Tokugawa clan and the site of a grand cathedral.

One of the smaller forty-eight attached temples built on Zōjōji's spacious grounds was Ankokuden. The following description of this temple can be found on the English-language version of the temple's contemporary website:

> Enshrined in this building is the Black Image of *Amida* Buddha, which was deeply worshiped by Tokugawa Ieyasu. This wonder-working image is said to have repeatedly saved Ieyasu from dangers and enabled him to win battles. Since the Edo period [1603–1868], it has been widely revered as a Buddhist image which brings victory and wards off evils.[3]

---

[3] Available online at www.zojoji.or.jp/en (last accessed August 20, 2018).

However, whether by design or accident, it is not until one reads Zōjōji's explanation of this "Black Image" *in Japanese* that one learns the process by which it became black:

> Tokugawa Ieyasu deeply revered the statue of *Amida* Buddha said to be the work of Eshin Sozu (aka Genshin) [942–1017]. Ieyasu carried it to battlefield campsites where he prayed for victory. After Ieyasu's death, it was presented to Zōjōji where, during the Edo period, it was widely believed to be a miraculous Buddha ensuring luck at winning and eliminating misfortune. Its name *"Kurohonzon"* (lit. black principal image of worship) comes from having been darkened by incense smoke offered at campsites over many years and is also due to *Amida*'s willingness to accept in his own body the wrongdoings and misfortunes of others, thereby contributing to turning his body black. Tradition states it was Ieyasu who named the statue.[4]

Unlike Minamoto Yoritomo's miniature *Kannon*, the black statute of *Amida* Buddha was full-sized, being so large that it had to be transported to battlefield camps in a special case mounted on wheels. Further, it became black due to the smoke emanating from countless campfires, not just incense. However, the most surprising feature of the above description, whether in English or Japanese, is that the contemporary Zōjōji-affiliated priests who placed this description on the temple's website did not hesitate to claim that *Amida* Buddha not only saved Ieyasu from dangers but "enabled him to win battles." In making this claim they clearly support the idea that *Amida* is a god of war.

As for Ieyasu, while yet alive he expressed the wish to be deified after his death in order to protect his descendants from evil. Accordingly, he was posthumously deified with the name Tōshō Daigongen, the "Great Gongen, Light of the East." This signifies, as previously noted, that Ieyasu regarded himself as nothing less than a Buddha appearing on Earth in the shape of a *kami* to save sentient beings. In this we can see that the emperor was not the only one who justified his rule through claiming linkage to cosmic Buddhist figures.

No doubt some would argue that – the preceding reference notwithstanding – it is incorrect to label *Amida*, let alone Hachiman or *Kannon*, as gods of war. After all, the vast majority of prayers made to them are for *protection* in battle, not killing or victory. In reality, this is exactly

---

[4] Available online at www.zojoji.or.jp/info/history.html (last accessed August 20, 2018).

the nature of the prayer political leaders and military chaplains of every faith, past and present, make to their respective deities as the faithful go into battle. For example, in ending his speech in Afghanistan on July 6, 2016, US President Barack Obama called on God to "bless our troops and all who serve to protect us." Would it be accurate to claim that in asking for God's blessing (i.e., divine protection), Obama had changed the Judeo-Christian God into a god of war?

As difficult as this question may seem, the answer is clear if one but considers how to determine whether the deity in question answered prayers for protection. Namely, those warriors who are the beneficiaries of the deity's protection return safely from battle while the enemy, who has no such protection (or protection offered by an ineffective/false deity), are all killed. In ensuring this result, the deity whose protection is sought has effectively been turned into a god of war. In the case of Buddhism, it would appear inconceivable – in light of the first precept proscribing killing – that Buddhas and bodhisattvas could act to ensure the deaths of large if not vast numbers of combatants who inevitably die in warfare. Yet, it must be admitted that, *historically speaking*, Buddhists in not only Japan but throughout Asia have long called on the aid/protection of Buddhas and bodhisattvas as they have engaged the enemy who were not infrequently Buddhists themselves.

THE EMERGENCE OF WARRIOR-MONKS (*SŌHEI*)

While it is possible to debate the question of whether deities, Shinto or Buddhist, to whom one prays for *protection*, not victory, should be labeled as "gods of war," there can be no doubt about the aggressive and violent nature of one group of Buddhists: the *sōhei* (lit. monk-warriors, but better known as warrior-monks). As oxymoronic as this term may appear in light of the Buddhist precept of nonkilling, there are historical precedents in China for the appearance of such belligerent clerics in Japan. For example, the monks of the now famous Chan (Zen) Shaolin temple in northern China began engaging in combat as early as the beginning of the Tang dynasty. It was in 618 that Shaolin monks are recorded as having fought on behalf of Prince Li Shimin (598–649) against rebel general Wang Shichong (567–621). Following Wang's defeat, Li went on to become Emperor Taizong, the second ruler of the Tang dynasty.

Thereafter, Shaolin monks would fight in a series of encounters, typically in support of the emperor of the day. By the 1500s, the monks of Shaolin were well-known for their staff-fighting skills, and in 1511, seventy monks are said to have died fighting bandit armies. In one of the earliest recorded clashes between Chinese and Japanese, Shaolin monks were mobilized to fight between 1553 and 1555 in at least four battles against (mostly) Japanese pirates who repeatedly raided China's coastal areas. This is not to claim that warrior-monks were a widespread phenomenon in China, but neither were they unknown despite the Buddhist prohibition against killing.

In Japan, warrior-monks as a distinct group can be traced back to the Heian period (794–1185). The Heian period began in 794 when Japanese Emperor Kanmu decided to move the capital from Nara to Heian-kyō, today's Kyoto. But why, if Buddhism had been introduced to Japan in the mid-6th century, had it taken more than two centuries for warrior-monks to emerge? Or, phrased alternatively, what happened at the beginning of the Heian period that resulted in the emergence of warrior-monks?

To answer these questions, we need to return to the previous Nara period (710–994) and even earlier. As previously mentioned, there was an initial – and sometimes bloody – struggle over the acceptance of Buddhism. However, once its proponents were successful, Buddhism grew at a rapid pace. In 624, for example, there were still only forty-six temples in all of Japan, but by 692, their number had grown to 545, a tenfold increase in just seventy years. The majority of these temples were built to ensure that the nation enjoyed the protection of the Buddhas and bodhisattvas that they enshrined. However, a few clan temples, known as *uji-dera*, were also built to ensure the well-being of a particular clan and its ancestors. Aside from officiating at clan temples, the Buddhist clergy's major role was to recite sutras and hold grand ceremonies to protect the state and ensure its prosperity, including the maintenance of its unity under imperial control.

In return for protecting the state, Buddhist priests (aka monks) were rewarded with high social status as well as special privileges, including exemption from taxation. But there was a cost associated with their status and privileges, namely the entire Buddha Sangha came under the strict control of the state. For example, the Clerical Code (J. *Sōniryō*) of 624 consisted of twenty-seven articles, the violation of which was connected to penalties of varying severity, up to and including expulsion from the Sangha. The government appointed high-ranking priests to oversee this system, with the result that every aspect of the Buddhist clergy's lives was the subject to intense scrutiny.

On the one hand, Buddhists priests during the Nara period accepted government control without complaint, for, after all, they benefitted from the system. Yet, within the Mahāyāna sutras, there was clear opposition to this kind of interference in or control over the Sangha's affairs by secular authorities. For example, the *Brahmajāla Sūtra* (J. *Bonmōkyō*) expressly forbids the establishment of civil codes regulating the clergy. Moreover, members of the clergy are admonished not to associate with the nation's sovereign or high-ranking officials. Further still, the *Brahmajāla Sūtra* urged Buddhist clerics to propagate the teachings of the faith among the masses, including establishing places where the faith could be practiced. Yet, the Japanese state forbade clerics from conducting missionary work among the masses.

If this latter restriction seems strange, it must be remembered that Japan as a centralized state under imperial control was still relatively fragile. That is to say, the unity of the state remained under threat from the various competing and powerful clans surrounding the throne, each controlling specific geographical areas. Overcoming clan animosities and internecine strife had, in fact, been one of the chief reasons for adopting Buddhism in the first place, for unlike clan-affiliated Shinto *kami*, the universal nature of Buddhas and bodhisattvas offered a clan-transcending locus in the spiritual world, just as the emperor filled a similar function in the secular world. Thus, propagating the Buddhist teachings among the common people threatened the development of mass movements that, like the clans, might endanger the unity of the state.

Buddhism in the pre-Heian period, and despite its teachings to the contrary, effectively became an appendage of the state to serve its purposes. Thus, Buddhism having military power of its own, as symbolized by warrior-monks, was simply unthinkable. Yet, this did not mean that Nara-period monks were no more than governmental ritualists. The monks also undertook academic study of the faith whose teachings were eventually formalized into six schools of scholastic study.[5] Importantly, however, these schools were not mutually exclusive, nor were they competing "sects." Instead, the six schools constituted the curriculum of Buddhist scholarship. Thus, it was typical for priests to study the doctrines of more than one school. Sectarian differences, and associated sectarian *rivalry*, had yet to emerge. But this would change.

---

[5] For a brief introduction to these six schools, see, for example, Tamura (2000: 44–47).

CHANGES DURING THE HEIAN PERIOD (794–1185)

The Heian period consisted of much more than changing the location of the capital. To some extent it represented the desire of the emperor to distance himself from the ecclesiastical interference of powerful Buddhist clerics in Nara. True, these clerics had no military power of their own, but that did not prevent their involvement in backstage intrigues and attempts to seek political power. As Tamura Yoshiro noted:

> The activities of the [Nara] clergy were not always above reproach. Their main occupation was to offer prayers and services for the protection of the nation and the health of the sovereign. With this came the rewards of rank and power, and some priests exploited these in a way most unsuited to their vocation .... [They] became involved in factional infighting, and lost sight of their true duties as members of the clergy.
>
> (Tamura 2000: 61)

The situation was so serious that when Emperor Kammu (735–806) ordered the relocation of the capital to Kyoto, he made sure the Nara temples were left behind. He also issued more than thirty edicts between 783 and 805 that restricted the activities and power of the Nara prelates. However, this did not mean that the emperor was opposed to Buddhism per se, for once the move had been made, he patronized Buddhism even more strongly than in the past, building many new temples to protect the new capital. However, he was always careful to do so in a manner that opposed the vested interests of the Buddhist institutions purposely left behind in Nara. At the same time, Kammu sponsored the travels of the monks Saichō and Kūkai to China, from where they returned to found what were the first true independent sects of Buddhism in Japan: Saichō (767–822) founded the Tendai sect and Kūkai (774–835) founded the esoteric Shingon sect.

One of the positive developments that occurred as a result the creation of sectarian Buddhism was that, a year after Saichō's death in 822, the Tendai sect finally acquired the emperor's permission to establish its own ordination platform at Enryaku-ji temple on top of Mount Hiei overlooking Kyoto. This meant that the Tendai sect was completely independent from the control of Nara prelates who heretofore had the only platform on which new priests could be ordained. Even more importantly, it signified the independence of Buddhism from secular authority, for during his lifetime Saichō based his efforts to establish an additional ordination platform on those Buddhist sutras that asserted it was wrong for a nation's ruler to govern the Buddhist Sangha.

Like Saichō, Kūkai also gained imperial patronage for the creation of a monastic complex centered on Kongōbu-ji temple, on Mount Kōya, near present-day Nagoya. However, unlike Saichō, Kūkai remained on friendly terms with the Nara prelates and succeeded in building a major temple complex in Kyoto, Tōji, where esoteric rituals for the protection of the state were conducted at the request of the court. Despite their sectarian differences, Saichō and Kūkai initially enjoyed cordial relations, though they eventually had a falling out and, by the time of their deaths, were no longer on speaking terms. The subsequent rivalry between the two sects would, in the following centuries, also contribute to the formation of warrior-monks seeking to protect their sect from the depredations of its rival. In addition, as these two sects grew in numbers and in power, there were also intra-sect conflicts, not to mention conflicts between the sects and secular authorities, including the imperial court.

The monks left behind in Nara did not readily accept their loss of power and influence. In fact, the first armed conflict occurred in 949, when fifty-six monks from Nara's Tōdai-ji temple came to protest an appointment made by a Kyoto official. Throughout the 10th century, protests of this nature took place on an ever more frequent basis, often turning into brawls and leading to the deaths of some of the participants. A major turning point occurred in 970, when, following a dispute between Enryaku-ji on Mount Hiei and the major Shinto Yasaka Shrine in Kyoto, the former created the first standing army of warrior-monks. According to the Matsunagas' description of these warrior-monks, "[t]- hese did not represent the real monks of Mt. Hiei, but rather miscellaneous duties such as maintenance and cooking. They were not spiritually motivated and easily aroused to champion mundane causes, frequently acting as mercenaries" (Matsunaga and Matsunaga 1974: 168).

Inasmuch as the members of the standing army came from the lower ranks of what was still a highly aristocratic priesthood on Mount Hiei, it is possible that the warriors were not fully ordained "monks" at all, but rather lay commoners in the service of elite monks. Sugiyama Shigeki notes:

> To enlarge their armies, temples recruited men to the priesthood solely to train them in warfare. These recruits were often peasants who had abandoned their farms or were petty criminals. The *sōhei* (warrior-monks or soldier priests) were formidable and their military skills were like those of the samurai. The priesthood had traditionally been

a gentleman's profession, although many upper class *gakusō* (scholar-priests) readily joined in battle if the need arose.

(Sugiyama 1994: 58)

Furthermore, the standing army of these warrior-monks was definitely not a rogue body, for the army's actions were directed by leading clerics on the mountain. For example, in 970, the year of the army's founding, Ryōgen, then abbot of Enryaku-ji temple, issued twenty-six articles prescribing how the army was to conduct itself as well as its weaponry. It is also noteworthy that whenever the army employed violence, the warrior-monks claimed to be doing so in order to *protect* the Buddha Dharma, a standard trope employed by Buddhists throughout Asia. Once again, as incongruous as this claim may sound, in the Mahāyāna *Mahāparinirvāṇa Sūtra* the Buddha is recorded as having said, "[a] person who upholds the Wonderful Dharma should take the sword and staff and guard *bhiksus* (monks)" (Yamamoto 1973: 45).

The need for monk armies became even greater as the Tendai sect grew in numbers and in power, for internecine conflict gradually engulfed the sect as it split into numerous subsects. This was because the Tendai sect, near to the capital as it was, enjoyed the patronage of successive emperors, aristocrats and government officials, all of which led to the establishment of new and larger temples scattered across Mount Hiei as well as branch temples in the capital itself. The struggle to be named abbot, especially of those temples with rich and powerful patrons, became a source of unending intrigue and conflict. It also led to increasing moral laxness and self-indulgence on the part of the clergy.

The result was that, by 981, a number of armed conflicts erupted between, for example, Enryaku-ji and Onjō-ji, popularly known as Mii-dera. Onjō-ji had originally been the clan temple of the powerful Ōtomo family, but it grew in importance until it became a Tendai subsect. These conflicts typically occurred when a priestly member of one subsect was chosen as the abbot of the other subsect's temple, causing the offended monks to protest. These conflicts continued, intermittently, throughout the 11th and well into the 12th centuries. During this period, the armies fielded by each subsect grew ever larger, with a concurrent increase in violence, until in 1121 and again in 1141 Onjō-ji was burned to the ground by warrior-monks from Enryaku-ji. Nevertheless, there were times when the two subsects united against a common enemy, including an attack on the Fujiwara's powerful clan temple of Kōfuku-ji in Nara in 1081. This attack was a retaliation for the warrior-monks of Kōfuku-ji who had destroyed the Mii-dera earlier in the same year.

In light of this background, it is not surprising that ex-Emperor
Shirakawa (1053–1129) is recorded as having lamented, while looking
out of his palace during an incursion by warrior-monks, "[t]hough I am
ruler of Japan, there are three things which are beyond my control: the
rapids of [Kyoto's] Kamo River, the fall of the dice at gambling, and the
[warrior-]monks of the [Hiei] mountain" (Sugiyama 1994: 59). If the
emperor's words are a commentary on the strength of Enryaku-ji's
warrior-monks, they also testify to the growing weakness of emperors
in the 12th century. Things had to change.

TRUE WARRIORS: THE SAMURAI TAKE CONTROL

In 1185, the growing samurai class seized the opportunity to take political control of the country, though they were careful to leave the emperor
as a figurehead in Kyoto so as to rule in his name. Ensconced in
Kamakura from 1192 onwards, the samurai's assumption of power did
not bring peace to Japan but, instead, a series of internecine wars, no
longer between competing Buddhist temples and sects but between competing warrior clans. However, the warrior-monk armies, now relegated
to the sidelines, did not disappear but were forced to choose sides even
prior to the emergence of the Kamakura period (1185–1333), for it was the
Genpei War of 1180–1185 that had led to the formation of the samurai
government in Kamakura. The Genpei War took place between two
powerful military clans, the Taira and Minamoto, both of which sought
the aid of the warrior-monk armies now found attached to temples in
both Nara and Kyoto. This time, however, warrior-monks were incorporated into one or another of the clans' already substantial samurai armies.

For example, in order to ensure that Enryaku-ji would not support
the Minamoto, Taira no Kiyomori (1118–1181) made them generous
gifts of rice and silk. The warrior-monks of Mii-dera, on the other hand,
chose to ally themselves with the Minamoto. In 1180, a major battle
took place between the two clans at the Uji River, located halfway
between Kyoto and Nara. The warrior-monks of Mii-dera were part of
a retreating force of about 1,500 Minamoto samurai who crossed over a
key bridge on the Uji River. In order to prevent the Minamoto's horse-
mounted samurai from pursuing them, the warrior-monks tore up the
bridge's planks behind them. The Taira force, however, found a place to
ford the river and soon caught up with the Minamoto. Although the
warrior-monks were well armed with bows and arrows, swords, daggers
and *naginata* (a long pole with a sharp blade at the tip), they were
ultimately defeated. Thereafter, Taira no Kiyomori took revenge by

ordering Mii-dera burned down yet again, as were a number of allied temples in Nara. Enryaku-ji, however, was spared.

As this incident, among many others, demonstrates, choosing the winning side was not only a matter of life and death for the warrior-monks involved, but their entire temple complex might be destroyed if their side lost. Things became even more complicated when there were internal struggles within clans over who was in control. An early example was the struggle between Minamoto no Yoshinaka (1154–1184) and his cousin, Minamoto on Yoritomo (1147–1199). Although nominally allied in their fight against the Taira, both men aspired to become clan leader, ultimately resulting in Yoshinaka's death at the hands of forces loyal to Yoritomo. During the lengthy struggle between the two, many of the warrior-monks in Kyoto, including those on Mount Hiei, aligned themselves with Yoritomo. This time, Kyoto's warrior-monks made the right choice, for not only did Yoritomo vanquish his rival, but he defeated the Taira in 1185. It was then that Yoritomo established the first samurai government (i.e., shōgunate) in Kamakura.

In the aftermath of the Genpei War, the major temples focused on rebuilding their temple complexes and restoring their political influence. Since the temples were successful in restoring their political influence without resort to violence, the warrior-monks played only very minor roles in the wars of the 13th and 14th centuries. Nevertheless, on occasion, violent conflict still broke out between temples or between a temple and the government due to decisions impacting the power and prestige of the temple or temples in question.

Things became more complicated when a split occurred within the imperial family itself in the 14th century. Known as the Nanboku-chō (Southern and Northern Court) period (1336–1392), two men, Go-Daigo and Kōgon, each with their samurai backers, claimed to be the legitimate emperor of Japan. During the struggle between the two factions, the warrior-monks on Mount Hiei took the side of Go-Daigo and offered protection to both him and his son. This protection, however, was ultimately to no avail, for in 1392 the Northern Court emerged victorious and the Southern Court disappeared.

ZEN'S EMERGENCE IN THE 13TH–14TH CENTURIES

Although the Northern Court and its successive emperors emerged the victors, in reality the emperors of that era had little real independence. They were controlled by the shōguns of the Ashikaga family, who, in 1336, moved the military capital back to Kyoto from Kamakura in order to ensure that the emperors followed their dictates. Like the earlier shōguns in Kamakura, the Ashikaga shōguns aligned themselves with the Zen sect that had been introduced to Japan in 1195. Needless to say, the Zen sect was regarded as an unwelcome competitor by the warrior-monks of Mount Hiei, as well as by those of other Tendai subsects. Thus, especially between the 1340s and 1360s, conflicts broke out between the Tendai warrior-monks and the Zen temples then being rapidly constructed in the capital with samurai backing. In 1367, for example, what began as a verbal dispute between the monks of Mii-dera and those of the major Rinzai Zen monastery of Nanzen-ji in Kyoto escalated two years later to the point that the warrior-monks of Mount Hiei attacked Nanzen-ji, destroying its massive main entrance gate.

Despite relatively isolated attacks on Zen temples like Nanzen-ji, on the whole Zen temples had no need to maintain their own armies of warrior-monks since their prestige and properties were protected by their samurai patrons. This does not mean, however, that Zen was not involved in violence, if only indirectly – "indirectly" because it was Zen priests who provided a number of valuable commodities to the samurai. One of the most important of these commodities was the samurai's ability, through the practice of meditation (i.e., zazen), to acquire a spiritual power called samādhi (J. zenjō), a highly concentrated state of mind. D. T. Suzuki quotes a samurai warlord by the name of Uesugi Kenshin (1530–1578) explaining the importance of samādhi:

> Those who cling to life die, and those who defy death live. The essential thing is the mind. Look into this mind and firmly take hold of it and you will understand that there is something in you which is above birth-and-death and which is neither drowned in water nor burned in fire. I have myself gained an insight into this Samadhi and know what I am telling you. Those who are reluctant to give up their lives and embrace death are not true warriors.
>
> (Suzuki 1938: 56)

In addition to acquiring the ability to "embrace death," Suzuki informs us of a second valuable commodity the samurai received from their Zen practice:

> Zen did not necessarily argue with them about immortality of soul [sic], or about righteousness of the divine way, or about ethical conduct, but it simply urged to go ahead with whatever conclusion rational or irrational a man has arrived at. Philosophy may safely be left with intellectual minds; Zen wants to act, and the most effective act is, once the mind is made up, to go on without

looking backward. In this respect, Zen is indeed the religion of the samurai warrior.

(Suzuki 1938: 64)

Although much more could be said about the importance of Zen to its samurai patrons, it can readily be seen from these two quotations that the spiritual power of *samādhi*, bestowing a fearless attitude on the battlefield, would have been of great value to the samurai, especially when coupled with freedom from any ethical concern for the killing they engaged in. However, once again, in light of the first Buddhist precept not to take life, whether this is the teaching of Buddhism's founder is, to say the least, debatable.[6]

CIVIL WAR (J. *SENGOKU-JIDAI*)

Like their aristocratic predecessors, the samurai class was plagued by conflicts surrounding the selection of the successor to ruling shōguns. Ideally, the successor would be the eldest son of the retiring shogun, but this was not always possible. For example, when, in 1467, Shōgun Ashikaga Yoshimasa had no heir, a struggle ensued that resulted in a full ten years of strife known as the Ōnin War (1467–1477). Kyoto was completely devastated, and without a power center, feudal lords throughout Japan contended with one another, singly or in ever-shifting alliances, to become the next shōgun. The end result was more than a century of continuous civil war. Surrounded by contending feudal lords, warrior-monks could no longer remain uninvolved in the ensuing secular power struggles, even had they wished to.

Initially, at least, the early years of the civil war period provided an opportunity for the warrior-monks of Enryaku-ji to regain their military strength. However, they decided to employ their restored strength to fight against yet another new sect in Kyoto, Nichiren-shū, created by the charismatic Japanese monk Nichiren (1222–1282). In this endeavor they were successful, at least in Kyoto, and they succeeded in burning down all of the city's Nichiren temples. However, in order to accomplish this, it had been necessary to ally themselves with the heads of the Azai (aka Asai) and Asakura clans. Unfortunately for them, both of these clans were the enemies of Oda Nobunaga (1534–1582), the first of three great warlords who successfully fought to reunify the country.

Inasmuch as they were allied with his enemies, Enryaku-ji's warrior-monks became Oda's enemies as well. Beginning on September 29, 1571,

---

[6] For my position on this question, see Victoria (2006a).

Nobunaga's army of 30,000 attacked Mount Hiei, burning some 300 buildings on the mountain to the ground, including all of Enryaku-ji on the mountaintop, and massacring an estimated 20,000 men, women and children (Turnbull 2003: 20). Enryaku-ji would soon be rebuilt, but on a smaller scale. One consequence was that it never again maintained a standing army of warrior-monks.

Even today, Enryaku-ji continues to commemorate all of those killed by Nobunaga's troops. Yet, at the same time, it has expressed regret or remorse for having employed warrior-monks in order to acquire additional lands, eliminate sectarian rivals or protest a perceived or real injustice against their temples on the part of a rival temple or the government. To do so would entail admitting that it once severely transgressed the spirit on nonattachment so fundamental to Buddhist teachings, let alone the precept proscribing killing. Given this, it is not surprising that Tendai sect leaders unreservedly supported Japanese imperialism in the modern era as the latter struggled to dominate not just Japan but Asia as a whole.

OTHER BUDDHIST FIGHTERS

In addition to traditional warrior-monks, a new type of Buddhist fighters formed in the countryside during the civil war era. Their movement became known as the *Ikkō-ikki*, and participants identified themselves with the Jōdo Shinshū (True Pure Land) sect. They are labeled here as "Buddhist fighters" instead of warrior-monks because their membership came from a wide swath of society, including lay-oriented priests unique to the True Pure Land sect as well as mostly low-ranking samurai, farmers and their families, all of whom fought to realize their religious, social and political ideals. The banners under which they fought bear witness to their religious motivations, such as "I take refuge in Amida Buddha" (J. *Namu Amida Butsu*) and "He who advances is sure of salvation [in the Pure Land of Amida Buddha], but he who retreats will go to hell" (Turnbull 2003: 42). In this, their struggles were significantly different from those of traditional warrior-monks, who, as we have seen, typically fought partisan struggles on behalf of their sect, chiefly but not exclusively the Tendai sect.

The movement's title is a combination of two words, *ikkō* and *ikki*. *Ikkō* may be translated as "single-minded" and was the designation, although originally mistakenly, used by outsiders to refer to the True Pure Land sect. *Ikki* refers to any type of uprising, of which there have been many in Japanese history, typically carried out by the oppressed peasantry.[7] However, a new form of uprising occurred at the end of the internecine Ōnin War in Kyoto in 1477. Taking advantage of the power vacuum accompanying the spread of civil war to the entire country, these uprisings were composed of a series of religion-based disparate and disorganized uprisings loosely based on the teachings of Rennyo (1415–1499), the eighth head of the True Pure Land sect. Rennyo had earlier been driven out of Kyoto into the countryside by the warrior-monks of Mount Hiei in 1465. After establishing a new branch temple of his sect in Echizen Province in 1471, Rennyo attracted a significant following among the peasantry and low-level samurai, who were attracted by the religious belief in the equality of all those held in Amida Buddha's embrace. Although Rennyo instructed his followers to obey established authority as a condition for good standing within the sect, he was ignored, and the first major organized uprising of the *Ikkō-ikki* began in 1473. By 1488, the uprising had succeeded, and for the next ninety-three years the uprising's leaders took administrative control of Kaga Province, the south and western portion of today's Ishikawa Prefecture on the Sea of Japan's coast. This marked a unique chapter in Japanese history, for it was the first time that a group of commoners had ruled an entire province.

The resistance to Rennyo, the acknowledged leader of the sect, raises the interesting question of what role True Pure Land Buddhist faith actually played in the uprisings. Was it marginal? One scholar, Michael Solomon, argues that it was not. He states:

> The doctrine that salvation is assured through faith in Amida and that all other practices are "extraneous" could provide not only the self-confidence but also the rationale for resistance to established authority and established religion, which served as its ideological buttress. Shinshū [True Pure Land] teaching, in other words, appealed to the spirit of resistance and rebellion that was widespread during much of the fifteenth century and into the sixteenth.
>
> (Solomon 1978: 64)

It is also notable that, at the time, Rengo, one of Rennyo's sons, facing the possible extermination of the sect's adherents in the Etchū and Noto districts, declared: "Out of gratitude for Amida's incomparable grace, is it not the fulfillment of our heart's desire to rush to battle and smilingly

---

[7] Sugiyama argues that *ikki* originally meant an association of persons for joint action – in other words, a "league." By extension, it came to describe the *activity* of a league and, in modern Japanese, a revolt or uprising. See Sugiyama (1994: 57).

sacrifice our lives?" (Solomon 1978: 62). By the time Rengo had uttered these words, his father, Rennyo, had died, but it was Rengo's words that would hold sway in the True Pure Land sect down to the modern era, being valid for both clerics and laity. Thus, a leading scholar-priest of that sect, Ōsuga Shūdō, wrote in 1905: "Reciting the name of Amida Buddha makes it possible to march onto the battlefield firm in the belief that death will bring rebirth in paradise . . .. Truly, what could be more fortunate than knowing that, should you die, a welcome awaits in the Pure Land [of Amida Buddha]?" (Victoria 2006b: 31–35).

Returning to Kaga, the *Ikkō-ikki* fought and won a number of battles that allowed them to establish powerful bases in three additional areas, including Nagashima and Ishiyama Hongan-ji temple in today's Osaka. Their success, however, led to their undoing, for when warlord Oda Nobunaga and his then subordinate, Tokugawa Ieyasu (1543–1616), launched their fight to reunite Japan, they recognized the threat that the *Ikkō-ikki* posed to their efforts. They also understood that it was their religious conviction – together with their strength and numbers – that made the *Ikkō-ikki* formidable enemies. In 1564, Tokugawa Ieyasu attacked a contingent of the *Ikkō-ikki* in Mikawa, but he failed to defeat them. He then recruited warrior-monks from his own Buddhist sect, the Jōdo-shū (Pure Land) sect, and renewed the attack. This time he was successful, and following their defeat, he burned all of the enemy temples to the ground.

Oda Nobunaga first attacked the *Ikkō-ikki* in their fortress-like temple compounds at both Nagashima and Ishiyama Hongan-ji. After initial failures in 1571 and 1573, and with the aid of naval forces commanded by Kuki Yoshitaka, Nobunaga's forces successfully blockaded the *Ikkō-ikki's* fortress at Nagashima in the summer of 1574, cutting off their food, water and other supplies. A large wooden palisade was constructed and set aflame, resulting in the complete destruction of the entire fortress complex, including its 20,000 defenders and their families. Nobunaga then turned his attention back to Ishiyama Hongan-ji, which he had first attacked in 1570, though unsuccessfully. Unable to breach its defenses, Oda placed the fortress under siege for a full ten years until he finally succeeded in wearing the defenders down to the point that they surrendered in August 1580.

There were, of course, other traditional warrior-monk armies associated with one or another major temple or sect, including both the Nichiren and esoteric Shingon sects. In the 1580s and 1590s, various factions of warrior-monks sided with one or more of the contending warlords, fighting in a number of battles and skirmishes. However,

Tokugawa Ieyasu ultimately emerged as the preeminent warlord of the day, defeating an alliance of feudal lords opposed to his rule at the Battle of Sekigahara in 1600. This left him in control of the entire country, and in 1603 he was appointed shōgun. Affiliated with the Pure Land sect as he was, Tokugawa was not opposed to Buddhism per se, but he would not countenance any other competing military force in the land, secular or religious. Thus, the era of warrior-monks, fighting Buddhists et al. finally came to an end.

CONCLUSION

The samurai government initiated by Tokugawa Ieyasu (i.e., the Tokugawa Shōgunate) lasted for more than two and a half centuries, ending with the return of political power to Emperor Meiji in 1868 (i.e., the Meiji Restoration). During the Tokugawa period, all Buddhist sects had been placed in an organizational straitjacket. On the one hand, temple financial support was assured by forcing all Japanese families to register with and support a Buddhist temple in their area. On the other hand, independent Buddhist temples were forbidden, with every temple forced to occupy a place within the pyramidal scheme of a major sect, stifling any action that might challenge the status quo. Thus, during the Tokugawa era, any form of resistance, especially military resistance, to the samurai government was impossible. Instead, with at least one temple located in every village, temples were turned into organs of the state at the local level, employed, among other things, to ensure the eradication of Christianity that had been introduced to Japan in 1549. By this time, it was recognized that Christianity served the interests of Western colonial powers.

Readers will not be surprised to learn that in the succeeding Meiji period (1868–1912) Buddhism, as well as Shinto, continued to support the state as it modernized and turned into the "Great Empire of Japan" (J. *Dai-Nihon Teikoku*), fighting numerous aggressive wars to enlarge and strengthen its empire. As for Buddhism, its role as a servant of the state, in one configuration or another, had been decided from the moment of its introduction in the mid-6th century. Although it is true that Buddhism was, for the first time in its history in Japan, suppressed by Shinto-inspired nationalists in the early years of the Meiji period, this suppression was short-lived and only served to reinforce Buddhism's increasingly slavish if not fanatical support of the state's imperial expansion. Interested readers may wish to look at three books that have been written on this topic (Victoria 2003, 2006b, 2020).

Needless to say, the story of Buddhism and war in premodern Japan is but one facet of Buddhism's multifaceted history in Japan. There are also many positive and inspiring stories to be told, something this author readily recognizes and whose own spiritual life has richly benefitted from. Sadly, the religions found in *all* countries have their "dark sides." It is only when these dark sides are honestly admitted and confronted that there can be hope of a brighter, less violent future. It is with this hope that this introduction to the premodern history of Buddhism and war in Japan has been written.

References

Anesaki, M. 1963. *History of Japanese Religion.* Tuttle.

Committee for the Celebration of the 70th Anniversary of the Introduction of Buddhism to America, ed. 1963. *The Teaching of the Buddha.* Tokyo Buddhist Center.

Keel, H. D. 1978. "Buddhism and Political Power in Korean History." *Journal of the International Association of Buddhist Studies* 1: 9–24.

Keyes, C. 2016. "Theravada Buddhism and Buddhist Nationalism: Sri Lanka, Myanmar, Cambodia, and Thailand." *Review of Faith and International Affairs* 14(4): 42–52.

Kubo, T. and A. Yuyama. 2007. *Lotus Sutra: Taishō 9, 262.* Translated from the Chinese of Kumārajiva. Bukkyō Dendō Kyōkai.

Matsunaga, D. and A. Matsunaga. 1974. *Foundation of Japanese Buddhism,* Vol. I. Buddhist Books International.

Miyata, K. 2001. "The Acceptance and Impact of the Lotus Sutra in Japan." *Journal of Oriental Studies* 11: 123–140.

Nelson, J. 2002. "From Battlefield to Atomic Bomb to the Pure Land of Paradise: Employing the Bodhisattva of Compassion to Calm Japan's Spirits of the Dead." *Journal of Contemporary Religion* 17(2): 149–164.

Solomon, M. 1978. "The Dilemma of Religious Power: Honganji and Hosokawa Masamoto." *Monumenta Nipponica* 33(1): 51–65.

Sugiyama, S. 1994. "Honganji in the Muromachi-Sengoku Period: Taking Up the Sword and its Consequences." *Pacific World Journal,* 10: 56–74.

Suzuki, D. T. 1938. *Zen Buddhism and Its Influence on Japanese Culture.* The Eastern Buddhist Society.

Tamura, Y. 2000. *Japanese Buddhism: A Cultural History.* Kosei Publishing.

Turnbull, S. 2003. *Japanese Warrior Monks AD 949–1603.* Osprey Publishing.

Victoria, B. 2003. *Zen War Stories.* RoutledgeCurzon.

   2006a. "Was It Buddhism?" In *Zen at War,* 2nd edition. Rowman & Littlefield. 192–231.

   2006b. *Zen at War,* 2nd edition. Rowman & Littlefield.

   2020. *Zen Terror in Prewar Japan: Portrait of an Assassin.* Rowman & Littlefield.

Yamamoto, K. 1973. *The Mahayana Mahaparinirvana Sutra.* Revised and edited by Tony Page. 2007. Available online at https://webzoom.freewebs.com/nirvana-sutra/convenient/Mahaparinirvana_Sutra_Yamamoto_Page_2007.pdf.

Part II

Just War

9 Judaism and the Ethics of War

REUVEN KIMELMAN

TYPES OF WARS

The Jewish ethics of war focuses on two issues: its legitimation and its conduct.[1] The Talmud classifies wars according to their source of legitimation. Biblically mandated wars are termed mandatory. Wars undertaken at the discretion of the Sanhedrin are termed discretionary.[2]

> There are three types of mandatory wars: Joshua's war of conquest against the seven Canaanite nations, the war against Amalek, and defensive wars against an already launched attack. Discretionary wars are usually expansionary efforts undertaken to enhance the political prestige of the government or to secure economic gain.[3]

The first type of mandatory war is only of historical interest as the Canaanite nations had already lost their national identity in ancient times. This ruling, which appears repeatedly in the Rabbinic literature[4] and is codified by Maimonides,[5] is part of a tendency to blunt the impact of the seven-nations policy. The Bible[6] points out that these policies were not implemented even during the zenith of ancient Israel's power. Indeed, the Midrash (i.e., classical Rabbinic exposition of the Bible) explicitly excludes the possibility of transferring the seven-

---

[1] For a recent survey of texts, commentary, and application, see Kimelman 1992: 233–255; Afterman and Afterman 2014: 8–75. The classical sources are all available in the original Hebrew with English translation at www.sefaria.org/texts.

[2] *Lekah Tov* to Deuteronomy, ed. S. Buber, 35a. Leviticus Rabbah 1,4 draws the distinction between David's wars "for Israel" and those "for himself." See Rashi to B. (= Babylonian Talmud) Gittin 8b and 47a, s.v. "*kibush yahid,*" and B. Avodah Zarah 20b, end.

[3] B. Berakhot 3b, Sanhedrin 16a, and Maimonides, *Mishneh Torah,* "Laws of Kings and their Wars," 5:1 (subsequently, "Laws of Kings").

[4] J. (= Jerusalem Talmud) Sotah 9:10, 23a, B. Berakhot 3b, Sotah 44b, Sanhedrin 16a, "Laws of Kings" 5:1; see Albeck 1958: 390f.

[5] "Laws of Kings," 5:4, ibid., *Sefer Mitsvot, Mitsvah* 187.

[6] 1 Kings 9:20f; 2 Chronicles 8:7–9.

nations ruling to other non-Jewish residents of the Land of Israel.[7] Limiting the jurisdiction of the seven-nations ruling to the conditions of ancient Canaan vitiated it as a precedent for contemporary practice.

The second category of mandatory war against Amalek has also been rendered operationally defunct by comparing them with the Canaanites, by postponing the battle to the immediate premessianic struggle, or by viewing them as a metaphor for genocidal evil.[8] In any case, according to 1 Chronicles 4:33, they were already eliminated in biblical times.

The two remaining categories – reactive defensive wars (which are classified as mandatory) and expansionary wars (which are classified as discretionary) – remain intact. So, for example, King David's response to the Philistine attack is termed mandatory, whereas his wars "to expand the border of Israel" are termed discretionary.[9] Intermediate wars such as preventive, anticipatory, or preemptive wars defy neat classification. The classifications are debated in the Talmud[10] and in classical commentary.[11]

The major clash occurs between the 11th-century Franco-German scholar Rashi and the 13th-century Franco-Provencal scholar Meiri. According to Rashi, the majority position considers preemptive action to be discretionary, whereas the minority position of Rabbi Judah considers it to be mandatory.

According to Meiri,[12] a preemptive strike against an enemy who it is feared might attack or who is already known to be preparing for war is deemed mandatory by the majority of the rabbis but discretionary by Rabbi Judah. Accordingly, Rabbi Judah defines a counterattack as mandatory only in response to an already launched attack. Maimonides also limits the mandatory classification to a defensive war launched in response to an attack.[13]

[7]   Following Hoffman 1908–1909: 121. On nontransferability, see Babad n.d.: 154f.
[8]   For both categories, see Kimelman 2020: 142–173.
[9]   For the ambiguities involved, see *Midrash Shmuel* 22.2, 2009: 71, 355–357.
[10] B. Sotah 44b, and J. Sotah 8:10; 23a.
[11] For recent analyses in English regarding primarily 20th-century Israeli rabbis, see Afterman 2014: 45–60; and Firestone 2012; Eisen 2017. The former focuses on law and theology, the latter on law.
[12] *Beit HaBehirah*, Sotah 42a, *Or Zaru'a* as cited in the gloss to the 16th-century Safdean, Joseph Karo, *Shulkhan Arukh, Orah Hayim* 329:6, also permits a preemptive strike against a hostile intention. Jaffe 2000, ad loc., limits this to defense of strategically vulnerable areas.
[13] "Laws of Kings," 5:1, according to Karelitz 1969: 841. Maimonides 1964: 8:7 lines up with Rashi.

In the light of the distinctions between mandatory and discretionary wars, this chapter will now take up the problematics of war by focusing on four issues: preemptive strikes as self-defense, the authorization to declare war, the ethical conduct of war, and exemptions from military service.

PREEMPTIVE STRIKES AS SELF-DEFENSE

Not only Machiavellians view the security and survival of the state as nonnegotiable. National self-defense is as much a moral right as is personal self-preservation. Whereas it is clear that offensive war cannot be subsumed under the inalienable right of self-defense, the moral status of preemptive attacks is not as clear. Is the moral category of self-defense limited to an already launched attack? The majority talmudic position, according to Rashi, and that of Rabbi Judah, according to Meiri, would answer in the affirmative. Their position is seconded by Article 51 of the United Nations Charter: "Nothing in the present Charter shall impair the inherent right of individual of collective self-defense if an armed attack occurs against a member."

The minority position of Rabbi Judah, according to Rashi, and the majority position, according to Meiri, however, hold that a preemptive strike against an enemy amassing for attack is close enough to a defensive counterattack to be categorized as mandatory. This position holds that to wait for an actual attack might so jeopardize national security as to make resistance impossible. Such an argument was championed by Lord Chancellor Kilmuir before the British House of Lords regarding Article 51: "It would be a travesty of the purpose of the Charter to compel a defending state to allow its opponents to deliver the first fatal blow."[14]

The judgment lies behind the endorsement by the United States House Appropriations Committee of the concept of a preemptive attack:

> In the final analysis, to effectively deter a would-be aggressor, we should maintain our armed forces in such a way and with such an understanding that should it ever become obvious that an attack upon us or our allies is imminent, we can launch an attack before the aggressor has hit either us or our allies. This is an element of

---

[14] Quoted in Feinstein 1976: 531.

deterrence which the United States should not deny itself. No other form of deterrence can be relied upon.[15]

This understanding of anticipatory defense allows for a counterattack before the initial blow falls.

Under the terms of modern warfare, for example, if an enemy were to launch a missile attack, the target country could legitimately retaliate even if the enemy's missiles were still inside their borders. The doctrine of anticipatory defense even allows for a preemptive strike as long as the order has been issued for their launching.

AUTHORIZATION TO DECLARE WAR?

A mandatory war is declared by the chief executive. A discretionary war requires the authorization of the Sanhedrin[16] or its judicial legislative equivalent. The Sanhedrin, also the high court, as the legal embodiment of popular sovereignty, is the *edah* in biblical terms.[17] Deeming it the legal equivalent of "the community of Israel as a whole,"[18] Maimonides uses interchangeably the expressions "according to the majority of Israel" and "according to the high court."[19] Similarly, former Israeli Chief Rabbi Shlomo Goren explained the requirement to secure the Sanhedrin's approval in a discretionary war as deriving from its representative authority.[20] The involvement of the Sanhedrin in the decision process of a discretionary war safeguards the citizenry from being endangered without the approval of their representative body. The Sanhedrin is also the authoritative interpreter of the Torah constitution. Since the judicial interpretation of the law is structurally separate from its executive enforcement, the Sanhedrin serves as another check on executive power.

The involvement of the Sanhedrin in discretionary wars helps explain the obligation of citizens to participate. Military obligation is

---

[15] Feinstein 1976: 533.
[16] M. (= Mishnah) Sanhedrin 1:5, 2:4, see B. Sanhedrin 16a, Berakhot 3b, with parallels. Similarly, the Dead Sea Temple Scroll (11 QT S S–21) allows for immediate mobilization in a defensive war but requires consultation with the High Priest and the Urim and Tumim, as does the Talmud when waging an offensive war. According to Soloveitchick 1984: 31, the requirement is applicable only when the institutions are extant.
[17] See Malamat 1970: 167ff.
[18] Maimonides 1964: 309: see Blidstein 1983: 58.
[19] Following Blidstein 1983: 247, n. 62.
[20] Goren 1983: 1:127–130. See Blidstein 1983: 58, n. 18, n. 19.

anchored in the biblical perspective that considers the people and the monarch to be bound by a covenant, each with its own obligations.[21] Presumably, modern statehood also entails a pact of mutuality. The people commit themselves to the support of the state and its ruler, whereas the ruler is forsworn to uphold the constitution and not to unnecessarily risk their lives. Allocating some war-making authority to the Sanhedrin guarantees the presence of a countervailing force to the ruler, helping to safeguard the inviolability of the social contract.[22]

Before granting authorization to wage war, the Sanhedrin must weigh the probable losses, consider the chances of success, and assess the will of the people. As David Bleich writes: "The Sanhedrin is charged with assessing the military, political and economic reality and determining whether a proposed war is indeed necessary and whether it will be successful in achieving its objectives."[23] Since wars are always costly in lives, the losses have to be measured against the chance of success. Preventive warfare is unwarranted if the number of lives saved does not significantly exceed the number of lives jeopardized. Calculations of victory alone are not determinative; the price of victory must be considered. The great 3rd-century Babylonian talmudic authority Mar Samuel deemed a government liable were its losses to exceed one-sixth of the fighting forces.[24] In addition to projecting future losses, a government should take precautions to limit them.

Nonetheless, precision in military projections is well-nigh impossible. The gap between plan and execution characterizes the best of military calculations. Linear plans almost always fail to deal with the nonlinear world that rules strategy and war. Rabbi Eleazar in talmudic times noted: "Any war that involves more than sixty thousand is necessarily chaotic."[25] Modern warfare has not significantly changed the

---

[21] See 2 Kings 11:17 and 2 Chronicles 23:3, along with 2 Samuel 5:3. On the problems involved in the term "covenant" for the Israelite polity, see Malamat 1970: 164–165; Tadmor 1971: 59–62; Cross 1972: 221.

[22] See the example in Josephus, *Antiquities* 9.7.4 (153).

[23] Bleich 1983: 25. Assessing the chances of victory falls within the province of the priestly Urim and Tumim, whereas the endorsement of a war policy falls within judicial jurisdiction; see B. Eruvin 45a with Rashi, Berakhot end of 3b. According to J. Sabbath 2:6, 5b, the chances of victory are assessed by the heavenly court.

[24] B. Shavuot 35b, following Tosafot, s.v., *deqatla*. See *Responsa Hatam Sofeir* to *Orah Hayyim* 208, p. 77a.

[25] *Song of Songs Rabbah* 4:4.

equation. In the words of Prussian Field Marshal Helmuth von Moltke: "No plan can survive contact with the battle."[26]

The Talmud and Midrash provide two considerations for the exclusion of the ruler from making these judgments alone: first, a ruler may be too prone to go to war; and second, they may be too hesitant to go to war. Regarding the former, a ruler may be insufficiently disinterested, being predisposed to perceive war as an opportunity for enhancing personal prestige, for stimulating the economy, or for consolidating their political base. As the Talmud notes, nothing diverts public attention and deflects the opposition while simultaneously creating the need for a strong leader as war.[27] Reflecting a similar insight, the 1st-century Josephus of Jerusalem and Rome, well aware of the machinations of opportunistic rulers, pointed out that the biblical laws of warfare are meant to deter conquest by preventing war "waged for self-aggrandizement."[28]

Regarding the latter, a ruler may be reluctant to commit their army for fear of incurring excessive financial burdens. The Talmud justifies excluding the ruler from some of the deliberations lest the expense of maintaining a standing army unduly influence their judgment. In a government where the executive is responsible for balancing the budget, similar considerations would obtain. There is also the concern that executive dillydallying might become a ruse to extend one's tenure in office.

In sum, before endangering the populace, the ruler's arguments for war have to be checked by the Sanhedrin's assessment of the people's interest. Being the more disinterested party, it is better positioned to assess the people's interest. Such a system of countervailing powers allows the interest of the ruler and the interest of the people to be part of the Sanhedrin's calculation to consent to war.

THE ETHICAL CONDUCT OF WAR

Who Is Subject to Immunity? What Is Subject to Destruction?[29]

The estimation of one's own losses and one's own interest is insufficient for validating discretionary war. The total destruction ratio required for

---

[26] For the so-called Clausewitzian friction that distinguishes the fluid and chaotic nature of real war from war on paper, see Craig 1986: 481–509; Lutwach 1987: 10–15.

[27] B. Temurah 16a. See Aristotle's observation: "The tyrant is also a warmonger so that they will always be ... in need of a leader (*Politics* 1313, l. 28f.).

[28] Josephus, *Contra Apion*, II.272, 292.

[29] For a survey of recent authorities, see Cohen 2010: 335–337.

victory must be considered. This assessment involves a "double intention"; that is, the "good" must appear achievable and the "evil" reducible. For example, before laying siege to a city, a determination must be made as to whether it can be captured without destroying it.[30] There is no warrant for destroying a town for the purpose of "saving" it.

The other rules for sieges follow similar lines of thought: Indefensible villages may not be subjected to siege. Negotiations with the enemy must precede subjecting a city to hunger, thirst, or disease for the purpose of exacting a settlement. Emissaries of peace must be sent to a hostile city for three days. If the terms are accepted, no harm may befall its inhabitants. If the terms are not accepted, the siege may not begin until the enemy has commenced hostilities. Even after the siege is laid, no direct cruelties against the inhabitants may be inflicted, and a side must be left open as an escape route.[31]

The early 1st-century Alexandrian Philo warns that national vendettas are not justifications for wars. If a city under siege sues for peace, it is to be granted. Peace, albeit with sacrifices, he says, is preferable to the horrors of war. But peace means peace. "If," he continues, "the adversaries persist in their rashness to the point of madness, they [the besiegers] must proceed to the attack invigorated by enthusiasm and having in the justice of their cause an invincible ally."[32] Although the purpose of an army at war is to win, both Philo and the ancient rabbis rejected the claim of military necessity as an excuse for military excess. Despite the goal of victory – indeed, victory with all due haste – aimless violence or wanton destruction is to be eschewed. As the 13th-century Spano-Jerusalem commentator Nahmanides makes clear, acts of destruction are warranted only insofar as they advance the goal of victory.[33] Weapons calculated to produce suffering disproportionate to the military advantage are not countenanced.

Excessive concern with moral niceties, however, can be morally counterproductive. When moral compunction appears as timidity and moral fastidiousness as squeamishness, they invite aggression. To ensure that moral preparedness be perceived from a position of strength, it must be coupled with military preparedness.

---

[30] *Sifrei Deuteronomy* 203, p. 239, with *Midrash HaGadol Deuteronomy*, p. 451
[31] See below, n. 41.
[32] Philo, *The Special Laws*, IV. 224.
[33] To Deuteronomy 20:19.

Philo, reflecting this concern for the military ambiguity of moral scruples, sounds a note of caution in his summary of the biblical doctrine of defense:

> All this shows clearly that the Jewish nation is ready for agreement and friendship with all like-minded nations whose intentions are peaceful yet is not of the contemptible kind which surrenders through cowardice to wrongful aggression.[34]

Much of the moral discussion of the conduct of the war derives from the prohibition in Deuteronomy 20:19–20 against axing fruit-bearing trees in the environs of a besieged city. The principal points deal with the issues of wanton destruction[35] and the immunity of the noncombatant. So, for example, Philo extends the prohibition against axing fruit-bearing trees to include vandalizing the environs of a besieged city:

> Indeed, so great a love for justice does the law instill in those who live under its constitution that it does not even permit the fertile soil of a hostile city to be outraged by devastation or by cutting down trees to destroy the fruits.[36]

In a similar vein, Josephus expands on the prohibition to include the incineration of the enemy's country and the killing of beasts employed in labor.[37] Despoiling the countryside without direct military advantage comes under the proscription of profligate destruction.

A millennium later, Abraham Ibn Ezra (1089–1164) on Deuteronomy 20:20 explained, as did Philo earlier, that fruit trees are singled out as a source of life. War is no license for destroying what is needed for human life. A century later, Maimonides[38] extended the prohibition to exclude categorically all wanton destruction:

> Also, one who smashes household goods, tears clothes, demolishes a building, stops up a spring, or destroys articles of food with destructive intent, transgresses the command "You shall not destroy" (based on Deuteronomy 20:19).[39]

---

[34] Philo, *The Special Laws*, 4, 224.

[35] See Novak 1992: 118–132.

[36] Philo, *The Special Laws*, 4, 226.

[37] Josephus, *Against Apion II*, 212 14.

[38] "The Laws of Kings," 6:10. See ibid., *Sefer Ha-Mitzvot*, negative mitzvah 57.

[39] This and Philo are the bases of the rulings of Hugo Grotius 1925: 3:12, 746f. See also 3:11, 739f.

For Maimonides, controlling the destructive urges provoked by war against nonhuman objects cultivates control of the destructive urge against humans. Thus, the 14th-century Spanish *Sefer HaHinukh* (*mitzvah* 529/530) states that the prohibition against wanton destruction was meant "to teach us to love the good and the purposeful and to cleave to it so that the good will cleave to us and we will distance ourselves from anything evil and destructive."[40]

The link between these two forms the basis of two a fortiori arguments for the immunity of noncombatants. The first argument for the immunity of noncombatants is grounded in the biblical prohibition against axing fruit trees during a siege. Since the prohibition against their destruction can be formulated in a rhetorical manner – to wit: "Are trees of the field human to withdraw before you under siege?" (Deuteronomy 20:19) – it is deduced that just as a tree – had it fled – would not be chopped down, so a person – were they to flee – should not be cut down. The logic of the argument is spelled out by the 16th-century Safedean exegete Moses Alshikh. After mentioning the prohibition against the wanton destruction of trees, he notes, "all the more so it is fitting that He have mercy on his children and on his creatures."[41]

The second argument is rooted in the ruling that a fourth side of a besieged city be left open,[42] either for humanitarian or tactical considerations.[43] Whatever the case, the opportunity to escape saps the resolve of the besieged to continue fighting. Otherwise, as the 15th-century Spanish–Italian exegete Abarbanel observes, they will out of desperation take heart "and seek to avenge themselves before they die . . . since one who despairs of life and well-being will risk his life to strike his enemy a great blow."[44] Thus, it is important to take measures to ensure that the chance to flee not be exploited for the sake of regrouping to mount rear attacks.

Now, if (unarmed) soldiers have the chance of becoming refugees, then surely noncombatants and other neutrals do. The principle may be stated as committing no harm to those who intend no harm. Thus, Abarbanel says with regard to the immunity of women and children: "Since they do not make war they do not deserve to die in it."[45]

---

[40]   Ed. Mossad Harav Kook, p. 647.
[41]   *Torat Moshe* to Deuteronomy 20:10.
[42]   See *Sifrei Numbers* 157, ed. Kahana, 2:523, l. 34f., with *Commentary* 4:1271f., n. 53f.; and *Midrash HaGadol, Deuteronomy*, p. 450, l. 3f., with n. 3.
[43]   See "The Laws of Kings," 6:7, ed. Rubinstein, 17:383, n. 31.
[44]   To Deuteronomy 20:10, the first *to'elet*, the third *ta'anah*.
[45]   To Deuteronomy 20:10, the third *to'elet*.

Similarly, the Midrash explains that the fear of Abraham, noted in Genesis 15:2, was due to him raising the possibility that among the troops he killed "there was an innocent man."[46] As noted, the principle of the immunity of noncombatants discriminates in favor of those who have done no harm. Even this principle that those who intend no harm should not be harmed is derived, according to Philo, from the case of the fruit tree: "Does a tree, I ask you, show ill will to the human enemy that it should be pulled up roots and all, to punish it for ill which it has done or is ready to do to you?" Obviously, the immunity of noncombatants cannot be sacrificed on the altar of military necessity.

In sum, as Philo notes:

> The Jewish nation when it takes up arms, distinguishes between those whose life is one of hostility, and the reverse. For to breathe slaughter against all, even those who have done very little or nothing amiss, shows what I should call a savage and brutal soul.[47]

From the limitations of sieges it can be extrapolated that weapons directed primarily at civilian targets would be proscribed. As such, the military option of counter-people warfare in conventional war as well as mutually assured destruction (MAD) in nuclear warfare would be precluded. Multi-megaton weapons whose primary goal is civilian slaughter and only secondarily military targets would be totally proscribed. As there are unacceptable weapons, so are there unacceptable targets.[48]

The Human Dimension in War: The Image of the Soldier and the Humanity of the Enemy

These ethical intrusions in the waging of war have two major foci: safeguarding the moral character of the soldier and preserving the human image of the enemy. Any system that appreciates the realities of both the moral life and the military life faces a dilemma in maintaining the moral conscientious of the individual while allowing for military involvement. Some systems forswear war as the price of moral excellence. Others apportion the moral life and the military life to different segments of the population. If the two are mutually exclusive, then a division of labor is a possible solution. Neither alternative is totally acceptable in Jewish ethical theory. Regarding forswearing war, Maimonides points out that it was "the neglect of the art of warfare that

---

[46] *Genesis Rabbah* 15.3.

[47] Philo, *The Special Laws*, 4, 224f., 7:14.

[48] For the issue of weapons of mass destruction, see Kimelman 2003: 36–56, esp. 41–52.

brought about conquest, destruction, and exile" at the time of the Second Jewish Commonwealth. Clearly, Maimonides would find it, in the words of Israel's 20th-century foreign minister Abba Eban, "hard to see why the advocates of unilateral renunciation are more 'moral' than those who seek to prevent war by a reciprocal balance of deterrents and incentives." Solutions to conflict have to be judged by their effectiveness as well as by their virtue. Indeed, there is no reason to concede, as Eban continues, "that prevention of conflict by effective deterrence [is] less moral than the invitation to conflict by avoidable imbalance."[49] For deterrence to be credible, the capacity to make war must be credible. Paradoxically, as the 20th-century Frenchman Raymond Aron notes, "the possibility of unlimited violence restrains the use of violence without any threats even being proffered."[50]

As noted, unilateral disarmament cannot be judged morally superior if it invites attack. A policy of abdication of power that results in condemning others to subjugation has a questionable moral basis. Since political naivete can result in moral sin, Maimonides concludes his critique of the political sagacity of ancient Israel's leaders by lamenting, "[o]ur fathers have sinned, but they are no more."

While a division of labor on ethical lines is always a possibility, those who reject solutions predicated on the exemption of the ethical elites from the maintenance work of society have struggled with the challenge of sustaining the moral stature of the soldier.

These ethicists have focused on the brutalization of character that inevitably results from the shedding of blood in wartime. Indeed, as mentioned, Philo explained the prohibition against slaying the defenseless out of concern with the savagery of the soul of the soldier, whereas the Midrash even condemned a king for the ruthless slaying of an enemy.[51] In the 13th century, Nahmanides, who elsewhere expressed his apprehension that "the most refined of people become possessed with ferocity and cruelty when advancing upon the enemy,"[52] opined that the Torah wants the soldier to "learn to act compassionately with our enemies even during wartime." In the 14th century, *Sefer HaHinukh* (*mitzvah* 527) explained the requirement to leave open a fourth side of a besieged city, saying, "the quality of compassion is a good attribute and it is appropriate for us, the holy seed, to behave

[49] Eban 1983: 325.
[50] Aron 1985: 345.
[51] Lamentations Rabbah, Introduction, 14, based on 2 Kings 6:22 with 1 Kings 20:31.
[52] To Deuteronomy 23:10.

accordingly in all our matters even with our idolatrous enemies." Isaac Arama of the 15th century noted that since "[w]ar is impossible without murder and hatred of humanity ... and there is nothing like it to undermine all sense of right and wrong," the Torah requires "the fighter be a man of peaceful intentions." In the 18th century, Hayyim Attar underscored how killing, however justified, "gives birth to a brutalization of sensibilities," requiring special divine grace to be palliated.[53]

In the 19th century, Samuel David Luzzatto argued that the Torah's purpose of strengthening the forces of compassion and of countering the natural drive for self-serving acts is concerned lest we become ingrates by casting stones into the well from which we drink. Such would be the case were one eat the fruit of a tree and then to chop it down.[54] The agonizing over the moral stature of the soldier was summed up in the 20th century in the words of former Justice Haim Cohen of the Israeli Supreme Court: "It seems that constant violence, even in self-defense, is not easily compatible with moral sensitivity."[55] All the more reason to promulgate an ethic of soldiery in order to limit any skewing of the balance between military and moral competence.

Regarding maintaining the human image of the enemy, referring to Deuteronomy 21:10ff., Josephus says the legislator of the Jews commands "showing consideration even to declared enemies. He ... forbids even the spoiling of fallen combatants; he has taken measures to prevent outrage to prisoners of war, especially women."[56] Apparently reflecting a similar sensibility, the 3rd-century R. Joshua claimed that his biblical namesake took pains to prevent the disfigurement of fallen Amalekites, whereas David brought glory to Israel by giving burial to his enemies. It is this consideration for the humanity of the enemy that forms the basis of Philo's explanation of the biblical requirement in Numbers 31:19 of expiation for those who fought against Midian. He writes:

> For though the slaughter of enemies is lawful, yet one who kills a man, even if he does so justly and in self-defense and under compulsion, has something to answer for, in view of the primal common kinship of mankind. And therefore, purification was needed for the slayers, to absolve them from what was held to have been a pollution.

---

[53] *Or HaHayyim* to Deuteronomy 13:18.

[54] Luzzatto 1965: 537–539.

[55] Cohen 1977: 332.

[56] Josephus, *Against Apion II*, 212f.

Since, alas, there are times when evil has to be used to hold evil in check, the problem, as the 20th-century Chief Rabbi of British Mandatory Palestine Abraham Kook noted, is how to engage in evil without becoming tainted. His solution involves constant acts of penance.[57] In a similar vein, Philo, as noted above, requires rites of expiation even after necessary evils. Since there is no war without evil – either because killing can never be deemed a good or because war inevitably entails unnecessary killing – there is no war that does not require penance. This explains the position that the slaying by the Levites after the Golden Calf episode required acts of expiation.[58]

The ongoing dialectic between the demands of conscience and the exigencies of the hour was spelled out by Kook's younger contemporary, the 20th-century German–Israeli Martin Buber:

> It is true that we are not able to live in perfect justice, and in order to preserve the community of man, we are often compelled to accept wrongs in decisions concerning the community. But what matters is that in every hour of decision we are aware of our responsibility and summon our conscience to weigh exactly how much is necessary to preserve the community, and accept just so much and no more; that we not interpret the demands of a will-to-power as a demand made by life itself; that we do not make a practice of setting aside a certain sphere in which God's command does not hold, but regard those actions as against his command, forced on us by the exigencies of the hour as painful sacrifices; that we do not salve, or let others salve our conscience when we make decisions concerning public life.[59]

Whatever the pretext, necessary evils remain evils subject to atonement.

THE PRINCIPLE OF PURITY OF ARMS

The concerns for the moral quotient of the soldier and the life of the enemy inform the "purity of arms" doctrine of the Israel Defense Forces. The doctrine of purity of arms limits killing to necessary and unavoidable situations. Although the expression was apparently coined

---

[57] See Kook 1985: 34f.

[58] See *Targum Ps. Yonatan* to Exodus 32:29.

[59] Buber 1997: 246f. The reluctance to attribute evil – however politically necessary – to divine command apparently lies behind the refusal to ascribe to God the Mosaic command of the Levites to slay their brethren; see Seder Eliahu Rabbah 1902: 17.

by the 20th-century Zionist idealogue Berl Katznelson, it was former Israeli Prime Minister David Ben-Gurion who made it a tenet of the Israel Defense Forces. How successfully it has been maintained under wartime conditions is illustrated by the following account of an Israeli unit entering Nablus during the Six-Day War:

> They entered first into Nablus after the tanks ... There were many people with guns ... I said to the battalion CO: "There are many people here with guns, to shoot or not to shoot?" Then he said to me, "Don't shoot." It could have been that several casualties could have been avoided afterwards if they would have gone straight into the city firing ... The battalion CO, furthermore, got on the field telephone to my company and said, "Don't touch the civilians ... don't fire until you're fired at and don't touch the civilians. Look, you've been warned. Their blood be on your heads." ... The boys in the company kept talking about it afterwards .... They kept repeating the words ... "Their blood be on your heads."[60]

According to Israeli colonel Meir Pa'il, the purity of arms doctrine maintains the moral stature of the soldier without seriously compromising their fighting capacity:

> There can be no doubt that the turning toward extreme and consummate humanism can endanger the I.D.F.'s [Israel Defense Forces] ability to function, but experience has proved that the proportions of this danger are extremely small and that it does not constitute a phenomenon that really endangers the operative capacity and the efficiency of the defense forces.[61]

In summary, a consistent thread weaves its way from biblical ordinance through medieval reflection to modern practice, as noted by exponents throughout the ages. Just because an army is legitimately repelling an aggressor does not allow it to wreak havoc with civilian life. The warrior is the enemy, not the noncombatant civilian. A just war does not justify unjust acts. There must be a consonance between means and goals. If peace is the goal, the reality of war is to be conditioned by the vision of the reconciliation between the warring populations. In this sense, education for peace forms part of military engagement.

---

[60] Shapira 1970: 132.
[61] Pa'il 1975: 215.

IMPOSING ON MANDATORY WARS THE LIMITATIONS
OF DISCRETIONARY WAR

Many of these considerations for maintaining the moral stature of the
soldier and the humanity of the enemy received their initial stimulus
from those biblical passages on wars that have been categorized as
discretionary. Nonetheless, many of them became applicable to mandatory wars. Although the better-known tendency distinguishes between
the two types of war, the inclination to underscore the overlap between
them figures significantly in the classical discussion.[62]

This drive toward moral convergence between the two types of war
finds its roots in the Bible. Thus, in 1 Samuel 15:6, provisions are made
to evacuate neutrals from the battle area even in the biblically mandated war against Amalek.

In addition to some moral considerations, the two types of war share
strategic considerations. As the statement by Rabbi Eleazar in the
Midrash about the chaotic nature of warfare derives from the numbers
involved in the conquest of the Land of Israel, it follows that even the
mandatory war of the original conquest of Israel required a weighing of
victory against losses not unlike those of discretionary wars.

The Midrash traces the blurring of the distinctions between the two
types of war back to the Torah. It finds in the following dialogue a way
of parrying the assumption that overtures of peace are limited to discretionary wars:

> God commanded Moses to make war on Sihon, as it is said, "Engage
> him in battle" (Deuteronomy 2:24), but he did not do so. Instead he
> sent messengers ... to Sihon ... with an offer of peace
> (Deuteronomy 2:26). God said to him: "I commanded you to make
> war with him, instead you began with peace. By your life, I shall
> confirm your decision. Every war upon which Israel enters shall
> begin with an offer of peace."[63]

Since Joshua is said to have extended such an offer to the Canaanites,
and Numbers 27:21 points out Joshua's need for applying to the priestly
Urim and Tumim to assess the chances of victory, it is evident that
divinely commanded wars are also predicated on overtures of peace as

[62] For Rashi and Nahmanides, see Girshuni 1984: 130–134. For Maimonides, see "Laws
of Kings," 6:1, 6:7, and 7:1, with Blidstein 1983: 221, n. 18, n. 34, and Soloveitchik
1984: 128–131.
[63] *Deuteronomy Rabbah* 5.13.

well as on positive assessments of their outcome.[64] Even in the mandatory war against Amalek, as mentioned, the fallen were not disfigured.
Finally, as discretionary wars require the assent of the Sanhedrin, so
mandatory wars require the concurrence of priestly appurtenances.
Obviously, chief executives lack carte blanche to commit their people
to war.[65]

The move to impose upon mandatory warfare some of the proced-
ural or moral restraints of discretionary warfare counters the sliding
scale argument – namely, the belief that "the greater the justice of one's
cause, the more rights one has in battle." The move from convictions of
righteousness to feelings of self-righteousness is slight. The subsequent
move of regarding the enemy population as beyond the pale of humanity
is even slighter. Since this tendency is especially pronounced in ideologically and religiously motivated wars, any countermove is salutary.

The greater the blurring of distinctions between discretionary and
mandatory wars, the greater the chance of removing from the military
agenda the option of total war. Strapping mandatory wars with some of
the restrictions of discretionary wars precludes them from becoming
holy wars.

According to John Yoder's *When War Is Unjust*,[66] holy wars differ
from just wars in the following five respects:

(1) Holy wars are validated by a transcendent cause.
(2) The cause is known by revelation.
(3) The adversary has no rights.
(4) The criterion of last resort need not apply.
(5) It need not be winnable.

The above discussion illustrates how the antidotes to (3)–(5) were woven
into the ethical fabric of mandatory wars. To repeat, the fallen of
Amalek were not to be disfigured, the resort to war even against the
Canaanites was only pursuant to overtures of peace, and even the
chances of success against Midian were weighed by the Urim and
Tumim. By replacing the category of holy war with that of mandatory
war and subjecting it to many of the limitations of discretionary war, all

---

[64] *Leviticus Rabbah* 17.6. The position that all wars must be preceded by an overture of
peace was accepted by a wide range of authorities including Maimonides, "Laws of
Kings," 6:5; Nahmanides to Deuteronomy 20:10; Coucy, *SeMaG*, positive mitsvah 11
8; *Sefer HaHinukh*, mitzvah 527 along with *Minhat Hinukh*, ad loc.; and possibly
Sa'adyah Gaon; see Perla 1973: 251f.

[65] For the issue of exercising discretion in a law-based system, see Blidstein 1992: 41–66.

[66] Yoder 1984: 26f.

war became subject to ethical restraint. Although a sliding scale of limited warfare is ethically feasible, an ethic of unlimited warfare is a contradiction in terms. It is therefore not surprising that the expression "holy war" is absent from the Jewish ethical or military lexicon.[67]

EXEMPTIONS FROM MILITARY SERVICE

The obligation of the citizen to participate in a mandatory defensive war flows from three assumptions. The first is that national defense is based on an analogue of individual self-defense. The second is that the duty of national defense is derived from the verse, "Do not stand idly by the blood of your neighbor."[68] The implication is that the duty to come to the rescue of compatriots under attack is comparable to the duty to intervene to rescue an individual from an assailant.[69]

These two assumptions alone prove inadequate. With regard to the first, if escape is available, self-defense is optional not mandatory. Thus, the domestic analogy on its own remains insufficient for extrapolating the right of national defense from the right of home defense. As for the second, while classical legal opinion is divided on the obligation of risking one's life for another,[70] it is agreed that there is no duty to save a life at the cost of life.

Justifying risk of life in the name of national defense requires the additional assumption that the duty to save the community mandates the risk of life, for if, as the Midrash states, "[i]t is preferable that one life be in doubtful danger than all in certain danger," then, as Maimonides notes, "[t]he public welfare takes precedence over one's personal safety."[71] "Indeed," according to Judah Halevy, "[i]t is proper for the individual to bear worse than death to save the community."[72] As the Midrash states: "It is preferable to risk one life to save all."[73] Responsibility to defend the

---

[67] Thus Firestone's title, "Holy War in Judaism," is an unfortunate misnomer, for he means, as he himself explains, "commanded war." Even "commanded war," however, does not mean a war that must be waged, only one that, when waged, a commandment is fulfilled.

[68] As Leviticus 19:16 was understood; see Kimelman 1983: 12–18.

[69] See Kimelman 1996: 6–11.

[70] This is a debate between two 16th-century authorities. David Ben Zimra, *Teshuvot Radbaz* 3: #1052, denies such a duty; Joseph Karo, *Kesef Mishnah* to *Mishneh Torah*, "Laws of the Murderer," 1:14, affirms it.

[71] End of The Epistle to Yemen.

[72] *Kuzari* 3.19.

[73] *Genesis Rabbah* 91.10.

community increases when the community is the state whose mandate includes the protection of the total citizenry.[74]

In a defensive war, the lives of the citizens are imperiled by the initial attack. Since the counterattack is undertaken to diminish the risk to life, it may be authorized by executive action. Such is not the case in discretionary wars, which, by seeking to extend the political or economic influence of the government, initially increase the peril to life. Even in a preemptive attack, according to one school of thought, the lack of imminent danger to the population precludes the executive from independently making the decision to endanger the lives of the citizenry. Thus, the endorsement of a policy of war is left to the discretion of the Sanhedrin.

Since discretionary wars initially increase the peril to life, the deliberations of the Sanhedrin are to weigh popular support in its endorsement. This does not imply a government by referendum. Even those who maintain that sovereignty ultimately rests with the community hold that, during their tenure, representatives are authorized to express the collective will.[75] Representative government is not government by the people, but government by their agents.[76]

Nonetheless, concurrent with theories of majority rule are provisions for minority rights.[77] As there is general agreement that the majority cannot impose unfair rules that discriminate against the minority, so there is a consensus that the majority has the right to impose on the minority in matters that are clearly for the benefit of the community. Legal opinion, however, is split on whether the minority can be imposed upon in those discretionary areas that, though desired by the majority, are not clearly for the benefit of the community as a whole.

Whether such provisions would apply in war is an open question. It would appear that once the government has complied with proper procedure, the individual would have no recourse but to fight. After all, if the duly constituted authorities have determined the necessity of

---

[74] See Kook 1964: 142–144.
[75] See Morell 1971: 87–119; Blidstein 1992: 225–227, n. 19. For the principle of representative government, see R. Solomon ben Aderet (Rashba) in his *Responsa* vol. l, #617, and vol. 3, #443, with Elon 1973: 2:588f.
[76] Waldenberg 1952: 3:90–97.
[77] See Morell 1971: 90–96, n. 75; Blidstein 1992: 235–237, 252–255, n. 19. For the principle of minority rights, see Rabbenu (Jacob) Tam, cited in Elon 1973: 589–587, n. 75.

war, who is the individual to second-guess the government's decision? This surely holds in defensive wars where no one is exempt from self-defense, the duty to rescue others, and the obligation to defend the state that secures the well-being of all.

The question is whether these considerations apply equally in a discretionary war or whether majority rule is limited by the discretionary nature of the war and thus must meet the requirement of benefit to the community as a whole. Although these considerations are not made explicit, they may help us understand the peculiar biblical rules of warfare with regard to exemptions from military service.

According to the Torah, before commencing hostilities, the officials are to address the troops as follows:

> Is there anyone who has built a new house but has not dedicated it . . . or planted a vineyard but has never harvested it . . . or spoken for a woman in marriage but has not married her . . . let him go back home, lest he die in battle and another . . . [do] it.
>
> (Deuteronomy 20:5–7)

The officials shall go on addressing the troops, saying:

> Is there anyone afraid and tender-hearted: Let him go back to his home, lest the courage of his comrades flag like his.
>
> (Deuteronomy 20:8)

All such are to report for duty before being assigned alternative service such as provisions and weapon supply, road repair, special security expenditures, or even oversight of defensive installations.[78]

Another category that not only is exempt from reporting for duty but is also excused from alternative service derives from the following verse: "When a man has taken a bride, he shall not go out with the army or be assigned to it for any purpose; he shall be exempt one year for the sake of his household, to give happiness to the woman he has married" (Deuteronomy 24:5). According to the Rabbinic code of Jewish law, the *Mishnah*, the absolute exemption of one year for one who has consummated his marriage applies also to "one who has built his house and dedicated it," as well as to "one who has planted a vineyard and harvested it."[79]

All of the exemptions are characterized by their universal access. There are no exemptions based on birth, on education, on professional

---

[78] Maimonides, "Laws of Kings," 7:11.
[79] M. Sotah 8:4.

class, or even on religious status.[80] This fits the moral purpose of conscription, which is to universalize or randomize the risks of war across a generation of men. By not creating a special exclusion even for religion, the Torah underscores that when life is at stake there can be no respecting of persons.

The purpose of all of the exemptions is not made explicit, although the value of removing from the field those who cannot concentrate on the battle is noted. The presence of such people increases fatalities resulting from disarray and failure of nerve. Other explanations for the exemptions include the need to mitigate individual hardship, to give courage to those who remain, to maintain the sanctity of the camp,[81] or to prevent depopulation of urban areas.[82]

The talmudic rabbis understood each case as illustrative of a principle and extended the exemptions to cover four categories of handicaps: the economic, the familial, the psychomoral and the physical.[83] Claims for economic and familial exemptions are subject to substantiation. The other two are assumed to be self-evident.[84]

Although the psychomoral exemption does not require independent confirmation, its meaning is far from self-evident. The Torah mentions two categories: "afraid" and "tender-hearted." According to Rabbi Yosi Hagalili, "afraid" means apprehensive about one's sins; "tender-hearted" means fearful of war lest one be killed. According to Rabbi Akiva, "afraid" means fearful of war; "tender-hearted" means compassionate or apprehensive lest one kill.[85] Taken together, there would be grounds for exempting the psychologically timid as well as the morally scrupulous.[86]

---

[80] Viewing the Levites as ideal types, Maimonides argued for their military exemption; see "Laws of Shemitah and Yovel" 13:12, followed by *Midrash HaGadol Numbers*, 1:49, p. 10 and n. 8. This position lacks a basis in classical rabbinic sources; see Zevin 1964: 27f; Girshuni 1984: 425. In any case, it would only apply were the Levites still serving in the Temple; see Arieli 1971: 37–42, and even then it would only be applicable in religiously motivated wars; see ed. Rubinstein, *Rambam Le-Am*, ad loc., p. 646, n. 54; Schneersohn 1985: 216–221. In any case, according to Maimonides ("Laws of the Sabbath" 2:23), when under attack, all able-bodied men are subject to the draft; see Waldenberg 1985: 3: siman 9.

[81] On the religious dimension of the army, see Waldenberg 1952: 197–216.

[82] *Sifrei Deuteronomy* 192, p. 233. See the Qumran Temple Scroll, 58.11.

[83] Goren 1982: 369.

[84] See *Sifrei Deuteronomy* 192, p. 233, with Kook 1959: 1:235–237.

[85] See Halivni 1968: 473f. Compare the contrasting comments of Ibn Ezra and Hizkuni to Deuteronomy 20:8.

[86] See Hein 1959: 1:36, 103.

Besides having to be substantiated, the economic and familial exemptions such as starting a house, planting the initial vineyard, or getting engaged mostly affect men in their prime, the age of maximum combat-readiness. Since in defeat these people have the most to lose, they would be most willing to fight a necessary war but most reluctant to engage in an unnecessary one. A large number of exemptions for this age group could so hamper mobilization efforts as to impair the military effort, as Nahmanides implies when he notes: "Were it not for [the requirement of substantiation], a majority of the people would seek exemption on false pretenses."[87] Nahmanides' fears were borne out by the experience of the biblical judge Gideon, who, upon making provisions for the psychomoral exemption, lost two-thirds of his fighting force (Judges 7:2f.).

But this is precisely the point. There is a loophole in the war legislation, one so gaping that it allows those dubious of the validity of the war to reassert their sovereignty through legal shenanigans. Doubts about the validity of a war stir up their own social momentum, inducing the seeking of wholesale exemptions. The result is a war declared by the executive and approved by the Sanhedrin, but one that sputters because of popular resistance.[88]

Mobilization fails without popular support. Many will express their half-heartedness by dragging their feet in the hope of being, as the Talmud says, "the last to go to war and the first to return."[89] When lives are at stake, people tend to reassert their sovereignty over their person. By impairing the mobilization process, they pass judgment on the necessity of the military venture and on the legitimacy of the political ends. Without popular support, political ends that endanger large parts of the population are *eo ipso* illegitimate.[90] In a similar vein, Abarbanel points out that those mobilized for war must go "willingly

---

[87] Nahmanides, Deuteronomy 20:8; see Bekhor Shor, ad loc.

[88] This helps explain why M. Sotah 8:7 and T. (= Tosefta) Sotah 7:24 locate the exemption specifically in a discretionary war. According to Meiri, the exercise of the exemptions is optional (see Lieberman 1973: 695, n. 38), and according to "Hazon Ish," "there should be no embarking on a discretionary war if it is impossible to fight without the exemptees" (Karelitz 1973: Eruvin, *siman* 6, 167b).

[89] B. Pesahim 113a.

[90] According to 1 Maccabees 3:56, draft exemptions were activated in the rebellion against the Syrians. It is possible that 1 Maccabees holds that the exemptions obtain in all wars, see Yadin 1957: 64. Alternatively, since the inception and timing of the war was at Maccabean initiative and initially increased the peril to life, it needed to allow for the exemptions.

without coercion or duress."[91] Isaac Arama also mandates "those who speak to the fighting forces to see whether they have accepted the risks of war."[92] That this populace principle, as it were, is a factor in legitimating acts of state is evinced in the ruling that for conquered territory to enter the public domain the military venture must have commanded the approval of the majority.[93] Notwithstanding the need to secure the approval of the Sanhedrin before incurring the risks of war, wars need to command popular legitimacy to be valid, whether politically or morally.

One of the reasons it is so difficult to justify a nondefensive war is that Judaism makes it difficult to forgo one's sovereignty. Life and liberty are divine gifts not to be squandered. According to the Torah (Exodus 21:6), a person who chooses to remain a slave is to have their ear pierced with an awl. Rabbinic tradition saw in the piercing of the ear a symbolic punishment for forgoing one's divinely given freedom:

> Because the ear heard on Mount Sinai: "For they are My servants, whom I freed from the land of Egypt; they may not give themselves over into servitude" (Leviticus 25:42), and it rejected God's authority and accepted human authority – let it be pierced.[94]

If such be the penalty for frittering away one's freedom, how much more so for frittering away one's life? Responsibility for one's life works to prevent one from signing it over nonchalantly to a government. The demand to live by the Torah rather than die by it ensures that the decision to wage war be handled with the requisite gravity by both government and individual.

The resort to military force requires a moral as well as a political raison d'être. Otherwise the war effort risks being undermined by the morale of the very community that constitutes the resource of power. As former Prime Minister David Ben-Gurion noted, "two-thirds of military prowess is popular morale."[95]

Since military success is as much a function of "staying power" as it is of "striking power," striking power is subject to both quantitative and qualitative assessments of military resources. Staying power, however, is a correlative of the strength of motivation, which itself derives from

---

[91] To Deuteronomy 19:1.

[92] *Aqeidat Yitshaq* 5, gate 97, 189b.

[93] See Maimonides, "Laws of Trumah," 1:2, "Laws of Kings," 5:6; and *Sifrei Deuteronomy* 51, p. 116, with n. 13, n. 16.

[94] T. Babba Qamma 7:5, ed. Lieberman, p. 29f.

[95] Ben-Gurion 1950: 5:292. For an American application of the "Clausewitzian trinity" of people, politicians, and army, see Summers 1982.

unity of purpose and popular consensus with regard to national aspirations. The result is that victory is a function of military might and national resources as well as the social fabric and the national will.

In sum, the issue is not just the proper use of force (*jus in bello*) but also the proper means of assessing whether to resort to force (*jus ad bellum*). Since such calculations exceed formal military considerations, official responsibilities for assessment lie with the body least to benefit from war – namely, the Sanhedrin. Nonetheless, since large numbers of lives are at stake, there exists a legal technicality in the mobilization process that allows for discerning popular sentiment. As the justification for a war loses credibility and the war itself loses popularity, so grows the likelihood of mass petitions for exemptions on dubious grounds. In the final analysis, the consent of those called upon to make the supreme sacrifice can outweigh the approval of the Sanhedrin. The greater the numbers of elements in the body politic needed to approve a war, the greater the check on unnecessary wars and their attendant abuses of power.[96]

EPILOGUE

In answer to the question of why the Torah records those occasions when God's orders on the conduct of war were rescinded in favor of Moses' counsel of restraint, the Midrash states: "Even war is recorded for the sake of peace."[97] If the reality of war is to be conditioned by the vision of peace, then restraint in both the recourse to and the conduct of war is imperative to keep ajar the openings for peace.

References

Abarbanel, Issac. 1964. *Peirush Al Ha-Torah*, 3 vols. Bene Arbe'al.

Afterman, Adam and Gedaliah Afterman. 2014. "Judaism." In *Religion, War, and Ethics: A Sourcebook of Textual Traditions*. Edited by Gregory Reichberg and Henrik Syse with Nicole Hartwell. Cambridge University Press. 8–75.

Albeck, Chanoch. 1958. *Seder Nashim*. Mossad Bialik.

Alsheich, Moshe. 1922. *Torat Moshe*, 2 vols. Levin Epstein Brothers.

Arama, Isaac. 2001. *Akeidat Yiṣḥak*. Lamda Publishers.

Arieli, Shmaryahu. 1971. *Mishpat HaMilḥamah*. Reuven Mass.

---

[96] For an assessment of the modern wars of Israel by the criteria herein, see Kimelman 1990: 247–294, esp. 282f.

[97] Midrash Tanhumah, Tsav 3.

Aristotle. 1941. *Politics, The Basic Works of Aristotle*. Edited by Richard McKeon. Random House.

Aron, Raymond. 1985. *Clausewitz: Philosopher of War*. Prentice-Hall.

Babad, Joseph. n.d. *Minhat Hinukh to Sefer HaHinukh*. Pardes.

Babylonian Talmud = B. Avodah Zarah, Berakhot, Eruvin, Pesahim, Sanhedrin, Shavuot, Sotah, Temurah.

Ben-Gurion, David. 1950. *BaMa'arakhah*. Green Brothers.

Bleich, David J. 1983. "Preemptive War in Jewish Law." *Tradition* 21(1): 3–41.

Blidstein, Gerald. 1983. "Individual and Community in the Middle Ages." In *Kinship and Consent: The Jewish Political Tradition and Its Contemporary Uses*. Edited by Daniel Elazar. Turtledove Publishing. 215–256.

　　1992. "'Ideal' and 'Real' in Classical Jewish Political Theory." In *The Quest for Utopia: Jewish Political Ideas and Institutions through the Ages*. Edited by Zvi Gitelman. Routledge. 41–66.

Buber, Martin. 1997. *Israel and the World: Essays in a Time of Crisis*. Syracuse University Press.

Cohen, Haim. 1977. "Law and Reality in Israel Today." In *Violence and Defense in the Jewish Experience*. Edited by Y. Aharoni, L. Goodman, S. Baron, and G. Wise. Jewish Publication Society of America. 323–336.

Cohen, Stuart. 2010. "'Invalid War' in Jewish Tradition: Sources and Implications" (in Hebrew). In *Jewish Political Tradition throughout the Ages: In Memory of Daniel J. Elazar*. Edited by M. Hellinger. Bar-Ilan University Press. 335–357.

Craig, Gordon. 1986. "The Political Leader as Strategist." In *The Makers of Modern Strategy from Machiavæli to the Nuclear Age*. Edited by Peter Paret. Princeton University Press. 481–509.

Cross, Frank Moore. 1972. *Canaanite Myth and Hebrew Epic*. Harvard University Press.

Eban, Abba. 1983. *The New Diplomacy: International Affairs in the Modem Age*. Random House.

Eisen, Robert. 2017. *Religious Zionism, Jewish Law, and the Morality of War: How Five Rabbis Confronted One of Modern Judaism's Greatest Challenges*. Oxford University Press.

Elon, Menachem. 1973. *Jewish Law: History, Sources, Principles* (in Hebrew). Magnes Press.

Feinstein, Barry. 1976. "Self-Defence and Israel in International Law: A Reappraisal." *Israel Law Review* 11: 516–562.

Firestone, Reuven. 2012. *Holy War in Judaism: The Fall and Rise of a Controversial Idea*. Oxford University Press.

Genesis Rabbah. 1965. Edited by J. Theodor and H. Albeck. 3 vols. Wahrmann Books.

Girshuni, Yehudah. 1984. *Sefer Mishpat HaMelukhah*. Moznaim Publishing Corp.

Goren, Shlomo. 1982. *Torat HaShabbat VeHaMoed*. WZO.

　　1983. "Meishiv Milhamah." *Jerusalem* 1: 127–130.

Grotius, Hugo. 1925. *The Law of War and Peace*. The Bobbs-Merill Co.

Halevy, Judah. 1972. *Kuzari*. Edited by Yehudah Even Shmuel. Dvir Co. Halevy.

Halivni, David. 1968. *Mekorot UMesarot, Nashim*. Dvir Co.

HaMeiri, Menahem. 1959. *Beit HaBehirah, Sotah.* 42a. Available at https:// hebrewbooks.org

Hein, Avraham. 1959. *BeMalkhut HaYahadut*, 2 vols. Mossad Harav Kook.

Hoffman, David. 1908–1909. *Midrash Tannaim ad Deuteronomy 20:15.* Ittskovski.

Jaffe, Mordechai. 2000. *Levush Malkhut, Levush Tekehelet.* n.p.

Jerusalem Talmud = J. Sotah.

Josephus. 1966a. *The Life against Apion.* Harvard University Press.

   1966b. *Antiquities.* Harvard University Press.

Karelitz, Avraham. 1969. *Hazon Ish Al HaRambam.* Grainiman.

   1973. *Orah Hayyim, Mo'ed*, Grainiman.

Karo, Joseph. n.d. *Kesef Mishnah to Mishneh Torah, "Laws of the Murderer".* 1:14. Available at www.sefaria.org/Kessef_Mishneh_on_Mishneh_Torah

Karo, Joseph, Shulkhan Arukh, and Orah Hayim. n.d. 329:6. Available at www .sefaria.org/Shulchan_Arukh

Kimelman, Reuven. 1983. "Judging Man by the Standards of God." *B'nai Brith International Jewish Monthly* 97: 12–18.

   1990. "The Ethics of National Power: Government and War in the Jewish Tradition." In *Authority, Power and Leadership in the Jewish Polity: Cases and Issues.* Edited by Daniel Elazar. University Press of America. 247–294.

   1992. "The Laws of War and Their Limits" (in Hebrew). In *Sanctity of Life and Martyrdom: Studies in Memory of Amir Yekutiel.* Edited by Isaiah Gafni and Aviezer Ravitsky. The Zalman Shazar Center for Jewish History. 233–255.

   1996. "Terrorism, Political Murder, and Judaism." *Journal of Jewish Education* 62(2): 6–11.

   2003. "Judaism, War, and Weapons of Mass Destruction." *Conservative Judaism* 56(1): 36–56.

   2020. "Israel's Election and the Moral Dilemma of Amalek and the Seven Nations of Canaan." In *Judaism's Challenge: Election, Divine Love, and Human Enmity.* Edited by Alon Goshen-Gottstein. Academic Studies Press. 142–173.

Kook, Avraham. 1964. *Mishpat Kohen.* Mossad Harav Kook. 142–144.

   1985. *Orot HaTorah.* Mossad Harav Kook.

Kook. Shaul Hannah. 1959. *Iyyunim UMehkarim.* Mossad Harav Kook.

Lekah Tov. 1960. *Tuviah b. Eliezer*, 2 vols. Edited by S. Buber. n.p.

Leviticus Rabbah 1.4. n.d. Available at www.sefaria.org/texts/Midrash

Lieberman, Saul. 1973. *Tosefta KiFshutah*, vol. 8. The Jewish Theological Seminary of America.

Lutwach, Edward N. 1987. *Strategy: The Logic of War and Peace.* Harvard University Press.

Luzzatto, Samuel David. 1965. *Commentary to the Pentateuch* (in Hebrew). Dvir Co.

Maimonides, Moses. 1962. *Mishneh Torah.* "Laws of Kings and their Wars," *Rambam LeAm*, 17:355–420. Edited by Shmuel Rubinstein. Mossad Harav Kook.

Malamat, Abraham. 1965. "Organs of Statecraft in the Israelite Monarchy." *The Biblical Archaeologist* 28(2): 33–65.

   1964. *Commentary on the Mishnah.* Edited by David Kapah. Mossad Harav Kook.

1985. *The Epistle to Yemen*. Edited by Abraham Halkin, Crisis and Leadership: Epistles of Maimonides. Jewish Publication Society.

Midrash HaGadol Deuteronomy. 1973. Edited by S. Fisch. Mossad Harav Kook.

Midrash Shmuel. 2009. Edited by Berachyahu Lifshitz. Schechter Institute of Jewish Studies.

Midrash Tannaim Al Sefer Devarim. 1909. Edited by David Hoffman. Itzkowski.

Mishnah. n.d. Available at www.sefaria.org/texts

Morell, Samuel. 1971. "The Constitutional Limits of Communal Government in Rabbinic Law." *Jewish Social Studies* 33: 87–119.

Novak, David. 1992. *Jewish Social Ethics*. Oxford University Press.

Pa'il, Meir. 1975. "The Dynamics of Power: Morality in Armed Conflict after the Six Day War." In *Modern Jewish Ethics: Theory and Practice*. Edited by Marvin Fox. Ohio State University Press. 191–220.

Perla, Yeruham. 1973. *Sefer HaMitzvot LeRav Sa'adyah*, 3 vols. Keset Publishers.

Philo, 1968. *The Special Laws*, vol, 8. Harvard University Press.

Responsa Chatam Sofer. n.d. Available at www.sefaria.org/Responsa Chatam_Sofer

Schneersohn, Menachem. 1985. *Ḥidushim UBiurim BeShas UBeDivrei HaRambam Z"L*. Kehat.

Seder Eliahu Rabbah. 1960. Edited by M. Friedmann. Bamberger & Wahrman.

Sefer HaḤinukh. 1974. Edited by Chaim Chavel. Mossad Harav Kook.

Shapira, Avraham. 1970. *The Seventh Day: Soldiers' Talk about the Six-Day War*. Simon Schuster.

Sifrei Deuteronomy. 1969. Edited by Louis Finkelstein. The Jewish Theological Seminary of America.

Sifrei Numbers. 2015. Edited by Menahem Kahana, 2 vols., Commentary, 4 vols. Magnes Press.

Sofeir, Ḥatam. n.d. *Responsa to Orah Ḥayyim*. 208. Available at https://hebrewbooks.org

Soloveitchick, Yosef Dov. 1984. *Kovets Ḥidushei Torah*. Zohar Publishers.

Song of Songs Rabbah. n.d. Available at www.sefaria.org/texts/Midrash

Summers, Harry, Jr. 1982. *On Strategy: A Critical Analysis of the Vietnam War*. Presidio Press.

Tadmor, Hayim. 1971. "The People and the Kingship in Ancient Israel: The Role of Political Institutions in the Biblical Period." In *Jewish Society through the Ages*. Edited by H. H. Ben Sasson and S. Ettinger. Schoken Books. 59–62.

Waldenberg, Eliezer. 1952. "The Religious Dimension of the Army of Israel" (in Hebrew). *HaTorah VeHaMedinah* 4: 197–216.

1985. *Responsa Tsits Eliezer*. Available at https://hebrewbooks.org

Yadin, Yigael. 1957. *The Scroll of The War of the Sons of Light against the Sons of Darkness* (in Hebrew). Bialik Institute.

Yoder, John Howard. 1984. *When War Is Unjust: Being Honest in Just-War Thinking*. Wipf and Stock.

Zevin, Shlomo. 1964. *LeOr HaHalakhah*. Abraham Zioni Publishing House.

Zimra, David Ben. 1882. *Responsa RaDBaZ*, 3 vols. Available at https://hebrewbooks.org

10 The Idea of Just War in Christian Thought from the Age of Augustine through the Early Modern Period

JAMES TURNER JOHNSON

INTRODUCTION: AUGUSTINE AND THE ORIGINS OF CHRISTIAN THOUGHT ON JUST WAR

The idea of just war has roots in both classical Greek and Roman thought and practice and in the Bible. Augustine of Hippo, widely cited as the first Christian just war thinker, was not fluent in Greek but drew on the thought of the Roman theorist Cicero and on the Hebrew tradition. But despite his reputation as the fount of Christian just war thinking, Augustine provided no systematic treatment of just war. Rather, his thoughts on just war appear as brief passages in a variety of works of various types written in different contexts and for different purposes throughout his career. Identifying and collecting these passages was the work of various compilations of canon law that began to appear about a century after Augustine's death. These were systematized into a coherent whole by the canonist Gratian in his *Decretum* (1149) and further developed by Gratian's two generations of successors, the Decretists and the Decretalists, in the late 12th and early 13th centuries. The result was the idea of just war in its classic form, which was in turn carried over into theological thought and summarized by Thomas Aquinas in his *Summa Theologiae* in the 1270s.

THE MEDIEVAL DEVELOPMENT OF THE JUST WAR IDEA IN CLASSIC FORM

Collectively, Gratian and his successors defined the concept of just war around three requirements: the authority of a sovereign ruler (a temporal ruler with no temporal superiors), a just cause (defense of justice and remediation of injustice), and a right intention (defined negatively in a passage from Augustine's treatise *Contra Faustum* listing evil intentions in war and positively by the end of peace defined by Augustine in various passages). These three requirements corresponded directly to the three ends of politics drawn from Roman law: order, justice, and peace. The canonical conception of just war was intentionally a practical application of statecraft.

The end of the period of consolidation and systematization of the idea of just war in the classic form defined by the work of Gratian and his successors was marked by Thomas Aquinas's adoption and summarization of this conception (Aquinas *Summa Theologiae*, II/II, Question 40, "On War"). Here, in line with the overall concern motivating the development of medieval canon law, Aquinas addressed whether war is always sinful; it is not, he argued in Article 1, provided that three necessary requirements are met – the three already defined by the canonists before him: princely (sovereign) authority, just cause, and rightful intention. The first he justified by reference to Romans 13.4: "[The prince] beareth not the sword in vain; for he is God's minister, an avenger to execute wrath upon him that doth evil," and by a citation from Augustine in *Contra Faustum* XXII, 75: "The natural order conducive to peace among mortals demands that the power to declare and counsel war should be in the hands of those who are princes" (Reichberg et al. 2006: 177). The requirement of just cause Aquinas defined and justified by a citation from Augustine's *Questions on the Heptateuch*: "A just war is wont to be described as one that avenges wrongs, when a nation or state has to be punished, for refusing to make amends for the wrongs inflicted by its subjects, or to restore what it has seized unjustly" (Reichberg et al. 2006: 177). The third requirement for a just war Aquinas similarly defined by appeal to Augustine: First, negatively, citing *Contra Faustum* XXII, 74: "The passion for inflicting harm, the cruel thirst for vengeance, an implacable and relentless spirit, the fever of revolt, the lust of power, and such like things, all these are rightly condemned in war" (Reichberg et al. 2006: 177); and second, in positive terms, by citing Augustine on the end of peace: "We do not seek peace in order to be at war, but we go to war that we may have peace" (Reichberg et al. 2006: 178). Textual analysis shows that Aquinas drew all the passages from Augustine from the *Decretum*.

Other medieval thinkers wrote on just war, but the conception developed by the canonists from Gratian through the Decretalists, then given a theological context by Aquinas, prevailed as the core concept. At this point it governed only the justice of resorting to war. But the canon law from this same period also included rulings from various episcopal councils establishing noncombatant immunity (the Peace of God), seeking to ban fighting in war on designated holy days (the Truce of God), and seeking to ban the use of particular weapons (siege weapons, bows and arrows, and crossbows; see further Johnson 1981: 124–131).

Within the world of the knightly class the development of the chivalric ideal contributed its own conception of noncombatant immunity based in the idea that knightly honor forbade directly and intentionally harming the types of persons who normally did not or could not bear arms. In the era of the Hundred Years War (1350–1450) this chivalric idea and the Church's canons on noncombatant immunity came together, importantly in the writings of Honore Bonet (or Bovet) and Christine de Pisan (or Pizan; Johnson 1975: 66–75; 1981: 131–150). The canonical weapons limits dovetailed with the chivalric interest in limiting the use of weapons to members of the knightly class and their immediate retainers. As a result of these developments, by the mid-15th century the earlier idea of just war, defining requirements for resort to just war, was supplemented by a consensual body of moral requirements having to do with how a just war should be fought. While the earlier requirements were not given the name *jus ad bellum* until the early modern period, the term *jus in bello* (the Latin translation of the chivalric French *loi d'armes*) was used coincident with its medieval coming together. From this time on the idea of just war included both requirements for going to war and limits on how to wage war. Today these are regularly described as "principles," but in the medieval context (as well as among the early modern just war thinkers) they were not principles to be reasoned from or debated but rules that defined a cultural consensus.

THE DEVELOPMENT OF THE JUST WAR IDEA IN THE MODERN PERIOD

The development of just war thought in the modern period took place in two different arenas. On one hand, thinkers from Vitoria to Grotius increasingly shifted the focus of the inherited just war tradition to reflect the changing nature of political communities and open the door to a new conception of the order among them. On the other hand, in the sphere of religion the just war idea carried over into Protestant thought in the Reformation era even while it continued to be advanced by Catholic thinkers. Neither of these developments took place overnight, and each is marked by its own complexity, but together they set the course for the just war idea in the modern period.

Francisco de Vitoria (1492–1546) was one of a number of scholars who wrote on just war from the late 15th through the early 17th centuries, prodded by the Spanish discovery of the New World and the wars of religion of the Reformation era. Four of these thinkers were Dominicans, Vitoria's older contemporary Thomas Cajetan (1468–1534) and three who taught at the University of Salamanca: Vitoria himself, Domingo de Soto (1494–1560), and Luis de Molina (1535–1600). Others had different backgrounds: the Italian Protestant legal theorist Alberico Gentili (1552–1608), the Spanish Jesuit theologian Francisco Suarez (1548–1617), various Continental and English Puritan legal and theological writers, and Hugo Grotius (1583–1645). Of these the contributions of Vitoria and Grotius are the most important. For the others mentioned, see Reichberg et al. (2006) for brief commentaries and selections from their writings, as well as Johnson (1975: chapters III and IV). Suarez is also discussed briefly below as exemplifying Catholic theological just war thought in the Reformation era.

Vitoria, though working from concepts and conventions of thought inherited from the Middle Ages, particularly Aquinas's treatment of just war, focused well beyond the concerns of Aquinas's era to problems of the age just beginning. Vitoria was Prime Professor of Theology at the University of Salamanca in Spain, which meant that his duty was to lecture at the monastic hour of prime, with his subject the whole sweep of the *Summa Theologiae* of the great Dominican theologian Thomas Aquinas. Once a year, however, he also lectured before the entire community of the university, taking as a point of departure some passage covered in the regular course syllabus and exploring it in ways that went beyond the usual exposition given in his class. This latter kind of address was termed a *relectio*, or "rereading." In 1539 he gave two such lectures, working from a question posed by Aquinas (*Summa Theologiae* II/II, Q. 10, A. 2) – "Whether it is licit to baptize the children of unbelievers against the wishes of their parents" – to address questions raised by the Spanish encounter with the Indians of the New World, extending his analysis to include implications for Spain's relations to other European states and Islam. The result was – as James Brown Scott has argued in *The Spanish Origin of International Law* (Scott 1934) – that Vitoria was effectively the first to discuss international law in the modern sense, though this new discipline did not fully emerge until after the thought of Grotius and the Peace of Westphalia a century and more later (1648).

Vitoria's two *relectiones* from 1539 were published in 1557, after his death, under the general title *De Indis* (Of the Indians), though customarily today this title is reserved for the first *relectio*, while the second is given a more pointed title reflecting its content, *De Jure Belli* (Of the

Law of War). Victoria made his major impact on the just war tradition through these *relectiones*, though his discussion of Aquinas's question "On War" from his classroom lectures was also published.

Vitoria's reasoning in the *relectiones De Indis* and *De Jure Belli* led to two interpretations of just war that later took root in international law: First, that war based in difference of religion is unjust; and second, that in some circumstances invincible ignorance of one or both parties to a conflict can lead to the possibility of a war believed just on both sides, so that as a result moderation should be emphasized in the fighting of war.

Vitoria's answer to Aquinas's question about baptism led directly to both these positions. He observed that Aquinas held that there is no such right to baptism in natural law. Others had argued that the Indians were in a state of ignorance from which the Spanish had the obligation to raise them, and that they might employ force as necessary to do so. This was in effect an argument that difference of religion – Christianity over the Indians' ignorance and paganism – justified war against them to introduce them to Christianity. Vitoria rejected this argument in *De Indis* in connection with his rejecting several other versions of the argument that the Spanish as Christians have a just cause for war against the Indians (Vitoria 1917: *De Indis*, section II, 10–16). He returned to this topic in the second *relectio*, stating his conclusion in simple language: "Difference of religion is not a cause of just war" (Vitoria 1917: *De Jure Belli*, section 10), continuing: "Nor is extension of empire or glory or advantage to the prince" (sections 11–12), and concluding: "There is a single and only just cause for commencing a war, namely wrong received" (section 13). This last is nothing more nor less than the definition of just cause found in Gratian and his canonist successors and in Aquinas's question "On War." Vitoria's context was the Spanish encounter with the Indians in the New World, but he concluded with a core proposition of classic just war thinking.

As to the possibility of justice on both sides in a war, in *De Indis* section II Vitoria observed that if the Spanish make war against the Indians to convert them by force, then the Indians have by natural law the right to defend themselves; therefore, if it is just to make war for religion, the paradoxical conclusion is that the resulting war is just on both sides, so that no one may kill anyone in it. He returned to the question of war that is just on both sides in *De Jure Belli* section 20, posing it there as the result of one party's belief that he is in the right even if he is not. Such is the case, argued Vitoria, when Turks and Saracens attack Christians to propagate Islam, believing they have a

just cause to do so. But the Christians in such a case have the natural
right to defend themselves, and thus they fight with a just cause, so that
each side appears to itself to have a just cause. In other contexts he
raised the same possibility for cases in which European princes go to
war over some dispute such as where a border lies: One prince,
following his own evidence, reaches one conclusion, while the other,
following his evidence, reaches another. Which is in the right and truly
has just cause (if either) is known to God, but the princes' reasoning is
clouded by invincible ignorance, which by definition cannot be overcome by reason. In *De Indis* Vitoria's logical conclusion in cases of a war
seemingly just on both sides is that neither side has the right to kill
persons on the other, and that therefore there should be no war. But in
De Jure Belli he moves in a different direction: "[T]he rights of war
which may be invoked against men who are really guilty and lawless
differ from those which may be invoked against the innocent and
ignorant" (*De Indis*, section 7). Thus, in prosecuting a war that
seems to be just on both sides, the *jus in bello* should be understood
as requiring moderation.

Subsequent thinkers developed this idea further, so that with
Grotius the idea that *all* wars should be treated as *de facto* just on both
sides moved into international law, with the corollary that this implies
the triumph of *jus in bello*, understood as restraints aimed at imposing
moderation, over *jus ad bellum*, which allows the just party the right to
determine the extent of punishment deserved by the guilty. Grotius's
position became that of the law of nations on war after him and carried
over into later customary and positive international law.

Grotius's *De Jure Belli ac Pacis* has from its first appearance exerted
a profound influence on the development of international law, early
being translated from the Latin into various European languages. The
citations below are from an early English translation published in 1682.

Grotius's thinking shows his deep indebtedness to the tradition on
just war, but he transformed the content of the just war idea in various
ways. While he, like the tradition before him, understood the just war
idea to be based in natural law, he defined the origin and nature of
natural law somewhat differently. Medieval thought had regarded
natural law as one of the stages in God's promulgation of law to his
creation: from divine law to the law of nature to the laws of particular
peoples. One's understanding of each lower stage could be checked by
the conformity of that understanding to the requirements of the stage
above it. Grotius worked in the opposite way, grounding natural law
in the behavior of the earliest historical cases he could identify: those

of classical Greece and Rome. Like his medieval predecessors, Grotius could represent Christian teaching on war, "the dictates of charity," as the perfection of the natural law. But viewed from his bottom-up perspective, what this meant for him was that Christian charity expressed the implications of natural law to their fullest extent. He thus made Christian morality over from something defined by divine revelation into a highly developed natural morality experienced and fleshed out in the secular world. The tradition on just war shared by the Christian nations accordingly became for Grotius the "law of nations," defined by common traditions of value and common consent.

Grotius developed the idea that all wars might be understood as just on both sides by defining just war as "solemn" war. In the framework of the law of nations the justice of a war depended on whether it adhered to certain formalities, not on moral considerations.

> Now that a war be solemn according to the Law of Nations, two things are requisite: First, that it be on both sides made by the Authority of those in their respective cities who have the sovereign power: And next, that it be waged with such rites and formalities as the Law of Nations requires.
>
> (Grotius 1682, bk. I, chap. III, 31–52)

The result of this thinking was to remove weight from the *jus ad bellum* while adding it to the *jus in bello*. The former, for Grotius, was defined for a just or "solemn" war by a formal declaration of war, including publication of the just causes for which the war was being fought, by the sovereign of a nation. That two sovereigns had to issue such formal declarations to make "solemn" war meant that Grotius, like Vitoria and others before him, had a concept of a war ostensibly just on both sides. But for him this shifted emphasis to the *jus in bello*, recharacterized by Grotius as the "rites and formalities" consensually agreed to by nations and to be observed as absolutely binding in fighting any wars between or among them. He described the content of these consensual rules for war-fighting with the words "modesty" and "moderation," understanding them as following from considerations of proportionality and equity: in other words, natural justice. The subsequent development of the law of war traces to this transformation of the *jus in bello* into rules rooted in an entirely secular basis, in a concept of justice rooted in the mutual consent of nations. It is no great step from this conception to that of the "customary" law of nations of the 19th century and then to the emergence of positive law, first as expressing and clarifying this customary law, then progressively as defined by the positive ratification of agreements among states regulating their conduct.

But Grotius did not see so far as this: His focus was on the Christian nations of Europe, whose common heritage defined norms of "charity" that he believed could translate into mutual consensus on limits ("modesty") in war-fighting. In the short term this was a highly optimistic expectation. Grotius wrote *De Jure Belli ac Pacis* during the Thirty Years War, whose conduct was marked by extreme violations of the sort of consensual international rules for war Grotius sought to put in place. But the Peace of Westphalia that ended this war established an international order that made possible the development of what Grotius had argued for. Over succeeding decades three thinkers – Samuel von Pufendorf, Christian Wolff, and Emerich de Vattel – built upon Grotius to establish and define the system of international law that has since expanded into a world system. In this system the heritage of just war tradition remains, but today it has been joined by traditions on statecraft and war from other cultures as well as that of the West, and the emphasis on the need for positive assent to the content of this law reflects this plural heritage. At the same time, this plurality introduces new tensions, taking the problems of war and international order far from the context Grotius assumed, that of the Christian nations of the West.

THE DEVELOPMENT OF JUST WAR TRADITION IN A DIVIDED CHRISTIANITY AFTER THE REFORMATION

Today references to the idea of just war as a "Catholic" teaching occur with some frequency. This is doubly wrong. On the one hand, as seen in the previous section, through the work of thinkers including Vitoria, Grotius, and others the idea of just war has been transformed into international law, increasingly conceived as without religious content. On the other hand, when European Christianity split into two faiths, Catholic and Protestant, both inherited the legacy of earlier Christian thought and practice, including the tradition of just war. The idea of just war belongs as much to Protestant Christianity as to Catholic.

In the Reformation era this shows up early in the writings of Martin Luther. The parameters of Luther's thought on war are defined by four of his writings: *Temporal Authority: To What Extent It Should Be Obeyed* (1523, in Luther 1962), *Against the Robbing and Murderous Hordes of Peasants* (1525, in Luther 1967), *Whether Soldiers, Too, Can Be Saved* (1526, in Luther 1967), and *On War Against the Turk* (1529, in

Luther 1967). The earliest and most fundamental of the listed writings, the treatise *Temporal Authority*, establishes the general framework of Luther's political theory around the concept of the two "kingdoms" (that of God and that of the world) with their respective "governments" (the spiritual and the temporal or secular). In Luther's thought on war, like that of Aquinas and the mainstream of the just war tradition Luther inherited, the question of authority is the most fundamental one for the justice of the use of the sword. Again and again in his discussion of matters bearing on the use of the sword he brings to bear the understanding of authority established in just war tradition.

In *Temporal Authority* Luther made his own this conception of authority to resort to the use of arms, doing so in the context of laying out his understanding of the extent of temporal and spiritual authority. The spiritual–temporal distinction came to Luther and his contemporaries as part of their common intellectual heritage from the Middle Ages. But Luther differed sharply from his Catholic adversaries on the meaning of this distinction. The latter held that the spiritual authority (embodied in the Pope) not only has its own exclusive sphere but also occupies a place of superiority over the secular. On this view the papacy could create and depose rulers or discipline them as needed. To do this the Pope had authority for use of the sword, both to protect true religion and to punish dissent and heresy, including the conduct of temporal rulers judged guilty of misgovernment, especially if that were manifest in opposition to the true religion of the Catholic Church. At the same time the papalists held to the traditional just war position that gave authority over the sword to temporal rulers. Together these two claims defined their so-called two swords doctrine. Luther rejected this position, holding to the "one sword" position first defined by the canonists: that only a prince, a temporal ruler without temporal superior, possessed the authority to take the sword in a just cause for the good of the commonwealth governed. Luther argued, against his Catholic adversaries, that the spiritual and temporal authorities occupy their own realms, with neither having authority over the other outside its own realm and each subject to the other's authority within its realm. This was his "two kingdoms" doctrine. In the worldly "kingdom," rightful authority belongs only to the secular powers, extending even to the external regulation of religious matters. This follows, Luther argued, from God's institution of government in the beginning of time.

In his treatise against the behavior of the German peasants in their 1524–1525 rebellion Luther turned this position not toward his argument with the papalists, but toward the peasants and their aristocratic

superiors. While Luther sympathized with many of the peasants' grievances, he believed them wrong to take arms against their superiors to
seek to achieve their aims: They did not have the authority to take the
sword, and their use of arms did wrongful harm up to and including
murder. This was not the case for the use of arms under legitimate
authority. For Luther (and the just war tradition before him) it was the
responsibility of the temporal authorities and their representatives to
put down the rebellion, restoring order and punishing the peasants for
usurping authority, and they might rightly use the sword to do so. His
argument against the peasants in rebellion illustrates the influence of
the just war idea he had inherited.

Whether Soldiers, Too, Can be Saved also reveals the influence of
just war tradition, though in a different way. Luther's argument here
was that so long as, in their use of arms, soldiers are acting on the orders
of those in temporal authority over them, they do not sin in using those
arms. This argument goes back to Augustine, who had compared the
roles of the public executioner and the soldier: Both do not sin in
carrying out their duties in service to the temporal order and the good
of the political community.

Finally, *On War Against the Turk* considers the matter of war
against unbelievers – a problem Vitoria also addressed when considering
the rights of the Spanish over the Indians of the New World. Though
these two men lived and wrote at the same time, they did not know
each other's work, and though they developed similar positions, they
did so independently. Both Luther and Vitoria argued against making
offensive war against the Turkish Empire on the grounds that neither
European rulers nor the Pope had authority over the Turkish ruler and
the political order he governed. Defensive war against a Turkish attack
was surely permitted, but offensive war was another matter entirely.
Vitoria's argument, discussed above, was that difference of religion is
not a cause of just war, while Luther's was a development out of his
"one sword" position: Both denied the papacy the authority to seek to
impose Christian faith on an unbelieving temporal power.

Luther's writings involving political authority and war show a clear
influence of the just war tradition he inherited. This continued in the
Lutheran movement after him.

John Calvin, the principal theologian of the second main branch of
the Protestant movement – the Reformed tradition – had little to say
directly about war, but when he did so, he addressed it succinctly. In his
Institutes of the Christian Religion, book IV, chapter 20, sections 11–12
(Reichberg et al. 2006: 276–277), section 11 summarizes the just war *jus*

ad bellum as Calvin inherited it, while section 12 summarizes the *jus in bello* as he knew it. He begins the former with these words: "But Kings and people must sometimes take up arms to execute ... public vengeance. On this basis we may judge wars which are so undertaken." The body of section 11 elaborates on this. Finally, in the conclusion to this section, Calvin sums up:

> Therefore, both natural equity and the nature of the office dictate that princes must be armed not only to restrain the misdeeds of private individuals by judicial punishment, but also to defend by war the dominions entrusted to their safekeeping, if at any time they are under enemy attack. And the Holy Spirit declares such wars to be lawful by many testimonies of Scripture.
>
> (Reichberg et al. 2006: 276)

In section 12 Calvin turns his attention to how armed force authorized and justified in such a way may be employed. The basic form of his position reflects the main line of the just war tradition before him, but what he says in this section also reflects the turn made in the just war *jus in bello* in his own age, initiated by Vitoria and echoed and developed by subsequent thinkers: Thus Calvin entitles the section on how to fight in a just war "Restraint and Humanity in War." He begins by adopting a basic just war understanding of the right to resort to arms: "[T]he reason for waging war which existed of old still persists today; and ... There is no reason that bars magistrates from defending their subjects" (Reichberg et al. 2006: 276–277). After further elaborating this Calvin turns to the subject previewed in the section title – restraint in the just use of arms – here making use of Augustine's language against what is evil in war from his *Contra Faustum*: For Calvin, magistrates are not to give vent to their passions, not to "be carried away with headlong anger" in their punishment of evildoing, "or be seized with hatred, or burn with implacable severity. Let them also (as Augustine says) have pity on the common nature in the one whose special fault they are punishing." He continues by counseling that the resort to arms not be undertaken "lightly" and should result only in cases of "extreme necessity" (Reichberg et al. 2006: 277). The earlier tradition had applied Augustine's passage to define right intention in the decision to wage war, but Calvin extended it to how to fight: the *jus in bello*. Calvin's position, and not least the title he gave this section, also reflects the development in early modern just war thought already highlighted above: the movement in just war tradition toward defining the *jus in bello* as implying restraint in the practice of war.

If Calvin treated just war only briefly, others in the Reformed tradition contemporaneous with him and later had a great deal to say revealing the influence of just war tradition. Many of these were English thinkers, writing in the context of the Protestant–Catholic wars of religion being waged from the time of Luther through the Thirty Years War. (See further Johnson 1975: chap. II.) The Puritan theologian William Ames, in treating war and other topics in his influential *Conscience, With the Powers and Cases Thereof* (1639), made extensive use of Aquinas's *Summa Theologiae*, and his position on war directly reflected that of Aquinas in his question "On War." Reformed thinkers on the continent also showed knowledge and influence of just war tradition in their work: A principal example is Grotius, who was educated in Reformed theology and worked with the inherited just war tradition out of deep knowledge of it.

Thinkers on the Catholic side of the new divide in European Christianity also made use of the inherited just war idea, with some, together with certain Protestants, seeking to turn it into a justification of holy war against the other (Johnson 1975: chap. II). But the main line of just war tradition, as exemplified by Vitoria, developed so as to reject war for religion, and for Catholic thought on war this is best exemplified by the work of the Jesuit theologian Francisco Suarez, mentioned earlier. His work *On War* held to the form established by Cajetan and Vitoria: a development of the idea of just war in Aquinas. Like Vitoria and other writers of the period, Protestant and Catholic, Suarez here explored the problems of war for religion and of doubt as to just cause.

Suarez devoted a full section of his *On War* to the question of whether difference of religion can provide a just cause for war. Rejecting the advocacy of war for religion advanced by proponents of holy war in his own time, he answered that just cause can be provided only by natural law, known by natural reason (Reichberg et al. 2006: 353–356). He thus affirmed the same conclusion as Vitoria and others in the main line of just war tradition before him, the position carried into the law of nations by Grotius.

On the question of whether both sides in a conflict may be just, Suarez's first answer is simply to say that the prince must examine the claims carefully so as to ascertain which is right. But then he continues, turning the matter into one of greater and less probability: "[W]hen the case of each side contains [an element of] probability," if the prince "finds that the opinion favoring his own side is the more probably true, he may, even justly, prosecute his own right; because ... The more probable opinion should always be preferred in passing judgment"

(Reichberg et al. 2006: 359). On the question of how war should be prosecuted, Suarez used similar reasoning, arguing that the prosecution of the war should reflect the degree of certainty of just cause: "[T]he punishment inflicted by war is of the severest kind; therefore, that punishment ought to be inflicted with the utmost restraint" (Reichberg et al. 2006: 362). Thus, Suarez reached a similar position to that held by Grotius and the law of nations after them both, a position that recognizes the possibility that neither side in a war may clearly have a monopoly on justice and that stresses that right conduct in war involves restraint.

After Suarez no Catholic theologian engaged in a major discussion of just war for over three centuries, though this idea, cast in the classic form given it by Gratian and his successors, remained in the canon law until early in the 20th century. Rather, discussion of war shifted, following the Enlightenment, to the possibility of an international order in which war might be eliminated, and in the late 19th century the advent of large national armies and more highly destructive weapons than seen earlier led to arguments against war itself. On the Protestant side attention to just war also waned as the modern period advanced, though here the main features were the shift toward regulating war by international law, and in the Enlightenment era by the development of thinking centered on human rights. Among both Catholics and Protestants, then, as the modern period developed, modes of thinking about war shifted away from religious language and concerns toward secular ones.

The present age, though, has seen a recovery of the idea of just war, including specifically Christian contributions by both Catholic and Protestant thinkers. This recovery began in the 1960s with two books by Protestant theological ethicist Paul Ramsey (1961, 1968). Michael Walzer's *Just and Unjust Wars* (1977) followed, and the US Catholic bishops' pastoral letter *The Challenge of Peace* in turn appeared in 1983. Two of these three, the contributions from Ramsey and the US Catholic bishops, were explicitly based in Christian reasoning, while Walzer's approach was secular, beginning with the idea of human rights and the model of international law on war. None of these sought to recover the historical tradition on just war but instead defined just war in their own ways. Subsequent writers, working from these beginnings, have followed one or another of these leads. Meanwhile, other writers have sought to recover attention to the historical tradition. As a result, contemporary just war thinking is marked by diversity, not the unity prevalent earlier.

References

Ames, William. 1639. *Conscience, with the Power and Cases Thereof.* n.n.

Grotius, Hugo. 1682. *The Most Excellent Hugo Grotius His three Books Treating of the Rights of War and Peace.* n.n.

Johnson, James Turner. 1975. *Ideology, Reason, and the Limitation of War: Religious and Secular Concepts, 1200–1740.* Princeton University Press.

  1981. *Just War Tradition and the Restraint of War: A Moral and Historical Inquiry.* Princeton University Press.

Luther, Martin. 1962. *Luther's Works,* vol. 45. Fortress Press.

  1967. *Luther's Works,* vol. 46. Fortress Press.

National Conference of Catholic Bishops. 1983. *The Challenge of Peace: God's Promise and Our Response.* United States Catholic Conference.

Ramsey, Paul. 1961. *War and the Christian Conscience: How Shall Modern War Be Conducted Justly?* Duke University Press.

  1968. *The Just War: Force and Political Responsibility.* Charles Scribner's Sons.

Reichberg, Gregory, Henrik Syse, and Endre Begby, eds. 2006. *The Ethics of War: Classic and Contemporary Readings.* Wiley-Blackwell.

Scott, James Brown. 1934. *The Spanish Origin of International Law.* Clarendon Press.

Victoria, Franciscus de. 1917. *De Indis et De Jure Belli Relectiones. Classics of International Law.* Edited by Ernest Nys. Carnegie Institute.

Walzer, Michael. 1977. *Just and Unjust Wars.* Basic Books.

11 Islam and the Just War Tradition: Postclassical Developments

DAVID COOK

INTRODUCTION

The postclassical just war tradition in Islam is important and continues to be influential to the present time. This period covers the point following the development of traditions and legal precedents concerning jihad (sacral warfare) during the 3rd–4th/10th–12th centuries. Development of traditions meant the collection and publication of the prophetic tradition concerning warfare, placing these traditions within the context of the Qur'ān,[1] and then formulating both of these legal bases into law (sharī'a), which could be applied to practical situations or used as an authority basis.

For the most part, the Muslim world during the classical period was at its apogee. In terms of control over territory, in terms of cultural and religious influence, and in terms of self-confidence, the Islamic world was at a high point. Such a high point enabled Muslim Sunni jurists to take a rather relaxed view of the role of sacral warfare. For the most part, those formulating the legal bases of Sunnism were physically divorced from actual battlefields, both in time and in space. That is to say, with regard to time, most of the precedents upon which they relied were deep in the Islamic past, and with regard to space, most of those then-contemporary battles being fought along the frontiers of Islam – the boundary between dār al-islām (House of Islam) and dār al-ḥarb (House of War) – were comparatively distant.

Sacral warfare had indeed acquired a high status as a result of the prophetic example (Muḥammad's battles enshrined inside the Qur'ān and his biography), as well as the historical memory of the great Muslim conquests' success during the period immediately following Muḥammad's death in 11/632. But sacral warfare was not a major factor while the great legal compendia of Sunni Islam were being compiled.

[1] Remembering that for Sunnis the Prophetic tradition had precedence over the Qur'ān.

These compilations were made when the Muslim Empire was at its height and exuded cultural superiority and self-confidence.

However, there were definitely fronts all along the Islamic world where warfare was persistent and had never ceased even after the conquests were over. Most of these fronts faced mountains or difficult terrain that the early Muslim conquerors had avoided. These regions included the area of northwestern Spain (where Spanish Christians had established themselves), the Caucasus mountains, the mountainous area of Afghanistan (where warfare against local tribes and the Turks was continuous), and most especially the mountainous region bordering northern Syria against the Christian Byzantine Empire.

It is to the conflict with the Byzantines that we must turn when we consider the question of postclassical just war developments. Whereas on other fronts Muslims fought entities with local aspirations at best, without being serious religious challenges, the religious and cultural challenge of the Byzantine Empire was on a different scale. As the empire that had previously controlled the eastern Mediterranean Basin, including the regions of Syria, Egypt, and parts of North Africa, the Byzantines from a historical point of view could contest the Muslims' right to rule those regions. As many of the inhabitants of those conquered regions, such as Syria and Egypt, were still Christians, there was a religious element to the struggle with the Byzantines as well. Those Christian populations might rise in revolt if the Byzantines were not kept in check.

The importance of the jihad against the Byzantine Christians is encapsulated in a (probably apocryphal) conversation between two of the postclassical greats: Abū Isḥāq al-Fazārī (d. 186/802–3), and ʿAbdallāh b. al-Mubārak (d. 181/797):

> Abū Isḥāq al-Fazārī said to Ibn al-Mubārak: "You left the frontiers of Khurāsān, al-Washajird and Qazwīn, when God most high said: 'Fight those unbelievers near you'." (Q9:123) But the latter said: "Abū Isḥāq, I have a verse more relevant than that: 'Fight those who do not believe in God and the Last Day, and (who) do not forbid what God and His messenger have forbidden'." (Q9:29)
>
> Then the latter said: "These are fighting about our world" meaning the Turks and the Daylamites, "whereas those are waging war against us about our faith," meaning the Byzantines. "So which is more worthy of defense: our world or our faith?"
>
> (Cook 1996:98)

This conversation lays bare the stakes in the Muslim warfare against the Byzantines. It was not merely concerning territory but the relative religious primacy of Islam as opposed to Christianity. This religious aspect was also present to some degree in the warfare against the Spanish Christians and the (as-yet non-Muslim) Turks, but it was nowhere near as urgent with the latter two groups, who were distant from the Muslim heartlands. During the 8th and 9th centuries, it was some time in the distant future before the Spanish Christians would seriously challenge the Spanish Muslims.

Just warfare, then, was that which was necessitated for the defense and aggrandizement of Islam during this early postclassical period. Muslims on these border regions, fighting those they called unbelievers, drove the discussions on jihad and just warfare. Ibn al-Mubārak, cited above, for example, authored the first independent book on jihad in Arabic. Later, the Byzantine menace became stronger during what is frequently called the Byzantine Revival – the period following 950 when the Byzantines, due to successive militarily talented emperors, managed to conquer or reconquer substantial sections of northern Syria from the Muslims. Such a conquest was a new sensation for the Muslims, used to centuries of victories and raiding adjacent territories.

The real test of postclassical just war came with the Crusades. The Crusades, lasting between 1095 and 1291, were a series of papally initiated invasions targeting the Levant, and most especially the holy city of Jerusalem, for Christian control. The Crusades, however, were not the only invasions that the Muslim world around the Mediterranean Basin faced. The popes also encouraged firstly the conquest of southern Italy and Sicily from the Muslims, and secondly the beginnings of the Spanish Reconquista.

Whatever the success of these various attacks upon the world of Islam – and their successes went up and down for some centuries – the very fact of Muslim territories being consistently attacked by non-Muslims, with the concurrent loss of Muslim self-confidence and the rollback of the world of Islam, necessitated new thinking about jihad and just warfare.

CRUSADES AND MONGOLS

The Crusaders exemplified a much more significant religious challenge to the Muslims than did the Byzantines. While the Byzantines threatened the heartlands of Islam and during the period 950–1075 controlled much of northern Syria – territory that the Muslims had once controlled – the Byzantines never actually invaded very deeply into the Muslim heartlands. Indeed, when the Byzantines had the opportunity during the early 11th century to conquer Jerusalem, they did not take it (under Basil II, who successfully attacked central and even southern Syria).

This is in stark contrast to the Crusaders, whose specific goal was the conquest of Jerusalem, and perhaps even the eventual conquest of the Muslim world. This latter goal might seem ludicrous to an outsider, given the Crusaders' tiny numbers; however, from a Muslim point of view, the possibility of Crusader conquest was emphasized by their continual attempts to conquer Egypt and other major tracts of territory in Syria and Anatolia (Hillenbrand 2000).

Prior to the appearance of the Crusaders, no major treatise on jihad had appeared in Arabic in several hundred years. Therefore, to a large extent the tradition of just warfare had to be recreated. The first writer who began to revive the jihad tradition was `Alī b. Ṭāhir al-Sulamī (d. 499/1106), who was a Damascene legal scholar. His work on jihad is highly theoretical and was singularly lacking in influence in the war against the Crusaders (Christie 2015).

That jihad was not influential in fighting the Crusaders is apparent from the manner in which the Muslim Turks pursued the war. Probably the best example of this disconnect between the jihad theory and the practicalities of war occurred with the Muslim victory at the Battle of the Field of Blood in 1119. This battle, during which the Turkish Il-Ghazi decisively defeated the northern Crusaders under Roger of Salerno, Prince of Antioch, who was killed during the battle, was not followed up, even though the entire Antiochene army was destroyed. The later memoirist Usāma Ibn Munqidh (d. 583/1188) recounts the reason:

> Now, when Il-Ghazi used to drink wine, he would be drunk for twenty days. And he took to drink, after destroying the Franks and killing them, going on a drunken spree, from which he never recovered until King Baldwin arrived in Antioch at the head of his army.
>
> (Ibn Munqidh, trans. Cobb 2007:12)

As we will see, one of the major bases for the postclassical Muslim just warfare is that there has to be a close connection between morality and victory. God supports the Muslim side as long as the Muslims act according to Islamic principles. Since Il-Ghazi habitually was drunk after a victory, he lost out on what could have been a complete victory over the northern Crusaders at this point.

Just warfare during the postclassical period against the Crusaders, and the other different western European Christians, then had to wait for Muslim leadership that was consistent in its application of Muslim laws and norms. The implicit accusation leveled against the Muslim rulers and dynasties that had suffered defeat first at the hands of the Byzantines and second at the hands of the Crusaders was that they were not sufficiently Islamic.

With the rise of Nūr al-Dīn (d. 571/1174), and especially with Saladin (d. 589/1193), this basis for the just war came to be realized. Both of these rulers were very ostentatious and devout Sunni Muslims, and both of them based their ruling legitimacy squarely upon jihad and success upon the battlefield (Bonner 2006:137–52).

Nūr al-Dīn utilized, among others, the great Damascene historian and religious figure Ibn ʿAsākir (d. 574/1176) to publish the jihad trad-itions that would support his just warfare against the Crusaders. Not surprisingly, Ibn ʿAsākir was very careful to give primacy to those traditions emphasizing the moral basis for warfare. For example, his very first tradition reads:

> The Messenger of God was asked: "Which aspect of belief is the best?" He replied: "The belief in God – glory and greatness belong to Him." He was then asked: "And what comes next?" He replied: "Next is jihad in the path of God – glory and greatness belong to Him" …
>
> (Mourad and Lindsay 2015:135)

This tradition is followed by those emphasizing that jihad in importance comes right after prayer – which is one of the five pillars of Islam – and various other good deeds, until the tenth tradition, which is the first that speaks purely about the experience of warfare and martyrdom.

All of these cited traditions are classical, and it is true that Ibn ʿAsākir did not actually add anything new here, but the moral emphasis as the basis for jihad is striking, especially when one considers the background of the relatively amoral (or at least un-Islamic) warfare that had been waged up until this period.

A further group of questions, especially when the war against the Crusaders was so difficult, queried: What are the outer limits of the tactics that are legitimate to utilize in a jihad? In general, classical Muslim jurisprudents had been quite conservative with regard to this issue. These jurisprudents had issued bans on killing civilians, burning their bodies, and other different types of terror tactics.

With the Crusaders, a number of explicitly terroristic tactics came to be used. The most controversial among these was the use of the mangonel. This type of a catapult, usually delivering a payload of rocks but sometimes primitive explosives or even biological weapons (such as dead or diseased bodies) into a city or fortress, raises a number of ethical questions. Because the mangonel's payload was indiscriminate in its nature, as it could not distinguish between fighter and civilian as it was being delivered, there was the very real possibility that its use might compromise the moral quality of the jihad.

Neither al-Sulamī nor Ibn ʿAsākir mentions mangonels, even though these weapons were known to have been used during the classical period against the Byzantines, and even supposedly during the Prophet Muḥammad's lifetime (against the city of al-Ṭā'if).[2] But the middle Crusader jurisprudent Ibn al-Munāṣif (d. 620/1223), writing on jihad a generation after Ibn ʿAsākir, includes a section discussing the use of terror tactics in warfare.

Questions relating to such tactics, for him, include whether it was permissible to kill those who are not causing the fighter immediate danger, whether it was permissible to kill women and children, and whether it was permissible to kill an enemy who was unarmed. Wanton burning of houses and farms and killing of herds are also discussed, as are killing of prisoners, taking them as slaves, and raping their women (Ibn al-Munāṣif 2003:185–220). To all of these questions, Ibn al-Munāṣif answers in the affirmative, either giving some type of prophetic example as a precedent or else stating that the enemy was using such tactics against the Muslims and needed to be terrorized.

With regard mangonels and other indiscriminate terror tactics, use of them, according to Ibn al-Munāṣif, should only be excluded from a legal point of view if there are Muslim prisoners among the enemy numbers or if Muslims are being used as human shields (Ibn al-Munāṣif 2003: 194f).

These views are considerably harsher than one finds in the classical Muslim legal literature and doubtlessly represent the technological changes that were occurring in warfare during the Crusader period. While mangonels had been utilized since the classical period of Islam, as previously noted, their use and accuracy and ability to deliver

---

[2] It is difficult to say whether Muḥammad's use of mangonels is historical or not. Wood for mangonel construction is difficult to obtain in Arabia, and one could speculate that there would have been no models available for the successful construction of such a device.

massive payloads expanded considerably during the Crusader period – an expansion that heralded the eventual rise of cannon centuries later. If Muslim jurisprudents had not been willing to allow for the large-scale use of the mangonel, it is possible that eventual victory over the Crusaders would not have occurred.

Thus, after the moral basis for jihad warfare, the postclassical Sunni literature emphasized the optimum means by which to obtain victory and was willing to finesse the prophetic traditions and earlier legal dicta in order to support the winning formula.

This winning formula was considerably tested by the appearance of the Mongols, which, from the Muslim point of view, began to occur during the 620s/1220s onwards (in Central Asian Transoxiania) and culminated with the sack of Baghdad and the murder of the ʿAbbāsid caliph in 656/1258. The Mongol advance through the eastern part of the Muslim world, while perhaps not as destructive as the Muslim chroniclers described it, was still a unique challenge to the Muslim community's identity. This challenge was due to the religious makeup of the Mongols and the nature of their invasions. While the Crusaders, being Christians, were believed by Muslims to adhere to an abrogated but monotheistic religion, the Mongols were mostly pagans or Buddhists (some were Nestorian Christians). Muslims had a long experience of up-and-down warfare against Christians, especially around the Mediterranean Basin. Therefore, some defeats at the hands of western Christians, while certainly problematic within the context of Islam's foreordained future victory, were not entirely unexpected.

However, the Muslim experience of warfare to the east until the Mongol invasions was entirely different. As Ibn al-Mubārak noted in the quotation cited above, the Muslims in the east were not really fighting about religion. For the most part, the trajectory of Islam in the east was an upward one, even if individual battles were sometimes lost. Warfare with the Turks or the Afghans, for example, resulted eventually in both groups converting to Islam and bolstering the Muslims' numbers.

At least initially this was not the case with the Mongols. Over the long haul, in fact, the Mongols did end up converting to Islam. During the critical period of 654/1256 to 700/1300, however, which is when most of the major jihad formulations were made, the Mongols were perceived by the Sunni Muslims as non-Muslims. This perception was due to the fact that the Mongols had killed the Sunni caliph, and even when they gradually converted to Islam – starting approximately during the 680s/1280s – they usually did not fully impose the *sharīʿa* upon their subjects, and in some cases could be quite tolerant of actions that flouted Islamic supremacy.[3]

There were a number of Mongol attempts to conquer the Sunni Mamluks, who were mostly Turkish by ethnicity, in Syria and Egypt. The Mamluks viewed themselves as being the defenders of Islam, which, given the fact that the Mongols ruled most of the eastern Muslim world and that much of the western Muslim world was either occupied by Christian Europeans or under attack by them, was not entirely an unjustified perception.

For the Mamluks, the development of a just war ideology to combat the Mongols was even more critical than it had been with earlier Islamic dynasties facing the Crusaders. This critical situation was due to the greatly superior numbers that the Mongols could bring to bear; the Crusaders, at least in the Levant, had never been able to enjoy anything remotely like numerical parity with their Muslim foes. The Mongols, on the other hand, were actually capable of conquest, a capability they had demonstrated when destroying Baghdad. Thus, for the Mamluks, the situation was an absolute one that required an absolute response.

RELIGIOUS CHALLENGE AND VICTORY

That absolute response had several ramifications for the development of just war. First of all, the doctrines concerning morality and warfare were tightened considerably. Usually, prior to battle, those Mamluk sultans facing either the Mongols or the Crusaders would make an ostentatious display of enforcing Muslim morality codes. Thus, Baybars al-Bunduqdari (d. 676/1277), who conquered a number of the Crusader cities and fortresses, prior to the conquest of the great Templar fortress at Safed (northern Israel) is said to have stated: "Anyone who brought in wine or was caught drunk would be hanged" (Ibn al-Furāt 1971: vol. VII:92).

Although this was during the holy month of Ramadan, so it is doubly understandable that Baybars did not want any forms of religious infraction, it is clear that, from the Mamluk point of view, the military–moralist formula was working. The account of Ibn al-Furāt also emphasizes Baybars' personal participation in the work, such as helping to drag the mangonels. The above threat to hang drunkards is considerably dissimilar from Il-Ghazi's drunkenness after the Battle of the Field of Blood.

---

[3] For example, their tolerance of Ibn Kammūna's writing a refutation of all monotheistic religions in 687/1288.

Similarly, Qalāwūn (d. 688/1290), who eventually succeeded Baybars, completed the latter's work by conquering many of the remaining Crusader fortresses. Prior to Qalāwūn's definitive battle with the Mongols – the Battle of Ḥimṣ during 679/1281 – he is said to have had all the wine in Damascus poured out. Morality was seen during this period as a key component to victory, which, in the case of both Baybars and Qalāwūn, seems to have been the case.

There was a second component to the just warfare theory during the Mongol period that was developed, and this was the question of how to relate to those Muslims who chose to fight on the other side. One should note that there is only minimal discussion of this question in the jihad literature from the Crusader conflict, in spite of the fact that it was not at all uncommon for both Muslims and Christians to fight together with those who were not their coreligionists.

In the case of the Mongols, from the Mamluk point of view, the sense that Muslims who fought on the Mongol side were not only traitors but actually apostates began to develop. Already during Qalāwūn's reign one sees discussion of the Sunni Muslim ruler of the northern Iraqi town of Mārdīn, who completely threw his lot in with the Mongols. Since we have no chronicler who documented the latter's point of view, we cannot say whether this choice was opportunistic or ideological.

For the Mamluks, it made no difference. In the immediate wake of the Battle of Ḥimṣ, Qalāwūn noted that "the [Muslims] of the east were helping the unbelievers ..." (Cook 2020:148, cited from Ibn ʿAbd al-Ẓāhir). He sought a religious ruling to permit him to raid them and to punish them for their collaboration with the Mongols. It is with this ruling that we can see during the postclassical period the need to redefine the boundaries between Islam and unbelief. Previously these boundaries were usually clear; there were few Muslims living in regions controlled by unbelievers (usually the Muslims were encouraged to emigrate upon being conquered), and so the issue of collaboration almost never arose.

But the ruler of Mārdīn and many other Muslims under the Mongols were perfectly good Muslims who fulfilled the basic ordinances of Islam. However, they were supporting a state that both was not imposing Muslim norms of *shariʿa* and was trying to destroy the major state – that of the Mamluks – that was imposing such norms.

Key to this debate is the Muslim jurisprudent Ibn Taymiyya (d. 728/1328), who was himself a refugee from the Mongols to the Mamluks and who had absolutely no mercy for those Muslims who fought on the side of the Mongols. When asked, Ibn Taymiyya made it clear that one who fights on the side of non-Muslims is himself a non-Muslim (Ibn Taymiyya 1991: vol. 2:160–2). This formula had the effect of once again clarifying the boundaries between belief and unbelief, and of how to wage just war. The just war was one that was fought by a Muslim state in order to impose (Sunni) Islamic norms upon the society.

MARTYRDOM AND MEANING

The just war also requires examples – martyrs – to exemplify the manner in which it is to be waged (Cook 2007). Classical Islamic martyrology is scattered through books on jihad, history books, as well as fine literature. Ideally these martyrs should be of exemplary character, and obviously they should be fighting on the Muslim side.

One of the classic martyrdoms from the postclassical period comes from the Second Crusade siege of Damascus (July 24–29, 1148). It is focused upon the elderly Mālikī jurisprudent al-Findalāwī and is cited by the historian and traditionalist Ibn ʿAsākir in his *Taʾrīkh madīnat Dimashq* (*History of the city of Damascus*):

> Al-Findalāwī was killed on Saturday, 6 Rabīʿ al-Awwal 543 [July 25, 1148] at the village of al-Nayrab under al-Rabwa. He had gone out to fight (*mujāhid*) the Franks, may God abandon them ...

Ibn ʿAsākir in this description uses all of the classical tropes in order to open up the martyrdom. Classical traditions emphasize the "going out" in the path of God (jihad), just as al-Findalāwī is said to have done, and the curses against the Crusaders emphasize their unbelief.

Al-Findalāwī fulfilled all of the criteria for being a martyr:

> It reached me that the emir ordered the one in charge to fight them that day, then met him prior to them going to battle. (al-Findalāwī) was clearly suffering from the march, so (the commander) said to him: "Shaykh, imam, return, you are excused because of your old age." But the former said: "I will not return. We have been sold, and He has bought from us" meaning God's Word, mighty and majestic "Surely God has purchased from the believers their lives and their wealth with (the price of) the Garden (in store) for them. They fight in the way of God." (Q9:111)
>
> (Ibn ʿAsākir 1995–8: vol. 74:235)

It is obvious that al-Findalāwī was suffering, no doubt because of his age, and he was given the opportunity to turn back. No Islamically legitimate accusation could have been leveled against him had he indeed turned back from the fighting. Instead, al-Findalāwī clearly stated the stakes: that the Muslims had been bought by God, and that he wanted to fulfill his side of the bargain so that he would obtain paradise.

In many earlier martyrdoms from the classical period it is not unusual for paradisical descriptions to be part of the martyrdom. With al-Findalāwī's martyrdom, these are supplied by a dream sequence:

> Before the day was over, he had gained the martyrdom that he wished, to the felicity he deserved.
>
> Aḥmad b. Muḥammad al-Qayrawānī said: I saw the shaykh, the imam, the Proof of the Religion in a dream, seated in his place, the one in which he used to sit, studying, in the [Damascus] Congregational Mosque. I approached him, and kissed his hand, and kissed his head. I said to him: "Master, shaykh, by God, I have not forgotten you" ... He said to me: "May God bless you." Then I said to him: "Master, shaykh, where are you?" He said: "In the Gardens of Eden 'on couches, facing each other'." (Q15:47)
>
> (Ibn ʿAsākir 1995–8: vol. 74:236)

Martyrdom was the ultimate proof that a war was a just one; the dream sequence serves here to absolutely confirm to the reader that the martyr, al-Findalāwī was rewarded in an appropriate manner.

However, the just war also raised questions about who exactly was a martyr and whether the circumstances of death in battle mattered when adjudicating the issue. These are significant questions, especially as Islam in all of its variants strongly prohibits suicide (cf. Q4:29). While in classical Islamic warfare there was little element of suicide in warfare, there was one category of fighting that bore some resemblance to suicide, which was the "single fighter attacking a (much larger) group."

During the Crusader and Mongol periods this category of fighting became more pronounced. Part of that development had to do with the fact that it was increasingly realized by Muslim fighters – and then later by jurisprudents – that there was some advantage to be gained by a single fighter who could penetrate a much larger number to cause damage – at the expense of his own life.

Immediately prior to the Crusades in Islamic history had been the rise of the Ismaili assassins. These assassins had been used to assassinate high-profile targets, usually political or religious opponents of the Ismailis throughout the Sunni Muslim world (Daftary 1990:352–6). Although their tactics caused Muslims, both Sunni and Shiʿite, to hate and fear the Ismailis, one has to grant that their actions were to some degree effective. Opponents of the Ismailis were more cautious as a result of the dangers of assassination, and the removal of prominent figures, usually Sunni, did have an effect upon the course of events.

If one extrapolates targeted killings to the field of battle, then there is a parallel with the Ismaili assassins. For example, during the Battle of Ḥimṣ between the Mamluks and the Mongols mentioned previously, one emir, ʿIzz al-Dīn Izdimur, charged right at the Mongol commander and managed to engage the latter right in the midst of his guard. The intrepid Izdimur was killed by the guard but managed to mortally wound the Mongol commander as well, who expired a few days later.

Such an action, while not precisely suicide, is suicidal, and as such the classical jihad literature tended to disapprove of it. However, by the Crusader and Mongol periods, improvements in warfare had made it possible that a single fighter could exact a terrible toll from the enemy at the cost of his own life. The later Mamluk jihad theorist (and practitioner) Ibn al-Naḥḥās (d. 814/1411) considered this very question in light of the development of combustibles and primitive Molotov cocktails that was occurring during the post-Crusader/Mongol period. He came to the conclusion – just as with the mangonels discussed above – that if there was some type of benefit to be gained from it, then such suicidal attacks could be considered legitimate and not suicide (Ibn al-Naḥḥās 2002: vol. 1:557–60).

As one reads over the jihad and martyrdom literatures from the postclassical period, it becomes apparent that gradually the heroic single brave fighter ideal that stands behind the early jihad literature is being supplanted by professionals. Already al-Findalāwī during this period was anachronistic, with his sacrifice being meaningless, as is apparent from the dialogue between him and the unnamed commander. His martyrdom, however, is paradigmatic, and it is cited in all of the major Syrian chronicles.

The ones who were winning wars are not even mentioned in the jihad literature or discussed by the jurisprudents. They are those such as the engineers constructing the mangonels, the professional siege-miners who tunneled under battlements and towers and caused them to collapse, and especially the archers who are often the ones to break a foe's resistance by shooting masses of arrows. In all the postclassical jihad literature there is not a single example of a martyrdom at sea, even though boats cutting off the enemy's supplies were often crucial in battle.

CONCLUSIONS

Jihad and just warfare in Islam during the postclassical period were characterized by the two strong imperatives of morality and the need to be victorious. The emphasis upon morality was due to the fact that most Muslims believed that divine favor would only be accorded to them if they were fighting on the basis of Islamic norms. Thus, the early Crusader period, characterized by Muslim defeats or ambiguous victories, was one that was unsatisfactory to Muslims in Syria and Egypt. The appearance of first the Zangid dynasty, especially under Nūr al-Dīn, and then the Ayyubid dynasty under Saladin, from a Sunni Muslim point of view, affirmed the moral character of the jihad and made it fully into a just war.

The need to achieve victory was a more difficult problem to solve. Muslim theories of war had been articulated in order to support a certain type of warfare – that of the light cavalry that enabled the early Muslim conquests of the 8th and 9th centuries. By the period of the Crusades and then that of the Mongols, while light cavalry warfare was far from being obsolete, it was definitely not always victorious in battle.

With the rise of other factors, such as the heavy cavalry favored by the European Crusaders, the development of siege warfare, the extensive use of mangonels, and the beginnings of primitive explosives, Muslim theories of just warfare were in danger of becoming obstacles in the path of victory. If one held to imperatives such as that noncombatants should not be killed in battle or that their bodies should not be burned, then both the use of mangonels and primitive explosives would be prohibited.

Muslims during the Crusader and Mongol periods desired victory, and they were willing to make the modifications necessary to jihad theory in order to both claim a just war and moral war as well as achieve victory. Indeed, the modifications described above served Sunni Muslims well over the several centuries following the Crusader/Mongol period, as this was the time of a massive Muslim expansion during the 1300s until the mid-1600s.

References

Bonner, Michael. 2006. *Jihad in Islamic History: Doctrines and Practice.* Princeton University Press.

Christie, Niall. 2015. *The Book of the Jihad of `Alī ibn Ṭāhir al-Sulamī (d. 1106).* Ashgate.

Cook, David. 1996. "Muslim Apocalyptic and *Jihād.*" *Jerusalem Studies in Arabic and Islam* 20: 66–104.

2007. *Martyrdom in Islam.* Cambridge University Press.

2020. *Chronicles of Qalawun and His Son al-Ashraf Khalil.* Routledge.

Daftary, Farhad. 1990. *The Ismailis: Their History and Doctrines.* Cambridge University Press.

Hillenbrand, Carole. 2000. *The Crusades: Islamic Perspectives.* Edinburgh University Press.

Ibn ʿAsākir. 1995–8. *Tāʾrīkh madīnat Dimashq.* Dār al-Fikr.

Ibn al-Furāt. 1971. *Ayyubids, Mamlukes and Crusaders: Selections from the Tāʾrīkh al-Duwal wa ʾl-Mulūk of Ibn al-Furāt.* Trans. U. and M. C. Lyons. Heffer.

Ibn al-Munāṣif. 2003. *Kitāb al-ijnād fī abwāb al-jihād.* Dār al-Gharb al-Islāmī.

Ibn Munqidh. 2008. *Book of Contemplation.* Trans. Paul Cobb. Penguin.

Ibn al-Naḥḥās al-Dimyāṭī. 2002. *Mashāriʿ al-ashwāq ilā maṣāriʿ al-ʿushshāq fī al-jihād wa-faḍāʾilihi.* Dār al-Bashāʾir al-Islāmiyya.

Ibn Taymiyya, Taqī al-Dīn Aḥmad. 1991. *al-Jihād.* Dār al-Jīl.

Mourad, Suleiman, and James Lindsay. 2015. *The Intensification and Reorientation of Sunni Jihad Ideology in the Crusader Period.* Leiden: E.J. Brill.

12 Is There a Hindu Just War?

TORKEL BREKKE

Comparing ideas and idioms across cultures and religions is difficult if we want to take local understandings seriously. If we look at Islamic, Hindu, Chinese or Aztec history we recognize practices, ideas and objects that relate to what we call "war" in English; however, without a deeper knowledge of the civilization in question we do not know whether its language and world view actually comport with the English concept. The Indian concepts of war are carried by different Sanskrit terms, which have little in common with the modern European concept of war, where the sovereign state is the prime actor. The Indian concepts advance unique ideas about sovereignty and the ethics of war.

Several scholars of Hinduism have asked if there is a Hindu just war theory (Clooney 2003; Brekke 2005; Balkaran and Dorn 2012). It seems that a minimum requirement for something to count as a just war theory is that we can find sophisticated ethical and/or legal thinking and arguing about rules dedicated to setting limits to the resort to war and to the manner of destruction and killing. Such ethical and/or legal thinking and arguing will often be expressed in literature, although just war thinking can also be expressed in art such as painting or theater. The enormous Hindu literary tradition contains countless references to war – in the Vedas, in epics, in the Puranas, in "scientific" treatises, in plays and poems – but we may limit our discussion to two concepts that are key to Hinduism's self-understanding: dharma and artha. This chapter will explore the tensions between these two concepts in Hindu literature on war.

On the most general level, Indian ethics can be analyzed as discourses and literatures concerning four key concepts: moksha, dharma, artha and kama. Moksha means salvation (i.e. liberation from the cycle of rebirth) and is what we may call a religious concept. Dharma refers to the right order of things in nature and in society and to the duties of all persons to different stakeholders that make up their social reality:

family, teachers, clan, caste and so on. Dharma is partly a religious and partly a secular concept. Artha is a secular concept, which refers to politics and worldly gain. We might equate artha with statecraft and political economy. Kama is also a secular concept, which is about worldly pleasures to be pursued by the upper-class Hindu. It has become famous in the West through the *Kama Sutra*, a Hindu book on sensual pleasure. These four concepts are the subjects of great traditions of literature.

WAR IN THE LITERATURE ON DHARMA

Dharma is a descriptive and prescriptive concept encapsulating the order of society, and for this reason understanding dharma is crucial for understanding Hindu political philosophy in general and the ethics of war in particular. Four ancient Hindu law codes survive to this day, all named after their mythical authors, Apastamba, Gautama, Baudhayana and Vasishta. The Sanskrit name of these law codes collectively is *Dharma Sutra*, which means that they are aphoristic and condensed expressions of dharma. They are designed to convey clear rules about the rights and obligations of persons according to social class, age and sex. They were probably composed by individual experts in legal and moral reasoning sometime between 400 and 100 BCE (Olivelle 1999b: xxv–xxxiv), but they were also culminations of a great tradition of learning that was crucial to regulating life in Hindu society. These texts give detailed rules about the lives of students and householders, men and women, inheritance and marriage, rituals for birth and for death and many other things.

The *Dharma Sutras* also discuss the duties and the rights of the warrior class (the *kshatriyas* in Sanskrit) in general and the kings (the *raja*) specifically, who, in theory, always hail from the kshatriya class. The right and duty to use violence to uphold social and political order is an essential aspect of the dharma of warriors and kings. In the *Dharma Sutra* of Gautama we can read that the king should protect his subjects, should travel in a chariot armed with a bow and should take proper measures to ensure victory in battle. However, he should also be careful not to kill the wrong people, such as Brahmins, or people who have lost their horses or those who have given up and fled the battlefield (Olivelle 1999b: 94). If we read the *Dharma Sutra* of Baudhayana, we find similar injunctions. The king must protect subjects and use violence when necessary, but he should not kill women, the old, children or Brahmins. Moreover, he should not kill those who have lost their armor, those who are mad or soldiers who surrender, and he should refrain from using barbed or poisoned weapons (Olivelle 1999b: 159). What we see here is what we may call the essence of a warrior code.

According to all authoritative Hindu texts, the most important duty of the king is to provide security for his subjects. Conversely, it is the duty of the subjects to pay a certain percentage of their wealth to the sovereign in return. It is often seen as a symbiotic relationship. The belief that a bad king is burdened by the sins of his subjects is common in Hindu literature (Scharfe 1989: 44; Lingat 1998: 236). Alongside the *Dharma Sutras*, an even more famous book about dharma is *The Laws of Manu*, composed sometime between 100 BCE and 200 CE. At the start of chapter 7 of this lawbook, the legendary author Manu states that protection of subjects is the most fundamental obligation of members of the warrior class. Manu has more to say about the moral status of the violence of the king, and we will soon return to this.

DHARMA AND WAR IN THE MAHABHARATA

The most important narrative literature in the Hindu tradition is contained in what we call the great epics: the Mahabharata and the Ramayana. The Mahabharata is a poem written in Sanskrit that developed over several centuries and probably found its current form around 400 CE. It is the longest epic poem in the world and has an immensely important role in literature, art, philosophy and religion not only in India but in many Asian cultures from Sri Lanka to Indonesia. The Mahabharata contains a great number of tales, but the main narrative framework is the war between two groups of cousins called the Kauravas and the Pandavas, all descendants of the mythic ancestor Bharata. At its heart, the Mahabharata is a poem about dharma, and it addresses key moral questions about killing and war. How can one justify a war against family members? How should the brave warrior fight? Is he allowed to use deceit in war, and what kinds of tricks are immoral? What is God's opinion on war and killing?

The Mahabharata's moral discussions about war often arise from events on the battlefield. Typically, after somebody is killed in a duel somebody will challenge the morality and bravery of the involved warriors and point out that rules or norms have been breached. Often God, in the form of Krishna, intervenes in such discussions with his own perspectives on these rules and norms. Clearly, for gods and men to discuss rules and norms there must be some shared idea about moral standards. The heroes often refer to the *kshatradharma*, the dharma belonging to the warriors (kshatriya) (i.e. the warrior code of ethics). There is never really a complete and systematic presentation of this system in the Mahabharata, but the references to the warrior code of ethics are so numerous that readers (or listeners) get a good sense of a set of specific rules. The most important thing to notice about this code is that it has very clear ideas about what in Western war ethics we call *discrimination* (i.e. delimiting classes of people or places that should be treated as protected from violence in war). For instance, old people, children, women and those who surrender must not be killed, and here I think we can see moral intuitions that come very close to being universal, as they can also be found in Christian and Islamic texts about war.

Specifically, the Mahabharata says that a soldier whose armor is broken, one who folds his hands or one who has thrown down his weapons may be taken prisoner but may not be killed. One must not kill those who are sleeping, are thirsty, are wearied, are disoriented or are confused, as well as those who have started out for liberation (i.e. ascetics), are on the move or walking, are drinking or eating, are crazy or are wounded. There are more rules, but the point should be clear: The literature on dharma is very keen to make distinctions between legitimate and illegitimate targets in war. A war fought in accordance with the code is a *Dharma Yuddha*, a just war. If we want to identify or evaluate a theory of just war, whether in Hinduism or anywhere else, this type of effort to institutionalize *discrimination* should be the most important criterion.

One short section of the Mahabharata has become so famous that it is often said to offer a synthesis of the manifold religious, mystical and ethical traditions that form Hinduism. This is the Bhagavadgita (Song of the Lord) – or the Gita for short. The Gita is a poem, like the rest of the Mahabharata, and it constitutes 700 verses out of 100,000, a relatively small part of Book 6 of the larger epic. The Gita brings together a number of different strands of religious ideals, not least the ideal of *bhakti*, or personal devotion to God. But the Gita is also fundamentally about war. It relates the conversation between the warrior Arjuna and the god Krishna on the battlefield as the war is about to start and the two mighty armies face each other with their flying standards and their war chariots. It takes place in Kurukshetra, a real place in Haryana, just north of Delhi.

In the Gita, the god Krishna has decided to become incarnate (an *avatara* in Sanskrit) as the charioteer of Arjuna in order to make sure that dharma prevails in the coming war. He reveals his divine nature in order to explain to Arjuna the moral and religious significance of the coming slaughter. Arjuna is distraught at the prospect of killing kinsmen, but Krishna explains that it is Arjuna's duty (dharma) as a warrior to fight. As long as he engages in battle without any thought of the fruit of his actions, he is in fact performing the religious act of *karmayoga*, the yoga of action. Fighting, then, becomes a religious act and a duty, according to the Gita. The Gita remains one of those classical works in Hinduism that all major philosophers from medieval to modern times have discussed and commented on. The basic lesson of *karmayoga* has animated moral and political debate in India right up to the present times.

Some of us, however, find our favorite part of the Mahabharata not to be the Gita, but rather Book 10, which in English bears the name "The Massacre at Night." The story here takes place closer to the end of the great conflict, which means that the anger and frustration of the warriors are at the boiling point and their moral standards are deteriorating, making for a number of highly ambivalent and rather dark episodes and discussions about the ethics of war. Book 10 starts with a striking image of a band of distraught and wounded warriors taking rest in a forest in the night. All fall asleep except for the hero Ashvatthaman, who is too angry at his enemies to find rest. In the dark he sees a great banyan tree containing thousands of sleeping crows. Suddenly a mighty owl comes flying stealthily through the dark and attacks the crows. With its terrible claws and beak it slashes the crows to pieces, and the mutilated birds pile up on the ground. Ashvatthaman reflects to himself in the night:

> This owl has tutored me in war. My thoughts are locked into my enemies' death, and now the time has come. ... In this, those who know treatises on statecraft prize certain means above those subject to doubt. It matters not at all what worldly blame and censure such an action draws: for a warrior following the warrior's code, it is a duty and must be done.
>
> (Johnson 1998: 8)

Then Ashvatthaman quotes several lines from a text on statecraft, which say that a good military leader should attack the enemy army when it is weakened and exhausted, even when the enemy army tries to rest and even in the dead of night. In other words, Ashvatthaman contradicts the aforementioned warrior code that animates many of the discussions of the Mahabharata. This episode in Book 10 is an excellent illustration of the deep ambivalence about dharma and the rules of war that are discussed throughout epic literature. It also illustrates that the epic literature is not entirely about high ideals. Instead, the hero reflects on verses from a book on statecraft, a cynical and pragmatic literature about grand strategy where morality is mostly seen as meaningless. This is the tradition to which we now turn.

WAR IN THE LITERATURE ON ARTHA

The literature on pragmatic statecraft and grand strategy is referred to in this chapter as the *artha* tradition. This was explained in a number of books composed in Sanskrit at different points in Indian history, the most important of which is Kautilya's Arthashastra, the greatest source for the study of politics in ancient India.

Authorship is generally hard to determine in ancient Indian literature, but Olivelle believes that Kautilya's Arthashastra is the work of one author and that it was composed between 50 and 125 CE (Olivelle 2013: 25–29). However, Kautilya clearly built on a broader Hindu tradition of statecraft or grand strategy that was developed as guidance for monarchs ruling the large states in northern India around 400 BCE. Kautilya's Arthashastra is an immensely rich text dealing with diverse issues concerning government. In Olivelle's analysis, Kautilya envisaged his work as addressing two main themes: the government of the king's own realm (Books 1–5) and its relationships with other states (Books 6–14). Kautilya's treatment of the organization of government in internal affairs is substantial and detailed. A key concern for Kautilya, as for all the writers in this tradition, was the selection and appointment of smart and loyal ministers and administrative personnel of different ranks. The book gives details about how much to pay them, how to secure their loyalty and how to murder them secretly if need be.

To understand Kautilya's political philosophy, and in particular his views on war and violence, we need to look at the crucial concept of *danda*. In its most basic and straightforward sense, the word *danda* means "stick" or "rod." However, the word means several other things in different contexts. It can mean violence – a bit like in the cynical saying "carry a big stick" – and it can mean punishment, but it can also refer to the army of the king. The word can also refer to a personification of legitimate violence, and in this sense it is identified with the person of the king. In order to maintain order and to protect his people the king uses *danda*, the rod of punishment. The execution of politics is equivalent to using the stick, the "wielding of *danda*" (*dandaniti*). A key passage from the *Law Code of Manu* Book 7 verses 16–18 reads:

Punishment (danda) is the king; he is the male; he is the leader; he is the ruler; and, tradition tells us, he stands as the surety for the Law with respect to the four orders of life. Punishment disciplines all the subjects, Punishment alone protects them, and Punishment watches over them as they sleep – Punishment is the Law, the wise declare.

(Olivelle 2009: 154–5)

Earlier in the chapter we discussed the *Laws of Manu* as an important work about dharma, but here we see that it is, at the same time, a very important source for what we call the artha tradition of politics. This should make the reader sensitive to the fact that the dharma and artha traditions are in tension in many places, while perspectives and ideals from both are often mixed into the same text, as we saw with reference to Book 10 of the Mahabharata.

What about war in this tradition of statecraft? Kautilya's Arthashastra treats war in Books 6–14, but anyone who looks for moral guidance there will be disappointed. Kautilya discusses the relationship between kings and their realms as an anarchic system, where the king must see himself in the middle of a circle of states and a circle of kings (*rajamandala*). The immediate neighbors are natural enemies and the neighbor's neighbor is a natural friend because he is the enemy of the enemy. Kautilya does not see the circle of kings as a map of an actual political situation but rather as a heuristic device that the king and his ministers use in order to analyze external relations. Kautilya explains:

Forming a circle all around him and with immediately contiguous territories is the constituent comprising his enemies. In like manner, with territories once removed from his, is the constituent comprising his allies.

(Olivelle 2013: 274)

This pattern of friends and enemies repeats itself in circles that the king must always strive to dominate. How exactly can the king dominate? There are six key tools in foreign policy according to Kautilya: peace, war, staying quiet, marching, seeking shelter, and dual policy (Olivelle 2013: 277). In other words, both war-making and peace-making are strategies employed to be successful in politics; no fundamental value is attached to either of them. Peace is a means to gain strategic goals, just like war. In fact, Kautilya never discusses the moral legitimacy of any of these strategies because such a discussion would strike him as irrelevant. There is no sense in which war needs to be justified on other grounds than for purely pragmatic reasons.

In other words, Kautilya's Arthashastra and the tradition of state-craft of which it is a part are not comparable to the just war tradition, with its focus on morally right causes, like self-defense, or the righting of wrongs. In this sense, we might say that Kautilya is to the Hindu ideology of war what Machiavelli is to the Christian just war tradition. To use a word from Western political science, Kautilya was a realist. He saw no need for justification because his book and the wider tradition of Hindu statecraft are about artha and not about moral rules associated with dharma.

ARTHA AND WAR IN ANIMAL FABLES

One of the most intriguing and entertaining aspects of the classical Indian literature of statecraft is the tradition of animal fables, crafted to convey central moral and political tenets. We find the earliest expression of this genre in the Pancatantra, a book that was composed in Sanskrit probably around 300 CE in an unknown part of India, although some scholars place it in the northern region of Kashmir. It is designed and written by an unknown author as an authoritative treatise (shastra) on how to conduct politics. It belongs to the genre of statecraft, just like Kautilya's Arthashastra, although the style of the text is very different. The animal fables of the Pancatantra are composed to be instructive and entertaining at the same time, and they contain layers of stories within stories to explain how things came about.

To get the gist of these animal fables, let us take a look at a story about birds that we find in Book 3 of the Pancatantra, which has the title "On War and Peace: The Story of the Crows and the Owls." This is the fable about a war between the crows, ruled by King Meghavarna, and the owls, ruled by King Arimardana. It starts with a terrible attack by the owls on the home of the crows in a great banyan tree, and then the king of crows assembles his five ministers of council to find a strategy to counter the aggressive policy of the owls. The relationship between the king and his senior ministers and advisers is a recurring theme in the literature on statecraft in India, and this is also the case for the animal fables. Several of the ministers offer bad advice, either calling for open war or suing for peace on the enemy's terms. However, the crow king happens to have one particularly intelligent minister called Ciramjivin, who designs a strategy for conquering the owls. He is able to infiltrate the fortress of the owls as a double agent and prepare a terrible attack by the crows. After a number of extraneous tales, the main story arrives at its climax when the crows are able to set fire to the fortress of the owls and burn all their enemies to death (Olivelle 1999b: 134).

It is instructive to present the fables of the crows and owls here because it resembles the episode we looked at from the Mahabharata, Book 10, above. In both cases, the story about the birds illustrates principles of deceit in war and breaks fundamentally with the norms associated with righteous war, or *Dharma Yuddha*. However, the metaphor of the great banyan tree with sleeping birds and the attacking owls has an even darker meaning. The owl is associated with evil and destruction in Indian culture. The episode alludes to the threat against the world by evil forces and the necessity to throw all moral constraints aside when confronting such a threat. It also alludes to the total destruction that ends the Mahabharata War.

The main character of many of the stories in the Pancatantra is the king's minister, and this is the case in the story of the crows and the owls. In fact, the kings of the Pancatantra universe, often represented by lions, are depicted as fearful, weak, confused and dependent on their chief minister for advice on how to run the kingdom and to solve political crises. The most famous of the chief ministers in this world of fables is the cunning jackal. Although the Pancatantra and the other collections in the genre are Hindu texts, they are not *religious* texts in the usual sense. On the contrary, these texts often display skepticism toward religion. In the fables of this genre, Hindu ascetics are always hypocritical liars and Brahmins are seen mostly as ridiculous and stupid characters. The human characters that come out in a positive light are the merchants, while barbers and other low-caste people are drunks and no-goods.

The animal fables of the Pancatantra have survived through the centuries. They have been told and retold to audiences throughout India, and they have entered folklore in other parts of the world, including in Europe and the Arab world. The most famous of the Indian reworkings of the fables is known as the Hitopadesha, a book composed probably in the 12th century and serving the same purpose of giving advice on statecraft and grand strategy. The fables were also very popular outside a Hindu audience and entered India's Muslim literature. Under several rulers the imperial Muslim court took great interest in the Hindu traditions of learning and employed Brahmins specializing in various branches of literature to make Sanskrit literature available to the Persian-speaking elites. This interest in learning and the arts was typical of Islamic imperial ideology. In imperial Baghdad of the 9th century under the Abbasid Caliphate there developed a translation movement that sought to translate and use ancient Greek philosophy and science, most notably the works of Aristotle, and enormous prestige and wealth were channeled into this scientific and educational endeavor (D'Ancona 2019). In the same spirit, the Indian animal fables and their political and moral ideas were translated and transmitted by Muslim rulers in India alongside other genres of Hindu literature, not least the Mahabharata. The Hitopadesha was translated into Persian around 1450 through the patronage of a local Islamic ruler in Bihar, almost a century before the establishment of the Mughal Empire. The translations of the Hitopadesha from the Sanskrit into premodern Hindi for the common people of north India and into Persian for an elite Muslim readership testify to the popularity of both this particular text and the genre of political advice in the form of animal fables (Auer 2018: 32).

WAR AND HINDUISM IN LATE COLONIAL INDIA

If the ideas that we have explored so far were only the stuff of ancient history, they would perhaps be interesting to a small group of historians comparing traditions of ethics. However, in reality, these ideas have continued to inform some aspects of Hindu politics through modern history. A complete overview is impossible here, but let us pick out one fascinating era of modern Indian history when Hindu ideas about war and violence were actualized by circumstances. This was the last days of British India, the time between 1900 and 1930 when the colonial power was challenged by waves of insurgencies by young Indian men often inspired by Hindu ideology.

The greatest and most famous proponent of resistance against the British at this time was Bal Gangadhar Tilak (1856–1920), a highly educated Brahmin from western India who was involved in a wide array of educational and political work from his youth. Tilak would be high up on any shortlist of the most important ideologues of the Indian independence movement. Tilak popularized the idea of *svaraj*, which he often translated as "Home Rule," but which more precisely means *self-government*. Tilak's main source for the justification of Home Rule was the Bhagavadgita, which he used in his speeches and writings throughout his life. In a speech in 1917 Tilak recalled how he started studying the Gita as a young man because he had grown up in the belief that this was the text that encapsulated the essence of Hinduism, and he hoped to find an answer there to a question that was fundamental to him: Did the religious life of the Hindu require him to renounce this world, to renounce politics? He explained how he came to be convinced that the Gita – and by extension Hinduism in general – never preached the renunciation of the world. On the contrary, even after reaching the highest religious realization, a Hindu should continue to act in society.

Tilak was fascinated by a new technology of violence that was used in the insurgency against the British colonial power: the homemade bomb. Importantly, he explored the philosophical significance of this new technology. Tilak pointed out that the bomb meant a completely new relationship between the oppressed and oppressor because the new bombs were so easy to make that they upset the normal balance of power between a strong state and a people who had been robbed of their weapons through legislation and thus stripped of their manliness and ability to resist tyranny (McQuade 2017; Upton 2017).

Tilak's public support for insurgency and bomb-throwing was very muted, but it nevertheless earned him several years in a colonial jail in Mandalay. During his prison term he wrote a thorough exposition of the message of the Gita, a long book called the Gita Rahasya. We should remember that for centuries one of the standard ways for Hindu philosophers to establish their own authority was to write commentaries on key texts like the Gita, so in this sense Tilak followed a long tradition. At the same time, his interpretation of the message of the Gita happened in the tense political context of the fight for Home Rule and self-determination, which meant that the essential ethical takeaway for Tilak was the call to war for a righteous cause. *Karmayoga* was the key message he found in the Gita.

In fact, this was the message that was read into the Gita by many Hindus throughout the subcontinent in this period. Among the revolutionary societies that were active in the first three decades of the 20th century many would use the text actively to forge a sense of higher religious meaning and purpose in the struggle against British oppression. Some of the terrorist groups that were established in Bengal would have new initiates swear allegiance to the cause while placing their hand on a copy of the Gita. However, there were other elements of Hindu religion that were perhaps even more important in Bengal, where revolutionary struggle was at its most intense. Much of Bengali Hinduism revolves around the cult of the Great Goddess in her various forms. She can be a benign mother dearly loved by her children; she can be the abstract power (*shakti*) underpinning all activity in the universe; and she can be the terrible and extremely violent Kali or Durga who slays the demons who threaten the world. Her terrible form is worshipped in the most essential of Bengali Hindu rituals, and she features as a main character in Bengali mythology and aesthetical expressions.

The image of the Great Goddess in her various forms became the most emotionally appealing religious symbol used by the newspapers and political pamphlets distributed by the tens of thousands in Bengal and in other parts of India in this period (1900–1930). Many of the publications would call for war against the British. They would give instructions for bomb-making and other tactics, but most importantly they would touch the feelings of Indians by couching the language of revolution in the well-known language of Hinduism, where the defense of the Mother Goddess as nation against the white demons from Britain was all-important (Sanyal 2008). To understand the great emotional impact of this religious revolutionary rhetoric we must note that Hindu social philosophy revolves around the concept of protection (rakshana), where the protection of the women in the family – mothers, wives, daughters – is the most fundamental duty of a man, and where political philosophy can be turned into a reflection of social philosophy when the humiliated nation takes the place of the violated woman (Brekke 2015).

CONCLUDING DISCUSSION

We have seen that the ethics and the ideology of war found in classical Hindu literature is not one unified whole but rather surfaces in several different traditions of literature. This chapter presented the literary tradition of dharma, which has much to say about the duties of kings and warriors, and we looked at the literary tradition of artha, which is concerned with the proper grand strategy to be followed by kings in relation to internal troublemakers as well as their external adversaries.

We touched on several different literary genres and traditions. We saw that the idea of war and warfare according to the high ideals of dharma could be found in terse and aphoristic form in the literature called the *Dharma Sutras*, as well as in narrative form in one of the two great epics, the Mahabharata. We did not include a discussion of the second great epic here – the Ramayana – simply for reasons of space, but an investigation of this text would have yielded similar insights. In both of these genres there appeared what we might call a warrior code of ethics setting limits and standards for how the warrior should fight, for what types of weapons and tactics were deemed just and lawful and for what types of persons should be considered immune from attack. A simple but striking comparative image would be to juxtapose authoritative texts from Hinduism, Islam and Christianity that describe the immunity of children, women, monks and ascetics from violence or the moral status of sieges and the use of fire.

We also looked at ideologies of war and warfare according to the more practical – or cynical – ideals of artha that can be found in treatises like the Arthashastra by Kautilya, as well as in narrative form in the folk tales about animals in the Pancatantra and other related collections of animal fables. We included a leap forward to the colonial period because it is instructive to see how ideals and concepts from the ancient tradition have animated moral debate about war and violence in modern times. In other words, we have explored quite different ideologies about war and violence expressed in fundamentally different genres of literature.

What can we make of this? First of all, it is clear that there is not one self-conscious tradition of just war thinking – nor one dominant just war theory – in the Hindu tradition. In the sense that we can talk about a Hindu theory of just war, this needs to be *reconstructed* from very different literatures spanning centuries. But this should not surprise us. It is crucial to keep in mind that the Christian tradition of just war is also, in some sense, a reconstructed or even "imagined" tradition. That is, modern Western writers who talk about a Christian just war tradition necessarily reconstruct a debate among Christian theologians and jurists from Augustine right through the Middle Ages and the early modern period up until today. This debate is reconstructed in the sense that it too includes various genres and spans many centuries. Many, or perhaps most, of the participants in this debate were not self-consciously contributing to such a large debate. If we realize that a just war "tradition" in any culture is always to some extent an anachronism, we will also realize that the Christian just war tradition is not a bedrock that other traditions should be measured against.

Having said that, one can say that to satisfy the criteria for a just war theory in any culture we should at least expect to find a relatively sophisticated treatment of questions pertaining to the legal and moral issues of going to war and to the rules of just warfare. We have discussed how several genres of literature mention or allude to a warrior code that clearly had the ambition of limiting how war is waged. This code discriminates between legitimate and illegitimate targets, and it gives opinions about just and unjust tactics and weapons. In other words, there is a parallel here with what scholars of the Christian just war tradition call *ius in bello*. However, *explicit* discussions of the circumstances under which waging war is allowed in the first place are harder to come by, but that is because many of the assumptions of right authority are implied in the Hindu ideology of kingship. In any case, the conclusion must surely be that the Hindu tradition does have a theory of just war, and that this theory is suspended in the incredibly productive tension that exists in Indian thought between dharma and artha.

References

Auer, Blain. 2018. "Political Advice, Translation, and Empire in South Asia." *Journal of the American Oriental Society* 138(1): 29–72.

Balkaran, Raj and Walter A. Dorn. 2012. "Violence in the Valmiki Ramayana: Just War Criteria in an Ancient Indian Epic." *Journal of the American Academy of Religion* 80(3): 659–90.

Brekke, Torkel. 2005. "The Ethics of War and the Concept of War in India and Europe." *Numen* 52(1): 59–86.

2015. "The Indian Tradition." In *Ashgate Research Companion to Military Ethics.* Edited by James Turner Johnson and Eric Patterson. Ashgate. 415– 27.

Clooney, Francis X. 2003. "Pain but Not Harm: Some Classical Resources toward a Hindu Just War Theory." In *Just War in Comparative Perspective.* Edited by Paul Robinson. Ashgate. 109–26.

D'Ancona, Cristina. 2019. "Greek Sources in Arabic and Islamic Philosophy." *The Stanford Encyclopedia of Philosophy.* Edited by Edward N. Zalta. Available at https://plato.stanford.edu/archives/fall2019/entries/arabic-islamic-greek

Johnson, W. J. 1998. *The Sauptikaparvan of the Mahabharata.* Oxford University Press.

Lingat, Robert. 1998. *The Classical Law of India.* Oxford University Press.

McQuade, Joseph. 2017. "Terrorism, Law, and Sovereignty in India and the League of Nations, 1897–1945." PhD dissertation, University of Cambridge. Available at www.repository.cam.ac.uk/bitstream/handle/1810/267882/McQuade-2017-PhD.pdf?sequence=1

Olivelle, Patrick. 1999a. *Pancatantra: The Book of India's Folk Wisdom.* Oxford University Press.

1999b. *Dharmasutras: The Law Codes of Ancient India: A New Translation by Patrick Olivelle.* Oxford University Press.

2009. *The Law Code of Manu – A New Translation by Patrick Olivelle.* Oxford University Press.

2013. *King, Governance, and Law in Ancient India: Kautilya's Arthashastra – A New Annotated Translation.* Oxford University Press.

Sanyal, Shukla. 2008. "Legitimizing Violence: Seditious Propaganda and Revolutionary Pamphlets in Bengal, 1908–1918." *The Journal of Asian Studies* 67(3): 759–87.

Scharfe, H. 1989. *The State in Indian Tradition.* E.J. Brill.

Upton, Robert E. 2017. "'Take Out a Thorn with a Thorn': B. G. Tilak's Legitimization of Political Violence." *Global Intellectual History* 2(3): 329–49.

13 Buddhist Just War Traditions

KRISTIN SCHEIBLE

Buddhism is no monolith but encompasses a vast variety of traditions, beliefs, textual resources, and practices spanning about 2,500 years of history, manifested in cultures across the globe. Attempting to essentialize Buddhist thought on just war does a particular kind of interpretive violence; is "just war" even a universally recognizable category, or is translation into disparate religious realms an incommensurable project? Even if the universal applicability of just war theory is debatable, might we gain something by juxtaposing familiar categories in just war theory to foundational categories of Buddhist thought and practice? And to what resources might we turn for our thought experiment to deliver the most comprehensive account of the salience of just war theory in Buddhist understanding even as we recognize there is no singular authoritative resource to construe a "Buddhist understanding."

For our project, we will look at the most commonly held conceptions, the dharmic current that runs through Buddhist thought pertaining to the human experience of war and how to comprehend it. For sources, we must self-consciously enter the pendular swings of academic Buddhist hermeneutics and discourse and try not to repeat biased, presumptive readings of Orientalists past while looking to canonical expressions that most closely conjure just war theory. In doing so, we do not undermine the lived experiences and understandings of Buddhists of our day wrestling with the reality of war; rather, we think alongside the Dharma, the teachings. The Dhammapada is in the Khuddaka Nikāya, one of the five collections of *suttas* (teachings) in the Pāli Tipiṭaka, the canon, and it is one among a plethora of authoritative sources. "In this world, hostilities are *never* appeased by hostility. But by the absence of hostility are they appeased. This is an interminable truth" (Wallis 2004: 4; emphasis in original). Consider the reverberations of the canonical wisdom in Thich Nhat Hanh's declaration after the violence of 9/11, which also helps prime us to encounter other core

principles of Buddhist thought salient for our project: coresponsibility
and the role of compassion, understanding, and justice:

> All violence is injustice ... Responding to violence with violence
> resolves nothing; it only escalates violence, anger and hatred, and
> increases the number of our enemies. It is only with compassion
> that we can embrace and disintegrate violence ... The violence and
> hatred we presently face has been created by misunderstanding,
> injustice, discrimination and despair. We are all co-responsible for
> the making of violence and despair in the world by our way of
> living, of consuming and of handling the problems of the world.
> Understanding why this violence has been created, we will then
> know what to do and what not to do in order to decrease the level of
> violence in ourselves and in the world, to create and foster
> understanding, reconciliation and forgiveness.
>
> (Nhat Hanh 2002)

Buddhist traditions attribute their foundation to the historical Buddha,
Siddhartha Gautama, born into the warrior/royal *kṣatriya* caste. Copious
biographical works depict his father, king of the Śakyas, anxiously preparing his son to take up his hereditary role as a *cakravartin* ("wheel turner," a
universal monarch) in spite of the prognostications that he would instead
become a *buddha* ("awakened"), a spiritual rather than temporal *cakravartin*. Several biographies illustrate his royal father's concerns and expectations that his son should be a king too, and the stories reveal a father who
went to great lengths to ensure Siddhartha would not be exposed to the
suffering of the world lest he be motivated to follow a spiritual track to do
something about it. The biographies dwell on Siddhartha's urge to see
beyond this protected environment; leaving the palace and coming across
the four sights (visions of an old man, a sick man, a corpse, and a renunciant
of society) catalyzed his own renunciation, awakening, and long teaching
career, lessons of which are made available to Buddhists today through the
Dharma (teachings). We turn to the authority of the Dharma to test the
conceptual appropriateness of just war theory.

The Dharma is theory and practice, experiential and didactic,
problem-based exempla and discourses on the amelioration of social
and personal ills. Dharma is one of the three jewels (Buddha, Dharma,
and sangha, the community of monks) in which Buddhists take ritual
refuge. At its root, at the very foundation of the tradition that the
Buddha initiated, are the four noble truths articulated in the Buddha's
First Sermon, the *Dhammacakkappavattana Sutta* (Turning the Wheel
of Dharma sutra): All life is *duḥkha/dukkha* (dis-ease); there is a cause

that is *tṛṣṇā/taṇhā* (craving); there is an end; the end being the practical noble eightfold path comprising a series of proper or balanced orientations (right view, right thought, right speech, right action, right livelihood, right effort, right mindfulness, and right concentration). *Duḥkha* is commonly translated as suffering, but as one of the three marks of all existence (the others being *anitya/anicca*, impermanence, and *anātman/anattā*, no pervasive self) it refers to both physical and mental unease. *Duḥkha* is rampant in *saṃsāra* (the "wandering on," the rounds of birth–life–death–rebirth and all it entails), and *duḥkha* is the cause, experience, and aftermath of war.

WAR IN A SUFFERING WORLD

In spite of the ubiquity of war and the comparability of suffering (cluster bombs, shelling of hospitals, disappeared persons in Sri Lanka or Ukraine), framing war as just has limited utility in Buddhist terms if the recognition of what is just is rooted in other theories of jurisprudence or soteriologies. The renowned anthropologist Gananath Obeyesekere says that unlike the Buddhist political tradition and historical record, in the doctrinal tradition and soteriology "there is little evidence of intolerance, no justification for violence, no conception even of 'just wars' or 'holy wars' that are important for systems of jurisprudence based on monotheistic values" (Obeyesekere 1995: 233–4). Yet we know from the historical record, from the abundance of stories about war, and from the frequent use of military metaphors that pepper all genres of Buddhist texts throughout history that war happens/happened, is explained, and is – frequently narratively – justified. An obvious case to explore would be the recent civil war in Sri Lanka, the appeal to the 5th-century *Mahāvaṃsa* for justification, and the religio-nationalistic just war rhetoric that stimulated and sustained it and continues today. Tessa Bartholomeusz writes of "the new refuge of political monks," who take refuge not in the three jewels (Buddha, *dhamma*, *saṅgha*) but in "'rata, jatiya, agama' ('country, nation/race, religion')" (Bartholomeusz 2002: 69), an aberration explained by the fraught circumstances of civil war.

William Scott Green once pointed out something obvious but very important: Wars and just war theorizing are species-specific activities (Green 2013: 386). All throughout Buddhist materials one encounters the refrain, "a human birth is precious indeed," meaning that in *saṃsāra* it is only in the troublesome human existence that one has the opportunity to make choices that have a bearing on soteriological aims and aptitudes. Only humans wage war, and only humans rationalize the impetus for war, justify actions during it, and make excuses and possible reparations afterward:

> The point made by the Buddha is . . . that people are psychologically incapable of forming opinions about what is right and wrong, just and unjust, righteous and unrighteous while being immersed in their defiled psychological condition. They may express strong convictions about what is just and right, but when objectively examined they turn out to be mere rationalizations of their preconceived notions, desires, cravings, likes and dislikes. When the unwholesome roots of motivation are removed conflicts and disputes no longer arise. When people make decisions about what is right and wrong, just and unjust while they are still affected by the roots of evil, greed, hatred and delusion their judgements are mere rationalizations. What we may conclude from this is that Buddhism allows no place for righteous wars.
>
> (Premasiri 2003: 159)

Conflict, the most extreme version of which is war, is endemic to the human condition, enmeshed as humans are in *saṃsāra*. If being situated in conflict further clouds one's judgment, how can something like war be recognized as just? And if narrativizing, theorizing, rationalizing, and justifying war relies on humans "immersed in their defiled psychological condition," can there ever be truly just war in Buddhist thought?

TERMS OF JUST WAR

There is a potential interpretive problem lurking in the application of "just war traditions," a category well-developed in Christian (primarily Catholic) and secular political thought, to Buddhist thought and practice. Comparativists have long been sensitive to the potential incommensurability of categories (Tambiah 1990) and to the obligation of scholars of religion to remain "relentlessly self-conscious" as we apply "imaginative acts of comparison and generalization" to interpret various data (here, doctrinal and narrative literature that sustains a varied and complex religious system heuristically recognized as Buddhism) (Smith 1982: xi). In spite of the heuristic challenge, the exercise of considering Buddhist just war traditions aligns with a central practical tenet of Buddhist thought. Buddhist thought and practice revolve around the investigation of root causes, examining the relationship of cause and effect, and ameliorating suffering, or at the very least minimizing harm. Buddhist thought also emphasizes the relationship (over vast swathes of time, even multitudes of existences) between the self and others.

War imagery abounds in the earliest layers of Buddhist doctrine, both as metaphor and as didactic exempla. Canonical and postcanonical sources can be profitably consulted for what might be recognized in a comparative sense as just war theory. "Just" as a category requires some concerted reflection. In a moral landscape where an adjudicator (God) presides and actions are weighed in this very lifetime, "just" carries a particular weight and temporal urgency. But in the Buddhist conception of time, predicated on the laws of *karma* (action), individuals' actions through many lifetimes carry various weights and have various consequences; what is "just" is deeply situational, subject to the shifting kaleidoscope of contexts. Just and unjust are concepts that are difficult to translate into Buddhist terms, but close analogs might be *kusala* (skillful, wholesome) and *akusala* (unskillful, unwholesome). All actions (*karma*) – which can be intentions, bodily actions, or words – can be considered skillful, unskillful, or neutral and have an effect on self and others.

Even noncombatant actions carry concomitant karmic weight. "Perpetrating or sanctioning the violence of war harms both self and others according to Buddhist text and tradition" (Harris 2003: 94). Nonharm, *ahiṃsā/avihiṃsā*, is the foremost of the *pañcasīla/pañcasīla*, the five moral precepts at the core of Buddhist ethics. *Avihiṃsā*, nonharm, is a synonym for compassion, and it "is the root of all virtues, especially the root cause of morality" (Bodhi 2000: 1183). In war, however, harm is unavoidable, but because harming (and, by extension, war) violates the very first precept, "just" in moral terms rings hollow. The mental and spoken act of justifying war itself is bound up in the perpetuation of *duḥkha*, as thinking and talking about it do little to eradicate war and ameliorate suffering. "Just" might serve as a term of expedience that addresses the slippery moral landscapes in which humans think, speak, and act, akin to Mahāyāna Buddhist *upāya*. Doyen of just war theory Michael Walzer might agree: "*[J]ust* is a term of art here; it means justifiable, defensible, even morally necessary (given the alternatives) – and that is all it means" (Walzer 2004: x, emphasis in original). And it is language for all experiencing "the moral reality of war" – monk, citizen, politician, soldier, combatant, or innocent – that is "not fixed by the actual activities of soldiers but by the opinions of mankind" (Walzer 2006 [1977]: 15). As we have just located the messy moral landscape of human birth in the *duḥkha*-drenched *saṃsāra*, speaking of war in terms of "just" seems heuristically useful if literally hollow.

"War," too, can be understood literally and metaphorically in the earliest Buddhist discourses. As *buddha* ("awakened," his most common epithet), the Buddha has vanquished the *kleśa* ("defilements," unskillful, unwholesome mental states), chief of which are *loba* (greed), *doha* (hatred), and *moha* (delusion/ignorance). This victory is why he is also called Jina ("conqueror, victor"), a battle-dependent moniker. In the biographical traditions, the Buddha/Jina is said to have defeated Māra, the antagonist who aspired to derail his awakening and subsequent teaching career. Central in Buddhist narratives and widely depicted in Buddhist art, the battle scene depicts a tranquil Buddha amidst Māra's grisly hordes and tempting daughters, touching the earth in a grounding gesture to call her to witness.

AT (JUST) WAR WITH ONESELF

The metaphor of war as a war to win over others with love, compassion, tolerance, and benevolence can be especially salient in terms of battling one's own inner demons. The Dhammapada is hyperbolic in making this point: "Though one might conquer in battle a thousand times a thousand men, the one who conquers himself alone is supreme in battle" (Wallis 2004: 23).

The roots of Buddhist pacifism are deep and varied, as are its approaches to mitigating harm. Buddhists do not subscribe to a singular moral theory; different situations call for different approaches (Hallisey 1996). A human birth, with its many attendant tensions and conflicts, need for community, but also frustrations with others, is the ideal location within the rounds of *saṃsāra* for ethical cultivation. When conflicts arise, large or small, they present the agent with an opportunity to make good, intentional decisions, to do good actions, and to reflect. One must make the right decisions when presented with such conflicts – avoidance of war, violence, and harm – in order to accumulate merit and eventually proceed to better births and the ultimate goal of nirvana.

The prolific 5th-century monk Buddhaghosa's manual *Visuddhimagga* (Path of Purification) advocates for personal culpability and transformation, where the *Brahmavihāra-niddesa* teaches the cultivation of the four *brahmavihārās* ("abodes of Brahmā," divine states) – loving-kindness, compassion, sympathetic joy, and equanimity – to supplant hatred and anger. Comparatively, we see that the orientation toward self-cultivation stands at odds to other religious considerations of just war. "By contrast with the Christian emphasis on not holding ill-will *against* someone, the Buddhist, particularly Theravāda, emphasis is on not holding it *within* oneself, because of its harmful effects" (Harvey 2000: 243, emphasis in original). The Dhammapada corroborates the primacy of the inner battle: "Whatever a rival might do to a foe, or a vengeful person to the one he hates, a wrongly applied mind would do more damage to him than that" (Wallis 2004: 11).

Jus ad Bellum

In just war theory, the concept *jus ad bellum* refers to the process of deciding to go to war as well as the justification – or understanding – of the right to be engaged in war. The problem of *jus ad bellum* from a Buddhist perspective is that violent thought, discourse, and action are inevitable for those involved, and "violence proceeds from malice and hatred whether it is motivated by the desire to achieve what is conceived as a just cause or not" (Premasiri 2003: 162). Buddhist teachings generally address the process of deciding to go to war with a primary appeal to conciliatory methods to avoid war altogether. Justifying the right to go to war prompts reflection on the ultimate ineffectiveness of war as a mechanism to redress harm.

A source to read while considering *jus ad bellum* would be the canonical tale of the battle between King Pasenadi of Kosala and King Ajātasattu of Magadha. Ajātasattu was the aggressor with his four-division army. Pasenadi mobilized a counter-march of a four-division army, and they then battled, with Ajātasattu victorious and Pasenadi in retreat to his capital, Sāvatthī. Alms-rounding monks brought word to the Buddha, whose response suggests neither participant was especially victorious:

> Victory breeds enmity,
> The defeated one sleeps badly.
> The peaceful one sleeps at ease,
> Having abandoned victory and defeat.
> (Bodhi 2000: 177)

To underscore the incessant repetition of war, the narrative repeats, but in the second instance Pasenadi reigns supreme and captures Ajātasattu alive, though he requisitions "all his elephant troops, all his calvary, all his chariot troops, and all his infantry" (Bodhi 2000: 178). Again, after the report from alms-rounding monks, the Buddha's response cuts critically to the heart of the matter:

> A man will go on plundering
> So long as it serves his ends,

But when others plunder him,
The plunderer is plundered.

The fool thinks fortune is on his side
So long as his evil does not ripen,
But when evil ripens
The fool incurs suffering.

The killer begets a killer,
One who conquers, a conqueror.
The abuser begets abuse,
The reviler, one who reviles.
Thus by the unfolding of kamma
The plunderer is plundered.
                              (Bodhi 2000: 178)

Elizabeth Harris explains that this is as close as canonical Buddhist texts get to proposing a just war theory, exemplifying "an empirical, context-dependent element in Buddhist ethics," where "the highest principles of Buddhism condemn war" even when the state may be justified to act in defense, and always with "an ethic of compassion" to stem the proliferation of war (Harris 2003: 100). But pulling back from the story, a larger "so what" emerges about the ultimate futility of war and the needless suffering war engenders. Donald Swearer, for example, considers the lesson of this sermon to be that aggression never solves the most fundamental problem:

> This and other stories of armed conflict in Buddhist texts make clear that today's victor is tomorrow's vanquished and vice versa and that karmic justice dictates there is no absolute victory or final solution brought about by armed conflict regardless of the scale of weaponry. The moral of these stories seems to be that armed conflict may or may not bring short-term benefit, but that there is no such thing as an absolute victory, a war "to end all wars."
> (Swearer 2004: 242)

In considering the right to engage and the process of conducting war and its concomitant, inevitable violence and harm, one must consider the cause in relation to probable outcomes and widen the lens to see the cyclical nature whereby those outcomes become future causes. Without eradicating the root cause of animosity and *duḥkha*, the wheel of *saṃsāra* is incessant. Just as the highest soteriological aim is to escape the wheel of *saṃsāra*, so the highest temporal goal is to prevent the suffering of war by cutting off its catalyst.

Jus in Bello

Jus in bello refers to the "how" during war, circumscribing the conduct of those conducting war. "The abhorrence of killing is a pervasive enough theme in Buddhist teachings that Buddhist involvement in war can never be routine or straightforward. It is doubtful that there is such thing as Buddhist warfare, if this means war waged in the name of a monolithic, universalist Buddhism and condoned by it unequivocally" (Sinclair 2014: 150). In other words, while Michael Walzer explains that it is "perfectly possible for a just war to be fought unjustly and for an unjust war to be fought in strict accordance with the rules," the very idea of "Buddhist warfare" is anathema (Walzer 2006 [1977]: 21).

As war is an inescapable experience for humans in *saṃsāra*, Buddhists have found themselves engaged in war and have imagined ways of mitigating harm. Several 7th- and 8th-century tantric Buddhist texts and plays illustrate effective war magic, "freezing" advancing and hostile armies in their tracks through the use of "stunning" magic in order to avoid bloodshed. Techniques included the use of incantations and the recitation of mantras – a relatively nonviolent way to overcome one's enemy. That said, if you freeze your opponent long enough, they might be exposed to the elements and die nonetheless (Sinclair 2014: 154–5). As we shall see, speech acts carry karmic weight, just as do negative intentions and physical acts of harm.

Just war theorists explain that *jus in bello* is "grounded in liability," when "combatants must confine their intentional attacks to legitimate targets," specifically other combatants who would do others harm (McMahan 2009: 11–12). "To say that a person is morally liable to be harmed in a certain way is to say that his own action has made it the case that to harm him in that way would not wrong him, or contravene his rights" (McMahan 2009: 11). The problem in Buddhist thought is the sense of karmic weight involved that exceeds a regular human's capacity to measure. One cannot know the actions of past lives that might have resulted in the precarities of the present, nor precisely how actions in this life might impact future existences. The moral liability aspect of *jus in bello* is complicated if the violation of the first precept, nonharm (*ahiṃsā/avihiṃsā*), is absolute.

Jus Post Bellum

Some just war theorists posit a third element, *jus post bellum*, or how to navigate postwar consequences (Stahn 2006). *Jus post bellum* includes reparations, articulations of new relationships between states, rebuilding infrastructure, housing refugees, prosecuting war crimes, and stabilizing the environment. In Buddhist terms, it might entail practices familiar to resolving all transgressions: acknowledging fault, articulating the resolve not to repeat it, apology, and reconciliation (Harvey 2000: 247). If war in all its manifestations is unethical because it entails harm yet is unavoidable and endemic in the human experience, *jus post bellum* might be the most compelling aspect of just war theory for Buddhist thought and practice. Postwar suffering requires concerted efforts to assuage those harmed and provides an opportunity for Buddhists to perform good acts with good intentions.

The iconic *cakravartin* Aśoka (268–239 BCE) is well-known for his edicts inscribed on pillars and rock faces throughout his empire where he proclaims his support for the Dharma, though here, in its broadest sense, Dharma constitutes a vast semantic field that includes law, order, morality, justice, what we recognize and categorize today as "religion," as well as particulars of Buddhist teachings such as *ahiṃsā*. Rock Edict XIII details his violent war campaign in Kaliṅga, where "one hundred and fifty thousand persons were carried away captive, one hundred thousand were slain, and many times that number died," and then immediate devotion to the study of Dharma and profound regret for the harm he had done (Nikam and McKeon 1959: 27). This was a particular event that had a transformative impact on Aśoka, according to his edict. But he says what weighs even heavier on his heart was that the harm done exceeds that done to the people directly maimed and killed. "The Brāhmaṇas and Śramaṇas [the priestly and ascetic orders] as well as the followers of other religions and householders – who all practiced obedience to superiors, parents, and teachers, and proper courtesy and firm devotion to friends, acquaintances, companions, relatives, slaves, and servants – all suffer from the injury, slaughter, and deportation inflicted on their loved ones … Thus all men share in the misfortune, and this weighs on King Priyadarśi's [Aśoka's] mind" (Nikam and McKeon 1959: 28). This is where our foray into just war theory gets interesting, because a critical element of Aśoka's navigation of postwar experiences (*jus post bellum*) is to dissuade future war thinking (*jus ad bellum*). The goal is to cut off the cycle of harm begetting further harm, or at least (in recognition of how difficult complete avoidance of harm in human existence is) moderating its impact. "This edict on Dharma has been inscribed so that my sons and great-grandsons who may come after me should not think new conquests worth achieving. If they do conquer, let them take pleasure in moderation and mild punishments. Let them consider moral conquest the only true conquest" (Nikam and McKeon 1959: 30).

CONCLUSION

On one "lesser" rock inscription directed to the Buddhist *saṅgha*, to whom it is known "how great is my reverence and faith in the Buddha, the *Dharma*, and the *Saṅgha*," Aśoka proclaims reading recommendations not just for monks and nuns, but to guide the actions of laymen and laywomen as well, "thus the true *Dharma* will be of long duration" (Hultzsch 1925: 173–4). The last of the seven texts mentioned is the *Lāghulovāda*, which refers to the *Ambalaṭṭhika-rāhulovāda Sutta* (Instructions to Rāhula at Ambalaṭṭhika) in the Majjhima Nikāya of the Tipitaka, and "which was spoken by the blessed Buddha concerning falsehood" (Hultzsch 1925: 174). The word for falsehood is *mūsāvadaṃ*, speech that is false or wrong – *mūsā* deriving from Vedic *mṛṣā*, "neglectful." In the *sutta*, the Buddha admonishes his son, Rāhula, then a novice in the *saṅgha*, to avoid the harm done by lies. He explains that bodily actions, actions by speech, and mental actions are to be done with repeated reflection, and that the focus for the tripartite reflection should be on the potential harm to self and others that the action might entail. The practice entails a temporal scope – there is to be consideration prior to the action, mindfulness during the action, and reflection after the action. Paraphrased, if cumbersome, the advice looks like this:

> Before, during, and after doing an action with the body, speech, or mind, you should reflect on it like this, "Would this [body/speech/ mind] action I want to do lead to self-harm, harm of others, or both? Would it be an unwholesome action, with painful consequences and results?" If so, don't do it. If not, continue. And if, on reflection, you know that it led to self-harm, harm of others, or both, and that it was an unskillful (*akusala*) bodily action "with painful consequences, painful results ... then you should confess such a bodily action, reveal it, and lay it open to the Teacher or to your wise companions in the holy life. Having confessed it ... you should undertake restraint in the future." But if on reflection you know that it did not lead to harm, your own or of others, and it was instead a skillful bodily action with pleasant consequences and results, "you can abide happy and glad, training day and night" in skillful states.
>
> (Bodhi and Ñāṇamoli 1995: 524–5)

Just war traditions are predicated on just war ideologies and pull decidedly political discourse and action into the realm of the moral. Training our attention on Buddhist sources – doctrinal, narrative, and historical – we see that the just war theoretical structure of *jus ad bellum, jus in bello,* and *jus post bellum* does not precisely align with foundational Buddhist thought on actions and consequences. A task of the comparative scholar is to recognize the varied moral landscapes that shape lived actions of the body, speech, and mind:

> In the act of stepping back and disentangling ourselves from the more visible assumptions of religion and violence, we find that one of the largest blind spots is the failure to recognize the religious subjectivity of violence, itself. The Buddhist treatment of violence is explicitly physical, mental, and emotional harm. Buddhists have been complicit in such violence as well as recipients of this violence.
>
> (Jerryson 2018: 15)

From the most foundational Buddhist perspective, the just way to think about war, conduct war, and repair harm from war is to avoid it altogether by accepting responsibility and addressing the harms that perpetuate it.

References

Bartholomeusz, Tessa J. 2002. *In Defense of Dharma: Just-War Ideology in Buddhist Sri Lanka.* RoutledgeCurzon.

Bodhi, Bhikkhu. 2000. *The Connected Discourses of the Buddha: A New Translation of the Saṃyutta Nikāya.* Wisdom.

Bodhi, Bhikkhu and Bhikkhu Ñāṇamoli. 1995. *The Middle Length Discourses of the Buddha: A Translation of the Majjhima Nikāya.* Wisdom.

Green, William Scott. 2013. "The Matter of Motive: Concluding Thoughts on Just War Theory." In *Just War in Religion and Politics.* Edited by Jacob Neusner, Bruce Chilton, and Robert Tully. University Press of America. 385–92.

Hallisey, Charles. 1996. "Ethical Particularism in Theravāda Buddhism." *Journal of Buddhist Ethics* 3: 32–43.

Harris, Elizabeth J. 2003. "Buddhism and the Justification of War: A Case Study from Sri Lanka." In *Just War in Comparative Perspective.* Edited by Paul Robinson. Ashgate. 93–108.

Harvey, Peter. 2000. *An Introduction to Buddhist Ethics: Foundations, Values and Issues.* Cambridge University Press.

Hultzsch, E. 1925. *Inscriptions of Asoka.* Clarendon Press.

Jerryson, Michael. 2018. *If You Meet the Buddha on the Road: Buddhism, Politics, and Violence.* Oxford University Press.

McMahan, Jeff. 2009, *Killing in War.* Oxford University Press.

Nhat Hanh, Thich. 2002. "Cultivating Compassion to Respond to Violence: The Way of Peace." Available at www.wagingpeace.org/cultivating-compassion-to-respond-to-violence-the-way-of-peace/

Nikam, N. A. and Richard McKeon, eds. and trans. 1959. *The Edicts of Aśoka.* University of Chicago Press.

Obeyesekere, Gananath. 1995. "Buddhism, Nationhood, and Cultural Identity." In *Fundamentalisms Comprehended*. Edited by Martin E. Marty and R. Scott Appleby. University of Chicago Press. 231–58.

Premasiri, P. D. 2003. "The Place for a Righteous War in Buddhism." *Journal of Buddhist Ethics* 10: 153–66.

Sinclair, Iain. 2014. "War Magic and Just War in Indian Tantric Buddhism." *Social Analysis* 58(1): 149–66.

Smith, Jonathan Z. 1982. *Imagining Religion: From Babylon to Jonestown*. University of Chicago Press.

Stahn, Carsten. 2006 "'*Jus ad bellum*', '*jus in bello*' ... '*jus post bellum*'? Rethinking the Conception of the Law of Armed Force." *European Journal of International Law* 17(5): 921–43.

Swearer, Donald K. 2004. "Buddhism and Weapons of Mass Destruction: An Oxymoron?" In *Ethics and Weapons of Mass Destruction: Religious and Secular Perspectives*. Edited by Sohail H. Hashmi, and Steven P. Lee. Cambridge University Press. 237–45.

Tambiah, Stanley Jeyaraja. 1990. *Magic, Science, Religion, and the Scope of Rationality*. Cambridge University Press.

Wallis, Glenn, trans. 2004. *The Dhammapada: Verses on the Way*. The Modern Library.

Walzer, M. 2004. *Arguing about War*. Yale University Press.

2006 [1977]. *Just and Unjust Wars: A Moral Argument with Historical Illustrations*, 4th edition. Basic Books.

Part III

Religious Nationalism

14 War in Religious Zionism

ROBERT EISEN

The state of Israel has had to grapple with the issue of war from the moment the United Nations (UN) voted for its establishment in 1947. For Jews, the creation of Israel was a momentous event; it represented a triumphant return to their ancient homeland after almost 2,000 years of exile that began with the destruction of the Jewish state by the Roman Empire in the 1st century CE. However, for Arab Palestinians who had been living in the land for generations, as well as for the surrounding Arab nations, the creation of Israel was an affront: Jews were foreign invaders claiming a land that was not rightfully theirs. Thus, the Palestinians and Arab nations united in going to war against Jews in Palestine even before the newly formed Jewish state formally declared its independence in May of 1948. Israel won that war, but there were several more wars to follow inspired by the same motives that caused the first one, and while Israel has managed to either win these wars or escape from them with a draw, the costs have been high for it in terms of lives lost and other forms of damage that war inevitably brings upon a nation economically, socially, and psychologically. At present, Israel's relationship with the Arab world has significantly improved, but war continues to be a threat along its borders with Gaza, Lebanon, and Syria. Moreover, Iran has now emerged as Israel's most dangerous enemy, issuing threats to destroy it on a regular basis. Israel has therefore never known a time when it was free of war or the threat of war.

Israeli writers in a number of disciplines have reflected extensively on the moral dilemmas associated with war. Legal specialists, philosophers, religious leaders, literary figures, and academics have all addressed these issues at length. Among these writers, one finds a wide range of approaches from hawkish to dovish, differences that reflect divisions within the larger Israeli society to which they belong. Israel has always been deeply torn over how to view the violence it had to use

to come into existence and that it continues to use for its survival
(Gorny 1987; Shapira 1992; Luz 2003).[1]

This chapter will focus on attitudes to war in the sector of Israeli
society most relevant to this volume: those who identify with religious
Zionism. It is this community in Israel that is most concerned with war
from a religious standpoint.

The religious Zionist community is relatively small. It has never
claimed the allegiance of more than a small fraction of Jews who identify with Zionism, and at present it makes up only about 10 percent of
Israel's population. However, studying the attitudes of this community
to war is very important for understanding how Israel in general deals
with this issue because of the influence this community has had on
Israeli society since the Six-Day War in 1967. In the political sphere, the
religious Zionist community has been at the forefront of the settlement
of the territories captured by Israel in the Six-Day War, most notably the
West Bank that Palestinians see as the location of their own future state.
Religious Zionism is thus a major factor in the ongoing violence
between Israelis and Palestinians and one of the primary roadblocks to
a peace agreement between the two sides. In the military sphere, religious Zionists are often more eager to perform military service than
their secular counterparts because of their high level of dedication to the
state of Israel. Thus, by the 1990s, religious Zionists made up 20 percent
of the soldiers in infantry brigades – twice the percentage of their
numbers in the general population – and among combat lieutenants
and captains the ratio of religious to secular is two to one. Religious
Zionism therefore permeates the culture of the Israeli army (Cohen
2007; Eisen 2017: 28).

There is an immense amount of material that pertains to the topic
at hand. Religious Zionist rabbis have produced an extensive literature
that has attempted to understand war from the standpoint of theology
and to formulate norms for war in accordance with Jewish law. Most of
this literature is only in Hebrew, though there is now a small body of
secondary literature that has made some of its contents available to
English readers. The task of this chapter will be to do the same, but
given the volume and complexity of the material, we will have to be

---

[1] Luz (2003) analyzes how early Zionist and later Israeli thinkers have grappled with
these issues. Gorny (1987) deals with the same issues but focuses exclusively on
Zionism prior to the establishment of Israel. Shapira (1992) narrows the focus even
further. Like Gorny, she examines how Zionism dealt with this issue before the
founding of the state, but her analysis deals exclusively with Labor Zionism, the
largest branch of the early Zionist movement.

selective about the issues covered. It will therefore focus mostly on how religious Zionists understand war from a theological perspective. This focus should provide the best insights into how religious Zionists approach war.

EARLY ZIONISM

The Zionist movement that led to the establishment of the state of Israel arose in the 1880s among European Jews who believed that there was no future for Jews in Europe, where the vast majority of Jews in the world at the time were located. Jews had been invited to become citizens of European states in a gradual process of emancipation that began just prior to the 1800s with the French Revolution, but despite the best efforts of Jews to contribute to European society, antisemitism remained widespread. Moreover, in the 1880s, the situation worsened; violence against Jewish communities in Eastern Europe began to erupt for the first time since Jews had been invited to become European citizens, a turn of events that shocked many Jews who had come to believe that this type of violence was a thing of the past. As a result of these developments, some Jews began to believe that Jews would never have a legitimate and secure place in European society. Compounding these sentiments was the fact that, even under the best of circumstances, many Jews did not feel that they could fully identify with the nations of which they were now citizens. This was an age of strong nationalism throughout Europe, and Jews often had difficulty developing a sense of belonging to nations of which they had only recently become part. Therefore, some European Jews began to feel that their future lay in reclaiming their ancient homeland in Palestine, where they could build a Jewish state and have control of their own security and destiny. Thus, "Zionism" was born, a movement dedicated to the implementation of this goal. The name of the movement came from the term Zion (*tisyon* in the Hebrew), a designation in the Hebrew Bible referring to a number of geographical locations, including the entire land of Israel, which Zionists saw as the Jewish homeland.[2]

Almost immediately upon its creation, the Zionist movement began sending Jews to Palestine, which was then under Turkish Ottoman rule, to build settlements for a future Jewish state. At the same time, Zionists began to raise funds for their enterprise and

[2] General histories of Zionism can be found in Laqueur (2003) and Sachar (2007).

organize themselves politically to convince the international community to support their cause. Eventually, Zionism succeeded in its quest, with the vote of the UN in 1947 partitioning Palestine into Jewish and Arab states. However, the path to statehood was by no means a smooth one for Jews. Violence erupted early on between the Jewish settlers and the Arab Palestinian population that opposed the Zionist enterprise, and it became a serious problem from the 1920s onward. That problem persisted well after the creation of the Jewish state, and it continues to this day.[3]

Zionism began as a staunchly secular movement and would remain so. Most Zionists rejected the traditional Jewish belief that Jews would return to their ancient homeland only if they observed God's 613 commandments as specified in the Bible and rabbinic literature and patiently waited for Him to reward them by sending His messiah to end the centuries of exile. In fact, many early Zionists did not believe in God at all, or if they did, they did not see him as a God who intervened in history. Thus, their view was that Jews would return to their homeland only if they took matters into their own hands by emigrating to the land, raising funds, and lobbying the international community to support their program. Moreover, the political state that secular Zionism envisioned was one in which religion would not play a central role. Religion had been critical for Jews during the centuries of exile in giving them a strong sense of identity that allowed them to bear their suffering, but it would no longer be needed in a modern state. Nationalism, not religion, would be the anchor for Jewish identity.[4]

EARLY RELIGIOUS ZIONISM

Not surprisingly, Orthodox Jews, who upheld the traditional beliefs that Zionists rejected, viewed Zionism with suspicion or outright hostility. However, a small number of Orthodox Jews supported the Zionist enterprise despite its secular character, and thus "religious Zionism" came into existence.

Two versions of this form of Zionism soon emerged. One was initiated by R. Isaac Jacob Reines (1839–1915), who supported Zionism for pragmatic reasons. He believed that Orthodox Jews should join the Zionist movement because Jews needed their own state as a refuge from

---

[3] See sources in note 2.
[4] General histories of Zionist thought can be found in Avineri (1981), Shimoni (1995), and Hertzberg (1997).

the physical and spiritual dangers that threatened them. A Jewish state would protect Jews from antisemitism and would help Jews stem the tide of assimilation into non-Jewish society by allowing Jews to build a state based on Jewish culture and values (Wanefsky 1970; Shapira 2002).

Of far greater influence in the long run was a more dramatic approach to religious Zionism initiated by R. Abraham Isaac Kook (1865–1935), the first Ashkenazi Chief Rabbi of the Jewish community in Palestine before the establishment of Israel. R. Kook believed that Zionism was not only compatible with Judaism in its traditional form – it was, in some sense, its fulfillment. The Zionist movement and its project of settling the land of Israel represented nothing less than the beginning of the messianic redemption, the time at the end of history when, according to Jewish tradition, God would send his messiah to bring the Jews back to their ancient homeland. The fact that Zionism was a mostly secular movement could be explained. R. Kook argued that secular Zionists were being compelled by the divine spirit to settle the Holy Land for messianic purposes, even though they were not aware of it, and eventually they would return to religion when they understood the significance of their actions. Underlying this way of thinking was the view that the messianic process was a gradual one. It would evolve slowly through the progress of normal historical events.[5]

Still, it must be emphasized that the vast majority of early Zionists were secular. Religious Zionism in both the forms that R. Reines and R. Kook envisioned was marginal to the Zionist movement as a whole.

On the issue of violence, early religious Zionists tended to be relatively moderate. Most believed that violence should not be used to establish a Jewish state; it should be employed only to defend Jewish communities from Palestinian aggression. Thus, during the period of the "Arab rebellion" (1936–1939), when Palestinians rose up en masse in protest against the growth of the Jewish community and engaged in violence against it that was more widespread and intense than ever before, most of the leading rabbis in the religious Zionist camp pleaded for Jews to exercise restraint (Gorny 1987: 242, 275; Don-Yehiya 1993: 155–190; Luz 2003: 205–207).

Secular Zionists had a much wider range of approaches to such violence. In the first few decades of Jewish settlement in Palestine, these Zionists took the same line on this issue that religious Zionists

---

[5] There is a vast literature on Kook's life and thought. Some general academic treatments include Gellman (1991), Ish-Shalom and Rosenberg (1991), Ish-Shalom (1993), Kaplan and Shatz (1995), Rosenak (2006), and Mirsky (2014).

did; violent force should be used only for defensive purposes. Yet, during the years of the Arab rebellion, the defensive ethos of the secular Zionist community began to give way to a more aggressive ethos characterized by militarism and nativism (Shapira 1992). Moreover, there had been a minority of secular Zionists since the inception of the movement that had always had militant views. The forefather of this branch of Zionism was Vladimir Ze'ev Jabotinsky (1880–1940), who headed the right-wing Revisionist Party in the early Zionist movement (Shavit 1988; Ben-Hur 1993; Katz 1996; Kaplan 2005). Jabotinsky believed that armed confrontation with the Palestinians was inevitable and that the question of who would rule Palestine would have to be settled by military force. Jabotinsky's thinking gave rise to even more extreme militant factions in secular Zionism, who employed terrorism to achieve their goals (Gorny 1987: 156–173; Sprinzak 1991: 23–27; Shapira 1992: 154–163, 242–248; Luz 2003: 177–182).

RELIGIOUS ZIONISM AFTER 1967

Significant changes occurred in religious Zionism after the Six-Day War in 1967. R. Kook's teachings were further developed by his son, Rabbi Tsevi Yehudah Kook (1891–1982), who applied his father's ideas to the momentous events his father did not live to see: the Holocaust, the establishment of the state of Israel, and its struggle for survival in the face of several wars with its Arab neighbors. The younger Kook also gathered around him a loyal group of disciples who had great success in disseminating his teachings in the religious Zionist community. During his lifetime, the elder Kook's views did not win large numbers of adherents, but his thinking, reshaped and popularized by his son, became dominant among religious Zionists in the decades after the Six-Day War in 1967 (Ravitzky 1996: ch. 3; Schwartz 1997, 1999, 2001, 2002).

Most importantly, R. Tsevi Yehudah Kook took his father's teachings in a more militant direction. The younger Kook followed his father's lead in believing that secular Zionism was unwittingly motivated by a divine impulse and was a vehicle for bringing about the messianic redemption, but he extended these ideas to the political reality of the state of Israel. Thus, the secular political state was now holy, and, most importantly for our purposes, so were its army and the wars it waged. The purpose of Israel's wars was to establish Jewish sovereignty over the geographical area that God had promised to Abraham in the Bible, for according to rabbinic tradition this land would belong to the Jews in the messianic period. There were disagreements in early rabbinic literature regarding what territory was included here, but according to most opinions it encompassed not only the entire expanse of land between the Mediterranean and the Jordan River, but also portions of present-day Jordan and Iraq (Ravitzky 1996: 80–84; Luz 2003: 223–224; Holtser 2007, 2009: ch. 6).

While the basic elements of R. Tsevi Yehudah Kook's thinking took shape after the 1948 War of Independence, it was further consolidated in the wake of the 1967 Six-Day War. Israelis were stunned by their seemingly miraculous victory in which several Arab armies were crushed in only six days and large tracts of territory were captured, including the West Bank, Gaza, the Golan Heights, and the entire Sinai Peninsula. For the younger Kook, the victory was nothing short of a miracle in the literal sense of the term. Israel now controlled a much larger portion of the territories promised to Abraham than ever before, and this course of events seemed to be proof that the messianic process was indeed heading toward completion. Moreover, the victory inspired the younger Kook and his followers to lobby the Israeli government for the settlement of the captured territories in order to secure Jewish sovereignty over them, to block attempts to trade land for peace, and to ensure that the messianic process would continue. *Gush Emunim* (the Bloc of the Faithful), an organization formed in 1974, became the leading force for this cause and was soon taken over by elite students of R. Tsevi Yehudah Kook, who used it as a means to implement their messianic program (Sprinzak 1991: 43–46).

This organization was remarkably successful. It raised the profile of religious Zionism from a relatively marginal force in Israeli society and politics to one that had a strong influence on the entire national agenda, and it was extremely effective in lobbying successive Israeli governments to support and implement its plans; it founded scores of settlements throughout the territories captured in 1967. *Gush Emunim* no longer exists today, but the settlements it established do, and they are populated by hundreds of thousands of Israelis (Sprinzak 1991: 46–55, 67–69; Ravitzky 1996: 129, 131–133).

It is important to clarify that R. Tsevi Yehudah Kook and his followers did not believe that Israel should wage war solely for the purpose of capturing territory meant for the messianic kingdom; war was only for defensive purposes. But they believed that if, in the course of defending itself, Israel conquered such territory, it should not return it as a part of a peace agreement; the conquest was part of God's messianic plan. The assumption here seems to have been that, given the depth of the hostility that the surrounding Arab nations had toward Israel, opportunities for Israel to fight defensive wars and gain land destined for the messianic kingdom would be ample. The Six-Day War was one such opportunity, and what a magnificent opportunity it turned out to be, according to this way of thinking (Ravitzky 1996: 86, 122–123; Luz 2003: 223–224).

Since the 1970s, when R. Tsevi Yehudah Kook's thinking was highly influential, religious Zionism has faced a number of daunting challenges, and it has become increasingly diverse as its followers have adopted different approaches to grapple with them. The idea that the state of Israel is the beginning of the messianic redemption has lost some of its luster. A number of events have raised doubts about whether the messianic redemption is indeed in process and, if so, whether it is in an advanced stage. Since its victory in the Six-Day War, Israel has fought several more wars, some of which have cost Israel dearly, and it has witnessed two Intifadas, or Arab uprisings. Israel also willingly gave land back to the Palestinians with the Gaza disengagement in 2005, which seemed to reverse the progress of the messianic process. Social realities have also been inconsistent with the messianic expectations of religious Zionists. The secular population in Israel has shown no greater interest in adopting Orthodox religious observance than it did at the time of the founding of the state, an indication that progress toward messianic times has been halted or was an illusion in the first place. And many Israelis of secular orientation have consistently supported the notion of trading land for peace that would allow for the creation of a Palestinian state on the West Bank and in Gaza. Such a plan, if successful, would constitute an enormous setback for the messianic process in the eyes of most religious Zionists. The Oslo Accords, which were signed in the 1990s, embodied this way of thinking among secular Israelis, and even though the accords ultimately failed, they were evidence that a substantial number of Israelis could be swayed to support territorial concessions in return for a peace agreement with the Palestinians.

A good portion of the religious Zionist community has held fast to R. Tsevi Yehudah Kook's original doctrines and continues to believe that the messianic process is on track and that the setbacks just outlined cannot derail what has been determined by God's will. However, other viewpoints have emerged. Some religious Zionists have taken positions even more militant than those of the younger Kook's followers, views that include xenophobic perspectives regarding

Palestinians, as well as Jews who disagree with them, and the belief that Israel needs no excuse to wage war in order to claim the land meant for the messianic kingdom. Other religious Zionists, however, have backed away from R. Tsevi Yehudah Kook's views and now believe that his predictions about the messianic period were premature. Finally, there is a small group of religious Zionists who were never convinced to support the younger Kook's views to begin with and whose positions are more in line with that of the early religious Zionists. This group holds not only that Israel should wage war solely for defensive purposes but that it should allow for the establishment of a Palestinian state in the West Bank and Gaza in return for peace with the Palestinians and the surrounding Arab countries. The religious Zionist community, at present, is therefore quite divided (Eisen 2011: 188–190; Inbari 2014).

THE TEXTUAL SOURCES

How is it that religious Zionism began with relatively moderate views on violence and war and moved toward more militant positions after the 1967 war? Clearly, one reason was the influence of historical events. Most significantly, R. Tsevi Yehudah Kook radicalized his father's teachings because he lived to see violence against Jews that his father had not witnessed, including the Arab rebellion of 1936–1939, the War of Independence in 1948, the Six-Day War in 1967, and spates of Palestinian terrorism that consistently plagued the Jewish state after its creation. Most important, R. Tsevi Yehudah Kook lived to see the Holocaust, the worst catastrophe that Jews had ever experienced and an event emblematic of the inhumanity of the modern era in general. It is therefore no surprise that the younger Kook would develop more favorable views regarding violence and war than his father did. For the younger Kook, Jews had no choice but to fight violence with violence.

Moreover, the Israeli victory in the Six-Day War, which resulted in Israel capturing large swaths of land, fueled speculations about the messianic import of the Jewish state, speculations that had originated with R. Tsevi Yehudah Kook's father and that the younger Kook and his followers adopted. As anyone who has studied religious violence knows, messianic speculations often bring violence in their wake, especially when they are coupled with the belief that the end of history is imminent. Religious believers who are convinced that the messianic period is at hand will often resort to violence against coreligionists and those outside their religion whom they perceive as obstacles to the final stages of redemption.[6]

We must also appreciate the malleability of the traditional textual sources upon which religious Zionists relied to formulate their views. As the author has shown in a previous study, biblical and rabbinic sources are highly ambiguous with respect to violence and war. In every period and in every major school of Judaism, there were sources that looked positively upon violence and war and sources that looked upon them negatively. Moreover, there were a good many sources in every one of these schools that may be interpreted both ways. This assessment applies not only to the biblical and rabbinic literature, but also to the literature of medieval Jewish philosophy and Kabbalah (Eisen 2011; Levin and Shapira 2012).

Many Jewish scholars have argued that Judaism underwent a major transformation in its attitude to violence and war in the transition from the Hebrew Bible to rabbinic Judaism in the first centuries of the common era. While the Bible often saw virtue in the waging of war, the rabbis consistently exhibited an aversion to it (Luz 2003: 21–24; Berger 2007; Cohen 2007: 35–36; Firestone 2012: part II). Yet, as I have shown in my previous study, this judgment is flawed. A careful analysis of rabbinic literature demonstrates that rabbinic Judaism was just as ambiguous on this matter as the Hebrew Bible (Eisen 2011: ch. 3).

Religious Zionist thinkers have therefore been able to draw on a significant body of authoritative Jewish sources to support a range of viewpoints on violence and war. Let us first look at how religious Zionists on the more militant end of the spectrum justified their positions on these issues – and here we include R. Tsevi Yehudah Kook and his followers, as well as religious Zionists who have taken even more extreme views. The conception of messianism that is supported in most traditional Jewish sources addressing the subject is passive in orientation. The messianic era will come about through God's sudden and miraculous intervention into history. But both the elder and younger Kook were inspired by a number of other sources in rabbinic literature espousing a more active, naturalistic messianism in which human initiative plays a significant role in bringing about the redemption, and they believed that Zionism was the embodiment of this type of messianism (Myers 1991: 4–7).

---

[6]   An excellent study that highlights this point and analyzes it in great depth is Hall (2009).

Most significant in this regard was the description of the messianic era provided by Maimonides (1138–1204), medieval Judaism's most famous rabbinic authority. Maimonides, in his massive legal compendium the *Mishneh Torah*, depicted the messianic period as an era that would evolve from normal historical events. The messiah would be a human political leader who would live and die as all mortal human beings do, and he would redeem the Jewish people from their exile and establish a messianic Jewish state in the land of Israel through military conquest. No miraculous assistance from God would be needed. Moreover, the ensuing messianic era would be no different from our own world except that Jews would reestablish a state in their ancient homeland, all nations would recognize the God of Israel as the one true God, and they would all live in peace with one another.[7] The initiatives of the Zionist movement and its ultimate success in establishing a Jewish state seemed to be, in critical ways, in harmony with Maimonides' naturalistic messianism.

Just as significant for religious Zionists who were inclined to militancy was a source from Nahmanides (1194–1270), another rabbi of great stature in the medieval period. Nahmanides took the unusual position that, in the biblical narrative, God's commandments to Joshua and the Israelites to conquer the land of Israel and settle it were not one-time imperatives; they were eternally in force. Thus, the original conquest of the land did not fulfill these commandments once and for all. Jews were required to conquer and settle the land in any subsequent period in which the land was ruled by non-Jews.[8] Zionism therefore provided the opportunity for fulfilling these imperatives.

Thus, sources in Maimonides and Nahmanides gave inspiration to religious Zionists who favored militancy. When combined, they seemed to support a positive approach to violence and war as means for Zionism to realize its messianic goals.[9]

Yet, religious Zionists who were not inclined to militancy found support in traditional Jewish sources as well, including those just cited. Maimonides may have envisioned a naturalistic messianism, but he did not take Nahmanides' position that the commandments to conquer and settle the land of Israel were eternal; these commandments were one-

---

[7] Maimonides, *Mishneh Torah, Hilkhot Melakhim*, chs. 11–12.

[8] Nahmanides, "Addenda to Positive Commandments," in Maimonides' *Sefer ha-Mitsvot*, addendum #4.

[9] R. Isaac Halevi Herzog (1888–1959) and R. Shlomo Goren (1917–1994), both of whom served as Ashkenazi Chief Rabbi of Israel, took this approach. For R. Herzog, see Eisen (2017: 87, 89, 100, 104); for R. Goren, see Eisen Eisen (2017: 112, 210, 220–221).

time imperatives for Joshua and the Israelites.[10] Furthermore, there were those who argued that, in Nahmanides' thinking, the commandment to settle the land of Israel was still in force, but his notion of conquering it militarily was not.[11]

It should also be pointed out that traditional Jewish sources could also be utilized to support the position of religious Zionist Jews, like the followers of R. Reines, who did not believe that Zionism or the state of Israel had any messianic significance whatsoever. As already noted, most traditional sources that dealt with the messianic period depicted it as an era that came about through God's initiative, not that of human beings. At best, Jews could observe God's commandments and pray for the coming of the messiah in order to bring about the final redemption, but they had no other role to play in the messianic process, and certainly not a military one.

We should also note that these sources were part of the reason why most ultra-Orthodox Jews both in Israel and abroad have steadfastly refused to accept Zionism in any form, secular or religious, and do not see the state of Israel as Jewishly meaningful. Some ultra-Orthodox Jews, in fact, believe that the state of Israel is a blasphemy and insult to God and that the Holocaust occurred because it was God's punishment for Zionism. Underlying this way of thinking is the view that Zionism cannot possibly have any messianic import given that it was initiated by secular Jews and that it is therefore an affront to God. Religious Zionists are not much better, according to this perspective, because they are not only in league with secular Zionists, but also demonstrate a lack of faith in God's redemptive power by adopting an active messianism (Ravitzky 1996: 13–26, chs. 2, 4, 5).

Ultra-Orthodox Jews in Israel constitute about the same percentage of the population as religious Zionist Jews do – about 10 percent –and if one wonders why ultra-Orthodox Jews live in Israel despite their beliefs, one has to be aware that their community long predates that of the modern state of Israel.[12] Thus, in their opinion, it is the state of Israel that is the interloper here, not they.

---

[10] Maimonides, *Mishneh Torah, Hilkhot Melakhim* 5:4.

[11] Such, for instance, was the opinion of R. Sha'ul Yisraeli; see Eisen (2017: 183–184). J. David Bleich, an American Orthodox rabbi, provides a thorough analysis of these sources in Maimonides and Nahmanides in light of their subsequent interpretation by premodern interpreters in Bleich (1983). Bleich himself sides with the view that the commandment to conquer the land of Israel militarily is no longer in effect.

[12] "Israel's Religiously-Divided Society," Pew Research Center (March 8, 2016), available at www.pewforum.org/2016/03/08/israels-religiously-divided-society/;

CONCLUSIONS

Religious Zionism has gone through dramatic changes in its attitude to violence and war since the inception of Zionism at the end of the 19th century. Religious Zionists began with views on these issue that were more moderate than those of their secular Zionist counterparts, who made up the vast majority of the early Zionist movement. But after 1948, R. Tsevi Yehudah Kook developed more militant views on the basis of his father's messianic theology that eventually became highly influential among religious Zionists, particularly after the Six-Day War in 1967. In this way of thinking, violence and war were seen as legitimate means to implement the messianic agenda. Events in the past twenty to thirty years have complicated that agenda, and as a result religious Zionism is now divided. However, it is by no means a spent force. Militant religious Zionists still make up a good portion of the population of settlements in the West Bank that have been an obstacle to peace, their political parties have been critical allies of Benjamin Netanyahu's Likud Party that has dominated Israeli politics for decades, and they are represented in the Israel's armed forces well out of proportion to their numbers in the general population. On the issues of violence and war in the Israeli–Palestinian conflict, religious Zionism will have to be reckoned with for some time to come.

References

Avineri, Shlomo. 1981. *The Making of Modern Zionism: The Intellectual Origins of the Jewish State*. Basic Books.

Ben-Hur, Raphaella Bilski. 1993. *Every Individual, a King: The Social and Political Thought of Ze'ev Vladimir Jabotinsky*. B'nai Brith Books.

Berger, Michael S. 2007. "Taming the Beast: Rabbinic Pacification of Second-Century Jewish Nationalism." In *Belief and Bloodshed: Religion and Violence across Time and Tradition*. Edited by James K. Wellman, Jr. Rowman & Littlefield Publishers. 47–62.

Bleich, J. David. 1983. "Judea and Samaria: Settlement and Return." In *Contemporary Halakhic Problems*, vol. 2. Ktav Publishing House. 289–221.

Cohen, Stuart A. 2007. "The Quest for a Corpus of Jewish Military Ethics." *The Journal of Israeli History* 26(1): 35–66.

Don-Yehiya, Eliezer. 1993. "Dat ve-Teror Politi: Ha-Yahadut ha-Datit u-Pe'ulot ha-Gemul be-Tekufat 'Ha-Me'or'ot'." *Ha-Tsiyonut* 17: 155–190.

Gilad Malach and Lee Cahaner, "2018 Statistical Report on Ultra-Orthodox Society in Israel," Israel Democracy Institute (December 19, 2018), available at https://en.idi.org.il/articles/25385.

Eisen, Robert. 2011. *The Peace and Violence of Judaism: From the Bible to Modern Zionism*. Oxford University Press.

  2017. *Religious Zionism, Jewish Law, and the Morality of War: How Five Rabbis Confronted One of Modern Judaism's Greatest Challenges*. Oxford University Press.

Firestone, Reuven. 2012. *Holy War in Judaism: The Fall and Rise of a Controversial Idea*. Oxford University Press.

Gellman, Ezra, ed. 1991. *Essays on the Thought and Philosophy of Rabbi Kook*. Fairleigh Dickinson University Press.

Gorny, Yosef. 1987. *Zionism and the Arabs, 1882–1948: A Study of Ideology*. Oxford University Press.

Hall, John R. 2009. *Apocalypse: From Antiquity to the Empire of Modernity*. Polity Press.

Hertzberg, Arthur. 1997. *The Zionist Idea: A Historical Analysis and Reader*. The Jewish Publication Society of America.

Holtser, Eli. 2007. "Attitudes Towards the Use of Military Force in Ideological Currents of Religious Zionism." In *War and Peace in the Jewish Tradition*. Edited by Lawrence Schiffman and Joel B. Wolowelsky. Yeshiva University Press. 357–372.

  2009. *Herev Pipiyot be-Yadam: Activizm Tseva'i be-Hagtuah shel ha-Tsiyonut ha-Datit*. The Hartman Institute.

Inbari, Motti. 2014. *Messianic Religious Zionism Confronts Territorial Compromises*. Cambridge University Press.

Ish-Shalom, Benjamin. 1993. *Rav Avraham Itzhak HaCohen Kook: Between Rationalism and Mysticism*. Translated by Ora Wiskind-Elper. State University of New York Press.

Ish-Shalom, Benjamin and Shalom Rosenberg, eds. 1991. *The World of Rav Kook's Thought*. Translated by Shalom Carmy and Bernard Casper. Avi Chai.

Kaplan, Eran. 2005. *The Jewish Radical Right: Revisionist Zionism and Its Ideological Legacy*. University of Wisconsin Press.

Kaplan, Lawrence J. and David Shatz, eds. 1995. *Rabbi Abraham Isaac Kook and Jewish Spirituality*. New York University Press.

Katz, Shmuel. 1996. *Lone Wolf: A Biography of Vladimir (Ze'ev) Jabotinsky*. Barricade Books.

Laqueur, Walter. 2003. *A History of Zionism*. Schocken Books.

Levin, Yigal and Amnon Shapira, eds. 2012. *War and Peace in the Jewish Tradition: From the Biblical World to the Present*. Routledge.

Luz, Ehud. 2003. *Wrestling with an Angel: Power, Morality, and Jewish Identity*. Translated by Michael Swirsky. Yale University Press.

Myers, Jody. 1991. "The Messianic Idea and Zionist Ideologies." In *Studies in Contemporary Jewry VII: Jews and Messianism in the Modern Era: Metaphor and Meaning*. Edited by Jonathan Frankel. Oxford University Press. 3–13.

Mirsky, Yehudah. 2014. *Rav Kook: Mystic in a Time of Revolution*. Yale University Press.

Ravitzky, Aviezer. 1996. *Messianism, Zionism, and Jewish Religious Radicalism*. Translated by Michael Swirsky and Jonathan Chipman. University of Chicago Press.

Rosenak, Avinoam. 2006. *A. I. Kook*. Merkaz Zalman Shazar.

Sachar, Howard M. 2007. *A History of Israel: From the Rise of Zionism to Our Time*, 3rd revised edition. Knopf.

Schwartz, Dov. 1997. *Erets Mamashut ve-Dimyon: Ma'amdah shel Erets Yisra'el be-Hagut ha-Tsiyonut ha-Datit*. 'Am 'Oved Publishers.

 1999. *Ha-Tsiyonut ha-Datit: Bein Higayon le-Meshihiyut*. 'Am 'Oved Publishers.

 2001. *Etgar u-Mashber be-Hug ha-Rav Kuk*. 'Am 'Oved Publishers.

 2002. *Faith at the Crossroads: A Theological Profile of Religious Zionism*. Translated by Batya Stein. E. J. Brill.

Shapira, Anita. 1992. *Land and Power: The Zionist Resort to Force, 1881–1948*. Translated by William Templer. Oxford University Press.

Shapira, Yosef. 2002. *Hagut, Halakhah, ve-Tsiyonut: 'Al 'Olamo ha-Ruhani shel ha-Rav Yitshak Ya'akov Reines*. Ha-Kibbuts ha-Me'uhad.

Shavit, Yaacov. 1988. *Jabotinsky and the Revisionist Movement, 1925–1948*. F. Cass.

Shimoni, Gideon. 1995. *The Zionist Ideology*. Brandeis University Press.

Sprinzak, Ehud. 1991. *The Ascendance of Israel's Radical Right*. Oxford University Press.

Wanefsky, Joseph. 1970. *Rabbi Isaac Jacob Reines: His Life and Thought*. Philosophical Library.

15 Christian Nationalism and Millennialism in the USA

ANGELA M. LAHR

In 1862, a southern Indiana man serving in the Union Army during the American Civil War wrote home from Arkansas. After praising his fellow Hoosiers and sharing his impressions of the South, the soldier cheered what he believed to be the coming of the end of the war:

> Well, God knows it is time, for this unnatural and unholy war to close. Our country has been drenched in blood long enough, and I think every man with a spark of humanity in his breast will rejoice when this struggle closes, and when peace shall once more spread her balmy wings, over this unhappy country, and will hail it as the dawn of a new millennium.
>
> (Jasper Weekly Courier 1862)

One-hundred years later, in October 1962, evangelist Billy Graham was in Argentina during the Cuban Missile Crisis. As Graham preached in Buenos Aires, he drew on Christian frameworks about the future: "Now the four horses of the apocalypse are preparing for action. The eventual showdown that is now on the horizon is inevitable. ... The Bible tells us that when world conditions are the worst ... then will Christ come" (Lahr 2007: 117).

While the two men referenced different aspects of Christian eschatology, both drew on it to understand American wars: a civil war and a cold war. The Civil War soldier believed that the war would bring about a millennium, a thousand years of peace. Graham saw the Cuban Missile Crisis as one sign of the end times, emphasizing the destruction of the apocalypse rather than a millennial utopia. Both men also blended their eschatological predictions with more worldly opinions about the USA. The soldier wrote that it was "fun" to track down rebel guerrillas, which implied that God was on the Union side, and stated with some pride that Confederates were "flocking" to swear allegiance to the USA (Jasper Weekly Courier 1862). Graham's tone was not quite so uncompromisingly nationalistic. He balanced pro-American sentiment with critique. In his Buenos Aires appearances during the Cuban Missile

Crisis, Graham noted that "the American people closed ranks behind the president," but he also stated that "whether the strong action of the American government has come in time remains to be seen" (Lahr 2007: 116–117).

The combination of Christian nationalism, political debate, and Christian eschatology has been present throughout American history, but in times of war it has been particularly evident. Millennialism and apocalypticism, the optimistic and pessimistic sides of the coin of American Christian eschatology, have provided a language and worldview to express hopes and fears about the future during times of trial. While the perspective often heightened Christian nationalism, that was not always the case. The millennialist outlook created a cultural space for political debate, a way for Americans to communicate and make sense of their wartime experiences by elevating the significance of the mundane and blending it with sacred paradigms.

DEFINITIONS AND DIVERSE MILLENNIAL TRADITIONS

The widespread use of the word "apocalypse" in pop culture reflects a fascination with end-times scenarios. Not only has "apocalyptic" become a common adjective, but "apocalypse" appears in film titles like *Apocalypse Now*, in dystopian fiction, and even in references to zombie apocalypses. A Greek word referring to the revealing of the previously hidden and obscure, "apocalypse" has come to mean an event, situation, or period – often occurring at some point in the future – that has changed the world as we knew it. In Christian eschatology, influenced by ancient traditions that include the Greek, Persian, Roman, and Jewish, among others, the apocalypse refers to the set of biblical prophetic beliefs found primarily in the books of Ezekiel, Daniel, and Revelation (Boyer 1992: 23, 21–45).

While "millennium" specifically denotes the period of 1,000 years of peace in the Christian eschatological timeline, "millennialism" is also used to reference end-times prophecy generally, even though theologians have interpreted the meaning of prophetic scripture differently based on their beliefs about the millennium and its timing. Amillennialists deny a literal era of peace, arguing that scripture depicts personal transformations figuratively. Postmillennialists and premillennialists, on the other hand, believe in a literal period of prosperity and righteousness, though they disagree about when that will happen in relation to Christ's return. Postmillennialists argue that believers will establish the millennium in the world and that Christ will return once that has been accomplished. Premillennialists maintain that Christ will return before the millennium in order to bring it about. Before the return of Christ, the world will experience a period of great trials, death, and destruction called the tribulation. Pretribulation premillennialists believe that Christians will be "raptured" – taken up to meet Christ – before the tribulation, sparing them from it. Post-tribulationists maintain that believers will live through the tribulation. After the Civil War, American evangelical Christians increasingly adopted a form of premillennialism known as "dispensationalism." Popularized by Plymouth Brethren missionary to North America John Nelson Darby and the *Scofield Reference Bible*, dispensational premillennialism divided human history and the end-times into ages – dispensations. The current dispensation – the church age – will end with a seven-year tribulation period (Weber 1987: 9–12, 16–24; Sutton 2014: 16–20).

Scholars have noted the ways by which postmillennial and premillennial perspectives have shaped American believers' worldviews over time. Postmillennial outlooks popularized in colonial America by Congregationalist Jonathan Edwards and others continued to inform reform movements prior to the Civil War, as postmillennialists believed that working toward the perfection of human society was not only possible but could help bring about the millennium (Moorhead 1998: 73–77). Premillennialists, however, who gained popularity among American evangelicals at the end of the 19th century, rejected the notion that the saints could establish the millennium. They more often sought out "signs of the times," events interpreted as the fulfillment of prophetic scripture and indications that the end-times were near. In the early Cold War, for example, many dispensationalists incorporated the atomic bomb into their prophetic timelines. While some continued to dabble in more specific speculations about the timing of the tribulation and the millennium, date-setting became largely discredited by the 20th century. This was partly due to the Millerite movement and the "Great Disappointment." Baptist minister William Miller used a historicist reading of prophecy to determine that Christ would return in the 1840s. When the calculated date came and went on October 22, 1844, the movement largely collapsed, though some maintained that God's kingdom had been established on that day, if not visibly (Boyer 1998: 145–147).

Apocalyptic worldviews were messier in the lived experiences of Protestants than these distinctions suggest. Miller's historicist premillennial movement took place during a time when postmillennial fervor was motivating Protestant reformers to turn the USA into a godly nation. Alexander Campbell, leader of the Christian (Disciples of Christ) movement, also argued for a more premillennial vision of the last days before the Civil War. Even premillennial dispensationalists in the 20th century who anticipated the imminent return of Christ refrained from completely despairing of worldly reform. Conservative evangelicals at the end of the 20th century created a "postmillennial window" by urging believers to work to oppose immorality within American culture (Harding 1994: 57–78). The lines separating pre- and postmillennialism have not always been clear, but the influence of these apocalyptic worldviews on American culture, during times of peace and war, is.

Fascination with the future survived even the most oppressive conditions. Slavery meant the loss of many African religious traditions in colonial America, but the enslaved continued to engage in divination practices common to African societies. Christian millennialism also reached some enslaved persons. While enslavers encouraged the circulation of religious messages that emphasized obedience and stifled preaching that may have empowered or offered the hope of freedom amongst their enslaved, Methodist and Baptist conversion efforts in the 1760s and 1770s promoted millennial beliefs in a future utopia (Butler 2008: 14, 104).

Despite some suppression of Native American religions, many Native American prophetic convictions also survived the arrival of Europeans and, later, the expansion of the USA. Contact brought syncretism as well, as was the case with the Ghost Dance movement at the end of the 19th century. Native American tribes across the west adopted a ritual meant to bring about the visions of Wovoka, a Paiute man who foresaw a brighter future for American Indians with the return of the bison and of Native American ancestors. The movement spread quickly, until Ghost Dancers gathered near Wounded Knee Creek clashed with soldiers in 1890. Wovoka's vision appealed to Native Americans struggling with changes that accompanied the westward expansion of the USA after the Civil War, but the Ghost Dance also reflected the blending of Native American and Christian traditions. Wovoka was rumored to be a "messiah," at one point revealing scars on his hands and feet that looked to some like Jesus' scars from hanging on the cross (Peterson 1990: 146). Wovoka's forecasting of a future period of paradise and peace for Native Americans paralleled the Christian millennium.

There are other similarities between Christian and Native American prophecies. Just as Christian millennialists expect Jesus' return, the Hopi await the return of Pahana, who will unite the people and bring about an era of peace (Peterson 1990: 234). The future arrival of the Jewish Messiah and the Twelfth (Hidden) Imam in Shi'i Islam play comparable roles. From the colonial period to the modern age, Native Americans responded to territorial and cultural threats from Americans of diverse religious (or nonreligious) backgrounds by adapting prophecy as a form of agency, drawing on traditional Native beliefs and practices and on some Christian ones (Johnson 1996: 583; Irwin 2008: 4). Eschatological narratives infused believers with a sense of their own transcendent significance. The stakes were high, and individuals and their communities could play a role in the end-times. This is what the diverse traditions shared, but 19th-century interactions between Natives and non-Natives have revealed the tension that also existed when millennial belief systems met in a context of racial inequality.

A shared eschatological vernacular encouraged an imperfect unity that contributed to American nationalism, especially in times of war. As the mainstream religion throughout most of American history, Christian (and particularly Protestant) nationalism dominated the millennial vernacular that promoted the USA as a special place with sacred purposes. Sociologists Andrew Whitehead and Samuel Perry define Christian nationalism as "an ideology that idealizes and advocates a fusion of American civil life with a particular type of Christian identity and culture" (2020: ix–x). Of the various tools of Christian nationalism that have sought to strengthen the connection between the state and an assumed divine plan, civil religion has been among the most studied. First coined by French philosopher Jean Jacques Rousseau, it was Robert Bellah's 1967 *Daedalus* article that touched off decades of inquiry into the meaning of the concept. Defined as a set of symbols, practices, and beliefs that promote and express patriotism within a nation, scholars have debated the degree to which religious institutions and principles have contributed to American civil religion. As historian Raymond Haberski, Jr. has pointed out, civil religion is "a hybrid of nationalism and traditional religion [with] an ideological flexibility that is intoxicating because it is so evocative, elastic, and deceptively complex" (2012: 5). Civil religion has reinforced the idea that the USA has a special place in the world. When infused with eschatological meaning, it promotes the view that the USA is special, God's "new Israel" (Wuthnow 1988: 395–399; Edwards and Valenzano 2016: xiii–xiv).

American exceptionalism, like civil religion, has served to advance Christian nationalism in the USA. Discussions of American exceptionalism typically begin more than a century before the founding of the country with John Winthrop's 1630 *Arabella* essay, which called for the new Massachusetts Bay colony to become a "city upon a hill," a godly example for the rest of the world. That sermon also expounded on two other concepts instrumental to both the Puritan worldview of the 17th century and the American exceptionalism that would survive until the 21st century: the covenant and the jeremiad. New England Puritans believed that their community had entered into a kind of spiritual agreement with God: a covenant (Miller 1956: 4–7; Gorski 2017: 40–44). If they followed God's will and laws, they could expect blessings. If, on the other hand, the Puritans broke their sacred covenant, God would turn from them (Winthrop 1630). The jeremiad is named after the biblical prophet Jeremiah. Atalia Omer and Jason A. Springs have defined it as "a form of address that laments and censures a set of status quo conditions and practices as inconsistent with, or contradictory to, what ought to be" (2013: 125). Puritan condemnation of those who had strayed from the sacred purpose was closely related to their belief in a covenantal relationship, creating a worldview that was deeply attuned to an understanding of the community in God's ultimate plan.

Taken together, the notion of the covenant, expressed after the USA's founding as the belief that the country was chosen by God as a "new Israel," and the jeremiad shaped American political culture over time by promoting American exceptionalism. In the 19th century, it justified American expansion in the form of manifest destiny. In the 20th century, as two world wars broke out, American exceptionalism appeared in arguments that rationalized both isolationism (with advocates making the case that the USA was geographically and culturally distinct from Europe, for example) and participation (the USA, because of its special role, could save the rest of the world). The jeremiad tradition also advocated American exceptionalism. Abolitionist reformers, sometimes motivated by postmillennial worldviews, warned the country about the consequences of continuing to allow slavery. The best-known and most-studied jeremiad political address in American history is Abraham Lincoln's second inaugural, in which he suggested that the Civil War had been God's punishment for slavery:

> Fondly do we hope, fervently do we pray, that this mighty scourge of war may speedily pass away. Yet, if God wills that it continue until all the wealth piled by the bondsman's two hundred and fifty

years of unrequited toil shall be sunk, and until every drop of blood
drawn with the lash shall be paid by another drawn with the sword,
as was said three thousand years ago, so still it must be said "the
judgments of the Lord are true and righteous altogether."

(Lincoln 1865)

In the American context, the jeremiad tradition has been used by the
powerful to wield and hold on to that power and by minority communities to call attention to injustice.

Millennialist thought reinforced both aspects of American exceptionalism: one that highlighted the country's unique relationship with
God and one that warned of the consequences of ignoring righteousness.
Examining how Christian nationalism has interacted with millennialism in key periods of war, moments when national myths, belief
systems, and institutions are scrutinized and reexamined, is one way
to tease out the intricate ways in which Americans imagined their
sacred and secular expectations for the future of the country.

DEFINING THE AMERICAN MILLENNIAL MISSION:
COLONIAL AMERICA AND THE AMERICAN REVOLUTION

Settlers in British North America, especially New England Puritans,
infused their colonial ventures with millennial significance. Scholars
disagree about the degree to which eschatological expectations motivated English Puritans to relocate to America, but by the time of the
American Revolution, postmillennial hopes of the coming millennium
on Earth – and specifically in the British colonies – would combine with
Christian nationalist rhetoric during the war. This would establish a
foundation for an American exceptionalism that would continue to
shape American political culture for years to come. The distinction
between pre- and postmillennialism, strands of which were both represented in colonial American theology, was blurred in the 1600s
(Smolinski 1998: 36–37, 39), but it has been theologian Jonathan
Edwards' postmillennial interpretations during the First Great
Awakening that have most captured the attention of scholars and
post-Revolutionary Americans eager to express the godly role of the
USA. In a 1742 sermon, "Some Thoughts Concerning the Present
Revival in New England," Edwards speculated about the realization of
the millennium in America. "This new world is probably now dis-
covered, that the new and more glorious state of God's church on earth
might commence there; that God might in it begin a new world in a

spiritual respect, when he creates the *new heavens* and *new earth"* (Cherry 1971: 56, emphasis in original). Edwards' anticipation of the colonies as God's future instruments is clear, and even if too much has been made of his postmillennialism in exclusion of other eschatological narratives, expectations of the millennium were also embraced by those seeking a unique role for an independent USA decades later.

As the American Revolution dawned, rhetoric promoting independence blended exceptionalist language with millennial tropes. In 1780, the *Maryland Gazette* printed a letter that blasted King George III: "Base tyrant! will he not be sensible, will he not acknowledge, that he himself is the source of all evils that, at the present time, tempest the earth. ... Let him withdraw his fleets and armies to his own island, and be bound like Satan for a thousand years, and we shall have a millennium on the earth" (*Maryland Gazette* 1780). For Christian patriots supporting independence, the king served as a stand-in for the diabolical actors in the eschatological scenario. By contrast, the new USA would defend liberty and fulfill God's righteous destiny on Earth.

Even Thomas Paine, whom evangelical believers would later denounce for his deist publication *Age of Reason*, used language that would later become familiar fodder for Christian nationalists. An independent USA, he wrote in *Common Sense*, could become a beacon of liberty: "O ye that love mankind! Ye that dare oppose, not only the tyranny, but the tyrant, stand forth! Every spot of the old world is overrun with oppression. Freedom hath been hunted round the globe. ... O! receive the fugitive, and prepare in time an asylum for mankind" (Paine 1776). Of course, not everyone in the British colonies supported independence. Loyalists also described a sacred cause, but it was one that would have kept the British Empire intact. In his response to *Common Sense*, James Chalmers expressed his "purest flame of patriotism" for the British "sacred cause," but also warned of the apocalyptic consequences of splitting from the empire ("Candidus" 1776).

Prophetic vernacular and religious-sanctioned nationalism were used on both sides of the war, then, but the Revolution's outcome elevated the American exceptionalist arguments that would serve as a template for future Americans who made a case for the USA's divinely sanctioned world role. As Yale president Ezra Stiles put it in a sermon delivered at the end of the war, the US population was to be the new chosen people. Stiles was confident in the "political welfare of God's American Israel" (Cherry 1971: 83). By the time of the Second Great Awakening in the early 19th century, the "conflation of sacred and secular metaphors" would "give mythic dimension to the new nation" (Smolinski 1998: 68).

The significance of this should not be misunderstood nor should these few examples be used to generalize too much. While Americans of the Revolutionary era drew on Christian nationalism, American exceptionalism, and eschatology to advocate for independence, this did not mean that the USA was founded as a "Christian nation" in the way that fundamentalists and conservative evangelical Protestants described it at the end of the 20th century (and beyond). Many of the founders, including Paine, held deist beliefs influenced by Enlightenment thought. Their God was an ecumenical one, but Christian millennialism was popular enough that it could be utilized as a vernacular to debate the future of the new country as a "visionary republic" (Bloch 1985). What was forged in the fires of the Revolutionary War was the idea, inspired by the struggle for independence and (in part) by postmillennial dreams of reform, that the USA was destined for greatness.

THE MILLENNIAL MISSION CHALLENGED AND REFINED: THE CIVIL WAR AND ITS AFTERMATH

Reformers and expansionists in the USA during the early 19th century drew on postmillennialism to work to perfect American society and to fulfill what they believed to be their country's "manifest destiny." The Civil War shattered some of that optimism, but millennialism continued to be a framework through which Americans on both sides of the war interpreted their individual realities and their political circumstances. Ironically, the Civil War both brought uncertainty about the country's future and reinforced Americans' belief in the USA's millennial role, even though Americans on opposite sides insisted that they were the proper guardians of that future. Anticipation of the future millennium and the apocalypse became common ways for Americans to understand the destruction and changes brought about by the war, and they also became a crucial part of a common vernacular used to debate everything from slavery to federalism to the economy.

Historian Jason Phillips' study of the various ways Americans conceptualized the future before and during the Civil War helps make sense of the complex applications of eschatology. He makes a distinction, for example, between two 19th-century "temporalities": anticipation and expectation. Americans with postmillennial outlooks anticipated a future in which they could make a difference, one that would advance progress. Premillennialism, in contrast, aligned more closely with expectation, based on the belief that the future had already been determined by forces outside of human control like providence and fate (Phillips 2018: 5–7). Americans relied on anticipation and expectation to interpret the changes brought on by the Civil War as both sides of the conflict adopted Christian nationalism.

Conflicting Union and Confederate causes were imbued with millennial significance. Convinced that God was on their side, Confederates insisted it was their destiny to carry out the prophetic mission forged during the American Revolution. Union officials, soldiers, and citizens claimed that mantle for themselves. Black and White abolitionists joined southern enslaved persons who flocked to Union camps in imagining a more just country free of slavery and moving closer to establishing a millennium. White northerners, who before the Emancipation Proclamation insisted that the war was not about slavery, embraced what they considered a sacred cause: keeping the Union together. As James Moorhead points out in his classic account of Protestant millennialism in the North:

> Protestants used the Scriptures eclectically, often juggling clearly eschatological ideas with other biblical motifs such as national election, covenant, or prophetic jeremiad. They also spoke of providential destiny in the context of contemporary problems. Their attitudes, for example, about slavery and the nature of democracy formed – an in turn were formed by – their understanding of America as a redeemer nation.
>
> (1978: xi)

Perhaps the best-known manifestation of the utilization of millennial themes to describe the Union cause is abolitionist Julia Ward Howe's "Battle Hymn of the Republic," written in the first year of the war. The ballad reflected many Americans' millennial hopes in the middle of an apocalyptic era with lines that included references to "the glory of the coming of the Lord" even as God "hath loosed the fateful lightning of His terrible swift sword." Here was not only an anthem that blended the anticipation of the millennium with the terrors of the apocalyptic; it also merged eschatological significance with temporal concerns, namely bringing about an end to slavery.

Howe was not alone in drawing connections between the war and Protestant prophecy. After Lincoln announced at the end of 1862 that the Emancipation Proclamation would go into effect in 1863, Joseph P. Thompson preached in a sermon at the Broadway Tabernacle Church in New York that "[t]he Proclamation of Emancipation has challenged all the powers of darkness to defeat it. ... We will still march on with the psalter in our hand; for soon the seventh angel shall 'pour out his vial into the air and there shall come a great voice out of the temple of heaven, from the throne, saying, IT IS DONE'" (Moorhead 1978: 96–97). The eschatological language of light versus darkness was easily adapted during the Civil War for political purposes.

For many African Americans, the millennial significance of the war and its aftermath could not have been clearer. The emancipation of southern enslaved persons was proof that God had blessed their communities and that they had a role in God's ultimate plan. Matthew Harper has pointed out that Black millennialism differed from White traditions. African American Protestants disagreed about the timing and meaning of the millennium as did White Protestants, but Black millennialism during and after Reconstruction also emphasized the "intersection of human history and divine history" by highlighting emancipation in Day of Jubilee celebrations and scripture that reflected freedom tropes (Harper 2013: 154–159). African Americans who celebrated emancipation were not blind to white supremacy. The language of the millennium was so widespread that it included use by those who opposed racial equality. One 1864 cartoon titled "Miscegenation – or the Millennium of Abolitionists" incorporated millennial sarcasm to negatively depict interracial marriage, stoking the fears of Whites who worried about the consequences of emancipation and Radical Republican Reconstruction policy (Blum 2013: 224). At the same time that examples like these existed, though, African American millennial traditions confronted white supremacy with eschatology that anticipated an end to racism and that predicted an important role for Blacks in the USA (Harper 2013: 169).

Despite being shaken, the millennial mission that shaped American exceptionalism did not die after the Civil War. It took different forms to justify western expansion, industrialization, and progressive reform efforts from the end of the 19th century to the beginning of the 20th. Christian nationalism fueled the expansionism of the Spanish American and Philippine wars as men like Theodore Roosevelt and Indiana Senator Albert Beveridge proclaimed it an American duty. The wars for American empire at the end of the 19th century began to shift the nature of the country's millennial mission from one of example to the rest of the world to one of world leader. The world wars further cemented that direction.

THE MISSION EXPANDED: THE WORLD WARS

Even before the USA's participation in World War I, President Wilson portrayed the USA as a "righteous neutral" (Jewett and Lawrence 2003), and his idealism reinforced the millennial mission shaped by American exceptionalism. In an address to the Senate in January 1917, a few months before the US Congress declared war, Wilson advocated for American involvement in peace discussions: "It is inconceivable that the people of the United States should play no part in that great enterprise. ... [T]hey set up a new nation in the high and honorable hope that it might in all that it was and did show mankind the way to liberty" (Wilson 1917). Some interpreted Wilson's speech as a religious one, including Atlanta minister Charles O. Jones, who believed the address was "not only one of the greatest state papers ever delivered, but that it has such a religious side, that it may be considered a prophecy of the millennium" (Atlanta Constitution 1917). Events further confirmed for many Americans the notion that the USA had saved the world when American involvement after April 1917 helped the Allies achieve victory by November 1918.

Those who supported Wilson's peace plan, the Fourteen Points and especially the creation of the League of Nations, also called upon the American millennialist vernacular to describe Wilsonian idealism. The power of the religious metaphor had its limits, however, as the failure of the US Senate to commit the USA to the League attests. The use of millennial sarcasm and skepticism revealed that a persistent realism about the possibility of permanent peace mitigated idealism. In one example, an article in the *Pittsburgh Gazette Times* questioned Wilson's lofty promises about the ability of the League to bring about peace and justice when the member powers continued to hold on to colonial territory. "[T]here is no sign," it concluded, "that the millennium is approaching" (Pittsburgh Gazette Times 1919). As had been the case in other wars, political realities tempered Christian nationalists' millennial hopes.

Despite the "good war" moniker applied to World War II, cynicism about the millennium could also be found in the early 1940s. In an address delivered near the end of the war, Republican Senator Owen Brewster (Maine) urged Americans to "move away from any silly sentimentality into a realistic recognition of the forces which are loose throughout the world and come to realize that the millennium may not be depended upon to dawn, whatever may be the arrangements that are made at the conclusion of this strife" (Indiana Evening Gazette 1945). The level of destruction unleashed during World War II tempered millennial optimism as well, especially at the end of the war when the horrors of the Holocaust and the extent of the power of weapons of mass destruction were revealed. Even so, Christian nationalist millennialism persisted. Cautious optimism drew on years of American exceptionalism even after the attack on Pearl Harbor. "While no millennium is in sight," an El Paso newspaper concluded, "a start has been made, with this country in the van and freedom's flag waving in breezes of liberty" (El Paso Times 1941).

The end of the war and the establishment of the United Nations revitalized millennial hopes similar to those sparked by the creation of the League of Nations, but the apocalypticism of World War II, especially in the aftermath of the bombing of Hiroshima and Nagasaki, also had a considerable impact on postwar American foreign policy. As Christian nationalism became part of the postwar effort to laud the American "way of life," premillennialist expectations of the end-times were boosted by the start of the nuclear age. World War II meant an end to an isolationist American foreign policy. The Cold War, accompanied by an anticommunism that characterized the USA as a godly country fighting godless Soviet communism, enhanced the American millennial mission.

THE MISSION REINFORCED: THE COLD WAR AND BEYOND

The dawning of the nuclear age and the simultaneous sharpening of the arms race raised the eschatological stakes for Protestant premillennialists, who believed that the atomic bomb was a sign of the end-times. They quoted II Peter 3:10, claiming that nuclear weapons were a fulfillment of prophecy: "[T]he heavens shall pass away with a great noise, and the elements shall melt with fervent heat, the earth also and the words that are therein shall be burned up." Evangelical believers, motivated by the sense of urgency that these predictions brought, encouraged conversion before it was too late. When the nuclear arms race quickly became an important battle in the Cold War, premillennial prophecy worked together with anticommunism to support American Cold War objectives (Lahr 2007: 26). Atomic apocalypticism, both Christian and secular, served as a language Americans used to consider the USA's place in history. Even influential Harvard historian of Puritan thought Perry Miller weighed in. In his 1956 book, Miller characterized the Puritan "errand into the wilderness," which became a framework to understand decades of American Christian nationalism, but he also asked about the consequences of reaching a point when a prophetic end of the world could be realized technologically. "What will America do – what *can* America do – with an implacable prophecy that there is a point in time beyond which the very concept of a future becomes meaningless?" (1956: 217, 239, emphasis in original; Boyer 1992: 120–121).

As Americans of many religious backgrounds mulled over the significance of the nuclear age, premillennialists looking for signs of the end-times in Cold War developments also closely watched Israel. For many Protestant evangelicals and fundamentalists, Christian Zionism merged with Christian nationalism during the Cold War. While Christian millennialists of earlier eras had proclaimed the USA to be God's "new Israel," dispensational premillennialists' eschatological timeline still depended on Jewish history. One of the most important prophecies involved the restoration of the nation of Israel in Palestine, so the establishment of Israeli statehood in 1948 stirred dispensationalists' imaginations. As Louis T. Talbot of the Bible Institute of Los Angeles put it, "I consider it the greatest event, from a prophetic standpoint, that has taken place within the last one hundred years" (Weber 2004: 173). As the Cold War guided American interests in the Middle East, premillennialists drew on prophecy and nationalism to react to events like the Six-Day War. The Cold War gave Christian nationalists a platform, and eschatology provided Christian Americans with a worldview to help them make sense of events like the nuclear arms race and Israel's founding.

During the Cold War and the subsequent "war on terror," rising and falling levels of immediate threats and a general acceptance of new "normals" meant that millennialist-inspired Christian nationalism also appeared more explicitly during certain crises such as the Cuban Missile Crisis or after events that had particular prophetic significance for Protestant leaders. Dispensationalists' fascination with Israel, however, has lasted beyond the end of the Cold War, as Christian Zionists continue to support the state of Israel as the Jewish homeland with conferences, prayer events, and lobbying efforts (Spector 2009).

CONCLUSION

This brief survey cannot possibly do justice to the web of millennial traditions that have shaped American worldviews over time. Even its

focus on Protestant Christian nationalism has revealed only an intro-
ductory glance at the complex ways in which end-times narratives have
influenced American political culture. What is clear is that war has
crafted circumstances in which Americans have debated their individual and their national destinies in light of chiliastic beliefs. The
Revolutionary War fused Christian prophecy and nationalism, laying
the foundation for exceptionalism in a manner that was ecumenical
enough to appeal to diverse Americans. By the time of the Civil War,
that national mythology was so widespread that, even as the country
was rendered in two, Americans on both sides of the war claimed to be
the true representatives of the mantle. African Americans adapted their
own millennialist interpretations to work to create a country that
fulfilled the lofty promises of its founding in the aftermath of the Civil
War and emancipation. As the 19th century ended, the American millennial mission to serve as an example to the world expanded. The USA
would lead the world. This cause justified American expansionism in
the Spanish American and Philippine wars, and Americans used it
during both world wars to represent the USA as a savior for the rest of
the world, even if some questioned the idealism that characterized it.
The millennial mission became an integral part of the Cold War strategy
of lauding and spreading the American way of life as a religious one, in
contrast to the Soviet Union's godless communism. That postwar conflict, exacerbated by nuclear competition, raised the eschatological
stakes for dispensational premillennialists. Even as the nature of the
national threat changed following the end of the Cold War and the
launching of the war on terror, millennialist-inspired nationalism continued to provide a framework through which Americans understood
the world.

References

Akenson, Donald Harman. 2018. *Exporting the Rapture: John Nelson Darby and the Victorian Conquest of North-American Evangelicalism.* Oxford University Press.
Atlanta Constitution. January 27, 1917. "In the Churches." *Atlanta Constitution* (Atlanta, GA).
Bloch, Ruth H. 1985. *Visionary Republic: Millennial Themes in American Thought, 1756–1800.* Cambridge University Press.
Blum, Edward J. 2013. "To Doubt This Would Be to Doubt God': Reconstruction and the Decline of Providential Confidence." In *Apocalypse and the*

Millennium in the American Civil War Era. Edited by Ben Wright and Zachary W. Dresser. Louisiana State University Press. 217–252.

Boyer, Paul. 1992. *When Time Shall Be No More: Prophecy Belief in Modern American Culture*. Belknap Press of Harvard University Press.

1998. "The Growth of Fundamentalist Apocalyptic in the United States." In *Apocalypticism in the Modern Period and the Contemporary Age*. Edited by Stephen J. Stein. Vol. 3 of The Encyclopedia of Apocalypticism. Edited by Bernard McGinn, John J. Collins, and Stephen J. Stein. Continuum. 140–178.

Butler, Jon. 2008. *New World Faiths: Religion in Colonial America*. Oxford University Press

"Candidus" (James Chalmers). 1776. *Introduction to Plain Truth*, 2nd edition. Edited by J. Almon. Accessed on Internet Archive. Available at https://archive.org/details/plaintruthaddresoocandrich/mode/2up

Cherry, Conrad, ed. 1971. *God's New Israel: Religious Interpretations of American Destiny*. Prentice-Hall.

Edwards, Jason A. and Joseph M. Valenzano, III. 2016. "Introduction: What Is Civil Religion?" In *The Rhetoric of American Civil Religion: Symbols, Sinners, and Saints*. Edited by Jason A. Edwards and Joseph M. Valenzano, III. Lexington Books. xi–xxii.

El Paso Times. December 16, 1941. "War Aspects More Optimistic." *El Paso Times* (El Paso, TX).

Garrett, Matthew. 2016. *Making Lamanites: Mormons, Native Americans, and the Indian Student Placement Program, 1947–2000*. University of Utah Press.

Gorski, Philip. 2017. *American Covenant: A History of Civil Religion from the Puritans to the Present*. Princeton University Press.

Haberski, Raymond, Jr. 2012. *God and War: American Civil Religion since 1945*, Kindle edition. Rutgers University Press.

Harding, Susan. 1994. "Imagining the Last Days: The Politics of Apocalyptic Language." In *Accounting for Fundamentalisms: The Dynamic Character of Movements*. Edited by Martin E. Marty and R. Scott Appleby. Vol. 4 of *The Fundamentalism Project*. University of Chicago Press. 57–78.

Harper, Matthew. 2013. "Emancipation and African American Millennialism." In *Apocalypse and the Millennium in the American Civil War Era*. Edited by Ben Wright and Zachary W. Dresser. Louisiana State University Press. 154–174.

Indiana Evening Gazette. January 31, 1945. "Americans Head the List as Illiterates on Int. Problems." Indiana Evening Gazette (Indiana, PA).

Irwin, Lee. 2008. *Coming Down from Above: Prophecy, Resistance, and Renewal in Native American Religions*. University of Oklahoma Press.

Jasper Weekly Courier. June 11, 1862. "Letter from a Dubois Volunteer." *Jasper Weekly Courier* (Jasper, IN).

Jewett, Robert and John Shelton Lawrence. 2003. *Captain America and the Crusade against Evil: The Dilemma of Zealous Nationalism*, Kindle edition. William B. Eerdmans.

Johnson, Willard. 1996. "Contemporary Native American Prophecy in Historical Perspective." *Journal of the American Academy of Religions* 64 (3): 575–612.

Lahr, Angela. 2007. *Millennial Dreams and Apocalyptic Nightmares: The Cold War Origins of Political Evangelicalism.* Oxford University Press.

Lincoln, Abraham. March 4, 1865. Second Inaugural Address. Avalon Project: Documents in Law, History and Diplomacy. Yale Law School. Available at https://avalon.law.yale.edu/19th_century/lincoln2.asp

Maryland Gazette. March 10, 1780. "The Honest Politician." Letter to the *Maryland Gazette* (Annapolis, MD).

Miller, Perry. 1956. *Errand into the Wilderness.* Belknap Press of Harvard University Press.

Moorhead, James H. 1978. *American Apocalypse: Yankee Protestants and the Civil War, 1860–1869.* Yale University Press.

    1998. "Apocalypticism in Mainstream Protestantism, 1800 to Present." In *Apocalypticism in the Modern Period and the Contemporary Age.* Edited by Stephen J. Stein. Vol. 3 of *The Encyclopedia of Apocalypticism.* Edited by Bernard McGinn, John J. Collins, and Stephen J. Stein. Continuum. 72–107.

Omer, Atalia and Jason A. Springs. 2013. *Religious Nationalism: A Reference Handbook.* ABC-CLIO.

Paine, Thomas. 1776. *Common Sense.* W. & T. Bradford and Project Gutenberg. Available at www.gutenberg.org/ebooks/147

Peterson, Scott. 1990. *Native American Prophecies,* 2nd edition. Paragon House.

Phillips, Jason. 2013. "The Prophecy of Edmund Ruffin: Anticipating the Future of Civil War History." In *Apocalypse and the Millennium in the American Civil War Era.* Edited by Ben Wright and Zachary W. Dresser. Louisiana State University Press. 13–30.

    2018. *Looming Civil War: How Nineteenth-Century Americans Imagined the Future.* Oxford University Press.

Pittsburgh Gazette Times. September 19, 1919. "The Millennium Not Yet." *Pittsburgh Gazette Times* (Pittsburgh, PA).

Smolinski, Reiner. 1998. "Apocalypticism in Colonial North America." In *Apocalypticism in the Modern Period and the Contemporary Age.* Edited by Stephen J. Stein. Vol. 3 of The Encyclopedia of Apocalypticism. Edited by Bernard McGinn, John J. Collins, and Stephen J. Stein. Continuum. 37–71.

Spector, Stephen. 2009. *Evangelicals and Israel: The Story of American Christian Zionism.* Oxford University Press.

Sutton, Matthew Avery. 2014. *American Apocalypse: A History of Modern Evangelicalism.* Belknap Press of Harvard University Press.

Weber, Timothy P. 1987. *Living in the Shadow of the Second Coming: American Premillennialism, 1875–1982,* enlarged edition. University of Chicago Press.

    2004. *On the Road to Armageddon: How Evangelicals Became Israel's Best Friend.* Baker Academic.

Whitehead, Andrew L. and Samuel L. Perry. 2020. *Taking America Back for God: Christian Nationalism in the United States.* Oxford University Press.

Wilson, Woodrow. January 22, 1917. Address before the Senate. Miller Center. Available at: https://millercenter.org/the-presidency/presidential-speeches/january-22-1917-world-league-peace-speech

Winthrop, John. 1630. "A Modell of Christian Charity." Hanover Historical Text Collections. Available at https://history.hanover.edu/texts/winthmod.html

Wuthnow, Robert. 1988. "Divided We Fall: America's Two Civil Religions." *Christian Century* 105(13): 395–399.

16 The Elusive Dream of Pan-Islamism

MOHAMMED M. HAFEZ

INTRODUCTION

Pan-Islamic solidarity has been a recurring theme in the modern Muslim world. From the early Islamic modernists to contemporary global Jihadists, the vision of pan-Islamism has been both a captivating aspiration and an elusive destination. Since the 1880s, confronted with the triple challenge of orientalism, imperialism, and colonialism, Muslim reformers have sought to harmonize their collective Islamic identity with notions of universal modernity. Pan-Islamism served as a defensive response to Western encroachment even as Islamic modernists sought to foster an indigenous modernization that took its inspiration from Western scientific and material progress (Aydin 2007: 47). The progressive themes promoted by Islamic modernists were coopted by an emergent secular nationalist elite in the first half of the 20th century. Anticolonial nationalist movements raised the banners of ethnic solidarity, social equality, and national independence in the face of Western imperialism. Their quest for pan-national unity and empowerment, however, was overshadowed by their governing failures and fractious movements. Postcolonial states thus opened the door to religious fundamentalism and, once again, the mantra of pan-Islamic unity (Dawisha 2003: 278).

The year 1979 was a particularly monumental one for pan-Islamic solidarity. The Iranian Revolution marked the beginning of Islamist ascendency after decades of marginalization and retreat and unleashed the power of the *mustad'afin* (oppressed) to challenge entrenched authoritarian regimes. The Soviet invasion of Afghanistan inspired a transnational movement of foreign fighters to aid the Afghans in their struggle against the communist occupiers, giving birth to a global jihadist movement that persists to this day. These new Islamist voices represented a radical search for unity, dignity, and empowerment in the face of illegitimate secular governments characterized by political exclusion, economic injustice, and military weakness (Hafez 2013: 86).

Yet, four decades after these momentous milestones, visions of pan-Islamism are once again in tatters. Sectarian fragmentation, factional infighting, and ideological hairsplitting characterize the state of Islamism today. Islamists are no better than their secular nationalist predecessors in forging unity across political and geographical barriers. The latest attempt to harness pan-Islamic unity is represented by the rise of Jihadi Salafism, which emerged from the broader Islamist movement in the 1990s. At its point of origin, Jihadi Salafism represented a clear alternative to prevailing forms of Islamism, principally the nationally based Islamism of the Muslim Brotherhood, the nonviolent activism of Salafist preachers, and the political quietism of Salafist scholars. Thus, from the moment of its birth, the Salafist movement was fragmented into three broad factions of *activists*, *quietists*, and *jihadists*.

The Jihadi Salafists are the most aggressive proponents of pan-Islamic unity today, rejecting any form of Islamism that confines itself to national borders and questioning the efficacy, and ultimately the legitimacy, of Salafists that do not embrace *jihad* in practice against both local regimes and in support of transnational Islamist causes. Yet, paradoxically, Jihadi Salafists do not represent a united front. Instead, they are divided by new ideological, strategic, and tactical differences. Specifically, Jihadi Salafists have diverged on critical issues such as collective *takfir* (excommunication of Muslims), sectarian targeting against Shiites and Sufis, and the importance of a *shariah*-governed territorial state. These disagreements produced distinct repertoires of violence among their adherents in important conflict zones such as Iraq and Syria, to name just a few (Gade et al. 2019). It also led to a violent rupture between Al-Qaeda and the Islamic State, two of the most important proponents of pan-Islamism today (Byman and Williams 2015). Thus, once again, the saliency of division over unity in Islamist movements renders pan-Islamism a utopian vision destined to disappoint its ideological adherents.

THE RISE OF ISLAMIST FACTIONALISM

Islamism aspires to a mythical golden age in which Muslims are ascendant, dignified, unified, and, above all else, ruled with justice. This utopian narrative, presumably anchored in actual golden ages of bygone days, contrasts with the palpable and complex reality of a diminished civilization struggling to forge its way forward after decades of imperial fragmentation, colonialism, and uneven modernization under secular authoritarian regimes.

Contemporary Islamic movements emerged as untainted critics of secularism and excessive Westernization in the Muslim world. No longer inspired by 19th-century notions of Western enlightenment and universal modernism, Islamists in the second half of the 20th century embraced an unapologetic return to Islamic traditionalism. The Islamic revival was characterized by the spread of public displays of piety, growing mosque attendance, and the spread of Islamic study circles, social movements, and political parties. Women donned their headscarves and men grew their beards. Young men and women gravitated toward Islamic social clubs in the universities, and Islamic activists reaped the benefits by expanding their representation in student union elections.

Islamists did not just offer a critique of the existing political order, they also advanced social and charitable projects to present a tangible alternative to secular governments. Networks of charity were created by Islamic activists who saw an opportunity to present viable public spaces free from the corrupting influence of the secular state, as well as to foster legitimacy for the Islamic movement through tangible provisions to the public (Wickham 2002; Clark 2004). Islamic groups, when possible, formed parties in order to challenge the hold of secular nationalists on government. Their ultimate aim was to establish governments bound by Islamic law (shariah). Those that were excluded from the political process sometimes organized violent rebellions (Hafez 2003).

Yet, despite their shared normative vision, Islamists disagreed about the proper goals, strategies, and tactics of their movement. Since the 1980s, at least three forms of Islamism emerged. *Political Islamism*, represented by the Muslim Brotherhood tendency, sought entry into state institutions through electoral politics and civic engagement. These political Islamists shunned violence against their regimes and instead pursued gradual, constitutional means even within authoritarian systems that heavily circumscribed democratic contestation. In contrast, *revolutionary Islamism* sought to overthrow the political system and establish an Islamic order in its place. Armed Islamic groups rebelled against the state, targeted its symbols of apostasy, and undermined its economic infrastructure. *Transnational jihadism* extended the radical ethos of revolutionary Islamists across national boundaries and attacked Western governments that supported their local regimes. Whereas revolutionary Islamists targeted the "near enemy," transnational jihadism placed strategic value on attacking the "far enemy" (Gerges 2005).

Jihadi Salafism, the ideology of transnational jihadism, is the latest attempt by militant Islamists to envision pan-Islamic solidarity. It seeks to transcend (even suppress) factional divides and pursue organizational coordination across national boundaries. Since its birth in the 1990s, adherents of this extremely puritanical Islamist movement have grown in number, strength, and geographical expanse.[1] Three of the bloodiest militant organizations in the last two decades – the Islamic State, Al-Qaeda, and Boko Haram – embrace this ideology and use it to rationalize mass atrocities against Muslims and non-Muslims alike. Their violence has far outstripped rival Islamist factions because of their innovative tactics and embrace of suicide bombings (Moghadam 2008; Hafez 2016). Jihadi Salafist networks have also been responsible for mobilizing tens of thousands of foreign fighters to several conflict zones, imperiling international security with the prospect of their homecoming (Hegghammer 2010).

JIHADI SALAFISTS AS THE NEW PAN-ISLAMISTS

The moniker Jihadi Salafism (al-salafiyya al-jihadiyya in Arabic) combines two concepts from the Islamic tradition.[2] Salafism is a form of Islamism that idealizes the first three generations of Muslims (or first 300 years of Islam). These formative generations lived through the prophetic mission of Muhammad; produced the Rightly Guided Successors (al-khulafa al-rashidun); witnessed the companions of the Prophet (sahaba) spread Islam beyond the Arabian Peninsula; collected prophetic traditions (ashab al-hadith); and produced erudite scholars

---

[1] In the mid-1990s, several jihadist groups in Algeria and Egypt began to identify themselves as Salafists. Additionally, radical ideologues like Abu Muhammad al-Maqdisi and Abu Qatada al-Filistini also identified their tendencies as both Salafist and Jihadist, although they did not merge the two words in a singular phrase. The term "Jihadi Salafist" garnered public notice in 2003 after a Moroccan group by that name carried out several suicide bombings in Casablanca, Morocco. It gained currency in Iraq as several groups identified their ideology as that of Jihadi Salafism. A recent study (Jones et al. 2018: 7–9) estimates that adherents of Jihadi Salafism increased by 270 percent between 2001 and 2018, numbering between 100,000 and 230,000. As of 2018, there were at least 67 Jihad Salafist groups worldwide, a 180-percent increase from 2001.

[2] Many specialists refer to this movement as "Salafist-Jihadist." However, this is a mistake in translation because Salafism is the noun and Jihadi is the adjective. The erroneous phraseology turns Salafist into an adjective that describes the singular noun Jihadist (alternatively, it contains two adjectives without a noun). The original phrase was intended to use "Jihadi" as the modifier of the plural noun "Salafists" to distinguish this faction from other, less militant Salafists.

that closely followed the way of the Prophet and his companions (*al-tabi'un*). Collectively, these categories of people are referred to as *al-Salaf al-Salih* (righteous predecessors or pious forbearers), hence the term "Salafism." Contemporary Salafists seek to follow closely in the footsteps of the Prophet and the traditions bequeathed by the pious ancestors; doing so is the best a Muslim can do to reach for perfection in the present and ensure salvation in the hereafter (Wagemakers 2016).

As for the second term, the adjective "Jihadi" refers to the tradition of *jihad* in Islam, an Arabic word that means "to strive, exert oneself, or take extraordinary pains" (Firestone 1999: 16). The Quran contains several references to *jihad* in conjugated form.[3] However, their meaning ranges from peaceful persuasion (verse 25:52) to fighting (verse 9:41).[4] Salafists, generally speaking, believe that *jihad* as combat is prescribed by God. They also agree that *jihad* is permissible when Muslim lands are attacked by external forces. However, they disagree about the conditions, requirements, and targets of *jihad* in the modern era. And they especially disagree about the legitimacy of *jihad* against regimes in the Muslim world. Quietist Salafists reject *jihad* against Muslim rulers, preferring to confer advice privately on leaders who deviate from the Islamic path. Political Salafists similarly reject *jihad* against their regimes, but they choose to challenge them publicly through their writings, speeches, or in elections (an option on rare occasions). Jihadi Salafists reject both of these options and insist that Muslim regimes that do not rule by Islamic law must be removed from power forcefully; advice and political contestation are insufficient to transform un-Islamic polities. To create genuinely Islamic states, *jihad* is necessary, hence their label "Jihadi Salafists."

Jihadi Salafists promote seven ideological concepts that have become the foundations for pan-Islamic rebellion against secular regimes in the Muslim world: *tawhid* (the oneness of God or monotheism), *hakimyat allah* (God's sovereignty), *takfir* (declaring Muslims to be infidels), *wala wal bara* (loyalty to Muslims and disassociation from unbelievers), *jihad* (striving in the path of God), *istishhad* (martyrdom), and *al-ta'ifa al-mansoura* (the Victorious Sect). Their intent is to compel Islamic solidarity and militancy against local regimes and their foreign allies.

---

[3] See, for example, verses 8:74 (*jahadu*); 9:24 (*jihadin*); 9:41, 9:86, and 22:78 (*Jahidu*); and 25:52 and 60:1 (*jahidahum, jihadan*).

[4] The Quran also refers to war (*harb*), combat (*qital*), and killing (*qatl*), all of which appear in defensive (verse 2:190) and offensive (verse 9:5) references. For an excellent exposition of the many meanings of *jihad* in Islam, see Bonner (2006).

Tawhid and *Hakimyat Allah*: Monotheism and God's Sovereignty

Salafists, including their Jihadist offshoot, place immense emphasis on the concept of *tawhid* ("oneness" of God or monotheism).[5] This emphasis is warranted because the first pillar of the Islamic faith is bearing witness that "there is no God but Allah, and Muhammad is His apostle." However, Salafists argue that *tawhid* is more than a confession of faith; it is a way of life. It is more than an utterance to gain acceptance into the community of believers; it is also sincere devotion in the heart and proper behavior in practice. All three can strengthen one's faith (*iman*), and the absence of one or more can diminish or even nullify it. The indivisibility of *tawhid*, therefore, can be thought of as a triangle of intersecting words, beliefs, and manifest acts that are mutually reinforcing.

Closely related to *tawhid* is the emphasis on God's sovereignty (*hakimiyyat allah*). God alone can define right and wrong, good and evil, permissible and forbidden. Abiding by God's commands as revealed in the scripture and as demonstrated by the Prophet's example is the ultimate form of *taqwa* (God-fearing piety) because it affirms God's sovereignty as the Lawgiver. Conversely, altering, suspending, or replacing God's revelation with some other law is violating *tawhid* by placing another authority on par with God. It is tantamount to disbelief as per the Quranic verse 5:44: "And whomever does not judge by what Allah has revealed – then it is those who are the disbelievers [*al-kafiroun*]."[6]

---

[5] *Tawhid* consists of affirming the unity of God's lordship in the universe (*tawhid al-rububiyyah*), which means that God is the only creator and provider. He has no partners, no intermediaries, and no offspring. *Tawhid* also consists of affirming worship of no one else but God (*tawhid al-uluhiyyah*). In other words, one cannot pray to anyone except God; those who pray to saints, idols, or grave sites are violating the unity of God. Finally, *tawhid* consists of affirming the uniqueness of God's names and attributes described in the Quran (*tawhid al-asma' wal sifat*). His nominal attributes are to be taken literally, not figuratively, although they are not equivalent to any human attributes.

[6] Verse 5:44 appears in two other forms that follow in quick succession, but the word "disbelievers" is replaced with "evildoers" (*al-dhalimoun*) in verse 5:45 and with "transgressors" (*al-fasiquun*) in verse 5:47. This variation has given rise to a debate between Salafists. One camp views the act of suspending God's laws as disbelief, evil, and transgression all in one. However, another camp holds that not ruling by God's laws could be a manifestation of acts of impiety, injustice, or disobedience – all of which are dreadful sins but insufficiently damning to exclude a Muslim from the community of believers (*kufr duna kufr*).

Salafists, moreover, do not believe it is necessary to apply something other than God's laws (*shariah*) to govern Muslim societies properly. Like other Islamists, they insist that the Quran and the Sunnah (Prophetic sayings and practice) are sufficient to guide Muslims in all aspects of life. They are comprehensive sources of law governing matters of creed (*'aqida*), ritual worship (*'ibadat*), and worldly conduct (*mu'amalat*), including taxation and commerce, marriage and divorce, war and peace, and crime and punishment. Therefore, Muslims who turn to positive law, Western legal systems, or alien ideologies such as Marxism, liberalism, or nationalism are disbelievers, evildoers, and transgressors in the eyes of God. For the Jihadi Salafists, it is nothing less than committing apostasy.

Takfir: Declaring Muslims Unbelievers

Salafists believe that it is both permissible and necessary to engage in *takfir* (the act of declaring a Muslim to be outside of the community of believers, the equivalent to excommunication in Catholicism). Certain beliefs and practices nullify one's status as a Muslim, leaving the pious no option but to label that person an infidel unless they repent and return to the right path. Otherwise, the lives and property of an apostate are no longer sacrosanct and can be expropriated without compunction.

The practice of *takfir*, however, is a subject of a major debate among Salafists, especially the controversy over general *takfir* – declaring entire categories of people as infidels (Hafez 2011). Nonetheless, Jihadi Salafists argue that existing Muslim regimes today are targets of *takfir* because they rule with secular laws, not Islamic ones. Consequently, it is permissible to reject them and rebel against them until they repent and apply Islamic law. *Takfir* is also invoked against any person working for the apostate regimes, including the police and security services, state-run media, and anyone supporting or giving legitimacy to these governments.

Al-Wala' Wal-Bara': Loyalty and Disavowal

Showing complete loyalty to Muslims and disassociating from unbelievers (captured in the Arabic phrase *al-wala' wal-bara'*) is an important behavioral requirement in the Jihadi Salafist worldview (Maher 2016: 111–141). When Muslims encounter *kufr* (unbelief), they must take the side of believers and disavow unbelievers. Neutrality is not an option. It is insufficient for Muslims to hate the unbelievers in their heart; they must outwardly demonstrate their hostility toward them. Loyalty to Muslims means supporting those who uphold

Muslim causes in civil conflicts by joining their *jihad*, fighting under their banner, giving them financial and material support, and praying for their success. Disassociation means turning away from those who fight against Islamists, refusing to aid them in anything minor or significant, and refraining from cutting deals with them.

Wala' wal bara' can also mean disavowing one's own family, friends, neighbors, tribes, or country. Jihadi Salafists cite the Quranic narrative of Abraham who disavowed his idolatrous father (verse 9:114). They also reference the Quranic verse 5:51: "O you who have believed, do not take the Jews and the Christians as allies. They are [in fact] allies of one another. And whoever is an ally to them among you – then indeed, he is [one] of them." This verse is used to justify attacks on Muslims who support foreign forces occupying Muslim lands. It is also used to recruit Western Muslims as foreign fighters in support of their coreligionists in conflict zones.

Jihad: Fighting in the Path of God

Jihadi Salafists believe that *jihad fi sabil allah* (fighting in the path of God) is an Islamic obligation against any state that does not apply Islamic law. They reject the notion that *jihad* is merely an internal struggle to lead a pious life. They also reject the argument that *jihad* is merely defensive. Although the Quran does make references to *jihad* as peaceful disputation with the unbelievers (verse 25:52) and defensive fighting when attacked (verse 2:190), these verses are said to have been abrogated (*nusikhat*) by subsequent verses that remove restraints on aggressive fighting against all unbelievers (i.e. 2:191, 9:5, and 9:29). *Jihad*, therefore, is not just an imperative to counter foreign aggression, it is also required to recapture all of the lands that were once in the abode of Islam and to further expand Islamic authority through new conquests. Jihadi Salafists reject modern nationalism and its concomitant system of sovereign states. Instead, they believe that *jihad* is continuous until all of humanity embraces Islam or submits to an Islamic authority, signifying that "religion is all for Allah" (partial Quranic verse 8:39).

Jihadi Salafists are plagued with several controversies that pertain to their application of *jihad*. The first relates to the permissibility of fighting Muslim regimes. In the classical Islamic legal tradition, *jihad* is permissible when conducted by a Muslim leader (*imam*) to bring non-Muslim territories under Islamic authority. It is also legitimate when Muslims are defending their lands from non-Muslim aggressors. In both cases, *jihad* is strictly against non-Muslims. Jihadi Salafists are thus accused of two errors: fighting without a recognized Islamic leader and fighting against their coreligionists. Their violent campaigns, therefore, do not qualify as *jihad*.

Jihadi Salafists reject these arguments and insist that the requirement for an *imam* applies when Muslims are fighting an offensive war (*jihad al-talab*). Today, however, Muslims are merely protecting their lands and faith against a new Western crusade aided by local lackeys. This is a defensive struggle (*jihad al-daf'i*) that is obligatory (*fard 'ayn*) on every capable Muslim until aggression ceases. Occasionally going on tactical offensives like the 9/11 attacks does not change the fact that jihadists are merely repelling Western encroachment with the few means at their disposal. As for fighting coreligionists, Jihadi Salafists insist that they are fighting regimes that have nullified their Islam by substituting God's law with secular law. They are fighting apostates, not Muslims.

Quietist Salafists argue that jihadists are sparking *fitna* (discord among Muslims) through their violence. Ruling regimes in the Muslim world, no matter how impious or tyrannical, must be obeyed as long as these rulers do not officially renounce their Islamic faith or justify positive law by declaring it to be superior to God's law. The best that pious people can do is advise their rulers privately and focus their efforts on instilling in the public the proper Islamic way through the socialization (*tarbiyya*) and purification (*tasfiyya*) of religious beliefs and practices. Jihadi Salafists counter that the greatest *fitna* is to govern by something other than what Allah has revealed.[7] By criticizing the jihadists, quietist scholars have become apologists for impious regimes that suppress the true believers. Jihadists refer to quietists as *ulema al-sultan*, a pejorative phrase that means "the sultan's scholars."

Another controversy relates to jihadist atrocities against civilians. The Quran and the Prophet Muhammad clearly gave immunity to noncombatants during warfare.[8] Jihadi Salafists counter that in their

---

[7] The word *fitna* carries multiple meanings. It could mean discord in the community; sedition; chaos and disorder; trials and tribulations; and temptation. It could also mean religious persecution intended to forcefully revert people from their embrace of Islam. Jihadists use the latter definition and argue, per verse 2:191, that "persecution [*fitna*] is worse than killing." In other words, fighting secular regimes that turn people from Islam is the lesser of two evils.

[8] The prohibition against killing noncombatants derives from Quranic verse 2:190: "Fight in the path of God those who fight you, but do not transgress limits, for God does not love transgressors." It is also found in an authentic Prophetic tradition: "It is narrated on the authority of 'Abdullah that a woman was found killed in one of the battles fought by the Messenger of Allah (may peace be upon him). He disapproved of the killing of women and children."

present context of defensive warfare attacking the civilians of adversarial states is a legitimate act because the other side kills Muslim civilians. The Quranic and Prophetic restrictions on harming civilians apply in the context of offensive warfare, when Muslims are leading the charge. Today, Muslims are in a state of weakness and are merely defending their lands and religion with the comparatively meager resources available to them. Furthermore, to the extent that civilian populations support their regimes and give them material assistance in the form of electoral votes and taxes, they are culpable in their nations' aggression against Muslims (Maher 2016: 46–59).

The most challenging controversy for Jihadi Salafists is their use of indiscriminate tactics that harm ordinary Muslims. As with civilians, the Quran and Prophetic traditions contain several clear prohibitions against killing believers.[9] Jihadi Salafists maintain that they do not intentionally harm Muslims, but in a context of a defensive warfare Muslim collateral damage is inevitable. Moreover, those killed are considered martyrs on Earth. Jihadists retrieved a historic ruling regarding the permissibility of killing Muslim human shields (qatl al-turse) if necessity requires it. Today, apostate regimes and foreign invaders place their institutions and forces in the heart of cities populated with Muslims. One cannot refrain from attacking these targets because of the harm that will come to innocent Muslims. When choosing between two evils, harming individual Muslims or suspending the jihad against the enemies of Islam, the latter is clearly the greater evil (Hafez 2010).

Istishhad: Martyrdom

Jihadi Salafists have justified and expanded the use of suicide attacks despite clear Islamic prohibitions against self-immolation.[10]

---

[9] Quranic verse 4:93 is the basis for this prohibition: "If a man kills a believer intentionally, his recompense is Hell, to abide therein (forever): And the wrath and the curse of Allah are upon him, and a dreadful penalty is prepared for him." In a commonly cited Prophetic tradition, Muhammad reminds his followers: "Everything belonging to a Muslim is inviolable for a Muslim; his honor, his blood, and property ..." Hadith in Jami' al-Tirmidhi, Book 1, Hadith 234 (https://sunnah.com/riyadussaliheen/1/234).

[10] Quranic verse 2:195 cautions, "cast not yourselves by your own hands into destruction." A Prophetic tradition cited in both sahih canons of Bukhari and Muslim offers the clearest expression against suicide: "And whoever commits suicide with a piece of iron will be punished with the same piece of iron in the Hell Fire." Hadith in Sahih al-Bukhari, Book 23, Hadith 117 (https://sunnah.com/bukhari/23/117).

To circumvent these prohibitions, they euphemistically label suicide as martyrdom (*istishhad*). They acknowledge that suicide is indeed rejected as religiously impermissible (*haram*) but insist that martyrdom – dying in battle – is venerated in several Quranic verses (2:154, 2:207, 3:169, 4:69, 4:74, 4:95–96, 9:111, 9:20–22, and 61:10–12). Jihadi Salafists argue that the so-called suicide attacks they employ are nothing short of martyrdom. The key distinction between suicide and martyrdom is the intention behind the act. Suicide is designed to kill oneself, while the chief aim of a suicide attack is to kill the enemies of Muslims. Human intentionality is the key to legitimating this direct form of self-sacrifice.

To overcome their critics, Jihadi Salafists have unearthed examples of the Prophet's companions eagerly charging the enemy (*inghimas fil-saf*) in order to hasten their own demise and earn the rewards of martyrdom. That is why suicide attacks are often called "*inghimasi* operations" (Hafez 2018: 127). Jihadi Salafists have also mythologized martyrdom. During the anti-Soviet *jihad*, Abdullah Azzam, the mentor of Usama Bin Laden, the founding leader of Al-Qaeda, glorified martyrdom by making it the personal choice and the highest aspiration of Muslim warriors (Hegghammer 2020). Azzam spoke of miracles on the battlefield, including Soviet bullets not penetrating fighters and angels literally fighting on the side of the jihadists. Through such stories, martyrdom was transformed from suffering and death into "an enchanted realm in which the original spirit of Islam had come back to life" (Edwards 2017: 104).

Jihadi Salafists have taken Azzam's myth-creation template and expanded it from the written form into online videos distributed through the Internet and social media. Weaving together emotional narratives of Western humiliation and local collaboration, jihadists are often presented as heroic figures who redeemed their nation through intentional acts of martyrdom. Their biographies are plastered across online forums, and poetry echoes their praises. The mythology surrounding individual suicide bombers appeals to potential recruits to make similar heroic sacrifices (Hafez 2007).

Al-Ta'ifa al-Mansoura: The Victorious Sect

Jihadi Salafists are often accused of being modern-day Kharijites, a reference to the historically detested sect known for its extremism and violence in Islam's formative period (Kenney 2006). Jihadi Salafists reject this comparison and instead argue that they constitute the

Victorious Sect (al-ta'ifa al-mansoura), the one about whom Muhammad prophesized:

> The Jews split into seventy-one sects, one of which will be in Paradise and seventy in Hell. The Christians split into seventy-two sects, seventy-one of which will be in Hell and one in Paradise. I swear by the One Whose Hand is the soul of Muhammad, my nation will split into seventy-three sects, one of which will be in Paradise and seventy-two in Hell.[11]

Claiming the label of the Victorious Sect has become the basis upon which some Jihadi Salafists differentiate their faction from rival Islamist groups. The Victorious Sect is defined by its adherence to Salafist orthodoxy; idealization of Islamic law as the perfect normative and legal system by which to govern Muslim and non-Muslim subjects; denunciation of creedal and ritualistic innovations; rejection of secularism as apostasy; elevation of *jihad* to one of the tenets of faith; and embracing martyrdom in the face of death. The Victorious Sect today is fighting to reestablish the Islamic caliphate without any regard to the modern system of sovereign states and without any support from non-Islamic forces.

The Victorious Sect is juxtaposed with all other Islamist movements that believe in establishing civil democratic states, those that reject violence as necessary to establish Islamic states, those that limit their fight for an Islamic order within the confines of the nation-state, or those that make alliances with secular factions or Western governments in the name of *realpolitik*. All of these pseudo-Islamists are insufficiently righteous to stake a claim to the title of the Victorious Sect. In practice, the Victorious Sect narrative is used to rationalize and publicly justify the factional suppression of rival Islamists (Hafez 2019).

---

[11] Hadith in *Sunan Ibn Majah* 3992, Book 36, Hadith 67 (https://sunnah.com/ibnmajah/36/67). A similar hadith is narrated by Abdullah bin 'Amr in *Jami' al-Tirmidhi* 2641, Book 40, Hadith 36 (https://sunnah.com/tirmidhi/40/36). Jihadists augment that tradition with another Prophetic report: "A group of people from my nation [*umma*] will always remain triumphant on the right path and continue to be triumphant (against their opponents). He who deserts them shall not be able to do them any harm. They will remain in this position until Allah's Command is executed." Hadith in *Sahih Muslim* 1920, Book 33, Hadith 245 (https://sunnah.com/muslim/33/245).

THE FRAGMENTATION OF JIHADI SALAFISM

Jihadi Salafism, despite its rapid growth and spread since 2001, no longer constitutes a single, unified faction. Instead, its ideologues and organizations often disagree about fundamental issues in the context of civil wars. Two disagreements in particular have become centrifugal, splintering Jihadi Salafists into opposing camps. The first pertains to the issue of collective *takfir* and sectarian killings. The second revolves around the importance of establishing Islamic states and the territorial limits of those states.

Collective *Takfir* and Sectarian Killings

Jihadi Salafists have been engaging in mass atrocities in which other Muslims are the primary targets. Sectarian killings of Shiites and Sufis in particular have increased substantially since 2003. It is no surprise, therefore, that these attacks have unleashed intense criticisms by other jihadists who are concerned about the permissibility of this violence and its political repercussions. The killing of coreligionists poses the greatest difficulty for jihadists from an Islamic jurisprudential perspective as well as a public relations standpoint.

As noted earlier, the principal ideological mechanism that enables extremists to justify killing their coreligionists is *takfir* – the act of Muslims declaring other Muslims to be infidels. However, *takfir* comes in two forms: collective (*kufr al-'aam*) and individual (*kufr al-mu'ayen*). Collective *takfir* involves declaring entire categories of people as infidels. For example, according to Salafists, Twelver Shiites are infidels because of their doctrine of a hidden *imam*. Similarly, Sufis who violate *tawhid* by seeking intermediaries with God are infidels, too. These are statements of collective *takfir*. They identify a certain practice or belief as nullifying faith and their adherents as having fallen from grace. These generalizations, however, are insufficient to justify attacks on the collective. Punishment stemming from the act of *takfir* can only apply against individuals, not entire collectives, following a rigorous due process that substantiates a charge of impiety and considers all possible mitigating circumstances for accused persons.

Punishing individuals for major impiety that nullifies their Islamic faith is permitted at the individual level as long as religious authorities follow a three-step process. Step 1 involves investigating whether the person accused of committing a major impiety has met the requirements of *takfir*. There are circumstances that preclude the application of *takfir* in individual cases. These include inadequate religious socialization, mental immaturity due to young age, disability, or coercion by unbelievers. The manifestation of major impiety does not automatically give religious authorities permission to engage in *takfir* because these mitigating circumstances diminish one's culpability. Step 2 involves exposing the major impiety to the culpable person and explaining the textual proof from the Quran and Sunnah to remove any doubt that the individual understands the violation. Step 3 requires that the accused person be given an opportunity to repent and return to the proper path. Only when these three steps have been exhausted can the unrepentant person be eligible for punishment.

The issue of collective *takfir* may appear esoteric, but its consequences are quite deadly. The important distinction between collective and individual *takfir* poses a problem for extremists who wish to engage in indiscriminate attacks against security institutions and the supporters of ruling regimes or rival factions. In Iraq, for instance, the Islamic State has engaged in mass killings of thousands of Shiites on the basis of their identity. Other Islamist factions, including militant Salafists, have condemned this violence as both Islamically illegitimate and politically damaging to the movement's cause. Sectarian targeting, therefore, has become a major divide among Jihadi Salafists on the battlefield.

Establishing Islamic States

Jihadi Salafists also disagree about when and where to establish Islamic states. Although they all share the ambition of establishing an Islamic caliphate that unites the *ummah* (Muslim nation) across borders, not all see this goal as immediately attainable. Therefore, they disagree about the strategic priorities necessary to achieve this long-term objective. One can discern three separate views on the issue of a territorial Islamic state.

The first view comes from Al-Qaeda, which holds that establishing Islamic states is not a priority under present circumstances. The priority is to support rebellions against secular regimes, establish Al-Qaeda's organizational presence in those conflict zones to grow its transnational network, and attack Western states that shore up their oppressive governments. This strategy involves making tactical alliances with local rebels, regardless of their ideological purity, and refraining from controversial policies that might alienate local factions, including sectarian killings, declaring an Islamic state, or governing with strict *shariah* codes.

The second view comes from local Jihadi Salafists mired in civil wars. They are fighting to topple their secular regimes in order to establish Islamic states within the framework of the modern nation-state. Their territorial vision is confined to their existing borders; they are not interested in abrogating their states' territorial integrity. Moreover, their ambition to rule over existing states that have multiple ethnic and religious communities drives them to exercise restraint in their targeting policy. They avoid overtly sectarian or ethnic killings, preferring instead to combine Salafism with local nationalism. Furthermore, local rebels invariably need external support – political, financial, and material – to topple their regimes. They pragmatically avoid rhetoric that can be viewed as threatening to neighboring states and other potential external allies. Thus, they refrain from talking about an Islamic caliphate that promises to upend the Westphalian system of sovereign states.

The third view comes from the Islamic State. It harbors the irredentist ambition of restoring an Islamic caliphate over territories that were divided by Western powers after the First World War (the so-called Sykes–Picot system). The Islamic State cares little about state sovereignty, the complex political considerations of local Islamist factions, or the interests of external powers. Whereas nationalist Salafists seek to work hand in hand with their beleaguered populations in order to *win* their hearts and minds, the Islamic State cares little about populism and, instead, advances a vanguardist vision that seeks to *mold* hearts and minds through compulsion. As a result, it seizes every opportunity to carve out a territorial state from within and across sovereign state boundaries and governs with a strict *shariah* code without regard to local conditions and habits. And it discards norms of human rights by expelling non-Sunni populations from its territories with genocidal violence.

These ideological, strategic, and tactical divides have fragmented Jihadi Salafists into multiple rival organizations that are increasingly competing over territory, fighters, and affiliates. In fact, they are killing each other in Afghanistan, Libya, Syria, and Yemen. Al-Qaeda and other Jihadi Salafists have denounced the Islamic State as modern-day Kharijites that kill Muslims simply for failing to give their oath of allegiance (*bay'ah*) to its caliph. The Islamic State retorts that it is the Victorious Sect that waves the banner of the authentic creed and banishes the pretentious and the hypocrites.

CONCLUSION

The development of Jihadi Salafism since the 1990s highlights a common truism held by experts of Islam and Islamism: Fragmentation is much more salient than unity. The fragmentation of Salafism into quietists, activists, and jihadists has been compounded by the intra-jihadist schisms over competing religious, ideological, and strategic considerations. Despite their shared normative commitments and mutual state adversaries, Jihadi Salafists have failed to overcome the challenge of factionalism. The stress of conflict and the urgency for survival did little to bind them into a singular unified movement. In fact, in the past three decades, Jihadi Salafists have descended into fratricidal violence against their brothers-in-arms. Instead of closing ranks, Jihadi Salafists have turned their attention away from near and far enemies and, instead, prioritized fighting with fellow Salafists, the nearest enemy of all. The diversity of tendencies within the militant Salafist camp means that the dream of pan-Islamism will remain elusive for years to come.

References

Aydin, Cemil. 2007. *The Politics of Anti-Westernism in Asia: Visions of World Order in Pan-Islamic and Pan-Asian Thought*. Columbia University Press.

Bonner, Michael. 2006. *Jihad in Islamic History: Doctrines and Practice*. Princeton University Press.

Byman, Daniel L. and Jennifer R. Williams. 2015. "ISIS vs. Al Qaeda: Jihadism's Global Civil War." *The National Interest*. Available at https://nationalinterest.org/feature/isis-vs-al-qaeda-jihadism%E2%80%99s-global-civil-war-12304

Clark, Janine A. 2004. *Islam, Charity, and Activism: Middle-Class Networks and Social Welfare in Egypt, Jordan, and Yemen*. Indiana University Press.

Dawisha, Adeed. 2003. *Arab Nationalism in the Twentieth Century: From Triumph to Despair*. Princeton University Press.

Edwards, David B. 2017. *Caravan of Martyrs: Sacrifice and Suicide Bombing in Afghanistan*. University of California Press.

Firestone, Reuven. 1999. *Jihad: The Origin of Holy War in Islam*. Oxford University Press.

Gade, Emily Kalah, Mohammed M. Hafez, and Michael Gabbay. 2019. "Fratricide in Rebel Movements: A Network Analysis of Syrian Militant Infighting." *Journal of Peace Research* 56(3): 321–335.

Gerges, Fawaz A. 2005. *The Far Enemy: Why Jihad Went Global*. Cambridge University Press.

Hafez, Mohammed M. 2003. *Why Muslims Rebel: Repression and Resistance in the Islamic World*. Lynne Rienner.

2007. "Martyrdom Mythology in Iraq: How Jihadists Frame Suicide Terrorism in Videos and Biographies." *Terrorism and Political Violence* 19(1): 95–115.

2010. "The Alchemy of Martyrdom: Jihadi Salafism and Debates over Suicide Bombings in the Muslim World." *Asian Journal of Social Science* 38(3): 364–378.

2011. "Debating *Takfir* and Muslim-on-Muslim Violence." In *Fault Lines in Global Jihad: Organizational, Strategic and Ideological Fissures*. Edited by Assaf Moghadam and Brian Fishman. Routledge. 25–46.

2013. "Illegitimate Governance: The Roots of Islamist Radicalization in the MENA." In *Governance in the Middle East and North Africa: A Handbook*. Edited by Abbas Kadhim. Routledge. 85–98.

2016. "The Ties That Bind: How Terrorists Exploit Family Bonds." *CTC Sentinel* 9(2): 15–18.

2018. "Apologia for Suicide: Martyrdom in Contemporary Jihadist Discourse." In *Martyrdom, Self-Sacrifice, and Self-Immolation: Religious Perspectives on Suicide*. Edited by Margo Kitts. Oxford University Press. 126–139.

2019. "Not My Brother's Keeper: Factional Infighting in Armed Islamist Movements." *Journal of Religion and Violence* 7(2): 189–208.

Hegghammer, Thomas. 2010. "The Rise of the Muslim Foreign Fighters: Islam and the Globalization of Jihad." *International Security* 35(3): 53–94.

2020. *The Caravan: Abdallah Azzam and the Rise of Global Jihad*. Cambridge University Press.

Jones, Seth G., Charles Vallee, Danika Newlee, Nicholas Harrington, Clayton Sharb, and Hannah Byrne. 2018. *The Evolution of the Salafi-Jihadist Threat: Current and Future Challenges from the Islamic State, Al-Qaeda, and Other Groups*. Center for Strategic and International Studies.

Kenney, Jeffrey T. 2006. *Muslim Rebels: Kharijites and the Politics of Extremism in Egypt*. Oxford University Press.

Maher, Shiraz. 2016. *Salafi-Jihadism: The History of an Idea*. Oxford University Press.

Moghadam, Assaf. 2008. *The Globalization of Martyrdom: Al Qaeda, Salafi Jihad, and the Diffusion of Suicide Attacks*. Johns Hopkins University Press.

Wagemakers, Joas. 2016. *Salafism in Jordan: Political Islam in a Quietist Community*. Cambridge University Press.

Wickham, Carrie Rosefsky. 2002. *Mobilizing Islam: Religion, Activism, and Political Change in Egypt*. Columbia University Press.

17 Killing for the Hindu Nation: Hindu Nationalism and Its Violent Excesses

KATHINKA FRØYSTAD

How could people who claim to represent one of the most nonviolent religions in the world become so eager to kill for the Hindu nation? Little epitomizes the impetus for violent defense of the Hindu nation better than the 2019 song that calls for everyone who does not hail Lord Ram, the divine king of the Ramayana epic, to be sent to the graveyard.[1] Similar incitements to violence were also heard in the early 1990s, when Hindu nationalist activists campaigning for the removal of a medieval mosque in the pilgrim town Ayodhya,[2] shouted that "there are only two places for Muslims: Pakistan or the graveyard."[3] With Hindu nationalism's spectacular ascent to power in 2014, such incitements became more brazen and frequent. Violent harassment and deadly lynching moreover became chronic risks for minority citizens and others suspected of defying Hindu sensitivities. How did Hindu nationalism reach that point? Drawing on established perspectives on the ideational logics that drive ethnonationalist violence, this chapter points to the increasingly collective anxiety that Hinduism will be endangered unless it secures political protection and keeps religious minorities in check. Phantasmagorical variations of this anxiety have been cultivated by Hindu nationalist organizations for decades and are now so widely internalized that they practically overshadow the thoughtful deliberations found within the Hindu traditions of how a "just war" (outlined in Chapter 12) may be fought. To understand the

---

[1] In Hindi: *Jo na bole jay sri ram unko bhej do kabristan.* The singer, songwriters and producers were arrested for violating India's hate speech laws (Iyer and Dubey 2019), but the song was nevertheless available on YouTube years later.

[2] More on this below.

[3] In Hindi: *Musalman ke do hi sthan, Pakistan ya kabristan* (cf. Pandey 2004: 61). Other versions begin with "there is only one place for Muslims (*Musalman ka ek hi sthan*)" or "*Musalman, Musalman*" before ending with "*Pakistan ya kabristan.*" Note the rhythm, which makes all versions suitable for use while marching and pounding fists in the air.

resonance of these anxieties, we begin by recapitulating the historical context in which Hindu nationalism began to grow forth while being mindful of what it shares with other nationalist ideologies.

HISTORICAL BACKGROUND AND THE GENERAL IN THE PARTICULAR

The roots of Hindu nationalism extend all the way back to the 1800s, when the Indian subcontinent was under British rule. Starting from Bengal and Bihar, the London-based East India Company acquired control over a growing number of provinces and kingdoms until it controlled most of the subcontinent. Following a dramatic violent uprising in 1857 that eventually was crushed, India became subject to direct British rule. Little by little, the influx of pale-complexioned soldiers, traders and plantation owners was followed by a growing presence of administrators, new architectural styles, racialized city planning, broader roads, churches, Western educational institutions, a new administrative language, newspapers, railway tracks, factories, new clothing styles and much more. Many Indians embraced the new opportunities, but the wide-ranging changes also gave rise to a feeling of cultural loss and annoyance. Numerous Christian missionaries had entered the country since the ban on missionizing was lifted in 1813 (Jones 1989: 27), and Indians who joined the army and administrative services had less scope for career advancement than British recruits. Though India already had ample experience with dramatic regime change, the emergence of an Anglicized elite, a civil society and a new public sphere now made it easier to respond.

The question of which homegrown modes of worship and everyday practices it was crucial to revitalize and which that had better be left behind was actively debated, particularly in Calcutta (now Kolkata), Bombay (now Mumbai) and Madras (now Chennai), where the colonial influence was strongest. Several religious reform movements sprang up in this period. Those that proved most consequential for Hindu revivalism were the Brahmo Samaj (founded in 1828) and the Arya Samaj (founded in 1875). Specific teachings aside, both promoted a collective identity as "Hindu" over sectarian and caste differences while "purifying" Hinduism by revitalizing its Vedic past and rejecting idolatry (Jones 1989). Frantz Fanon's legendary advice to colonized intellectuals across the world to help articulate a "national culture" that enables resistance (Fanon 1963) was thus prefigured in India by more than a century.

The independence movement that grew out of these developments was spearheaded by the Indian National Congress (INC), founded in 1885. Though the violent uprising of 1857 is often referred to as India's First War of Independence,[4] it lacked the organization, strategizing and future vision required to bring the growing desire for independence to fruition. Yet even as the independence movement matured in the early 20th century, fissures emerged. Should the fight for independence involve violent resurgence[5] or should it be strictly nonviolent, as Mohandas Gandhi (later known as "Mahatma," great soul) insisted when he took charge of the INC's freedom campaigns from the 1920s? And should independent India be a country for everyone irrespective of religious denomination, as argued by the INC? Or should it rather reflect the tenets of the religious majority, as desired by the less influential Hindu Mahasabha, founded in 1915 (Bapu 2013: 75)? Or should India's Muslims even strive for a state of their own, as the Muslim League (founded in 1906) came to demand in the late 1930s (Jalal 1985: 4)? The 1921 Census had shown British India to count 68.6 percent Hindus and 21.7 percent Muslims,[6] which made it increasingly difficult to agree on a unanimous vision for independent India. The decennial census exercise that the colonial government had implemented since 1881 had reified pan-Indian religious identities and given rise to concerns with majority/minority relations, exemplifying how enumeration unwittingly transforms the society it attempts to reflect.[7]

India ended up being divided the minute it gained independence in August 1947. The Muslim-majority provinces in the west and east were carved out to form Pakistan, along with half of Punjab and Bengal.[8] For contemporary Hindu nationalists, India was dismembered in a way that still gives phantom pain. The chaos of Partition made matters even worse. The territorial division had been poorly planned, and the uncertainty, frustration and fear that ensued unleashed a mutual interreligious carnage. Between 200,000 and 2 million people were killed and

---

[4] See Chakravarty (2013) for a discussion on terminology.

[5] While most historians portray India's path to independence as nonviolent, Kama MacLean (2015) suggests that the scarcity of written sources about the revolutionary factions within the independence movement may have given its use of violence less attention than it deserves.

[6] Calculated from The Census of India 1921, table IV: The Population by Religion (Marten 1923: 40–44).

[7] See Kertzer and Arel (2002) for general reflections and Jones (1981), Frykenberg (1987), Appadurai (1993) and Bhagat (2013) for India-specific considerations.

[8] In 1971, East Pakistan broke free to form Bangladesh.

about 15 million were displaced. Countless women were raped and around 100,000 women from both sides were abducted (all figures from Talbot and Singh 2009: 2–3). The memories of these horrors still resound in Indian politics. For Hindu nationalists, they gave rise to an enduring conception of Pakistan as a malicious neighbor and of Muslims – including those who remained in India – as potential violent marauders and sexual predators in addition to offspring of Mughal "invaders." Consider the words of M. S. Golwalkar, who headed the Rashtriya Swayamsewak Sangh (RSS) from 1940:

> Has their old hostility and murderous mood which resulted in widespread riots, looting, arson, raping and all sorts of orgies on an unprecedented scale in 1946–47, come to a halt at least now? It would be suicidal to delude ourselves into believing that they have turned patriots overnight after the creation of Pakistan. On the contrary, the Muslim menace has increased a hundredfold by the creation of Pakistan which has become a springboard for all their future aggressive designs on our country.
>
> (Golwalkar 1968 [1966]: 167)

Though such views were not commonly voiced at the time, they indicate the daunting challenge of initiating a nation-building process that could heal the wounds of Partition.

Independent India's first Prime Minister, Jawaharlal Nehru, and his Congress-dominated parliament advanced a civic nationalism, which is a nationalist ideology that treats all inhabitants as equal members of the nation irrespective of their ethnic origin, religion, language or other cultural traits (Ignatieff 1993: 5–6). The Constitution enacted in 1952 promoted equal citizenship and extensive religious freedom symbolized by Nehru's "unity in diversity" slogan and the tricolor flag in saffron, white and green.[9] Until the mid-1980s, this recipe worked well. Though many Congress politicians were biased towards Hinduism (Khalidi 2008; Basu 2018), there was so little interreligious animosity that India gained a global reputation as a model for interreligious coexistence. Granted, state suppression helped. On three occasions the RSS was banned for suspected involvement in political violence and its activities were periodically restricted (Andersen and Damle 1987: 3).[10]

---

[9] See Roy (2006) for an in-depth discussion of the development and symbolism of the tricolor flag.

[10] The first ban (1948–1949) was precipitated by an RSS member's assassination of Mahatma Gandhi, the second (1975–1977) by Indira Gandhi's crackdown on

India's proscription of hate speech and religious offences moreover minimized antiminority rhetoric (Rollier et al. 2019: 8–15). Besides, people of different religious denominations still lived side by side and had little option but to try to get along. Yet, in the late 1980s, Hindu nationalism began its move towards the center stage of Indian politics.

TOWARDS THE CENTER STAGE

Two nationwide controversies were crucial for transforming Hindu nationalism from a fringe movement to a major political force. The first was the Shah Bano case, which helped direct a critical spotlight at India's plural legal system and the so-called vote-bank politics of the Congress Party. At Independence, India had retained a legal system in which all family laws were religion-specific. In 1985, the Supreme Court nevertheless ruled that the elderly Shah Bano should receive maintenance from her separated husband according to a law applicable to all citizens rather than to Muslim Personal Law. Fearing for their religious autonomy, conservative Muslims withdrew their support from the Congress Party. Keeping the next election in mind, the Congress-dominated government then enacted a new law that absolved Muslim husbands of all responsibility after the two-year Islamic waiting period (Philips 2011). Ever since then, the Congress Party has been vulnerable to Hindu nationalist critique for "appeasing" the Muslim minority and supporting a legal plurality that encourages identity politics and has questionable outcomes for women (cf. Agnes 2007).

In the Ayodhya case, Hindu nationalist organizations successfully invoked the trope of temple-destroying Mughals to expand their followings. The crux of the matter was a medieval mosque in Ayodhya in Uttar Pradesh erected at the order of Babar (1483–1530), who founded the Mughal Empire that ruled substantial parts of the Indian subcontinent prior to the British period. Yet at least since the 1850s, local Hindu lore had claimed this mosque to have been constructed atop the ruins of a temple commemorating the birthplace of Lord Ram, the avatar king in the Ramayana epic (van der Veer 1994: 2), which pious Hindus hold to be factual history (*itihas*). In the late 1980s, Hindu nationalist organizations initiated a countrywide campaign to "reclaim" the mosque, shouting slogans such as "Ram, we are coming, we will build a temple

political opponents during the Emergency and the third (1992–1993) by the RSS's involvement in the demolition of the Babri Masjid and the violence that ensued.

right there" (*Ram ham aenge mandir vahin banaenge*),[11] in addition to
the incitements to violence mentioned at the beginning of this chapter.
In December 1992, Hindu nationalist activists demolished the mosque
as the police watched, which unleashed widespread Hindu–Muslim
riots that killed around 2,000 people (Guha 2007: 582–598). Though
these events resulted in a temporary electoral setback, the campaign
succeeded in entrenching the historical narrative about the Mughal
Empire as a 250-year-long period of temple destruction, forced conversion and other assaults against Hindus, in addition to popularizing
stereotypes of Indian Muslims as violence-prone, child-breeding fanat-
ics (cf. Frøystad 2005).

The ascent of Hindu nationalism was uneven and underwent several setbacks. By 2014, however, the landslide electoral success of its
political wing, the Bharatiya Janata Party (BJP), in the general elections
made it abundantly clear that India's civic nationalism had a serious
rival in Hindu nationalism. Judging from the BJP's even more impressive electoral success in 2019, the latter may even be its successor.
Briefly explained, Hindu nationalism strives to transform India to a
Hindu state (*rashtra*) by aligning the polity more closely with Hindu
sensibilities and "correcting historical wrongs," as Hindu nationalists
sometimes express it. In terms of analysis, Hindu nationalism is thus a
case of religious nationalism (cf. Juergensmeyer 1993; van der Veer
1994), which is an ethnic nationalism or majoritarianism in which the
main fault lines are pan-religious identities rather than, say, linguistic,
cultural or occupation-related ones. While not even the most civic of
nationalisms is entirely free from religious biases (Omer and Springs
2013), Hindu nationalism is self-consciously identarian in terms of
religion. Yet exactly how its proponents would position their desired
Hindu state on an imagined civic–theocratic continuum remains to be
seen. Golwalkar's wish to revoke citizenship rights for those who do not
"respect and hold in reverence Hindu religion" (Golwalkar 1939: 47–48)
has now been disowned by RSS (Mukul 2006), and BJP representatives
protest strongly against criticism that they are converting India into a
"Hindu Pakistan" (cf. Special Correspondent 2018). Yet, according to
Jaffrelot, India has already become a de facto Hindu state by virtue of its

---

[11] More dramatic but less common versions of this slogan begin with "whether we must
face bamboo sticks or bullets" (*lathi goli khaenge*) or "whether we must kill or die"
(*marenge mar jaenge*), before ending with "we will build a temple right there"
(*mandir vahin banaenge*). All versions have the same rhythmic "shoutability" as
the slogans mentioned in Note 3.

underrepresentation of religious minorities in elected bodies and the police, and it may well be about to develop into a de jure Hindu state with unequal citizenship along the lines of Israel (2019: 66–67).

COMPLICATING THE NARRATIVE

Describing Hindu nationalism as a well-defined political ideology that faced a humiliating defeat in 1947, began to move towards the center stage in the late 1980s and captured state power in 2014 is, of course, a simplification. Consider some of the complexities. First, Hindu nationalism is fronted by a number of different organizations (see Katju 2019 for a useful overview), and though most are closely related and have a clear-cut division of labor, they hardly speak with a single voice. Second, the intellectuals who helped shape this ideology explain their views differently, and their priorities have changed over time (cf. Jaffrelot 2007). In fact, they even differ with regard to whom they define as Hindus. While RSS's founder Veer Savarkar included everyone who considered India his "holyland" (Savarkar 1989 [1923]: 113), thus excluding Muslims and Christians, RSS's leader since 2009, Mohan Bhagwat, claims every child of Mother India to be Hindu irrespective of religious denomination and other differences (Pandey 2019). In practice, however, Hindu nationalists frequently vilify Muslims and treat marginalized low castes and tribals as imperfect Hindus so much that they spend considerable resources on schools that inculcate them in "proper" Hindu worship. Third, Hindu nationalism has had a far stronger foothold in certain federal states (notably Maharashtra, Uttar Pradesh and Gujarat) than in others (such as Kerala and West Bengal). And fourth, Hindu nationalist rhetoric is multilayered and multimodal. Its official rhetoric is typically more restrained than what can be expressed between friends, in publications intended for limited circulation or suggested in images, audiovisual material and, since around 2010, social media (as exemplified by Manuel 1993; Brosius 2005; Frøystad 2005; Anand 2011; Ghassem-Fachandi 2012; Udupa 2018, 2019; and many others). This is partly attributable to the vernacularization of Hindu nationalism (Reddy 2011, 2018) but also to the strategy of communicating in different ways to different people without coming into too direct conflict with the law. Some BJP politicians are, moreover, deft at dog whistling (Gopalakrishnan 2016).

Differences like these have made several scholars distinguish between "soft" and "hard" Hindu nationalism. Some have developed more refined typologies, such as the 2018 study that distinguishes between three types of Hindu nationalist supporters: (1) conservatives, mainly consisting of elderly people dedicated to ritual observances who resist cultural erosion and change; (2) progressives, consisting of younger people who embrace new technologies, food styles and gender roles but want to preserve their religious identity and help restore the country to its lost glory; and (3) warriors, who are driven by anxieties about identity loss and cultural dilution and who display a profound anti-other stance (Chakrabarti et al. 2018: 47–53). To emphasize such differences is crucial as most supporters of Hindu nationalism neither vilify their religious others directly nor endorse violence, let alone commit it. Yet a growing minority do, and to understand the anxieties that drive them, we now shift to a more ideational – others might say structural, ontological or even essentialist – mode of analysis that distills the logic behind their rhetoric and political priorities.

ANXIETIES, DYSTOPIA AND RETROTOPIA

Despite the fear of rapid cultural change, the anxiety that Hinduism is endangered is primarily rooted in a fear of minoritization and its dreaded dystopian consequences: repeated Muslim/Christian conquest or loss of additional territory. To avert these perceived dangers, Hindu nationalists monitor religious demographics closely, both for India as a whole and for the federal states and union territories. Census reports showing the Muslim or Christian populations (nationally counting 14.2 and 2.3 percent respectively in 2011) as growing faster than the Hindu population are treated with grave concern. Phantasmagoric scenarios are constantly invoked to alarm fellow Hindus of the consequences that would ensue unless such developments are reversed, and "disadvantageous" religious demographics are frequently exaggerated to make these dangers seem more immanent. These anxieties have been remarkably consistent since the time of Golwalkar, but tireless activism and new communication technologies have now made them more explicit, elaborate and widespread. Following the BJP's ascent to power in 2014, they have also been promoted by the energetic social media activists organized by the party's so-called IT cell (Chaturvedi 2016), which by 2017 numbered over 100,000 members (Udupa 2019).

Consider the following excerpt from a lengthy WhatsApp message circulated in December 2019 to garner understanding for the BJP government's controversial decision to fast-track the naturalization of non-Muslim refugees from Bangladesh, Pakistan and Afghanistan:

In 2035 India will look like this:

- Muslims now comprise 50% of the population. Today the election result of the central government shows that Asaduddin Owaisi [a politician from the regional party All India Majlis-e-Ittehad-ul-Muslimeen] has become prime minister . . ..
- Today . . . Hindustan [a common term for India] was declared as a Muslim state as per the party's election promise.
- Throughout the country, temples are being broken and mosques constructed.
- The law is in the hands of Muslims. Hindus are killed on the streets.
- Slum dwellers are taking over the bungalows and Hindu girls of large houses made into concubines or sold in the markets.
- Till today, the Hindu "leaders" remained secular. Many converted to Islam and went to foreign countries with huge amounts of money.
- But middle-class and poor Hindus are being eaten by these devils. Their wives and daughters are raped and killed on the roads or taken as mistresses . . ..
- How did you find it? Was your soul not shaken by reading this?

(Translated from Hindi by the author, explanations added in square brackets)

The message then proceeded to list a number of atrocities committed against Hindus in the past before concluding: "Some impotent Hindus will not even share this. Hail Lord Ram." The message was enhanced by emoticons: Each bullet point was a green flag associated with Muslim statehood, whereas the final sentences were interspersed with triangular saffron flags of the kind that signify Hindu shrines as well as the desired Hindu state. In principle, the anxiety over a non-Hindu takeover also extends to Christians, as a volunteer from the BJP's social media cell exemplified to Chaturvedi:

People like you have no idea of the reality of India. You don't know these Muslims and nuns just want to rule us again. Well, at least the nuns are not doing love jihad [demographic conquest by interreligious marriage]. Muslim men only want to corrupt Hindu women and have mixed breed children with them.

(Chaturvedi 2016: 89; explanation added)

Yet as this statement indicates, the scenario of a Christian takeover is far less phantasmagoric than the imagination of what it would be like to be ruled by Muslims again.

Two additional issues are worth noting. First, Hindu nationalist anxieties about non-Hindu takeover rarely make reference to international events. Not even the ghastly atrocities of the Islamic State in Syria and Iraq find much explicit mention. The reference point is invariably India's own past or, rather, an academically erroneous Hindu nationalist interpretation that portrays the Mughal and British empires as unequivocally destructive (Thapar 2007; Truschke 2020). Second, these anxieties are heavily gendered. Though hard-line nationalists across the world commonly imagine how "they" come to snatch "our" women (cf. Mostov 2000: 92), the gender dimension is intensified in India given the factual historical occurrences of abduction, whether following military conquest (cf. Chapter 6) or during Partition. These atrocities are nurtured and mythologized by Bollywood films that heroize Hindu women who threw themselves to the flames to escape being sullied by the enemy.[12] According to Anand, the gendering is further enhanced by what he terms "pornosexuality": Many Hindu nationalist foot soldiers live in conservative environments and enjoy sharing stories about what their religious others purportedly can do to women that they cannot do themselves, which gives them "pleasure through displacement" (2011: 77).

Hindu nationalists are equally worried about regional minoritization. True, this anxiety is widely shared across the political spectrum and enshrined in the Constitution as a duty to protect the unity of India (Raju 1988). Nevertheless, Hindu nationalists excel in worrying about germinating "new Pakistans." States in which Hindus lack a comfortable majority are constantly monitored for nascent insurgencies. India has already experienced some of these. In the 1980s, Sikh militants in Sikh-majority Punjab fought for an independent state named Khalistan. In the 1990s, Kashmiri Muslim separatists fought for the liberation of Kashmir. The northeastern states have experienced insurgencies grounded in tribal identities. Though these have all been struck down, suspicions about reinvigorated or novel insurrections with alleged support from activists, political opponents, academics or journalists have virtually become a hallmark of Hindu nationalism.

---

[12] A prime example of this genre is Sanjay Leela Bhansali's film *Padmaavat* (2018), based on a poem about the legendary queen Padmini in 13th- or 14th-century Chittor in today's Rajasthan.

Since 2016, such suspicions grew so pervasive that political critics were frequently discredited as a *"tukde-tukde* gang," a conspiracy of people aiming to divide the country into fragments. Yet the worst dystopia within this genre is perhaps Mughalstan, an imagined corridor of land from Pakistan to Bangladesh across the Indo-Gangetic plain and Kashmir allegedly intended as a homeland for South Asia's Muslims. According to Anand, however, Mughalstan is more of a Hindu nationalist nightmare than a plan that anybody is working towards (Anand 2011: 56–63).

Hindu nationalists of all hues share the anxieties about minoritization and territorial dismemberment, but their notions of intentionality differ. While the conservatives and progressives tend to conceptualize these dreaded scenarios as "natural" outcomes of divergent fertility rates, religious conversion and illegal immigration from Muslim-majority neighboring countries, warriors – or "hard-liners," as this chapter prefers to call them – attribute them to sinister intentions. This line of thinking is epitomized by R. V. Bhasin's 2003 book *Islam: A Concept of Political World Invasion*. Consider the following passage:

> The Muslims within India after 1947 have recommended a plan of action for all Muslims in India to use the following 10 methods for immediate implementation: 1. Convert Hindus by every mean to embrace Islam. 2 By polygamy. God himself divinely allows you this. 3. By thwarting any family planning programme. 4. Infiltrate into India from all directions to grow fast as servants of Allaha. 5. Form Muslim majority geo-political areas within India. 6. Force mass expulsion of Hindus when they come close to being a religious minority. 7. Jehad is the duty of every Muslim. Be Allahas own soldiers to fight & kill those who oppose his diction as said in Quran. 8. Let no non believer dare settle where you have come into close majority. 9. Abduct women of Hindus to breed out of them your children. Hindu abducted woman are delivered to you as MALE GANIMAT [booty]. 10. Attack the foundation of Hindu culture in India, their temples and their books. They will then automatically follow Allaha's ordainment and convert to ISLAM. Know thus, that India is under attack of ISLAM.
>
> (Bhasin 2003: 154; cf. Anand 2011: 22–23)

This passage is as rare in its explicitness as the WhatsApp message about the imagined Muslim takeover in 2035. Though the Maharashtra government promptly banned Bhasin's book, central passages are still available digitally, and similar messages about an alleged

Muslim conspiracy to Islamicize India frequently shine through in the BJP's rhetoric and policies. For instance, India's Home Minister Amit Shah openly explained his government's initiation of a National Register of Citizens as a strategy to weed out "infiltrators" (IANS 2019) once non-Muslim illegal immigrants had been offered fast-track citizenship. Likewise, interreligious marriages are increasingly suspected of being cases of "love jihad" (Frøystad 2021), and several BJP-ruled states have now enacted anticonversion laws to curb this practice (Nielsen and Nilsen 2021).

Hindu nationalist suspicions about sinister Muslim or Christian intentions to gain control over India region by region are, however, only half the story. Granted, such suspicions are central to Western Islamophobia and have been more than sufficient in motivating violence (cf. Gardell 2014: 33). But in the case of Hindu nationalism we would also do well to follow Appadurai (2006) in considering the gap between the perceived incompleteness of the present and the pristine purity of the envisioned future. The former refers to the worries that if the imperfect conditions of the present are allowed to develop unchecked their dystopias will sooner or later come true. The latter is not directly reducible to the future Hindu state discussed in constitutional terms but has closer affinity with what Bauman (2017) terms "retrotopia": a mirage-like vision of the future grounded in an idealized imagination of the past. To understand how Hindu nationalism drives and legitimates violence, we also need to look at the antithesis to their dystopias.

Hindu nationalists conceptualize India's past in terms of three distinct phases: the long and glorious Hindu period, the tyrannical Mughal period and the oppressive colonial period. Interestingly, this periodization is heavily orientalist: Besides being factually simplistic, it reflects the colonial tendency to portray their predecessors as barbarians (Thapar 2007; Truschke 2020). Prior to the Mughal period, Hindu nationalists infer, everything was good, beautiful and just. To them, pre-Mughal India represents a golden age. Gone are the violent rivalries between neighboring monarchs, stark social inequality, gender disparity and competing religious traditions, despite these being thematized in most of the religious scriptures Hindu nationalists eulogize. Gone is even the passage of time: By emphasizing continuity from the Indus Valley Civilization of 3300 BCE until the beginning of the Mughal Empire, the Hindu Nationalist conceptualization of history is eerily ahistorical (Truschke 2020). Hindu nationalists further claim that ancient Hindus excelled not only in art, architecture, philosophy and medicine, but also in science, with many believing plastic surgery, airplanes and the Internet to have been prefigured in ancient India (Nanda 2003). Central Hindu nationalist priorities have thus been to reclaim this knowledge, document India's ancient glory and, when in power, rewrite the textbooks to make the population more aware of Hindu India's magnificent past. Following the BJP's ascent to power in 2014, this history has begun to be materially engraved into cityscapes. Massive deity figures, gargantuan statues of historical heroes, sprawling new Hindu temples and new pilgrim destinations now bring India's pre-Mughal past to life in new ways (Gandhi 2020), as if indicating what the country would have been like if it had remained unsullied by uninvited religious others.

The ideological effect of the dystopian scenarios of Muslim take-over and territorial loss lies in their contrast to this golden age retro-topia rather than in their difference from the perceived reality or even from the civic nationalism of their political opponents. The retrotopian yardstick doubles the gap, which makes every act of violence that can be construed as being committed for the Hindu nation morally justifiable as self-defense. Hindu nationalist hard-liners see themselves as fighting a slow, ideological and virtually metaphysical war for the future of Hinduism, and though they are still restrained by constitutional propriety and law, they increasingly overstep the limits.

NEW FORMS OF VIOLENCE AND IMPUNITY

Following the BJP's ascent to power in 2014, scholars of religious vio-lence in modern India have had to adjust to an expanded repertoire of violence and its justification. Leaving aside the insurgencies in which ethnoreligious communities fought for independence, the academic archive had been mainly filled with interreligious riots and pogroms until then. Central questions were whether such violence erupted spon-taneously or was engineered by vote-hungry politicians, whether the police and paramilitary forces did their duty as suppressors, acted as mute spectators or joined the perpetrators and what role the state played in potential orchestration and postviolence redress.

While these lines of research will continue to remain important, the change of guard at the center has emboldened hard-liners to initiate additional forms of violence. One is the assassination of vocal critics and rationalists who openly challenge Hindu or Hindu nationalist modes of thought. Between 2013 and 2017, Narendra Dabholkar, Govind Pansare, M. M. Kalburghi and Gauri Lankesh were assassinated outside their homes or during their morning walks by shooters on motorcycles. Investigations are still underway, but some of the suspected assassins claimed to have been inspired by a hard-line Hindu nationalist organization, and Lankesh's murderer claimed to have acted "to save my religion" (Kalkod 2018).

Another trend is an increase in cow violence. Many Hindus treat cows as divine mothers, and cow slaughter is dissuaded in scriptures from The Laws of Manu to the Mahabharata. Yet it was not always so (Jha 2002), and neither Muslims, Dalits nor tribals necessarily share these religious ideas. Cows that no longer give milk have thus frequently been sold to butchers for leather and meat. But by 2020, the proscription of cow slaughter had been strengthened in most of India's federal states and union territories (Human Rights Watch 2019: 16). This gave Hindu nationalist vigilantes a new mission, and between 2015 and 2018 at least forty-four people – predominately Muslims – suspected of clandestine cow slaughter or beef consumption were killed, often with impunity (Human Rights Watch 2019). A hard-line BJP MP from Unnao, Sakshi Maharaj, commented that "[i]f somebody tries to kill our mother, we are ready to kill and be killed" (TRT World 2019), while another BJP MP, Jayant Sinha from Jharkhand, garlanded convicted cow vigilantes upon their release on bail (The Wire Staff 2018). In short, killing those who are rumored to kill cows is increasingly justified as an acceptable way of fighting for the Hindu nation.

The third novel mode of violence is less deadly but leaves little doubt about Hindu nationalist hard-liners' opinion about freedom of religion in the country. In a number of instances, young Muslim men and Christian tribals were harassed and badly beaten by groups of young male Hindu vigilantes unless they would say "hail Lord Ram" (*jay sri ram*), which is heretical for pious Muslims and Christians. Originally a respectful veneration of the avatar-king Lord Ram, these words became a common slogan during the Ayodhya movement, and they metamorphosed further around 2016 into a battle cry in the fight against Muslims and other unwelcome non-Hindus (Us Salam 2019). Several perpetrators uploaded videos of their harassment, which suggests an expectation to be celebrated rather than reprimanded or charged. Songs that call for everyone who fails to hail Lord Ram to be sent to the graveyard encourage such actions, as do songs with refrains such as "[t]hose who want to live in India must say Sri Ram"[13] or "the day my blood boils, I wish to show you your place. Then I will not speak, only my sword will."[14]

The expectation of escaping legal sanctions merits a comment about impunity, which many observers seemingly attribute to the rise of Hindu nationalism. But impunity is hardly a Hindu nationalist invention. For instance, very few of the Congress politicians involved in the anti-Sikh riots of 1984 have been punished (Human Rights Watch 2014), and scholars document a "Mafia-esque" nexus between the police, representatives of the law and politicians, irrespective of party (Michelutti et al. 2019; Michelutti 2020). What is new is that the BJP's ascent to power increasingly enables Hindu nationalist representatives, activists and vigilantes to excel in such practices as well. By filling top positions within the judiciary, the police and other institutions of power with "their" people – just like US presidents do (cf. Gramlich 2021) – the likelihood of prosecution and damning verdicts diminishes. Granted, some assassins, cow vigilantes and hate-mongers have been charged and imprisoned, but many have not. The leader of a cow protection organization in Haryana, for instance, claimed support from the police and administration to such an extent that his "boys" were trained by the home guard and received gun licenses from the administration (Anand 2018). If perpetrators nevertheless are taken to court, friendly lawyers and judges can obfuscate individual culpability with such an excessive proceduralism that nobody can be held liable in the end. According to Chatterjee (2017), this was the strategy employed following the massive anti-Muslim pogrom in Gujarat in 2002, and we know the result: One of the accused became prime minster of India.

CONCLUDING REMARKS

Some scholars of Hindu nationalism use terms such as "fundamentalism" or "fascism" to accentuate its antiminority dimensions. They have reason to do so: If hard-line Hindu nationalists could have their way, their most unwanted religious others could well be stripped of their minority rights, voting rights and perhaps even citizenship, which would unleash a humanitarian catastrophe that would surpass even

---

[13] In Hindi: *Bharat me rahna hoga jay sri ram kahna hoga.* Several such songs can be found on YouTube and Gaana.com.

[14] In Hindi: *Jis din khola khun mera, dikha denge aukat teri. Fir to ham nahin bolenge, bas bolegi talwar meri.* This song provoked serious disturbances in Rajasthan in April 2022 (Iyer 2022).

Partition. However, negatively loaded concepts such as fundamentalism or fascism are rarely helpful for understanding the appeal of this political ideology. To this end, this chapter emphasized its ideational universe, focusing particularly on the contrast between its deepest anxieties and long-term future visions. Without engineering religious demographics, Hindu nationalist propaganda infers, India will sooner or later experience a new Muslim takeover or repeated loss of territory. Hence the need to "do something" and, as a long-term project, revive the imagined Hindu golden age. It is the urge to "do something" that occasionally translates into unprovoked violence to "save Hinduism," which results in the paradox that perpetrators frequently claim victimhood. The fact that many Hindu traditions thrive and have shown a remarkable ability to adapt to new political circumstances throughout the centuries is ignored.

Despite thematizing how hard-line Hindu nationalists see themselves as participating in an ideological if not mythological war for Hinduism that occasionally motivates unprovoked violence against minorities, it is worth reiterating that most Hindu nationalists are decent people. They care for their families, work hard, are regular in their worship, treat subordinates politely and never speak harshly to Muslim or Christian strangers, though they do not necessarily want them as neighbors or in-laws. It is just that Muslims and Christians have no place in their ideal India of the future. That said, it is equally true that Hindu nationalism would not have been able to come to power without its many gentle supporters.

References

Agnes, Flavia. 2007. "The Supreme Court, the Media, and the Uniform Civil Code Debate in India." In *The Crisis of Secularism in India*. Edited by Anuradha Dingwaney Needham and Rajeswari Sunder Rajan. Duke University Press. 294–315.

Anand, Dibyesh. 2011. *Hindu Nationalism in India and the Politics of Fear*. Palgrave Macmillan.

Anand, Madhureeta. 2018. "Armed Men, Friendly Cops, Underfed Cows: My Visit to a Haryana Gaurakshak Office." *DailyO*, June 10, 2018. Available at www.dailyo.in/politics/gau-rakshak-hindutva-lynching-hate-crimes-junaid-khan-pehlu-khan/story/1/24772.html (accessed March 4, 2021).

Andersen, Walter K. and Sridhar Damle. 1987. *The Brotherhood in Saffron: The Rashtriya Swayamsewak Sangh and Hindu Revivalism*. Vistaar Publications.

Appadurai, Arjun. 1993. "Number in the Colonial Imagination." In *Orientalism and the Postcolonial Predicament*. Edited by Carol A. Breckenridge and Peter van der Veer. Pennsylvania University Press. 314–339.

2006. *Fear of Small Numbers: An Essay of the Geography of Anger*. Duke University Press.

Bapu, Prabhu. 2013. *Hindu Mahasabha in Colonial North India, 1915–1930: Constructing Nation and History*. Routledge.

Basu, Amrita. 2018. "Whither Democracy, Secularism, and Minority Rights in India?" *Review of Faith and International Affairs* 16(4): 34–46.

Bauman, Zygmunt. 2017. *Retrotopia*. Polity Press.

Bhagat, R. B. 2013. "Census Enumeration, Religious Identity and Communal Polarization in India." *Asian Ethnicity* 14(4): 434–448.

Bhasin, R. V. 2003. *Islam: A Concept of Political World Invasion*. National Publications.

Brosius, Christiane. 2005. *Empowering Visions: A Study on Videos and the Politics of Cultural Nationalism in India*. Anthem Press.

Chakrabarti, Santanu, Lucile Stengel and Sapna Solanki. 2018. "Duty, Identity, Credibility: 'Fake News' and the Ordinary Citizen in India." *BBC News*. Available at http://downloads.bbc.co.uk/mediacentre/duty-identity-credibility.pdf (accessed February 19 2021).

Chakravarty, Gautam. 2013. "Mutiny, War or Small War? Revisiting an Old Debate." In *Mutiny at the Margins: New Perspectives on the Indian Uprising of 1857*, vol. IV. Edited by Gavin Rand and Crispin Bates. Sage. 135–146.

Chatterjee, Moyukh. 2017. "The Impunity Effect: Majoritarian Rule, Everyday Legality, and State Formation in India." *American Ethnologist* 44(1): 118–130.

Chaturvedi, Swati. 2016. *I Am a Troll: Inside the Secret World of the BJP's Digital Army*. Juggernaut.

Fanon, Frantz. 1963. *The Wretched of the Earth*. Grove Press.

Frøystad, Kathinka. 2005. *Blended Boundaries: Caste, Class and Shifting Faces of "Hinduness" in a North Indian City*. Oxford University Press.

2021. "Sound Biting Conspiracy: From India with 'Love Jihad'." *Religions* 12 (12): 1–23.

Frykenberg, Robert Eric. 1987. "The Concept of 'Majority' as a Devilish Force in the Politics of Modern India." *Journal of Commonwealth and Contemporary Politics* 25(3): 267–274.

Gandhi, Supriya. 2020. "When Toppling Monuments Serves Authoritarian Ends." *Foreign Affairs*, July 13, 2020. Available at www.foreignaffairs.com/articles/india/2020-07-13/when-toppling-monuments-serves-authoritarian-ends?utm_medium=email_notificationsandutm_source=reg_confirmatio nandutm_campaign=reg_guestpass (accessed February 15, 2021).

Gardell, Mattias. 2014. "Crusader Dreams: Oslo 22/7, Islamophobia, and the Quest for a Monocultural Europe." *Terrorism and Political Violence* 26(1): 129–155.

Ghassem-Fachandi, Parvis. 2012. *Pogrom in Gujarat: Hindu Nationalism and Anti-Muslim Violence in India*. Princeton University Press.

Golwalkar, M. S. 1939. *We, or Our Nationhood Defined*. Bharat Publications. 1968 [1966]. *Bunch of Thoughts*. Sharda Press.

Gopalakrishnan, Amulya. 2016. "Dog-Whistling, the BJP's Art-Form of Choice." *Times of India*, October 13, 2016. Available at https://timesofindia

.indiatimes.com/blogs/to-name-and-address/dog-whistling-the-bjps-art-form-of-choice (accessed February 19, 2021).

Gramlich, John. 2021. "How Trump Compares with Other Recent Presidents in Appointing Federal Judges." *Fact Tank*, January 13, 2021. Available at www.pewresearch.org/fact-tank/2021/01/13/how-trump-compares-with-other-recent-presidents-in-appointing-federal-judges (accessed March 4, 2021).

Guha, Ramachandra. 2007. *India after Gandhi: The History of the World's Largest Democracy*. Ecco.

Human Rights Watch. 2014. "India: No Justice for 1984 Anti-Sikh Bloodshed." Available at www.hrw.org/news/2014/10/29/india-no-justice-1984-anti-sikh-bloodshed (accessed March 4, 2021).

2019. "Violent Cow Protection in India: Vigilante Groups Attack Minorities." Available at www.hrw.org/report/2019/02/18/violent-cow-protection-india/vigilante-groups-attack-minorities (accessed July 1, 2020).

IANS. 2019. "'Infiltrators' Will Be Extradited within 2024 Using NRC: Amit Shah." *The Hindu*, December 2, 2019. Available at www.thehindu.com/elections/jharkhand/infiltrators-will-be-extradited-by-2024-using-nrc-amit-shah/article30139667.ece (accessed 1 March 2021).

Ignatieff, Michael. 1993. *Blood and Belonging: Journeys into the New Nationalism*. Farrar, Straus and Giroux.

Iyer, Aishwarya. 2022. "'The day my blood boils': How songs incited hate at a Navratri rally in Rajasthan's Karauli." *Scroll*, April 11, 2022. Available at https://scroll.in/article/1021548/the-day-my-blood-boils-how-songs-incited-hate-at-a-navratri-rally-in-rajasthan-s-karauli (accessed November 16, 2022).

Iyer, Aishwarya S. and Vikrant Dubey. 2019. "Bahar and 3 Others Arrested for 'Jai Shri Ram ... Kabristan' Song." *The Week*, July 26, 2019. Available at www.thequint.com/news/hot-news/varun-bahar-detained-for-jo-na-bole-jai-shri-ram-controversial-song#read-more (accessed January 20, 2021).

Jaffrelot, Christophe. 2007. *Hindu Nationalism: A Reader*. Princeton University Press.

2019. "A De Facto Ethnic Democracy? Obliterating and Targeting the Other, Hindu Vigilantes and the Ethno-State." In *Majoritarian State: How Hindu Nationalism Is Changing India*. Edited by Angana P. Chatterji, Thomas Blom Hansen and Christophe Jaffrelot. Oxford University Press. 41–67.

Jalal, Ayesha. 1985. *The Sole Spokesman: Jinnah, the Muslim League and the Demand for Pakistan*. Cambridge University Press.

Jha, D. N. 2002. *The Myth of the Holy Cow*. Verso.

Jones, Keith W. 1989. *Socio-Religious Reform Movements in British India*. Cambridge University Press.

Jones, Kenneth J. 1981. "Religious Identity and the Indian Census." In *The Census in British India: New Perspectives*. Edited by N. Gerald Barrier. Manohar. 73–102.

Juergensmeyer, Mark. 1993. *The New Cold War? Religious Nationalism Confronts the Secular State*. University of California Press.

Kalkod, Rajiv. 2018. "I Killed Gauri Lankesh to Save My Religion: Waghmore to Sit." *Times of India*, June 16, 2018. Available at https://timesofindia

.indiatimes.com/india/i-killed-gauri-lankesh-to-save-my-religion-wagh
more-to-sit/articleshow/64608133.cms (accessed March 3, 2021).

Katju, Manjari. 2019. "The History of Hindu Nationalism in India." In
Modern Hinduism. Edited by Torkel Brekke. Oxford University Press.
203–215.

Kertzer, David I. and Dominique Arel, eds. 2002. *Census and Identity: The
Politics of Race, Ethnicity, and Language in National Censuses.*
Cambridge University Press.

Khalidi, Omar. 2008. "Hinduising India: Secularism in Practice." *Third World
Quarterly* 29(8): 1545–1562.

MacLean, Kama. 2015. *A Revolutionary History of Interwar India: Violence,
Image, Voice and Text.* Hurst.

Manuel, Peter. 1993. *Cassette Culture: Popular Music and Technology in India.*
University of Chicago Press.

Marten, J. T. 1923. *Census of India 1921, Part II: Tables.* Superintendent
Government Printing.

Michelutti, Lucia. 2020. "Electoral Manipulation and Impunity: Ethnographic
Notes from Uttar Pradesh." *Commonwealth and Comparative Politics* 58
(1): 21–42.

Michelutti, Lucia, Ashraf Hoque, Nicolas Martin, David Picherit, Paul Rollier,
Arild E. Ruud and Clarinda Still. 2019. *Mafia Raj: The Rule of Bosses in
South Asia.* Stanford University Press.

Mostov, Julie. 2000. "Sexing the Nation/Desexing the Body: Politics of National
Identity in the Former Yugoslavia." In *Gender Ironies of Nationalism:
Sexing the Nation.* Edited by Tamar Mayer. Routledge. 89–112.

Mukul, Akshaya. 2006. "RSS Officially Disowns Golwalkar's Book." *Times of
India*, March 9, 2006. Available at https://timesofindia.indiatimes.com/
india/rss-officially-disowns-golwalkars-book/articleshow/1443606.cms
(accessed February 19, 2021).

Nanda, Meera. 2003. *Prophets Facing Backward: Postmodern Critiques of
Science and Hindu Nationalism in India.* Rutgers University Press.

Nielsen, Kenneth Bo and Alf Gunvald Nilsen. 2021. "Love Jihad and the
Governance of Gender and Intimacy in Hindu Nationalist Statecraft."
Religions 12(12): 1–18.

Omer, Atalia and Jason A. Springs. 2013. *Religious Nationalism: A Reference
Handbook.* ABC-Clio.

Pandey, Ashish. 2019. "For Sangh, All 130 Crore Indians Are Hindus, Says RSS
Chief Mohan Bhagwat." *India Today*, December 26, 2019. Available at
www.indiatoday.in/india/story/for-rss-all-130-crore-indians-are-hindus-
says-mohan-bhagwat-1631485-2019-12-26 (accessed February 18, 2021).

Pandey, Gyanendra. 2004. *Remembering Partition: Violence, Nationalism and
History in India.* Cambridge University Press.

Philips, Amali. 2011. "Sharia and Shah Bano: Multiculturalism and Women's
Rights." *Anthropologica* 53(2): 275–290.

Raju, K. H. Cheulva. 1988. "Indian Federalism and the Integrity of the Nation."
Indian Journal of Political Science 49(1): 1–13.

Reddy, Deepa. 2011. "Hindutva as Praxis." *Religion Compass* 5(8): 412–426.

2018. "What Is Neo- About Neo-Hindutva?" *Contemporary South Asia* 26(4): 483–490.

Rollier, Paul, Kathinka Frøystad and Arild Engelsen Ruud. 2019. "Introduction: Researching the Rise of Religious Offence in South Asia." In *Outrage: The Rise of Religious Offence in Contemporary South Asia*. Edited by Paul Rollier, Kathinka Frøystad and Arild Engelsen Ruud. UCL Press. 1–47.

Roy, Srirupa. 2006. "'A Symbol of Freedom': The Indian Flag and Transformations of Indian Nationalism, 1906–2002." *Journal of Asian Studies* 65(3): 495–527.

Savarkar, Veer. 1989 [1923]. *Hindutva: Who Is a Hindu?* Bharati Sahitya Sadan.

Special Correspondent. 2018. "Shashi Tharoor Kicks up a Row with 'Hindu Pakistan' Jibe." *The Hindu*, July 12, 2018. www.thehindu.com/news/national/shashi-tharoor-kicks-up-row-with-hindu-pakistan-jibe/article24399540.ece (accessed February 18, 2021).

Talbot, Ian and Gurharpal Singh. 2009. *The Partition of India*. Cambridge University Press.

Thapar, Romila. 2007. "Secularism, History and Contemporary Politics in India." In *The Crisis of Secularism in India*. Edited by Anuradha Dingwaney Needham and Rajeswari Sunder Rajan. Duke University Press. 191–207.

The Wire Staff. 2018. "BJP Minister Jayant Sinha Felicitates 'Gau Rakshasks' Convicted for Ramgarh Murder." *The Wire*, July 7, 2018. Available at https://thewire.in/communalism/bjp-minister-jayant-sinha-gau-rakshaks-convics-ramgarh-lynching (accessed March 3, 2021).

TRT World. 2019. "India's Cow Protection Mobs." May 23, 2019. Available at www.youtube.com/watch?v=xe4zb3JCP8o (accessed March 3, 2021).

Truschke, Audrey. 2020. "Hindutva's Dangerous Rewriting of History." *SAMAJ: South Asia Multidisciplinary Journal* 2020(24/25): 1–15.

Udupa, Sahana. 2018. "Enterprise Hindutva and Social Media in India." *Contemporary South Asia* 26(4): 453–476.

2019. "Nationalism in the Digital Age: Fun as a Metapractice of Extreme Speech." *International Journal of Communication* 13(1): 3143–3163.

Us Salam, Ziya. 2019. "'Jai Sri Ram': The New Battle Cry." *Frontline*, August 16, 2019. Available at https://frontline.thehindu.com/the-nation/article28758718.ece (accessed March 3, 2021).

van der Veer, Peter. 1994. *Religious Nationalism: Hindus and Muslims in India*. University of California Press.

18 Nationalism, Violence and War in Myanmar's Theravāda Buddhist Context

MATTHEW J. WALTON

Contemporary Myanmar has seen the rise of a phenomenon labelled by many observers as "Buddhist nationalism." While there is indeed some justification for this label, a closer look at the dynamics of interaction between Buddhist and national identities and motivations paints a more complicated picture. This chapter argues that this ambivalence stems from the way that a pre-modern Buddhist organizing principle, the *sāsana*, cuts, intrinsically, against national boundary markers. In other words, there is an abiding tension between the theoretical universality of *sāsana* (as a collective understanding that potentially includes *all* Buddhists and is not temporally anchored to the present) and, in practice, its particularity, as it has been localized in specific contexts, including the nation-state.

The chapter begins with an extended consideration of the category of *sāsana*, especially its vague utility as a principle of collective identity, even as it has provided a common religious vernacular and ostensive sense of community for Theravāda Buddhists over millennia. It considers how *sāsana* has interacted with pre-modern Buddhist polities and modern nation-states, acting as a point of reference and motivation for the defence of religion, but also generating an imperfect overlap with contemporary political boundaries and identities. It then looks at several instances in early modern Burma where *sāsana* acted as a justification for both wars of conquest against co-religionists and defensive wars against an invading, non-Buddhist colonial power. Finally, the chapter turns to contemporary Myanmar to consider how the tension between *sāsana*'s scope and existing national and sub-national identities have shaped the ways in which Buddhism is invoked in violent conflicts.

SĀSANA AND BUDDHIST IDENTITY

While it might seem odd or anachronistic to begin a discussion of Buddhism, violence and nationalism several millennia before the nation-state even appeared, it is argued here that one of its socio-religious precursors, the *sāsana*, has fundamentally shaped contemporary Buddhist conceptions of and actions in relation to national identities. On the one hand, appeals and framings that position the nation as contiguous with *sāsana* and acting on its behalf can strengthen Buddhists' identification with and support for the nation, including during episodes of large-scale violence. On the other hand, the universal pretension of *sāsana* makes any national claims on it contingent, destabilizing national identities in one of two ways: either recognizing nation as secondary to *sāsana* in Buddhist doctrinal contexts or bolstering subnational identities through their imbrication with *sāsana* defence and propagation. First, it is necessary to see the ways in which scholars have understood and analysed *sāsana* – especially its persistence and resonance into the modern period – and to examine a few competing arguments about its relationship to the nation.

Alicia Turner describes *sāsana* as "the life of the Buddha's teachings after he is gone; it is the condition of possibility for making merit and liberation" (2014: 1). This capacious understanding can capture the teachings themselves, as well as commentaries and related texts, but would also necessarily include their lived practice among Buddhists. It includes the whole community of Buddhists, as well as the institutional boundaries within them, along with the processes for joining and distinguishing between different types of people (for example, monastic ordination ceremonies). It also includes the full range of material elements associated with Buddhism beyond texts, such as "properties, shrines, statutes, temples, other material objects, and [sacralised] geographic spaces" (Schonthal 2016).

According to the very teachings that constitute the *sāsana*, it is subject to impermanence. That is, while it reflects what are understood to be ultimate and abiding truths of existence, the awareness of those truths is predicated on the emergence of a Buddha who can discover and reveal them, which happens in a recurring cycle but necessarily implies that there will be periods of ignorance regarding these truths, where *sāsana* ceases to exist or exists only as potentiality. This fact introduces a fundamental uncertainty and anxiety into Buddhist practice, where *sāsana* is understood to have an "end date" but conscientious activities by Buddhists to support or defend it can extend its existence (albeit not indefinitely) through more robustly embodying its truths.

The anthropologist Gananath Obeyesekere sought to challenge contemporary assessments of non-European nationalisms as derivative by arguing that, in South and South-East Asia, they were also re-imaginings of a more loosely situated pre-modern collective religio-political identity, namely *sāsana*. Speaking specifically of modern Thai nationalism and responding to Benedict Anderson's (2006) argument about its derivative nature, Obeyesekere claimed that the modern practices and beliefs "had their family resemblances in Thailand's past and that past, in conjunction with European models, constituted [King] Vajiravudh's remaking of nationhood" (2004: 9–10).

To further develop his argument, Obeyesekere turned to pre-modern Sri Lanka, claiming that disparate polities were understood as ideologically connected and integrated through a common salvation idiom provided by Theravāda Buddhism as well as common practices of ritual and pilgrimage. It was particularly through pilgrimage that adherents recognized themselves as holding common beliefs and practices with others who were not part of their immediate familial or political communities. Obeyesekere concluded that "Sinhalas had no term that could be translated as 'nation'; they had a term that belonged to the same polythetic class as nation, namely sasana" (2004: 22).

Steven Collins' related conception of the "Pāli imaginaire" is less tied to the sense of common purpose or identity that Obeyesekere seems to imply (1998). As such, it situates people similarly within a literary tradition that contains both discursive and practice-based elements but does not necessarily argue that this contributed to or determined the formation of political communities, especially prior to the modern era. In this way, it probably more effectively describes the *limited* potential pull that *sāsana* can have on someone's identity or loyalty, at least in general terms, when not linked with other, more localized identities.

Sāsana, then, was for centuries one of the important ways in which many Theravāda Buddhists understood themselves and their practice. It would have gestured to a broader, shared positionality, but probably primarily was understood or experienced with regard to more local communities and identities. *Sāsana* would have interacted with other existing and emerging political and cultural identities, including those associated with various Buddhist kingdoms and, eventually, nation-states. But because of the particularities of these interactions, it is probably not adequate to follow the normal scholarly convention of talking about Buddhism and nationalism becoming 'intertwined' over the course of the late 19th and early 20th centuries. We need to recognize at least two consequential axes of discontinuity that persist in this overlapping space: first, the partial identification with a given national community, furthered by the persistence of sub-national identities in many Theravāda Buddhist-majority countries; and second, the tension between the theoretically more universal or capacious *sāsana* identity and more bounded and mundane national identities.

One of the consequences of these overlapping – and often prioritized – identities is that, despite the seeming centrality of *sāsana* to many Buddhists' self-understandings and everyday practices, the category has only been able to generate a limited sense of pan-Theravādin fellow-feeling. Of course, this shared religious space has not prevented large-scale violence between Theravāda Buddhist polities, whether the many conflicts between Burmese and Thai polities or the Burman conquest of the Kingdom of Arakan in the 18th century. In fact, it seems like *sāsana* has only been effective in this respect when deployed in response to a perceived collective threat. Even then, its appeal has been limited by national borders and interests. The next section turns to several events in early modern Myanmar that demonstrate the variable ways in which national interest has interacted with *sāsana*-orientated concerns.

BUDDHISM, NATIONALISM AND VIOLENCE IN EARLY MODERN MYANMAR

Prior to the emergence of modern nation-states in South-East Asia, kingdoms in the region made use of Theravāda Buddhist symbolism and the trope of defending or purifying the *sāsana* in order to justify their conquests and defensive struggles. One of the conflicts that demonstrates the ways in which this purifying impulse could be used to validate a war between co-religionists was the conquest of the Arakanese kingdom of Mrauk U by the Konbaung king Bodawphaya in 1784–1785. Similarly, when rallying his subjects to defend the Konbaung monarchy against British annexation, the final Konbaung king Thibaw couched his appeal in terms of defence of the religion and the nation. And, while the colonial-era monk Ledi Sayadaw did not advocate for violence, his exhortation to his fellow citizens to attend to their moral conduct as a necessary step in the struggle for political independence placed nation in a related but subservient position to the *sāsana* and its moral force.

The ethnic Rakhine Buddhist kingdom of Mrauk U was founded in the 15th century. The ethnic Burman king Bodawphaya (r. 1782–1819) was well-known for his attention to monastic conduct, and he expressed concern for what he saw as the wider destabilizing effects of laxity in discipline among Arakanese monks. Seeing an opportunity to expand his territory *and* develop the religion, "the king intended to put an end to the country's anarchy and to re-establish the purity of the *sāsana*, the Buddhist religion" (Leider 2008: 413). While his mission to standardize religious practice across Arakan was largely successful, large parts of the population fled after the conquest, making political stability more elusive. What is remarkable about this conflict is that *sāsana* defence was used to justify an offensive war against a co-religionist population. Jacques Leider argues that, even if we do not classify these warring kingdoms as "nations," we should remain aware of their distinctive differences of culture and practice, even if they existed within a common "Pāli imaginaire" (2008: 410). Indeed, although Bodawphaya's reasoning did not refer to ethnic differences, the conquest has loomed large since that time in the Arakanese imagination of seeing the central Burman state as oppressive, despite a shared Theravāda belief system.

As the British began chipping away at Konbaung territories throughout the 19th century, the Burmese kings sought to strengthen themselves and their nation through moral practice and *sāsana* reforms. King Mindon (r. 1853–1878), realizing that his country's military might was no match for the British soldiers and their weaponry, sought to reorganize the *sangha*, although his efforts had the unintended effect of encouraging several debilitating schisms among different monastic sects (Mendelson 1975: 112–144). The final Konbaung king, Thibaw (r. 1878–1885), about to be deposed, issued a royal proclamation that read: "These heretics, the English ... have most harshly made demands calculated to bring about the injury of our Religion ... To uphold the Religion, to uphold the national honor, to uphold the country's interest ... will gain for us the notable result of placing us on the path to the celestial regions and to Nibban [*nirvana*]" (Scott and Hardiman 1983 [1900]: 110). Here he sacralised the defence of the nation in the face not just of foreign invasion but of non-Buddhist, heretical takeover, again equating the defence of the nation with the defence of Buddhism.

Finally, although he eschewed violent means, the influential colonial-era monk Ledi Sayadaw helped to further link the fortunes of Buddhism and the Burmese nation through his writing and activism following the British annexation in 1886. In a famous public letter, he castigated his fellow Buddhists, suggesting that they had been colonized because they had let their moral conduct lapse. Only exemplary moral actions – such as abstaining from eating beef – would lay the groundwork for a stronger Buddhist community that, in the future, would be positioned to be able to become politically independent (Braun 2013: 75–78). Building on Ledi Sayadaw's logic, moral campaigns formed the bulk of social and political activism among Burmese Buddhists in the first two decades of the 20th century (Turner 2014). In all of these examples, the well-being of the *sāsana* was the spur to action. But *sāsana*-orientated action could be directed in different ways: towards violent conquest of fellow Buddhists for the sake of religious purification or for defence of the country against non-Buddhist colonial incursions. These ambivalent dynamics have continued in contemporary Myanmar.

BUDDHISM, NATIONALISM AND VIOLENCE IN CONTEMPORARY MYANMAR

Given the ways in which the practice of war has expanded in the 20th and 21st centuries to include broader topical or ideological struggles that are often carried out through violent means if not through clearly delineated battles (e.g., the War on Terror or the War on Drugs), it seems appropriate to consider the ways in which three major ongoing conflicts in Myanmar have been framed in terms of a Theravāda Buddhist national or collective identity. The first of these, Myanmar's protracted civil war, has primarily been framed in terms of ethnic divisions, but it is argued here that a partially shared Buddhist identity between the ethnic majority and several (but not all) minority groups has influenced the dynamics of the conflict over its many decades, especially the circumstances under which common religious identity can override ethnic division. The second relates to several recent decades of intensified anti-Muslim popular sentiment and violence, which has been particularly directed at the Rohingya population through genocidal means. Here, violence is justified by narratives of a perceived threat to the nation but primarily articulated as a threat to the nation's asserted Buddhist character. Interestingly, this seems to be an instance where a shared threat narrative articulated in national terms has been sufficiently strong to (at least provisionally) overcome a history of conflict and exclusion based in large part on ethnic and religious identities. Finally, the military coup of February 2021 sparked immediate resistance and civil disobedience that, in response to increasingly brutal tactics of oppression and terror from the military, generated a widespread armed civilian resistance movement. The military – especially through a few loyal proxy monks – has continued to frame itself as a protector of Buddhism and its opponents as enemies of the faith, while many in the civilian opposition have self-consciously sought to decentre Buddhism and decouple it from national identity, citing the exclusionary and violent dynamics it has legitimized in recent decades.

Ethnic, Civil Conflict

Prior to independence in 1948, Myanmar was already faced with a range of low-level civil conflicts, arranged along ethnic, religious and ideological spectrums, the latter being fought among various shades of leftists. Throughout the 1950s, as the state gradually gained control over the country, largely through increased militarization, ethnic resistance movements coalesced and grew, becoming the primary axes of this ongoing conflict. At the same time, protection of Buddhism remained a strong part of the military's justification of its violent campaigns, and Buddhist identities affected internal dynamics within the ethnic armed groups.

Military-controlled media outlets regularly ran articles reinforcing the necessarily intertwined nature of Buddhism and the Burmese nation, as well as the military's leading role in protecting both. Through the 1950s and 1960s, as leftist resistance remained a threat, pamphlets portrayed communism as an existential threat to Buddhism (Walton 2016: 122). This assertion of the need to project Buddhist-grounded authority became more prominent through the 1980s and 1990s, as military leaders embarked on ambitious building projects of stupas and monasteries, alongside other forms of enhanced support for the *sāsana* (Schober 1997).

This process was further extended by the creation of the State Sangha Maha Nayaka Committee (Ma Ha Na, in its Burmese acronym) in 1990, establishing a central Buddhist authority after several years of consultation and negotiation. Notably, this effort faced strong grass-roots resistance from monks, who have historically seen state-led attempts to centralize and control the *sangha* as an inappropriate extension of political power over one of the core institutions of *sāsana*. Overcoming those objections through arguments about reforming monastic conduct and more effectively promoting Buddhism – as well as through disciplinary measures and coercion – Ma Ha Na was a creation of the Burmese state, becoming another tool in the standardization of Buddhist practice, as it was spread through contested conflict areas (Tin Maung Maung Than 1988).

Finally, the role of Buddhist identity was prominently on display in one of the most destructive and consequential internal splits among the ethnic armed groups. The ethnic Karen population in modern Myanmar has been difficult to accurately describe demographically. While the ethnic armed resistance movement – led by the Karen National Union (KNU) – has presented a predominantly Christian identity, the entire Karen population in the country is likely majority Buddhist. This has been challenging to measure because the Karen population has always been located not only in Karen State, but also in Mon State and across several of the ethnic Burman-majority regions. The inadequate accounting of Karens overall has been a persistent source of grievance, but these circumstances have also failed to capture the range of stances towards the Burmese state and the Burman Buddhist majority, what Ardeth Maung Thawnghmung has called the "Other Karen" (2011).

Of relevance to this discussion is the 1994 fracture in the KNU that led to the creation of the Democratic Karen Buddhist Army (DKBA; later renamed the Democratic Karen *Benevolent* Army) and the fall of the KNU stronghold at Manerplaw, which not only split the KNU but hobbled a nascent alliance of ethnic armed forces opposed to the military. The split was fuelled partly by grievances of non-Christian Karen soldiers against their predominantly Christian leadership, and the religious implications of the dispute were amplified by a prominent monk, U Thuzana. The faction that he supported was induced to defect, and it became a powerful and effective proxy for the military in Karen State, fighting against the KNU intermittently for decades. What this example demonstrates is that, far from being a unifying force, the presumed intertwining of a singular national and Buddhist identity narrative in Myanmar was itself an axis of conflict, swinging Buddhist Karen from prioritizing ethnic identity in the early decades of the resistance movement, to stoking religious grievance (and co-religious identity with the Myanmar military) as part of a split with the KNU, to eventually establishing a more moderated relationship with both entities, which has seen Buddhist Karen interests as distinctive from both the Buddhist majority of the country and the Christian majority of the KNU leadership.

Anti-Muslim Violence and Rohingya Genocide

One of the most jarring aspects of Myanmar's much-lauded (albeit short-lived) democratic "transition" from 2011 to 2021 was that it happened alongside widespread anti-Muslim discrimination and violence, including the genocidal repression and large-scale expulsion of ethnic Rohingya Muslims. Myanmar's contemporary Rakhine State, on the country's western border with Bangladesh, has long been a religiously plural region, with extended periods of both Islamic and Buddhist kingship and traditions of political rule that integrated elements of both religions (Charney 1999). The Konbaung conquest and incorporation of the Arakanese kingdom of Mrauk U described above fuelled several generations of ethno-centric narratives that defined

Arakanese political aspirations *against* the central Burman-led state, despite having a shared religion. British colonization complicated the demographic picture, expanding the number of Muslims present in Rakhine State and heightening tensions. A small, pre-independence Islamic separatist movement had limited political impact at the time but provided fodder for later anti-Muslim narratives that tried to paint a secessionist threat. Although the descendants of people currently identifying as Rohingya have lived in the region for centuries – under a variety of different ethnonyms – the coalescing of that identity around the common label of Rohingya set the contemporary tensions in Rakhine State along those lines.

The spark for the most recent period of conflict was the rape and murder of a Rakhine woman in May 2012 by several Muslim men. Retaliatory violence followed on both sides, and the period between 2012 and 2014 saw sporadic riotous violence in cities across Myanmar and several extended periods of violence in Rakhine State. Muslims were primarily the victims in these events, and the whole period saw a rise in general anti-Muslim rhetoric and religio-political organizing among Buddhists, including the formation of Ma Ba Tha (the Organization for the Protection of Race and Religion) and related groups, described in more detail below. Major violent clearance operations by the Myanmar military in 2016 and 2017 – as well as local vigilante and paramilitary forces – caused two periods of mass exodus of Rohingyas to Bangladesh. Today, there are still up to a million Rohingya and other refugees in Bangladesh and over 100,000 displaced people within Rakhine State.

Two aspects of this conflict are particularly relevant in the light of questions of nation and *sāsana*. First is the attempt by Ma Ba Tha to frame its efforts in terms of the protection of both *sāsana* and nation. The organization's name in Burmese refers to protecting *a-myo* (understood in this context to refer to ethnic identity, and specifically the 135 ethnicities formally recognized by the Myanmar government), *batha* (a generalized Burmese term for religion) and *thathana* (the Burmese rendering of *sāsana*, obviously referring specifically to Buddhism). The invocation of this phrase as a shorthand not only indicates the ways in which Ma Ba Tha's leaders saw religious and national identities to be connected, but also the ways in which the appeal to a common *sāsana* identity was intended to overcome any perceived ethnic differences. Ma Ba Tha was not entirely successful in this respect, as it never effectively made inroads into Rakhine communities. By contrast, the ethnic Karen State Ma Ba Tha chapter was one of the most successful and militant, even refusing multiple government orders to disband and rename. But its identity was established as more specifically ethnic Karen Buddhists struggling to defend the *sāsana*, underscoring the utility of *sāsana* as a common reference point but also its inability to fully overcome existing ethnic divisions.

The second aspect is that the contemporary Rohingya crisis occasioned at least a temporary ratcheting down of ethnic tensions between Rakhines and the majority Burmans, in terms that made reference both to shared religious identity and values as well as common national interests. Ethnic Burman military and political leaders made regular reference to the historically established role of Rakhines in protecting the country's "western gate" (Wade 2017). Nationalists monks such as U Wirathu regularly visited Rakhine State, praising efforts to marginalize and exclude the Rohingya. Rakhine nationalists – monks and laypeople – parroted anecdotes that sought to reinforce a general stereotype of rapacious and predatory Muslims as a threat against Buddhist women in general and Rakhine women in particular.

At the height of the second military campaign against the Rohingya in 2017, the influential Burmese monk Sitagu Sayadaw gave a sermon to a group of Burmese soldiers in which he lauded the example of the Sinhalese king Duttagamani (Walton 2017). In this commonly cited tale from the *Mahavamsa*, the king, feeling remorse at having won a battle that caused the deaths of many people, is assured by his advisors that the karmic demerit is limited because, not being Buddhists, his foes were not fully human. Not only this, his broader intent – to fight for the *sāsana* – was of infinitely more value in determining the moral effects of his actions. Not only did this sermon have the effect of issuing an absolution to soldiers being sent to commit violence against Muslims in Rakhine State, it also provided a higher moral purpose for this violence committed on behalf of the nation, thus positioning Rakhine Buddhists as being on the front lines of the noble task of protecting both *sāsana* and nation.

However, even though anti-Muslim and anti-Rohingya sentiment would persist across Myanmar, a shared role in the protection of *sāsana* did not prove able to overcome the ethnic political tensions between Rakhines and the central Burman-led government. A heavy-handed security response to public events supporting Rakhine national identity and culture in January 2018 resulted in seven deaths and hardened some aspects of Rakhine political rhetoric away from recognition of co-religionist status and back towards the terms of ethnic division (Beech and Saw Nang 2018). In a moment of perceived crisis of Buddhism and the Myanmar nation on the part of the Buddhist majority, a shared *sāsana*-orientated identity provided some grounds for common action, but this was limited, both temporally and in its extent.

2021 Military Coup and Resistance

Early on the morning of 1 February 2021, hours before a newly elected parliament was scheduled to be sworn in, the Myanmar military launched a series of arrests of leaders of the government, including State Counsellor Daw Aung San Suu Kyi and many members of her National League for Democracy (NLD) party. The military claimed – with no evidence – that there were severe irregularities in the November 2020 election and quickly moved to install an interim government. Within days, citizens launched widespread strikes across virtually every major employment sector, complemented by massive public protests. While the military regime initially showed restraint in its responses, by March it had become more brutal, arresting protesters and critics, using torture to procure confessions and information and deploying violent tactics against demonstrators. Since the coup, a shadow government-in-exile has arisen – the National Unity Government – alongside other political consultative bodies. These have been complemented by a range of underground resistance groups and locally organized People's Defence Force (PDF) units across the country, as citizens in Myanmar continue to defy this illegal and violent overthrow of an elected government.

In contrast with the 2007 monastic protests (which the media dubbed the "Saffron Revolution"), a number of prominent and influential monks have remained public supporters of the military, in almost every case justifying their position with regard to military support for Buddhism, its presumed capacity to maintain security and stability in the country and various implausible conspiracy theories that posit that the NLD was controlled by global Islamic forces (Artinger and Rowland 2021). Military propaganda has tried to undercut the armed grassroots opposition by claiming that PDF groups have killed monks and by decrying the reduced status of Buddhism under the previous NLD government (Mendelson 2022). Its leaders have also drastically increased their public donations to monks and *sāsana*-orientated activities, such as building pagodas and other religious structures (Ford and Zarchi Oo 2021). All of this is proceeding according to the standard *sāsana*-building monarchical model that previous regimes of Buddhist rulers have attempted to implement, seeing the health and strength of the nation as grounded on the moral authority of the monastic community and the *sāsana*.

By contrast, many voices in the opposition movement have seized this moment to open a more critical public discussion on the role of Buddhism in the Myanmar state and in Myanmar national identity (Hayward 2021). Social media discussions regularly address not only ethnic discrimination and systemic ethnic Burman supremacy, but also the negative effects of Buddhist hegemony in the country. Many Burman Buddhists have even expressed apologies and remorse for not having defended the Rohingya during the persecution of the last decade (Hölzl 2021), making public declarations to act against religious and ethnic discrimination and to use the opportunity of the coup to envision new institutions not grounded in Burman or Buddhist norms. Led by youth voices and primarily taking place on social media, it is hard to discern the extent or impact of this critical perspective, but it has certainly influenced the stances and policies of the National Unity Government, which has made remarkably progressive and inclusive promises in this regard.

It is unlikely that the *sāsana* will cease to be an important part of most Myanmar Buddhists' identities, along with ethnicity and other axes. But these contemporary examples demonstrate that, while *sāsana* persists as an organizing principle, it only acts inconsistently as a rallying point, just as often being overcome by ethnic or national interests. Equally, while we can discern a strong narrative that sees the flourishing of the Buddhist *sāsana* as essential to the health of the Myanmar nation, this has also been a contingent connection. Moments of collective violence in particular have revealed the ways in which the alignment of *sāsana* and nation are, in practice, impermanent and subject to change as Buddhists in Myanmar reassess and prioritize different aspects of their identities.

References

Anderson, Benedict. 2006. *Imagined Communities: Reflections on the Origin and Spread of Nationalism*. Verso books.

Artinger, Brenna and Michael Rowland. 2021. "When Buddhists Back the Army." *Foreign Policy*, 16 February.

Beech, Hannah and Saw Nang. 2018. "Myanmar Police Gun Down Marchers in Rakhine Ethnic Rally." *New York Times*, 17 January.

Braun, Erik. 2013. *The Birth of Insight: Meditation, Modern Buddhism, and the Burmese Monk Ledi Sayadaw*. University of Chicago Press.

Charney, Michael Walter. 1999. "Where Jambudipa and Islamdom Converged: Religious Change and the Emergence of Buddhist Communalism in Early

Modern Arakan (Fifteenth to Nineteenth Centuries)." Unpublished PhD dissertation, University of Michigan.

Collins, Steven. 1998. *Nirvana and Other Buddhist Felicities: Utopias of the Pali Imaginaire*. Cambridge University Press.

Ford, Billy and Zarchi Oo. 2021. "Myanmar Coup: Military Regime Seeks to Weaponize Religion." *United States Institute of Peace*, 16 December.

Hayward, Susan. 2021. "Beyond the Coup in Myanmar: Don't Ignore the Religious Dimensions." *Just Security*, 3 May.

Hölzl, Verena. 2021. "Myanmar Coup Protesters Regret Silence Over Rohingya Genocide." *Vice*, 25 February.

Leider, Jacques P. 2008. "Forging Buddhist Credentials as a Tool of Legitimacy and Ethnic Identity: A Study of Arakan's Subjection in Nineteenth-Century Burma." *Journal of the Economic and Social History of the Orient* 51: 409–459.

Mendelson, Allegra. 2022. "Myanmar's Military Turns to Buddhism in Bid for Legitimacy." *Al-Jazeera*, 30 January.

Mendelson, E. Michael. 1975. *Sangha and State in Burma: A Study of Monastic Sectarianism and Leadership*. Cornell University Press.

Obeyesekere, Gananath. 2004. *Buddhism, Nationhood, and Cultural Identity: The Premodern and Pre-colonial Formations*. International Centre for Ethnic Studies.

Schober, J. 1997. "Buddhist Just Rule and Burmese National Culture: State Patronage of the Chinese Tooth Relic in Myanmar." *History of Religions* 36(3): 218–243.

Schonthal, B. 2016. "Securing the *Sasana* through Law: Buddhist Constitutionalism and Buddhist-Interest Litigation in Sri Lanka." *Modern Asian Studies* 50(6): 1966–2008.

Scott, James George and J. P. Hardiman. 1983 [1900]. *Gazeteer of Upper Burma and the Shan States*. AMS Press.

Thawnghmung, A. M. 2011. *The "Other" Karen in Myanmar: Ethnic Minorities and the Struggle without Arms*. Lexington Books.

Tin Maung Maung Than. 1988. "The *Sangha* and *Sāsana* in Socialist Burma." *Sojourn* 3(1): 26–61.

Turner, A. 2014. *Saving Buddhism*. University of Hawai`i Press.

Wade, Francis. 2017. *Myanmar's Enemy Within: Buddhist Violence and the Making of a Muslim 'Other'*. Zed Books.

Walton, Matthew J. 2016. *Buddhism, Politics and Political Thought in Myanmar*. Cambridge University Press.

2017. "Religion and Violence in Myanmar: Sitagu Sayadaw's Case for Mass Killing." *Foreign Affairs*, November 6.

Part IV

Featured Conflicts

19 Christian Crusading, Ritual, and Liturgy

M. CECILIA GAPOSCHKIN

On July 8, 1099, more than three years into their campaign and a week before the final victorious assault on Jerusalem, the Franks who had set out on what would come to be known as the First Crusade performed a penitential procession around the walls of the holy city. They had begun the siege in early June, but, short on food and water, constantly harassed when foraging for supplies, and defeated in several skirmishes, things were going badly. Peter Tudebode, a French cleric who had accompanied the campaign and who left us an account of the expedition, recounted the following:

> When our lords saw these atrocities, they were greatly angered and held a council in which the bishops and priests recommended that the crusaders hold a procession around the city. So the bishops and priests, barefooted, clad in sacred vestments, and bearing crosses in their hands, came from the church of the Blessed Mary, which is on Mount Zion, to the church of Saint Stephen the Protomartyr, singing and praying that the Lord Jesus Christ deliver his holy city and the Holy Sepulchre from the pagan people and place it in Christian hands for His holy service. The clerks, so clad, along with the armed knights and their retainers, marched side by side ... The Christians came to the church of Saint Stephen and there took their stations as is customary in our processions.[1]

What Peter described here was a classic litanic procession, a long-standing liturgical ritual in which the community, recognizing that misfortune (in this case, the inability to take the city of Jerusalem) was the result of Christian sin, ritually performed penance before God. The rite had biblical authority, especially in the story of the Ninevites (cf. Jonah 3:5–9). They were performed regularly during the liturgical

---

[1] Tudebode 1974: 115.

year but could also be organized by clerical authorities on an ad hoc basis when necessitated by calamity or distress. Townspeople and clergy were supposed to come together as one in supplicant humiliation to beg God for forgiveness and beseech Him to grant the Christian community worldly needs and heavenly salvation. In 1099, the procession circled the entire city, stopping at all of the principal holy sites outside the city walls: the Churches of Saint Stephen, Mary of Zion, the Ascension, and the Dormition.[2] The participants – clergy and laity alike – chanted the litany, a long list of petitions that may well have included prayers known in the West such as "Please deign to destroy the pagan people" and "Please deign to humiliate the enemies of the church."[3] As told in all of the accounts of the First Crusade, the procession was followed a week later by the glorious capture of the city, in which God granted the Franks their military success. "For they did not ascribe this victory to their own strength," wrote Peter's contemporary, Baldric of Bourgeuil, "but attributed it entirely to God who had worked in them both to want it and to achieve it."[4]

The episode reveals the role that liturgical prayer and ritual played in the tactical prosecution and devotional meaning of crusading, both as a means for communicating with God and effecting outcomes and as the ideological framework for connecting the events on the ground to the Divine will. Models for this type of liturgical intercession were found throughout the Old Testament (the Hebrew Bible[5]), which, in this and many other ways, provided the template for holy war activated in the Crusades. Indeed, the crusaders understood themselves explicitly as the new Israelites, their Muslim opponents as "pagans" and "heathens," and the crusade itself as fought on the model of Moses and Joshua's battle for the Promised Land, and later that of the Maccabees against the Seleucids.

---

[2] Peter does not identify all of the sites of the procession, which can be reconstructed using further sources. See Gaposchkin 2018: 454–468.

[3] We do not know what precise litany was performed on July 8, 1099, though these prayers are preserved in the earliest Sacramentary known to survive reflecting the Latin rite in Jerusalem after 1099, Rome Angelica ms. 477, 62r–v. Versions of these prayers were known in the West from the end of the 11th century. See examples in Lapidge 1991.

[4] Bourgueil 2014: 111; 2020: 149.

[5] The Franks/Crusaders called the books of the Hebrew Bible the Old Testament, and I retain this usage here because the distinction between and relationship between the "Old" and the "New" Testaments represent fundamental parts of their interpretation and structuring of history and their own roles in it.

The First Crusade culminated after three years of travel, sieges, victories, and setbacks on July 15, 1099, with the Christians' bloody capture of the holy city of Jerusalem. In the moment, the unlikely victory was considered an extraordinary miracle, a sign that the Franks were fulfilling God's will. As traditionally narrated, the First Crusade had been launched by Pope Urban II on November 27, 1095, with a public address in which he called upon the military class of Latin (Western) Christendom to take up arms and go to the Holy Land in order to recapture the Holy Sepulcher from Muslim domination.[6] The broader geopolitical goals included defending the Byzantine Empire against the incursion of Seljuk Turks in Anatolia and Syria and protecting (or what they called "liberating") Christians in the East from persecution, but the heart of the project was control of Jerusalem, which had been under Muslim control since the 7th century. It was from the very start a religious enterprise, conceived of largely in religious terms, the fighting of which had religious meaning and entailed spiritual credit (ultimately known as an indulgence).[7] Because of the focus on Jerusalem, participants understood themselves to be pilgrims, a quasi-juridical category infused with devotional and penitential meaning.[8] Urban decreed that the emblem of the crusader would be the cross, which crusaders would wear upon their garments as a sign of their devotion to Christ;[9] in time these pilgrims would come to be called *crucesignatus* (Latin for "signed with the cross") and thus crusaders.[10] The enemies – in this first phase Muslims, both Arab and Turkic – were called pagans (*paganos*), heathens (*gentes*), and "Saracens," and also, in a phrase that came with scriptural authority, "the enemies of cross" (*inimicos crucis*, Philippians 3.17).

By 1109, the Franks had established four political territories, known as the Principalities of the Latin East, or sometimes in older historiography "the Crusader States." The largest and most important of these was the Latin Kingdom of Jerusalem, the prestige of which

---

[6]   There are a great many accounts of both the First Crusade and the Crusades in general. Reliable scholarly narratives in English include Mayer 1988; Madden 1999; Tyerman 2006. On the First Crusade in particular I still consider indispensable Riley-Smith 1986. Riley-Smith must now be read alongside Rubenstein 2011.

[7]   This has been a contested question, but the current consensus favors an understanding of crusading as a religious movement. For example, see Constable 2008b; Purkis 2008.

[8]   Garrisson 1965: 1165–1189.

[9]   Constable 2008a: 45–91.

[10]   Markowski 1984: 157–165; Tyerman 1998: 27–29.

was nourished by biblical echoes of the Kingdom of David and eschatological resonances of the new Jerusalem. Jerusalem was important as the place that Christ had lived, died, and risen, and as the prophesized site of the Second Coming.[11] The holy city was thus in one sense a gateway – or an imprint – of the Heavenly Jerusalem, the future peace of providential salvation.[12] Recent scholarship has emphasized the Apocalyptic undertones and expectations that attended the First Crusade and its interpretation. Quite quickly, the Capture of Jerusalem was understood as a critical juncture on the providential march towards the End of Time. Robert of Reims, one of the First Crusade's early interpreters writing within a decade of 1099, claimed that the Capture of Jerusalem was the most important event since Creation – with the single exception of Christ's redeeming sacrifice on the Cross itself.[13] The event was commemorated in the liturgical calendar both East and West with a feast for "the Liberation of Jerusalem," which framed the conquest as an event of biblical significance itself pointing forward to the Second Coming.[14]

The First Crusade inaugurated a tradition of fighting holy war in the Levant centered on control of the Holy Land that lasted more than four centuries, followed by the spread of crusading to other regions and against other types of religiously defined enemies.[15] Throughout the high and later Middle Ages, the ideal of crusade – a religious war, fought for religious reasons, against religious enemies (usually) on the authority of the pope, the fighting of which garnered religious merit and thus had religious meaning – was deployed against any variety of what were deemed the enemies of the Cross (*inimicos crucis*), of Christ (*inimicos Christi*), and of the Church (*inimicos ecclesie*). In time, Crusades were called against pagans in the Baltic, heretics in the south of France, Hussites in Eastern Europe, Muslims in Spain (known traditionally as the *reconquista*), Eastern Christians in Constantinople, and even political enemies of the pope.

---

[11] Rubenstein 2011; 2019; Buc 2015.

[12] Schein 2005.

[13] Reims 2005: 78; 2013: 4.

[14] Linder 2003a: 46–64; Gaposchkin 2015: 127–181. 2017a: 130–164; 2017b: 34–48; John 2015: 409–431; Aspesi 2017: 278–296.

[15] Historians disagree about whether to the term "Crusade" should be reserved for campaigns focused on Jerusalem or whether it can be used for the broad array of military ventures that gained papal support and spiritual reward aimed a religious enemies or, more broadly, "enemies of the church."

Undergirding these many military campaigns was a sophisticated religious ideology, regularly nourished with religious rituals, that connected and reconciled these practices with the crusaders' understanding of Christianity. Central to this set of beliefs were the ideas that the Crusades were God's wars, fulfilling His will, part of His broader eschatological plan; that the enemy was both the devil (in the eschatological battle) and also the devil's minions and agents on Earth, who were in turn also identified as the *inimicos Christi* and *inimicos crucis*; that any earthly battle was a singular manifestation of God's greater battle; and that success or defeat in these battles was a measure of Christian worthiness. In this, the First Crusade (and by extension all crusading) was no different from any other war or battle, the outcomes of which even in the pre-Christian period were understood to reflect God's (or, before that, the gods') judgment and thus moral virtue.[16] A letter thought in the Middle Ages to be Augustine's articulated this clearly: "Take up your arms with your hands, and let the prayers strike the ears of The Creator, because, when a battle takes place, God looks down from the heavens and, observing which side is just, grants there the palm [of victory]."[17] But the theology of victory that underpinned this logic was heightened by the explicitly religious, biblical, and eschatological framework of crusading, which thus invited attention to the relationship between the crusaders, God, and history. A central axiom of crusading theology was that loss and defeat were always the results of Christian sin.[18] And following the biblical model articulated repeatedly in the Old Testament, sin was a collective responsibility of the religious community, expiated ritually and communally.

Liturgical rituals played an important role within this complex matrix of religious belief and its battlefield practice, in Christian interpretation of the Crusade as holy war, and in Christians' communications with God about holy war. The liturgy was (is) the formal and ritualized worship performed by the clergy on behalf of the Christian community. It took many forms – the mass, the office, prayers, processions, blessings, and so forth. The Eucharistic mass was the most important of these, since it constituted the central defining ritual of the Christian religion, the celebration of which, in enacting Christ's sacrifice on the Cross, brought humankind into iterative communion with God. The core symbolism of the Eucharist became increasingly

[16] Rufus 1981: 736–826; McCormick 1986; Heim 1992; Stephenson 2018: 25–58.
[17] Migne 1844: 33:1098 (ep. 13).
[18] Siberry 1985: 69–108.

important to the penitential aspects of crusading.[19] But all of the liturgy, like the mass, collapsed time, brought the earthly in line with heaven, and connected the present, the specific, and the particular to the Christic, the salvific, and the providential.

Historians have long noted the importance of the liturgy in the prosecution of the Crusades.[20] Crusaders took the Eucharist before battle, military priests chanted prayers on the battlefield, and armies fasted and did processions like the one described by Peter throughout the history of the Crusades. The narrative accounts of the First Crusade in particular are infused with references to liturgical rites performed along the journey and in battle.[21] The eminent Jonathan Riley-Smith spoke of the First Crusade as "military monastery on the move, constantly in prayer."[22] The goal was to invite God's intervention on Earth. Peter Tudebode's account of the liturgical procession of 1099, in which both clerics and armed knights chanted and prayed that Christ would "deliver His Holy City and Holy Sepulcher from the pagan people and place it in Christian hands for His holy service," is an extended example of the widespread phenomenon of the crusader's use of liturgical intercession on behalf of military goals.

In fact, throughout the history of the Crusades, from 1095 through the end of the Middle Ages, the liturgy was deployed ritually and ideologically, on behalf of Crusading objectives, in ways that endowed crusading with meaning and in turn permitted the interpretation of its outcomes. In this sense, the liturgy articulated the field of crusading action within a salvific register. The sacralizing and transforming capacity of its rituals endowed and reendowed crusading with sacramental force. Its prestigious, scripturally informed language provided a hermeneutical framework that permitted the singular crusader or particular battle to be connected with the broader salvific narrative of Christian history. Intercessions and liturgical rites were performed both in real time on the field but also more broadly on the home front, in support of faraway campaigns, whereby the entire Christian community was responsible for the success of any particular Crusade. In this, the liturgy can also be understood as a mechanism of propaganda, enveloping the broader community into the ideological imperatives of Crusade. The

[19] Maier 1999.
[20] Erdmann 1977 (original published in German in 1935); Delaruelle 1980; Riley-Smith 1986: 82–86. McCormick 1992: 209–240; Maier 1997: 628–657; Linder 2003b.
[21] Riley-Smith 1986: 82–86; Gaposchkin 2017a: 93–129.
[22] Riley-Smith 1986: 84.

ritualized prayers were understood, as Pope Honorius III explained in 1217 in one directive relating to the Fifth Crusade, as "invisible weapons," every bit as important to victory as the visible weapons used by knights on the battlefield. "We are instructed by Ancient example to fight the visible enemy with invisible weapons – that is, prayers ... Behold, now is the time that all of the faithful must fight with weapons. This is the time they must sprinkle their heads with ashes. This is the time they must cry to heaven with tears and the sound of their prayers."[23] The Ancient examples, repeatedly evoked and explicitly recalled here, were the Ninevites, who repented before the Lord in sackcloth and ashes and were reprieved, and Moses, whose prayers to the Lord were credited with permitting Joshua and the Israelites' victory over the Amalekites.[24]

From the very start, the liturgy was implicated at every stage of crusading. Special liturgical rites were quickly confected for crusaders as they prepared to leave home and undertake the journey of the armed pilgrim. These rites of departure were built on preexisting ceremonies for pilgrims. Initially, these involved a series of prayers with which the priest or bishop would bless the insignia of the pilgrim – the scrip (wallet) and walking staff. In its pre-Crusade form, these departure rites assumed that the pilgrims undertaking their sacred journeys were often fulfilling a penitential obligation. The departure liturgy thus enveloped the pilgrim into the sacred aura of a penitent, establishing his identity for the length of his journey as that of a quasi-religious. These devotional ideals were in turn absorbed into the rituals and ideology of crusading, which always had a strongly penitential tenor, thus producing the sacralized status of the armed pilgrim fighting in God's army.[25] Our earliest evidence for the adaptation of the pilgrimage rites for Crusades, speaking of the year 1101, has crusaders submitting to a blessing, not of scrip and staff, but of sword and staff.[26] Sword blessings, as discussed below, bestowed upon the sword's owner the authority to enforce God's justice through its power, underscoring this new category of pilgrim – the armed pilgrim, known subsequently as the crusader.

With the institutionalization of crusading in the later 12th century, probably around the time of the Third Crusade (1189–1192), the

[23] Bouquet et al. 1738–1904: 19:639.
[24] For Moses and prayer, see Exodus 17:8–13. Honorius evoked both later in his letter. Bouquet et al. 1738–1904: 19:640.
[25] An axiom of much of the literature on crusading. See, for example, Riley-Smith 2008: 29–44.
[26] Schmale 1972: 142.

departure rite coalesced around the blessing of the scrip, the staff, and the Cross (rather than the sword). As noted above, from the outset the Cross had been the singular symbol of both the crusader (who was "marked by the Cross," and who "took up the Cross" and fought in "the army of the Cross") and crusading itself. For the most part, the confection of these ceremonies simply incorporated one of many pre-existing Cross benedictions into the pilgrimage rite, sometimes further pairing it with a mass for travelers or a mass for the Cross. These Cross prayers, many of which go back to the earliest layer of evidence we have for the Latin liturgy, expressed the idea that the Cross symbolized both penitence and eschatological victory. On the one hand, the Cross was the mechanism of Christ's suffering and passion, fed by the scriptural line that the true Christian should deny himself and "take up the Cross and follow me [that is, Christ]" (Matt 16.25). This verse was central to an ideology of crusader suffering as Christic passion, particularly as it developed in the 13th century in the face of successive crusader defeats and the development of Eucharistic piety. On the other hand, the Cross was the mechanism of Christ's victory over death, the world, and the devil, and as such was understood as the protection and weapon within the eschatological battle of which any single Crusade battle was simply the earthly reflection. For example, a departure rite from southern Italy dating from the last third of the 12th century drew its Cross prayers from the Feast of the Exaltation of the Cross. It enjoined: "Oh God, free us from our enemies by the sign of the cross . . . the sign of the cross will be in the sky when the Lord will come to judge us," and it asked God "with the standard of the holy cross to destroy the crimes of our enemies, so that we can attain the port of salvation."[27] The enemies (plural) of the prayer's original context were the devil and his minions, and here, within the expanded context of the Crusades, they would surely have included the Crusade opponents, those ubiquitous *inimici crucis* of Crusade propaganda. The incorporation of the Cross blessing into the departure rite was part of broader developments in both crusader piety and crusader theology, promoting the twin and interrelated ideals of Christic suffering on the one hand and eschatological triumph on the other.

Although the liturgy of departure, strictly speaking, was increasingly focused on the Cross, a series of other liturgical rites were developed in this period that sacralized the arms of war, including most

---

[27] Pennington 1974: 433–434.

prominently the sword (as above) and the military banner (the *vexillum*), but also including the knight's shield, helmet, breastplate, and spurs.[28] These rites were often found in liturgical ceremonies for blessing a new knight. They were not strictly speaking limited to crusade warfare over and above other types of warfare in the sense that, as above, at one level all military engagements were tests of God's favor. But they were part of the process by which chivalric knighthood was constructed partly out of devotional ideals of service to Christ.[29] Their use in crusading constituted further elements in which liturgical forms continually resacralized holy war as a central tenet in the flourishing ideology of the military class. Although they came in many forms, these blessings all sacralized the sword as the means of enforcing God's justice, delegating to the knight God's power (*virtus*) on Earth. One called the sword's owner the "newly girded servant of Christ" who would protect the Church, widows, and orphans against the "cruelty of pagans," that typical descriptor for the crusader-enemy. The knight, with his sword, should "oppress visible enemies beneath his feet, and through victory over all things, remain always unharmed."[30] We witness the application of this idea in real time with an episode from the Albigensian Crusade in the early 13th century. In 1213, the leader of the crusader forces, Simon de Montfort, stopped at the Cistercian abbey of Boulbonne in Saverdun in southern France "to pray and to commend himself and his soldier to the prayers of the monks." The account proceeds:

> After prolonged and devoted prayer he drew the sword he was wearing and placed it on the altar, saying: "loving Lord, Bountiful Jesus! You have chosen me, unworthy as I am, to fight your battles. Today I take my arms from your altar, so that as I prepare to fight Your battles, I receive from You the instruments of battle."[31]

The sword blessings in this way sanctified the means of earthly warfare within the framework of providential battle. This was God's battle, and the sword, so blessed, was the sword given to the crusader by God to achieve His ends.

Perhaps the most evocative was the blessing of the battle standard since it was often equated with the Cross. Strictly speaking, in Latin the

---

[28] Franz 1909: 2:289–306; Flori 1986: 369–386. Discussed in Rivard 2009: 155–179.
[29] Flori 1978; 1979; 1983; 1986. See also Keen 1984; Lieberman 2015: 391–423.
[30] Vogel and Elze 1963: 2:379 (CCXLIV).
[31] Vaux-de-Cernay 1926: 143; 1998: 205.

term for the military standard was *vexillum*. Blessings for the *vexillum bellicum* asked God to sanctify the battle standard "so that it might prevail against adversaries and rebellious nations ... may it be terrifying to the enemies of the Christian people," since "You are indeed the God who crushes wars and gives the aid of celestial protection to those who have hope in You."[32] Another one asked God to sanctify the standard "so that it could be borne in defense of the holy church against the fury of the enemy ... and that the people of God following it might rejoice to acquire triumph and victory from the enemies through the power of Your holy cross."[33] The evocation here of the power of the Holy Cross (*virtus sancte crucis*) added layers of meaning to the blessing of the battle standard since the Cross, as Christ's battle standard in his fight with the devil, was also called the *vexillum*. Moreover, military standards were often marked by the sign of the Cross, and the Cross itself (in the form of a relic) was carried into battle as a battle standard.[34] The Holy Sepulcher's relic of the Holy Cross, discovered in the days after the city's conquest, immediately became the army's battle standard. Of their first major sortie after that, one account stated that the Franks "set out for battle ... armed with the *vexillo sanctae crucis*, which went before the troops, and directed the army to Ascalon where they intended to meet the opposing side."[35] The most famous example of this practice was in 1187 when the King of Jerusalem carried the great Jerusalem Cross relic into the battle of Hattin, losing it to Saladin.

Up until that point, liturgical support of the Crusade was largely performed on an individual and ad hoc basis, in the crusader's home town, on the field outside a siege, or right before a battle. This changed in 1187. The loss of the Holy Cross on the field of battle in that year, followed within weeks by the loss of the holy city itself, was such a blow that the papacy quickly organized Christendom-wide liturgical intercessions to beg God for forgiveness and plead for His help in reversing these losses.[36] The sense was that such a catastrophic loss – Pope Urban III was said to have died upon hearing the news[37] – could only be explained by Christian unworthiness. Urban's successor, Gregory VIII, immediately issued an encyclical calling the Third Crusade, in which success was predicated upon a complete reform of

[32] Vogel and Elze 1963: 2:378 (CCXLIII).
[33] Gaposchkin 2013: 88.
[34] Murray 1998: 217–238.
[35] Gesta Francorum Iherusalem Expugnantium, ch. 38:517.
[36] Linder 2003b; Gaposchkin 2017a: 192–225.
[37] Morgan 1982: 83–84 (ch. 74); Edbury 1998: 75.

Christian society.[38] "We ought not to believe," the pope wrote, "that these things [the defeats in the Holy Land] have happened through the injustice of a violent judge, but rather through the iniquity of a delinquent people." His successor, Clement III, in turn ordered all churches throughout Christendom to perform special prayers and a clamor during mass begging God to come to the aid of the Christian army.[39] A clamor was a special entreaty to God, inserted into the mass, beseeching Him to redress, through the power of His terrible vengeance, a wrong. Clement's clamor was based on the aptly chosen Psalm 78:

> O God, the heathens [gentes] have come into Your inheritance, they have defiled Your holy temple, they have made Jerusalem as a place to keep fruit [v.1] ... How long, O Lord, will You be angry forever [v.5] ... Pour out your wrath upon the infidel [gentes] that have not known You [v.6] ... Remember not our former iniquities [v.8] ... Help us, O God, Our Savior, and for the glory of Your name, O Lord, deliver us, and forgive us our sins for the sake of your name. [v.9] ... Lest they should say among the gentiles [gentibus]: Where is their God? And let him be made known among the nations before our eyes, By the revenging the blood of thy servants, which hath been shed [v.10].

Psalm 78 was keyed perfectly to the religious and military situation in which the crusaders found themselves after the loss of Jerusalem. And its sustained use from 1188 onwards further linked the crusading effort to secure the Holy Land to Old Testament models of holy war on the one hand and the broader drama of biblical history on the other. Clement's instructions do not survive, but we know that at this stage a number of institutions also took up a prayer known from earlier collections as one used in times of war (or against pagans) to ask God for help in defeating the enemy:

> Almighty and everlasting God, in whose hands are the power and rule of all kingdoms, in Your mercy look down in support of

---

[38] A good translation of the encyclical, *Audita tremendi*, can be found at Bird et al. 2013: 4–9. Mine differs somewhat and is based on the Latin provided in two different medieval versions of the document reproduced by two different chroniclers. These can be found at Hoveden 1868–1869: 2:326–329; Chroust 1928: 6–10.

[39] Our best evidence for the 1188 effort comes from Hoveden 1868–1869: 2:359–360. There are other echoes in the sources, which have been reviewed by Linder 2003b: 8–12.

Christians, that the heathen [*gentes*] who put trust in their own ferocity may be vanquished by the power of your right hand.[40]

The prayer dated to the 7th or 8th century, probably composed within the context of Frankish conquests of non-Christian territories, but the reference to heathens (*gentes*), like the reference in Psalm 78, was readily adaptable to the crusading context. It was already in use at Holy Sepulcher itself for their votive mass against pagans.[41] As it was, it became a standard of Crusade liturgy, adopted widely in spiritual warfare to support individual campaigns, and it would be used consistently through to the end of the Middle Ages.[42]

Another important prayer was composed in the second decade of the 13th century during the preparation for the Fifth Crusade (1217–1221). This prayer was part of an even wider liturgical effort to repent and beg God for aid. In 1213, Pope Innocent III (1198–1216), in his effort to shore up spiritual support for the Crusade at home, issued far-ranging instructions for liturgical intercessions throughout Christendom. In addition to the recitation of Psalm 78, Innocent both prescribed a new prayer, which asked God specifically to "seize the land that Your only begotten son has consecrated with His own blood from the hands of the enemies of the cross, [. . . and to] restore it to Christian worship," and ordered penitential processions to be enacted by both men and women, clergy and laity, on a monthly basis.[43] Innocent said clearly that the procession was to ask "merciful God to take away the opprobrium and confusion, to liberate from the hands of the pagans that Land in which he had established all the sacraments of our redemption, restoring it to the Christian people to the praise and glory of his holy name."[44] Like the penitential procession performed outside of the walls of Jerusalem in 1099, the point here was to expiate sin, demonstrate worthiness, and entreat God for worldly aid. But organized in this way across all of Christendom, the program was designed also to promote

[40] We know minimally that the prayer was used in London and by the Cistercians. Whether it was part of Clement III's instructions is not clear. The prayer is *Omnipotens sempiterne deus*, which has a long history before 1188. See Moeller and Clément 1992: 6:67 (no. 3846B, with many variants).

[41] Rome Angelica ms. 477, 166r, *Missa contra paganos*. On the Latin liturgy of the Holy Sepulcher, see Dondi 2004.

[42] Linder 2003b: see index listing at p. 405. And see discussion at Gaposchkin 2017a: 198–199, and throughout.

[43] A translation of the encyclical, *Quia Maior*, can be found in Bird et al. 2013: 107–112. For the Latin, see Migne 1844: 216:817–821.

[44] Bird et al. 2013: 111.

widescale social reform of Christian society and the broad mobilization of spiritual support for the targeted effort in Egypt (since the initial target of the Fifth Crusade was Cairo, the center of Ayyubid power). That is, as Gregory VIII had noted a generation earlier, the unworthiness was not that of the crusaders alone, but extended to all of Christianity society, and thus all of Christian society needed to reform and demonstrate expiatory penance before the Lord. To the extent that Innocent instructed all of Christendom to participate in these processions, this liturgical program was one way of inculcating the ideals of Crusade and Christian reform beyond the clerics and the crusaders themselves. That is, the regular performance of these invisible weapons and the expectation that the duty to pray for the success of the Crusade was incumbent upon all members of Christian society were also mechanisms of ideological propagation.

The evidence for the use of broad-based liturgical supplication increases in the liturgical, the narrative, and the documentary record from about 1220 onwards.[45] Popes and local ecclesiastical authorities issued prescriptions with increasing regularity throughout the 13th century. In the early 14th century, within a generation of the collapse of the Latin political presence in the Levant, as the papacy was looking to shore up a targeted military effort against the Mongols in Armenia, Clement V instructed every priest in Christendom to include three special prayers for Crusade success at every single mass recited.[46] By asking for these prayers to be recited at every single Eucharistic service, the pope had coopted the central rite of the Christian faith for military goals.

Those three prayers, what Amnon Linder dubbed "the Clementine triple set," were reproduced in a dizzying number of liturgical books throughout the next two centuries, with rubrics such as "Mass against the pagans," "Mass against the Turks," "Mass against the infidel," and as heretics (such as the Hussites in Bohemia) increasingly became the object of Crusade, "Mass against heretics." Linder documented an explosion of liturgical rites in the 14th and 15th centuries directed, especially after the fall on Constantinople in 1453, against the Ottoman Turks.[47] Based on the Clementine triple set, most of these included a whole new set of biblical readings and newly composed prayers in which the fear and dread of the Ottoman Turk as the agent

---

[45] Gaposchkin 2017a: 219–222, 309–323.
[46] Linder 2003b: 118–136.
[47] Linder 2003b: 175–273.

of the End-Times reverberated. Where earlier prayers enjoined God to
bring his terror down upon the enemy, many of these later liturgical
rites understood the Ottoman advance – and its threat to the Christian
political community in Christendom itself – as the onset of the
Apocalypse. In Eastern Europe especially, Christians used the mechanism of the liturgy to beg God for help and to implore Him that He might
once again come to the aid of His people as He had in ancient times.

By this point, prayers for crusading success, for the defeat of the
religious enemy on the battlefield, and for Christian victory were
included in liturgical books throughout Christendom. With the advent
of printing, these rites were further disseminated in early printed
missals and pontificals. By the 15th century, the ideal of religious
warfare against a religious enemy had been injected into the blood-
stream of Christian ritual, routinely reified through liturgical rites that
endowed the crusading project with sacramental meaning and salvific
potential. In this sense, the liturgy was one of the vectors in the long
development of Christian militantism and Christian holy war. It was in
this way that Crusade liturgy became, in a sense, one of the strategic
considerations of the papacy's military aims. It was also one measure of
the extent to which crusading and its prejudices insinuated themselves
into the very heart of Christian identity in the later Middle Ages.

References

Aspesi, Cara. 2017. "The Contribution of the Cantors of the Holy Sepulchre to
   Crusade History and Frankish Identity." In *Music, Liturgy, and the Shaping
   of History (800–1500).* Edited by Margot Fassler and Katie Bugyis. York
   Medieval Press. 278–296.
Bird, Jessalyn, Edward Peters, and James M. Powell, eds. 2013. *Crusade and
   Christendom: Annotated Documents in Translation from Innocent III to
   the Fall of Acre, 1187–1291.* University of Pennsylvania Press.
Bouquet, Martin, et al., eds. 1738–1904. *Recueil des historiens des Gaules et de
   la France,* vol. 19. Victor Palmé.
Bourgueil, Baldric of. 2014. *The Historia Ierosolimitana of Baldric of Bourgueil.*
   Edited by Steven Biddlecombe. Boydell & Brewer.
   2020. *"History of the Jerusalemites": A Translation of the "Historia
   Ierosolimitana."* Edited by Susan Edgington and Steven Biddlecombe.
   Crusading in Context. The Boydell Press.
Buc, Philippe. 2015. *Holy War, Martyrdom, and Terror: Christianity, Violence,
   and the West.* University of Pennsylvania Press.
Chroust, Anton. 1928. *Historia de expeditione Friderici imperatoris et quidam
   alii rerum gestarum fontes eiusdem expeditionis. MGH SS rerum
   Germanicarum, NS 5.* Weidmannsche Buchhandlung.

Constable, Giles. 2008a. "The Cross of the Crusaders." In *Crusaders and Crusading the Twelfth Century*. Ashgate. 45–91.

2008b. *Crusaders and Crusading in the Twelfth Century*. Ashgate.

Delaruelle, Etienne. 1980. *L'idée de croisade au moyen âge*. Bottega d'Erasmo.

Dondi, Cristina. 2004. *The Liturgy of the Canons Regular of the Holy Sepulchre of Jerusalem: A Study and Catalogue of the Manuscript Sources. Bibliotheca Victorina XVI*. Brepols.

Edbury, Peter W., ed. 1998. *The Conquest of Jerusalem and the Third Crusade, Crusade Texts in Translation*. Ashgate.

Erdmann, Carl. 1977. *The Origin of the Idea of Crusade*. Translated by Marshall W. Baldwin. Edited by Walter Goffart. Princeton University Press.

Flori, Jean. 1978. "Chevalerie et liturgie." *Le Moyen Age* 84: 266–278, 409–442.

1979. "Les origines de l'abouement chevaleresque: étude des remise d'armes et du vocabulaire qui les exprime." *Traditio* 35: 209–272.

1983. *L'idéologie du glaive: préhistoire de la chevalerie*. Librairie Droz.

1986. *L'Essor de la chevalerie, XIe–XIIe siècles*. Droz.

Franz, Adolph. 1909. *Die kirchlichen Benediktionen im Mittelalter*. 2 vols. Herder. Reprint, Verlag nova & vetera, 2006.

Gaposchkin, M. Cecilia. 2013. "From Pilgrimage to Crusade: The Liturgy of Departure, 1095–1300." *Speculum* 88(1): 44–91.

2015. "The Feast of the Liberation of Jerusalem in British Library Additional MS 8927 Reconsidered." *Mediaeval Studies* 77: 127–181.

2017a. *Invisible Weapons: Liturgy and the Making of Crusade Ideology*. Cornell University Press.

2017b. "The Liturgical Memory of 15 July 1099: Between History, Memory, and Eschatology." In *Remembering Crusades and Crusaders*. Edited by Megan Cassidy-Welch. Routledge. 34–48.

2018. "The Pre-Battle Processions of the First Crusade and the Creation of Militant Christian *Communitas*." *Material Religion: The Journal of Objects, Art and Belief* 14: 454–468.

Garrisson, Francis. 1965. "A propos des pèlerins et de leur condition juridique." In *Études d'histoire du droit canonique dediées à Gabriel Le Bras*, vol. 2. Sirey. 1165–1189.

Heim, François. 1992. *La théologie de la victoire: de Constantin à Théodose. Théologie historique 89*. Beauchesne.

Hoveden, Roger of. 1868–1869. *Chronica magistri Rogeri de Houedene*. Edited by William Stubbs. Vol. 4. Longmans, Green, Reader, and Dyer.

John, Simon. 2015. "The 'Feast of the Liberation of Jerusalem': Remembering and Reconstructing the First Crusade in the Holy City, 1099–1187." *Journal of Medieval History* 41: 409–431.

Keen, Maurice. 1984. *Chivalry*. Yale University Press.

Lapidge, Michael. 1991. *Anglo-Saxon Litanies of the Saints.H enry Bradshaw Society 106*. The Boydell Press.

Lieberman, Max. 2015. "A New Approach to the Knighting Ritual." *Speculum* 90: 391–423.

Linder, Amnon. 2003a. "A New Day, New Joy: The Liberation of Jerusalem on 15 July 1099." In *L'idea di Gerusalemme nella spiritualità cristiana del Medioevo: atti del Convegno internazionale in collaborazione con l'Instituto della Görres-Gesellschaft di Gerusalemme: Gerusalemme, Notre Dame of Jerusalem Center, 31 agosto–6 settembre 1999*. Libreria Editrice Vaticana. 46–64.

2003b. *Raising Arms: Liturgy in the Struggle to Liberate Jerusalem in the Late Middle Ages. Cultural Encounters in Late Antiquity and the Middle Ages 2*. Brepols.

Madden, Thomas F. 1999. *A Concise History of the Crusades. Critical Issues in History*. Rowman & Littlefield.

Maier, Christoph T. 1997. "Crisis, Liturgy and the Crusade in the Twelfth and Thirteenth Centuries." *Journal of Ecclesiastical History* 48(4): 628–657.

1999. "Mass, the Eucharist and the Cross: Innocent III and the Relocation of the Crusade." In *Pope Innocent III and His World*. Edited by John Moore. Ashgate. 351–360.

Markowski, Michael. 1984. "*Crucesignatus*: Its Origins and Early Usage." *Journal of Medieval History* 10: 157–165.

Mayer, Hans Eberhard. 1988. *The Crusades. Translated by John Gillingham*, 2nd edition. Clarendon Press.

McCormick, Michael. 1986. *Eternal Victory: Triumphal Rulership in Late Antiquity, Byzantium, and the Early Medieval West*. Cambridge University Press.

1992. "Liturgie et guerre des Carolingiens à la première croisade." In *Militia Christi' e crociata nei secoli XI–XII: atti della undecima settimana internazionale di stuiod Mendola*. Vita e pensiero. 209–240.

Migne, J.-P., ed. 1844. *Patrologia cursus completus*. 221 vols., *Series latina*. Paris.

Moeller, Eugene, and Jean-Marie Clément, eds. 1992. *Corpus Orationum*. 14 vols., *Corpus Christianorum Series Latina 160*. Brepols.

Morgan, Margaret Ruth. 1982. *La Continuation de Guillaume de Tyr (1184–1197)*. Librairie orientaliste P. Geuthner.

Murray, Alan V. 1998. "'Mighty Against the Enemies of Christ': The Relic of the True Cross in the Armies of the Kingdom of Jerusalem." In *The Crusades and Their Sources: Essays presented to Bernard Hamilton*. Edited by John France and William G. Zajac. Ashgate. 217–238.

Pennington, Kenneth. 1974. "The Rite for Taking the Cross in the Twelfth Century." *Traditio* 30: 429–435.

Purkis, William J. 2008. *Crusading Spirituality in the Holy Land and Iberia, c. 1095–1187*. The Boydell Press.

Reims, Robert of. 2005. *Robert the Monk's History of the First Crusade = Historia Iherosolimitana*. Translated by Carol Sweetenham. *Crusade Texts in Translation 11*. Ashgate.

2013. *The Historia Iherosolimitana of Robert the Monk*. Edited by Damien Kempf and Marcus Bull. The Boydell Press.

Riley-Smith, Jonathan. 1986. *The First Crusade and the Idea of Crusading*. University of Pennsylvania Press.

2008. *The Crusades, Christianity, and Islam*. Columbia University Press.

Rivard, Derek A. 2009. *Blessing the World: Ritual and Lay Piety in Medieval Religion*. Catholic University of America Press.

Rubenstein, Jay. 2011. *Armies of Heaven: The First Crusade and the Quest of the Apocalypse*. Basic Books.

2019. *Nebuchadnezzar's Dream: The Crusades, Apocalyptic Prophecy, and the End of History*. Oxford University Press.

Rufus, Fears J. 1981. "The Theology of Victory at Rome: Approaches and Problems." *Aufstieg und Niedergang der römischen Welt II* 17(2): 736–826.

Schein, Sylvia. 2005. *Gateway to the Heavenly City: Crusader Jerusalem and the Catholic West (1099–1187)*. Ashgate.

Schmale, Franz Josef, ed. 1972. *Frutolfs und Ekkehards Chroniken und die anonyme Kaiserchronik*. Wissenschaftliche Buchgesellschaft.

Siberry, Elizabeth. 1985. *Criticism of Crusading: 1095–1274*. Oxford University Press.

Stephenson, Paul. 2018. "The Imperial Theology of Victory." In *A Companion to the Byzantine Culture of War, ca. 300–1204*. Edited by Yannis Stouraitis. *Brill's Companions to the Byzantine World 3*. Brill. 23–58.

Tudebode, Peter. 1974. *Historia de Hierosolymitano itinere*. Memoirs of the American Philosophical Society v. 101. American Philosophical Society.

Tyerman, Christopher. 1998. *The Invention of the Crusades*. Macmillan Press.

2006. *God's War: A New History of the Crusades*. Belknap Press of Harvard University Press.

Vaux-de-Cernay, Peter of les. 1926. *Petri Vallium Sarnaii monachi Hystoria albigensis*, 3 vols. Edited by Pascal Guébin and Ernest Lyon. Champion.

1998. *The History of the Albigensian Crusade*. Edited by W. A. Sibly and M. D. Sibly. The Boydell Press.

Vogel, Cyrille, and Reinhard Elze, eds. 1963. *Le Pontifical romano-germanique du dixième siècle*, 2 vols. *Studi e testi 226–227*. Biblioteca apostolica Vaticana.

20 A Paradigm of Pious *Jihād* in the Muslim Ethos

OSMAN LATIFF

One of the premier points of the Qur'ānic message is the development of inner qualities of piety that culminate in closeness to God (*al-qurbatu ila-Allāh*). The Qur'ān instructs the faithful to be mindful of the workings of one's *nafs* (inner self) and the way it can both resonate with pietistic sentiments as well as undercut our potential to attain that closeness to God (Picken 2005: 119). It instructs on the development of inner qualities such as the fear or consciousness of God (*taqwa*), steadfastness (*istiqāma*), and patience (*ṣabr*). These can be pursued in a range of ways and for various ends. For example, the Qur'ān mentions the importance of abiding by *taqwa* in a diverse range of instances, such as fulfilling rights of inheritance (2:180), the establishing of prayer (6:72), the act of fasting (2:183), the pilgrimage of *Ḥajj* (2:197), in keeping company with the pious (43:67), in relation to marriage and divorce (2:241), in the law of contracts and discharging trusts (2:282–283), and others. One such time when *taqwa* is ordained for believers is during conflict as a kind of spiritual law governing the practice of *jihād*. God reminds the faithful: "for, indeed, God did succour you at Badr, when you were utterly weak. Remain, then, conscious of God, so that you might have cause to be grateful" (3:123).

THE PARADIGMATIC BATTLE OF BADR

The Battle of Badr (2 H/624 CE) noted in the above verse is paradigmatic in many ways. It represents the first physical confrontation and subsequent victory against the polytheists of Makkah and symbolises the potential of strong faith and the promise of God when such faith is upheld. What the verse stresses is that believers should remain steadfast in remembering God in the course of their engagements with an enemy, that they should rely on God during the battle, and to remember that victory against an enemy is essentially predicated on triumphing over one's inner self. The victory at Badr was a subsequent reminder that the early community, in spite of its fewer numbers and weaponry, overcame a larger and better-equipped adversary because of the community's devotion to the spirit of *jihād*, seen as a culmination of the strength of their faith and piety.

Later Muslims demonstrated how the *ummah* (Muslim community) could profit continuously from divine assistance if it remained true to both the outer struggle against an adversary and the inner struggle against one's *nafs*. In this light, the instructions of the second caliph 'Umar b. al-Khaṭṭāb (r. 13–23 H/634–644 CE) to his military general Sa'd b. Abī Waqqāṣ (d. 674 CE) who led the Muslims against the Sasanian army in the Battle of Qādisiyya (15 H/636 CE) further advance this *jihād* ethos. The letter demonstrates how inner preparation constituted a form of "spiritual armament" : "I instruct you to be weary of the sins of your army, for the sins of your army are more deadly to them than their enemy" (Al-Nuwayrī 1925: 6:168–170). That religious misdemeanours would inhibit progress in a military setting underlines the ways in which military leaders framed their struggles as cosmic ones in which personal acts of piety would call in divine assistance and in which there was a social acknowledgement that spiritual distance from God would result ultimately in loss in earthly and heavenly terms. These ideas come through clearly in the *Kitāb faḍāil al-jihād* (A Book on the Merits of Jihad) of Ṣalāḥ al-Dīn's biographer Abū-l Maḥāsin Yūsuf ibn Shaddād, a text he authored and presented to Ṣalāḥ al-Dīn in 1188 (Ibn Khallikān 1977: 7:88). A section of his text provides a hermeneutical discussion on a Qur'ānic verse from Surah al-Baqarah: 153. The verse instructs believers not to think of the martyred as dead, "but they are alive though you do not perceive." Ibn Shaddād explains that this is not a matter that is understood in a physical sense but instead in metaphysical terms:

> God instructed us in the preceding verse that we remember Him through obedience, with respect to all that has been prescribed for us, and that we thank Him for all that He has blessed us with of bounties. And we seek His assistance with the performance of our obligations which includes remembrance of God, gratitude, patience and prayer, in light of what God said: 'So remember me and I will remember you and be grateful unto me and do not deny me. O you who have attained to faith! Seek aid in steadfast patience and prayer: for, behold, God is with those who are patient in adversity' (3:170).
>
> (Ibn Shaddād 2007: 192)

What was therefore expected of the *jihād* participant was a devoted-
ness to God. Ibn Shaddād draws upon the structural relationship
between a verse on martyrdom and a preceding verse on one's spiritual
connection to God developed through His remembrance, through the
exhibiting of gratitude, and by upholding patience and prayer. These
situate the *jihād* in the frame of a holistic endeavour purposed for both
political and spiritual regeneration.

Though the Qur'ān therefore granted believers permission to physically engage with the Meccans of Quraysh as a defensive step to
safeguard the early Muslim community, it was regarded as a measure
of true faith that a believer should 'struggle' with his life and wealth to
draw closer to God, to "struggle" against the temptations of life, and to
fight the enemies of the faith. The Prophet is reported to have said: "The
mujāhid is he who struggles against himself in obedience to God" (al-
Albānī 1985: 2:81).

In the course of armed struggle as a physical response to the
Crusades, a major incentive for participants was the pursuit of martyrdom (*ṭalab al-shahāda*) as a way to attain heavenly favour (Cook 2007).
Such a pursuit gained new momentum following the Muslim capture of
the crusader state of Edessa in 538 H/1144 CE, and perhaps the most
noted example of this pursuit is that found with the Mālikī jurist Yūsuf
al-Findalāwī (d. 543 H/1148 CE) (Latiff 2018: 61–66). Al-Findalāwī was a
khaṭīb (sermoniser) at Bānyās, then a teacher of the Mālikī *madhhab* in
Damascus. In the chronicles, al-Findalāwī is recounted as a worthy
shahīd (witness/martyr), and this, importantly, is due to his elderly
age and physical weakness. A senior jurist from Damascus and a devout
ascetic, despite being encouraged to stay behind in the defence of
Damascus in the failed crusader siege of the city in 543 H/1148 CE, he
preferred instead to participate in the *jihād*. His devotion underscores
the *ṭalab al-shahāda* as an altruistic endeavour. Al-Findalāwī is victorious because of the honour that is accorded to him as a *shahīd* (witness/
martyr). His witnessing is for him as well as for God. His burial as a
martyr further ensures that he will be remembered as such, and it serves
posthumously as a lesson for those committed to the *jihād* and for those
still negligent in participating. Further still, through his martyrdom al-
Findalāwī was believed to be assigned a place in paradise – itself a form
of heavenly witnessing.

Dreams of the *shahīd* are also a form of witnessing. Such dreams are
common in the Muslim martyrdom tradition and are a way of confirm-
ing the status of martyrs after their deaths; the "witnessing" of the
martyr adds weight to his martyrdom. He also serves as a witness to

the splendour of God's bounty and stands as a proof for others. Ibn al-Athīr cites Ibn 'Asākir: Al-Ḥāfiẓ Abū l-Qāsim b. 'Asākir has mentioned in his *Tārīkh Dimashq* that one of the *'ulamā'* (religious scholars) related to him that he saw al-Findalāwī in a dream. He asked him: "How has God treated you? Where are you?" Al-Findalāwī replied: "He has forgiven me. We are in the Gardens of Eden, face to face on couches" (Ibn al-Athīr 2006: 9:158–160). Such heavenly comfort finds its description in the Qur'ān (37:44).

In Usāma b. Munqidh's account, his attention to the spiritual components that made up his sacrificial struggle are underscored: "Among men there are those that go to battle just as the Companions of the Prophet (may God be pleased with them) used to go to battle: to obtain entrance to Paradise, and not to pursue some selfish desire or to gain a reputation. Here is an example ..." (Abū Shāma 2002: 1:205–206; Ibn al-Qalānisī 2002: 284; Ibn Munqidh 2008: 108). This instance of an old man relinquishing his religiously sanctioned permit to abstain from fighting must be understood in light of the *jihād al-nafs* (struggle against one's self) paradigm. In this respect, al-Findalāwī exercised a kind of *zuhd* (abstention) in his insistence; he was, in the minds of the faithful, unconcerned about the comforts of this world and hoped through his martyrdom to "purchase" a place in the hereafter. Predictably, such an ideal was also employed in the *Kitāb al-Jihād* of 'Alī b. Ṭāhir al-Sulamī (430–431 H/1039 CE to 499–500 H/1106 CE). Al-Sulamī was a Shāfi'ī Damascene grammarian who taught in the Umayyad Mosque of Damascus. His *Kitab al-Jihād* (Book of *Jihād*) (498 H/1105 CE) is believed to be the first treatise on *jihād* to be produced after the arrival of the Franks in the Near East. He was a source of much discussion because of his rapid assimilation of the aims of the crusaders. Unlike some contemporaries, he did not confuse the crusaders with Byzantines; rather, he described the assault on Jerusalem and the crusader expansion as a Christian "*jihād*." For al-Sulamī, the capture of Jerusalem was part of a wider Christian military scheme that began with conflicts in Sicily and Spain. Al-Sulamī's treatise is of immense significance for the information it provides about the Muslims' moral condition and political weakness, which he saw as reasons for the crusader victories. He dedicated a short, albeit important section to these aspects entitled: "The joining of struggle against the self and struggle against the enemy – hoping for a good reward and recompense." In this section, al-Sulamī cited an incident in which some inhabitants of Damascus approached a certain Abū Muslim, "a fighter in the land of the Romans," who was fasting during his travels. The Damascenes questioned him: "What makes you fast while you are travelling, and [you know that] eating has been permitted for you during fighting and travelling?" Considering his state of fasting as an act of purification that would have a significant bearing on the act of his physical struggle, he replied: "When the fighting is ready, I eat, and then I will be prepared for it and [be] strong; indeed horses do not run to far ends while they are stout but they run while they are lean" (al-Sulamī 2007: 135). These examples were purposeful in demonstrating the twin nature of the *jihād* and the pious intent intrinsic to its execution and success.

As the aforementioned verse from Surah al-Baqarah: 153 underscores, one of the repeated themes in the Qur'ānic discourse therefore is the importance of exhibiting reliance on God through prayer. Supplications, both Qur'ānic and those taught by the Prophet, are encouraged throughout the day and night and constitute a form of *dhikr* (remembrance of God), and these pertain to morning and evening invocations, to times of joy and distresses, on entering and leaving one's residence, on travelling, on settling, and also to military engagements – to call upon God for patience, protection, and victory. An example of a supplication for victory in battle that made its way as a poetic appeal is found in the context of early Frankish interest in Egypt and the Frankish recognition of its vital geographical and economic position. This aroused the fears of poets such as the Yemeni poet and historian and loyal Fāṭimid supporter 'Umāra al-Yamanī (d. 571 H/1175 CE), who, upon hearing of crusader interest in Egypt, particularly during Shāwar's[1] alliance with Amalric in the early 1160s, composed a prayer-like poem in which he beseeches God for the protection of Islam:

> O Lord, I see that Egypt is beginning to notice the enemy, after it was previously asleep.
> So let the path of Islam remain in Egypt, and protect its decades of guidance so that it does not go astray.
> And grant us from yourself support that will protect us from this trial that only intensifies its flame.
> (Badawī 1979: 478; Latiff 2018: 198)

There is a tone of desperation running through the verses of the poem. Though the threat was a real one, the poet does not divulge the fears extant in the Muslim population, nor does he highlight the strengths of the formidable approaching Frankish army. The poet

---

[1] For more information on Shāwar, see Ibn Khallikān 1977: 2:418–422.

stresses that it is Islam itself that is threatened by the enemy's occupation, and that God is most concerned with His religion and its adherents. This type of entreaty resembles that made by the Prophet himself
at the Battle of Badr mentioned earlier, wherein he prayed to God for the
survival of the Muslims: "O God, they are barefooted, so carry them;
naked, so clothe them; O God if this contingent from the nation of Islam
is destroyed, then you will not be worshipped on earth" (Al-Wāqidī
2006: 54). The Frankish threat in 'Umāra al-Yamanī's poem is described
as a *fitna*, a trial. *Fitna* often denotes a religious trial and temptation – a
real danger to the Muslim body analogous to punishment and social
tumult (Qur'ān 2:193, 5:71, 8:73).

Poems such as 'Umāra al-Yamanī's served as important stimuli for
the anti-Frankish *jihād*. Poetry was a rousing literary vehicle, and the
one most closely connected to the *jihād* rulers in that it drew on the
public image they wanted to project to their subjects. The poetry of this
period was more than an art form; it was also a form of political
commentary, and one that was integral to reinforcing the place of
Islam, its sacred destinations, its enemies, and its champions during a
period of spiritual and physical upheaval. The *jihād* poetry was functional in that it could be recited at key historical moments.

NŪR AL-DĪN ZENGĪ AND THE CONQUERING OF ONE'S *NAFS* (SELF)

Where Islam was about individual piety, humility, and a taking of refuge
from the trappings of the worldly life as shown through al-Findalāwī, it
was Nūr al-Dīn Zengī in the course of the anti-Frankish struggle who
stands out as uniting both pietistic concern and military struggle.
Described by one poet as a possessor of two *jihāds*, one against himself
and the other against the enemy, he was very much presented as such by
his admired contemporaries (Abū Shāma 2002: 1:128). The pietistic
focus in Nūr al-Dīn served the purpose of making authentic the
examples of Islam's past champions, upon which he based his *jihād*.
The flourishing of Sufism at this time allowed for Nūr al-Dīn and his
entourage of holy men to generate a pious warrior ethos that was
pertinent in shaping the spirit of the anti-Frankish *jihād*. As Lapidus
notes, 'the equation of holy men and martyrs with the spiritual universe
became an inherent aspect of Islamic religious culture' (Lapidus 2002:
176). Nūr al-Dīn's social practice was sometimes questioned by the
poets of his time, who perhaps sought to inspire in him a piety that

would have complemented the new spiritual focus of the 5th/11th century (Latiff 2018: 150–156).

On one occasion, Nūr al-Dīn was severely censured for misappropriating taxes and for overlooking displays of religious negligence in his army. He was once queried: "How can you be supported when you have wine and drums in your army?" (al-Mutanabbī 1975: 189; Ibn Kathīr 2004: 12:299). Such an idea, predicated on ensuring divine approval in military undertakings, is also found in the *Dīwān* of al-Mutanabbī[2]: "And do not think that glory is found in alcohol and female singers; there is no glory except in a sword and in fighting" (al-Mutanabbī 1975: 189).

Texts like al-Mutanabbī's *Dīwān* and Abū Tammām's *Ḥamāsa* were memorised in their entirety by rulers who sought to draw inspiration from ideals of courtly virtue, chivalry, and religious mores. Ṣalāḥ al-Dīn, for example, was believed to have memorised the *Ḥamāsa* in full. The poem cited by Ibn Kathīr that severely scorns Nūr al-Dīn and calls on him to consider the consequences of his actions in light of the hereafter reflects a requirement that taps into pietistic concern: "And though you have finished drinking wine, you have recklessly drunk from the cup of oppression" (Ibn Kathīr 2004: 12:299).

It was expected that Nūr al-Dīn would live up to the reputation of his predecessors in line with instructions found in the Baḥr al-Fawāʾid, anonymous treatises mostly written in Persian in the middle of the 6th/ 12th century. It belongs to the "mirrors for princes" genre that was popular in the mediaeval Islamic period. These texts were compiled to provide indispensable Islamic instructions for those invested with political authority, making use of anecdotes, maxims, and prophetic traditions attributed to kings and saints (Latiff 2018: 10). The Baḥr al-Fawāʾid teaches:

> Even though the renown of the might of a son of Adam reach east and west, and men from east to west acknowledge his rule and pay taxes to his diwan, he yet must die alone, be laid in the grave alone, and pay his accounts alone.
>
> (Meisami 1991: 50)

---

[2] Al-Mutanabbī was a professional poet who travelled through Syria seeking patronage; he found it most illustriously with the Hamdanid ruler of Aleppo, Sayf al-Dawla. The Arab prince fought dozens of battles against the Byzantines and became an inspiration for later *jihād* leaders. It was during the time al-Mutanabbī spent with his patron that he composed his most celebrated verses extolling the *jihād*, verses containing imagery that was utilised repeatedly by poets in the age of the crusades. For more information on al-Mutanabbī, see Issawi 1972: 236–239; Heinrichs 1990: 120–139; Larkin 2006: 542–544.

The aforementioned instruction from the Baḥr al-Fawā'id evokes the kind of pietistic sentiments found in the chronicles that established Nūr al-Dīn's reputation as a devout warrior committed to the Islamic cause. While these chronicles provide examples of his magnanimity and piety, the poetry also commemorates him as one inspired by Islam's early and illustrious predecessors. Although many of these texts, mainly those composed in Arabic, served largely literary functions, some of those written in Persian emanated from the period of Saljūq political ascendancy and are particularly relevant to understanding how ideas about governance may have filtered through to *jihad* leaders of the 6th/12th and 7th/13th centuries. In light of the date of the text's composition – which coincides with the promotion of Nūr al-Dīn's *jihād* programme – the Baḥr al-Fawā'id is particularly relevant for its sections on *jihād* and *taṣawwuf* (Sufism).

> The above poem, cited by Ibn Kathīr and censuring Nūr al-Dīn, continues:
>
> (4) You prevented cups, and now upon you is the sin of the distribution of forbidden cups.
>
> (5) What would you say on a day when you are carried to the grave by yourself? And Munkar and Nakīr [angels of the grave] come to you.
>
> (6) What would you say if you stood on the station of the Day of Judgement by yourself, humiliated, and with a heavy account?
>
> (7) And clinging to you are the rights of others [whom you have wronged], and on the day of judgement you become a chained criminal.
>
> (8) And your soldiers desert you, and you lie in the narrowness of the grave.
>
> (9) You would wish that you were not a guardian and that people would not have called you an *amīr* [leader].
>
> (10) And know that after having been honoured, you will be subject to a pit in the world of the dead, and you will be despicable.
>
> (11) And you will be gathered without clothes, sad, crying, and worried, and you will not find anyone from creation there to help you. ...
>
> (14) [So p]repare for yourself a witness that can deliver you on the day of appointment, and on the day when there is no concealment.
>
> (Ibn Kathīr 2004: 12:299; Latiff 2018: 159–160)

This poem is similar to the *zuhdiyya* (poem of asceticism) type of poetry that contains several motifs evocative of the ephemeral nature of life, the drawing close of death, and the *akhirah* (next life) – namely, the interrogation of the occupants of the grave and divine accountability. In the poem directed to Nūr al-Dīn, mention of the *ḥisāb* (account), *yawm al-ḥisāb* (day of reckoning), and *qabr* (grave) are striking forms of religious imagery and are intended to appeal directly to Nūr al-Dīn's pietistic sentiments – that he not be hindered hereafter by his lack of spiritual concern – and the way such inattentiveness might negatively shape his political policies. The simple message was intended to strike a chord with Nūr al-Dīn and to remind him that it was essential that the *jihād* fighter did not transgress religious boundaries. Though we might ascribe *jihād* sentiments to much of such poetry, as this poem shows, some of this poetry ties in with other religious undercurrents like spirituality and the *jihād al-nafs* paradigm.

The Sufi foci on the hereafter and on self-accountability – invigorated by the 5th-/11th-century theologian and ascetic Abū Ḥāmid al-Ghazālī (d. 505 H/1111 CE) – were in fact deemed imperative for everyone, especially an *amīr* (leader). An anecdote, for example, in al-Ghazālī's *Naṣīḥat al-mulūk* sounds strikingly similar to the verses addressed to Nūr al-Dīn: "Adorn yourself with righteousness, for at the tribunal of the resurrection no man will lend you his adornment" (al-Ghazālī 1964: 73).

Nūr al-Dīn likely found solace in his spirituality, and much of the poetry written for him addresses this notion. One of the main poets who composed numerous adulatory verses for him was Abū 'Abdallāh Muḥammad al-Ḥalabī b. al-Qaysarānī, better known as Ibn al-Qaysarānī (Latiff 2018: 14). Born in the port city of Acre, he later moved to Caesarea and was also well-versed in astronomy and philology. He later travelled to Damascus and then to Aleppo and found favour and fortune in the patronage of 'Imād al-Dīn Zangī and later his son, Nūr al-Dīn. For Ibn al-Qaysarānī, Nūr al-Dīn is "as a worshipper, succour for the *abdāl*, and in fighting, the king of lions" (Abū Shāma 2002: 1:264). The *abdāl* are believed by Sufis to be an enigmatic group who come to the aid of Muslims in times of difficulty. Ibn Kathīr corroborates Nūr al-Dīn's attention to such reproaches by narrating an episode in which a group of Sufis recount what they heard from some Franks in the kingdom of Jerusalem. The jurist Abū l-Fatḥ Banjīr al-Ashtarī (d. 579 H/1183 CE), who was said to have composed an abridged life history of Nūr al-Dīn, said:

We heard that he turned to a group of Sufis regarding what they said when they entered Jerusalem for *ziyāra* [visitation] in the days when the Franks had taken Jerusalem, and he heard them say that al-Qusaym b. al-Qusaym thinks that Nūr al-Dīn is being helped by God in secret, for [otherwise] he will not triumph and will not be victorious over us with the size of his army and soldiers, but he will indeed triumph over us and be victorious with supplication and night prayers for indeed he prays in the night and raises his hands to God and beseeches Him, and indeed He answers him [Nūr al-Dīn] and gives him what he asks for and so he triumphs over us. He said: This is the true speech of the unbelievers.

(Abū Shāma 2002: 1:118; Latiff 2018: 162)

This anecdote is valuable not for its historical accuracy, but for the religious sentiments that the author intended to arouse among the Muslim population of Syria. In light of the presentation of Nūr al-Dīn, the idea of personal and public reform (*iṣlāḥ*) becomes a vital feature for social and military success. Such an accommodating and utilising of Sufis to play an important role in the spirit of the anti-Frankish *jihād* is revealing for what it highlights about divine assistance assured through public and private displays of piety and the paying of homage to holy men by whose presence and supplication the *jihād* would succeed. The emphasis on secrecy of devotion, on night prayers, and on supplication underscores the ways in which Muslims believed victory was made possible.

Together with the *'ulamā'*, Sufis therefore were a popular group that congregated in the courts of Nūr al-Dīn and Ṣalāḥ al-Dīn. The Ayyūbids, a dynasty founded by Ṣalāḥ al-Dīn that ruled Egypt, Syria-Palestine, and parts of northern Mesopotamia, endowed numerous Sufi lodges (*khānqāhs*), and Ṣalāḥ al-Dīn further demonstrated his commitment to Sufis by allotting them travel stipends. Because the "power and appeal to the masses of everyday Muslim believers came from faith in the miraculous power of saints" (Lapidus 2002: 254), the closeness of saints to temporal rulers served to legitimise the latter's authority and provide the religious conditions necessary for divine assistance. An outstanding example of this can be observed in a scene in which Nūr al-Dīn's men advised him to cease the stipends distributed to the jurists, the poor, the Sufis, and Qur'ān reciters in favour of the army. Nūr al-Dīn retorted:

By God, I do not hope for victory except by those men, for indeed you are provided and given support by your weak ones. How can I stop favours for a people who fight for me with arrows that do not

miss while I am asleep in my bed and change them for those who do
not fight for me except when they see me with arrows that miss and
hit? Those people [the first group] will have a portion of the *bayt al-
māl* [royal treasury] and I will spend from it for them, how can I give
it to other than them?

(Ibn Wāṣil 1953: 1:136; Latiff 2018: 21)

His critics were silenced. These displays of piety revealed that both
personal and public *jihāds* were sought. They emphasised the spiritual
ethos of the *jihād* and showed the depth and meaning of the relationship
between religious and military leaderships (Latiff 2018: 17–27).

A SYMBOLIC STRUGGLE OF SACREDNESS

What the Muslim/crusader struggle generated is a theological confrontation framed around the sacred symbols of the two faiths in which each
side legitimised its encounter by underscoring the preponderance of its
connection with the sacred. This might be in relation to land, sacred
sites, symbols, and personalities. This is reflected in a telling description by the 13th-century influential Damascene teacher and preacher
Abū l-Muzaffar Sibṭ b. al-Jawzī (d. 654 H/1256 CE) in his account of the
siege of Damascus during the Second Crusade in 543 H/1148 CE. He
recounts that "[t]he whole population, men, women, and children,
assembled in the Great Mosque and 'Uthmān's Qurʾān was displayed,
and the people sprinkled their heads with ashes and wept and humbled
themselves. And God heard their prayers" (Sibṭ ibn al-Jawzī 1952:
8:198). The spiritual aura that surrounded the Qurʾānic copy of
'Uthmān' ibn 'Affān (656 CE), martyred whilst engaged in its recitation,
is brought out vividly by Ibn Jubayr:

> In the east corner of the New Maqsurah, inside the mihrab, is a large
> cupboard containing one of the Korans of (the Caliph) 'Uthman –
> may God hold him in His favour. It is the copy (of the definitive
> recension) which he sent to Syria. This cupboard is opened daily
> after the prayers, and people seek God's blessings by touching and
> kissing the Book; and the press around it is very great.

(Ibn Jubayr 1952: 279; 2001: 209)

Though overt displays of penitence on the Muslim side were certainly not lacking, and whilst the sprinkling of ashes is not customary
religious practice, it may, however, say something about the kind of
humility that the community deemed necessary for spiritual success
and divine favour. Chamberlain notes that "where we may never know

whether particular people in fact had the 'honour' or 'piety' that a particular source attributed to them, these anecdotes are likely to have been 'true' in the sense that these stories were believed by their contemporaries" (Chamberlain 2002: 19). Such symbolic acts of penitence can also be observed in Sibṭ b. al-Jawzī's own participation in a raid on Frankish settlements after a sermon he delivered in Nablus in the summer of 606 H/1210 CE. There, Sibṭ b. al-Jawzī dramatically awarded al-Muʿaẓẓam ʿĪsā (d. 624 H/1227 CE) with the hair he had collected from penitents in Damascus; the raid followed (Talmon-Heller 2007: 133).

References

Abū Shāma, Shihāb al-Dīn. 2002. *Kitāb al-Rawḍatayn fī akhbār al-dawlatayn al-nūriyya wa-l-ṣalāḥiyya*, 4 vols. Edited by Ibrāhīm Shams al-Dīn.. Dār al-Kutub al-ʿIlmiyya.

al-Albānī, Muḥammad. 1985. *Silsilat al-aḥādīth al-ṣaḥīḥa*. Muʾassasat al-Kutub al-Thaqāfiyya.

al-Ghazālī, Abū Ḥāmid Muhammad. 1964. *Naṣīḥat al-mulūk (Ghazālī's Book of Counsel for Kings)*. Translated by F. R. C. Bagley. Edited by Jalāl Humāʾī and H. D. Isaacs. Oxford University Press.

al-Mutanabbī, Abū al-Ṭayyib Aḥmad. 1975. *Dīwān al-Mutanabbī*. Dār Bayrūt lil-Ṭibāʿa wa-l-Nashr.

Al-Nuwayrī, Shihāb al-Dīn. 1925. *Nihāyat al-arab fī funūn al-adab*. Dār al-Kutub.

al-Sulamī, ʿAlī ibn Ṭāhir. 2007. "Kitāb al-Jihād." In *Arbaʿa kutub fī l-jihād min ʿasr al-ḥurūb al-ṣalībiyya*. Edited by Suhayl Zakkār. Dār al-Takwīn. 41–165.

Al-Wāqidī, Abu ʿAbd-Allāh Muḥammad. 2006. *Kitāb al-Maghāzī*. Edited by M. Jones. ʿAlam al-Kutub.

Badawī, Aḥmad Aḥmad. 1979. *Al-Ḥayāt al-adabiyya fī ʿasr al-ḥurūb al-ṣalībiyya bi-Miṣr wa-l-Shām*. Dār Nahdat Miṣr.

Chamberlain, Michael. 2002. *Knowledge and Social Practice in Medieval Damascus, 1190–1350*. Cambridge University Press.

Cook, David. 2007. *Martyrdom in Islam*. Cambridge University Press.

Heinrichs, Wolfhart. 1990. "The Meaning of Mutanabbī." In *Poetry and Prophecy: The Beginnings of a Literary Tradition*. Edited by J. L. Kugel. Cornell University Press. 120–139.

Ibn al-Athīr, Abū al-Ḥasan ʿAlī. 2006. *Al-Kāmil fī l-tārīkh*, vol. 9. Edited by ʿUmar ʿAbd al-Salām al-Tadmurī. Dār al-Kutub al-ʿArabī.

Ibn al-Qalānisī, Abū Yaʿlā Ḥamzah. 2002. *The Damascus Chronicle of the Crusades*. Translated by H. A. R. Gibb. Dover Publications.

Ibn Jubayr, Abū al-Ḥusayn Muḥammad. 1952. *The Travels of Ibn Jubayr*. Translated by Roland Broadhurst. J. Cape.

——— 2001. *Tadhkira al-akhbār ʿan ittifāqāt al-asfār*. Edited by ʿAlī Aḥmad Kanʿān. Dār al-Maʿārif.

Ibn Kathīr, ʿImād al-Dīn Ismāʿīl. 2004. *Al-Bidāya wa-l-nihāya*, vols 12 and 13. Dār al-Taqwā.

Ibn Khallikān, Aḥmad. 1977. *Wafayāt al-a ʾyān wa-anbā ʾ abnā ʾ al-zamān*, 8 vols. Edited by I. ʿAbbās. Dār Ṣādir.

ibn Munqidh, Usāma. 2008. *The Book of Contemplation: Islam and the Crusades*. Translated by P. M. Cobb. Penguin Classics.

Ibn Shaddād, Bahā ʾ al-Dīn. 2007. "Kitāb faḍāʾil al-jihād." In *Arbaʿa kutub fī l-jihād min ʿaṣr al-ḥurūb alṣalībiyya*. Edited by S. Zakkār. Dār al-Takwīn. 183–273.

Ibn Wāṣil, Muḥammad. 1953. *Mufarrij al-kurūb fī akhbār Banī Ayyūb*, vols 1–2. Edited by Jamāl al-Dīn al-Shayyāl. Dār al-Kutub.

Issawi, Charles. 1972. "Al-Mutanabbī in Egypt (957–962)." In *Medieval and Middle Eastern Studies: In Honor of Aziz Suryal Atiya*. Edited by S. A. Hanna. E. J. Brill. 236–239.

Lapidus, Ira. 2002. *A History of Islamic Societies*. Cambridge University Press.

Larkin, Margaret. 2006. "Al-Mutanabbī, Abūʾl-Ṭayyib Aḥmad b. al-Ḥusayn al-Juʿfi." In *Medieval Islamic Civilization*. Edited by Josef W. Meri. Routledge. 542–544.

Latiff, Osman. 2018. *The Cutting Edge of the Poet's Sword: Muslim Poetic Responses in the Crusades*. Brill.

Meisami, Julie Scott. (trans. and ed.). 1991. *The Sea of Precious Virtues (Baḥr al-Fawā ʾid): A Medieval Islamic Mirror for Princes*. University of Utah Press.

Picken, Gavin N. 2005. "*Tazkiyat al-nafs*: The Qurʾānic Paradigm." *Journal of Qurʾanic Studies* 7: 101–127.

Sibṭ ibn al-Jawzī, Shams al-Dīn. 1952. *Mirʾāt al-zamān fī tārīkh al-aʾyān*, vol. 8, parts 1 and 2. Maṭbaʿat Majlis Dāʾirat al-Maʿārif al-ʿUthmānīyah.

Talmon-Heller, Daniella. 2007. *Islamic Piety in Medieval Syria: Mosques, Cemeteries and Sermons under the Zangids and Ayyūbids (1146–1260)*. Brill.

21 Fierce Goddesses of India: Durga and Kali

JUNE MCDANIEL

While the warriors of India through the centuries have been primarily male, the great deities of war have been female. Durga is associated with kings and armies, warhorses and weapons and great battles between kingdoms and countries. Kali, on the other hand, tends to be associated with more personal concerns, with the inner warfare between devotion and desire. She is the goddess of *tantrikas* at the burning ground and yogis, devotees and magicians. While Durga emphasizes ethics and moral virtue, Kali is more ambiguous, and people may call upon her for helpful or destructive ends. Durga is a goddess who comes down to help in earthly difficulties, while Kali is goddess of life, death and rebirth, and her realm is primarily the supernatural.

DURGA

Durga was adopted into the Hindu pantheon as a warrior goddess – there are images of her slaying a buffalo by the 4th century CE, and there are many descriptions of her in the puranic texts by the 6th century CE (Kinsley 1988). While she has several origin stories in the *Puranas* (as a form of Parvati or as Vishnu's power of illusion), her major story comes from the *Markandeya Purana*, in the section popularly known as the "*Devi Mahatmyam*" In this story she is both a created being, given power by the gods to defeat a demon who had a special power (that he could never be killed by a man), and a preexisting force, the supreme, primordial Prakriti, the active opposite of the inert Purusha. As the *Devi Mahatmyam* describes her: "She creates this entire universe, both moving and unmoving. It is she who, when propitious, becomes a boon-giver to human beings for their final liberation. She is the supreme knowledge, the cause of final liberation, and eternal; she is the cause of the bondage of transmigration, and the sovereign over all lords" (*Devi Mahatmyam* 1955: I.54–58). Though she is created in this story, she herself also emanates other goddesses, such as Kali and the fierce *matrika* goddesses or Mothers. Accompanied by these goddesses, she conquers the demon armies (which are exclusively male).

The story of Durga in the *Devi Mahatmyam* revolves around three battles with demons: Durga fought with Madhu and Kaitabha, with Shumbha and Nishumbha and their armies and with Mahishasura and his armies. Her role was a minor one in the first battle – she merely emerged from Vishnu's body, so that he would wake up and kill the demons (which he did).

In the second battle, which is best known, there was a war between the gods (*devas*) and their ruler, Indra, and the demons (*asuras*) and their ruler, Mahishasura. The demons won, and Mahishasura became the lord of heaven, expelling the gods. Brahma, Vishnu and Shiva concentrated their anger into a great light, and they were joined by the other gods; this light shone like a blazing mountain and then coalesced into a woman's form. The lights from the various gods became her limbs, and she was given weapons, jewelry and armor by the gods, as well as a lion to ride. Her crown touched the sky, her feet shook the earth. She conquered the armies of demons, even those who danced and fought after their heads had been chopped off. She was called various names and titles in the battle: Chandika, Durga, Ambika, Bhadrakali, Ishvari, Bhagavati, Shri and Devi. She fought the demon king Mahishasura, who could shift forms at will. Though he became a lion, an elephant and a buffalo, she conquered each form, and finally he emerged from his slain buffalo form as a man and was killed in that form. She is again praised by the gods as the origin of the worlds, as primordial Prakriti, as supreme knowledge, the cause of liberation and the origin of the Vedas. Pleased by the hymns, she promised future gifts, especially help in times of danger.

This help is shown in the next chapter. The demon kings Shumbha and Nishumbha also conquered Indra's heaven. The gods remembered that the goddess had offered to return, and they again sang hymns to her. She came down in the form of Parvati and divided into two bodies: a dark one called Kalika and bright one called Ambika. The lower demons Chanda and Munda saw Ambika and reported back to the demon kings that they should possess this woman. When a matchmaker came, Ambika/Durga responded that she could only marry the man who conquers her in battle. The demon kings sent their armies, which she conquered, and then sent the demons Chanda and Munda. When Durga saw them, her skin became black with anger, and Kali emerged from her forehead (it is not clear if this is the earlier Kalika or a different goddess). Kali devoured elephants and riders, ate weapons and killed Chanda and

Munda (Durga then gave her the name Chamunda, as she was the conqueror of Chanda and Munda).

Then the demon kings and their remaining armies came out and surrounded Durga. At that moment, the creative energies (*saktis*) of the various gods came forth in female form as an army to fight the demons. When drops of blood from the demon Raktabija fell to the earth and created new demons, Kali drank all of the blood so that no new demons would arise, and Raktabija was conquered. When Shumbha accused Durga of being dependent upon her female army to win the battle, she absorbed them all back into herself, saying that they were only her own powers. Both demon kings were slain in the battle.

Durga saved the gods and the world and stated that she would incarnate on other occasions when necessary. She would respond to the prayers of her devotees in times of danger, such as forest fires, wars, capture by enemies, storms at sea, threats by wild animals or generally affliction by pain, as well as if the devotee is robbed, imprisoned or in danger of execution (*Devi Mahatmyam* 12.24–28). She shows her willingness to give gifts to disciples by granting one devotee kingship and another liberation after they prayed to her for three years (and offered their own blood). She has power over creation and destruction, protecting the world now but destroying it at the end of the age (*Devi Mahatmyam* 12.40). The word "Durga" in Sanskrit literally means "impassable," "invincible, unassailable," "beyond defeat." It is related to the Sanskrit root *durg*, which means "fortress, something difficult to defeat or pass." She is the defender who will not let enemies defeat her.

Durga is a goddess with many faces. During her annual Durga Puja festival (the Navaratri or nine nights *mela*), Durga is often worshipped as a different warlike deity on each night (largely following her roles in the *Devi Mahatmyam*). Over time, the warrioress Durga came to represent the power of good over evil in mainstream Hindu society, of dedication to virtue over such weaknesses as lust and desire for power. Many informants have told me that this is the real meaning of the statues displayed on Durga Puja, showing how a woman's virtue can conquer the lust of even an all-powerful demon. Sometimes there is an ethical explanation and sometimes a more allegorical one. Durga is fair and beautiful in her statues and images, with perfect features, beyond earthly lust and desire.

Durga Puja or Navaratri (nine nights) is one of the biggest annual festivals in India. Durga is worshipped both in public, with large statues and crowds, and in private through home services in which smaller statues are set up. She is portrayed as strong and beautiful, with ten arms, carrying weapons, riding a lion and conquering the buffalo demon.

Durga Puja is celebrated throughout India. In the Punjab, Durga Puja was a royal festival of the war goddess, in which Durga presided over military activities, and ancient rulers started military operations following the festivities. There were processions with maharajahs, elephants, infantry, trumpets and drums, as well as animal sacrifices. However, this style of celebration largely disappeared with Indian independence (Thomas 1960: 5). Today, there are political and social problems shown in the Durga shrines that one finds at many street corners during the annual holiday of Durga Puja, especially in West Bengal. While many are simply images for worship, showing a beautiful goddess defeating the evil and lustful demon Mahishasura, others display social commentary. Durga may be shown as Mother Earth getting rid of the demon Pollution, made of recycled waste to show the problems of garbage collection and recycling, as a goddess liberating the elderly left in old age homes, as a liberator of sex workers from bondage, as a tribal woman fighting for her rights or as a savior of refugees who are symbolized by shuttlecocks and a badminton net. The demon may be shown to represent black money (money that is not declared to the Indian government and taxed), corrupt landlords, dishonest businesspeople, violent neighbors, greedy politicians and illiteracy, censorship and repression. While many problems cannot be discussed openly, in newspapers or in public, their symbolic presence in religious art allows special leeway for problems to be discussed. It is artistic condemnation, a subtle form of warfare.

Durga has had a political role in Indian history, from the worship by kings for success in battle to symbolizing the land that needs to be freed; she became Mother India, Bharat Mata or Bharat Devi. She suffers when her children do, and she calls upon them to rescue her. They do so through protest, war, terrorism, revolution or other political actions. From the mid-19th century, the goddess had become a symbol of Indian nationalism, the Divine Mother who is herself the land of India. This was seen especially vividly in Bankimchandra Chatterji's novel *Anandamath*, based upon the sannyasi rebellion of the 18th century. From this novel came the "Bande mataram" (Bow to the Mother) anthem, in which the country is identified with the goddess. It was sung by those opposing the partition of India and by those in favor of self-rule (*swaraj*) for India. It became the battle cry of the freedom fighters and later the national song of India, as important as the national anthem. Devotion to the goddess showed patriotism and the willingness to fight.

By the end of the 18th century, Durga Puja became a front for training freedom fighters in the use of weapons, as well as in martial arts, wrestling and boxing. The British were told that these were religious rites. By 1906, Calcutta housed arms caches that were worshipped during Durga Puja, with spears, swords and knives substituting for the clay figure of the goddess. The worship of weapons was called *birashtami puja*, the ritual of honoring heroes. This began the trend of social protest during Durga Puja, along with statues of Durga depicting her killing colonial soldiers in military uniforms.

Though India is no longer ruled by kings, the political worship of weapons for Durga Puja still continues; there have been reports of the Jharkhand police worshipping AK-47 rifles and other firearms and of Narendra Modi, the current Prime Minister of India, worshipping machine guns, swords and axes as *shastra* (weapon) *puja* while he was Chief Minister of Gujarat (Bapat and Mabbett 2017: 174). Images were published online of him performing the worship of guns, swords and other weapons in 2013, and he also stated: "While the weapons are an integral part of the lives of security personnel, its worship keeps them distant from its misuse" (www.narendramodi.in/narendra-modi-per forms-shastra-puja-on-vijayadashmi-5619). On a recent trip to northern India, I was shown a temple to Durga Gorkheshwari where antique weapons (rusty swords, muskets, old rifles) were being secretly worshipped to empower a future revolt. Durga Gorkheshwari would lead the young fighters in their cause of independence.

Durga has also become the unofficial goddess of Indian feminism. In a Hindu culture where the ideal woman is devoted and submissive to her husband and family, the warrior Durga of the *Devi Mahatmyam* has neither parents, children nor husband, and she is independent and strong. There are books and websites that talk about "how to become a Durga" and that tell girls and women to "put on the Durga *rupa*" (put on Durga's personality or act like Durga). Durga is described as being present in a woman who can defend herself, who is the first to rise to any situation and who can help women and children. Durga is present in any woman's "boundless compassion for other women around her," as Priya Varadarajan states; she is "an ever-reliable source of strength and support."[1]

Durga workshops give girls an opportunity to openly discuss taboo issues like sexual harassment with other girls in the same situation.

[1] See pamphlet, "Be A Durga: Take control over your safety." [Print Replica] Kindle Edition, n.d.

This sort of alternative community is justified with reference to the goddess's actions when conservative parents might object. It can be described as an approach to help women assert themselves at home and work and reclaim their lives. There are Durga support groups, Durga champions and Durga prizes and celebrations. A recent movement called "Abused Goddesses: Save Our Sisters" shows Durga with a slashed face, Lakshmi with a broken jaw and Sarasvati with a black eye. It discusses the high rate of violence against women ("more than 68% of women are victims of domestic violence"; Kohli 2013) and the necessity for action. In these images, Durga is the only goddess shown who holds a sword (Jha 2013). This is another kind of warfare: the war between the sexes.

Some of this approach has been adopted in the West. For example, a recent *Yoga Journal* article discusses meditating on Durga as a warrior to slay the metaphorical demons of fear, greed and anger, to find inner ferocity and to win the battles in the warfare of everyday life. Durga's transformative power can turn a woman into a warrior (Kempton 2018).

Durga is also found in Indonesia as Devi Durga, but here she is a terrifying deity for Balinese Hindus. She is a patroness of black magic, the goddess of witches (*leyak*) and sorcerers. To avoid invoking her presence, she is called by other names, such as Ratu Ayu and Ida Betari. She has absorbed the darker aspects of the goddess Kali, and like Kali she lives in graveyards; she brings death and disease and can curse people and devour their enemies.

While Durga is both a protective mother and warrior in India, she went through a process of demonization as her worship reached Java and Bali. She was adopted by kings in order to destroy their enemies, and they worshipped her through tantric rites. There were Durga curse rituals to call down attacks on invaders by tigers, lightning and illness, and she was portrayed with skull ornaments as goddess of the *satkarmas*, the tantric magical powers that include the subjugation of enemies. As Durga Mahabhairavi, she had four arms, and she would destroy the weapons of enemies by burning them to ash and swallowing them. She wore a sacred thread made from skulls and had wild hair and sharp teeth.

Her major origin story involves a curse. When the god Shiva (Bhatara Guru) heard that his wife had committed adultery with the god Brahma, he was furious and cursed his wife, Uma, to become a terrifying demoness named Durga. At his words, Uma because a monstrous figure with fangs and long nails. She had to dwell in a cremation ground called Setra Gandamayu for twelve years until her husband came to exorcise the evil from her. She would then be called Ra Nini, or Honorable Mother (Ariati 2016: 130).

In the Balinese *lontar* texts (written on palm leaves), Durga is called Bhatari, Bhadrakali, Kalaratri and Chamunda. She entered the Javanese pantheon in the 12th century CE and was prominent during the Majapahit dynasty. As a warrior goddess and destroyer of enemies, she was worshipped in the death temples (*pura dalem*) by kings who wanted the powers of black magic. As Durga-Kalika, she was the protectress of royal lands who cursed trespassers and fought enemies. She was given offerings of flesh and alcohol. She was portrayed as huge in stature, reaching to the top of the sky, with fangs, sunken eyes and nostrils like wells, and her voice was like thunder. She could bless all beings, but she rejoiced in the terrible fire that destroys the worlds. With her magic, warriors gained the power to transform their own bodies into terrifying forms, to become *"anak sakti,"* full of destructive supernatural power (Ariati 2016: 148).

Today, she is seen most often in the Calon Arang dance drama, in which her devotee Rangda/Calon Arang, queen of the witches, fights against the Barong, leader of good earth spirits and protector of villages. Rangda was first portrayed in medieval texts as an angry widow who wished to destroy the kingdom of Airlangga through black magic. Rangda later became a personification of evil in general, and the dance shows the eternal struggle between good and evil. It became famous later as a trance dance in which dancers would stab themselves with wavy *kris* knives.

KALI

Kali is an important deity in eastern India, especially in West Bengal. Though Kali is now a mainstream Hindu goddess, she has also been worshipped by a variety of different tribal groups. She ranges from being a local village goddess who protects a small area and an ancestress who blesses to a tantric goddess who gives liberation to her devotees and a protective mother giving entrance to heaven, as well as being a goddess of death and destruction.

As a village goddess, she tends to be a protectress of a particular city or locality. Among many Adivasi or tribal groups, she is called Kali *bonga* and is offered goats as sacrifices. Among the Oraons of the Sunderbans swamps, she is called Bankali, the forest goddess, and she is invoked before cutting trees, collecting honey and performing other work there. But she is the goddess of *tantrikas* and *bhakti* devotees as well. While her most popular image portrays her with a necklace of skulls and a belt of hands, she has many other forms.

Most historians seek the origin of the goddess Kali in the Sanskrit great tradition. In the Vedic texts, Kali has been associated with the goddess of night, Ratri (based on the "Ratrisukta" of the Rig Veda) and with the fearful Nirrtidevi of the Brahmanas. The name of Kali is first found in the Mundaka Upanishad, where Kali is one of the seven tongues of the sacrificial fire or *yajna*. Kali is later mentioned in the Mahabharata, being seen by Asvatthama when he entered the Pandava camp at night to kill the soldiers. Here she had bloodshot eyes and dark skin, and she carried nooses and was of terrifying appearance. There is some question as to whether this image came with the earliest writings of the text or whether it was a later addition (Dasgupta 1985: 64).

In early Sanskrit literature, Kali is negative and devouring. As Bana's *Harsa-carita* describes her: "The tongue of the goddess of Doom's night, black like the charcoal of the funeral piles and covered with blood, licks up the lives of living beings, like a cow that licks her calf's shoulder – eager to swallow all creation as a mouthful" (The Harsa-carita of Bana 1961: 256). In the *Khila Harivamsa*, we find a goddess fond of meat and wine who is worshipped by Adivasi and low-caste groups, and in Bhavabhuti's *Malatimadhava*, Kali is a terrifying goddess who is worshipped with human sacrifice. She is dark and violent (*ugra*), and her temple is in a burning ground (Dasgupta 1985: 66).

There are many stories of her origin in the puranic texts. Kali is described as an emanation from the goddess Durga in the *Devi Mahatmyam*. When Ambika/Durga became angry, her skin turned dark, and from her forehead came Kali, armed with a sword and noose:

> Bearing the strange skull-topped staff, decorated with a garland of skulls, clad in a tiger's skin, very appalling owing to her emaciated flesh, with gaping mouth, fearful with her tongue lolling out, having deep-sunk reddish eyes and filling the regions of the sky with her roars, and falling upon impetuously and slaughtering the great asuras in that army, she devoured those hosts of the foes of the devas.
>
> (*Devi Mahatmyam* 7.7–9)

In the *Linga Purana*, Shiva asks Parvati to destroy the demon Daruka, who can only be killed by a woman. Parvati enters Shiva's body and takes the poison that is stored in his throat. With this, she is transformed into the terrifying Kali. Accompanied by cannibalistic spirits (*pisacas*), she attacks Daruka and his armies. Kali defeats them, but she gets so maddened by the battle that she threatens to destroy the world. Shiva comes to calm her, and the world is saved. Later in the text, Kali is part of Shiva's army as he goes off to defeat another demon. She wears skulls and drinks the blood of demons (Kinsley 1988: 118).

There are many visualizations or *dhyanas* of Kali, which describe different aspects for the devotee to contemplate. According to one visualization in the tantric encyclopedia *Tantrasara*, the four-armed Kali is smiling and full of blood, with three red eyes, and she stands on Shiva's heart. He is lying like a corpse, yet he is involved with her in reverse (*viparita*) intercourse, in which the woman squats over the man. In other descriptions she is soaked with a shower of nectar, her hair matted, and she is making a loud roaring noise. Sometimes she stands on an ordinary corpse and sometimes she stands on Shiva as a corpse (Bhattacharya 1986).

According to the *Skanda Purana*, Shiva told Devi to destroy the world at the time of universal destruction. She hesitated to do this because of her feminine compassion, and Shiva yelled at her to do it with a great roar. She took the form of Mahakali, expanding like thunder and lightning. She became full of lightning; her eyes were like burning pits of fire, and she was difficult to look at. Her giant figure covered the three worlds. She roared, breathed fire and laughed, wearing a tiger skin and a snake for a sacred thread. In this form, she destroyed the universe. In the *Devi Gita*, the goddess is huge, with a thousand heads, a thousand eyes and a thousand pairs of feet (Bhattacharya 1986). This is one of her tantric forms, which we see in the *Devibhagavata Purana* as well: As the gods looked at Devi, she appeared to have a thousand eyes, a thousand hands and a thousand feet (*Sri Mad Devi Bhagavatam* III.3.48).

While the goddess Kali traditionally threatens order and stability, she also represents a transcendent order, beyond the expectations of an earthly life. Her inner beauty is beyond human understanding. While in many older texts she is ugly, with a black and emaciated body, matted hair and covered in snakes, in many of her modern statues and posters she is young and beautiful, with flirtatious eyes, large breasts, a narrow waist and a big smile. She may be deep blue, sky blue or even white – all colors representing beneficent and auspicious forms of the goddess. This reflects the rise of Shakta *bhakti*, devotion to the goddess through love (McDaniel 2004). From the modern Kali *bhakti* perspective, this beautiful form is her real and inner form, with the ugly image is only to frighten those who are unworthy and evil. If you are her enemy or do not respect her, the black Kali of the burning ground will drink your blood. But if you are devoted, her graceful form will come to you at the time of your death, and she will smile lovingly as she takes you to dwell on her lap forever. According to the *Devi Bhagavata Purana*, Kali's heaven of Manidvipa is a beautiful place, and, interestingly, is open only to women. When a male Kali devotee dies, he must take on the form of a woman to enter. Even the male gods must take on a female form to enter her heaven (*Sri Mad Devi Bhagavatam* III.5.13–15).

As a devotional goddess, Kali is Mother of the Universe and the beloved parent of Shakta poets like Ramprasad Sen. She is described with love, and her dark side is justified by the presence of death in nature – Kali represents what is true, not what people would like to see. She is described as loving in her poetry, but she is also capable of saving her devotees from their own karma, sweeping them out of the ghostly worlds between incarnations and taking them to her paradise. Ramprasad emphasized the importance of a personal relationship with the goddess:

> Because you love the burning ground
> I have made a burning ground of my heart
> So that you, dark goddess, can dance there forever.
> I have no other desire left, O Mother
> A funeral pyre is blazing in my heart.
> Ashes from corpses are all around me, my Mother
> In case you decide to come.
> Prasad prays, "O Mother, at the hour of death
> Keep your devotee at your feet ..."
>   (Sen n.d.: 46, translated from the Bengali)

The most popular songs by Ramprasad show a goddess who is beyond human concerns of good and evil, sorrow and joy. The devotee must accept the experiences that the goddess gives them in order to perceive her true nature. In sorrow and terror, the devotee's limited scope revealed, their karma is purged and they can see beyond the finite world. Death is the embrace of the Mother, so it should be valued, not feared.

Another famous poet of Kali is the Bengali writer Kazi Nazrul Islam. Nazrul is perhaps most famous for his writings on the *rasa* or poetic mood of the terrible, in which he expresses both passion and patriotism. He writes of the Mother as the Motherland who is hungry and ragged, who cries from door to door for her sons. She has been abused (by the British colonialists), and she is angry and violent. He calls her "[n]ot the goddess of pity, but the goddess of terror," who is "fierce, belligerent, serpent-toothed." Kali is the Mother who gives apocalyptic birth to the new universe:

The deluge will soon overtake the universe.
The final hour is fast drawing near
The old and rotten will be wiped out ...
Why should the sight of destruction frighten you?
All of this upheaval is but the birth pains
Of a new creation.

(Kazi Nazrul Islam, A New Anthology
1990: 48–49, rephrased)

Kali also has a tantric side which focuses on the more frightening aspects of death, especially in her worship by means of the corpse ritual. In the typical *sava-sadhana* rite, the *tantrika* should go to a burning ground or some other lonely spot on the night of a new moon. They should bring a corpse – young and attractive, usually low caste – of a person who died by violence, drowning or snakebite. The body is washed and placed on a blanket or deer or tiger skin. The *tantrika* should worship it and then sit on the corpse and contemplate the goddess. If they are successful, they may gain the power to use a mantra (*mantrasiddhi*) or receive a vision of the goddess. She may appear to possess the corpse, and the corpse's head is said to turn around and begin speaking to the *tantrika*. Or she may appear in a vision. When the *tantrika* asks for supernatural powers, the goddess cannot refuse (McDaniel 2004: 123–131).

Kali is known for being morally ambiguous – supporting wishes from all sorts of devotees. She was known as the goddess of criminals because she was the patron goddess of the Thuggee cult in colonial India, an organized band of thieves and murderers. The Thugs were both Muslim and Hindu, and her worship as Kali Bhavani became an excuse for killing for profit. They acted in organized gangs for generations, for the Thuggee role was largely hereditary. Some writers claim that the Thuggee group is the best example of Hindu–Muslim unity to date.

One major regional form of the goddess Kali is Bhadrakali, also known as Bhagavati. She is the patroness of war and martial arts in Kerala, south India, and she blesses weapons and shields as a part of the Kalari warrior tradition. She is a Hindu goddess, but she is associated with the tribal goddess Kottavai, a warrior who wears a necklace of tigers' teeth, rides a tiger into battle and devours the flesh and blood of her enemies. Bhadrakali has blue-black skin and three eyes, and she is both beautiful and fierce. She goes into battle carrying weapons and the head of a slain demon, accompanied by an army of ghosts and demon women.

Her most famous story in Kerala is similar to the story of Durga in the *Devi Mahatmyam*. The demon Darika received a boon from the god Brahma to conquer the universe and overcome death, and every drop of his blood would give birth to a thousand demons. No man could kill him; however, he could be killed by a woman. He conquered the heavens, and the god Shiva was enraged. He opened his third eye, and its blazing fire became Bhadrakali, with thousands of heads, arms and legs. She took on human form, and the gods created Durga to find Darika's secret mantra. Using this mantra, Bhadrakali beheaded Darika and drank his blood, so no new demons could be formed. The heavens and the Earth were saved (Caldwell 2000: 19).

Bhadrakali also possesses people (primarily women) who have inner conflicts. There are shrines for the mad in Kerala where people dance, scream and leap in the air. The goddess's presence can drive away the spirits that afflict the person in a battle for their soul.

Today, we also see the figure of Kali in Western New Age religion, following Jungian psychology in which she is an archetype of female rage. She is the personification of anger, used for women who are too hesitant or weak to defend themselves in difficult situations; she is a symbolic warrior goddess who can feel rage, a cathartic image for women and an expression of conflicting fear and desire for men.

CONCLUDING THOUGHTS

As we look at the symbolism of these goddesses, we can see that Durga tends to be associated with warfare as military conflict, representing the force of good against evil. She blesses armies and weapons, acting as the patron goddess of kings, countries and armies, guiding their weapons and war elephants into battle. She is the great goddess of the universe, but she will incarnate to save people in trouble. She empowers the virtuous and helps the weak, and she is immune to corruption and desire. More recently, she has been invoked to help the weak fight against the strong in the war between the sexes.

Kali, on the other hand, is willing to serve both good and evil worshippers. Her powers are not limited to the virtuous, for she reflects the overwhelming power of nature, in which good and evil are smaller and subjective categories. She is beautiful and terrible, the frightening power of death that can yet lead to her heaven. While Kali may occasionally act as patron goddess to a group, she is primarily an individualistic goddess who responds to a devotee's personal love and sacrifice.

Though she dances upon the chest of the Lord of Death, her battleground is the heart.

References

Ariati, Ni Wayan Pasek. 2016. *The Journey of the Goddess Durga: India, Java and Bali*. International Academy of Indian Culture.

Bapat, Jayant Bhatchandra and Ian Mabbett, eds. 2017. *Conceiving the Goddess: Transformation and Appropriation in Indian Religions*. Monash University Press.

Bhattacharya, Hamsanarayana. 1986. *Hinduder debadebi* (in Bengali). Firma KLM.

Caldwell, Sarah. 2000. *O Terrifying Mother: Sexuality, Violence, and Worship of the Goddess Kali*. Oxford University Press.

Dasgupta, Shashibhushan. (1985). *Bharater sakti-sadhana o sakta sahitya* (in Bengali). Sahitya Samsad.

Devi Mahatmyam or Sri Durga Saptasati. 1955. Translated by Swami Jagadiswarananda. Sri Ramakrishna Math.

The Harsa-carita of Bana. 1961. Translated by E. B. Cowell and F. W. Thomas. Motilal Banarsidass.

Jha, Rega. 2013. "India's Incredibly Powerful 'Abused Goddesses' Campaign Condemns Domestic Violence." Available at www.buzzfeed.com/regajha/indias-incredibly-powerful-abused-goddesses-campaign-condemn

Kazi Nazrul Islam, A New Anthology. 1990. Translated by Rafiqul Islam. Bangla Academy.

Kempton, Sally. 2018. "How to Channel Durga During Challenging Times." Available at www.yogajournal.com/yoga-101/how-to-channel-durga-during-challenging-times

Kinsley, David. 1988. *Hindu Goddesses: Visions of the Divine Feminine in the Hindu Religious Tradition*. University of California Press.

Kohli, Karnika. 2013. "Bruised, battered goddesses feature in campaign against domestic violence." Available at https://timesofindia.indiatimes.com/india/bruised-battered-goddesses-feature-in-campaign-against-domestic-vio lence/articleshow/22461046.cms?utm_source=contentofinterest&utm_medium=text&utm_campaign=cppst

McDaniel, June. 2004. *Offering Flowers, Feeding Skulls: Popular Goddess Worship in West Bengal*. Oxford University Press.

Sen, Ramprasad. n.d. *Ramprasadi Sangit* (in Bengali). Rajendra Library.

Sri Mad Devi Bhagavatam. n.d. Translated by Swami Vijnanananda. Bhuvaneswari Asrama.

Thomas, Paul. 1960. *Hindu Religion, Customs and Manners: Describing the Customs and Manners, Religious, Social and Domestic Life, Arts and Sciences of the Hindus*. D. B. Taraporevala Sons and Co.

Varadarajan, Priya. 2016. "Every Woman Needs to Become a Durga and Fight for her Rights." Available at https://yourstory.com/2016/07/women-become-durga?utm_pageloadtype=scroll

22 The Demonological Framework of the Heavenly Kingdom of Great Peace

BAREND TER HAAR

The 19th-century civil war of the Heavenly Kingdom of Great Peace (*taiping tianguo* 太平天國 or Taiping) was one of the most violent events in human history, with estimates of its victims ranging from 20 to over 70 million direct and indirect deaths among an estimated population of 400–450 million people (Cao 2001: 455–553; Meyer-Fong 2013). It lasted formally from 1851 to 1864, with a prehistory going back to 1843 and a bloody aftermath until 1871 when the last armies were defeated. It was inspired in part by the first translated Christian texts by Protestant missionaries and their converts in the 1830s. They were active around Guangzhou (or Canton) in the southern province of Guangdong. A central role was played by the visions of a failed student studying for the lowest civil service examinations, a man of Hakka background known to us as Hong Xiuquan 洪秀全 (1814–1864). The movement took on its final form around Thistle Mountain, a marginal location in the north of the neighboring province of Guangxi. This area was full of ethnic, social and economic tensions but lacked the kind of long-established mechanisms for brokering social peace and state control that Guangdong had built up over the previous centuries (Faure 2007). The Qing state failed to suppress the movement in its early stages, after which its armies burst out in 1851 and fought their way through the provinces of Hunan and Jiangxi to conquer Nanjing and its surroundings in 1853. Here they established their Heavenly Capital and were eventually exterminated in 1864. The movement initially attacked the statues of local cults, as well as the tablets for worshipping ancestors or Confucius. They saw these representations as demons. They subsequently redefined the demons as their local enemies in Guangxi and then as the Manchus themselves who ruled the empire from faraway Beijing.

The movement has long been a source of fascination for Chinese, Japanese, and Western historians, each with their own agendas (Wagner 2016). Chinese observers at the time saw it as an example of the dangers of Christianity. For later Chinese historians, it was a proto-nationalist precursor and anti-Manchu movement for nationalists or a proto-communist precursor for communist historians (Xia 2016). For many Western Christian observers at the time, the movement held out the hope of a rapid conversion of China, but they were bitterly disappointed by the mix of indigenous and Christian beliefs and practices. The movement produced its own printed record, which has survived in Western libraries thanks to the missionaries who took many of these texts home with them. Just how important the Christian dimension was depends to some degree on one's point of departure. Coming from missionary history, one tends to stress Christian theology and the figures of Hong Xiuquan and Hong Ren'gan 洪仁玕 (1822–1864), who were most influenced by Christianity (Spence 1996; Reilly 2004; Kilcourse 2016). Coming from the study of traditional Chinese religious culture, as does the present author, one can only be struck by the predominance of indigenous motives and narratives. Traditional beliefs and practices were crucial in creating the violent scenario that guided the Heavenly Kingdom leaders, as well as those of their followers, in their attempt to conquer the world, or rather the All-under-Heaven as most Chinese at all social levels imagined it at the time (Wagner 1982; Weller 1994; ter Haar 2002). For them, the Qing Empire more or less equaled the civilized world, being not so different from Western views about their own world at the time.

The religious framework of the Heavenly Kingdom made followers willing to accept great personal sacrifice in fighting their enemies. Their war served the higher purpose of reshaping the world as they knew it, following a script that was influenced both by indigenous utopian ideas from classical texts often identified as Confucian and Christian narratives derived from an incomplete exposure to parts of the Bible. Their awareness of Christian ritual practice and exegesis was limited. The way to attain their Heavenly Kingdom, however, was derived from the demonological undercurrent of Chinese culture, with some remarkable additions such as the promise of ascent to Heaven after dying in meritorious battle and a distinctly Old Testament vengeful Yahweh and an only slightly less vengeful Jesus.

The discussion below is divided into two sections, starting with the original visions of Hong Xiuquan in which he took on the role of the Younger Brother of Jesus, and followed by its local interpretation in Guangxi by Yang Xiuqing 楊秀清 (ca. 1820–1856) and Xiao Chaogui 蕭朝貴 (ca. 1820–1852) as the vessels for the Heavenly Father or Yahweh and the Heavenly Elder Brother or Jesus, respectively. For reasons of space, much detail must be left out of this discussion, including the reception of the message(s) by Heavenly Kingdom followers (ter Haar 2002) and the genocidal suppression of the rebels by the Qing state, which was interpreted by many educated elites as an eschatological event foreshadowing the end of time (Goossaert 2016).

VISIT TO HEAVEN: THE YOUNGER BROTHER OF JESUS

Hong Xiuquan was of Hakka provenance, today seen as one of the main Han-Chinese regional cultures. He came from Hua County, close to the provincial capital of Guangzhou. We know nothing on his religious ideas and practices before his visions of 1837. But we do know that the county had been founded in 1686 in an attempt to control a marginal and hilly area known for robbery and general instability (Hua xianzhi 1687: 4: 54a–57a). Its first magistrate describes lineages formed around ancestor worship and common property and briefly refers to annual festivals, Daoist and Buddhist rituals as well as mediumistic practices, and religious healing based on exorcism above classicist (ru 儒) medicine based on Yin/Yang and other abstract concepts (Hua xianzhi 1687: 1: 30a–35b). State-sponsored rituals were practiced in the county capital, which were irrelevant to most, but not to people such as Hong Xiuquan, who were studying for the imperial examinations. Important in these rituals was the intimidating figure of Confucius, an ancient sage who was worshipped as the ultimate teacher but, unlike ordinary deities, did not provide personal assistance to petitioners (Hua xianzhi 1687: 1: 37a–47a).

   Hong's ancestors had moved to Hua County three generations before him, coming from Jiaying Prefecture (or Meizhou) on the Jiangxi–Fujian–Guangdong border (Hamberg 1855: 3). At this time, the Hakka identity was still in the process of becoming, including the now familiar belief that this group had once come from northern China, a theory first formulated in late 18th-century educated Hakka circles (Hamberg 1855: 2–3; Leong 1997: 76 and passim). These migrants probably belonged to the same "bandits" or even "barbarians" who were the main reason for founding the county – that is, outsiders who were hard for the thinly spread imperial bureaucracy to control. The now familiar label "Hakka" (kejia 客家 or "guest people") essentially means people from elsewhere without local land rights. The founding magistrate of Hua County did not yet have this label available to him and used other derogatory qualifications such as "bandit" or "barbarian." He devoted much of his effort to setting up the appropriate institutions for Sinitic enculturation, including the cult of Confucius (*Hua xianzhi* 1687: 1: 37a–47a, 4: 54a–57a). Hong thus grew up in a tension between imperial enculturation through participation in state rituals that included Confucius as a major focus of worship and local religious practices that involved the exorcist mastery of uncertainty through the war on demons. Hong Xiuquan was the hope of his family for a jump in social status and a corresponding increase in economic wealth, making his failure to do so, however common at the time, a cause of great personal stress.

In 1837, Hong failed in the examinations for a third time. During his stay in Guangzhou, he heard a Protestant missionary lecture, assisted by an interpreter, and obtained a Christian tract in simple Chinese that introduced parts of the Bible and the faith. It was entitled "Good Words to Exhort the World" (*Quanshi liangyan* 勸世良言), taking up the Greek term for the gospel, or εὐαγγέλιον/*euangélion*, meaning the "good message." During his mental and physical breakdown that soon followed, whatever he had heard and read got intermingled with traditional beliefs and expressed in waking dreams or visions spread out over several weeks. Our access to the resulting narrative is through much later interpretations. The earliest extant version was given by his cousin, Hong Ren'gan, to the missionary Theodore Hamberg (1819–1854) in 1852 (Hamberg 1855); I will draw upon it here. Even late in the war, leading participants remained engaged in interpreting the visions' meanings (Wagner 1982: 44–46; Spence 1996: esp. 262–267). Dreams and visions were commonly interpreted as significant on all social levels, and they often featured a life-changing encounter with a deity who provided cryptic advice. Their purport usually became clear only much later – or never at all. For men participating in the examinations, such divine messages dealt with the uncertainty of success in their degrees and their subsequent job prospects as career officials (ter Haar 2017: 194–198). Initially, Hong may well have interpreted his visions along those lines.

In the original visions, the Christian dimension is quite limited (Wagner 1982: 44–45). At first, he thought he was going to die and enter the kingdom of Yanluo 閻羅 (King Yama's underworld), but then the visions took a very different turn. As Hamberg has translated the account, "[h]is soul was acted upon by a peculiar energy, so that he not only experienced things of a very extraordinary nature, but afterwards retained in memory what had occurred to him." After a ritual washing and obtaining a new heart and other organs, he entered a large hall in which a man "venerable from his years, with a golden beard, and dressed in a black robe, was sitting in an imposing attitude in the highest place." The man complained to Hong that human beings worship demons and rebel against him. He gave him a sword to exterminate demons, a seal to overcome evil spirits, and a sweet-tasting yellow fruit. The old man also made him look down from above, where he saw "such a degree of depravity and vice, that his eyes could not endure the sight, nor his mouth express their deeds" (quotations from Hamberg 1855: 16–18). Originally, these episodes make far more sense as a reflection of common exorcistic ritual practice at the time, partially influenced by the undigested Christian message from his Canton visit and from leafing quickly through the booklet that he had gotten there. Many elements can be interpreted very well in both traditions, such as the ritual washing that may relate to Christian baptism but is equally common in indigenous confession rituals (for an example, see Pregadio 2008: 753).

Let us briefly consider some crucial non-Christian background. The belief that humankind had declined morally was widespread among new religious groups with a primarily Buddhist background since at least the 16th century, but it also appeared in long-established millenarian and messianic lore that we would classify as Daoist. This lore had become increasingly popular in the preceding centuries. Several waves of new texts were produced through spirit writing on the imminent apocalypse caused by the moral decline of the world. Depending on the revelation, different deities take it upon themselves to rescue humankind. These moralistic concerns were expressed on a social level that was literate, ranging from the highest elite to at best the sub-elite, since most ordinary people would have lacked the requisite literacy. We have no explicit evidence that Hong was aware of these traditions beyond the fact that they and his visions were strikingly similar in structure. He certainly could have picked up knowledge of them during his visit to the Guangzhou metropolis, where we know that such prophecies were circulating at the time (Goossaert 2014; ter Haar 2017: 233–243). In 1850, Hong had settled in Guangxi and concretely predicted the advent of pestilences sent down by the Heavenly Father (the bearded man from his vision), warning his relatives at home that they should join him now. At the same time, several counties in Guangxi were actually hit by pestilences, causing locals to join the movement in the expectation that they would be safe (Hamberg 1855: 73). As not-yet-converted, these people were not operating according to any form of Christian logic, but that of indigenous traditions. For them, martial exorcism of the type that Hong Xiuquan claimed could protect against diseases, since these were commonly imagined as demonic attacks (Katz 1995).

Another strand was Hong's encounter with the old man with the golden beard, who is emphatically not yet labeled more specifically as God or Yahweh. The golden color remained a problem of exegesis throughout the movement's history, since Chinese were accustomed only to black and especially white beards on old men or deities, such as the Lord of the Soil, who was the omnipresent deity of a locality. This man bestowed Hong with a sword (*jian* 劍, with two sharp edges) and a seal (*xi* 璽, using the term for the imperial seal), which are the foremost ritual objects of any ritual specialist, exemplified best by the Daoist Heavenly Master Zhang Daoling 張道陵 (Wagner 1982: 4, 34–36, using an 1862 version of this account). We know that Hong's family first attempted an exorcist ritual healing, which traditionally uses a sword and seal as part of the fight against the demons of illness. The family only resorted to theory-driven medical approaches at the very end.[1] The bestowal of a sweet yellow fruit might in fact go back to parallel attempts to feed the patient with healthy food, perhaps an orange, which is traditionally used in medical recipes as well.

The second important encounter in the vision was when Hong met a "man of middle age, whom he called his elder brother, who instructed him how to act, [and] accompanied him in his wanderings to the uttermost regions in search of evil spirits, and assisted him in slaying and exterminating them." The old man reproached Confucius for having expounded the true doctrine insufficiently clearly, making the latter feel ashamed and guilty. During his illness, Hong often ran around his room "leaping and fighting like a soldier engaged in battle. His constant cry was ... Slay the demons (*yao* 妖)! slay the demons!" Despite an attempt at ritual healing to drive out evil spirits, Hong persisted in his behavior, causing people in the wider surroundings to consider him mad. He clearly saw himself in the role of exorcist and therefore quite normal (Hamberg 1855: 19–21). His Confucius bashing reflected his frustrations as a student of the conventional examination curriculum, which included the *Analects* ascribed to Confucius himself. Hong Xiuquan had a fully moralistic point of view in line with his classicist

---

[1] Although related to the modern practices of so-called Traditional Chinese Medicine (TCM), real traditional practices largely abstained from the acupuncture that is so common today in TCM, and they differ in other respects as well. What they both have in common is a strong dependency on theories regarding the circulation of Qi and the correct balance of Yin and Yang.

or Confucian studies but also in tune with the indigenous eschatological literature of that time. In short, this meant that only morally upright people could be saved, which is different from those approaches in which possessing a protective talisman or talismanic scripture might be enough (ter Haar 2015). Moreover, his demonological view of the world certainly did not stem from the classicist tradition or the practices of worshipping Confucius or his own ancestors, which were essential parts of what missionaries at the time had begun to call Confucianism (ter Haar 2016). Instead, this view originated in local religious practice during festivals, healing rituals, funerals and so on. The much later Chinese version of the vision is even more explicit on his exorcist mission, mentioning the assistance of divine armies or Heavenly Generals and Heavenly Soldiers and his summoning of the famous Yang Family 楊家將 generals fighting the Jürchen (proto-Manchus) and the divine general Zhao Xuanlang 趙玄朗 (TPTG, 510–511; also see Huan 2018). The target as well as the instruments of the fight against demons were not yet ordinary humans at this point in time.

Following his 1837 visions, Hong Xiuquan also produced lengthy poems, and a mysterious prophecy was found stuck beside the door of his house. Chinese anecdotal records abound with poetic predictions that are communicated by deities in dreams or obtained from temple oracles. They acquired meaning only afterwards when something occurred in real life that could somehow be linked to these poems (Smith 1991; Strickmann 2005). Hong's poems contained numerous references to the ultimate imperial animal, the dragon, but also to defeating the demons (Hamberg 1855: 21–22). At this stage, nobody could explain these words, and initially his visions were largely forgotten.

It is only after a fourth examination failure in 1843 that he read the tract he had received six years before more carefully. He now identified the old man in his vision as the Heavenly Father (tianfu 天父) or Yahweh (yehuohua 也火花) and the man of middle age or his Heavenly Elder Brother (tianxiong 天兄) as Jesus (Hamberg 1855: 31). He then baptized himself and promised to stop worshipping evil demons (in Hamberg's translation "spirits"). He threw away the statues of the deities he worshipped and removed the tablet of Confucius from the school where he was teaching, declaring all of them demons (Hamberg 1855: 31–33, 37). In the light of his fourth examination failure, this must have been tremendously satisfying. The appellations Heavenly Father and Heavenly Elder Brother remained current in Heavenly Kingdom lore and were not corrected to orthodox Christian forms. The initial models for the Heavenly Father were not yet (and certainly not only) the figure of Yahweh in the Old Testament, but the much more familiar Jade Emperor (*yuhuang shangdi* 玉皇上帝) and/or the Northern Emperor (*beidi* 北帝, also known as the Emperor of Dark Heaven [*xuantian shangdi* 玄天上帝]). The Northern Emperor was in fact a major regional deity where Hong had grown up (Faure 1990). In the eschatological traditions of the 18th and 19th centuries, the Jade Emperor plays a central role in punishing humankind for their moral decline and then dispatching various deities to rescue those who want to mend their ways. The use of the term *shangdi* (God/Emperor on High) or just *di* (Emperor) in texts produced by the Heavenly Kingdom allowed new followers to combine different modes of understanding, traditional and Christian inspired, both at the same time.

Hong later acquired more knowledge of the Bible but continued to read it largely to confirm his own sense of mission and not to correct (or change) it. The demonological scenario remained the basic structure of his beliefs, much to the dismay of the missionaries (Hamberg 1855: 35–37). As he was one of the very few participants in the Heavenly Kingdom who had read this text, its influence on the larger following of the movement was always mediated through his particular understanding. After their self-baptism, he and a friend had two "demon-exterminating swords" (*zhanyaojian* 斬妖劍) made for themselves, despite their very limited means, attesting to the significance of exorcist practice to them (Hamberg 1855: 38). With Hong being out of a job as a teacher, and with him and his close followers isolated from their community due to their iconoclasm, they went on a journey to Guangxi to find refuge with distant Hakka relatives. They started spreading Hong's teachings and temporarily settled down at Thistle Mountain in modern Guiping County (Hamberg 1855: 41–43). Hong himself soon returned home and even stayed with a Baptist missionary in Guangzhou for two months. In the middle of 1847, he returned again for a while to Guangxi, where one of his closest early followers, Feng Yunshan 馮雲山 (1815–1852), had continued to proselytize and had founded the "God/Emperor-on-High Society" (*shangdi hui* 上帝會) (Xia 2016: 25–29). Subsequently, Hong returned home one more time to resume work as a teacher, and he only returned to Thistle Mountain permanently in 1849. As a result of his frequent absences, he was not able to control the reception of his vision by local communities, as we will see below. Moreover, his absences also indicate that he still aimed to make a regular career at home rather than embarking on an uncertain future in Guangxi.

All the same, from 1843 onwards Hong and his followers continued to practice his iconoclastic message (Hamberg 1855: 33). In 1848, they even destroyed the statue of King Gan that was worshipped in a prominent temple of competing ethnic groups in Xiangzhou County, not far from Thistle Mountain. Hong followed this up with a verbal attack on yet another local temple, while his followers engaged in real attacks on other cults. Since the organizations around these cults formed the fabric of local society, the attacks caused severe social tension and led a local magistrate to intervene by arresting one of their leaders (Hamberg 1855: 56–59). This iconoclasm was directly inspired by the demonological message of the movement and their identification of such deities as demons, but it also fitted rather well with the growing and often violent tensions between the newly arrived Hakka ("guest people") and the people already living here, identified rather generically as Punti (*bendi* 本地 or "locals"). After the attack, the King Gan cult was restored and has continued to flourish to this day, indicating its importance as a node of a local community network (Tang 2010, 2011). In 1840s Guangxi, this religious message and socio-ethnic conflict came together in an explosive mixture. Thus, the initial trigger that set the area alight was a violent conflict between the Punti and the Hakka in 1850 that led to the massacring of Hakka villages (Hamberg 1855: 73–89; Leong 1997).

DIRECTLY FROM HEAVEN: THE HEAVENLY FATHER AND THE HEAVENLY ELDER BROTHER

Among the earliest converts in Guangxi were two local men by the names of Yang Xiuqing 楊秀清 (ca. 1820–1856) and Xiao Chaogui 蕭朝貴 (ca. 1820–1852). Yang was a charcoal burner and illiterate of Hakka provenance. Xiao was a poor farmer and most likely also of Hakka background and illiterate (TFTX, 67, 83; Brine 1862: 89–90). During the prolonged absence of their religious leader Hong Xiuquan and his principal missionary Feng Yunshan in 1848, numerous members of the community started being possessed by a variety of divine figures. Among them, Yang claimed to be possessed by the Heavenly Father, with Xiao claiming several months later that he was possessed by the Heavenly Elder Brother. Some of the statements that Yang, Xiao and other converts made during possession were written down, and they were inspected by Hong Xiuquan when he returned from one of his trips back home to Guangdong. He rejected most of them as demonic except those by Yang and Xiao, since possession was as real to Hong as it was to most Chinese at the time (TFTX, 29, 32; TPTG, 7, 59; Hamberg 1855:

69–71). Like all regional cultures, the Hakka were fervent believers in the possibility of communication with the deceased through female shamans and with deities usually through male mediums (Hamberg 1855: 58; Chan 2013). The role of Yang and Xiao in the movement was crucial, although Western historiography has privileged the figure of Hong Xiuquan, with his more elaborate exposure to Christianity. Part of their mediumistic records was published by the movement itself as a form of propaganda.

Even more than Hong Xiuquan, the illiterate Yang Xiuqing interpreted the figure of the Heavenly Father in line with general beliefs in supreme deities such as the Jade Emperor. Their role was to punish moral transgressions, which is also why someone like the Jade Emperor is so important in late imperial eschatological traditions such as those mentioned above. More generally, Chinese folklore is also very clear about the role of the Jade Emperor as a moral judge who punished wrongdoing directly in the present by sending down afflictions and disasters both individually and collectively rather than the underworld gods, who punished only individually in the afterlife (ter Haar 2017: 140, 157–160). This is also the interpretation of the role of the Heavenly Father that Yang Xiuqing adopted, albeit with one curious twist. He claimed to possess the gift of curing people, in itself a normal medium practice, but in Christianity more typical of the figure of Jesus than of Yahweh. As the Heavenly Kingdom record describes it, he "redeemed [people] from their sins" (*shuzui* 贖罪) by taking their guilt upon himself, after which they would be cured (Hamberg 1855: 71). Part of this healing process was always a confession, and the mediumistic records contain several cases in which followers were pressurized at length to confess their crimes before they could be tried. For Jesus or the Heavenly Elder Brother, the indigenous model is less clear. Xiao Chaogui not only took on his role of savior (*jiushizhu* 救世主) or redeemer of sins like his "father," but also of exorcist of evil demons (Hamberg 1855: 93). Both Yang and Xiao may have adopted central roles from Christianity, but they did so in an entirely indigenous way.

Early mediumistic records are preserved only for the Heavenly Elder Brother or Xiao Chaogui. They allow us to trace the changing identifications of the demons that Hong Xiuquan and his followers had to destroy. In the late summer of 1850, the ongoing tensions with non-Hakka communities around them escalated into continuous violence. From August 29 onwards, the Heavenly Elder Brother started to identify the Punti enemy as "demon(s)" (*yao* or *yaomo* 妖魔) and "demons creating abnormalities" (*yaozuoguai* 妖作怪). These are all highly conventional terms for demons haunting a place or person, which would normally be expelled through the enactment of violent combat in rituals or operatic performances (TFTX, 58–60, 62–63, 65, 67–69, 71, 75–76, 78, 80–83, 87–91, 93, 97).[2] While they are fighting to escape their encirclement in Guangxi, the vocabulary for "demon" is transferred to the Qing armies as well (TPTG, 65–66, 68). In the same vein, the Heavenly Elder Brother sends "Heavenly Soldiers and Heavenly Generals" (tianbing tianjiang 天兵天將) to protect Hong or even to punish Xiao Chaogui's own brother-in-law (TPTG, 61, 67, 84, 90). This kind of divine army is a standard ritual resource in fighting the demons that threatened humankind and again attests to a demonological world-view (ter Haar 2019). The change that now took place is a crucial development, since until then the demons had been identified as statues or spirit tablets that needed to be destroyed, and now the same frame-work was applied to real people (TPTG, 11).

Within the movement, strict order was maintained, and the mediumistic sessions of Yang Xiuqing as the Heavenly Father and Xiao Chaogui as the Heavenly Elder Brother played an important role in this. Transgressions of the Heavenly Rules (tiantiao 天條, a promin-ent term in the Christian tract mentioned above) were punished severely by beatings with sticks, wearing a cangue and potentially even execution. Particularly striking is how even the Heavenly King himself (i.e. Hong Xiuquan) was subject to violent sanctions by the Heavenly Father. During a session in late 1851, the latter even ordered that Hong and others receive forty beatings with a stick. Hong was only spared because he submitted to his punishment and the Heavenly Father then relented (TPTG, 29–32; see also TPTG, I, 33, 36).

At some point in early 1851, the demonological viewpoint was further generalized to the claim that the Heavenly Elder Brother has seen that many in the ordinary world are deluded and harmed by demons. He stated that normally he would be happy if just one of them could be saved, but now the movement had grown so large that many would be saved, and so he no longer needed to worry. He promised his audience that those "who cultivated well" (liande haohao 練得好好) would receive good fortune. He listed several dozen leaders whose "souls would ascend to Heaven," a welcome promise during the ongoing battles in which many lost their lives, including Xiao

---

[2]   The term yao is common in indigenous demonological thinking. The much more theological term xie 邪 or "heretic" that is used in Hong Xiuquan's original Christian source is not used in these sessions.

Chaogui or the Heavenly Elder Brother himself (TFTX, 80–81; see also TFTX, 89, 92, 107; TPTG, 512, 777). Using conventional terms here derived from indigenous religious discourse such as "cultivate" (*lian* 錬) and "good fortune" (*fu* 福) made his message easy for followers to comprehend, the majority of whom would have had very little knowledge of Christianity as such. While we nowadays often label the notion of "cultivation" as Daoist, this is a modern label that suggests a theological background and exclusiveness that does not fit premodern discourse. "Cultivation" here refers to the proper practice of the "Heavenly Rules" (*tiantiao*) mentioned above.

The Heavenly Kingdom combined their demonological framework with biblical stories as well, such as in their account of the three outbursts of anger (*nu* 怒) of the Heavenly Father. The first time he caused a terrible flood (*hongshui* 洪水, using the same Hong as in Hong Xiuquan), which lasted forty days and nights (taking up the story of Noah and the Ark). The second time was when he took the people of Israel out of the country of Mizraim (the story of Moses leading his people from Egypt). The third time was when he sent down Hong to "execute the demons (*zhuyao* 誅妖)" and "save people" (*jiuren* 救人), which was their interpretation of the story of Jesus, who frequently practiced the exorcism of demonic creatures according to the Gospels. He was motivated by his sadness that people "were deluded and entangled by demons" (*bei yaomo zhi michan* 被妖魔之迷纏). The Heavenly Father wished the destruction of these demons through the instrument of his two sons, Xiao Chaogui and Hong Xiuquan. Both of them are conceptualized as master exorcists rather than benevolent saviors (TPTG, 159–160). Such an account fitted perfectly within the indigenous messianic traditions that were increasingly current in the 19th century, in which a divine figure would be mandated by the Jade Emperor to rescue the chosen few and the immoral rest of the world would be violently destroyed. Even the tripartite structure fitted very well with these traditions in which the present chance is always the third and last one (Seiwert 2003: 393–394).

CONCLUSION

As the cases of Yang Xiuqing and Xiao Chaogui show even more clearly than that of Hong himself, the latter's vision was received within a traditional religious framework in which the world was largely interpreted in terms of demonic threats that needed to be counteracted through exorcistic violence. Contact with the divine was sustained through possession by the highest deities: the Heavenly Father and Heavenly Elderly Brother. Targeting their attacks at local cults as well as the worship of Confucius and ancestors shows the significance of local religion in providing a frame of reference. The basic demonological framework of local religious life, however, was not changed. This Christianity was derived from the Old Testament, with its frequent genocides by Yahweh directly (think of the Flood or the destruction of Sodom and Gomorra) or by his chosen people (think of Joshua and the inhabitants of Jericho). Such a worldview fitted perfectly within the demonological view of traditional Chinese culture as well as within the ongoing violent conflicts in which Hakkas and Puntis found themselves.

We have stressed the non-Christian, demonological side of the Heavenly Kingdom because this side was crucial in shaping its path towards violent action and its willingness to fight merciless battles with enemies. Christian resources were used to confirm the vision and explain remaining points of doubt. There was no attempt to become Christian, or at least not in the way that the missionaries hoped for, even though the imperial system certainly qualified the Heavenly Kingdom supporters as such, and this view contributed considerably to the imperial system's negative perception of Christianity overall. Precisely for this reason was the role of the two mediums Yang Xiuqing and Xiao Chaogui so important, since they provided hermeneutic flexibility thanks to the undisputable authority of the Heavenly Father and Heavenly Elder Brother. As Rudolf Wagner has pointed out, after their deaths, the movement soon ran out of steam (Wagner 1982: 112–113).

To Christian missionaries at the time and Christian researchers now, the attacks on idols may have seemed completely reasonable, but this was not very common among traditional Chinese religious groups. A rare lay movement that rejected ancestor worship and kept a distance from the meat-eating and spirits-drinking local cults can be found in the Buddhist-inspired Non-Action Teachings, but while this movement was iconoclastic within its own circles, it never engaged in attacks on other religious groups or local communities (ter Haar 2014). What made the Heavenly Kingdom of Great Peace violent was the translation of conventional exorcist discourse into a messianic message in which the demons were identified first as local deities and ancestral images and then reidentified as their Punti enemies and finally as the Manchu state.

References

Brine, Lindesay. 1862. *The Taeping Rebellion in China.* J. Murray.

Cao, Shuji 曹樹基. 2001. *Zhongren renkou shi* 中国人口史, vol. 5. Fudan daxue chubanshe.

Chan, Margaret. 2013. "The Spirit-Mediums of Singkawang: Performing 'Peoplehood' of West Kalimantan." In *Chinese Indonesians Reassessed: History, Religion and Belonging.* Edited by Sai Siew-Min and Hoon Chang-Yau. Routledge. 138–158.

Faure, David. 1990. "What Made Foshan a Town? The Evolution of Rural–Urban Identities in Ming–Qing China." *Late Imperial China* 11(2): 1–31.

2007. *Emperor and Ancestor: State and Lineage in South China.* Stanford University Press.

Goossaert, Vincent. 2014. "Modern Daoist Eschatology: Spirit-Writing and Elite Soteriology in Late Imperial China." *Daoism: Religion, History and Society (Daojiao yanjiu xuebao: zongjiao, lishi yu shehui* 道教研究學報: 宗教, 歷史 與社會) 6: 219–246.

2016. "Guerre, violence et eschatologie. Interprétations religieuses de la guerre des Taiping (1851–1864)." In *Guerre et Religion.* Edited by Jean Baechler. Hermann. 81–94.

Hamberg, Theodore. 1855. *The Visions of Hung-Siu-tshuen, and the Origin of the Kwang-si Insurrection.* Walton and Maberly.

Hua xianzhi 花縣志. 1687. Reprint from 1866.

Huan, Jin. 2018. "Authenticating the Renewed Heavenly Vision: The Taiping Heavenly Chronicle (Taiping tianri)." *Frontiers of History in China* 13(2): 173–192.

Katz, Paul R. 1995. *Demon Hordes and Burning Boats: The Cult of Marshal Wen in Late Imperial Chekiang.* State University of New York Press.

Kilcourse, Carl S. 2016. *Taiping Theology: The Localization of Christianity in China, 1843–64.* Palgrave Macmillan US.

Leong, Sow-theng. 1997. *Migration and Ethnicity in Chinese History: Hakkas, Pengmin, and Their Neighbors.* Stanford University Press.

Meyer-Fong, Tobie S. 2013. *What Remains: Coming to Terms with Civil War in 19th Century China.* Stanford University Press.

Pregadio, Fabrizio. 2008. *The Encyclopedia of Taoism.* Routledge.

Reilly, Thomas H. 2004. *The Taiping Heavenly Kingdom: Rebellion and the Blasphemy of Empire.* University of Washington Press.

Seiwert, Hubert (with Ma Xisha). 2003. *Popular Religious Movements and Heterodox Sects in Chinese History.* Brill.

Smith, Richard. 1991. *Fortune-Tellers and Philosophers: Divination in Traditional Chinese Society.* Westview Press.

Spence, Jonathan D. 1996. *God's Chinese Son: The Taiping Heavenly Kingdom of Hong Xiuquan.* Norton.

Strickmann, Michel. 2005. *Chinese Poetry and Prophecy: The Written Oracle in East Asia.* Edited by Bernard Faure. Stanford University Press.

Tang, Xiaotao 唐晓涛. 2010. "Qingzhong houqi cunluo liangmengde xingcheng ji qi dui defang shehui yiyi 清中后期村落联盟的形成及其对地方社会的意义." *Qingshi yanjiu* 清史研究 3: 90–105.

唐晓涛. 2011. "Shenmingde zhengtongxing yu she, miao zuzhide diyuxing–Baishangdi hui huimiao shijiande shehuishi kaocha 神明的正统性与社、庙组织的地域性——拜上帝会毁庙事件的社会史考察." *Jindai shi yanjiu* 近代史研究 3: 4–26+160.

ter Haar, Barend J. 2002. "China's Inner Demons: The Political Impact of the Demonological Paradigm." In *China's Great Proletarian Revolution: Master Narratives and Post-Mao Counternarratives*. Edited by Woei Lien Chong. Rowman & Littlefield. 27–68.

2014. *Practicing Scripture: A Lay Buddhist Movement in Late Imperial China*. Hawai`i University Press.

2015. "The Sutra of the Five Lords: Manuscript and Oral Tradition." *Studies in Chinese Religions* 1(2): 172–197.

2016. "From Field to Text in the Study of Chinese Religion." In *Religion and Orientalism in Asian Studies*. Edited by Kiri Paramore. Bloomsbury. 85–105.

2017. *Guan Yu: The Religious Afterlife of a Failed Hero*. Oxford University Press.

2019 *Religious Culture and Violence in Traditional China*. Cambridge University Press.

TFTX and Wang Qingcheng 王慶成. 1986. *Tianfu tianxiong shengzhi* 天父天兄聖旨. Liaoning renmin chubanshe.

TPTG. 1952. "Tianfu xiafan zhaoshu 天父下凡詔書." Republished in Wang Zhongmin 王重 and Xiang Da 向達, *Taiping tianguo* 太平天国. *Shenzhou guoguang she* I: 1–69.

Wagner, Rudolf G. 1982. *Reenacting the Heavenly Vision: The Role of Religion in the Taiping Rebellion*. Institute of East Asian Studies, University of California.

2016. "Taiping Civil War." Last modified 27 October 2016. Available at https://doi.org/10.1093/obo/9780199920082-0139

Weller, Robert. 1994. *Resistance, Chaos and Control in China: Taiping Rebels, Taiwanese Ghosts and Tiananmen*. University of Washington Press.

Xia, Chuntao 夏春濤. 2016. *Tianguo de yunluo: Taiping tianguo zongjiao zaiyanjiu zengdingban* 天國的隕落：太平天國宗教再研究增訂版. Zhongguo renmin daxue.

23 War Outside the State: *Religious Communities, Martiality, and State Formation in Early Modern South Asia*

ANNE MURPHY

War is generally associated with states: these are the entities with both the ability and, to some, moral right to pursue war. Yet, our world today and in the past has been shaped by conflicts involving diverse kinds of non-state actors. As Eric Heinze and Brent Steele asked in a 2009 volume that addresses non-state actors in war in contemporary contexts, "[g]iven that our moral vocabulary about war is primarily equipped to apply to the conduct of states, how are these state-centric normative frameworks impacted by the presence and practices of these *non*-states?" (2009: 1, emphasis in original). Although the authors grant that not all entities that might engage in armed conflict seek statehood, they tie their broadened understanding of war – meant not to assume the state and defined as "the actual, organized, and widespread use of armed force to compel an enemy to submit to one's will" – to "political communities," which they subsequently define as "organized associations of people with a political purpose, who may aspire to statehood, or at least wish to influence governance in a particular territory" (Heinze and Steele 2009: 10–11). Statehood, then, is here posited as a goal, if not an existing reality, of conflict-as-war. We see a similar privileging of the state in a recent discussion of the idea of sovereignty by Naomi Goldberg and her notion of religions as "vestigial [sic] states," which she defines as "the institutional and cultural remainders of former sovereignties surviving within the jurisdictions of contemporary governments" (2015: 280). She also calls such entities "once and future states" (Goldberg 2015: 282).

There are limitations, however, of a definition of "political community" that necessitates the state, as reality or as aspiration, and consideration of the relationship of religion with war invites us to consider the utility of an expanded notion of a political community that might act

I am grateful to Dr Julie Vig (York University) and the editor for insightful suggestions.

with violence outside of the logic of statehood. First of all, sovereignty itself is not a solid thing; it is, in the words of Thomas Blom Hansen, more of "a performative ideal, an aspiration toward effective on-the-ground authority, ownership (whether legal or symbolic), and de facto impunity that states, private corporations, rulers, private armies, and many other 'de facto sovereigns' strive to project and maintain" (2021: 41). Eric Lewis Beverley's term *minor sovereignty*, used to describe princely state rule under the British (Beverley 2015), is deployed by Hansen to understand more broadly the terms of subordination that accompany sovereignty and to give a wider sense of the nuance and gradation needed to make "sovereignty" a descriptive rather than prescriptive term (cited in Hansen 2021: 42; on this issue more broadly, see Benton 2009).

These issues have historical as well as contemporary significance, and indeed, since Goldberg's argument hinges on the supposed prior state-ish-ness of what are now called "religions," the historical generation of these social formations is key. The example of the East India Company, which established territorial sovereignty and statehood in India in the mid-17th century, seems to provide an important historical example of the teleology assumed above, whereby a non-state actor was able to "achieve" sovereignty through war with a sovereign state in Bengal in 1757, and acted as ruler and sovereign until being displaced in 1858 by the British state itself after the 1857 rebellion that almost cost Britain its Indian territories, at which time these were brought under the Crown and Parliament. Yet, Philip Stern's 2011 work on the early formations of the East India Company, *The Company-State*, reveals that the Company was, in short, "acting like a state" *before* it had achieved territorial power: focus on the Battle of Plassey in the tale of the rise of East India Company sovereignty neglects this broader dynamic. Looked at more closely, this example provides more clearly an alternative dynamic of a non-state actor participating in and perpetrating war in different kinds of contingent relationships with "state," an example of Hansen's description of the "vast array of intermediate forms of domination, property, and claims to overlordship and suzerainty" that characterized the Indian Ocean world in the early modern period (2021: 43; see also Stern 2011: 3). This was broadly characteristic of the "early modern construction of sovereignty as spatially elastic," in the words of Lauren Benton (2009: 288), and "shared and layered," in the words of Sugata Bose (2006: 25, see also 41–43, 69–71).

This early modern world in South Asia and the various communities that comprised its martial landscape in the context of the greater social and political fabric of the Mughal Empire (1526–1858) are the focus of this chapter, aiming to understand the constitution of violence in a context where the absolute – but often not actually so – sovereignty of the state was not assumed and martialized communities of various types, many of them undergirded by religious affiliations, operated in complex relation to states and state-driven forms of organized aggression that we call "war." This examination allows us to discern the complexity of war both between states and within and beyond them, and the ways in which multiple operators worked within a larger system of political forces that do not map simply to state forms. Religion and war, it will be seen, operate in a complex dynamic in the early modern domain, both as functions of the state and in differentiated autonomous and semi-autonomous relations with it. The "political community" that Heinze and Steele (2009) speak of, therefore, must be decoupled from the state and allowed a constitution and domain of action that operate outside of the state form as well as in relation to it. This also allows us to return to questions of sovereignty that have continuing significance today to assess their historical constitution and to see the limitations of a preoccupation with the state as the sole articulation of political community.

MARTIAL RELIGIOSITY IN EARLY MODERN SOUTH ASIA

If we seek to understand the relationship between "war" and "religion," therefore, we must seek to understand how these are configured in particular moments and places. This allows us to do two things: to recognize the martial dimensions of religious cultural formations that have in many cases been shorn of such elements in modern times; and to see that martial endeavours should not been seen as necessitating a quest for kingship and sovereignty. Instead, war and martiality had diverse relationships with political and religious communities of different kinds. This allows us, further, not to equate the activity of religious martial communities as seamlessly equivalent to state formation and to see that the system of layered sovereignty allowed for martial action and participation by religious communities in complex ways that elude modern notions of the all-encompassing power of the state and its monopolization of violence. This is not to glorify the dispersal of violence into the hands of multiple actors but to recognize that our understanding of the role of violence in relation to religious communities requires further examination of the multiple sites of its articulation and understanding of the multiplicity of form of the "political community" beyond the state. This, in turn, allows us to assess ideas of "sovereignty" more carefully, and – it is hoped – it allows us to move towards a more careful and precise use of its language.

The locus of our discussion here is the Mughal Empire. The sovereignty of the Mughal Empire in South Asia was complex in its forms and has been rendered in diverse ways in scholarship. The Empire can be said to have begun in 1526 with the defeat by its founding emperor, Babur, of the sultan of Delhi, Ibrahim Lodi, at the Battle of Panipat, and did not cease as a political entity until the failed 1857 rebellion that sought to reinstate it fully, after which the imperial sovereign's role was formally ended by the British in 1858; its reach and influence waned significantly, however, after the death of the emperor Aurangzeb in 1707. In earlier literature, the Empire was portrayed as extractive and absolutist in control. In the words of Tapan Raychaudhuri, "[t]he empire, held together by force, needed a vast machinery of coercion and, hence, adequate resources to sustain it" (1982: 172; see Hasan 2004: 'Introduction' for a useful overview of the literature). More recent work has added far greater nuance to the ways in which imperial power depended and built upon local powers, whereby "the system of rule, in its 'everyday form,' represented and involved, reinforced and integrated the local structures of power" (Hasan 2004: 1); work has also opened up awareness of how diverse groups of people engaged with the state and with politics, such as in Abhishek Kaicker's important recent work on the political actions of the "urban masses" of Delhi and the "potential of Delhi's urbanites for concerted action in extraordinary circumstances" (2020: 16). This more recent work has allowed us to appreciate both the diverse ideological underpinnings of Mughal sovereignty, such as Muzaffar Alam (2004) has explored, and their diverse articulations, applications, and inhabitations, as well as the ways in which other forms of political community – sometimes quasi-sovereign, sometimes not cast in such terms – could emerge in relation to Mughal sovereignty.

Recent work on the 16th to 18th centuries in north India more broadly has also significantly enriched our understanding of the complex cultural and political field within which religious communities were configured both within and at the periphery of the Mughal Empire. This was a crucial period in particular for the development of new martial religious communities in diverse forms, building on and expanding earlier precedents. Such communities represent the kind of 'cacophony of enclaved, self-governing communities, from city-states to merchants, mercenaries, masons, mendicants, and many others ... an interlocking matrix of commonwealths, churches, associations, communities, office-holders, agencies, and families' that Stern describes as the context for the East India Company's emergence (2011 : 9). Dirk Kolff's (1990) work on the military labour market in northern parts of South Asia sets the stage for a broader understanding of the domains within which martial religious groups operated from the late mediaeval and into the early modern periods. In this ground-breaking work, Kolff demonstrates the vibrancy of the market in military labour in early modern South Asia and the ways in which diverse members of the peasantry participated in it. He also calls attention to the deep affinities between martial and ascetic communities in this period in particular. More broadly, he offers the important insight that it is a mistake to conflate the shape of martial communities in this period with the interests of the state. For example, referring to a census taken in Abu Fazl's famous 16th-century text, the *Ā'in-i-Akbarī*, on the administration of the Mughal Empire under Akbar (r. 1556–1605), Kolff notes that a large number of foot soldiers and horsemen are listed, but "the state could never employ all these men" (1990: 3). Instead, the list betrays the concern over this population of martial persons, "essentially as free to become rebels as they were to turn auxiliaries" (Kolff 1990: 3). As Kolff further argues:

> In such as society, no government, however powerful, could even begin to think of achieving a monopoly on the use of arms. In some respects, the millions of armed men, cultivators and otherwise, that government was supposed to rule over, were its rivals rather than its subjects.
>
> (1990: 7)

It is in this period that we see the rise, in particular, of martial ascetic communities across religious community boundaries, as Kolff demonstrates. While this may seem like something of an oxymoron to modern readers unfamiliar with the social landscape under examination here, a martial comportment and allied practices were closely linked to both ascetic and religious forms of social organization in the early modern period in South Asia and beyond.

David Lorenzen broke early ground in recent understanding of the martial ascetic communities that came to the fore in the early modern period; he cites the following work from the approximately mid-16th century Bījak of Kabīr as evidence:

Never have I seen such yogīs, Brother.

They wander mindless and negligent ...
To markets and bazaars they bring their meditation,
False *siddha*s, lovers of *māyā* [worldly illusion]
When did Dattatreya attack a fort?
When did Śukadeva join with gunners?
When did Nārada fire a musket?
When did Vyāsadeva sound a battle cry?
These make war, slow-witted.
Are they ascetics, or archers?

(Lorenzen 1978: 61)

This description of martial ascetics resonates with diverse communities across the subcontinent, as peasants took up arms and religious persons took to war. Matthew Clark's important synthetic work on the emergence of the *Daśanāmī Saṃnyāsīs*, which featured a prominent martial ascetic order, takes us further, detailing the diverse and multi-devotional aspects of martial asceticism in late mediaeval and early modern South Asia, with most being formed and organized between the mid-16th and 18th centuries (2006: 228–9; see also Bhattacharyya 2014: 159ff.). Clark includes among these a wide range of groups: 'the early Sikh *khālsā*, the Udāsin and Nirmala orders, Dādūpanthī, Rāmānandī (Bairāgī), Nimbarkī and Rādhāvallabhī *nāgā-s*', as well as the *Daśanāmī* order that he argues was formed and consolidated in the late 16th century (2006: 228–9). This list is instructive in that it incorporates a range of distinct religious communities – Sikh (the *Khālsā*, *Udāsin* and *Nirmala* communities), Vaishnava (*Rāmānandī* and *Rādhāvallabhī*), and Śaivite (*Daśanāmī* and *Nāth*) orders – religious positions distinguished theologically and historically but yet shared this same martial dynamic and positioning. Clark argues that "[t]he organisation of *saṃnyāsī*-s and other ascetics into military *akhāṛā-s* [units] can be understood as a relatively seamless transition between the two lifestyles of the *nāgā* [or ascetic] and soldier: both require rigorous self-discipline, and an adaptability to harsh conditions" (2006: 231). These religious formations did not emerge out of nowhere; as Clark notes, "[f]rom references in the *Mahābhārata* and Kauṭilya's *Arthaśāstra* (c. second century CE) it is ... apparent that ascetics had a reputation for being useful to the state for a variety of nefarious activities, including spying and assassination" (2006: 11). In the 17th and 18th centuries, he shows us, "[m]any thousands of militant *nāgā saṃnyāsī*-s (also known as *gosain*-s) were involved as mercenaries in numerous political conflicts in north India during this period, becoming wealthy as bankers and traders, and acquiring substantial property," having emerged in the mid-16th century and consolidated into military units (2006: 14, 25). While some of the conflicts Clark describes might seem religious and sectarian in derivation, he notes well that even the seemingly "simply religious" issue of the order in which different groups would bathe at the sacred *sangam* or confluence of sacred rivers, an important pilgrimage site, was not fundamentally a "religious" issue at prominent sites like Haridwar, where martial ascetics came to gather in numbers in the 18th century. Instead, it was linked to other kinds of social activity, such that "dominance of trade and taxation by one sect or another led to bathing privileges" (Clark 2006: 65; see also Maclean 2008: 12, 22ff.).

We see a wide range of theological and communitarian commitments among martial communities. As Monika Horstmann tells us, the *Dādūpaṅthī nāgās* were warrior ascetics within the *Dādūpaṅthī* community who "counterbalanced" the *Daśanāmī* community's ascetic warriors whom Clark focuses on (1991: 255; see also Hastings 2002). The *nāgās* are generally understood to represent a *Nirgun* orientation that focused on the indescribability of God, beyond the realm of form, but they also exhibited strong Vaishnava leanings, embracing a *Sagun* orientation that celebrates the world of form and representation. As Horstmann notes, the "Nāgās confirm strongly a dual identity of bhakti [or devotionalism] and militancy alike" and "present-day *nāgā* identity is articulated as '*śastra-śāstra-vyavahār*'; 'Practice of Sword and Scripture'" (1991: 255–6). William Pinch (2006) suggested that the transformations that we see in this period represent a move from a martial ascetic religiosity to one characterized by devotion, or *bhakti*; but as Horstmann well notes, martial and ascetic religiosity were not opposed to devotion: the *Nāgās* themselves see no contradiction, and fully "reconcile world renouncing bhakti and warfare" (1991: 256). Muslim religiosity could also be martially configured; as Nile Green has argued: "*Faqīrs* themselves became an important part of India's armed brigades through the militant flexibility of their renunciation of family ties and their mobility alongside their command of supernatural powers" (2009: 25).[1] Lorenzen highlights the *Madārī faqīr* community, which, in the account given in the 17th-century overview of religions in Mughal India, the *Dabistān-i Maẕāhib* (*The School of Religions*), is portrayed as being very similar to *sannyāsīs*; in the 18th century, "[t]he

---

[1] Clark and Lorenzen, indeed, credit different kinds of interactions with Islamic institutions and individuals with inspiring the institutionalization of ascetic warrior groups.(Lorenzen 1978: 68; Clark 2006: 269).

animosities built up between the British and both the Madārīs and Dasnāmīs eventually seem to have caused the fakirs and sannyāsīs to join together to resist the new order" in the so-called Sannyasi Rebellion (Lorenzen 1978: 74).[2]

Julie Vig has called attention to the strong parallels between Sikh and Dādūpanthī martial traditions in this period (2019: 184–91). Indeed, Clark is careful to count Sikh martial social formations among the "radical militant ascetics" who emerged in the 16th and 17th centuries (2006: 25). The Sikh Khalsa is often portrayed today as unique in its articulation of a martial ethos. This has led the notion of sovereignty to operate centrally in both scholarly and community accounts of the tradition. Exemplary of this is Louis Fenech's discussion of the Zafarnāmah, attributed to the final human-embodied Guru of the Sikh tradition; Fenech portrays sovereignty as something central to the constitution of Sikh communities (2013).[3] We see this elsewhere: Hardip Singh Syan, for example, has argued that "the Sikh community developed sophisticated ideas on violence, sovereignty and social order" and "evolved from its genesis as a gentry (zamindari) movement to a movement dedicated to political sovereignty" (2013: 2). This representation of the Sikh community as being uniquely martial and engaged with political concerns requires reconsideration, however, given the number and diversity of communities engaged in parallel pursuits, as discussed here. It is also the case that the nature of the political community in question is less clear than the claims above suggest. Purnima Dhavan (2011) has shown in detail, for example, how the political field of Sikh chiefs and militias was complex and shifting in the 18th century, involving an array of relationships with and among other powers (Mughal, Afghan, and Pahāṛī, from what is now Uttaranchal and Himachal Pradesh and their environs in India) demonstrating both ideals regarding Sikh political articulation and their accommodation to political realities of the time; Syan (2013: 250) notes this as well. As Dhavan argues, "far from reflecting the uncomplicated binary of Sikh–Mughal struggle, this period instead was marked by a complex web of alliances between various regional powers as each group attempted to buttress its own position" (2011: 79). We must also see this struggle in the context of a larger struggle, signalled by Kolff, between the state and rural martialized communities. As he notes, "many peasant communities left their rulers with no choice but to consider an attack upon

---

² On the *Dabistān-i Maẕāhib* overall, see Behl (2011).
³ See discussion of this element in the text in Murphy (2015).

them" (1990: 13): martial activity by peasants was significant enough to be considered a threat to the state. Further, as Clark details, Sikh martial formations were not only expressed within the Khalsa: the *Udāsī* and *Nirmala* orders functioned in a way parallel to other military ascetic orders (2006: 55, 61, 228–9).

There were, therefore, complex and multiple forms of martial community articulated in the early modern moment in South Asia. Such groups engaged in diverse relationships with the state and with state formation. At times, they were organized in alliance to state power (but not necessarily supplanting it), such as under the centralizing campaign of the Kachvāha king Sawai Jaisingh of present-day Rajasthan, who sought to endorse, strengthen, and enforce orthodox religious social and ideological formations among diverse sectarian groups (Hastings 2002; Horstmann 2011; Vig 2019: 185). As Pinch (2006) has shown so vividly, such martial groups might also gain control of territory as sovereigns and control considerable military forces, as he demonstrates with his in-depth portrait of Anupgiri Gosain, also known as Himmat Bahadur, a Śaivite ascetic warlord. At other times, such community formations operated entirely separately from the state or might be linked to decentralized challenges to state power, as we see in the 18th century in Punjab, which Purnima Dhavan (2011) has shown in her account of the rise of Sikh militia leaders and communitarian political formations among Sikhs.

For this reason, we must take care in how we interpret the languages of power associated with the state and/or contesting it. As Alexis Sanderson (2009: 261–2) has shown well, the association of royalty with Śaiva religious institutions and leaders was well established in the mediaeval period; this extended to the martial realm, and inscriptional evidence provides clear support for the role played by Śaiva leaders in martial pursuits, in conjunction with state interests, within the states where they had become prominent. Along these lines, Sanderson argues that "the Śaiva rites by which the Guru assumed his office ensured that he, as Śiva's agent among men, was imbued with the numen of royalty" (2009: 260). We see the same model followed among early modern religious communities across the subcontinent in how the language of worldly power was inscribed within the religious community. This is broadly visible in relation to Sufi charismatic figures and their shrines in the early modern period, which were deeply engrained with the symbolism of courtly power. Sufi and secular powers, Nile Green argues, "often shared the symbolic and linguistic vocabularies through which their power was expressed" (2006: 38); indeed, Aditya Behl's

(2012) more recent work and Simon Digby's (1990) now classic work have explored at some length the ways in which Sufi shrines both shared in and contested power in the form of the state through their conceptualization of their "*vilayat*" or "spiritual rule" (Digby 1990: 71) over territory, where "sovereignty over the realm was theirs [the Sufis] to grant" (Moin 2012: 74). Thus, Green notes, "sufi and political texts did not so much borrow from one another's distinct spheres, but were rather both part of a wider literary and cultural ecumene in which kings and saints shared centre-stage together" (2006: 28).

We can see this dynamic more broadly, as interconnected phenomena.[4] Louis Fenech (2008) has detailed the ways in which imperial languages of power were engaged in the Sikh tradition to honour the Guru and to establish the domain of his influence. The history of the Vallabha *sampraday*, a prominent Vaishnava sect, as described by Shandip Saha (2006, 2007) provides another important example from the same period.[5] There were seven "houses" designated for the male descendants of Vittalnath, one of the sons and successors of founder of the *sampraday*, Vallabhacarya. The leaders of these houses were known as *maharajas*, or "great kings," and they achieved not only wealth but also temporal control of extensive lands under the patronage of royalty in Rajasthan. In 1672, indeed, those designated as *tilkāyat*, the descendants of Vitthalnath's eldest son, were established in a small, autonomous kingdom within Mewar (Saha 2007: 304–5), such that, according to Edwin Allen Richardson, "the goswamis exerted total control over commerce, local industry, and taxation, Nathdwara operated as a veritable Vatican, levying fees on pilgrims who entered its gates, assessing all goods produced in the market place, and controlling the services instituted for the maintenance of the god" (1979: ix). "Thus," Saha tells us, "by the early nineteenth century, the Nāthdvārā *tilkāyats* had amassed sufficient land and wealth to be formally made members of the Rājpūt nobility with unfettered spiritual and temporal control over their estates" (Saha 2006: 229, 2007: 304–5). Indeed, it is not therefore surprising to learn that the elaborate *seva* or ritual services of the *Pustimārg* sect that followed from Vallabha were initiated at the time

---

[4] Recent scholarship has demonstrated the deep connections between Sufi and Yogi worlds. See, for example, Ernst (2005), Green (2008), and Behl (2012). As Ernst (2005: 41) points out: 'Sufis and yogis alike both felt the need periodically to take account of the other group, and this acknowledgement took the form of competing narratives.' I have described an 18th-century Sikh account that establishes a comparative rubric between Sikh and Islamic thought/practice (Murphy 2012).

[5] This paragraph draws on Murphy (2009).

of Vitthalnath rather than the time of the founder, Vallabha – this reflected the relative power and status of the community as these grew in Vitthalnath's time (Peabody 1991: 731; Saha 2007: 308). Within two generations, the form and function of worship reflected changed social and institutional circumstances through different languages of power as the community came to be dominated by merchant communities.

Our interpretation of warfare in religious contexts and the languages of power that are engaged in them must therefore be grounded in an understanding of the intersection of royal and religious articulations of power, martial practices and positionalities among diverse actors, and the relative independence of religious communities within a loose broader political system. "Political community," to use the terminology referenced at the opening of this chapter, here operates outside of or in diverse relations to state power and is not identical to it; it is not always and inevitably about state formation. Louis Fenech's (2008: 64ff.) discussion of *khil'at* – the ritual exchange of gifts between subordinate and superior – in the Sikh context provides one example of the multiple symbolic registers of certain practices.[6] Such exchanges of gifts took place between sovereign and subject, as Fenech highlights – Finbarr B. Flood tell us that such objects functioned as 'an incarnated sign of sovereign authority' (2009: 76) – and Fenech sees this as an indication of an articulation of sovereignty in the Sikh context. However, this kind of exchange was also prominent in Sufi and other religious contexts and did not always function as a marker of sovereign relations. Even such exchanges in the state setting are impossible to designate as "non-religious," as revealed by Sudipta Sen's (1999) work on the construction of history in Indo-Persianate contexts in north India. Interaction with the Mughal emperor was engaged within religious modes, particularly but not exclusively in relation to the emperor Akbar, adding a particular importance to the remembering of interactions with the emperor within historical accounts, such that "it is no surprise then that the memory of imperial association added transcendental significance to the past, particularly among a heterogeneous nobility which was not necessarily bound by the same religious sensibility" (1999: 250). Broadly, the court mirrored the world of the religious, as argued by Nicholas B. Dirks, who found *pūjā* or worship to act as the 'the root political metaphor' in south Indian state formation: in the Tamil context, "[o]n the one hand, ritual was a pervasive political

---

[6] This and the next paragraph draw on Murphy (2015). For further discussion of *khil'at* and its multiform roles in the Sikh tradition, see Murphy (2012: 48ff.).

fact; on the other, politics was permeated by ritual forms" (Dirks 1987: 47, 129). *Pūjā* or worship as a core metaphor for political relations does not mean that all politics were religious: "the deity was not so much the paradigmatic sovereign as worship was the paradigmatic exchange" (Dirks 1987: 289). As Caleb Simmons has shown more recently in his work on the 18th- to 19th-century Mysore State, in what is now Karnataka, "in early modern and early colonial Indian kingship ... religion was a site on which sovereignty could be grounded, even as it transformed" (2020: 11), and rulers engaged the language of religious devotion in the face of territorial contestation and British encroachment "to provide an idiom through which they could articulate their unique claims to kingship in the region" (2020: 4).

Recognition of the diverse and decentralized nature of martial formations among religious communities helps us to understand in new ways these religious communities and their diverse relationships with war and with state formation. Returning to the Sikh tradition, it was Lorenzen who first suggested that the Sikhs be considered a kind of ascetic warrior tradition (1978: 62–3, 70–1); Sikhism, and the other traditions described here, all, as Pinch well noted, "bear the imprint of the Mughal experience," and were decidedly not world-denying (2006: 57, 65–6). As Dhavan makes clear, throughout the 18th-century, Sikh chiefs had to "negotiate a fine balance between asserting individual sovereignty and acknowledging the right of the community to curb or censure their actions," in effect spreading "Khalsa practices to all parts of Punjab while simultaneously broadening and transforming them" (2011: 9). Sikh political philosophy, according to Syan, developed from the Guru's embrace of the idea of the "householder-sovereign," but such ideas also reflected much broader debate about the relationship between householder and renouncer that was prevalent in Indian culture in general and did not operate in binary opposition (2013: 151). Again, Saha's discussion of the householder orientation of the Vallabha *sampraday* provides a strong parallel, albeit one that is located strongly within the caste-conscious *varnāshrama* order that the Sikh tradition generally rejected (2006: 226).[7] The political communities thus formed could occupy diverse political positions, both adhering to and challenging conventional political and social hierarchies. Vocabularies and practices associated with sovereignty were present within these many different religious institutional formations.

---

[7] For discussion of Sikh positions on caste within this period in relation to other parallels, see Murphy (2018).

THE RELIGIOUS AND THE POLITICAL

Our understanding of the nexus of martiality, religion, and state formation in the northern reaches of early modern South Asia must be located within a Mughal polity that featured complex and layered articulations and administrations of sovereignty and power and a broader fusion of the political and religious in the rhetoric of power.[8] As A. Azfar Moin's *Millennial Sovereign* (2012: 5) demonstrates so beautifully, among the Mughal emperors (and beyond, in Safavid Persia), "the institution of kingship became locked in a mimetic embrace with the institution of sainthood." It was tied to a "widespread messianic myth [that] was clearly a 'political' one" and that depended on a complex synthesis of Sufi thought and practice with devotional loyalty to 'Ali (Moin 2012: 28).[9] Sanjay Subrahmanyam argued that millenarianism was a defining feature of that period we call the "early modern," which "saw the emergence of a new set of material conditions within which millenarianism could arise, and propagate itself both as a current that embraced a large geographical space, and as a phenomenon that had specific, and even unique, local manifestations" (1997: 749–50); he has thus argued that this millennial personification was part of a language of sovereignty from India to Portugal in the 16th century (Subrahmanyam 2005). The parallels are striking: he notes, for instance, that 'the epistemological subsumption of older traditions into a newer one' was a consistent feature of millenarian ideologies, which could "open out into other, often far more ancient, traditions and incorporate them in an implicitly subordinate position" (2005: 129). Along such lines, Samira Sheikh has argued that "groups and states who professed a millennial mode of discipleship and authority emerged as a profound challenge to the Mughal monopoly on millenarianism" (2018: 560–1); they were then conceived as representing a kind of threat to the state. This can be revealing when returning to the example of the Sikhs: we can see the martyrdom of the fifth and ninth Sikh Gurus as mirroring a pattern established for millenarian competitors of the Mughal emperor, as described by Sheikh: being called to account for themselves before the Mughal throne and asked to recant, with execution to follow for those

---

[8] This and the next paragraph are developed from Murphy (2015).

[9] On the Sufi–Shi'i synthesis, see Moin (2012: 40ff.). In Moin's account, this millennial orientation was strongly tied to astrology (throughout, but see, for example, p. 102). See Gilmartin (2017) for an insightful discussion of sovereignty in relation to Moin's book.

who did not.[10] Such millennial discourses were certainly broadly present in Punjab: we see this in the language of Shaikh Ahmed Sirhindi, for instance, a Naqśbandī Sufi contemporary of Guru Arjan's who was temporarily detained himself by Jahangir for the challenge he posed (Subrahmanyam 2005: 110; Moin 2012: 135–6, 183ff.). Sirhindi was identified as the *mujaddid-i alf-i thānī*, the renewer of the second millennium, and was a controversial figure who expressed the sense of expectation, urgency, and fulfilment that characterized millennial discourses, seeking to, in the words of Arthur Buehler, "intensify the process of collapsing time through contemplative practice and [restructure] one's life according to Prophetic guidelines" (2011: 28). Indeed, it may be that the challenge of the Gurus to the Mughal court should be construed as a millennial ideological one rather than as a political one: the Gurus were generally treated in the same way as Shi'a charismatic figures, for example, as Sheikh has described.

The nature of the connection (and disconnection) of religious discourses with state power is crucial to our understanding of the ways violence was enacted in the early modern period: as Pinch (2006: 8ff.) has noted, criticism of the artificial division between "the religious" and "the political" in the formation of early modern religious communities in South Asia has generally resulted in a privileging of only the *political*. We therefore see in this period a broad engagement of religious figures and institutions with war and martiality, at the intersection with millennial discourses and relatively loose connections to state formation. We can see Akbar's 1567 encounter with warrior ascetics, so beautifully portrayed by Pinch (2006: 28ff.), Lorenzen (1978: 68–9), and others, as a confluence of the rise of both martial mendicancy and messianic religiosity across religious traditions and political formations. State formation is not at the centre of these "political communities," which instead articulate a divergent set of relationships to state power – at times subverting it, at times collaborating with it, and at times claiming it – and to each other.

RELIGION AND WAR

War was, simply put, religious business for many in early modern South Asia, and we see synergies in broad terms between the religious and the political in various kinds of relationships to state sovereignty. This

---

[10] See description of the Sufi building of forts (parallel to the Sikh pursuit of the same) in Moin (2012: 83, on charges of heresy, see 210).

helps us to understand the religious communities that have emerged out of this nexus, such as the Sikh tradition, which we can see as characteristic of various forms of early modern religious communitarian mobilization, representing a convergence of the commitments and forces that characterized the early modern period – a millenarian expectation and communitarian devotional ethos, wedded to a martial form at the conjunction of the religious and the political – that has carried forward into our present in a way that few other such convergences have. Pinch argues that this was impossible for many other groups in this period, which could not integrate martial sensibilities and practices with a new devotional orientation where religion was "private, devotional and depoliticized," and which were demilitarized by the British as they gained power in the subcontinent.[11]

What does all of this tell us about the relationship between religion and war in early modern South Asia? Ananda Bhattacharyya has noted that "the existing historiography mainly portrays the Dasanami Sannyasis either as dacoits, bandits, plunderers or as participants in peasant uprising in the second half of 18th-century Bengal" (2014: 152, 170–1; see also Clark 2006: 252). Our current moment finds it difficult to understand the relationship between devotion and asceticism and between both of these and martiality, which Horstmann (1991) describes as unexceptional for her *Dādūpanthī* interlocutors and which we see across the many different communities discussed in this chapter. And, as has been discussed, assumptions about statehood and sovereignty in exclusive terms do not allow for political and social formations of other kinds. Goldberg seeks to "de-spiritualize" the notion of religion with her approach, but in so doing she has simply equated any organization that claims jurisdiction over its membership with a kind of a would-be state (2015: 281). Surely there are other forms of social and political formation that deserve our attention. Interestingly, in Arvind-Pal Mandair's extension of Goldberg's ideas to understand the place of Sikhs in the world, he utilizes her critique to focus on a notion of sovereignty as "the ability to freely express one's life-world" and "the struggle of the self to overcome itself while paradoxically retaining itself" (2015: 115, 118). In keeping with the argument developed here, he argues that there is the "possibility that the concept of sovereignty was always already plural and heterogenous in essence, and that its meaning became homogenized with the rise of the modern nation state

---

[11] See Pinch (2006: 259); on demilitarization of *sannyāsīs*, 84ff. (and ch. 2 in general); on depoliticization, 237; on the Sikh avoidance of demilitarization, 145, n. 117.

and tied to the emerging religion–secular binary" (2015: 116). But what he calls "heteronomic sovereignty," which operates outside of the absolutist sovereignty of the nation-state, is cast fully outside of the language of the state (and therefore the conventional notion of "sovereignty") as "one whose fundamental rule is the self's relationship to the other; the notion that the self exists in the world only on the basis of its tangible relation to its other (ego-loss)" (2015: 118). This language of self-transformation as the core of an alternative notion of "sovereignty" supports an understanding of resulting social formations outside of the frame of the state (and returns us to the domain of the "religious" or the "spiritual," as problematic as these terms may be).

Things did change with the onset of British rule in South Asia, with the eventual establishment of a stronger monopoly of power by the state and less room for independent-operator martial formations outside of the direct control of the state or in contingent relation to it. As Lauren Benton has shown so well, British rule in India was itself marked by "theoretically vibrant notions of divided sovereignty [that] permitted experiments in partial or mixed sovereignty" (2009: 281). Within this complex field, the "Princely States," as they were known, negotiated diverse forms of sovereign relation to the British Empire, for example. Still, this was the time during which, as Sugata Bose tells us, "wandering peoples on land were either forcibly settled or branded "criminal tribes" and their counterparts at sea termed 'pirates'" (2006: 25) and the nature of warfare changed, with the institution of a massive standing army (2006: 24, 123–4). Within the complicated matrix of complex imperial sovereignty and martial domination, most warrior ascetic communities in South Asia did not find a clear place within the colonial order, except in rare cases where they were successfully integrated into East India Company and then British Indian military formations, such as with the Sikhs and the Coorgi/Kodava community of present-day Karnataka. In these cases, martiality was sanctioned by the state – but it was never controlled by it, and its logic was not determined solely by its usefulness to the state, much as the state might seek to fully control and direct it.[12] The connection here between war and religion in the earlier moment explored here, in contrast, bore multiple and divergent relationships with state formation. We need to think across and within both war and

---

[12]   This is the deep flaw with Richard Fox's (1985) early influential account of the making of Sikh martiality in the British military order: it places agency and control with the army and the British and pays insufficient attention to Sikh martial articulations in their own and historical terms.

religion to understand the formations of early modern religious communities in South Asia and the legacies of these formations for our present, outside of the box of the state.

References

Alam, Muzaffar. 2004. *The Languages of Political Islam: India 1200–1800.* University of Chicago Press.

Behl, Aditya. 2011. "Pages from the Book of Religions: Encountering Difference in Mughal India." In *Forms of Knowledge in Early Modern Asia: Explorations in the Intellectual History of India and Tibet, 1500–1800.* Edited by Sheldon Pollock. Oxford University Press. 210–239.

2012. *Love's Subtle Magic: An Indian Islamic Literary Tradition, 1379–1545.* Oxford University Press.

Benton, Lauren. 2009. *A Search for Sovereignty: Law and Geography in European Empires, 1400–1900.* Cambridge University Press.

Beverley, Eric Lewis. 2015. *Hyderabad, British India, and the World: Muslim Networks and Minor Sovereignty, c. 1850–1950.* Cambridge University Press.

Bhattacharyya, Ananda. 2014. "Dasanami Sannyasis: Polity and Economy in the Eighteenth-Century India." *Studies in History* 30(2): 151–77.

Bose, Sugata. 2006. *A Hundred Horizons: The Indian Ocean in the Age of Global Empire.* Harvard University Press.

Buehler, Arthur. 2011. *Revealed Grace: The Juristic Sufism of Ahmad Sirhindi (1564–1624).* Fons Vitae.

Burchett, Patton. 2019. *A Genealogy of Devotion: Bhakti, Tantra, Yoga, and Sufism, in North India.* Columbia University Press.

Clark, Matthew. 2006. *The Daśanāmī-Saṃnyāsīs: The Integration of Ascetic Lineages into an Order.* Brill Academic Publishers.

Dhavan, Purnima. 2011. *When Sparrows Became Hawks: The Making of Sikh Warrior Tradition, 1699–1799.* Oxford University Press.

Digby, Simon. 1990. "The Sufi Shaykh and the Sultan: A Conflict of Claims to Authority in Medieval India." *Iran* 28: 71–81.

Dirks, Nicholas B. 1987. *The Hollow Crown: Ethnohistory of an Indian Kingdom.* Cambridge University Press.

Ernst, Carl. 2005. "Situating Sufism and Yoga." *Journal of the Royal Asiatic Society* 15(1): 15–43.

Fenech, Louis. 2008. *The Darbar of the Sikh Gurus: The Court of God in the World of Men.* Oxford University Press.

2013. *The Sikh Zafar-Nāmah of Guru Gobind Singh: A Discursive Blade in the Heart of the Mughal Empire.* Oxford University Press.

Flood, Finbarr B. 2009. *Objects of Translation: Material Culture and Medieval "Hindu–Muslim" Encounter.* Princeton University Press.

Fox, Richard. 1985. *Lions of the Punjab: Culture in the Making.* University of California Press.

Gilmartin, David. 2017. "Imperial Sovereignty in Mughal and British Forms." *History and Theory* 56(1): 80–8.

Goldberg, Naomi. 2015. "The Category of Religion in the Technology of Governance: An Argument for Understanding Religions as Vestigial States." In *Religion as a Category of Governance and Sovereignty*. Edited by Trevor Stack, Naomi R. Goldberg, and Timothy Fitzgerald. Brill. 280–92.

Green, Nile. 2006. *Indian Sufism since the Seventeenth Century: Saints, Books and Empires in the Muslim Deccan*. Routledge.

2008. "Breathing in India, c. 1890." *Modern Asian Studies* 42(2/3): 283–315.

2009. *Islam and the Army in Colonial India: Sepoy Religion and the Service of Empire*. Cambridge University Press.

Hansen, Thomas Blom. 2021. "Sovereignty in a Minor Key." *Public Culture* 33 (1): 41–61.

Hasan, Farhat. 2004. *State and Locality in Mughal India: Power Relations in Western India, c. 1572–1730*. University of Cambridge.

Hastings, James. 2002. "Poets, Saints and Warriors: The Dadu Panth, Religious Change, and Identity Formation in Jaipur State Circa 1562–1860 CE." PhD dissertation. University of Wisconsin at Madison.

Heinze, Eric and Brent Steele. 2009. *Ethics, Authority and War: Non-State Actors and the Just War Tradition*. Palgrave Macmillan.

Horstmann, Monika. 1991. "On the Dual Identity of Nagas." In *Devotion Divine: Bhakti Traditions from the Regions of India*. Edited by Diana L. Eck and Francoise Mallison. E. Forsten. 255–73.

2011. "Theology and Statecraft." *South Asian History and Culture* 2(2): 184–204.

Kaicker, Abhishek. 2020. *The King and the People: Sovereignty and Popular Politics in Mughal Delhi*. Oxford University Press.

Kolff, Dirk. 1990. *Naukar, Rajput, and Sepoy: The Ethnohistory of the Military Labour Market in Hindustan, 1450–1850*. Cambridge University Press.

Lorenzen, David. 1978. "Warrior Ascetics in Indian History." *Journal of the American Oriental Society* 98(1): 61–75.

Maclean, Kama. 2008. *Pilgrimage and Power: The Kumbh Mela in Allahabad, 1765–1954*. Oxford University Press.

Mandair, Arvind-Pal. 2015. "Sikhs, Sovereignty and Modern Government." In *Religion as a Category of Governance and Sovereignty*. Edited by Trevor Stack, Naomi R. Goldberg, and Timothy Fitzgerald. Brill. 115–42.

Moin, A. Azfar. 2012. *The Millennial Sovereign: Sacred Kingship and Sainthood in Islam, South Asia Across the Disciplines*. Columbia University Press.

Murphy, Anne. 2009. Review of The Darbar of the Sikh Gurus: The Court of God in the World of Men, by Louis Fenech (Oxford University Press, 2008). *Indian Historical Review* 27(1): 154–8.

2012. "The Gurbilas Literature and the Idea of Religion"." In *Punjab Reconsidered: History, Culture, and Practice*. Edited by Anshu Malhotra and Farina Mir. Oxford University Press. 93–115.

2015. "A Millennial Sovereignty? Recent Works on Sikh Martial and Political Cultures in the Seventeenth and Eighteenth Centuries." *History of Religions* 55(1): 89–104.

2018. "Thinking beyond Aurangzeb and the Mughal State in a Late 18th Century Punjabi Braj Source." *Journal of the Royal Asiatic Society* 28(3): 537–54.

Peabody, Norbert. 1991. "In Whose Turban Does the Lord Reside?: The Objectification of Charisma and the Fetishism of Objects in the Hindu Kingdom of Kota." *Comparative Studies in Society and History* 33(4): 726–54.

Pinch, William. 2006. *Warrior Ascetics and Indian Empires*. Cambridge University Press.

Raychaudhuri, Tapan. 1982. "The Mughal Empire." In *The Cambridge Economic History of India*. Edited by Dharma Kumar and Meghnad Desai. Cambridge University Press. 172–93.

Richardson, Edwin Allen. 1979. "Mughal and Rajput Patronage of the Bhakti Sect of the Maharajas, the Vallabha Sampradaya, 1640–1760 A.D." PhD dissertation. University of Arizona.

Saha, Shandip. 2006. "A Community of Grace: The Social and Theological World of the *Puṣṭi Mārga vārtā* Literature." *Bulletin of SOAS* 69(2): 225–42.

——— 2007. "The Movement of *Bhakti* along a North-West Axis: Tracing the History of the Puṣṭimārg between the Sixteenth and Nineteenth Centuries." *International Journal of Hindu Studies* 11(3): 299–318.

Sanderson, Alexis. 2009. "The Śaiva Age: The Rise and Dominance of Śaivism During the Early Medieval Period." In *Genesis and Development of Tantrism*. Edited by Shingo Einoo. Institute of Oriental Culture. 41–349.

Sen, Sudipta. 1999. "Imperial Orders of the Past: The Semantics of History and Time in the Medieval Indo-Persianate Culture of North India." In *Invoking the Past: The Uses of History in South Asia*. Edited by Daud Ali. Oxford University Press. 231–57.

Sheikh, Samira. 2018. "Aurangzeb as Seen from Gujarat: Shi'I and Millenarian Challenges to Mughal Sovereignty." *Journal of the Royal Asiatic Society* 28 (3): 557–81.

Simmons, Caleb. 2020. *Devotional Sovereignty: Kingship and Religion in India*. Oxford University Press.

Stern, Philip. 2011. *The Company-State: Corporate Sovereignty and the Early Modern Foundations of the British Empire in India*. Oxford University Press.

Subrahmanyam, Sanjay. 1997. "Connected Histories: Notes towards a Reconfiguration of Early Modern Eurasia." *Modern Asian Studies* 31(3): 735–62.

——— 2005. "Sixteenth Century Millenarianism from the Tagus to the Ganges." In *Explorations in Connected History: From the Tages to the Ganges*. Oxford University Press. 102–37.

Syan, Hardip Singh. 2013. *Sikh Militancy in the Seventeenth Century: Religious Violence in Mughal and Early Modern India*. I.B. Tauris.

Vig, Julie. 2019. "Participating in Other Worlds: Locating Gurbilās Literature in the Wider World of Brajbhasha Traditions." PhD dissertation. University of British Columbia.

Index

CAMBRIDGE COMPANIONS TO RELIGION (*continued from page ii*)

Other Titles in the Series

Printed by Printforce, United Kingdom